Nonverbal Communication,
Interaction, and Gesture

Approaches to Semiotics

41

MOUTON PUBLISHERS · THE HAGUE · PARIS · NEW YORK

Nonverbal Communication, Interaction, and Gesture

Selections from Semiotica

General Editors
Thomas A. Sebeok
Jean Umiker-Sebeok

Volume Editor
Adam Kendon

MOUTON PUBLISHERS · THE HAGUE · PARIS · NEW YORK

ISBN 90 279 3489 4 (cloth bound)
ISBN 90 279 3089 9 (paperback)
Jacket design by Jurriaan Schrofer

Printed by Krips Repro Meppel.
Printed in the Netherlands.

Preface

Since its inception in 1969, *Semiotica* has played a dynamic role in the formation and development of semiotics around the world. As the only globally-oriented, multilingual outlet for articles on all conceivable semiotic subjects, representing a vast array of scientific and humanistic approaches and methodologies, *Semiotica* has helped shape the growing international community of semioticians. For some topics, being newly explored at the intersection of several traditional fields, *Semiotica* has provided the only forum for the exposition and airing of a host of controversial issues. For other subjects, where other outlets are now available, *Semiotica* has published many path-finding papers by major world figures.

Over the years, *Semiotica* has responded in size to the phenomenal increase in the production of first-rate articles on semiotic topics. While this has enabled the journal to maintain its position as the foremost periodical publication in the field, it has now become financially inaccessible to many individual scholars and their students. For those persons, as well as for those whose interest in semiotics is focused only on one or two segments of the whole, Mouton will be publishing a number of collections of *Semiotica* articles, each devoted to a unified semiotic theme such as art and aesthetics, conversation, mythology, narrative, poetics, and text analysis, to name only a few. Taking articles from *Semiotica* as camera-ready copy, it will be possible to present relatively inexpensive, paperbound editions which are within the reach of individual academics, whether for use in research or as textbooks in the ever more numerous semiotics courses being taught in many countries.

Volumes in this project will be under the general editorship of the undersigned and will appear in the *Approaches to Semiotics* series. Each book will also have a Volume Editor — a leading expert in the particular field treated in the book — who will contribute a special Introduction, the purpose of which is to set each *Semiotica* piece within the field(s) to which it belongs, both synchronically and diachronically, discuss the scope of the volume vis-à-vis that of relevant wider areas of research, and provide a reasonably full and up-to-date reference apparatus or further guide to the literature.

Nonverbal Communication, Interaction, and Gesture, the first of these collections, addresses itself to an important and timely field of investigation. With Adam Kendon's masterful introductory chapter — which will stand as a classic in its own right — the book serves as an excellent introduction to the study of human nonverbal communication, including gesture and interaction, for students or specialists in other disciplines, as well as a convenient compilation of significant contributions to the field, for experts.

National Humanities Center,   Thomas A. Sebeok
Research Triangle Park, North Carolina   Jean Umiker-Sebeok
December, 1980

Contents

ADAM KENDON

Introduction: Current Issues in the Study of "Nonverbal Communication"

1.0. Introduction

The articles collected together in this volume comprise a selection from those articles published in *Semiotica*, up to the end of 1979, which may be regarded as being concerned with the phenomena of what has come to be termed 'nonverbal communication'. In selecting them an attempt has been made to include those articles that have proved to be particularly seminal over the years and to ensure that the full range of issues and approaches that have been dealt with in *Semiotica* are represented. The result is a collection which, we believe, presents a good cross section of the work currently being done in this field.

In Part I, four articles have been included the import of which is primarily theoretical or methodological. In the first of these, Ekman and Friesen not only propose a classificatory scheme for different aspects of behavior from a communicational perspective but also discuss a number of general issues. Poyatos discusses the uses that novelists make of 'nonverbal communication' in their characterizations and in their descriptions of encounters. This raises several interesting issues of theory and method. For instance, it raises the question of how features of voice and movement are to be described in words. It raises the question of how the function of 'nonverbal' information in human behavior is perceived by the novelist and what uses he makes of it in developing narrative and characterization. The other two articles in Part I, by Freedman and Seaford, address questions of the description and measurement of behavior. Freedman's article, a review of Bouissac's *La Mesure des Gestes*, touches on a number of different ways in which the problem of 'measuring' bodily movement has been approached and deals with the important question of what is to count as a unit of action. Seaford's article is an argument for developing descriptions of facial action based upon an analysis of the visible consequences of muscular action, the descriptions to be cast in terms of the actions of the muscles themselves. Included in this paper is an account of a study of 'facial dialects' to date the only such discussion to have appeared anywhere.

In Part II of this selection we have grouped articles in which instances of interaction are examined and an attempt is made to give an account of how the behavior that can be observed in them functions in the interaction process. The section begins with papers by Collett, et al. and by Givens, which are concerned with how people behave with respect to one another when they are in each other's presence, but not engaged in some joint activity, such as conversation. Next comes an article by Schiffrin, which deals with the uses of the handshake. Then follow four articles (by De Long, Argyle, et al., Beattie, and Kendon) which deal with various aspects of behavior within ongoing interaction and how it serves in the regulation of the actions of the participants. Finally, in a paper by Rosenberg, an analysis is presented which shows how speech, gesture, and action are all integrated within interaction. This paper further shows how one may look upon the patterning of action in interaction from the point of view of how the participants, through this action, continually renegotiate or reconfirm the nature of their relationship and how their actions are to be defined.

In Part III we present articles on what may broadly be referred to as 'gesture'. Here we have a set of articles which deal with specific actions, mostly of the forelimbs, which are usually deemed to have specific significance. Poyatos reviews three works that are concerned with providing inventories of gestures and in the course of doing so provides a useful outline of several of the different issues that are involved. Johnson, et al., Sparhawk, and Kirk and Burton deal with one kind of gesture, widely known as an 'emblem'. Rosenfeld, et al. show how minor movements of the head and face, though not usually recognized as 'gesture', may nevertheless convey quite specific information. The paper by Smith, et al. illustrates yet another approach to finding out the communicational significance of a specific action, in this case the action of protruding the tongue.

In the discussion to follow, an attempt will be made to place these articles in the wider context of studies of this sort. In this way, the significance of each article as a contribution to the development of an understanding of how human visible behavior functions communicatively may be made more apparent. This discussion will also contribute, it is hoped, to an assessment of the present 'state of the art' in the field.

2.0.   The concept of 'nonverbal communication'

2.1.   *The purview of 'nonverbal communication'*

We have said that we have sought to include in this volume just those articles from *Semiotica* that have addressed the phenomena of what is commonly referred to as 'nonverbal communication'. Anyone taking this term literally, however, might reasonably ask why it is that this collection does not include such papers as Taylor's 'Nonverbal communication systems in Native America' (Taylor, 1975) or why it does not include papers on such nonverbal communication systems as national flags (Weitman, 1973; Pasch, 1975), architecture (Eco, 1972; Wallis, 1973; Ghioca, 1975), traffic signs (Studnicki, 1970) or dancing (Ikegami, 1971; Lasher, 1978; Hanna, 1979). In fact articles on these matters were not even considered for inclusion in this collection, nor were such papers as those by Stokoe (1974a), Cicourel and Boese (1972), or Williams (1977) on sign languages. This is because we have been guided by a certain usage that the term 'nonverbal communication' has come to have. A brief consideration of the nature of this usage and how it has come about will prove a useful way of opening up some of the fundamental theoretical issues with which this field of inquiry must be concerned.

The term 'nonverbal communication', as it is currently employed, is most frequently used to refer to all of the ways in which communication is effected between persons when in each other's presence, by means other than words. It refers to the communicational functioning of bodily activity, gesture, facial expression and orientation, posture and spacing, touch and smell, and of those aspects of utterance that can be considered apart from the referential content of what is said. Studies of 'nonverbal communication' are usually concerned with the part these aspects of behavior play in establishing and maintaining interaction and interpersonal relationships.

It will be seen from this that there are three main limits governing the use of the term, its literal meaning notwithstanding. First, it is used mainly in reference to communications between persons who are directly present to one another. That is to say, it is used mainly in reference to communication that occurs when people are able to respond directly to each other's actions and are able to directly affect one another through such responses. It generally has not considered the various ways that people can communicate with one another when they are not copresent (cf. Sigman, 1979 for a discussion of communication between absent persons and Basso, 1974 for a discussion of the uses of writing for such communication).

Second, 'nonverbal communication' is generally considered to refer to communication as it is effected through behavior whose communicative significance cannot be achieved in any other way. From the point of view of the propositional significance of an utterance such as 'the cat is on the mat' it makes no difference whether I speak this or whether I present you with the proposition in written form. Furthermore, just the same information may be conveyed, whether I say it in Chinese, French, or Warlpiri. However, the communicative significance of the tone of voice in which I produce this utterance, the timing what I employ in making it in relation to the timing of the utterances of the others with whom I am in conversation, of the speed with which I pronounce the words, and so on, depends upon my recipient's apprehension of just those features. Whereas the proposition 'the cat is on the mat' is, one might say, 'detachable' from the means by which it may be conveyed to another, the messages conveyed by the features of the act of utterance itself are not detachable. It is to these 'undetachable' or 'embodied' aspects of communication that the term 'nonverbal communication' has usually been applied.

A third characteristic of 'nonverbal communication' is that messages that are at the center of interest (whether in fact conveyed by words or not), are typically those messages that are not given explicit formulation. They are the messages that may be inferred from or are implied by a person's actions. It is for this reason, in particular, perhaps, that such 'nonverbal' codes as sign language are not usually regarded as being part of the purview of 'nonverbal communication' studies. Sign language, like spoken language, is a vehicle for highly 'detachable' messages and it no more seems to 'embody' what it conveys than spoken language does. It can be considered abstractly, in its own right, and it is employed consciously for explicit communicational purposes.

2.2.   The emergence of 'nonverbal communication'

The term 'nonverbal communication' made one of its earliest appearances in the usage we have just outlined, as the title of a book by Ruesch and Kees (1956). This book was an attempt to present for the general reader the implications for the understanding of communication in human interaction of the conceptual discoveries of cybernetics and the mathematical theory of information. Cybernetics and the mathematical theory of information were developed in the context of computer technology and telecommunications engineering. However, the concepts involved were of sufficient generality that they had applications far beyond these particular fields. Wiener (1948), who pioneered cybernetics, and Weaver (Shannon and Weaver, 1949), who was an important contributor to the development of information theory, participated from an early date in discussions with physiologists, psychiatrists, psychologists, and other social scientists in which the implications of these ideas were explored (Von Foerster, et al., 1949–1953; Heims, 1977). Ruesch, a psychiatrist, was much influenced by this and, together with Gregory Bateson, an anthropologist, produced a pioneering discussion of human communication in these terms (Reusch and Bateson, 1951; see also Ruesch, 1953, 1955). Cherry (1957) provides a very useful survey of the development of information theory.

The notion of 'quantity of information' which the mathematical theory of information had evolved in the course of an endeavor to measure the efficiency of telephone lines, required a way of thinking about information without any

yes

reference to the nature of the messages transmitted. This meant that the information value of something could be considered regardless of the sorts of messages involved and regardless of whether any deliberate attempt to transmit messages had been made. This idea became important for the study of communication in human interaction for it led to the idea that *all* aspects of behavior that are detectable could be treated in information theory terms. *yes, even the patho-logical*
That is to say, the perspective of information theory, when applied to human behavior suggested that not only are such actions as speech and gesture to be considered as a signal, but all other aspects of behavior may be considered from this point of view as well, whether or not intended or designed to transmit messages. Weaver, one of the pioneers of information theory makes this quite clear when he writes (in Shannon and Weaver, 1949: 95): 'The word communication will be used ... in a very broad sense to include all of the procedures by which one mind may affect another. This , of course, involves not only written and oral speech, but also music, the pictorial arts, the theatre, the ballet, *and in fact all human behavior*' (italics added).

This realization, that any aspect of human behavior could be treated as a source of information, led to an expansion of what, in human action, could be considered relevant for an understanding of communication in interpersonal relations. It is not only what A *says* to B that sends messages to him, but it is also what A does. Ruesch appears to have been one of the first authors to make this explicit. He makes it quite clear that he does so as a result of his attempts to apply notions from information theory to human behavior in interaction (Ruesch and Bateson, 1951; Ruesch 1953, 1955).

As Ruesch also pointed out, however, although ordinary practical actions can be viewed as conveying information just as utterances and gestures may do, it is also clear that they do so in a different way. Ruesch suggested that this difference could best be expressed in terms of the notions of encoding that information theorists had proposed. Messages can be encoded either *digitally* or *analogically*. In digital encoding discrete units, such as numbers, are employed. In analogic encoding (sometimes referred to as iconic encoding) there is a continuous relationship between the events serving to convey information about something and whatever it is that is being conveyed. Words and other discrete symbol systems, it seems clear, convey their messages digitally. Actions, whether practical or expressive, convey their messages analogically. Emotional expressions seem to vary continuously with the intensity of the emotion. However, verbal statements about emotion, though they can encode differences in intensity of feeling, must do so in a discrete, arbitrary, and therefore digital, fashion. Ruesch (1955) provided a detailed comparison between what he termed 'nonverbal codification' and 'verbal codification'. He not only pointed out that humans could transmit information to one another according to these apparently quite different principles, but he also suggested that the kind of information transmitted analogically (or non-verbally) was different from the information transmitted in words. Thus Ruesch supposed that analogically encoded information pertained to the immediate state of feeling of the individual. It served to provide information about the state of the relationship between interacting individuals, whereas digitally or verbally encoded information pertained to propositions about states of affairs that were not necessarily tied temporally and spatially to the prevailing interaction. Ruesch maintained, as many others also came to do (cf. Sebeck, 1962; Watzslawich, et al., 1967; Wilden, 1972) that nonverbal or analogic codifications were the first kinds of codifications to be mastered in the developmental sequence, that they were more closely related to phylo-genetically older modes of codification and that they were less fully subject to conscious control.

The view of 'nonverbal communication' that emerged from this line of thought has been very succinctly expressed by Gregory Bateson. He has written:

> ... our iconic communication serves functions totally different from those of language and, indeed, performs functions which verbal language is unsuited to perform. ... it seems that the discourse of nonverbal communication is precisely concerned with matters of relationship — love, hate, respect, fear, dependency, etc. — between self and vis-a-vis or between self and environment and that the nature of human society is such that falsification of this discourse rapidly becomes pathogenic. From an adaptive point of view it is important therefore that this discourse be carried on by techniques which are relatively unconscious and only imperfectly subject to voluntary control (Bateson, 1968: 615).

2.3.   Some consequences of the concept

The formulation of the notion of 'nonverbal communication' in these terms had several consequences. First of all, as we have suggested, it led to the investigation from a communicational point of view of many aspects of be-havior that hitherto had been overlooked. Not only did it provide a new perspective for the long tradition in psychology of studies of 'expression', expecially facial expression, but it also meant that aspects of behavior such as gaze direction, posture, and interpersonal spacing came to be studied. It came to be realized, as a consequence of this notion, that the way in which one person came to adjust or alter his behavior when in the presence of another was to be understood neither in purely practical terms nor in terms of some notion of 'expression', where this is thought of simply as the translation into external forms of inner states. It came to be realized that persons in each other's presence guided their behavior in relation to one another in the light of information the behavior of each provided. Thus actions of all sorts came to be viewed in terms of their possible significance as message in interaction. All aspects of behavior, it appeared, could function communicationally.

The notion of 'nonverbal communication' has also encouraged the view, however, that communication by actions can be studied independently of words. It has suggested that there is a great divide in human communication, with words on one side and all else on the other. Yet, as soon became apparent, the sharp distinction which the concept of 'nonverbal communication' proposes is impossible to sustain. It is impossible to establish consistent criteria by which to distinguish 'words', and what they convey, from everything else (cf. Lyons, 1972). Furthermore, from a functional point of view, as developments in the analysis of the pragmatics of language (Bates, 1976; Ochs and Schiefflin, 1979), 'conversation analysis' (Schenkein, 1978), and 'discourse analysis' (Coulthard, 1977) have made abundantly clear, verbal utterance plays as crucial a role in the establishment and maintenance of interactive relationships as nonverbal aspects of human action do. At the same time, as studies of gesture show, aspects of human action that are definitely not 'verbal' may nevertheless serve in the place of words or may serve as an essential component in referential communication (see 5.0 below).

3.0. Theoretical and methodological issues

A further drawback of the concept of 'nonverbal communication' is that it tempts one to think of it as one sort of communication only. Yet in fact, as Ruesch pointed out in his early discussions, there are many different kinds of 'nonverbal language'. Ruesch (Ruesch and Kees, 1956) suggested that a distinction should be drawn between what he called *sign language, action language*, and *object language*. Sign language for him 'includes all those forms of codification in which words, numbers and punctuation signs have been supplanted by gestures'. *Action language* refers to the communicative consequences of ordinary actions. Object language 'comprises all intentional and nonintentional displays of material things'. Ruesch goes on to point out that not only do these different 'languages' differ from one another in mode of codification and in whether they comprise actions or the results of actions but they also differ in terms of the kinds of information they convey. He suggested, for example, that the kinds of messages which 'action language' convey are different from the kinds of messages that are conveyed by the explicit use of gestures (or 'sign language', in his terms).

The paper by Ekman and Friesen, which is the first in the present collection, addresses just this issue. Ekman and Friesen suggest that their article 'may make it more difficult to conceive of nonverbal behavior as a simple, unified phenomenon'. In this paper they set out to suggest that in considering any action (by implication from a communicational perspective) one must see that it may differ in how it was acquired, the circumstances in which it may be employed, and in how it encodes whatever message it may convey. They further propose five 'types' of nonverbal behavior: 'emblems', 'illustrators', 'affect displays', 'regulators', and 'adaptors'.

In several respects, as we shall explain shortly, this paper has been superseded by later work by Ekman and his colleagues. We reprint it here, however, both because it has some historic importance and because it touches on several theoretical issues that are still very much with us. Several of these issues will now be discussed.

3.1. Intentionality and the concept of communication

We may begin with the question of how the term 'communication' is to be used. Ekman and Friesen suggest that behavior should only be considered 'communicative' if the person providing it *intended* thereby to convey some message, regardless of whether or not anyone else is able to receive the message. Ekman and Friesen suggest that behavior, from the point of view of its meaning, may be either idiosyncratic (its meaning known only to one person) or shared. Behavior which has shared meaning is said to be *informative*, insofar as it conveys information to someone other than the producer, but such behavior will only also be *communicative* if the producer intended to send the information that was received. Ekman and Friesen further suggest that behavior may be said to be *interactive* if, within the context of an interaction, it can be shown to influence the behavior of the other.

Ekman and Friesen offer these terms and these distinctions in opposition to a use of the term communication which they attribute to Birdwhistell and Scheflen (cf. Birdwhistell, 1970; Scheflen, 1973) in which it is supposed that 'all behavior is communication'. This way of using the term 'communication' arose, as we have seen, as a consequence of developments in information theory which showed that, from this point of view, any event can be treated as signal. Writers such as Birdwhistell and Scheflen, and also Bateson and Ruesch, use the term 'communication', thus, to refer to the process of conveying information in any form whatever. This is the sense of the term intended by Shannon and Weaver (1949) and other information theorists. In this sense of the term, the focus is entirely upon the effect of the behavior upon a perceiver of it. No reference is made to the intentions or motives or causes that may lie behind the behavior that is perceived to occur. Ekman and Friesen, however, are proposing to include in the definition of the term 'communication' a reference to what was intended by the person in producing the behavior in question. This is a different, and more restricted, sense of the term than the usage of it that had come to be proposed by those influenced by communication theory.

Ekman and Friesen are not alone in wishing to make this restriction. MacKay (1972) and Wiener, et al. (1972) have advanced a very similar argument. If 'communication' is conceived as the general process of information transfer, however, the question of the intention that governs the production of any item of behavior is irrelevant. Furthermore, a little consideration shows that the 'message intended' is not determinable. The communicative intent of an action is thus not suitable as a criterion for deciding what should and what should not be considered as 'communication'. *yes*

The question of intentionality is irrelevant because, as we have seen, to witness a behavioral event is to receive information and the process of communication has, accordingly, taken place, regardless of what was intended by the production of the behavior. The question of intentionality is not determinable because whatever message an actor may have intended to convey there are always messages at other levels that are conveyed simultaneously. Which of these the actor may have intended can never be known for certain. If P thumbs his nose at Q, not only does he thereby convey an insult to Q but also, insofar as it is recognized as a deliberate act, the nose thumbing conveys the message that P intended to address Q and, that he did address him is itself a message, when this is taken in contrast to its absence (cf. Ruesch and Bateson, 1951: 213). In addition, actions never occur except within a context both of other actions and of a situation, and the relationship an act bears on its context is itself a source of message. If the nose thumbing is done at a party in the context of a jocular conversation it will have a very different significance from its occurrence in the course of an argument in the street. There are, thus, many 'layers' of message for any distinguishable act, and many of these layers cannot be part of the actor's intent, at least not as he is able to report it. Certainly, we can never be in a position to determine the extent to which they are. Thus for those writing from an information theory perspective, because the issue of whether or not a certain meaning was intended or not cannot be determined it cannot be put forward as a criterion for deciding which sort of action is to be admitted as 'communicative' and which is not.

If analysts of behavior from a communicational perspective cannot use the intention that may or may not lie behind any action as a criterion for considerating the action's relevance for communication, it nevertheless remains that participants in interaction themselves act as if such intentions are readily discernible. Participants in interaction continually distinguish actions that are 'intentional' from those that are not. Actions that are considered 'intentional' are responded to very differently from those considered to be involuntary or merely done in the course of something else and not designed to send any particular messages. Goffman (1963) makes this point very clearly in his useful discussion of the differences between what he calls 'given' and 'given off' information. Information that is 'given', according to this discussion, is information that is provided through actions such as utterances and gestures that are regarded by those who receive them as fully intentional. The messages of such actions are considered to be fully the consequences of the other's intentional action. He is held fully responsible for them and he may be challenged and held to account. Information that is 'given off', however, is information which is, as Goffman puts it, 'gleaned' from another. It is picked up from the other, regardless of whether he intended it or not. The individual from whom information is gleaned is not deemed to be fully responsible for it and he is not liable to be challenged about it and if he is, he is often able to deny having any intention of providing it. Information that is treated as 'given off' by someone includes information that is provided by his bodily size, shape and coloring, his clothing and adornments, his manner of moving and speaking.

Information that is made available in this way, though not treated as being provided deliberately in the same way that information provided by spoken utterance or gesture is treated, may nevertheless be under some degree of control of the individual. People often go to considerable lengths to insure that their clothing, appearance, and manner will create the right 'impression'. It will be seen, thus, that what is actually intentional and what is not need not by any means be the same as the way it is treated by others. Accordingly, although it is fruitless to try to decide what messages a person *actually* intends to convey and what he does not, how people treat each other in this regard should nevertheless be carefully attended to. That is, it is very important to consider what aspects of the flow of information participants treat *as if* they have been provided intentionally and what aspects they treat *as if* they are unintentional. As a corollary to this, it then becomes a matter of great interest to investigate which features actions must have to be treated as intentional and which they must have to be treated otherwise. To the best of my knowledge, this question remains one to be investigated systematically, although Weiner, et al. (1972) offer some interesting suggestions that are relevant here.

3.2.   *Origins, codes, and categories*

A second issue Ekman and Friesen refer to is the issue of the 'origins' of behavior. By this they mean the question of how a pattern of behavior came to be established in an individual's repertoire: has it arisen because it is 'wired in' or has it been acquired through a process of learning? An important part of the work Ekman has done, much of it subsequent to the publication of this article, has been concerned with this question. In particular, he has sought to answer this question with respect to facial expressions of emotion. His basic position on this issue is discussed at some length in the paper we reprint here in the section devoted to 'affect displays'. The thrust of the work has been to argue that facial expressions of emotion are manifestations of biologically determined patterns of action. He distinguishes six basic patterns which are considered to be discretely different from one another, which he suggests can occur in certain blends or combinations to generate a wide range of complex affect displays. Ekman offers in the present paper an early version of what he has come to refer to as the 'neurocultural' theory of affect display in terms of which cultural variations in facial expressions are to be explained in terms of cultural variations in 'display rules' – rules which govern when and how affect displays may be manifested. Ekman's work on this issue may be found in Ekman, Friesen, and Ellsworth (1972) and Ekman (1973), which also contains useful reviews of many aspects of work on facial expression. The most recent statement of the neurocultural theory of affect is provided in Ekman (1977). A detailed discussion of the whole issue of the origins of facial expression in relation to evolutionary theory is to be found in Ekman (1980).

The other issue of theoretical importance which Ekman and Friesen discuss is that of 'coding' by which they mean the 'principle of correspondence between the act and its meaning'. This issue is, of course, central to the development of any theory of communication; we have already seen that the distinction between 'analogic' and 'digital' encoding provided the starting point for the whole concept of 'nonverbal communication'. We shall delay any further discussion of it until section 5.0 of this Introduction, however, when we shall deal with some of the issues of coding in reference to gesture. The discussion of coding which Ekman and Friesen offer in the paper reprinted here, it will be seen, has relevance chiefly to the phenomena of gesture.

Ekman and Friesen's paper is perhaps most well known for its definition of five categories of nonverbal behavior termed 'emblems', 'illustrators', 'adaptors', 'affect displays', and 'regulators'. A critique of these categories would be out of place in this Introduction. However, it will be noted that in setting up such categories Ekman and Friesen appear to believe that it is possible to assign actions to such categories on an exclusive basis. For example, of their category 'regulator' they write: 'though a whole variety of behaviors can serve regulatory functions, we reserve the lable *regulators* for those behaviors which do not fit into one of our other categories; that is, for behaviors which seem only to regulate' (p. 90).

I would like to point out how markedly such an approach differs from the one suggested by the theory of communication initiated by Ruesch and Bateson under the influence of information theory. From this approach it would be argued that a final assignment of any item of behavior to an absolute category of communicational function cannot be accomplished because any distinguishable act participates simultaneously in a multiplicity of communicational functions. From this point of view, absolute behavioral types cannot be established. From Ekman and Friesen's paper one comes away with the view that people have repertoires of sharply distinguishable types of acts that can, independently of the contexts of their occurrence, be labled exclusively as either an emblem or an illustrator or an adaptor, or the like. However, from the point of view of a communications theory approach, no action can be understood to 'be' anything, apart from the context in which it occurs, including the perspective in terms of which it is dealt with by its recipient. No action can ever absolutely be a regulator, an emblem, an illustrator, and nothing else. To refer once again to P thumbing his nose at Q: such an act is indeed highly coded and when shown outside of any context of discourse it may be recognized as an insulting gesture (Morris, et al., 1979). Yet, though P, in using this gesture in an address to Q, may insult him, he is also performing an act which takes its place in whatever turn structure the interactional event in which it occurs may have, and it thereby participates in regulating the interaction. It will also be performed in a particular manner or style which will certainly convey information about P's affective state, among other things. Rather than establish it in an absolute category, therefore, the alternative approach we here refer to would recommend that it be considered in terms of how it participates in the multiplicity of communicational functions which the situation calls for.

We have considered Ekman and Friesen's paper at some length because it ranges over so many of the theoretical issues that are quite central to the field we are concerned with here. It is perhaps surprising to note that efforts comparable in scope to that of Ekman and Friesen are rather few. Ruesch's papers we have already mentioned and, as we have already indicated, the discussion in Ruesch and Kees (1956) remains one of the most comprehensive theoretical discussions in the field. Other essays on a comprehensive theoretical treatment for 'nonverbal communication' include the discussion by Wiener, et al. (1972), discussions by Scheflen (1963, 1964, 1966, 1973, 1979, 1980), by Birdwhistell (1970), and in Sebeok, Hayes, and Bateson (1964). Important treatments may also be found in Hinde (1972), especially in the chapters in that volume by MacKay, Lyons, and Leach. Gregory Bateson's general position may be found in Ruesch and Bateson (1951), Bateson (1970), and in Bateson, Weakland, Haley, and Jackson (1956). Bateson addresses himself explicitly to the phenomena of nonverbal communication in Bateson (1968). Lipset (1980) provides a useful guide to Bateson's thinking as a whole.

3.3. *Differential functions of 'nonverbal communication'*

Ekman and Friesen, by proposing that behavior may be classified into several different categories, imply that different aspects of human behavior convey different kinds of information. The kinds of information conveyed by gestures — well-bounded, short-lived actions, perceived as fully deliberate — are different from the kinds of information conveyed by bodily posture, for example. A systematic treatment of this point has not been attempted anywhere, although it would seem well worth an exploration. The article by Poyatos on 'The forms and functions of nonverbal communication in the novel' is relevant to this, however. He discusses the uses that novelists make of descriptions of various nonverbal aspects of behavior of their characters. He shows how this may be used in a variety of ways to convey certain kinds of information about the characters. A further exploration of this, for which Poyatos' article merely provides a beginning, might be quite illuminating from the point of view of this question. Folklorists interested in gesture have made use of literary sources (e.g., Taylor, 1971) and there are a few papers that have looked at the use of nonverbal communication by writers (e.g., Marks, 1971, 1974). The present article offers, however, a systematic exploration of the many different uses which novelists make of nonverbal communication and it provides a starting point for more extensive investigation of this question.

Poyatos also discusses the question of the technical problems faced by a writer who would like to portray manners of speech, nuances of facial expression, or gesture. He points out that there are few devices available to the writer, other than verbal description, by which an author may portray various aspects of speech, such as pauses, hesitancy, rapidity, and volume, and by which he can indicate certain aspects of intonation and stress, and these are all quite limited. Furthermore, there are no conventional devices by which kinesic aspects of behavior can be written down.

Poyatos seems to consider this a lack, and he sees no reason why conventional written forms for at least some of the extralinguistic aspects should not be invented (cf. Poyatos, 1975). However, one may perhaps also approach this observation from another point of view. One may ask why it should be that there are well-established devices for writing down the verbal aspects of speech as well as a limited set of devices for other aspects of speech which are essential to a clear comprehension of the written text, but no devices for anything else. To convey tone of voice, pattern of facial expression, mode of gesture, the author can only resort to written description. To accompany one's written text with a kinetic and paralinguistic score might be a device useful for playwrights, but it seems that this would not at all be in the interests of the improvement of literary power. This is because scores or notation systems are instructions for action. A written text has a different function to perform. It serves as a means of transmitting images and concepts by way of language.

3.4. *Problems in the description of behavior*

Any attempt to analyze how the behavior of participants in interaction functions communicatively necessarily involves an analysis of the behavior itself. Some means have to be found of giving an account of the body movements, orientations, and patterns of facial actions that occur with a view to specifying which dimensions and which variations in such actions are significant. A major branch of the study of language, *phonetics*, is concerned with the analysis of the nature of the acoustic signal of speech and how it is produced. One can envisage an analogous development for the study of other aspects of behavior that function communicationally. How is such a task to be approached? There have been numerous attempts to develop notation systems for various aspects of behavior besides speech, including gesture (Austin, 1806; Birdwhistell, 1952; Stokoe, 1960; West, 1960) and facial expression (Kendon, 1975b; Blurton-Jones, 1971, Birdwhistell, 1952). Choreographers, perhaps, have advanced the art of movement notation the farthest. Labanotation, developed by Rudolf Laban (Laban, 1950, 1956; Hutchinson, 1966) is one widely used system which is quite comprehensive and may well prove capable of adaptation to any situation where there is a need for the transcription of bodily movement. Eshkol-Wachmann (Eshkol and Wachman, 1958) is another system that is also comprehensive and developed for choreographic purposes. It has been applied to the study of behavior of interaction among animals, notably jackals (Golani and Zeidel, 1969; Golani, 1976) and it has also been used for the description of signs in Israeli sign language (Cohen, Namir, and Schlesinger, 1977). Key (1977) provides a useful compilation, with a very extensive bibliography, of the many different attempts that have been made in the notation of bodily movement. Rosenfeld (in press) provides a recent critical survey.

The article by Freedman that is reprinted here is a review of Paul Bouissac's *La Mesure des Gestes* which, as Freedman makes clear, is a very useful discussion of many different movement notation systems. It is also an attempt to argue for an approach to the recording of movement in a completely objective and digital form by way of a mechanical recording device. The device that Bouissac proposes in this book is a device that would serve, for him, as an ideal solution to the problem of the recording of bodily movement as a preliminary to the analysis of its communicational function. As explained by Freedman, Bouissac maintains that any notation system is bound to distort the phenomena being notated. Particular aspects are bound to be given emphasis because of the biases the investigator's theoretical outlook impose on his perceptions. Furthermore, a notation system involves an analysis of the behavior in terms of units of some sort. Since behavior is actually continuous, the segmentation of this continuous flow into units which any notation system will involve constitutes another way in which the theory implicit in the notation system is imposed upon the phenomena to be studied. Many writers have been concerned with this problem, of course, and numerous attempts to find a way of making unbiased notations have been made. Bouissac reviews and criticizes many of these attempts and offers a solution of his own.

Freedman provides a very perceptive discussion of the problems inherent in any project of this sort. He points out that, for example, quite apart from the fact that it is probably impossible to devise a machine that will objectively record all aspects of behavior, if something like this were to be achieved we would have no way of interpreting such a record. Bouissac's totally objective record, it appears, seeks to describe bodily movement as a succession of spatial volumes. Freedman reminds us that the human body is organized into distinguishable anatomical systems that tend to be employed differentially with respect to different communicational functions. A totally nonselective recording system that did not make such anatomical discriminations would present insuperable problems for interpretation.

Second, Freedman points out that the significant units of behavior in terms of which people respond to one another are units of action of which bodily motion may only be a part. Thus he suggests that the significance of a given movement of, say, an arm or hand movement may depend upon whether it is embedded within a spoken discourse structure or not. No sense could be made of any purely objective recording of movement in itself, separate from everything else, until we are able to establish its context with respect to whether or not it is focused interaction, for instance, and whether or not it is produced by the recipient of an utterance or by the producer, and how it may be integrated with the verbal content of the utterance that is produced.

This last point relates to Freedman's conclusion in which he argues that the first step in any analysis of behavior is not to record everything as objectively as possible. Rather, our first step must be to seek to establish through 'naturalistic observation' those aspects of behavior that appear to be most relevant for a given functional system. Once this step has been taken, but only then, does it become appropriate to engage in some kind of precise measurement. For example, it becomes appropriate to undertake precise quantitative analyses of spatial arrangement in interaction only after naturalistic observation has suggested how in different kinds of interaction of situations different spatial arrangements are employed. Only when we have established the relevance of studying patterns of action in the face does it become appropriate to devise a means of recording facial action in greater detail.

In short, in approaching the phenomenon of behavior in interaction, one must first develop an hypothesis about its organization and use this hypothesis to specify which aspects of behavior are relevant and which are not. Greater precision of analysis, involving refined techniques of recording of selected aspects of behavior, comprises a later step in the analytic process. The first step in analysis is not to record 'everything' objectively. The first step in analysis is to develop some notions about its organization.

The last paper included in Part I of this collection is also concerned with the problem of behavioral description, in this case that of the behavior of one functional — anatomical system (or 'instrument' of human communication) — the face. The face has always been recognized as an instrument of human communication second only to that of the voice and it has attracted scientific attention at least since the work of Sir Charles Bell (1847). Bell, an anatomist, sought to establish by what muscular movements the different emotional expressions of the face were produced. Such a project was also pursued by Duchenne (1862) who, by stimulating the muscles of the face electrically (first in the faces of recently guillotined criminals, later in the face of a man who could feel no pain) provided a photographic atlas of all of the different facial expressions produced by different muscular contractions.

The cues by which people recognize emotion in the face has been a persistent theme of subsequent investigations, given special impetus by the work of Darwin (1872) who claimed that facial expressions were the products of evolution by natural selection and that therefore both the production of expressions and their recognition was a matter of instinct rather than of learning.

The relevance of the face to the study of human communication is thus not in doubt. However, it presents enormous problems of description, as Seaford indicates. Seaford reviews a number of the schemes that have been developed for the description of the face but concludes that none of these allow for the replication of description. If the descriptions are given in terms of the actions of the facial muscles, however, such replicability, he argues, can be achieved.

Since Seaford's paper was published, Ekman and Friesen have published a very detailed system for describing facial action, firmly grounded in an analysis of the visible effects of muscle contractions. They have specified some 35 'action units', defined in terms of the actions of specific groups of facial muscles, and it is in terms of these that their descriptions are made. Their system is notable for the great detail in which the criteria for the recognition of these 'action units' have been spelled out, making it possible for analysts of facial action to be systematically trained. Ekman and Friesen acknowledge that it was Seaford who finally convinced them that an anatomically based description was both feasible and necessary (Ekman and Friesen, 1976: 4). Their system replaces earlier attempts which had not been based on the musculature (for example, the so-called FAST system reported by Ekman, Friesen, and Tomkins, 1971). Accounts of Ekman and Friesen's Facial Action Coding System (FACS) may be found in Ekman and Friesen (1976, 1978). Studies making use of it have only begun to appear quite recently. They include Oster (1978) and Liddell (1978). For a review see Ekman and Oster (1979).

Seaford's paper also includes a study of a 'facial dialect'. It has often been suggested that people in different cultural regions or people who belong to different subcultural groups have characteristically different ways of holding their faces. Seaford's study, highly preliminary though it remains, is in fact the only one so far to have been published that deals with this aspect of facial behavior. It remains an intriguing field for further study.

4.0. Organization of behavior in face-to-face interaction

It is to the study of how human action functions communicationally within the context of the face-to-face social encounter that most of the work on 'nonverbal communication' has been directed and, as we have suggested, this area of concern seems to be a defining feature of the field. In Part II we present eight papers which together cover a representative sample of the various problems that have been tackled.

The limit of the concern with face-to-face interaction may be taken to be the limit of *copresence*, a term used by Goffman (1963) to refer to any occasion where two or more persons are able to detect each other's presence by their unaided senses. Goffman has further proposed a useful distinction between 'unfocused' and 'focused' interaction. 'Unfocused' interaction refers to the mutual adaptation in behavior that people display whenever they are merely copresent to one another. 'Focused' interaction refers to any instance, however fleeting, where two or more individuals come to jointly sustain a common focus of attention.

4.1. Strangers in public places

We begin the present Part with two papers that are concerned mainly with unfocused interaction. They are both concerned with how people adjust to one another as they pass by one another in pedestrian settings.

Such passings by represent one kind of minimal interaction and have attracted attention for this reason. As Collett and Marsh point out, managing to avoid collisions with others is necessary for efficient living in urban environments. It thus presents itself as an issue for investigation.

The starting point of all of the recent studies of pedestrian interaction is

Goffman's discussion (Goffman, 1963, 1971). In this discussion Goffman proposed a specific pattern of gaze management by which people could both acquire information about the direction of movement of the other and also avoid indicating to the other that they were an object of special curiosity or design. This presents a point of particular interest to students of interaction: the eyes, as has been widely observed, are of great salience, being at once the principle means by which we acquire information about the environment around us, including others, and also the principle clue by which someone else may gather the direction of our attention and interest. For this reason the management of the glance in the pedestrian setting seems to be a matter of particular delicacy. One must look at others so as to avoid bumping into them. However, in these circumstances, we must not look at them too directly, lest they think they are of special interest.

Collett and Marsh report a pattern of gaze in pedestrians in the setting which they studied which suggested that passers by picked up information about each other's direction of movement from the movement of their body and they did not, as Goffman suggested, assess each others intentions by exchanging glances. Givens selected for observation only those pairs of pedestrians who had either already looked at one another or who had actively begun to avoid the other as they approached on the sidewalk. He thus confined his observations to how people handled one another when each had already been noticed. His findings suggested that, in these circumstances, when persons unacquainted with one another behaved in a way that indicated definite attention to the other, avoidance displays could be observed.

Studies of patterns of gazing and facial expression in passing pedestrians using film analysis have been conducted by Carey (1978, 1979). He shows that there is considerable variation in looking patterns in these circumstances. He finds that there is little difference between the way pedestrians behave when passing one another and the way they behave when by themselves. He does find, however, that when males and females pass by one another they are more likely to look at one another than are same-sex passers by.

It should be pointed out that no one has systematically compared settings in studies of this sort. Carey's observations were conducted on the campus of a large university. Givens' observations were conducted in several different settings, but all of them crowded and urban. Goffman does not specify any particular settings for his observations. Yet, as Goffman's discussion also reminds us, the way in which unacquainted individuals are likely to treat one another as they pass one another in public tends to vary considerably with circumstances. In lonely places passers by often offer each other gestures of greeting and in very lonely places, such as the North African desert, passers by, who are very rare, are under an obligation to approach and greet one another (Youssouf, Grimshaw, and Bird, 1975). This has been interpreted in terms of the idea that in such circumstances people need to reassure each other about their intentions. Further studies of how passing strangers deal with one another should include systematic comparisons of settings.

4.2. Greetings

Greetings, which may most simply be defined as an exchange of actions by which two individuals acknowledge that they have seen each other and by which each provides the other with information about how the other will be treated, have received considerable attention in recent years. They offer themselves as a seemingly well-defined unit of interaction and they are, of course, functionally important. It is through the ritual of the greeting that people define their social access to one another. Schiffren's paper on the handshake is a fine example of how a single ritual act, commonly part of greetings, but found in other (related) contexts as well, can be traced out in its various usages. It may be compared with Goffman's treatment of hand-holding as a 'tie-sign' (Goffman, 1971) and MaCannell's treatment of hat-tipping (MaCannell, 1973). Schiffrin's article may be said to exemplify an approach to the study of a particular behavioral form and the contexts in which it occurs. Other studies of particular behavioral forms that are used in greetings include Eibl-Eibesfeldt's studies of the eyebrow flash (1972, 1975). Descriptions of other greeting gestures may be found in H. Ling Roth (1889), Firth (1973), and Eibl-Eibesfeldt (1974).

There are also a number of studies which have analyzed the structure of the greeting encounter as it unfolds in time. Thus Kendon and Ferber (1973) and Kendon (1980b) have proposed that greeting encounters may be divided into a number of stages. For example, it is pointed out that the accomplishment of a 'close salutation' such as a handshake depends upon the accomplishment of a number of preceding steps. To begin with the two parties to the greeting must sight one another. Following this, there must be a step which serves as a pregreeting agreement to greet. This is often explicitly ratified in a 'distance greeting'. This will then be followed by a phase in which the participants must cooperate with one another to establish the appropriate spatial and orientational relationship for carrying out the 'close salutation', whatever it is to be. They must also exchange signals by which they can agree on the sort of close salutational ritual that is to be performed. Youssouf, Grimshaw, and Bird (1975) have offered an analysis of the greetings that occur between Tuareg travellers when they pass one another by in the desert. They show how these greetings likewise go though a number of steps which are very similar to those proposed by Kendon and Ferber (1973) and Kendon (1980b), whose studies were done largely with greetings filmed at a garden party near

New York City. Schiffrin (1977) has offered an analysis of encounter openings based on encounters in urban situations. She has confined herself mainly to a consideration of the verbal exchanges of such encounters but once again the steps she suggests are closely comparable to those suggested by Kendon and Ferber (1973) and Youssouf, Grimshaw, and Bird (1975).

Most studies of greeting have concentrated on what Kendon and Ferber (1973) refer to as the *close salutation*. There are many scattered descriptions of such salutations which, as the compilation of H. Ling Roth shows, display a remarkable diversity. Discussion by Firth (1973) and Eibl-Eibesfeldt (1974b, 1980), however, do suggest that there are certain principles by which this diversity can be accounted for. In particular, the close salutation serves as a means whereby relative status between greeters is expressed. Despite superficial differences, the underlying principle, the greater the disparity of status, the greater the asymmetry of the performances of the respective participants, seems to be widely upheld. Studies of variations in greeting rituals within a particular society, relating this variation to specific kinds of social relations have been presented by Kommenich (1977) and Goody (1972).

Greetings, as Goffman (1971) has shown, may be regarded as a species of access ritual of which departure rituals are the converse. There are far fewer studies of departure than of greeting, however. Apart from the descriptions that may be found in ethnographic reports, departures have been studied systematically by Sacks and Schegloff (1973), Knapp, et al. (1973), Albert and Kessler (1976, 1978), Laver (1975), Lockard, et al. (1978), and Deutsch (1979).

4.3. Coordination of action in interaction

Greetings have a number of functions. While they always can be interpreted as serving to mark an increase in social access, they also serve as a way of establishing a common frame or perspective for the focused encounter. This shared frame may be established in a number of ways but the ritual of greeting exchanges provides an important way of doing this. The focused encounter, of which conversation is an instance, is the locus of most of the work that has been done on the communicational functions of behavior. One issue that has attracted particular attention is that of the coordination of turns at talk. One approach to this question has been to suppose that such coordination may be achieved through a mutual adjustment of the temporal pacing of utterances. Chapple (1940), in his pioneering work on the measurement of the temporal patterning of utterances in conversation, proposed that coordination is achieved through the mutual adjustment of each participant's interactional rhythm. Chapple's work led to the development of diagnostic studies of 'interaction styles'. Such styles were measured in terms of the temporal patterning of utterances in conversation and in terms of the way in which individuals differed in how they responded to changes in the temporal patterning of utterances of their partners. Accounts of this work are to be found in Chapple, Chapple, and Repp (1955) and in Chapple (1949, 1970). Readers interested in this approach should also consult the work of Matarazzo and his colleagues (e.g., Matarazzo, Wiens, Matarazzo, and Saslow, 1968). For more recent work see Jaffe and Feldstein (1970) and the collection of papers in Seigman and Feldstein (1979).

A second approach to the problem of coordination of action in interaction is one that begins by considering features of behavior in an interactant that could serve as cues to another as to whether a participant was about to begin an action such as a turn at talk, whether they were to shortly bring it to an end, whether they were to continue it, or whether they were to pass by an opportunity to take their turn at talk. Kendon (1967), for example, reported observations on the regularity of patterning of gaze direction changes in two-person conversations and presented evidence that such patterning functioned in the process of coordinating 'floor apportionment' or 'turn taking' as it is now usually referred to. Duncan, in a series of papers (Duncan, 1972, 1973, 1974, 1975), has pursued the issue of turn-taking cues with great thoroughness and has shown that several different aspects of both bodily movement and speech may function as turn-taking cures, either singly or in combination. This work is well summarized in Duncan and Fiske (1977). Other contributors to this line of investigation include Wiemann and Knapp (1975), Beattie (1978, 1979) and Rutter and Stephenson (1977) and Rutter et al. (1978). These last two authors have continued the investigation of the turn-taking function of gaze. Their findings suggest that Kendon's widely quoted conclusions on this point may need considerable modification.

De Long's study, which we include here, is of interest because it is one of the few studies of turn-taking cues in children (another study is by Dittman, 1977). De Long's study is also of interest because he provides detailed case by case analyses which show the diversity of kinesic action that can function as a turn-taking cue. He finds that the four- and five-year-old children he studied did not offer turn-initiation cues as much as they signalled turn-termination cues. Whether or not this is a general phenomenon for children of that age is not known. However, it is of interest in that it suggests that children of that age may not monitor the turn-taking structure of the conversation they are engaged in in the same way that older individuals do. There is room here for a considerable amount of study.

It should be observed that all of the studies of turn-taking cues hitherto have been confined to studies of two-person interactions. In encounters of three or more participants one is immediately confronted by new problems.

For example, where there are two or more potential speakers competing for the same stretch of time for talking, devices for establishing turn-queues may arise. A particular individual may have to establish a recipient for himself from among the several that are potentially available. Individuals will also have to indicate to whom their utterance is addressed. None of these arise in the two-person situations that have so far been the locus of turn-taking studies.

4.4.   *Direction of gaze in interaction*

We have already mentioned the study by Kendon (1967) in which changes in gaze direction in relation to the occurrence of spoken utterances in conversation was studied. This paper suggested not only that interactants thereby signaled their intent with regard to beginning or ceasing to speak but it also suggested a number of other functions of gaze in conversational interaction. This paper, along with the work of Nielsen (1964), Exline (1963), and Argyle and Dean (1965) comprise the beginnings of the systematic study of gaze in interaction. Since that time, the study of gaze has grown very considerably indeed. Argyle and Cook's (1976) survey lists some 400 references. Another recent survey, Harper, Wiens, and Matarazzo (1978), which is somewhat less comprehensive, covers 243 references.

The peculiar feature of gaze, which is part of what makes it so attractive for researchers is that it is at once the means by which persons gain important information about what is going on around them and also, because they can be seen by others to be looking, a means by which others can tell from where in an environment an individual is deriving visual information. The direction in which the eyes are pointing provides an index of the direction of the individual's attention.

The paper by Argyle, et al. seeks, by measuring under different conditions the amounts of time P spends looking in the direction of a conversational partner, to assess the extent to which gaze serves in six different functions that the authors' outline. By using a one-way screen the authors are able to vary who can see whom during the conversation. Assuming that all six of the different functions suggested may be operating at once, the authors are able to make predictions about how the amount of time spent looking in the direction of the interlocutor will vary from one circumstance to another.

Argyle, et al.'s paper illustrates a highly experimental approach to the study of the functions of gaze. Beattie's paper that follows represents what can be achieved through the close analysis of naturally occurring interaction sequences that have been recorded on video-tape. In this paper, Beattie reviews the various functions of gaze that have been distinguished and he then focuses on the issue of how speakers pattern their lookings and lookings away in relation to features of their speech which can be related to the planning processes that underlie speech production. In general he finds that the cycling of looking-at–looking-away from one's interlocutor is coordinated with the organization of planning and production phases of the utterance. During planning phases, indicated by pausing, the speaker looks away. During speech production the speaker looks at the interlocutor. He also finds that listeners offer head nods or other listener responses at the boundaries of speech units preceded by planning pauses, indicating that speech is dealt with by the recipient in units that are similar to those in terms of which it is produced. Beattie's findings are in accord with those reported by Kendon (1967) and Allen and Guy (1977).

It will be clear from several places in Beattie's discussion, however, that it is insufficient to treat gaze merely as a symptom of inner processes. Its fluctuations cannot be accounted for on the basis of this alone. Since, as we have seen, gaze is taken by others to be an index of direction of attention, individuals come to deploy their gaze as a means of signalling their attention. Gaze direction becomes a device for displaying attention direction. Focused interaction is characterized by a jointly sustained focus of attention between the interactants. Accordingly, rules arise governing the ways in which gaze direction (among other aspects of behavior) is to be deployed in interaction if a proper show of attention in the situation is to be sustained (cf. Goffman, 1957). Thus patterns of gaze direction in interaction must also take into account the rules that govern the use of gaze within interaction and they must also take into account the strategies that the participants are following in interaction. As Duncan and Fiske (1977) have argued, if there are rules that govern behavior, participants in interaction will relate to those rules in various ways. How they pattern their behavior in relation to what is expected in the situation is part of the way in which interactants establish and sustain a particular 'line' (cf. Goffman, 1955). A full account of the use of gaze in interaction, thus, as indeed for other behavior as well, requires that these rules of usage be made explicit.

4.5. *Multiple levels in communicational functioning*

The last two papers included in Part II, though very different from one another in several respects, are both thoroughly interactionist in their outlook. That is to say, they attempt to look upon the behavior that may be observed in a strip of social interaction strictly from the point of view of how it serves the interaction in question. Rosenberg establishes this as the second of his two methodological tenets. Kendon is less explicit but he presents his paper as an attempt to approach patterns of action in the face from the point of view of their interactive functions rather than as symptoms of emotions or feelings. Second, in both of these papers a single specimen of interaction is analyzed for its internal structure. In both cases it is supposed that the interactional event that has been recorded is highly structured and it is the aim of the analysis to display that structure.

The paper by Kendon (which is unusual because it is one of the few studies of a kind of interaction *other than* conversation), seeks to show, by examining the patterning of action in a kissing round in relation to the pattern of changes in the facial expressions of the participants, that it is possible to see how these changes in facial expression appear to function as signals regulating the progress of the action. The analysis deals with facial expression, thus, not from the point of view of its functions as a symptom or manifestation of emotion but from the point of view of how facial expression may function interactionally. There are still few papers that take this approach to the face and much remains to be done in this regard. Kendon offers a brief discussion of this issue and he refers to a number of previous studies of the face which have approached it from this point of view. More recent papers on the face which include discussions of its interactional functions include papers by Zivin (1977a, 1977b) and Ekman (1980).

In considering the 'kissing round' it was found that several different phases or subroutines of interaction could be distinguished. The question was raised as to how the two individuals moved from one subroutine of action to another. It was shown that these changes in interactional routines are joint accomplishments of the two participants and that they are achieved through the operation of patterns of action that serve to presage or forewarn of the impending change of action. Each, thus, is given the opportunity to be appraised of how the other would like to change the interaction before the interaction actually changes. Of particular interest is the suggestion, in this analysis, of how, as changes in interaction routines are negotiated, the action that serves to forewarn of these changes can be seen both to refer to what pattern of action the participant would next like to move to, and also to the context or organizing frame within which the action is to be approached. Specifically, in this case, it is found that actions which presage a change of interactional routine carry with them a reference to the frame 'kissing' if the kissing round is to continue, but they carry with them a reference to a frame of action beyond kissing, or separate from it, if the interaction is to change from kissing to some other activity.

The issue that underlies this discussion is fundamental for the understanding of human interaction. Human beings are not constrained to respond to each other's actions in specific ways, as courting sticklebacks or herring gulls are said to be constrained. For humans, any action of P can be interpreted in a number of possible different ways by another. Therefore by doing X, P is in no position to be sure that Q will do Y. Yet is it impossible for P to formulate a coherent program of action without some basis for supposing that it will be responded to in a particular way. Thus the establishment of conditions in which one may be able to expect particular responses in one's partner seems to be a fundamental condition of coherent interaction. A basic problem for interactants, therefore, is to become assured of what sort of action they can expect from another. A common organizing perspective or 'frame' must be established, a context of interpretation which both can share (Goffman, 1961, 1974). It is a feature of human interaction, accordingly, that in producing an action a participant not only thereby responds to the other, but he also conveys information about what sort of a response his response is and thus he informs the other as to what sort of an action he took the other's action to be. Participants in interaction may be said to be continuously instructing each other in what they take the other's frame of interpretation to be, at the same time as they instruct the other in how their own actions are to be taken. This aspect of communicative functioning has been referred to as 'metacommunication', a concept first formulated by Bateson (Ruesch and Bateson, 1951).

Rosenberg, in his paper, makes explicit use of the concept of metacommunication. In his analysis, Rosenberg suggests how statements or actions by one participant in the interaction at once can be seen as 'responses' to the previous action or statement by the other, but simultaneously they can be seen to refer to the common framework in terms of which the interaction is now being governed. They also can refer to the framework in terms of which P expects his action to be interpreted. Thus, for Rosenberg, anything Q does in the context of an interaction situation serves both as a contribution to the interaction and as a contribution to the definition of the situation. Rosenberg's analysis provides us with a vivid illustration of the way in which actions in interaction serve to refer to a multiplicity of levels of meaning. This, as we have stressed more than once, seems to be a fundamental feature of human interaction.

It is also to be noted that Rosenberg shows how both verbal utterance, gesture and expressive action, and practical actions, such as drinking coffee or reading, are fully orchestrated in the communicational structure. His paper is a nice demonstration of how there is no separate 'nonverbal communication', only a number of distinguishable infracommunicational systems.

4.6. *Further issues in methodology*

The papers by Kendon and Rosenberg both proceed on the assumption that human action is interpreted in interaction as if it functions communicationally at multiple levels simultaneously. They also both propose that meaningful conclusions can be drawn from the analysis of very short stretches of interaction. Rosenberg's analysis is built upon a study of a ninety-second stretch. Kendon's analysis is based upon two segments, each approximately two minutes in length. It could be argued that no conclusions of any sort could possibly be drawn from such short samples. Since the intensive analysis of short specimens of interaction constitutes a particular tradition in human interaction study (cf. McQuown, 1971; Birdwhistell 1970; Bateson and Mead 1942; Scheflen 1963, 1964, 1966, 1973; Kendon 1970, 1972b, 1977; Mc-Dermott, Gospodinott, and Aron 1978; McDermott and Roth, 1978) it is worth briefly dwelling on the justification for it.

First of all it is assumed by those who work in this tradition that all aspects of behavior are potentially functional in communication, a point already dealt with in our discussion of the paper by Ekman and Friesen. It will be seen that if this assumption is made, then it becomes important to be able to examine as many aspects of behavior as possible. This means that one must rely upon specimens of interaction, that is, films or video-tapes of interactional events, which allow one to examine and reexamine the behavior which constitutes them.

It is further supposed that in human communication the interactional significance of an action, how it is dealt with by a coparticipant, cannot be understood except when it is considered in context. This means that, in approaching the analysis of the specimens at hand, rather than singling out one or more aspects of behavior for separate measurement and analyzing their patterning statistically over a large sample, one proceeds by examining several different aspects of behavior to see how they pattern in relation to one another in the context of a given interactional event.

It is assumed that human interaction is highly organized. It is assumed that people in interaction behave in highly organized, patterned ways. If we can dissect the pattern into a single episode, we thereby illuminate the way in which this pattern manifests itself in other episodes that are comparable. Rather as a critic may seek to display how a poem works by a careful analysis of the way in which its various components have been organized in relation to one another, so one may take an interactional episode and show how it works by analyzing the patterning of its component parts.

The critic, in analyzing a poem, presupposes that there is a separable unit, a poem, that is distinguishable for analysis. In the same way, the analyst of the structure of interaction presupposes that a structural unit, an 'interactional episode', of some sort can be distinguished for analysis. Rosenberg is not explicit about the criteria he followed in deciding what segment of the fifteen-minute video-tape to select for his analysis, however it is clear that he begins it when the conversation is initiated and he terminates it when something new has begun. Kendon was not free to select his own material but, being provided with footage collected by someone else, finds episodes within it. In fact the cameraman who took the footage in question undertook his own segmentation: he started the camera whenever he saw 'action' and stopped it when the 'action' was over.

The question of how to distinguish episodes of interaction is one of the fundamental questions of the field. Discussions of the problems involved with proposals for various kinds of solutions may be found in Barker and Wright (1955), Barker (1963), Pike (1967) and Frake (1964, 1975). For an attempt to investigate the segmentation of behavior as a problem in perception see From (1971) and Newtson (1976a, 1976b).

The assumption must always be made, it will be seen, that 'episodes' may be selected which have a certain recognizability as a unit and that these episodes have a structural coherence. A detailed analysis of what goes on inside the episode will reveal the nature of this structural coherence and will thus show how human action is deployed in its production. Thus the analysis of single episodes can be highly illuminating for our understanding of how human action is meaningful in face-to-face interaction.

A further, and final, point may now be made. Just as the analyst relies upon his common understanding, initially, in selecting an episode for analysis, so he also relies upon it in carrying out the analysis. The assumption that human action is intelligible for the analyst in just the same way that it is intelligible for the participants in the interaction being analyzed runs right through papers such as those by Rosenberg and Kendon. In this respect the method employed is reminiscent of the central methodological tenet of 'conversation analysis' (Schenkein, 1972; Schegloff and Sacks, 1973; Sacks, Schegloff, and Jefferson, 1974). Here the analyst seeks to establish the procedures or methods which the conversationalists themselves are following as they construct conversations with one another that are, for them, intelligible. This is done by looking at how the conversationalists themselves interpret one another's utterances. Such interpretation is revealed, according to this view, in the very responses that the participants provide one another. This method can only be followed, however, if the analysts themselves share the very same procedures of the conversationalists they are studying. What is sought after is a detailed account of the methods being followed by an appeal to specific examples. This is just the method that Rosenberg himself is following (cf. McDermott and Wertz, 1976, for another discussion of this point).

5.0. Gesture

5.1. Background

A *gesture* is usually deemed to be an action by which a thought, feeling, or intention is given conventional and voluntary expression. Gestures are thus considered to be different from expressions of emotion, involuntary mannerisms, however revealing, and actions that are taken in the pursuit of some practical aim, however informative such actions may be. Gestures have been studied somewhat separately from other aspects of behavior and in recent years they have attracted relatively little attention. This may be because they are perceived as being too close to language to command the interest of most students of 'nonverbal communication'. Linguists, however, find gestures altogether quite different from language and although several have recognized their interest and importance (cf. Sapir, 1949; Pike, 1967; Bolinger, 1968) none have undertaken to investigate them.

In some circumstances gestures can become elaborated into a more or less fully developed linguistic system. In these instances we speak of a sign language. Sign languages are most widely used by the deaf (Stokoe, 1980a). However, they have also developed in circumstances where speech is proscribed by social custom, as among Australian aborigines (Meggitt, 1954; Umiker-Sebeok and Sebeok, 1978; Kendon, 1980c) or among Cistercian monks (Barakat, 1975). They have also developed as a *lingua franca* in situations where many different languages come into contact, as appears to be the case among the Plains Indians of North America (Taylor, 1975). For most people most of the time, however, gesture seems to serve only as an adjunct to speech. In relation to verbal expression, it appears to be used as a means of decoration or dramatization, occasionally as a substitute, but only in a sporadic and seemingly unsystematic way.

In the present collection we have only included papers which deal with everyday gestures. Papers on sign language and other gesture systems which have appeared in *Semiotica* have not been considered because, as we explained in (1.0) above, the field of 'nonverbal communication', as it has emerged in recent years, does not comfortably contain them. However, any collection dealing with sign languages and gesture systems would also have to include papers on 'everyday' gestures such as those considered here. Sign languages are but special elaborations of gestural expression. They do not constitute a completely separate phenomenon.

Studies of gesture are very old. The earliest tradition concerned with them is that associated with the Classical and Mediaeval study of Rhetoric. Rhetoric was, since Quintilian (1922 [100]), divided into five divisions, of which the fifth, *pronunciatio*, was concerned with the actual conduct of the orator as he delivered his speech. This included a careful consideration of gestures and Quintilian's treatise on rhetoric includes an extensive discussion. The first book to have been devoted entirely to gesture appears to have been the volume by Bulwer (1969 [1644]). This book includes not only detailed recommendations on how the orator should conduct himself but also, in the first part of the volume, an attempt to establish a natural history of gesture. In this, Bulwer was inspired by Francis Bacon who had proposed in his *Advancement of Learning* that a science of gesture should be established.

The influence of Bulwer's treatise is not clear (Cleary, 1959, 1974), but a later work by Gilbert Austin (1966 [1802]), which probably is indebted to Bulwer, was very influential in the development of Rhetoric in the nineteenth century (Robb and Thorssen, 1966). By that time, Rhetoric was almost exclusively confined to matters of delivery, or Elocution, as it was termed (Howell, 1959). Austin's book, which included a well developed notational system for gesture, was important as a source for the development of the teaching of gestures.

Gesture was also of considerable interest to philosophers concerned with the question of the nature and origin of language, especially in France during the Enlightenment. Condillac, for example, urged that gesture, especially as it was used by the deaf, provided an important key to the understanding of this question. He considered gesture to have been the foundation of the first form of language (Condillac, 1974 [1756]; Aarsleff, 1976). In France, at that time, there was also widespread interest in the possibility of a universal language and the natural language of gesture seemed to offer itself as a possible candidate for such a language (Knowlson, 1965, Seigel, 1969).

This interest in gesture was preserved and extended in the late nineteenth century in the work of anthropologists and psychologists when the whole question of language origins was reopened under the impact of Darwin's work (Stam, 1976). Both E. B. Tylor, a 'founding father' of modern anthropology, and Wilhelm Wundt, who was perhaps the first experimental psychologist, devoted considerable attention to gesture. Both of them gave careful consideration to the use of gesture by the deaf. Both thought that, in the study of gesture, it was possible to observe a kind of transition from natural expression to conventionalized symbolic action, and thus to glimpse the process by which language could have arisen (Tylor, 1878; Wundt, 1973 [1921]). Mention should also be made of the work of Mallery. He made a thorough study of the sign language of the North American Plains Indians, but he had a broad concern with the whole phenomenon of gesture, and indeed with the whole phenomenon of the representation and expression of thoughts in media other than words. His best known publication (Mallery, 1888) remains one of the best general discussions of this topic.

After the beginning of the twentieth century the systematic study of gesture appears to have gone into decline. Although a large number of scattered and unsystematic accounts of specific gestures have accumulated (Hayes, 1957), there appear to be only six scholarly books on gesture published in English between 1900 and 1979. Of these, Critchley (1939), Efron (1941), and Morris, et al. (1979) are the most important.

Critchley's (1939) volume is a short survey of the whole field containing much valuable reference to the Classical interest in gesture (a second edition, Critchley [1977], has appeared but its usefulness is gravely impaired for it completely lacks a bibliography). Efron's book is justly famous for it provided the first and, until recently, it remained the only thorough observational study of gesture. Efron's concern was to examine gesturing styles in two contrasting U. S. immigrant cultural groups — East European Jewish and Southern Italian — and to compare their styles with the gesturing styles employed by assimilated descendants of these two groups. He showed not only that the Italians and the Jews differed markedly in their style and use of gesture, he also showed that the assimilated descendants had lost much of their distinctive styles and had adopted the style of the majority culture. In the course of this study, which was well ahead of its time in methodology (and in some ways has yet to be equalled), Efron offered many acute observations on the nature of gesture. He provided an initial classification of gestures which has formed the basis for the distinctions that Ekman and Friesen offer in their own classification of gesture. Morris, et al. (1979) is a study of a small selection of 'symbolic gestures' or emblems in which geographical variations in their usages and meanings have been studied in various places in Western Europe. It is a pioneering attempt to examine systematically the cultural variations found in this form of communication.

Efron, a student of Boas, approached the study of gesture from the perspective of cultural anthropology. He saw it as a cultural product, part of the shared system of communication codes of a culture. In this he proved to be a precursor of the tradition later developed by Birdwhistell who, in founding the field of kinesics (Birdwhistell, 1952), must be seen as the next most influential figure in the development of the study of gesture (See Kendon, 1972a for an assessment). Birdwhistell's program was to establish the study of bodily movement as a communicative code, analogous to language. He proposed to use the concepts and methods then employed in the analysis of languages to this purpose. He hoped to show that the kinesic code could be seen as an hierarchically organized system of kinemes, kinemorphs, and kinemorphic constructions. He thus resisted the idea that one could isolate a set of 'gestures' and treat them separately, as many authors have sought to do. Though his work has remained largely programmatic, it has nevertheless exerted considerable influence in serving to draw attention to the possibility of studying body motion communication codes. Recent students of gesture, such as Saitz and Cervenka (1972) and Green (1968) have clearly been much inspired by Birdwhistell, even if they have not followed his method.

Interest in the phenomenon of gesture has lately begun to revive. Hewes (1973a, 1973b, 1977) has restated the view that language-like communication first emerged in the course of human evolution in gestural form, speech being a later development. His well-argued essays on this topic have provided an important impetus to the recent reopening of discussion on the question of language origins (Harnad, Steklis and Lancaster, 1976; Hockett, 1978). Interest in gesture has also revived as a consequence of the recent surge of studies in sign languages of the deaf, especially American Sign Language. The linguistic study of sign language was pioneered by Stokoe (1960), but it is only within the last five years or so that sign language studies have really developed (Klima and Bellugi, 1979; Wilbur, 1979; Siple, 1978; Lane and Grosjean, 1980; Stokoe, 1980a, 1980b). The climate now seems ripe for some major advances in our understanding of this mode of expression.

Efron, as we have already mentioned, distinguished between a number of different types of gesture. On the one hand, he distinguished gestures which are produced concurrently with speaking. These included ideographic gestures which are said to diagram the logical structure of what is being said; indexical gestures, in which something being referred to is pointed at; pictorial gestures, in which something that is being referred to is sketched out or in which an action is referred to by a pattern of movement; and batons, in which movements are made that beat time to the rhythm of the speech. On the other hand, he recognized symbolic gestures or emblems which can be produced in the absence of speech and stand for something in their own right and can function as an utterance. Ekman and Friesen offer a slightly revised version of this classification (and Ekman [1977] offers a further revision) but they, like Efron, retain the distinction between gestures which can serve independently of speech and those which only occur in close association with it. Those which occur in association with speech have been termed *illustrators* by Ekman and Friesen and under this term they subsume ideographs, pointers, pictorial gestures, and batons as subtypes of this general category. Gestures which can function independently of speech, which have a stable form, they term *emblems*.

The first four papers in Part III of this collection are concerned mainly with emblems as these would be defined by Ekman. The last two papers are concerned with well-circumscribed acts which have many of the functions of gesture but which do not really fit well with any of the categories that have so far been offered. We include them here, for not only are they useful studies in their own right but they also allow us to raise the question as to what is and what is not to count as a 'gesture'.

5.2.   *Emblematic gestures*

The first article in this section is a review by Poyatos of Saitz and Cervenka's *Columbian Gestures* which serves a useful discussion not only of this book and of a similar book on Spanish gestures by Green but also of Efron's work. Poyatos is concerned with pointing out the various considerations of method that should guide anyone who sets out to construct an inventory of emblematic gestures. There are now a number of such inventories available. Besides those mentioned by Poyatos, lists of emblems have been published for Italy by di Jorio (1832), Munari (1963), and Cocciara (1932); for North African Arabic by Barakat (1973a); for France by Wylie (1977); for Western Kenya by Creider (1977), and for Iran by Sparhawk (1978), whose paper is reprinted here. Poyatos' comments on method would apply to most of these inventories. The ways in which these lists have been constructed are quite diverse and usually only sketchily referred to. Systematic comparative studies of emblematic gestures, which are much needed, will require a greater degree of systematicity in the elicitation of these gestures.

The paper by Johnson, Ekman, and Friesen, which follows the paper by Poyatos, offers a systematic procedure for the elicitation of emblems and for establishing an estimate of the degree to which knowledge of such gestures is shared within a given population. Inventories collected by this method from different societies could, perhaps, be usefully compared. So far, only Sparhawk has published results using this method and her findings are discussed in the paper reprinted next. It should be noted that, in addition to following the kind of systematic procedure which Ekman and his colleagues outline, it will be important to address in detail the question of how samples of informants are to be constructed. Poyatos' remarks on this and other problems are well worth taking into account.

Sparhawk's study offers an important advance in the study of emblematic gestures. In this paper she seeks to establish a description of Persian emblems in terms of the set of features which discriminate them from one another. She attempts to establish the repertoire of 'cheremes' which the Persian emblem collection makes use of in their formation. In following this approach, she is adopting a mode of analysis which is borrowed directly from the analysis of the 'cheremic' structure of American Sign Language pioneered by Stokoe (1960). This enables Sparhawk to make some specific comparisons between an emblem repertoire and the system of gestures in sign language. The differences that she reveals she suggests arise because American Sign Language relies far more upon 'digital' encoding principles than do emblems, which, she says, are largely 'iconic'. She suggests that American Sign Language is 'digital' because it is a 'main' communication system. She implies that a 'main' communication system is more likely to employ 'digital' encoding principles because it has a larger repertoire of items that must be kept distinct from one another. This means that the features that serve to distinguish signs in a sign language tend to have contrastive significance only. They are not governed by the meaning of the sign. On the one hand, since emblems tend to occur separately from one another and not in complex sequences, and since there are fewer of them, they can still be formed according to 'iconic' principles. The features that characterize them in this case are retained because of their 'pictorial' value. In a sign language, on the other hand, a premium is placed upon making sure that the various signs in the repertoire are distinguishable from one another. Features which serve to do this will be retained, then, regardless of their 'pictorial' value. In this way a sign language, evolving out of a system of emblematic gestures, may be seen to change increasingly into a digital code.

The linguistic study of sign languages has grown markedly in recent years, as already mentioned. Despite the early writings on the subject of Tylor (1878), Mallery (1888) and Wundt (1973 [1921]), until the work of Stokoe (1960) it was widely supposed that sign languages were merely artificial devices for representing spoken language. It is now quite clear that a sign language such as American Sign Language follows its own principles of organization, largely independent of spoken language. Important sources for the modern study of sign language are Stokoe (1960, 1972, 1974a,b, 1980a, 1980b), Stokoe, Casterline, and Croneberg (1965), Friedman (1977), Siple (1978), Klima and Bellugi (1979), Wilbur (1979), and Grosjean and Lane (1980).

All of the work just cited has been concerned with American Sign Language, but other sign languages are now also being described including French (Sallagoity, 1975), French Canadian (Mayberry, 1978), Chinese (Yau, 1977), and Danish (Hansen 1975) and others. Besides such national sign languages, sign languages that have emerged locally have also been described. Washabaugh, et al. (1978) has reported on a sign language from Providence Island and Kendon has reported on a sign language from Papua New Guinea (Kendon, 1980a, in press a, b). Kuschel (1973) describes the remarkable case of a single deaf man on Rennell Island (British Solomans) who invented his own sign language so that he could communicate with those around him.

Many have recognized that when people are deprived of the capacity for speech they will resort to gesture and early students of sign language, such as Epée, Condilliac, Tylor, and Wundt, recognized that highly systematized gestural languages were the result. Recent work by Goldin-Meadow (Goldin-Meadow and Feldman, 1977) has not only revealed something of the processes by which such gestural communication emerges in children but also indicates that it will do so at a very early age.

There can be little doubt, then, that the propensity to use gesture as a means of linguistic communication is basic. The modern studies of sign language

show that when gestures are employed as the sole means of linguistic communication they quickly become organized into an autonomous system which
has properties that are strictly analogous to those found in spoken languages,
although differing in substance in important respects. Such gesture systems it
seems clear, however, are further elaborations of gestural usage. They are not
completely separate systems. Sparhawk by showing the applicability of a
'phonological' analysis of an emblem repertoire contributes to this point.
Sparhawk also shows, however, that an analysis of Persian emblems in terms
of a set of features that are fully contrastive throughout the entire system
cannot be achieved. With respect to some features, these serve to contrast
certain gestures with one another only when they are related to the meaning
of the gesture. She finds, furthermore, that with regard to movement patterns,
for which Stokoe, in his analysis of American Sign Language, established
twenty-four distinct movement cheremes, for her analysis it was more useful
to consider movement in terms of a limited number of parameters. This, she
suggests, is due to the fact that emblems are often 'iconic' or 'analogic' and
not encoded in a purely 'digital' fashion.

5.3.   The problem of 'iconicity'

Sparhawk's work on Persian emblems, it turns out, as well as recent work on
American Sign Language by Friedman (1977), Mandel (1977), and DeMatteo
(1977) and work by Washabaugh (1980) on Providence Island sign language,
contributes to the recent revision in thinking that has developed with respect
to the notion of 'iconicity'. This work has called into question the sharp distinction that is often proposed between 'arbitrary' or 'digital' encoding and
'iconic' or 'analogic' encoding. As we saw in the opening section of this essay,
Ruesch, following the conceptualization then current in information theory,
proposed two modes of symbolization in humans — analogic and digital —
which came to be equated with 'nonverbal' and 'verbal' communication, respectively. Ekman and Friesen, in their discussion of coding suggest that we
should consider three types of coding: 'intrinsic', 'iconic', and 'arbitrary'. It
is now becoming clear, however, that sharp distinctions of this sort are not
sustainable. As we shall see in a moment, indeed, the very notion of 'iconicity'
as a principle of coding has been called into question.

It is usually said that a gesture is 'iconic' if it in some way resembles that
to which it refers. Leaving aside, for the moment, the question of what might
be a proper criterion of 'resemblance', as Washabaugh (1980) has lately pointed
out, such a way of talking must, at best, be considered to be very loose. The
referent of a gesture is not to a specific object or particular action. It is always
a concept and concepts do not have concrete characteristics. A gesture in

which the index and middle fingers are extended forward away from the gesturer, with the hand held so that the palm faces toward the gesturer's median plane, the remaining fingers folded to the palm, occurs as an item in Sparhawk's list and it is said to refer to 'gun'. One is at once tempted to conclude that such an emblem is 'iconic' because it 'resembles' a gun. However, what the gesture refers to is the concept 'gun' and not to any particular object. Although it is true to say that there are certain features in common between the shape the hand here assumes and the shape of, say a revolver (the extended fingers 'modeling' [Mandel, 1977] the barrel of the revolver), there is no particular revolver which is serving as the object this gesture resembles. Furthermore, a revolver has many other features, and any one of these could have been selected as a basis for the gesture. The recognition that it was 'gun' that was intended by the gesture does not depend upon the gesture being 'like' any particular gun. It depends, rather, upon the fact that it serves to remind us of one of the features by which guns may be represented. However, that such a feature serves to denote 'gun' is purely a matter of convention. It does not come about through any connection of resemblance between gesture and referent, as the notion of 'icon' would have us believe.

When words fail us, or they cannot be used, we may resort to a variety of actions in an effort to produce one which will call forth the recipient's recognition of the concept we wish to convey. Gestural expression may, thus, employ highly variable forms. However, once agreement is reached about what was intended, the gestural form that was successful may become standardized. To the extent that it does so, it ceases to denote its referent in virtue of the recognition it induces in its recipient. It comes to denote its referent in virtue of a rule of agreement between user and recipient. (See Tervoort [1961] for some excellent examples of this process). Once this happens, the features which such gestures come to have are those featues that are needed to ensure that the gesture is recognized and distinct from others with which it might be confused. In form, thus, they are no longer 'motivated' by any relationship of resemblance and their apparent 'iconicity' is irrelevant to their semiotic functioning.

Because of the difficulties that have been shown to arise with the concept of iconicity (cf. Eco, 1976), Washabaugh has suggested that it be replaced with a concept of variability of expression or codedness (Washabaugh, 1980). Gestures that are highly coded, in this sense, are produced in the same way each time and they must possess specific features to be regarded as being correctly produced. Gestures with these properties can be described in terms of combinations of sets of contrasting features, as we have already seen. Gestures which show a low degree of coding, however, vary extensively in their form and serve to convey the concepts which they refer to in virtue of reminding the recipient of the features shared by the concept in question, as just explained above.

In the light of these considerations, it will be seen that it is no longer appropriate to speak of 'iconic' coding, on the one hand, and 'arbitrary' coding, on the other. Rather, one must recognize a dimension of codedness. Comparing items at either end of this dimension will suggest a sharp contrast, of course. However, it is possible to show, as we have seen, that gestures may occupy intermediate positions along this dimension. It also appears that once a gesture becomes established, it quickly moves up the scale of codedness. One of the intriguing features of the study of gestural communication is that it allows one to observe this transformation toward codedness taking place. It seems to offer itself as a model for the processes by which such highly coded systems as spoken language, with their apparently highly arbitrary sets of symbols, could have come to be established (cf. Frishberg, 1975).

5.4. Gestures, speech, and language

A systematic survey of emblems in different cultures will make possible the investigation of cultural variations in gestural forms. It will be seen that if emblems are highly coded forms it is likely that there will be considerable variation from one community to another. Johnson, et al. offer a few comments on some of these issues but neither they, nor Sparhawk, provide a thoroughgoing comparative study. We must await the accumulation of more data before such a study can be begun. Interested readers are referred, however, to the excellent pioneering study of Morris, et al. (1979), already mentioned. This has received discussion in Kendon (in Press c).

The paper by Kirk and Burton, however, opens up the question of comparing emblems between different cultural groups in a particularly interesting way. They seek to compare how members of two East African groups, the Kikuyu and the Masai, classify a set of emblems and the set of verbal glosses that are given for these emblems. They argue that if it is found that gestures themselves and the verbal glosses attached to them are classified in the same way, this would be good evidence that the gestures and the verbal glosses are both treated as labels for semantic units. However, if the gestures are classified in terms of their physical form, this would suggest that they function as meaningful actions only in context and they cannot be considered to be the functional equivalents of verbal forms. Kirk and Burton employ the triads test as a means of getting informants to provide judgements of degrees of similarity between the items studied. Nine Kikuyu and nine Masai emblems were studied. The authors find that, for both groups, gestures and verbal glosses are classified in closely similar ways. They conclude, accordingly, that gestures function in the same cognitive system as expressions for the same ideas as the verbal glosses. However, they find, in comparing the Kikuyu and the Masai groupings, that though the gestures and the verbal expressions are classified in the same way within each language group, each language group differs from the other in the organization of this classification. They conclude

... what appear to be the same emblems in terms of physical performance and elicited verbal labels are in fact distinct in the two language groups in terms of their cognitive organizations. That is, it appears here to be relatively inconsequential what the particular manifestation of the language: whether written, spoken or emblematic — the cognitive organization seems to be consistent within languages and inconsistent across languages. (p. 484)

Kirk and Burton's paper is the only one to my knowledge that explicitly addresses the question of the relationship between emblematic gestures and spoken expressions in this way. It shows clearly that more studies which do make this comparison are badly needed. The implication of Kirk and Burton's findings appears to be consonant with the view that, in our conceptualization of language we must consider, on the one hand, its cognitive organization, and, on the other, its various possible modes of manifestation. Until recently it has been widely held that speech is essential to any concept of language and that nonspeech forms of expression, such as writing and sign language, are but derivatives of spoken language structures. Studies of these nonspeech forms, however, now strongly suggest that they have their own properties. In the case of sign languages, as we have seen, it is quite clear that these need not be modeled on spoken language in any way. Teodorrson (1980) has recently proposed that we recognize that language be regarded as a system of several interrelated components of which the component concerned with its expression (the *delological* component, to use Teodorrson's term) must be considered to be as fundamental as all the others. From this point of view, then, gestural expression is but one of a number of alternate modalities of linguistic expression (delological forms) that a person has available. Speech is not to be regarded as a prior form of expression in all respects.

The question of the relationship between gesture and spoken language has also been approached through the study of gesturing that co-occurs with speech, or gesticulation, as we shall here term it. Efron provided the first attempt at a classification of the various ways in which such gesturing can relate to speech, as we have already mentioned. Detailed studies of the relationship between gesticulation and speech have been undertaken by Freedman and his colleagues (Freedman, 1972, 1977) by Baxter, Winters, and Hammer (1968), Sainsbury (Sainsbury 1955; Sainsbury and Wood 1977), among others. These studies are from the point of view of how gesticulation may be symptomatic of cognitive styles, modes of thought, or psychiatric condition. Kendon (1972b, 1975a, 1980d) has offered analyses of the way in which speech concurrent gesturing is organized in relation to the phrasal organization of speech and has argued that such gesturing must be considered a fundamental mode of utterance. McNeil (1979) and McNeil and Levy (in press) have developed this point of view further in studies which show that gesturing while speaking serves to express the underlying cognitive representations from which meaningful utterance units or 'syntagmata' (to use McNeil's term) are constructed.

From the point of view of how gesticulation functions in communication, curiously enough, little seems to be known. Graham and Argyle (1975) suggest an experimental approach to this question and they have shown, with respect to gestures that people make when they are describing the shapes of objects or figures, that such gestures can make a contribution to the understanding of such descriptions. Observational studies, such as those of Birdwhistell (1970), Slama-Cazacu (1976, 1977), and Sherzer (1973) have also demonstrated the communicative importance of speech-concurrent gestures.

Gestures have also been studied developmentally. The emergence of gesturing in the child is taken as an indication of the emergence of the child's capacity for symbolization. There have been studies of pointing (Werner and Kaplan, 1963; Anderson, 1972; Bates, et al., 1975; Scaife and Bruner, 1975; Murphy and Messer, 1977; and Lempers, 1979). Enactive and depictive gestures have been studied by Werner and Kaplan (1963), Kaplan (1968), Klapper and Birch (1969), Overton and Jackson (1973), and Jackson (1974). See also Michael and Willis (1968), Anderson (1972), Trevarthen (1977), and the papers in Lock (1978) by Clark, Lock, Nokony, Trevarthen and Hubley and Feldman, Goldin-Meadow, and Gleitman. Jancovic, Devoe, and Wiener (1975) report a study of the emergence of different types of speech associated gestures in children.

5.5.   What is a gesture?

The last two papers in this section differ from the others in that neither deals with actions that are usually classed as gestures. Yet they deal with specific actions which have clear communicational consequences.

Rosenfeld, et al. established a situation in which a 'teacher' conveyed feedback to a 'student' on whether the student's responses in a word-association task were correct or not by way of foot pedals that purportedly sent signals to the 'student'. In fact these pedals were inoperative, but the 'student', who could see their 'teacher' by way of a video channel, nevertheless learned the word-associations rapidly. Evidently the 'teachers' were indicating to the 'students' by subtle facial actions and head movements whether they were right or wrong. Rosenfeld, et al. set out to establish what these subtle cues were. They also went on to explore ways in which one might measure individual variation in sensitivity to such subtle cues. This paper is relevant to a number of issues. To begin with, it is a clear demonstration that people provide information to one another even when they are not aware of doing so. In itself this demonstrates the difficulty of employing a criterion of intentionality to establish what is and what is not a matter of communication (see the discussion in 3.2., above). Second, Rosenfeld, et al.'s study suggests the kind of methodology that one has to resort to when one is dealing with behavior that cannot be easily reenacted (because the people who produce the behavior were not aware of doing so). As a way of systematically establishing which aspects of action were serving to provide information in this situation, this study suggests a useful approach. Finally, Rosenfeld raises the question of sensitivity to the information provided by others. This is an issue that Rosenthal has explored in the development of his so-called PONS test (Rosenthal, 1979; Rosenthal, et al., 1979), however in this work the interest has been in developing a measure of general sensitivity to 'nonverbal communication' and exploring this as a personality trait. Rosenfeld, in contrast, is here seeking to establish the repertoire of subtle, but nevertheless conventionalized, acts that people produce and then to find ways of training people to recognize them.

Smith, et al., in their study of tongue-showing, are dealing with an action that is not recognized as a 'social' act at all. Whereas the facial movements Rosenfeld, et al. describe appear to be incipient versions of facial gestures such as smiling or turning the mouth down which are recognized by everyone as communicationally specialized, tongue-showing seems to belong to that class of action that is overlooked or regarded as 'autistic' or in any event is not recognized as a specialized communicational action. Smith, et al., by carefully observing the contexts in which tongue-showing occurs, suggest, nevertheless, that it does appear with some consistency. People show their tongues, according to Smith, et al., when they are engaged in a delicate operation of some sort and do not wish to be addressed socially. The authors conclude that the common thread of information that an observer could derive from observing tongue-showing is that the tongue-shower does not wish to be engaged in interaction. It is a mildly forestalling action, they suggest, which will serve to inhibit social approaches in others.

One general point that both of these papers raise is the question of where one is to draw the line in deciding what to count as a gesture. Rosenfeld includes in his analysis explicit gestures, such as headshake and headnod, but, as we have just noted, the subtler forms of action that were also highly informative to 'students', though provided by the 'teachers' out of awareness, nevertheless appear to be subdued versions of actions that would have been recognized as explicit gestures. Smith, et al.'s tongue-showings do not seem to fall into the class of gesture, although the reason is perhaps not immediately clear.

One approach to this problem is to consider it from the point of view of how a fellow participant in interaction makes the distinction. Kendon (1978) has suggested that participants in interaction readily sort out the behavior of others into behavior that is deliberate, fully intentional, and other behavior which they do not regard in this light. As Goffman's discussion of the issue of 'given' versus 'given off' information reminds us (see above in section 2.0), this is a distinction which is consequential for participants. It is a distinction that they make on the basis of manifest features of the behavior they are able to observe. One might do well to attempt to set about systematically exploring what these features are. The category 'gesture' is, in fact, a 'folk' category. Perhaps our question should not be: how can we establish clear criteria by which observers agree as to what is and what is not a 'gesture'? Rather we should ask: what are the ways in which interactants, in practice, classify behavior in others? We should seek first to explore the distinctions that participants themselves employ, and then investigate the features upon which such distinctions are based.

6.0. Conclusions

In the foregoing we have sought to bring forward the various issues that are raised by the eighteen papers included in this volume and to show their relevance to current discussions within the field of what has come to be known, almost by default, as the study of 'nonverbal communication'. We have sketched in the way in which the concept of 'nonverbal communication' arose and have suggested some of its drawbacks. We have dealt with the question of how 'communication' is to be conceived in the context of interaction and the important issue of deliberateness. We have reviewed some of the problems attendant upon the description of behavior and we have identified many of the leading matters of investigation in the structure of interaction. Finally, we have dealt with 'gesture' and some of the issues of coding that it raises.

It is hoped that it will be clear that this field of study, however it may be labeled, is very active and is but on the threshold of exciting theoretical and empirical explorations.

7.0. References

In addition to the references cited in the text we include below references to several of the more useful bibliographies that have appeared in recent years.

Davis (1972) deals with studies of human movement from several different points of view, including many references to the performing arts. Each paper listed is concisely abstracted. It is soon to appear in a revised and expanded version. Hore and Paget (1975) also provides abstracts for the papers it lists. It draws mainly from the recent literature of experimental social psychology. Key (1977) is the most comprehensive of all, listing over 2000 references, including many that are out of the way or of historic interest. It is preceded by several short chapters intended to guide the reader through the material. Ciolek, Elzinga, and McHoul (1979) is a selective bibliography organized with a view to showing that the study of the organization of face-to-face interaction may be seen as a distinct field. A substantial body of literature is considered, including many references to 'conversation analysis' and to pertinent literature in sociolinguistics as well as work that deals with the role of visible behavior in interaction. It is well indexed and it is preceded by a survey of the field by Kendon. Hayes (1957) is an older compilation of papers concerned with gesture. It includes many references to anecdotal accounts and to work on gesture by folklorists.

References

Aarsleff, H. (1976). Outline of language origins theory since the Renaissance. In *Origins and Evolution of Language and Speech*, S. R. Harnad, H. D. Steklis and J. B. Lancaster, (eds.), 4–13. (*Annals of the New York Academy of Sciences* 280).

Albert, S. and Kessler, S. (1976). Processes for ending social encounters: The conceptual archaeology of a temporal place. *Journal for the Theory of Social Behavior* 6: 147–170.

– (1978). Ending social encounters. *Journal of Experimental Social Psychology* 14: 541–553.

Allen, D. E. and Guy, R. F. (1977). Ocular breaks and verbal output. *Sociometry* 40: 96–99.

Anderson, J. W. (1972). Attachment behavior out of door. In *Ethological Studies of Child Behavior*, Cambridge: Cambridge University Press.

Argyle, M. and Cook, M. (1976). *Gaze and Mutual Gaze*. Cambridge: Cambridge University Press.

Argyle, M. and Dean, J. (1965). Eye contact, distance and affiliation. *Sociometry* 28: 289–304.

Austin, G. (1966 [1802]). *Chironomia or a Treatise on Rhetorical Delivery*. Carbondale and Edwardsville: Southern Illinois University Press.

Baker, C. and Padden, C. A. (1978). Focusing on the nonmanual component of American Sign Language. In *understanding Language Through Sign Language Research*, P. Siple (ed.). New York: Academic Press.

Bär, E. (1974). Context analysis in psychotherapy. *Semiotica* 10: 255–282.

Barakat, R. A. (1973a). Arabic gestures. *Journal of Popular Culture* 6: 749–793.

– (1973b). *Cistercian Sign Language*. Kalamazoo, Michigan: Cistercian Publications.

Barker, R. G. (ed.) (1963). *The Stream of Behavior*. New York: Appleton-Century-Croft.

Baker, R. G. and Wright, H. F. (1955). *Midwest and Its Children*. New York: Harper and Row.

Barroso, F., Freedman, N., Grand, S. and Van Meel, J. (1978). Evocation of two types of hand movements. *Journal Experimental Psychology: Human Perception and Performance* 4: 321-329.

Basso, K. H. (1974). The ethnonography of writing. In *Exploration in the Ethnography of Speaking*, R. Bauman and J. Sherzer (eds.). Cambridge: Cambridge University Press.

Bates, E. (1976). *Language and Context*. New York: Academic Press.

Bates, E., Camaioni, L. and Volterra, V. (1975). The acquisition of performatives prior to speech. *Merrill-Palmer Quarterly* 21: 205-226.

Bateson, G. (1968). Redundancy and coding. In *Animal Communication: Techniques of Study and Results of Research*, T. A. Sebeck (ed.). Bloomington and London: Indiana University Press.

— (1970). *Steps to an Ecology of Mind*. San Francisco: Chandler.

Bateson, G., Jackson, D. D., Haley, J. and Weakland, J. (1956). Toward a theory of schizophrenia. *Behavioral Science* 1: 251-264.

Bateson, G. and Mead, Margaret (1942). *Balinese Character: A Photographic Analysis*. New York: Special publications of the New York Academy of Science, volume II.

Baxter, J. C. Winters, E. P., and Hammer, R. E. (1968). Gestural behavior during a brief interview as a function of cognitive variables. *Journal of Personality and Social Psychology* 8: 303-307.

Beattie, G. (1978). Floor apportionment in conversational dyads. *British Journal of Clinical and Social Psychology* 17: 7-16.

— (1979). Contextual constraints on the floor apportionment function of gaze in dyadic conversation. *British Journal of Social and Clinical Psychology* 18: 391-392.

Bell, Sir Charles (1847). *The Anatomy and Philosophy of Expression as Connected with the Fine Arts*, 4th edition. London: John Murray. (Reprinted 1971 by Gregg International Publishers, Farnborough, England).

Birdwhistell, R. L. (1952). *Introduction to Kinesics: An Annotation System for Analysis of Body Motion and Gesture*. Washington, D.C.: Foreign Service Institute, U.S. Department of State/Ann Arbor, Michigan: University Microfilms.

— (1966). Some body motion elements accompanying spoken American English. In *Communication and Culture*, H. G. Smith (ed.). New York: Holt, Rinehart and Winston.

— (1970). *Kinesics and Context*. Philadelphia: University of Pennsylvania Press.

Burton-Jones, N. G. (1971). Criteria for use in describing facial expressions. *Human Biology* 43: 365-413.

Bolinger, D. L. (1968). *Aspects of Language*. New York: Harcourt, Brace and World.

Bulwar, J. (1969 [1644]). *Chirologia: or the Natural Language of the Hand and Chironomia: or the Art of Manual Rhetoric*. Carbondale and Edwardsville: Southern Illinois University Press.

Butterworth, B. and Beattie, G. (1978). Gesture and silence as indicators of planning in speech. In *Recent Advances in the Psychology of Language: Formal and Experimental Approaches*, R. N. Campbell and P. T. Smith, (eds.). New York: Plenum.

Carey, M. S. (1978). Does civil inattention exist in pedestrian passing. *Journal of Personality and Social Psychology* 36: 1185-1193.

— (1979). Gaze and facial display in pedestrian passing. *Semiotica* 28: 323-326.

Chapple, E. D. (1940). Measuring human relations. *Genetic Psychology Monographs* 22: 3-147.

— (1949). The interaction chronograph: Its evolution and present application. *Personnel* 25: 295-307.

— (1970). *Culture and Biological Man: Explorations in Behavioral Anthropology*. New York: Holt, Rinehart and Winston.

Chapple, E. D., Chapple, M. F. and Repp, J. A. (1955). Behavioral definitions of personality and temperament characteristics. *Human Organization* 13: 34–39.

Cherry, C. (1957). *On Human Communication*. Cambridge, Massachusetts: MIT Press.

Cicourel, A. and Boese, R. J. (1972). The acquisition of manual sign language and generative semantics. *Semiotica* 5: 225–256.

Ciolek, T. M., Elzinga, R. H. and Mchoul, A. W. (eds.) (1979). Selected references to coenetics. *Sign Language Studies* 22: 2–6, 23–72.

Cleary, J. W. (1959). John Bulwer: renaissance communicationist. *Quarterly Journal of Speech* 45: 391–398.

— (1974). Introduction. In *Chirologia . . . and Chironomia*, J. W. Cleary (ed.) Carbondale and Edwardsville: Southern Illinois University Press.

Cocchiara, G. (1932). *Il Linguaggio del Gesto*. Turin: Bocca.

Cohen, A. and Harrison, R. P. (1973). Intentionality in the use of hand illustrators in face-to-face communication situations. *Journal of Personality and Social Psychology* 28: 276–279.

Cohen, A. A. (1977). The communicative functions of hand illustration. *Journal of Communication* 27: 54–63.

Cohen, E., Namir, L. and Schlesinger, I. M. (1977). *A New Dictionary of Sign Language*. The Hague: Mouton.

Collis, G. M. and Schaffer, H. R. (1975). Synchronization of visual attention in mother-infant pairs. *Journal of Child Psychology and Psychiatry* 16: 315–320.

Condillac, E. B. de (1974 [1756]). *An Essay on the Origin of Human Knowledge: Being a Supplement to Mr. Locke's Essay on the Human Understanding*. New York: AMS Press.

Coulthard, M. (1977). *An Introduction to Discourse Analysis*. London: Longman.

Creider, C. (1977). Toward a description of East African gestures. *Sign Language Studies* 14: 1–20.

Critchley, M. (1939). *The Language of Gesture*. London: Edward Arnold.

— (1975). *The Silent Language*. London: Butterworth.

Darwin, C. (1872). *The Expression of the Emotions in Man and Animals*. London: John Murray.

Davis, Martha (1972). *Understanding Body Movement: An Annotated Bibliography*. New York: Arno Press.

— (1979). Laban analysis of nonverbal communication. In *Nonverbal Communication: Readings with Commentary*, S. Weitz (ed.). New York: Oxford University Press.

DeMatteo, A. (1977). Visual imagery and visual analogies in American Sign Language. In *On the Other Hand: New Perspectives in American Sign Language*, L. A. Friedman (ed.). New York and London: Academic Press.

Deuchar, Margaret (1978). Doing without word order and inflections: The case of British Sign Language. Paper presented to the fourth annual meeting of the Berkeley Linguistics Society, February 19.

Deutsch, F. (1947). Analysis of postural behavior. *Psychoanalytic Quarterly* 16: 195–213.

— (1949). Thus speaks the body: An analysis of postural behavior. *Transactions of the New York Academy of Science* 12: 58–62.

— (1966). Some principles of correlating verbal and non-verbal communication. In *Methods of Research in Psychotherapy*, L. A. Gottschalk and A. H. Auerback (eds.). New York: Appleton-Century-Croft.

Deutsch, R. D. (1979). On the isomorphic structure of endings: An example from everyday face-to-face interaction and Balinese Legong dance. *Ethology and Sociobiology* 1: 41–58.

di Jorio, A. (1832). *Mimica Degli Antichi Investigata nel Gestire Napolitano*. Naples: Stamperia del Fibreno.

44   Adam Kendon

Dittman, A. (1977). Development of conversation. In *Communicative Structures and Psychic Structures*, N. Freedman and S. Grand (eds.). New York and London: Plenum.

Duchenne, G. B. A. (1862). *Mechanisme de la physionomie humaine: ou analyse electro-physiologique de l'expression des passions applicable à la pratique de arts plastiques.* Paris: Renouard.

Duncan, S. (1972). Some signals and rules for taking speaking turns in conversations. *Journal Personality Social Psychology* 23: 283–292.

– (1973). Toward a grammar for dyadic conversation. *Semiotica* 9: 29–46.

– (1974) On the structure of speaker-auditor interaction during speaking turns. *Language in Society* 2: 161–180.

– (1975). Interaction units during speaking turns in dyadic face-to-face conversations. In *Organization of Behavior in Face-to-Face Interaction*, A. Kendon, R. M. Harris and M. R. Key (eds.). World Anthropology. The Hague: Mouton.

Duncan, D., Jr. and Fiske, D. W. (1977). *Face-to-Face Interaction: Research, Methods and Theory* Hillsdale, N.J.: Erlbaum.

Eco, U. (1972). A componential analysis of the architectural sign *column Semiotica* 5: 97–117.

– (1976). *A Theory of Semiotics.* Bloomington and London: Indiana University Press.

Efron, D. (1941). *Gesture and Environment.* New York: King's Crown Press. (Republished in 1972 as *Gesture, Race and Culture.* The Hague: Mouton).

Eibl-Eibesfeldt, I. (1972). Similarities and differences between cultures in expressive movement. In *Nonverbal Communication*, R. A. Hinde (ed.). Cambridge: Cambridge Unversity Press.

– (1974). *Love and Hate.* London: Methuen.

– (1975). *Ethology: The Biology of Behavior*, 2nd edition. New York: Holt, Rinehart and Winston.

Ekman, P. (1957). A methodological discussion of nonverbal behavior. *Journal of Psychology* 43: 141–149.

– (1976). Movements with precise meanings. *Journal of Communication* 26: 14–26.

– (1977). Biological and cultural contributions to body and facial movement. In *The Anthropology of the Body*, J. Blacking (ed.). London and New York: Academic Press.

– (1980). About brows. In *Human Ethology: Claims and Limits of a New Discipline*, M. Von Cranach, K. Foppa, W. Lepenier and D. Ploog (eds.). Cambridge: Cambridge University Press.

Ekman, P. (ed.) (1973). *Darwin and Facial Expression: A Century of Research in Review.* New York: Academic Press.

Ekman, P. and Friesen, W. (1972). Hand movement. *Journal of Communication* 22: 353–374.

– (1976). Measuring facial movement. *Environmental Psychology and Nonverbal Behavior* 1: 56–75.

– (1978). *Facial Action Coding System.* Palo Alto, Calif.: Consulting Psychologists Press.

Ekman, P., Friesen, W. V. and Ellsworth, P. (1972). *Emotion in the Human Face: Guidelines for Research and an Integration of Findings.* New York: Pergamon.

Ekman, P., Friesen, W. V. and Tomkins, S. S. (1971). Facial affect scoring technique: A first validity study. *Semiotica* 3: 37–58.

Ekman, P. and Oster, H. (1979). Facial expression of emotion. *Annual Review of Psychology* 30: 527–554.

Erickson, F. (1979). Talking down: Some cultural sources of miscommunication in interracial interviews. In *Nonverbal Behavior: Applications and Cultural Implications*, A. Wolfgang (ed.). New York: Academic Press.

Eshkol, N. and Wachmann, A. (1958). *Movement Notation*. London: Weidenfield and Nicolson.

Exline, R. V. (1963). Explorations in the process of person perception: Visual interaction in relation to competition, sex and need for affiliation. *Journal of Personality* 31: 1-20.

– (1978). Applications of semiosis to the study of visual interaction. In *Nonverbal Behavior and Nonverbal Communication*, A. Siegman and B. Pope (eds.). Hillsdale, N.J. Erlbaum.

Feldman, S. S. (1959). *Mannerisms of Speech and Gesture in Everyday Life*. New York: International Universities Press.

Feldman, H., Goldin-Meadow, S. and Gleitman, L. (1978). Beyond Herodotus: The creation of language by linguistically deprived deaf children. In *Action Gesture and Symbol: The Emergence of Language*, A. Lock (ed.). London: Academic Press.

Feleky, A. M. (1914). The expression of the emotions. *Psychological Review* 21: 33–41.

Firth, R. (1973). *Symbols: Public and Private*. London: George Allen and Unwin.

Frake, C. (1964). How to ask for a drink in Subanum. In *The Ethnography of Communication*, J. J. Gumperz and D. Hymes (eds.), 127-132. (*American Anthropologist* 66).

Frake, C. (1975). How to enter a Yakan house. In *Sociocultural Dimensions of Language Use*, M. Sanches and B. Blount (eds.). New York and London: Academic Press.

Freedman, N. (1972). The analysis of movement behavior during clinical interviews. In *Studies in Dyadic Communication*, A. Siegman and B. Pope (eds.). Elmsford, N.Y.: Pergamon.

– (1977). Hand, word and mind: On the structuralization of body movement during discourse and the capacity for verbal representation. In *Communicative Structures and Psychic Structures: A Psychoanalytic Approach*, N. Freedman and S. Grand (eds.). New York and London: Plenum.

Freud, S. (1914). *The Psychopathology of Everyday Life*. London: Ernest Benn.

From, F. (1971). *The Perception of People*. New York: Columbia University Press.

Friedman, L. (1977). *On the Other Hand: New Perspectives on American Sign Language*. New York: Academic Press.

Frishberg, N. (1975). Arbitraniness and iconicity: Historical change in American Sign Language. *Language* 51: 696-719.

Ghioca, G. (1975). A comparative analysis of architectural signs (applied to columns). *Semiotica* 14: 40-51.

Goffman, E. (1955). On facework. *Psychiatry* 18: 213-231.

– (1957). Alienation from interaction. *Human Relations* 10: 47-59.

– (1959). *The Presentation of Self in Everyday Life*. Garden City, N.Y.: Doubleday.

– (1971). *Encounters*. Indianapolis: Bobbs-Merrill.

– (1963). *Behavior in Public Places*. New York: The Free Press of Glencoe.

– (1971). *Relations in Public*. New York: Basic Books.

– (1974). *Frame Analysis*. New York: Harper and Row.

Golani, I. and Zeidel, S. (1969). *The Golden Jackal*. Tel Aviv: Movement Notation Society.

Goldin-Meadow, S. and Feldman, H. (1977). The development of language-like com-

Golani, I. and Zeidel, S. (1969). *The Golden Jackal*. Tel Aviv: Movement Notation in Society.

Goldin-Meadow, S. and Feldman, h. (1977). The development of language-like communication without a language model. *Science* 197: 401–403.

Goody, E. (1972). 'Greeting', 'begging' and the presentation of respect. In *The Interpretation of Ritual: Essays in Honour of A. I. Richards*, J. S. Fontaine (ed.). London: Tavistock.

Graham, J. A. and Argyle, M. (1975). A cross-cultural study of the communication of extra verbal meaning by gestures. *International Journal of Psychology* 10: 57-67.

Grant, E. C. (1968). Human facial expression. *Man* 4: 525-536.

Green, J. R. (1968). *Gesture Inventory for the Teaching of Spanish*. Philadelphia: Chilton Books.

Hanna, J. L. (1979). Toward a semantic analysis of movement behavior: Concepts and problems. *Semiotica* 25: 77-110.

Hansen, B. (1975). Varieties in Danish sign language and grammatical features of the original sign language. *Sign Language Studies* 8: 249-256.

Harnad, S. R., Steklis, H. D. and Lancaster, J. (1976). *Origins and Evolution of Language and Speech*. From a conference held in New York at the New York Academy of Sciences, September 1975. *Annals of the New York Academy of Sciences* 280: vii + 914.

Harper, R. G., Wiens, A. N. and Matarazzo, J. D. (1978). *Nonverbal Communication: The State of the Art*. New York: Wiley.

Hayes, F. (1957). Gestures: A working bibliography. *Southern Folklore Quarterly* 21: 218-317.

Heims, S. P. (1977). Gregory Bateson and the mathematicians: From interdisciplinary interaction to societal functions. *Journal of the History of the Behavioral Sciences* 13: 141-159.

Hewes, G. W. (1973a). Primate communication and the gestural origins of language. *Current Anthropology* 14: 5-24.

– (1973b). An explicit formulation of the relationship between tool-using, tool-making and the emergence of language. *Visible Languages* 7: 101-127.

– (1977). A model for language evolution. *Sign Language Studies* 15: 97-168.

Hinde, R. A. (ed.) (1972). *Nonverbal Communication*. Cambridge: Cambridge University Press.

Hockett, C. F. (1978). In search of Jove's brow. *American Speech* 53: 243-313.

Hore, T. and Page, N. S. (1975). *Nonverbal Behaviour: A Select Annotated Bibliography*. Hawthorn, Victoria: Australian Council for Educational Research.

Howell, W. S. (1959). Sources of the elocutionary movement in England 1700-1748. *The Quarterly Journal of Speech* 45: 1-18.

Hutchinson, A. (1966). *Labanotation: The System for Recording Movement*. New York: Theatre Arts Books.

Ikegami, Y. (1971). A stratificational analysis of the hand gestures in Indian classical dancing. *Semiotica* 4: 365-391.

Jaffe, J. and Feldstein, S. (1970). *Rhythms of Dialogue*. New York: Academic Press.

Jancovic, M., Devoe, S. and Weiner, M. (1975). Age related changes in hand and arm movements as non-verbal communication: Some conceptualizations and an empirical exploration. *Child Development* 46: 922-928.

Kaplan, E. (1968). Gestural representation of implement usage: An developmental study. Ph.D. dissertation, Clark University, Worcester, Massachusetts.

Kendon, A. (1967). Some functions of gaze direction in social interaction. *Acta Psychologia* 26: 22-63.

– (1970). Movement coordination in social interaction: Some examples described. *Acta Psychologia* 32: 100-125.

– (1972a). Review of R. L. Birdwhistell's *Kinesics and Context*. *American Journal of Psychology* 85: 441-445.

– (1972b). Some relationships between body motion and speech: An analysis of an example. In *Studies in Dyadic Communication*, A. Seigman and B. Pope (eds.). Elmsford, N.Y.: Pergamon.

— (1973). The role of visible behaviour in the organization of face-to-face interaction. In *Social Communication and Movement in Man and Chimpanzee*, M. Von Cranach and I. Vine (eds.). London: Academic Press.

— (1975a). Gesticulation, speech and the gesture theory of language origins. *Sign language Studies* 9: 349-373.

— (1975b). Some functions of the face in a kissing round. *Semiotica* 15: 299-334.

— (1977). *Studies in the Behavior of Face-to-face Interaction*. Lisse: Peter de Ridder Press.

— (1978). Differential perception and attentional frame in face-to-face interaction: Two problems for investigation. *Semiotica* 24: 305-315.

— (1979). Some methodological and theoretical aspects of the use of film in the study of social interaction. In *Emerging Strategies in Social Psychological Research*, G. P. Ginsburg (ed.). Chichester and New York: Wiley.

— (1980a). A description of a deaf-mute sign language from the Enga Province of Papua New Guinea with some comparative discussion. Part I: The formal properties of Enga signs. *Semiotica* 31-1/2: 1-34.

— (1980b). Gesticulation and speech: Two aspects of the process of utterance. *The Relationship of Verbal and Nonverbal Communication*, Mary R. Key (ed.). The Hague: Mouton.

— (1980c). Sign language of the women of Yuendumu: A preliminary report on the structure of Warlpiri sign language. *Sign Language Studies* 27: 101-112.

— (1980d). Features of the structural analysis of human communicational behavior. In *Aspects of Nonverbal Communication*, W. Von Raffler Engel (ed.). Lisse: Swets and Zeitlinger.

— (in press a). A description of a deaf-mute sign language from the Enga Province of Papua New Guinea, etc. Part II: The semiotic functioning of Enga signs. *Semiotica* 32-1/2.

— (in press b). A description of a deaf-mute sign language from the Enga Province of Papua New Guinea, etc. Part III: Aspects of utterance construction. Appendix: A description of Enga signs. *Semiotica* 32-3/4.

— (in press c). Geography of gesture. *Semiotica*.

— (in press d). The organization of behaviour in interaction: observations on the development of a methodology. In *Methods of Research in Nonverbal Behaviour*, K. Scherer and P. Ekman (eds.). Cambridge: Cambridge University Press.

Kendon, A. and Ferber, A. (1973). A description of some human greetings. In *Comparative Ecology and Behaviour of Primates*, R. P. Michael and J. H. Crook (eds.). London and New York: Academic Press.

Key, M. R. (1977). *Nonverbal Communication: A Research Guide and Bibliography*. Metuchen, N.J.: Scarecrow Press.

Klapper, Z. and Birch, H. G. (1969). Perceptual and action equivalence to objects and photographs in children. *Perceptual and Motor Skills* 29: 763-771.

Klima, E. and Bellugi, V. (1979). *The Signs of Language*. Cambridge, Mass.: Harvard University Press.

Knapp, M. L., Hart, R. P, Friedrich, G. W. and Shulman, G. M. (1973). The rhetoric of goodbye: Verbal and nonverbal correlates of human leave-taking. *Speech Monographs* 40: 182-198.

Knowlson, J. R. (1965). The idea of gesture as a universal language in the XVIIth and XVIIIth centuries. *Journal for the History of Ideas* 26: 495-508.

Komnenich, P. (1977). Decision making aspects of greeting behavior among Serbians and Montenegrins. *Internatoinal Journal of Psycholinguistics* 4: 31-50.

Krout, M. H. (1935). Autistic gestures, an experimental study in symbolic movement. *Psychological Monographs* 46 (208).

– (1937). Further studies on the relation of personality and gesture: A nosological analysis of autistic gestures. *Journal of Experimental Psychology* 20: 279-287.

– (1954). An experimental attempt to determine the significance of unconscious manual symbolic movements. *Journal of General* 51: 121-152.

Kuschel, R. (1973). The silent inventor. *Sign Language Studies* 3: 1-26.

Laban, R. (1950). *The Mastery of Movement*. London: Macdonald and Evans.

– (1956). *Principles of Dance and Movement Notation*. London: Macdonald and Evans.

Laban, R. and Lawrence, F. C. (1947). *Effort*. London: Macdonald and Evans.

Lane, H. and Grosjean, F. (1980). *Recent Perspectives on American Sign Language*. Hillsdale, N.J. Erlbaum.

Lasher, M. D. (1978). The pause in the moving structure of dance. *Semiotica* 22: 107-126.

Laver, J. (1975). Communicative functions of phatic communion. In *The Organization of Behavior in Face-to-Face Interaction*, A. Kendon, R. M. Harris and M. R. Key (eds.). World Anthropology. The Hague: Mouton.

Lempers, J. D. (1979). Young children's production and comprehension of nonverbal deictic behavior. *Journal of Genetic Psychology* 135: 93-102.

Liddell, S. K. (1978). Nonmanual signs and relative clauses in American Sign Language. In *Understanding Language Through Sign Language Research*, P. Siple (ed.). New York: Academic Press.

Lipset, D. (1980). *Gregory Bateson: The Legacy of a Scientist*. Englewood Cliffs, N.J.: Prentice-Hall.

Lock, A. (1978). *Action, Gesture and Symbol: The Emergence of Language*. London New York: Academic Press.

Lockard, J. S., Allen, D., Schiele, B., and Wiemer, M. (1978). Human postural signals: stance, weight shifts and social distance an intention movements to depart. *Animal Behaviour* 26: 219-224.

Lyons, J. (1972). Human language. In *Nonverbal Communication*, R. A. Hinde (ed.). Cambridge: Cambridge University Press.

MaCannell, D. (1973). A note on hat tipping. *Semiotica* 7: 300-312.

McDermott, R. P., Gospodinoff, K. and Aron, J. (1978). Criteria for an ethnographically adequate description of concerted activities and their contexts. *Semiotica* 24: 245-276.

McDermott, R. P. and Roth, D. R. (1978). The social organization of behavior: Interactional approaches. *Annual Review of Anthropology* 7: 321-346.

McDermott, R. P. and Wertz, M. (1976). Doing the social order: Some ethnographic advances from communicational analysis and ethnomethodology. *Reviews in Anthropology* 3: 160-174.

McGrew, W. C. (1972). *An Ethological Study of Children's Behavior*. New York: Academic Press.

MacKay, D. M. (1972). Formal analysis of communicative processes. In *Nonverbal Communication*, R. A. Hinde (ed.). Cambridge: Cambridge University Press.

McNeil, D. (1979). *The Conceptual Basis of Language*. Hillsdale, N.J.: Erlbaum.

McNeil, D. and Levy, E. (in press). Conceptual representations in language activity and gesture. In *Speech, Place and Action: Studies of Language in Context*, R. J. Jarvella and W. Klein (eds.). Chichester: Wiley.

McQuown, N. A. (1974). Natural history method: A frontier method. In *Creative Developments in Psychotherapy*, A. R. Mahrer and L. Pearson (eds.). New York: Jason Aronson.

McQuown, N. A. (ed.) (1971). *The Natural History of an Interview*. Microfilm collection of manuscripts on Cultural Anthropology, fifteenth series. Chicago: The University of Chicago Joseph Regenstein Library of Photoduplication.

Mahl, G. (1968). Gestures and body movements in interviews. In *Research in Psychotherapy*, J. M. Shlien (ed.). Washington, D. C.: American Psychological Association.

— (1977). Body movement, ideation and verbalization during psychoanalysis. In *Communicative Structures and Psychic Structures*, N. Freedman and S. Grand (eds.). New York and London: Plenum.

Mallery, G. (1880). *Sign Language Among the North American Indians Compared with that Among Other Peoples and Deaf-Mutes*. Washington, D. C.: Smithsonian Institution Bureau of Ethnology. (Reprinted 1972, The Hague: Mouton).

Mandel, M. (1977). Iconic devices in American Sign Language. In *On the other Hand*: *New Perspectives in American Sign Language*, L. A. Friedman (ed.). New York and London: Academic Press.

Marks, S. P. (1971). The sound and the silence: Nonverbal patterns in *The Wings of the Dove*. *The Arizona Quarterly* 27.

— (1974). A silent morality: Nonverbal expression in *The Ambassadors*. *South Atlantic Bulletin* 39: 102–106.

Matarazzo, J. D., Wiens, A., Matarazzo, R. G. and Saslow, G. (1968). Speech and silence behavior in clinical psychotherapy and in laboratory correlates. In *Research in Psychotherapy: Proceedings of the Third Conference*, J. M. Schlein (ed.). Washington, D. C.: American Psychological Association.

Mayberry, R. I. (1978). French-Canadian sign language: A study of inter-sign language comprehension. In *Understanding Language Through Sign Language Research*, P. Siple (ed.). New York: Academic Press.

Meggitt, M. (1954). Sign language among the Walbiri of Central Australia. *Oceania* 25: 2–16.

Meissner, M. and Philpott, S. B. (1975). The sign language of sawmill workers of British Columbia. *Sign Language Studies* 9: 291–347.

Michael, G. and Willis, F. (1968). Development of gestures as a function of social class, education and sex. *Psychological Record* 18: 515–519.

Morris, D., Collett, P., Marsh, P. and O'Shaughnessy, M. (1979). *Gestures: Their Origins and Distribution*. London: Jonathan Cape / New York: Stein and Day.

Munari, B. (1963). *Supplemento al Dizionario Italiano*. Milan: Muggiani.

Murphy, C. M. and Messer, D. J. (1977). Mothers, infants and pointing: A study of a gesture. In *Studies in Mother-Infant Interaction*, H. R. Schaffer (ed.). London: Academic Press.

Newtson, D. (1976a). The process of behavior observation. *Journal of Human Movement Studies* 2: 114–122.

— (1976b). Foundations of attribution: the perception of ongoing behavior. In *New Directions in Attribution Research*, J. Harvey, W. Ickes and R. Kidd (eds.). Hillsdale, N.J.: Erlbaum.

Nielsen, G. (1964). *Studies in Self-Confrontation*. Copenhagen: Munksgaard / Cleveland, Ohio: Howard Allen.

Ochs, E. and Schiefflin, B. (1979). *Developmental Pragmatics*. New York and London: Academic Press.

Oster, Harriet (1978). Facial expression and affect development. In *The Development of Affect: Genesis of Behavior*, vol. I, M. Lewis and L. A. Rosenblum (eds.). New York: Plenum.

Overton, W. F. and Jackson, J. P. (1973). The representation of imagined objects in action sequences: A developmental study. *Child Development* 44: 309–314.

Pasch, G. (1975). Drapeaux nationaux. *Semiotica* 15: 285–295.

Philips, S. U. (1976). Some sources of cultural variability in the regulation of talk. *Language in Society* 5: 87–95.

Pike, K. L. (1967). *Language in Relation to a Unified Theory of the Structure of Human Behavior.* The Hague: Mouton.

Poyatos, F. (1975). Cross cultural study of paralinguistic 'alternants' in face-to-face interaction. In *Organization of Behavior in Face-to-Face Interaction*, A. Kendon, R. M. Harris and M. R. Key (eds.). The Hague: Mouton.

— (1977). The morphological and functional approach to kinesics in the context of interaction and culture. *Semiotica* 20: 197–228.

Quintilian, M. F. (1922 [100]). *Quintiliani Institutiones.* English translation by H. E. Butler. London: Heinemann.

Robb, M. M. and Thorssen, L. (eds.) (1966). Critical Introduction. In *Chironomia or a Treatise on Rhetorical Delivery*, G. Austin. Carbondale and Edwardsville: Southern Illinois University Press.

Rosenfeld, H. M. (1966a). Instrumental affiliative functions of facial and gestural expressions. *Journal of Personality and Social Psychology* 4: 65–72.

— (1966b). Approval-seeking and approval-inducing functions of verbal and nonverbal responses in the dyad. *Journal of Personality and Social Psychology* 4: 597–605.

— (1967). Nonverbal reciprocation of approval: An experimental analysis. *Journal of Experimental Social Psychology* 3: 102–111.

— (in press). Article in *Methods of Research in Nonverbal Behaviour*, K. Scherer and P. Ekman (eds.). Cambridge: Cambridge University Press.

Rosenthal, R. (1966). *Experimenter Effect in Behavioral Research.* New York: Appleton-Century-Croft.

Rosenthal, R. (ed.) (1979). *Skill in Nonverbal Communication: Individual Differences.* Cambridge, Mass. Oegeschlager, Gunn and Hass.

Rosenthal, R., Hall, A., Dimatteo, M. R., Roger, P. L. and Archer, D. (1979). *Sensitivity to Nonverbal Communication.* Baltimore, Maryland: John Hopkins University Press.

Rosenthal, R. and Rubin, D. B. (1978). Interpersonal expectancy effects: The first 345 studies. *The Brain and Behavioral Sciences* 3: 377–415.

Roth, H. L. (1889). On salutations. *Journal of the Royal Anthropological Institute* 19: 164–187.

Ruesch, J. (1953). Synopsis of the theory of human communication. *Psychiatry* 16: 215–243.

— (1955). Nonverbal language and therapy. *Psychiatry* 18: 323–330.

Reusch, J. and Bateson, G. (1951). *Communication: The Social Matrix of Society.* New York: W. W. Norton.

Ruesch, J. and Kees W. (1956). *Nonverbal Communication: Notes on the Visual Perception of Human Relations.* Berkeley: University of California Press.

Rutter, D. R. and Stephenson, G. M. (1977). The role of visual communication in synchronizing conversation. *European Journal of Social Psychology* 7: 29–37.

Rutter, D. R., Stephenson, G. M., Ayling, K. and White, P. A. (1978). The timing of looks in dyadic conversation. *British Journal of Social and Clinical Psychology* 17: 17–21.

Sacks, H., Schegloff, E. A. and Jefferson, G. (1974). A simplest symtematics for the organization of turn-taking for conversation. *Language* 50: 696–735.

Sainsbury, P. and Wood, E. (1977). Measuring gestures: Cultural and clinical correlates. *Medicine* 17: 458–469.

Sainsbury, P. and Wood, E. (1977). Measuring gestures: In cultural and clinical correlates. *Psychological Medicine* 7: 63–72.

Saitz, R. L. and Cervenka, E. J. (1972). *Handbook of Gestures: Colombia and the United States.* The Hague: Mouton.

Sallagoity, P. (1975). The sign language of southern France. *Sign Language Studies* 7: 181–202.

Sapir, E. (1949). Selected writings of Edward Sapir. In *Language, Culture Personality*, D. G. Mandelbaum (ed.). Berkeley: University of California Press.

Scaife, M. and Bruner, J. S. (1975). The capacity for joint visual attention in the infant. *Nature* 253: 265–266.

Schaffer, H. A. (1977). Early interactive development. In *Studies in Mother-Infant Interaction*, H. A. Schaffer (ed.). London: Academic Press.

Scheflen, (1963). Communication and regulation in psychotherapy. *Psychiatry* 26: 126–136.

– (1964). The significance of posture in communication systems. *Psychiatry* 27: 316–331.

– (1966). Natural history method in psychotherapy: Communicational research. In *Methods of Research in Psychotherapy*, L. A. Gottschalk and A. H. Auerback (eds.). New York: Appleton-Century-Croft.

– (1973). *Communicational Structure: Analysis of a Psychotherapy Transaction.* Bloomington and London: Indiana University Press.

– (1979). On communicational processes. In *Nonverbal Behavior: Applications and Cultural Implications*, A. Wolfgang (ed.). New York: Academic Press.

– (1980). Systems in human communication. In *Aspects of Nonverbal Communication*, W. Von Raffler-Engel (ed.). Lisse: Swets and Zeitlinger.

Schegloff, E. A. and Sacks, H. (1973). Opening up closings. *Semiotica* 8: 289–327.

Schenkein, J. (1972). Towards an analysis of natural conversation and the sense of *heheh*. *Semiotica* 6: 344–372.

Schenkein, J. (ed.) (1978). *Studies in the Organization of Conversational Interaction.* New York and London: Academic Press.

Schlosberg H. (1954). Three dimensions of emotion. *Psychological Review* 61: 87–88.

Schriffrin, D. (1977). Opening encounter. *American Sociological Review* 42: 679–691.

Sebeok, T. A. (1962). Coding in the evolution of signalling behavior. *Behavioral Sciences* 7: 430–442.

Sebeok, T. A., Hayes, D. and Bateson, M. C. (eds.) (1964). *Approaches to Semiotics.* The Hague: Mouton.

Seigel, J. P. (1969). The enlightenment and the evolution of a language of signs in France and England. *Journal of the History of Ideas* 30: 96–115.

Seigman, A. and Feldstein, S. (1979). *Of Speech and Time.* Hillsdale, N.J.: Erlbaum.

Shannon, C. E. and Weaver, W. (1949). *A Mathematical Theory of Communication.* Urbana, Ill.: University of Illinois Press.

Sherzer, J. (1973). Nonverbal and verbal deixis: The pointed lip gesture among the San Blas Cuna. *Language and Society* 2: 117–133.

Sigman, S. J. (1979). The neglected situation. *ETC: A Review of General Semantics* 36: 85–93.

Siple, P. (1978). *Understanding Language through Sign Language Research.* New York: Academic Press.

Slama-Cazacu, T. (1976). Nonverbal components in message sequence: 'mixed syntax'. In *Language and Man*, W. Mc Cormack and S. Wurm (eds.). The Hague: Mouton.

– (1977). Le concept de 'syntaxe mixte' recherches autour d'une hypothèse, *Etudes de Linguistique Appliquée* 27: 114–123.

Stam, J. H. (1976). *Inquiries into the Origin of Language: The Fate of a Question.* New York: Harper and Row.

52   Adam Kendon

Stokoe, W. C., Jr. (1960). Sign language structure: An outline of the visual communication system of the American deaf. Occasional paper No. 8, *Studies in Linguistics*. Buffalo, N.Y.: University of Buffalo.

– (1972). *Semiotics and Human Sign Languages*. The Hague: Mouton.

– (1974a). Motor signs as the first form of language. *Semiotica* 10: 117–130.

– (1974b). The classification and description of sign languages. In *Current Trends in Linguistics*, vol. 12, part I, T. A. Sebeok (ed.). The Hague: Mouton.

– (1980a). Sign language and sign languages. *Annual Review of Anthropology*, vol. 9.

Stokoe, W. C. (ed.). (1980b). *Sign and Culture*. Silver Spring, Maryland: Linstok Press.

Stokoe, W. C., Casterline, D. and Croneberg (eds.). (1965). *A Dictionary of American Sign Language on Linguistic Principles*. Washington, D. C.: Gallaudet College Press.

Studnicki, F. (1970). Traffic signs. *Semiotica* 2: 151–172.

Sullivan, H. S. (n.d.). *Collected Works of Harry Stack Sullivan*, volumes I and II. New York: W. W. Norton.

Taylor, A. (1956). The shanghai gesture. *Folklore Fellows Communications* 166: 1–76.

– (1971). Gestures in an American detective story. *Estudios del Folklore* 25: 295–300.

Taylor, A. R. (1975). Nonverbal communications systems in native North America. *Semiotica* 13: 329–374.

Teodorrson, S. T. (1980). Autonomy and linguistic status of nonspeech language forms. *Journal of Psycholinguistic Research* 9: 121–145.

Tervoort, B. T. (1961). Esoteric symbolism in the communication behavior of young deaf children. *American Annals of the Deaf* 106: 436–480.

Trevarthen, C. (1977). Descriptive analyses of infant communicative behavior. In *Studies in Mother: Infant Interaction*, H. R. Schaffer (ed.). London: Academic Press.

Tylor, E. B. (1878). *Researches into the Early History of Mankind*. London: John Murray.

Umiker-Sebeok, D. J. and Sebeok, T. A. (1978). *Aboriginal Sign Languages of the American and Australia*, vol. II. New York and London: Plenum.

Vine, Ian (1973). The role of facial-visual signaling in early social development. In *Social Communication and Movement: Studies of Interaction and Expression in Man and Chimpanzee*, M. Von Cranach and J. Vine (eds.). London and New York: Academic Press.

Von Foerster, H. (ed.). (1949–1953). *Cybernetics: Circular Causal and Feedback Mechanisms in the Biological and Social Sciences*, 5 volumes. New York: Josiah Macy Jr. Foundation.

Wallis, M. (1973). Semantic and symbolic elements in architecture: Iconology as a first step toward an architectural semiotic. *Semiotica* 8: 220–238.

Washabaugh, W. (1980). The manufacturing of a language. *Semiotica* 29: 1–38.

Washabaugh, W., Woodward J. and DeSantis, S. (1978). Providence island sign language: A context dependent language. *Anthropological Linguistics* 20: 95–109.

Watzlawick, P., Beavin, J. H. and Jackson, D. D. (1967). *Pragmatics of Human Communication*. New York: W. W. Norton.

Weitman, S. R. (1973). National flags: A sociological overview. *Semiotica* 8: 328–367.

Werner, H. and Kaplan, B. (1963). *Symbol Formation: An Organismic Developmental Approach to Language and the Expression of Thought*. New York: Wiley.

West, La Mont (1960). The sign language. Ph.D. Dissertation, Indiana University, Bloomington.

Wieman, M. and Knapp, M. L. (1975). Turn-taking in conversations. *Journal of Communication* 25: 75–92.

Wiener, M., Devoe, S., Rubinow, S. and Geller, J. (1972). Nonverbal behavior and nonverbal communication. *Psychological Review* 79: 185–214.

Wiener, N. (1948). *Cybernetics or Control and Communication in the Animal and the Machine*. New York: The Technology Press, Wiley.

Wilbur, R. (1979). *American Sign Language and Sign Systems*. Baltimore, Maryland: University Park Press.

Williams, D. (1977). The arms and hands with special reference to an Anglo-Saxon sign system. *Semiotica* 21: 23-73.

Wilden, A. (1972). Analog and digital communication. *Semiotica* 6: 50-82.

Wundt. W. (1973). *The Language of Gestures*. The Hague: Mouton. (Translation of *Volkerpsycholgie: Eine Untersuchung der Entwicklungsgesetze von Sprache, Mythus und Sitte*, Vol I, 4th edition, part I, chapter 2. Stuttgart: Kroner, 1921).

Wylie, L. (1977). *Beaux Gestes: A Guide to French Body Talk*. Cambridge, Mass.: The Undergraduate Press.

Yau, S. C. (1977). *The Chinese Sign Language*. Hong Kong: Chin Ming.

Yngve, V. (1970). On getting a word in edgewise. Paper from the Sixth Regional Meeting, Chicago Linguistic Society. Chicago: Chicago Linguistic Society.

Youssouf, I. A., Grimshaw, A. D. and Bird, C. S. (1975). Greetings in the desert. *American Ethnologist* 3: 797-824.

Zivin, G. (1977a). On becoming subtle: Age and social rank changes in the use of a facial gesture. *Child Development* 48: 1314-1321.

– (1977b). Facial gestures predict preschoolers encounter outcomes. *Social Science Information* 16: 715-730.

Part One

Theoretical and Methodological Issues

PAUL EKMAN and WALLACE V. FRIESEN

The Repertoire of Nonverbal Behavior: Categories, Origins, Usage, and Coding[1]

If we are to understand fully any instance of a person's non-verbal behavior — that is, any movement or position of the face and/or the body — we must discover how that behavior became part of the person's repertoire, the circumstances of its use, and the rules which explain how the behavior contains or conveys information. We will call these three fundamental considerations ORIGIN, USAGE, and CODING.

The interrelationships among and the differences within these three aspects of nonverbal behavior are extremely complex. The task of unraveling nonverbal behavior in these terms is enormously difficult; and it becomes impossible if we fail to consider the possibility of multiple categories of nonverbal behavior.

The need to develop such a categorical scheme has emerged from the results of our empirical studies over the past eight years, and has been crystallized by our two current research projects, the study of cross-cultural differences in nonverbal behavior, and the study of nonverbal leakage of information during deceptive situations. We will briefly trace how some of the findings raised questions which led us to attempt to

[1] Part of this paper was given at the Symposium: "Communication Theory and Linguistic Models in the Social Sciences" at the Center for Social Research of the Torcquato Di Tella Institute, Buenos Aires, Argentina, October, 1967.

The research reported in this paper was supported by research grants from the Advanced Research Projects Agency, administered by the Air Force Office of Scientific Research (AF-AFOSR-1229-67), the National Institute of Mental Health (MH-11976-03) and a Career Development Award (1-K3-MH-6092-02).

The authors are indebted to Patricia W. Garlan for her helpful suggestions on content and editorial criticisms of style.

specify the usage, origin, and coding of five categories of nonverbal behavior.

SUMMARY OF OUR PAST RESEARCH

In studies designed to determine what kinds of information could be derived from observing facial or body behavior we found that inferences about emotions, attitudes, interpersonal roles, and severity of pathology can be made by observers who have had no specialized training (Ekman, 1964; Ekman, 1965a; Ekman and Friesen, 1965, 1968). Such inferences are usually accurate, in that they coincide with independent assessments of the person's total behavior, life circumstances, *etc.* But, how do observers decode the nonverbal behavior to make judgments about emotion, attitude or personality? Is there a language of the body, much like verbal language, in which specific meanings, denotative or connotative, are associated with specific movements? Or, are the meanings of nonverbal behavior more diffuse or less specific, and the interpretation global and intuitive? Are the nonverbal acts which are informative about emotion also informative about personality or pathology? If observers are able to interpret information accurately, can we infer that nonverbal behaviors are intentional efforts to communicate? Although our research had not been directed to answer these questions, our studies forced us to the observation that there must be essentially different types of nonverbal behavior, some types providing very specific information, others providing more diffuse information, some obviously intended to transmit messages, others in no way designed as communication, some providing information about emotion, others conveying information about traits, attitudes and interpersonal styles.

In another set of studies we attempted to determine the kind of affective information which could be derived from different body areas by observers (Ekman, 1965b; Ekman and Friesen, 1967a). The face was found to convey more information about the nature of an emotion (whether the person felt sad, angry, afraid, *etc.*), than about the intensity of the emotional state. Information derived from observing the body differs for ACTS (movements of the hands and arms, legs and feet, shoulders, or total posture) and still POSITIONS. Body acts were found to provide information both about intensity and about the nature of the emotion. Still positions of the body typically provide information about intensity of emotion, but sometimes also about what we call the gross affective state, whether the person felt pleasant or unpleasant. What might account for these differences between face, body acts and positions; might it be anatomy, socialization processes, clothing? Where does the o bserver learn how to interpret nonverbal behavior; or DOES he learn how to interpret these cues?

In another set of investigations we studied the meaning of the specific act, which was defined as a class of movements distinguishable from another class of movements by its distinctive visual appearance (Ekman and Friesen, 1966, 1968). Covering the eye would be one act, rubbing the temple another, caressing the forehead another. We found that such acts have fairly specific meaning; their frequency of occurrence varies with the psychological state of the sender; they can be related in a number of different ways to the associated speech, and they convey quite specific messages to observers. Among psychiatric patients the eye-cover act, for example, is shown most often by individuals who are depressed, particularly if their depression involves withdrawal and shame, but not by these same individuals when their depression has lifted. The eye-cover act will often be preceded or followed by turning away from the other interactant, and sometimes by crying. Observers who see only the eye-cover act will infer shame and general unhappiness. Certainly the overall context, the physical setting, the age, sex, body size and role of the person showing the act, and the rest of the nonverbal and verbal behaviors modify the meaning of such an act, much as the verbal context, voice tone and speaker characteristics modify the meaning of a word; however, the act, like the word, has a distinct set of meanings different from the meanings associated with another act. But, is an act like the eye-cover unique to depressive patients; or, if it is shown by normal people as well, in what way does its occurrence relate to the psychological state of the sender? Is the meaning associated with an act always dependent upon observing what the act accomplishes or does to some part of the body, as is the case with the eye-cover act; if so, what then of gesticulations in space? Does the person who covers his eye do so to EXPRESS his shame, or to COMMUNICATE to others his shame, or ADAPTIVELY to hide his shame? Our tentative answers to these questions were that the movements shown by depressive patients are not unique to them, and that the differences associated with pathology are shown in the frequency of occurrence, range of behavior manifested, and extent to which the behavior is governed by social norms, rather than in a peculiar class of movement. Many acts can be decoded by interpretation of what the act is accomplishing, like the eye-cover; but other acts seem to illustrate the words rather than do anything to a body part. Again we were impressed with the very different types of nonverbal behavior shown, some which seem designed to transmit information, others which appear to be expressive or adaptive.

We have become increasingly curious about what nonverbal behavior can tell us which verbal behavior does not (Ekman and Friesen, 1967b, 1968, 1969). One of our first thoughts was that nonverbal behavior provides valuable information when we can't trust what we are told in words, either because the speaker is purposefully trying to deceive us, or because he has blocked or repressed the information we want. We have developed a theory to explain why nonverbal behavior seems to escape efforts to deceive (Ekman and Friesen, 1967b, 1969) providing either deception clues, *i.e.*, information that deception is in progress, or leakage, *i.e.*, the betrayal of the withheld information. But, we know that nonverbal behavior can lie — if not as well perhaps as verbal behavior — and one cannot trust everything one sees. Our theory has specified major differences among the face, hands, and feet, in the type and frequency of both leakage and deception clues, and has looked to differences in the anatomy and in socialization processes as the source of these differences. But this raises questions about the censoring or control of information, and we have had to postulate that some types of nonverbal behavior can be easily controlled while other types of nonverbal behaviors escape control and provide leakage.

Our initiation of two cross-cultural studies required the formulation of a theory of both the origin and coding of nonverbal behavior. The first of these studies involved examination of the encoding, or display, and the decoding, or recognition, of facial displays of emotion in different cultural settings. The methods used in such a study, the selection of specific emotions and techniques for analyzing encoding and decoding, and the development of hypotheses about pan-cultural elements as well as cultural differences required the explicit formulation of a theory of both the origins and coding of this form of nonverbal behavior. The second study involved another type of nonverbal behavior, where major cultural differences were predicted: those actions which are almost always employed as intentional communicative signals (which we will later define as emblems). Thus, we were required to begin to specify the basic differences between various forms of nonverbal activity. And this required consideration of three fundamental issues mentioned at the outset: the usage, origin and coding of nonverbal behavior.

USAGE, ORIGIN AND CODING

Usage

The term 'usage' refers to regular and consistent circumstances surrounding the occurrence of a nonverbal act. Usage includes (1) the external conditions found whenever the act occurs, (2) the relationship of the act to the associated verbal behavior, (3) the person's awareness of emitting the act, (4) the person's intention to communicate, (5) feedback from the person observing the act, and (6) the type of information conveyed by the act.

(1) EXTERNAL CONDITION refers to any of the environmental circumstances which customarily coincide with, inhibit or occasion an act, or qualify its meaning. Setting is one such external condition; for example, the act could be customary in home, office, interviews, conversations, dyadic or group interactions, *etc*. The act might be more frequent in one role than another: *e.g.*, within settings, husband or father in the home, supervisor or supervisee for an employee located in the middle of a business hierarchy; across settings, in the roles of listener, authority, *etc*. The emotional tone of the interaction might also be related to the occurrence of an act; *e.g.*, angry, formal, warm, stressful moments, or more enduring characteristics of the particular relationship between interactants.

(2) RELATIONSHIP TO VERBAL BEHAVIOR refers both to the temporal sequence or coincidence of the nonverbal and verbal behaviors, and to interrelationships between the meanings conveyed by each channel. The nonverbal act can repeat, augment, illustrate, accent, or contradict the words; it can anticipate, coincide with, substitute for or follow the verbal behavior; and it can be unrelated to the verbal behavior.

(3) AWARENESS, or internal feedback, refers to whether the person knows he is engaging in a particular nonverbal act at the moment he does it, or whether he can recall with any ease what he has done. A person can be aware of his nonverbal behavior whether or not he engages in the act as an intentional attempt to communicate a specific message.

(4) INTENTIONALITY [2] refers to the deliberate use of a nonverbal act to communicate a message to another interactant. This definition does not

---

[2]   Intentionality is a concept traditionally avoided by psychologists interested in human communication on the grounds that it is not possible to operationalize intentions, or that the investigator will become lost in questions of levels of intention or unconscious intention. We believe that there are some nonverbal behaviors which the sender usually consciously intends as communicative signals to convey messages (soon to be defined as emblems), and that through naturalistic or experimental methods it

include behavior which is considered to be unconsciously intended; intentional nonverbal behavior must be, by our definition, within awareness and the sender must want to send a message through his act.

(5) EXTERNAL FEEDBACK refers to the information regarding a nonverbal act which the observer, or receiver provides to the sender. Such feedback may consist of direct verbal comments on the sender's activity, or obvious visual attention to a particular nonverbal act, or to the receiver's verbal and nonverbal behavior which clearly is reactive to the sender's nonverbal actions. External feedback is thus not identical with what the observer perceives, but is more narrowly defined to include only the observer's activity which clearly informs the sender that his nonverbal action is being perceived and evaluated.

(6) TYPE OF INFORMATION CONVEYED refers to a basic distinction between idiosyncratic and shared information, and definitions of INFORMATIVE, COMMUNICATIVE and INTERACTIVE nonverbal behavior. An act has idiosyncratic meaning if there is some regularity in the information associated with its occurrence but the association is peculiar to a single individual. An act has shared meaning if the information associated with it is common across some specifiable set of individuals. Idiosyncratic or shared meaning can refer to either the encoding or decoding of an action. An act has idiosyncratic encoded meaning if it is emitted under similar environmental or stimulus conditions by one individual, but not by others. A particular hand movement might frequently occur when the individual is exhausted, or anxious, or confronted with humiliating rejections or under the influence of dexedrine. The act has an encoded meaning in terms of the regularity of its occurrence with those stimulus events which precede, accompany or typically follow it or with consistently associated ideation. The encoded meaning is idiosyncratic if the meaning is peculiar to one person, and shared if the meaning is common to a set of persons. An act has idiosyncratic DECODED meaning if it consistently conveys a particular item of information to a single receiver, but not to others. A parent to his child, a wife to her husband, a psychoanalyst to his patient might be such special privileged receivers who have learned the private decoding of specific acts of another person; but that decoding is not known by other observers who have not shared such intimate contact with the sender. Shared decoded meaning occurs when any specifiable set of observers

is possible to differentiate these acts from other forms of nonverbal behavior. At the same time, we do admit that the intentionality of other nonverbal behavior is problematic, and it may not be possible to determine the intentionality of every instance of nonverbal behavior.

usually agree about the information conveyed by an act. Idiosyncratic and shared meaning does not exhaust the possibilities. We must admit that there may be actions which are meaningless — random activity or noise, movements which have no regularities in either their encoding or decoding, not even for a single person.

It is important to note that we do not speak of an act as idiosyncratic or shared. These terms refer instead to the meaning associated with an act. Almost any act can have either or both kinds of meaning, and if an act is classified into one of the five categories of nonverbal behavior to be described, certain differences in the proportion of idiosyncratic to shared meaning can be expected. Having made a distinction between two layers of meaning (idiosyncratic and shared) in regard to two types of meaning (encoded and decoded) let us now introduce our way of formulating the difference among 'informative', 'communicative' and 'interactive' nonverbal behavior.

INFORMATIVE nonverbal behavior encompasses those acts which have some shared decoded meaning, in that such acts elicit similar interpretations in some set of observers. The use of this term does not imply that the act was intended to convey the information it does, nor does it imply that the act was intended to convey any information at all, though it does. The term informative refers only to decoded meaning; if that decoding is idiosyncratic rather than shared the act would not be considered informative. The shared meaning is not, however, a sufficient criterion for our use of the term informative; an act could have shared encoded meaning but still not have shared decoded meaning. For example, a twitch of the facial muscles, which reliably occurred in association with hostile assaults by an interviewer; this association might be reliable across some set of individuals thus having shared encoded meaning, and yet the acts might not convey consistent information about anything to any given set of observers and thus they would not be informative. An informative act is not necessarily one which conveys correct or accurate information about the sender; what the observers decode may be quite mistaken when compared with any criteria; *e.g.*, stereotypes. The meaning conveyed by an informative act could vary enormously; it could be such simple messages as *hello* or *goodbye*, or emphasis on particular words, or the speaker's wish to have the receiver respond, or, the act might convey information about the transient or enduring affect state, or about personality or attitude.

COMMUNICATIVE nonverbal behavior encompasses those acts which are clearly and consciously intended by the sender to transmit a specifiable message to the receiver. We are excluding thereby much informative behavior. That is, many acts which convey shared decoded meaning are not, by our definition, communicative; these would be acts which while informative were not intended consciously by the sender to transmit a message. Communicative acts are not necessarily accurate conveyors of information. We are not restricting the term to only those instances where the decoded information fits the information intended by the sender; those instances we would call accurate communication and there can be miscommunicative or inaccurate communicative behavior as well. Communicative acts need not necessarily have a shared decoded meaning; there could be non-informative communicative acts where the sender intended to transmit a message but no one understands him. Presumed unconscious intentions to transmit a message are also excluded from our definition, as is any criterion that the receiver's interaction with the sender must be influenced by the sender's communicative act.

INTERACTIVE nonverbal behavior encompasses those acts which meet this last criterion: They are acts by one person in an interaction which clearly modify or influence the interactive behavior of the other person(s). If this influence upon the interactions is shared, in that more than one receiver who decodes the sender's act responds to it interactively in a similar fashion, it would be informative-interactive; if the act's influence is for only one other interactant, or varies with each interactant, then the act would be considered idiosyncratic-interactive. Not all informative behavior is interactive; many informative acts may not influence or modify the interaction, at least in detectable ways. Interactive behavior need not be communicative; many informative acts will influence the interaction and yet not be the result of an intent to communicate.

Figure 1 illustrates the relationships among these terms. Interactive behavior may be also informative (b), it may be both informative and communicative (f), or it may be idiosyncratic (c) (the latter may refer to acts which regularly influence the behavior of a wife in regard to her husband, but those acts have no such influence on the interactive behavior of his other interactants). Some communicative behavior is interactive and informative (f), some is informative but not interactive (d) and there could be some communicative behavior which is neither interactive nor informative (e) (an example of the latter might perhaps be those schizophrenic acts consciously intended to communicate but which are not informative to observers and do not influence the interaction of even one receiver). Finally, there would be much informative behavior which is neither interactive nor communicative (a).

We have developed this terminology in order to clarify our own think-ing and illuminate possible differences between our approach and those of Birdwhistell, of Scheflen and of Mahl. Birdwhistell and Scheflen have applied a communication framework to nonverbal behavior, based largely upon the argument that much of the nonverbal behavior they observe

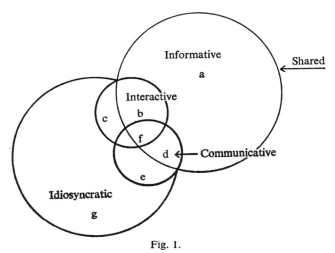

Fig. 1.

influences the behavior of the other interactants. We believe that their use of the term 'communicative' is too broad; it fails to distinguish among that behavior which has a shared decoded meaning (informative), that which influences the other person's interaction (interactive), and that which intended to transmit a message (communicative). Many nonverbal behaviors may have interactive effects, but not be intended to communi-cate nor best be considered as analogous to verbal communication. Similarly, nonverbal behavior with a shared decoded meaning may not be intended to communicate, nor be best considered as analogous to linguistic phenomena.

Mahl had this in mind when he suggested that the term 'informative' is more applicable than 'communicative' for shared decoded meaning, and we have changed our terminology accordingly, reserving the word 'communicative' for instances in which the sender consciously intends to transmit a message. Mahl's distinction between AUTISTIC and COM-MUNICATIVE behavior, while valuable, can be improved upon. His concept of autistic action — those behaviors which have only idiosyncratic mean-ing, presumably in both encoding and decoding — while valid for some behavior, includes much behavior which also has a layer of related shared meaning. Further, we think that the level of meaning, idiosyncratic or shared, is an inadequate basis for distinguishing fundamental categories of nonverbal behavior. In our opinion, such categories of nonverbal behavior (which we will soon describe) must be based upon differences in origin, coding and other aspects of usage in addition to level of meaning.

Another difficulty with Mahl's division of behavior into autistic and communicative actions, is that it has left much nonverbal behavior out. The term 'communicative', as he (and we) define it, refers to only part of what is not autistic; it applies only to those actions which are consciously intended to transmit a message. There are two other kinds of shared decoded meaning which need not be communicative; informative and interactive.

We again must emphasize that the distinction between idiosyncratic and shared, or among informative, communicative and interactive, refers to level or type of meaning, not to categories of behavior. Thus, a given act can have both idiosyncratic and shared levels of meaning (we will give examples of this when discussing the categories of emblems and adaptors). An act which is informative might or might not be interactive or communicative in any given instance. The categorical scheme to be presented here distinguishes nonverbal behavior in part in terms of the relative prevalence of informative, communicative and interactive meaning; the categories differ in the ratio of idiosyncratic to shared meaning but not all of the behavior in any category is exclusively one of these. Although we will speak of behavior as informative, or communicative or interactive, these terms cut across our five categories and refer to the information or type of meaning associated with a behavior, in any category, not a category of behavior itself.[3]

---

[3] In our past writing (Ekman, 1965a; Ekman and Friesen, 1968) we have not utilized these terms in the same way as we have now proposed. We used the terms 'indicative' and 'communicative' to refer to methods of research aimed at determining the encoded or decoded meaning of nonverbal behavior. But the use of the word 'communicative', even though we specified that it did not imply intention to communicate, may have been confusing, and so we now suggest reserving the term only for instances where there is evidence that the behavior was consciously designed to transmit a message. We had used the phrase 'communicative value' in discussing the decoded meaning associated with an act; now, for the same reasons, we suggest the term 'informative'. Finally, we had (Ekman and Friesen, 1965, 1967a) used the term 'interactive' to refer to any nonverbal behavior which occurs during an interpersonal interaction. Now we are proposing a much more restricted usage of that term, *viz.*, to refer to acts whose meaning can be shown to influence the interaction of the person perceiving it, in order to distinguish behavior of this sort from behavior which is also communicative, also informative, or only informative or only communicative, but not interactive.

Origin

The term 'origin' refers to how the nonverbal behavior originally became part of the person's repertoire, that is, the source of the action. Not all of the conditions involved in the origin are necessarily repeated in the later usage of an act. For example, a steering-wheel-arm-rotation act may have been originally learned as part of the instrumental task of driving a car, but be used conversationally with no car present to refer to problems of management or direction. At least three types of origin can be distinguished.

One origin of nonverbal behavior is a relationship between stimulus events and nonverbal activity which is built into the nervous system of every intact member of the species. A reflex is the most obvious example, and some authors have argued that facial expressions of emotion are also based upon inherited neurological programs.

A second origin is experience common to all members of the species; this differs from the first origin in that one need not assume that the non-verbal behavior is inherited, but rather that it is acquired as part of the species-constant experience of the human equipment interacting with almost any environment. For example, regardless of culture the hands will be used, with or without an implement, to place food in the mouth.

A third origin of nonverbal behavior is experience which varies with culture, class, family or individual. Some nonverbal behaviors are learned as part of an instrumental task in which the goal is mastery of a particular activity such as farming, driving, swimming, and in learning particular styles of eating, defecating, *etc.* Other nonverbal acts are learned as part of a social interaction, where the goal is the establishment or maintenance of a type of social interaction. Some nonverbal behaviors are learned explicitly with conscious attention from learner and tutor, or from only the learner; others are acquired more implicitly with less focus upon the acquisition process. Imitating the posture or facial expression of a favorite movie star may be quite explicit and practiced, while the acquisition of the posture or other movements of the same-sex parent may occur with less awareness on the part of the learner. Imitation can also be relevant to learning NOT to resemble another person's nonverbal behavior. The parent can explicitly caution the child about not talking with his hands or to smile when uncle and aunt visit; or the parental reinforcements can be more subtle, with neither child nor parent specifically aware of the reinforcement contingency.

Coding

The last of the three aspects of nonverbal behavior which must be examined is the principle of correspondence between the act and its meaning. The code which describes how meaning is contained in a nonverbal act, that is, the rule which characterizes the relationship between the act itself and that which it signifies, may be EXTRINSIC or INTRINSIC. An extrinsic code is one in which the act signifies or stands for something else, and the coding may be arbitrary or iconic.[4] An intrinsic code is in a sense no code in that the act does not stand for but IS its significant; the meaning of the act is intrinsic to the action itself. We will characterize these as three coding principles: ARBITRARY (extrinsic) codes, ICONIC (extrinsic) codes, and INTRINSIC codes.

Acts which are arbitrarily coded bear no visual resemblance to what they signify. In this they are like words, most of which do not sound like what they mean; exceptions are words like *slush* and *buzz*. When the opening and closing of the raised hand signifies greeting or departure, we have an example of an arbitrary coding of nonverbal behavior, since the movement does not intrinsically show what it signifies.

Acts which are iconically coded carry the clue to their decoding in their appearance; the nonverbal act, the sign, looks in some way like what it means, its significant.

Acts which are intrinsically coded are, like iconically coded behavior, visually related to what they signify. But unlike the iconically coded act, the intrinsically coded act does not resemble its significant; it IS its significant, at least in part.[5] If one person hits another during conversation, that is not similar to aggression; it is one form of aggression; the act is the significant.

Let us explore a little further the differences between the iconically

---

[4]   Our use of the term iconic is taken from Morris (1946), who said "An iconic sign, it will be recalled, is any sign which is similar in some respect to what it denotes. Iconicity is thus a matter of degree... the strength of the iconic sign lies in its ability to present for inspection what it signifies...." Ruesch (1956) said that the distinction between digital and analogic codification was relevant to nonverbal behavior; the former is more characteristic of verbal and the latter of nonverbal behavior. This distinction is very similar to the way we have described arbitrary and iconic coding. The terms, analogic and digital, moreover, involve further specifications of the mathematics relevant to modeling information processing, and the question of continuities in items of information, which are not necessary to our distinction here. For further discussion of analogic and digital coding, with special reference to nonverbal behavior in infrahuman organisms see Sebeok (1963) and Diebold (1968).

[5]   The recognition of the need to distinguish intrinsically coded from iconic behavior grew out of a discussion with Silvan Tomkins.

and the intrinsically coded act. When a person waves his fist menacingly, but laterally and with a particular tempo and position of the fingers, the movement of the hand resembles an aggressive act; but it is not that act; rather, depending on its visual appearance, it could be part of a politician's victory speech, an athletic coach's encouragement to ferocity, *etc.* However, if a person waves his fist, not to show something similar or analogous to what he will do, but literally to enact the movement involved in aggression, even if he does not touch another person we have something closer to an intrinsically coded act.

If a person runs a finger under his throat to signify 'having one's throat cut' or more figuratively, 'an unfortunate outcome', this is iconic coding since one cannot cut a person's throat with the finger, and the finger is standing for the knife. Similarly, a trigger finger movement made in the usual manner is an icon, since the hand is used in a way that makes it look like a gun, but the hand is not a gun, and the action of the fingers has nothing to do with the action involved in pulling the trigger of a gun. However, if one holds his hand just as one would with a gun in it, and moves his finger as if to pull a trigger, then we have an action which does not resemble the significant, but is the action involved in the significant. If the hand held a gun, we would have a clear example of an intrinsically coded act; if the hand formed the shape of a gun, we would have a clear example of an icon. But, even when the hand performs only part of the act of firing a gun, if that performance is part of the literal action involved in the total act, it is intrinsically coded, though its meaning may be obscured by the absence of a gun.

The line between the iconic and intrinsically coded act may appear to be a fuzzy one particularly in the case of an act which is only a part of a total action; (*e.g.*, forming the hand as if it held a gun requires that one infer the presence of a gun in order to comprehend this act). The iconically coded act is often easier to comprehend and simpler to utilize as a communicative signal; it is more stylized, starker, perhaps more abstract, and will leave out many of the details involved in the intrinsically coded act which it may resemble.

Let us now refine further the ways in which a nonverbal act is related to its significant, both when the relationship is an iconic code and when the meaning is shown in an intrinsic code. This discussion is not relevant to the arbitrary code, because we will only discuss different types of visual relationships between act and significant.

PICTORIAL. A pictorial relationship is one in which the movement shows its meaning by drawing a picture of an event, object or person (*e.g.*, using the two hands to show the size or shape of an object). By definition, pictorial behavior is iconic.

SPATIAL. A spatial relationship is one in which the movement indicates distance between people, objects or ideas (*e.g.*, placing the hands close together to show intimacy, or how the car nearly hit the pedestrian). By definition, spatial behavior is an iconic code, which depicts spatial distance without actually changing it. For example, bringing the two hands together to propose greater intimacy is a spatial iconic code. However, moving closer to a person to indicate the same thing is not a spatial iconic code, but an intrinsically coded, kinetic act (see below).

RHYTHMIC. A rhythmic relationship is one in which the movement traces the flow of an idea or accents a particular phrase, or describes the rate of some activity. It carries no message content apart from information about tempo, and is by definition iconic. (Not included in this definition is behavior in which rhythmic elements are part of a kinetic code and do have message content.)

KINETIC. A kinetic relationship is one in which the movement executes all or part of an action performance, where that performance either signifies or is the meaning, at least in part. This action performance can signify a meaning by resembling another action (*e.g.*, the throat-cut movement); in this case it is an iconic code. Or, it can actually be part or all of the action it signifies (*e.g.*, fist-waving or the more extreme behavior of hitting); in this case the behavior is a kinetic, intrinsically coded act.

POINTING. A pointing relationship is one in which some part of the body, usually the fingers or hand, points to some person, to some part of the body, to an object or place. Or, the referent may be a more abstract attitude, attribute, affect, direction, or location. Pointing is always intrinsically coded; the act means 'to show something'; the something is the target or referent of the point and, of course, can vary.

In sum, pictorial, spatial and rhythmic relationships between movement and meaning are always iconic. Kinetic relationships may be either iconic or intrinsic. Pointing is always intrinsically coded. It should be noted that, typically, nonverbal behavior combines elements of more than one code. For example, a pictorial code may include spatial elements; a spatial code may include rhythmic elements.

FIVE CATEGORIES OF NONVERBAL BEHAVIOR

As mentioned earlier, and as the examples should have made clear, nonverbal behavior is not a single, unified phenomenon with but one type of usage, one origin and one form of coding. Instead, facial and body behavior involve a number of quite different kinds of behavior which will be described in terms of five categories distinguished by the particulars of usage, origin and coding. This categorization of nonverbal behavior owes most to the writings of Efron (1941) and to a series of discussions with Mahl in which we attempted to clarify some of the issues implicit in his dichotomization of nonverbal behavior (Mahl, 1968). We have attempted, where possible, to avoid inventing new terms, and have therefore taken from Efron, even though frequently we have defined them differently to avoid contradictions.

Emblems

The first type of nonverbal behavior is what we have previously defined with the term 'gesture'. But that word in common usage is too inclusive; let us substitute a term proposed by Efron (1941), 'emblems'.[6] Emblems differ from most other nonverbal behaviors primarily in their usage, and in particular in their relationship to verbal behavior, awareness and intentionality. Emblems are those nonverbal acts which have a direct verbal translation, or dictionary definition, usually consisting of a word or two, or perhaps a phrase. This verbal definition or translation of the emblem is well known by all members of a group, class or culture. While we usually think of emblems as general, at least within a culture or language group, clearly for groups within a culture such emblems as secret signs for fraternal orders fit our definition. An emblem may repeat, substitute, or contradict some part of the concomitant verbal behavior; a crucial question in detecting an emblem is whether it could be replaced with a word or two without changing the information conveyed.

People are almost always aware of their use of emblems; that is, they know when they are using an emblem, can repeat it if asked to do so, and will take communicational responsibility for it. Similarly, the use of an emblem is usually an intentional, deliberate effort to communicate; but there are exceptions. We have seen people make a fist, which within our culture is an emblem for anger or hitting, and yet be quite unaware of having done so; we have similarly seen obscene gestures shown during

[6]   Efron used this term only for those gestures which are not morphologically related to what they signify; emblems could only be arbitrarily, not iconically coded. Our use of the term is broadened to include both. Ruesch (1956) used the word gesture to cover what we are calling emblems, noting their conscious intentional use to communicate; but he also included as gestures the category which we will describe as illustrators, and further emphasized that the gesture must be symbolic, a requirement which to us seems relevant to the arbitrary, but not to the iconic gestures or emblems.

a conversation, with absolute denial by the sender that he used such an emblem. The fact that an emblem is shown without awareness on a particular occasion does not bear upon the question of whether the action is an emblem; emblematic status is determined by the shared decoded meaning and the conscious intentional usage across some group of individuals. There can be emblematic slips, much like slips of the tongue, where the sender just does not know what he has done. But in determining whether an action is emblematic, again we want to emphasize that unconscious intent is not sufficient for our definition.

Emblems occur most frequently where verbal exchange is prevented by noise, external circumstance (*e.g.*, while watching a play), distance (between hunters), by agreement (in the game of charades), or by organic impairment (the deaf mute). In such instances, emblematic exchange carries the bulk of messages which would typically be communicated through words. Emblems, of course, also occur during verbal exchange. We are not certain why they are used at one point in a conversation and not another; might it be that emblems are used around the more ritualized aspects of conversation, such as greetings and departures, or changes in status or topic; or might it be that emblems occur when matters get heated; or might it be that emblems are used to derogate the impact of what is said verbally?

Emblems are the most easily understood nonverbal behavior; by our definition they have a quite specific, agreed-upon meaning. We would expect that they are the most frequently attended to nonverbal behaviors, simply because they have been so explicitly defined. Receiver feedback, direct comment by the other interactant on an emblem, its meaning or implication, is within U.S. culture quite acceptable.

In a sense, emblems seem to carry less personal information than other categories we will later discuss, perhaps because emblems are so much more intentional and within awareness than other nonverbal behaviors, and like words, the time and place to use an emblem is usually chosen with some care. Emblems usually have a much higher proportion of shared than idiosyncratic meaning, although it is possible, as Mahl (1968) pointed out, for emblems to have an idiosyncratic level of meaning in addition to their shared meaning. Emblems are communicative behavior, although there are rare instances when they are emitted without awareness. Emblems often are interactive in that their usage tend to draw the perceiver's attention, and their shared decoded meaning would increase the probability that they would affect the other interactants' behavior.

We have been considering the usage of emblems; let us now consider their origins. Emblems originate through learning, much of which is culture-specific. Efron's study of the nonverbal behavior of Jewish and Italian immigrants to the U.S. and of their offspring showed major differences between the immigrant groups in emblematic behavior. Saitz and Cervenka (1962) have catalogued differences in emblematic behaviors between Colombia and the U.S.

We would expect that emblems are usually learned much like verbal materials. Emblems can be shown in any area of the body, although in the U.S. emblems are primarily shown by the face and hands. Emblems can be based upon what we will later describe as affect displays and adaptor nonverbal behaviors; for example, the raising of the brows and horizontal forehead wrinkle which are usually part of the surprise affect display can be emblematic, if the culture pays specific attention to and prescribes a very specific meaning to that facial behavior, although the emblematic meaning might be different from the affect.

Some emblems are arbitrarily coded, in that the action does not look like what it means. The sign alphabet language of the deaf contains a number of finger movements where the fingers do not look like the shape of the letter; these are arbitrarily coded. Other finger signs are iconically coded, in that the fingers are placed into a position which closely resembles the alphabet letter they stand for. The 'body-signs' of the deaf which employ an action to convey a word or phrase are iconic (resembling their significant visually). The tracing of the body outline of a woman is an iconic-pictorial emblem in which the hands draw a picture of a shapely woman to state sexual attractiveness. The making of a fist, or shaking of a fist, is usually an iconic-kinetic emblem. While an intrinsically coded act could be an emblem, it seems likely that if an act achieves emblematic status it will become highly stylized for convenient use as a communicative signal, with some elements of the act altered or deleted for ease of performance and clear discriminability, and thus the act would be better considered as iconically coded.

RESEARCH IN PROGRESS: Our research on emblematic behavior is directed to three types of questions.

(1) Is there a set of emblematic 'words' which can be arranged to create emblematic phrases or sentences? Is the size of the emblematic vocabulary similar across cultures; if not, what are the factors correlated with variations in size? Our focus is descriptive, to map the emblematic vocabulary of specific cultures, and to determine the syntax of emblematic statements.

(2) Are the same message domains emblematic in various cultures? Do the same types of information become emblematic in all cultures;

do all cultures have, for example, emblems for greetings and departures, for statements of hunger or satiation? Peculiarities in the environmental conditions in which communication occurs, and the state of development of the technology of communication might lead to the production of a large number of emblems for a specific message domain in one culture but not in another. For example, a warring society which conducts guerrilla warfare but which lacks the technology for quiet verbal communication among its members, and where the terrain permits line-of-sight observation over fairly long distances, might develop a large number of emblems to convey information back and forth between warriors as they approach their prey.

(3) Are there pan-cultural emblems; what would distinguish these from culture-specific emblems? We expect that arbitrarily coded emblems will probably not have the same meaning across cultures, because by definition the act does not visually show its significant; for example, one does not know which letter is signified by arbitrary finger signs unless one has memorized the language. Iconically coded emblems will tend to elicit the same decoding across cultures, simply because at least part of the significant is visually shown in the movement. Just because iconic emblems will be decodable across cultures, such similarity in decoding of emblems is not a sufficient criterion for claiming an emblem is pancultural. It must also be shown that the action is encoded as an emblem within each culture being examined. Our hypothesis is that pan-cultural emblems will tend to be primarily those which refer to or show the activity of a body function such as eating, lovemaking, and those which refer to the simplest human activities, such as walking, sleeping, sitting, touching, building. Such emblems will be pictorial-iconic, or kinetic-iconic, or pointing-intrinsic in their coding. Culture-specific emblems will tend to be those which refer to more complex human activities, those which refer to cognitive events, and those which include reference to tools or to unique features of the ecology. All arbitrarily coded emblems will be culture-specific; some iconically coded emblems will be culture-specific in encoding, but understandable by members of another culture.

We have developed a rather simple method for beginning our study of emblems, in collaboration with Carleton Gajdusek [7] and Richard

[7]   This research on emblematic behavior in the South Fore of New Guinea is a joint endeavor between our research group at Studies in Nonverbal Behavior of the Langley Porter Neuropsychiatric Institute, the University of California Medical School, and the Center for the Study of Growth, Development and Disease in Primitive Cultures, of the National Institutes of Neurological Diseases and Blindness, directed by Carleton Gajdusek.

Sorenson. While working among the South Fore of New Guinea we compiled an *a priori* list of messages which might be emblematic within any culture. As we thought about it and checked with a few highly acculturated informants, the list grew to about 60 messages, such as *Hello, I am hungry, It's going to rain, You stay here, etc.* We then sat down with subjects and explained the concept of talking with your hands and body, and took motion picture films of the subject's attempt to show an emblem for each message on our list. Even in work with informants who had seen very few Caucasians and spoke no pidgin, we found that in less than a half hour they understood what we were interested in, and would not only perform emblems for us, but volunteer ones not on our list. The main problem we encountered was the subject's wish to please us; it was obvious that we were interested in this behavior and most subjects wanted to give us an emblem for each message, even when they did not know what to do and had to invent and essentially perform a charade. Emblems can be distinguished from charades by reaction time between instruction and performance, which is very short for an emblem, and usually much longer while the subject innovates for a charade; and safeguards are provided by comparison of nonverbal behavior performed for the same message by different subjects, which is identical if the message is emblematic and quite different if the behavior is a charade.

Our analysis of these films is directed toward uncovering the basic emblematic units through comparisons across filmed subjects, and across messages comprised of the same set of verbal words but in different syntaxes, *e.g., You go, I stay, I stay, you go, We stay, then go.* The second step is to draw comparisons between cultures of the message domains which have been found to be emblematic. A third step in the analysis is to test our hypothesis about the basis for pan-cultural emblems by isolating these emblems through comparisons of the New Guinea films with films of other cultures,[8] showing the emblems to observers in various cultures, and checking the similarity in their decoding. We are in the first phase of this research, and can report that there seem to be both minimal emblematic units, emblem phrases, and an emblem syntax; there are pan-cultural emblems — actions which fit our definition of emblems and which are identical among the people of the U.S., the South Fore of New Guinea and Argentinians. It appears that our hypothesis

[8]   We have begun a study of emblematic behavior among Spanish origin and Italian origin Argentinians as a joint research project with the Centro de Investigaciones Psychiatriquas, Buenos Aires, directed by Carlos Sluzki.

Sorenson. While working among the South Fore of New Guinea we compiled an *a priori* list of messages which might be emblematic within any culture. As we thought about it and checked with a few highly acculturated informants, the list grew to about 60 messages, such as *Hello, I am hungry, It's going to rain, You stay here, etc.* We then sat down with subjects and explained the concept of talking with your hands and body, and took motion picture films of the subject's attempt to show an emblem for each message on our list. Even in work with informants who had seen very few Caucasians and spoke no pidgin, we found that in less than a half hour they understood what we were interested in, and would not only perform emblems for us, but volunteer ones not on our list. The main problem we encountered was the subject's wish to please us; it was obvious that we were interested in this behavior and most subjects wanted to give us an emblem for each message, even when they did not know what to do and had to invent and essentially perform a charade. Emblems can be distinguished from charades by reaction time between instruction and performance, which is very short for an emblem, and usually much longer while the subject innovates for a charade; and safeguards are provided by comparison of nonverbal behavior performed for the same message by different subjects, which is identical if the message is emblematic and quite different if the behavior is a charade.

Our analysis of these films is directed toward uncovering the basic emblematic units through comparisons across filmed subjects, and across messages comprised of the same set of verbal words but in different syntaxes, *e.g., You go, I stay, I stay, you go, We stay, then go.* The second step is to draw comparisons between cultures of the message domains which have been found to be emblematic. A third step in the analysis is to test our hypothesis about the basis for pan-cultural emblems by isolating these emblems through comparisons of the New Guinea films with films of other cultures,[8] showing the emblems to observers in various cultures, and checking the similarity in their decoding. We are in the first phase of this research, and can report that there seem to be both minimal emblematic units, emblem phrases, and an emblem syntax; there are pan-cultural emblems — actions which fit our definition of emblems and which are identical among the people of the U.S., the South Fore of New Guinea and Argentinians. It appears that our hypothesis

---

[8]   We have begun a study of emblematic behavior among Spanish origin and Italian origin Argentinians as a joint research project with the Centro de Investigaciones Psychiatriquas, Buenos Aires, directed by Carlos Sluzki.

Efron pointed out that the first two types of illustrators, batons and ideographs, have no independent meaning or connotation when viewed without hearing the words, while the other illustrators have meaning independent of the words, and would convey something of the speech content if viewed without hearing the speech. But all of these illustrators share the attribute of being intimately interrelated with the concomitant verbal behavior on a moment-to-moment basis; they are directly tied to content, inflection, loudness, etc.[10] Illustrators can repeat, substitute, contradict or augment the information provided verbally.

Illustrators are quite similar to emblems in terms of both awareness and intentionality. The person using an illustrator may be slightly less aware of what he is doing, and his use of illustrators may be somewhat less intentional. Most illustrators would be informative, providing shared decoded meaning which is intimately related in one of the ways we described to the verbal behavior. Some illustrators could be considered communicative as well; they are probably at least as intentional as the words spoken when the speaker is excited and not exercising forethought and care about his choice of words. Illustrators could be interactive, but whether they are or not would depend on the total context in which they are shown.

Illustrators receive some external feedback from the observer, who will usually pay obvious visual attention, although he may not verbally comment as often on illustrators as on emblems.

Illustrators are socially learned, primarily through imitation by the child of those he wishes to identify with or resemble. Public speaking courses can teach the use of specific illustrators, although this practice was much more common 40 years ago in the days of eloquent oratory.

The type of illustrators used will vary with the ethnic background of the individual, as Efron found between Italian and Jewish immigrants (the Jewish immigrants used more of the batons and ideographs, the Italians more of the kinetographs and pictographs; assimilated first generation offspring no longer showed these differences while those who maintained closer contact with the traditional customs still showed the differences in illustrators).

All of the illustrators are either iconically coded or intrinsically coded, most usually the former. The deictic illustrator is a pointing movement

---

[10]   Dittmann's (1966) finding that certain head and hand movements are related to phonemic clauses in speech may be pertinent to the illustrators, although his measures did not differentiate among categories of nonverbal behavior except in terms of body area involvement.

and therefore intrinsically coded. The batons and ideographs are forms of rythmic-iconic coding. They tell no message, in the sense of conveying message content; Efron said they were logical-discursive. They are still iconically coded, but in terms of the rhythm. The spatial illustrators are iconic if they represent spatial relationships, intrinsically coded if they actually change spatial relationships. Pictographs, described earlier as pictorial codes, are iconic because by definition a picture must resemble but cannot be its significant.

Kinetographs are kinetic behavior, iconic if they represent the movement of a natural force or mechanical action, or if they resemble a human action, and intrinsically coded if they reproduce a human action, at least in part.

RESEARCH IN PROGRESS: We are currently applying our classification of illustrators to a collection of 120 sound motion picture films of interviews with psychiatric inpatients. The interviews were standardized, covering a limited number of topics; each patient was usually interviewed three times, once upon admission, once during hospitalization, and finally shortly before discharge. We are comparing the frequency of occurrence of the six types of illustrators with another type of nonverbal behavior, hand-to-face self-adaptors, which will be discussed later. Our first aim is to determine whether our classification of illustrators actually can be operationalized in application to motion picture film records. We are also testing a number of hypotheses: (1) Frequency of illustrator actions will increase as the patient moves from the acute phase of a psychiatric disorder to the remitted state, while the reverse correlation with psychopathology will be found for hand-to-face self-adaptors. (2) The type of illustrator movement shown will be constant for a given person regardless of degree of psychopathology, although we are predicting changes in frequency of occurrence (this hypothesis is based upon Efron's findings which suggest that the type of illustrator is related to ethnicity). (3) Particular types of hand-to-face movements (grooming, autoerotic, and attacking), more than illustrators coincide with breaks in inter-ocular contact between patient and interviewer. We are also investigating the relationship of both illustrators and hand-to-face movements to phonemic aspects of speech.

Affect Displays

Our discussion of affect displays begins with consideration of the site of this category of nonverbal behavior (the face), and then proposes the universality of one aspect of affect displays, the movements of the facial muscles in association with primary affects. The concept of primary affects, a tentative list of what they may be, and some of the factors which might account for pan-cultural elements in such displays, will then be discussed. We will turn from these considerations largely about the origin of affect displays to a discussion of their usage in which we will distinguish and separately consider the evoking stimuli, the display rules which modify the movements of the facial muscles, the occurrence of affect blends, and the behavioral consequences of affect displays. We then consider coding, and finally report research in progress on affect displays.

We agree with Tomkins (1962, 1963, 1964) that the face is the primary site of affect displays. Some facial behaviors, however, such as mouth movements which result from talking, lip bites and eye closures are better characterized as 'adaptors', to be described later. Some body movements are affective displays, such as the startle response and, perhaps, trembling; but generally body movements occur in response to affect and are relevant to how the person will cope with the facially displayed affect; they are the behavioral consequence of the affect, rather than display of affect itself (the relationship of body movement to affect is discussed at some length in Ekman and Friesen, 1967a).

We agree with Tomkins and with Darwin that there are distinctive movements of the facial muscles for each of a number of primary affect states, and these are universal to mankind. There has, of course, been considerable disagreement about what the PRIMARY AFFECTS are. Despite differences in theoretical orientation, methods, nationality of the subjects studied, and decade when the investigation was performed, the studies of Frijda (1963), Nummenmaa (1964), Osgood (1966), Plutchik (1962), Schlosberg (1941), Tomkins (1964), Woodworth (1938) and ourselves (Boucher and Ekman, 1965; Ekman and Friesen, 1967a) reveal some consistencies which suggest a tentative, perhaps partial, list of primary affects: happiness, surprise, fear, sadness, anger, disgust and interest.

Each of these affective states can easily be distinguished by observers of facial displays within this culture, and we have found that most of these affects can be just as readily distinguished by observers in other cultures,[11] although language difficulties in translating or finding a correct word to describe an affect, and the strangeness in some cultures of the task of looking at a photograph or film and judging affect may introduce

---

[11] Working independently, Izard (1968) has recently obtained data on similarities in the recognition of affect displays across cultures.

errors which might be misinterpreted as cultural difference. Other problems which make it difficult for an investigator to demonstrate pancultural elements in the recognition of facial affect displays will be discussed later in connection with evoking stimuli, behavioral consequences, display rules, and blends.

If observers can distinguish among these seven affective states when viewing the human face, then there must be some specifiable cues in a facial display which could be coded or quantified to measure affect. Later, when discussing our research in progress on affect displays we will briefly mention an attempt to develop a facial affect scoring technique.

We are not certain what might account for similarities across cultures in particular facial muscles which move when a particular affect is aroused. Darwin claimed that affect displays have evolved from the functional activities associated with these facial muscular movements. This explanation would require inherited mechanisms which relate affective arousal to specific distinctive patterned movements of the facial muscles. Tomkins has proposed a theory of how such mechanisms might work, and believes that at least some of the evoking stimuli which elicit an affect are built into the organism. While not disagreeing with Tomkins, we have become interested in alternative explanations which do not presume an inherited association between evoking affective stimuli and distinctive patterned facial muscular movements for each primary affect. It might be that affective facial displays evolve in the same way for each individual during the course of his development; these affective facial displays might be elaborations of or in part initially based upon constants in the human equipment involved in performing rudimentary activities, or upon certain reflexes. The disgust affect display, for example, might evolve in each person's development from the movements of the mouth and nose involved in ejecting a bad taste or smell; but simple regurgitation or spitting would not be considered an affective display although this would be the constant in the human equipment which facilitates the development of similar disgust displays. Anger affective displays might evolve from the muscular movements in the mouth and eye areas necessary to preventing rupturing of capillaries in the eyes and lungs, whenever major physical exertion is undertaken, or perhaps from biting movements; the constants would be the strain-exertion or biting movements, which facilitate the similar development of anger displays. Sadness might develop from the lax state of exhaustion, perhaps with some of the features associated with the long term endurance of physical pain; the pain contractions and the lax state would be the constants. Fear might evolve from a combination of the startle reflex and the pain contractions. We are not satisfied with this account (it is particularly weak in explaining the facial affect display of happiness; but Darwin also had trouble with providing a functionally based evolutionary explanation of this display and had to invent his principle of antithesis). Clarity on this question requires further research. Of particular value would be a close study of visual records of the development of affect displays in the first few years of life across two cultures with blind and sighted children.

The assertion that there are universal distinctive movements of the facial muscles for each of a number of primary affect states is not as yet a proven fact, and many would disagree. We believe that some of the impressions of cultural differences in affect display have arisen from a failure to distinguish adequately the pan-cultural elements from the circumstances governing the display of affects which are markedly influenced by social learning and vary within and between cultures. We believe that, while the facial muscles which move when a particular affect is aroused are the same across cultures, the evoking stimuli, the linked affects, the display rules and the behavioral consequences all can vary enormously from one culture to another. Figure 2 illustrates the various aspects of facial affect displays which we will consider.

The EVOKING STIMULI which elicit an affect may well differ from one culture to another. Tomkins has argued that while there are at least some unlearned affect evokers, social learning teaches the individual a number of associations between events, memories, anticipations and affect. For example, when a person is angry the facial features will show a given configuration, but what provokes anger is at least in part determined by social learning, and will vary among cultures. A common pitfall in cross-cultural research on affect display is to infer a common emotional state simply because the same event is being compared in two cultures; in actuality the event may evoke a different affect in each culture, and the differences in facial behavior may reflect those differences rather than differences in the facial muscles associated with affect in each culture. For example, culture X might show up-turned lips, nasolabial folds, and almost closed eyes at funerals, while culture Y might show down-turned lips, stretched lower lip, partially closed eye lids, nostril dilations at funerals. Before stating that the facial display of sadness varies across cultures it would be necessary to verify that the stimulus "funeral" normatively evokes the same affect in the two cultures, rather than being a stimulus for joy in one culture and for sadness in another.

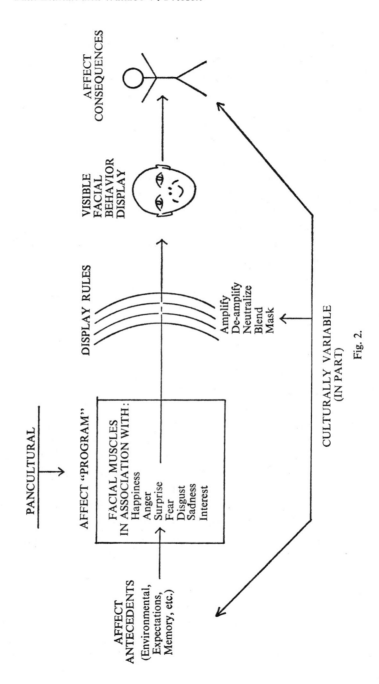

Fig. 2.

DISPLAY RULES are socially learned, probably quite early in life, and prescribe different procedures for the management of affect displays in various social settings, roles, *etc.* We can distinguish at least four display rules. One rule is to de-intensify the appearance clues to a given affect; for example, when one is extremely fearful he must attempt to look only moderately or slightly fearful. A second display rule is to over-intensify: for example, when one is slightly fearful he must attempt to look extremely fearful. A third display rule is to look affectless or neutral; for example, when one is fearful, he must attempt to look as if no affect were being experienced. A fourth rule is to mask the felt affect as completely as possible by dissimulating it with another affect; for example, when one is fearful, he must attempt to look happy.

We believe that there are well-established social norms about which display rule is appropriate for each affect when experienced by individuals of varying status, role, sex, age, physiognomy, *etc.* These display rule norms take into account not only the characteristics of the displayer, but also those of any other persons present when the display is evoked, and of the social context. Such display rule norms are over-learned, and will vary from one culture to another. In cross-cultural comparisons of affect displays it is important not to interpret evidence as showing a basic difference in the muscles involved in an affect display when the difference was due to the application of display rules differently in the cultures being compared. Returning to our example of a funeral, let us suppose that we are comparing two cultures where this event has the same evoking characteristic of sadness; it is still possible that in one culture the display rule will be to over-intensify the affect, while in the other the display rule will be to mask it with a pleasant demeanor. Without highspeed photography and slow motion inspection of the films to see the initial sad movements in the one culture, the observer may gain the impression that sadness produces different facial muscle movements in the two cultures.

Tomkins' (1964), Plutchik's (1962), Nummenmaa's (1964), and our own studies have suggested that at any given instant in time the face typically conveys AFFECT BLENDS (multiple emotions), rather than a single emotional state. The map of the facial features is sufficiently complex to allow the display of mixtures of two or more emotions simultaneously. Affect blends may be dictated by the evoking circumstances; or, they may be dictated by learned habits which associate one emotion with another. The particular affects which are blended can vary for individuals, families and social classes, or may be common within a culture. We should note that these affective combinations can occur not only simultaneously as blends, but in rapid sequence.

Blends also may lead to confusions in cross-cultural comparisons of affect display. If for one culture the sadness evoked by a funeral is normatively blended with fear, but in another culture sadness is blended with anger, there will be differences in the facial displays. We are arguing that these differences should not be interpreted as signifying that the movements of the facial muscles in association with affect are completely variable from one culture to another, but should be attributed to differences in the habitually blended affect.

A last variable to be considered is the BEHAVIORAL CONSEQUENCE of an affective display. The behavioral consequence of an affect display can be most readily determined from the body posture and movements, although the face may show the affect associated with a given behavioral consequence. We interpret the movements and postures of the body which coincide with and follow a facial affect display as coping with the facially displayed affect. Such movements often do not differentiate one facial affect from another; for example, the behavioral consequence of flight may occur as a coping procedure for anger, fear, or even disgust in particular social contexts. The fact that people show very different body movements after displaying the same facial affect should not be interpreted as meaning that the facial affect is meaningless, or inconsequential.

We have been arguing that the movements of the facial muscles are the basic building blocks of affect displays, and that these are the pancultural elements of affect. Yet, such movements are embedded in a context; they may be elicited by different stimuli, be operated upon by different display rules, be blended with other affects, and be followed by different behavioral consequences. We do not mean to belittle these factors; in actuality we want to focus attention on these factors as the major sources of cultural differences in affect display. But our argument has been to emphasize the difficulty in uncovering the pan-cultural elements, and to caution against the danger that they may be obscured by a failure to isolate each of the variables listed in our figure.

Although we usually are aware of our facial affect displays, they may occur with or without a deliberate intention to communicate. Similarly, inhibition of facial display, control of facial display, or dissimulation of an affect (looking cool even when tense), may or may not be intentional. Because we have such good feedback about our facial behavior, we usually are aware of what happens the moment we change facial movements; we can monitor, inhibit and dissimulate with our faces. The problem for the observer of facial affect displays, if there is any suspicion that deception may be in progress, is to detect which affect displays are lies, and which are more involuntary leakage (Ekman and Friesen, 1969).

Facial behavior in general, and affective displays in particular, receive great attention and external feedback from the other interactant, in terms of direct comments on facial behavior. While people do not continually look at each other's faces, for to do so would be to start flirtations, power struggles or questions of suspicion or distrust, the face receives more visual attention from the other person than any other part of the body, and we are more likely to comment on a facial expression. We are not certain whether observations about the external feedback given to facial behavior are limited to the U.S. or Western cultures.

Affective displays carry more personal information than illustrators or most emblems. The most personal or idiosyncratic information comes not just from the display of a particular emotion, but from the affective blends, the affective sequences, and the extent to which the affective display is influenced by the setting. In the U.S., the norms about what affects are allowable or expected in different social settings are rather well known. Affective displays are appropriate in certain public places, not in others; *e.g.*, at funerals, weddings, athletic events, but not in restaurants.[12] The appropriateness of affective displays is also governed by the role position, age and sex. The mapping of norms in different cultures for affective displays, affect blends, affect sequences and affective behavioral consequences, in different social settings, interpersonal roles, age levels and sexes, is a central problem.

Affect displays can be related to verbal behavior in a number of ways. They can repeat, qualify or contradict a verbally stated affect, or be a separate, unrelated channel of communication. Affect displays can be emblems, in that a particular social group or culture may select an entire affective display or an element of an affective display and code it so explicitly that it is recognized and used as an emblem; the smile in many cultures is such an emblem.

Most affect displays are informative, particularly if they are of sufficient duration to be easily observed. Much of the confusion in the perception of affect displays, we believe, may be due to the presentation of seemingly contradictory blends of affect simultaneously or sequentially. Affect displays often have interactive consequences, modifying the behavior of the other interactant. Much affect display would not be commu-

[12] Goffman, Erving, *Behavior in Public Places* (London, Collier-MacMillan Ltd., 1963).

nicative; much of it is emitted without intention to transmit a message. Even the operation of the display rules to modify affective displays usually occurs below the level of awareness, based on deeply rooted habits, with little intention to transmit a message. But, there can be communicative affective displays in which the sender purposely emits a muscular movement to send a message. Elsewhere (Ekman and Friesen, 1969) we have discussed the differences between communicative and non-communicative displays. We have emphasized the shared level of meaning associated with the muscular movements of the face. These affective displays also have an important level of idiosyncratic meaning; the particular blends, the particular display rules employed in particular circumstances, the particular affect evokers, and the imagery, expectations and past events associated with particular affect displays would provide idiosyncratic information.

The coding of facial affect displays is not at all obvious. Both Darwin's explanation of the evolution of such displays, and our account of how certain displays may naturally develop in the course of each person's life, would suggest that some affect displays are either intrinsically coded or iconic. This may be so only for some affects; if we accept Darwin's principle of antithesis as the explanation of the happiness display, then it would be arbitrarily coded.

RESEARCH IN PROGRESS: In collaboration with Silvan Tomkins we have been developing a Facial Affect Scoring Technique (FAST), a coding scheme for the various facial cues associated with each of the primary affects. FAST is designed to be applied to either still photographs or motion picture film, and the scoring shows which affects are present. No attempt, as yet, is made to distinguish between felt and simulated affect. Our development of FAST borrows most heavily from the work of Duchenne, whom Darwin had quoted extensively. We are now conducting our first direct validity test of FAST. However, preliminary and partial use of FAST, in the experiment to be reported next, has given us some indirect evidence.

We have been comparing observers' interpretations of the same set of facial affect displays across different cultures. The stimuli used in this experiment were selected by ourselves and Tomkins, partially on the basis of FAST. We scanned over three thousand still photographs, with the FAST scoring system in front of us; but we did not systematically apply FAST to all stimuli and then pick those which fit our scores for each affect. Instead, our judgment was more subjective, although we believe it was guided by FAST. Our major basis for rejecting stimuli was the occurrence of blends of two or more affects in a given photograph; we chose only 'pure', single affect photographs. Our final set of stimuli included 34 pictures of males and females, some children, many adults, professional actors, amateur posers, and spontaneous photographs of mental patients. These stimuli were shown to observers (college students) in the U.S., who were instructed to pick from a list of 8 terms the affect which fit the photograph (we had included pain stimuli and pain as a judgment choice for another study we won't report here, although we do not consider pain an affect).

The results are remarkable, in three respects: very high agreement among observers in their recognition of affect displays; the observers decoded almost all the facial stimuli as we had predicted; and, the stimuli were decoded the same in more than one culture. There was more than 70 % agreement among American observers on a particular affect label (when choosing from a list of 8 terms), for 32 of the 34 stimuli. The majority affect label chosen for the stimuli was as we had predicted for 30 out of the 34 stimuli, thus providing indirectly some evidence for our selection of stimuli, and encouragement that FAST may be validly describing the cues associated with the recognition of affect displays. The four pictures where the observers decoded affects we had not predicted involved minor errors (which can be either considered ours or the observers). Two stimuli we considered to show disgust were called contempt by about half the judges, while the remainder said disgust. Two stimuli which we had called slight pain, were labelled sad.

Our results from showing these stimuli to college students at the National University in Brasilia are almost identical. The same high level of agreement among observers, and their interpretation of the affect shown by each stimuli differed from the U.S. on only one of the 34 stimuli, a disgust photo in the U.S. called contempt in Brazil.

While we would like to interpret the similarity in the decoding of affect between Brazilian and U.S. observers as evidence of the pan-cultural aspects of affect displays, there is a major problem in such an interpretation. The Brazilian and U.S. observers both share some of the same visual input, they both see some of the same people in motion picture films and television who may serve as models of affect display to be imitated, they both see tourists from the other country. Perhaps both groups have learned the recognition of affect from the same sources. In order to meet this criticism, we initiated studies of affect display in New Guinea where we were able to obtain observers who had not seen any movies, television, and where some had seen very few Caucasians.

This investigation in collaboration with Sorenson and Gajdusek has primarily focused on a South East New Guinea highland culture, the South Fore. We showed the 34 stimuli, which had been used with U.S. and Brazilian observers, to a variety of subjects who varied in extent of acculturation from those who wore western clothes and had learned Pidgin or English in a mission or government school, to those who had never gone far from their village, wore traditional clothes, spoke no Pidgin, and had seen less than ten Caucasians. In one study, mission educated Fore subjects translated the other subjects' responses from Fore, to Pidgin and to English. The acculturated subjects were able to choose from a list of terms a particular word to describe the photograph. The less acculturated subjects seemed unable to do this, perhaps because of the language barrier, so we instead obtained stories which described what had been happening that lead up to and/or followed the expression shown in the photograph. In another study, we were able to obtain, with the aid of a linguist, the South Fore words for different affects, and all subjects were able to label the photographs in their own language. In another study we had subjects pose affects, described in their own language, and we then showed these New Guinea photographs to other South Fore observers, who decoded the affect shown. Finally, we took cinema of the posing of affect and were analyzing the particular muscles which are involved in each pose utilizing our facial coding procedure, FAST.

The same decoding of the same facial behaviors was found across three literate cultures (U.S., Brazil, and Japan), for happy, anger, fear, surprise, sadness and for a single category combining both disgust and contempt (Ekman, Sorenson and Friesen, 1969). Since that time we have obtained the same results in Chile and Argentina. The literate culture results were compared with data from two preliterate cultures, the most acculturated persons of the South Fore of New Guinea, and the Sadong of Borneo. The level of agreement was generally lower, although evidence was obtained that the same facial stimuli are decoded as the same emotions for happiness, anger, and fear. In subsequent work, completed in the last few months, a new task procedure was employed which overcame some of the difficulties in translation and the novelty of task. In this second study of the South Fore of New Guinea, the results from both the encoding and decoding of emotion were the same as had been obtained in literate cultures. Thus we have obtained reasonable evidence for a pan-cultural element in affect displays—the association of particular facial muscles wiht particular emotions.

In the course of this work in New Guinea we have been intrigued with the affect stories we obtained in response to our photographs. These stories can be analyzed to reveal the social contexts in which affect is displayed; many of the themes are similar across subjects, revealing the age, sex, usual evoking stimuli and behavioral consequences of particular affects. Information derived in this way would of course have to be compared with information gathered from field observations and from other informants, in order to determine the generality of these affect stories. It does appear, however, that the use of such stimuli to elicit information from an informant may prove to be a useful anthropological tool when the stimuli have been standardized within a culture.

Our last cross-cultural study of affect displays is utilizing a different method of study; we are focusing upon the elicitation of affect, or affect encoding, and within a traditional laboratory framework. This research is being conducted in collaboration with Lazarus, Averill and Opton,[13] utilizing their stress-inducing procedure. Subjects are shown one of a number of stress-inducing films, most of which are concerned with different forms of body mutilation, or one of a series of bland, mildly interesting films. In previous work, Lazarus' group verified, both in the U.S. and in Japan, that these are stressful stimuli, by analyzing verbal reports after the films, and self-ratings during and after the films, and by taking physiological measures of arousal.

In our study we take motion pictures of the subject's facial expressions and hand movements without his knowledge, while he watches a stress film and a neutral film. We have collected pilot data, utilizing very brief samples of nonverbal behavior both in Japan and in the U.S. Our analysis of these records involves both the application of FAST and the collection of Japanese and U.S. observers' interpretations of the affect shown in the Japanese and U.S. films. The FAST analysis is designed to determine whether the same muscles move in response to stress in both cultures, and whether the same display rules are exhibited in the two cultural groups. The observers' interpretations of the stimuli will reveal whether both cultures interpret similarly the stress reactions of members of their own and of another culture. It is too early to report results from this study, other than the impressions that the procedures have worked and information is obtainable from the experiments.

---

[13]   University of California, Berkeley.

Regulators

The next category of nonverbal behavior is what we are calling REGU-LATORS. These are acts which maintain and regulate the back-and-forth nature of speaking and listening between two or more interactants. They tell the speaker to continue, repeat, elaborate, hurry up, become more interesting, less salacious, give the other a chance to talk, *etc.* They can tell the listener to pay special attention, to wait just a minute more, to talk, *etc.* Regulators, like illustrators, are related to the conversation, but while the illustrators are specifically interlaced with the moment-to-moment fluctuations in speech, the regulators are instead related to the conversational flow, the pacing of the exchange. The most common regulator is the head nod, the equivalent of the verbal *mm-hmm*; other regulators include eye contacts, slight movements forward, small postural shifts, eyebrow raises, and a whole host of other small nonverbal acts.

Most regulators, like the categories of batons and ideographic illustrators, carry no message content in themselves, but convey information necessary to the pacing of the conversation. They differ from batons and ideographic illustrators in that the regulators manage the exchange between the conversationalists, and do not accent a word or trace the development of a speech. But affect displays, and our last category of nonverbal behavior, adaptors, can also serve as regulators. Almost anything that one individual does and another observes has a regulative function, in that it can influence the communicative behavior of the other. But as Mahl (1968) has pointed out, simply the fact that a nonverbal behavior can influence another person does not mean that regulation is the sole, or even the primary, intent of the behavior. Thus, though a whole variety of behaviors can serve regulative functions, we reserve the label REGU-LATORS for those behaviors which do not fit into one of our other categories; that is, for behaviors which seem only to regulate.

Regulators seem to be on the periphery of awareness; a person can perform a regulative act without knowing that he does so, but if asked can easily recall and repeat it. Similarly, the other interactant seems quite sensitive to regulators if they are removed, but rarely aware of them when they are present. As a game we have suggested to friends that they try to inhibit all such regulators during a conversation. Most people find this very hard to do, but if they succeed in withholding regulators, their fellow interactant becomes quite disturbed, and communication stops. Regulators are not as intentional as either emblems or illustrators; people do not knowingly perform them in order to manage the communication system. They are usually not deliberate, but almost involuntary, highly over-learned habits.

We suspect that the frequency and type of regulators vary considerably with role, setting, and demographic characteristics of the person. We further suspect that the particular regulators and their frequency of occurrence are related to ethnicity, social class and culture, and that their misuse or misinterpretation is one of the more perplexing sources of misunderstanding between members of different groups. Regulators are taken for granted, and so typically occur out of explicit awareness that when someone does not emit the expected regulators or misinterprets our regulators, one is less likely to be able to isolate the source of the problem than if the miscommunication stemmed from emblematic or illustrator misunderstandings. People are likely to attribute regulator differences to rudeness or unmannerliness, rather than to a regulator system different from their own. We are not at all certain about the coding principles involved in regulators; some are obviously intrinsically coded, like shifts in posture to bring about greater or lesser attention, or more or less distance. But we suspect that there are many iconic and arbitrarily coded regulators.

Scheflen (1963, 1964, 1965) has been primarily concerned with what we are calling regulators. He has also written about the regulative aspect of the illustrators, affect displays, emblems, and our last category, adaptors. In our terms, regulators are always interactive-informative, but not often communicative. Scheflen has seemingly regarded any behavior which has interactive consequences as primarily functioning to regulate the relationship between interactants, and best comprehended from a communication or linguistic framework. Earlier we criticized this view, and while we recognize by our use of the term interactive that many other kinds of nonverbal behavior, emblems, affect displays, adaptors, can be interactive, we are reserving the use of the term regulator to describe only behaviors which do not readily fit into one of the other categories. Scheflen has made a major contribution to the understanding of such regulators in his distinction between three levels of regulators: points, positions, and presentations.

POINTS occur every few sentences; they are movements of the head, neck and/or eyes to mark the end of a structural unit, which is at a level higher than a single sentence. A point corresponds to the making of a point in a conversation. Different types of points may be used with explaining, interpreting, interrupting and listening. Earlier we described regulative acts primarily in terms of movements which, like Scheflen's points, pace or manage the back-and-forth nature of the communication. Scheflen seems to imply also that points state something about the content of the last few sentences of speech, providing decoding clues to the observer.

A POSITION, a large unit composed of several points, corresponds to a point of view taken in a conversation. Scheflen concentrates on posture, but also mentions how spatial distance between interactants can serve as a position.

A PRESENTATION is the totality of positions within an interaction; it is primarily composed of body movements which remove the person from the scene of interaction, at least temporarily. Scheflen discusses how overall posture and distance defines the inclusiveness of an interaction, in this sense defining the intimacy of the conversation. Body orientation, whether vis-à-vis or in parallel, defines whether the interaction is one of exchange of information or feeling (conversing, arguing, courting) or is one where the members are focused on a third party or object. Similarity in posture between two interactants, or what Scheflen calls congruence, is related to similarity in what is being said by both persons, or similarity in their perceived status. Scheflen would agree with our assumption that all of these regulators are culture-specific and vary within a culture with the demographic characteristics of the person. We are not conducting any research on regulators.

Adaptors

The last category of nonverbal behavior is the most difficult to describe, and involves the most speculation. We use the term ADAPTORS because we believe these movements were first learned as part of adaptive efforts to satisfy self or bodily needs, or to perform bodily actions, or to manage emotions, or to develop or maintain prototypic interpersonal contacts, or to learn instrumental activities. Thus we distinguish and will separately discuss self-adaptors, alter-adaptors, and object-adaptors.

The confusing aspect of these adaptors is that while they were first learned (usually in childhood) as part of a total adaptive pattern where the goal of the activity was obvious, when these actions are emitted by the adult, particularly during social conversation, only a fragment of the original adaptive behavior is seen. These fragments or reductions of previously learned adaptive acts are maintained by habit. When originally learned the adaptor was associated with certain drives, with certain felt emotions, with expectancies, with types of interpersonal interaction, or in a given setting. When the adaptor appears in the adult it is because something in the current environment triggers this habit; something has occurred currently which is relevant to the drive, emotion, relationship or setting originally associated with the learning of the adaptive pattern. But the original total adaptive activity is rarely carried through to completion; and when seen without knowledge of the origin of the activity, it may appear as random or noisy behavior. By this reasoning, adaptors when emitted by the adult are habitual, not intended to transmit a message, and usually without awareness.

This view of adaptors is basically similar to Darwin's explanation of certain body movements and facial expressions, except that we are postulating that the evolutionary development is ontogenetic rather than phylogenetic. Darwin hypothesized that such movements originally had serviceable functions, relevant to the survival of the organism, and that they were, through selection, preserved and maintained over the course of evolution, although in man they are no longer related to their original function. We assume that these adaptors are learned anew by each person early in life, and that they evolve over the course of his development with gradual modification and reduction of the total adaptive pattern so that by adulthood, and particularly in social conversation, only a fragment of the earlier learned adaptor may be seen, and not necessarily in obvious relationship to the original purpose served by the movement.

SELF-ADAPTORS are learned around the mastery or management of a variety of problems or needs. Some self-adaptors are learned in order to facilitate or block sensory input through hearing, seeing, smelling, tasting or touching. Some self-adaptors are learned for the proper performance of ingestive or excretive functions. Others are learned for the safe performance of autoerotic activity (those regarding sexual relations with others we will consider as alter-adaptors). Self-adaptors are also learned to properly groom, cleanse, or modify the attractiveness of the face and body. And, some self-adaptors are first learned to facilitate or block sound-making and speech.

Most self-adaptors are taught by the child-training practices of the parent and shaped by socialization processes. The grooming self-adaptors are re-learned during adolescence when there is a repeated, intensified focus upon appearance and changes in appearance. Each of these self-adaptors can involve learning to use the body or a facial feature in a specific way, OR learning to use the hands in relation to the face or body. When first learned, these adaptors were associated with drive states, with particular felt emotions or emotion blends, with interpersonal events, and with particular settings. When these adaptors are repeated later in adult life, it can EITHER be in order to perform the relevant adaptive activity, OR because some aspect of the current situation triggers the adaptive habit. It is the latter case which most often accounts for the adaptors shown by the adult in conversation. Only a fragment or a reduced version of the adaptor appears, probably because of later learned inhibitions about performing these activities in public places.

With high levels of emotional arousal, in more private places, during the most intimate relationships, or when there is personality disorganization, a fuller version of the self-adaptor may be manifest.

These self-adaptors are usually performed with little awareness, and no intention to communicate. The grooming self-adaptors may be the major exception, although people pretend that they do not know when they are grooming in public, particularly when they attend to body orifices; this may be a pretense to cover the behavior rather than actual lack of awareness. Self-adaptors have no intrinsic relationship to speech; but they may be triggered by, or related to, the motives, or affects, which are being verbalized. Generally self-adaptors receive little external feedback; other people don't directly comment on them, and rarely wish to be caught looking at them. It was only our parents who commented on the improper performance of self-adaptors in public places. We are not necessarily mannerly, avoiding the performance of such behaviors, but we are polite observers. If we notice someone engaged in a self-adaptor, we will look away, and pretend it is not occurring. Rudeness resides just as much in the person who continues to observe a self-adaptor as in the person who engages in the behavior.

An example of a self-adaptor seen in adult conversation would be the wiping of the lips with the tongue or, in particular, with the hand. Although chapped lips or a dryness of the mouth may be relevant to the appearance of this movement, if it also includes a clicking or slapping of the tongue against the roof of the mouth it may be a self-adaptor originally learned to clear away debris from the mouth and lips after a satisfying meal. It may appear in adult conversation when nothing is being eaten, but when the person feels satisfied over something he has just figuratively swallowed or devoured. The hands may wipe around the corners of the eye, a self-adaptor which would remove tears; but it may be shown by the adult with no tears present when grief or sadness is felt or anticipated. A person may squeeze his legs, exerting pressure in the genital region, a self-adaptor originally learned as a covert prelude to masturbation; if this action was originally associated with the sudden termination of parental affection, it may reappear when the adult experiences rejection by authority figures.

The interpretation or decoding of these self-adaptors is difficult, often speculative and uncertain. We presume that if they were not decayed by time and fragmented by inhibitions, but were instead totally performed, their meaning would be obvious. But this is seldom the case, except with children, and imagining the childhood origin of the movement can be an area for quite varied and wild inferences. Yet our own findings show that at least some of these self-adaptors convey very specific attitudinal information to observers, with high consensus among observers; and that when an individual who engages in a self-adaptor is asked about it, if he is able to provide information about the action, it will often refer backwards in time to childhood occurrences.

Probably the easiest self-adaptors to decode are ones in which the hands touch the face. Such hand-to-face adaptors are a particularly rich source of information, partially because the face contains differentiated organs, and where the hand goes and what it does to a facial feature can provide information. But there is another reason for the importance of hand-to-face adaptors. The face symbolizes, at least for people in the U.S., the self; people identify with their faces; if asked for a representation of another person they will show a picture of the face, not of the hands or legs; and when in scientific experiments we wish to preserve anonymity, we do so by disguising the face, although people can be recognized from the body as well. When a person touches his face, the action can be conceived in terms of what the person has had done to him, what he wants done to him, or what he is doing to himself. Activities such as picking or scratching may be forms of attacking the self; holding may be giving nurture or support; rubbing or massaging may be caress or reassurance. Since location of the activity is important also, and locations are generally relevant to the sensory input and output already discussed, this notion of the face as self overlaps with our earlier commentary.

Yet, parts of the face may represent self-properties which are not relevant to the organs involved in sensation, ingestion, or speech. The forehead and back of the scalp may be an example, since they often connote thinking activities. The head may be scratched almost as an emblem of ongoing thinking or wondering, the forehead wiped almost as an emblem of difficult or tiring thought. Another reason for the importance of hand-to-face adaptors, and for their comparative ease in decoding, is that such hand movements may follow and be interpreted in terms of how they handle a facial affect display.

Self-directed adaptors have rich psychological meaning, more personal in nature than is typical of regulators, illustrators and most emblems. Part of this personal meaning is shared among at least a group of persons, part is quite idiosyncratic to a given individual. We believe that many self-adaptors are informative, providing similar information across persons from the same social class or from sub-cultures with similar child-rearing practices. A large part of the idiosyncratic meaning is related to the conditions which trigger the emission of a self-adaptor — the particular motive, emotion, interpersonal event or expectancy which might have been associated with the particular self-adaptor; and this, of course, will vary considerably with the life history of each person. For example, the eye-cover act in which the hand covers but does not dig, scratch or rub the eye has a shared meaning relating to preventing sensory input or avoiding being seen, and is relevant to shame. More generally the act may have the meaning of support or help, needed or received, if the head leans down upon the hand which is covering the eye. But the conditions which trigger this act, which determine when it is shown, will vary for each individual; it may be a habit associated with crying, with intense anger, with excitement, or it may more particularly be associated with such an emotion in regard to a particular type of other person, a maternal surrogate, a sibling surrogate, *etc.* The most idiosyncratic meaning is thus related to the associational links between the adaptor and other events, feelings, and drives; these links reach back in time, were usually formed in childhood, vary with the life history of each person and are relevant to understanding why an adaptor is shown at a given point in a conversation.[14]

The ALTER-DIRECTED ADAPTORS originate in movements learned in early, perhaps prototypic, interpersonal contacts. They include movements necessary to giving to or taking from another person; movements relevant to attacking or protecting oneself from attack; movements

[14] Freedman and Hoffman's (1967) category of body-focused movements is quite similar to our description of self-adaptors. They limited their initial work to actions in which the hands touch the body, and have considered these movements as relevant only to sensory experience, but assume that such actions are relevant to need gratifying ideas. We would expect that they would concur in our description of self-adaptors which are relevant to ingestion, excretion, autoerotic activity, and grooming, in addition to the sensory self-adaptors. Rosenfeld's (1966) category of self-manipulation is described as actions in which one part of the body contacts another; his examples are scratching, rubbing, or tapping. Rosenfeld interprets these movements as indications of discomfort; while we would agree that this is true for some self-adaptors, other self-adaptors, particularly those which involve attacking movements directed against the self, and certain restless-looking movements (which we consider as alter-adaptors) can be related to other need states, or to emotions which are in no way necessarily discomforting.

necessary to establishing affection and intimacy, or withdrawal and flight; movements relevant to establishing sexual contact, such as invitations, flirtations, and courtship; and movements necessary to establishing sexual relationship (the last may be learned later). As with the self-adaptors, alter-adaptors are not necessarily shown in a total or complete fashion when they occur during adult conversations, although they may be in less public settings or in more pressured or intimate conversations. Instead, fragments or reductions of these movements occur, as habits linked to particular types of interpersonal events, expectancies, emotions.

Many of these alter-adaptors involve the use of the hands, often in space, but sometimes in contact with the body. Alter-adaptors which involve hand-in-space movements may be difficult to distinguish from illustrators, and actually may be completely redundant with the kineto-graphic illustrators if they actually illustrate in action what is being said verbally. Hand movements which touch the body must be distinguished from self-adaptors, although the two may be contained in a single move-ment, the distinction being thus artificial in that instance; *e.g.*, a protective movement which holds or conceals part of the body from attack, or a movement which stimulates part of the body, may at the same time draw attention and be an invitation for or rejection of contact with the other. Total postural movements, as well as changes in spatial distance, are alter-adaptors, although Scheflen would consider them presentations, which we previously described as relevant to regulators. An alter-adaptor has a regulative aspect, of course, if it is perceived; but we have attempted to reserve the term "regulator" for those movements which exclusively or primarily serve to regulate the back-and-forth conversational flow.

Leg movements can often be alter-adaptors, showing residues of kicking aggression, sexual invitation, or flight. Many of the restless movements of the hands and feet which have typically been considered indicators of anxiety we believe to be residues of alter-adaptors necessary for flight from the interaction.

While the alter-adaptors, like the self-adaptors, can be engaged in voluntarily, with full awareness, and perhaps might even be used inten-tionally to communicate, more often they occur with limited or no aware-ness, and with no intention to communicate. They may receive external feedback and generally people will be more willing to comment on an alter-adaptor than on a self-adaptor.

A fascinating example of an alter-adaptor was suggested by Washburn (1967), from his studies of baboon behavior. He had noted that during adult threat behavior, the baboon will often turn his head to the side;

and this action was unusual in that unlike the other behaviors found during threat, it seemed to have no functional value. A clue came from examining the situation when the baboon first learned to fight and attack. At those times, the baboon would attack another member of the group, but since he was not fully developed, he would only do so in the presence of his mother. Looking laterally was thus learned as a necessary part of aggressive behavior, to check whether mother was there. It is maintained by habit, although it no longer serves such a purpose in the adult threat behavior.

A last form of adaptor is the OBJECT-ADAPTOR, a movement originally learned in the performance of some instrumental task: driving a car, smoking, wielding a tool, *etc.* This movement will be repeated, again only in part, during conversations if the emotional or attitudinal component associated with the adaptor is triggered. The object-adaptors differ from the self- and alter-adaptors in that many are learned later in life. Object-adaptors may often be within awareness, which was not so for either self- or alter-adaptors, and some may be intended to communicate. Generally there are fewer social taboos about the performance of object-adaptors than self-adaptors, or even alter-adaptors.

All three categories of adaptors — self-, alter- and object- — are either iconically coded or intrinsically coded; they are not arbitrarily coded. If the movement is only a residue or a fragment of the original adaptive behavior, it approaches being iconic, but could be considered intrinsically coded if the residue has not been altered. If the movement reproduces all of the essential elements for the movement to have an adaptive consequence, we would consider it intrinsically coded adaptive behavior. It seems likely, however, that with time, fragmentation will occur, and that with fragmentation, alteration will also occur. The coding of adaptors is primarily kinetic. That is, the movement executes part of an action or performance, and meaning either is associated iconically with that performance or is that performance. By implication, there should be considerable variation in adaptors across cultures. Those adaptors which are common across cultures will chiefly be those which are most relevant to sensations and to the body functions of ingestion, excretion and reproduction, since the human anatomy necessitates some commonality in the performance of these activities.

The adaptors will usually have a rich level of idiosyncratic meaning as well as shared meaning, particularly the self-adaptors. This idiosyncratic meaning will generally refer to the stimuli which trigger the self-adaptor, the history of how the adaptor was learned and parental reactions to the movement, and associated ideational material. Most adaptors are emitted with little awareness and no intention to transmit a message; only in exceptional circumstances or with exceptional senders would we expect to find adaptors communicative. But, their shared level of decoded meaning would suggest that many adaptors are informative. Some may also be interactive, changing the behavior of the other interactant, but this will not be as frequent as for other categories of nonverbal behavior, such as emblems or illustrators, as there is a selective tendency to not attend to adaptors, particularly the self-adaptors. The self-adaptors are probably what Mahl had in mind with his term autistic actions, although, as we described much earlier, we believe his ideas are best interpreted as describing a layer of idiosyncratic meaning which can be found with any action, rather than as descriptive of an exclusive category of behavior.

RESEARCH IN PROGRESS: Our past work (Ekman and Friesen, 1968, 1969) has examined the meaning of self- and alter-adaptors in psychiatric patients, and noted changes in the frequency of these movements as the patients change from an acute disturbance to a remission of symptoms. In one of our present studies of adaptors we are examining this type of nonverbal behavior as a major form of leakage of withheld information during deceptive interactions. We have described elsewhere why this form of nonverbal behavior escapes efforts to conceal or withhold information, and is rarely employed as part of a dissimulation.

In another study of self-adaptors, we are comparing the frequency of such movements and their coincidence with linguistic phenomena, with facial affect displays, with interocular contact, and with another class of nonverbal behavior, the illustrators. This study employs our films of psychiatric patients; it was described earlier in the section on illustrators, (p. 74).

We are also looking at self-adaptors in our Japanese-U.S. study of nonverbal reactions to stress films (see affect displays, p. 77). While some of the behaviors are clearly affect displays, a number are self-adaptor movements in response to stress, and we are determining the differences in the repertoire of self-adaptors shown by both Japanese and Americans.

A last study of adaptors was quite limited in scope, but had the virtue of being conducted in New Guinea, where the subjects would have little opportunity to learn such movements from exposure to the style of body movements in Western culture. We investigated the body movements associated with embarrassment, flirtation and shame. Two methods of study were employed to investigate encoded and decoded meaning.

Photographs of adaptors were made from cinema previously taken of the South Fore, and these photographs were shown to South Fore informants who were asked to interpret the meaning of the movement — agreement among informants would show that the movement was informative, that is they had shared decoded meaning. *Ad lib* cinema was also taken of spontaneous instances of embarrassment, flirtation and shame, to study particular movements encoded in such circumstances. The class of movements studied included self-adaptors (hiding the face, covering the eyes, or mouth) and alter-adaptors (flirtatious display and concealment of body parts to another person). Both the encoding and decoding of many of these movements were found to be the same as it occurs in the U.S. These results are in agreement with a report by Eibl-Eibesfeldt which appeared in the popular press on similar flirtation movements in different cultures.

SUMMARY

In the table we have summarized some of the discussions of each of the five categories of nonverbal behavior in terms of origins, coding and usage. Limitations of space mean that the information given is brief and many of the qualifications have been left out; some points are overstated, and others which are important are ignored. The table should, however, facilitate comparisons between categories on a particular topic, such as awareness. The table should also reveal that different aspects of usage, and sometimes of coding or origin may be more salient in defining one category than another. The table should also show the gaps in our present thinking.

Let us emphasize that this categorical scheme is not complete or final. There are nonverbal behaviors which probably don't fit very well into any of the five categories — for example, an enduring postural feature such as holding the head in a forward, angular position .The five categories are not exclusive; the same nonverbal act can and sometimes must be placed within multiple categories. The emblems can include affect displays or adaptors which have been isolated by the culture and given explicitly defined meaning. The illustrators can include adaptors as kinetographic illustrators, and often will. Illustrators may also use an emblem which is kinetographic or pictographic to illustrate what is being said verbally. Affect displays which repeat or augment the affect being described verbally could be considered to illustrate the words, but we have not called such affect displays illustrators. Almost any of the categories can have a regulative influence, if observed, but we have tried to label as regulators only those acts which are not emblems, adaptors, affect displays or illustrators.

We wish to emphasize that many of the ideas put forward here are incomplete. We regard this paper as a report of progress rather than a final statement. Most troublesome, perhaps, is our treatment of coding. We are not happy with the term 'intrinsically coded behavior'. While the distinction between arbitrary and iconic codes seems clear to us, and the distinction between iconic codes and what we have called intrinsically coded behavior is important, we are dissatisfied with our present account of the differences between iconic and intrinsically coded behavior. A further problem is the distortion resulting from our treatment of nonverbal behavior as isolated units; we have attempted to map the elements of nonverbal behavior and have yet to specify sequential interrelationships either for the flow of an individual's behavior or for the interaction of two or more persons.

We think that the answers to many of the questions which were outlined at the beginning of this discussion when reviewing our past research are provided by the reasoning involved in this categorization of nonverbal behavior, although it would take another paper of this length to detail this. While this account is not supported by systematic evidence, and rests on examples, logical argument, and reference to isolated bits of data, we believe that it contains many hypotheses susceptible to test and we have described how our own research in progress is making use of this framework.

Perhaps the main value of this scheme is that it may make it more difficult to conceive of nonverbal behavior as a simple unified phenomenon, best explained by a single model of behavior, whether that model be neurophysiological, linguistic or psychoanalytic. If we have succeeded, then you should also be persuaded that even a dichotomization of nonverbal behavior does not do justice to the complexities and variety of body movements and facial expressions found in this domain.

University of California Medical Center
Langley Porter Neuropsychiatric Institute

	EMBLEMS	ILLUSTRATORS: Batons, Ideographs, Deictic, Spatial, Kinetographs, Pictographs	REGULATORS	AFFECT DISPLAYS	ADAPTORS: Self, Alter- & Object-
USAGE: external conditions	Most frequent when verbal channel blocked; also related to demographic variables	May vary with enthusiasm or excitement; varies with setting and demographic variables	Vary with and partially define roles, orientation of interaction; vary with demographic variables	Culture, social class & family define affects appropriate for certain settings; display rules incorporate social norms about affect displays	Self adaptors inhibited by conversations, but still prevalent. Adaptors triggered by a feeling, attitude
relation to words	high agreement about verbal definition; can be replaced by word or phrase	directly tied to speech, illustrate message content, or rhythmically accent or trace ideas	maintain and regulate back-and-forth conversational flow, not tied to specifics of speech	can repeat, augment, contradict or be unrelated to verbal affective statement	can be triggered by verbal behavior in present situation which is associated with conditions when adaptive habit first learned
awareness	usually as aware as choice of words	within awareness, not as explicit as emblems	periphery of awareness; difficult to inhibit	often highly aware of affect once displayed, but can occur without any awareness	typically not aware of adaptors, although tend to conceal and inhibit
intention to communicate	usually intended to communicate	intentional to help communicate, not as deliberate as emblems	over-learned habits that are almost involuntary	often not intended to communicate but can be; subject to inhibition; can be dissimulated	rarely intended to communicate
receiver feedback	visual attention and direct comment.	visual attention and some direct comment or response	other interactant very responsive to, but rarely directly comments on	greater receiver attention; can or cannot be direct comment on	other interactant rarely comments on, and politeness implies lack of attention to

information	syncratic. typically communicative, informative & interactive	syncratic; informative, often interactive & communicative	syncratic; by definition interactive, usually informative, not often communicative	cratic; informative, can be interactive, communicative only in simulations	cratic; often informative, not usually interactive, rarely communicative
CODING:	Some arbitrarily; some iconic (pictorial, kinetic, spatial) usually not intrinsic. Iconic can be decoded, at least in part, by a foreign culture.	Batons & ideographs: rhythmic/iconic: pictographs: pictorial/iconic; deictics: pointing/intrinsic; spatial & kinetographs: iconic or intrinsic. Vary with culture, social class, etc.	Arbitrary, iconic or intrinsic; we have not clearly specified. Vary cross-culturally and source of misunderstanding which is often not recognized.	Some intrinsic, may be iconic as result of display rules; perhaps some arbitrary. Some evokers, blends, display rules & consequences vary within and between cultures.	Intrinsic/kinetic or tend to be iconic when fragmented by time. Some similar, some differ across cultures.
ORIGINS:	Culture specific learning; specifically taught as verbal language taught.	Socially learned by imitation; vary with ethnicity; cultural and social class differences in type and frequency	Learned but we have not specified when.	Relationship between facial musculature & affect and some of the evokers neurophysiologically programmed. Some evokers, blends, display rules, consequences socially learned	Habits first learned to deal with sensation, excretion, ingestion, grooming, affect; or to maintain prototypic interpersonal relationships; or to perform instrumental task.
OVERLAP:	Can be based on affect display, or adaptors.	Kinetographs can include an adaptor.	All other categories can serve as regulators; but we call acts regulators only if they are not part of another category.		

type of information	more shared than idiosyncratic, typically communicative, informative & interactive	more shared than idiosyncratic; informative, often interactive & communicative	more shared than idiosyncratic; by definition interactive, usually informative, not often communicative	both shared & idiosyncratic; informative, can be interactive, communicative only in simulations	both shared & idiosyncratic; often informative, not usually interactive, rarely communicative
CODING:	Some arbitrarily; some iconic (pictorial, kinetic, spatial) usually not intrinsic. Iconic can be decoded, at least in part, by a foreign culture.	Batons & ideographs: rhythmic/iconic: pictographs: pictorial/iconic; deictics: pointing/intrinsic; spatial & kinetographs: iconic or intrinsic. Vary with culture, social class, etc.	Arbitrary, iconic or intrinsic; we have not clearly specified. Vary cross-culturally and source of misunderstanding which is often not recognized.	Some intrinsic, may be iconic as result of display rules; perhaps some arbitrary. Some evokers, blends, display rules & consequences vary within and between cultures.	Intrinsic/kinetic or tend to be iconic when fragmented by time. Some similar, some differ across cultures.
ORIGINS:	Culture specific learning; specifically taught as verbal language taught.	Socially learned by imitation; vary with ethnicity; cultural and social class differences in type and frequency	Learned but we have not specified when.	Relationship between facial musculature & affect and some of the evokers neurophysiologically programmed. Some evokers, blends, display rules, consequences socially learned	Habits first learned to deal with sensation, excretion, ingestion, grooming, affect; or to maintain prototypic interpersonal relationships; or to perform instrumental task.
OVERLAP:	Can be based on affect display, or adaptors.	Kinetographs can include an adaptor.	All other categories can serve as regulators; but we call acts regulators only if they are not part of another category.		

Haggard, E. A., and F. S. Isaacs,
    1966 "Micromomentary Facial Expressions as Indicators of Ego Mechanisms in Psychotherapy". In L. A. Gottschalk, and A. H. Averback (Eds), *Methods of Research in Psychotherapy* (New York, Appleton-Century-Crofts).

Izard, C. E.,
    1968 "The Emotions and Emotion Constructs in Personality and Culture Research". To be published in R. B. Cattell (Ed.), *Handbook of Modern Personality Theory,* Chap. 23 (Chicago, Aldine).

Mahl, G. F.,
    1968 "Gestures and Body Movements in Interviews". Paper presented at the Third Research in Psychotherapy Conference (Chicago, June 1966); in Vol. III, American Psychological Association).

Morris, C. W.,
    1946 *Signs, Language and Behavior* (New York, Braziller).

Nummenmaa, T.,
    1964 "The Language of the Face", *Jyvaskyla Studies in Education, Psychology and Social Research* (Jyvaskyla [Finland], Jyvaskylan Yliopistoyhdistys).

Osgood, C. E.,
    1966 "Dimensionality of the Semantic Space for Communication via Facial Expressions", *Scandinavian Journal of Psychology,* 7, 1-30.

Plutchik, R.,
    1962 *The Emotions: Facts, Theories, and a New Model* (New York, Random House).

Rosenfeld, H. M.,
    1966 "Approval-seeking and Approval-Inducing Functions of Verbal and Nonverbal Responses in the Dyad". Unpublished manuscript.

Ruesch, J., and W. Kees,
    1956 *Nonverbal Communication* (University of California Press).

Saitz, R. L., and E. J. Cervenka,
    1962 *Colombian and North American Gestures: An Experimental Study* (Bogota, Centro Colombo Americano).

Scheflen, A. E.,
    1963 "The Significance of Posture in Communication Systems", *Psychiatry,* 26, 316-331.
    1964 "Communication and Regulation in Psychotherapy", *Psychiatry,* 27, 126-136.
    1965 "Quasi-courtship Behavior in Psychotherapy", *Psychiatry,* 28, 3, 245-257.

Schlosberg, H. A.,
    1941 "A Scale for the Judgment of Facial Expressions", *Journal of Experimental Psychology,* 29, 497-510.

Sebeok, T. A.,
    1963 "Coding in the Evolution of Signalling Behavior". In P. L. Garvin (Ed.), *Natural Language and the Computer* (New York, McGraw-Hill), 430-442.

Tomkins, S. S.,
    1962 *Affect, Imagery, Consciousness,* Vol. 1, *The Positive Affects* (New York, Springer).
    1963 *Affect, Imagery, Consciousness,* Vol. 2, *The Negative Affects* (New York, Springer).

Tomkins, S. S., and R. McCarter,
    1964 "What and Where are the Primary Affects? Some Evidence for a Theory", *Perceptual and Motor Skills,* 18, 119-159.

Washburn, S.,
    1967 Personal Communication.

Woodworth, R. S.,
    1938 *Experimental Psychology* (New York, Holt).

FERNANDO POYATOS

Forms and Functions of Nonverbal Communication in the Novel: A New Perspective of the Author-Character-Reader Relationship*

> The rank on his rounce him ruched in his sadel,
> And runischly his reden he reled aboute,
> Bende his bresed browes, blicande grene,
> Wayved his berde for to waite whoso wolde rise.
> *Sir Gawayne and the Grene Knight*, 303-6**

Mr. Weller, the elder, gave vent to an extraordinary sound, which being neither a groan, nor a grunt, nor a gasp, nor a growl, seemed to partake in some degree of the character of all four.

> (Dickens, *Pickwick Papers*, LII, 770)

Tom laughed. "Jesus, are we gonna start clean! We sure ain't bringin' nothin' with us." He chuckled a moment, and then his face straightened quickly. He pulled the visor of his cap down low over his eyes. And the truck rolled down the mountain into the green valley.

> (Steinbeck, *The Grapes of Wrath*, XVIII, 204)

1. NONVERBAL COMMUNICATION IN THE PRINTED NARRATIVE TEXT

1.1 A cursory reading of a page in a novel, where both the writer and his characters speak (they among themselves, he to us), that is, where an interactive conversational encounter takes place alternating with the author's own observations about it, shows that if we were to rely exclusively on what words those characters say — depicted on paper as printed lexemes — and on a few punctuation marks, plus some instances of extralinguistic communicative features, a good part (perhaps the most important one) of the total human message would be simply lost, even though not so in the mind of the novelist.

A page picked at random from the end of chapter eight in Huxley's *Point Counterpoint*, for instance, in which a dialog is carried out among Spandrell, George Rampion, and Mary Rampion,[1] appears to be constructed of the following elements:

(a) a printed morphologico-syntactical exchange whose morphemes and lexemes express a present situation with evocations of the last fifteen years, and a series of intellectual concepts and of references to the social relationship of marriage; to which the author added a few structural punctuation marks, some quotation marks to indicate direct speech, periods that limit complete sentences, and commas that suggest juncture points, pauses, and pitch variations;

(b) two exclamation marks, one question mark and two suspension points, symbolizing – and unsatisfactorily representing – certain suprasegmental elements which complement the reader's imagined paralinguistic features concomitant with the linguistic ones;

(c) three paralinguistic descriptions concerning: Spandrell's peculiar way of laughing on two occasions (later used as a recurrent identification), and George Rampion's way of interrupting "with impatience" (a cultural, and not necessarily universal, quickening of the speech rhythm, and pitch raising);

(d) eleven descriptions of the kinesic behavior of the three participants in their face-to-face conversation, of which two describe the way Spandrell throws back his head before laughing, and one the way he looks from Mary to Rampion "almost triumphantly"; two more, Rampion's frowning at what is being said, one his "staring into his coffee cup", and one his looking at Spandrell "distatefully"; and two Mary's glancing at her husband, once "enquiringly", one her lighting a cigarette, and one her shutting her eyes to think of her youth.

(e) the author's exclusive comments on the characters' interrelationships, on their feelings towards each other, now and at other times, and on their very thoughts.

Another passage might have had fewer, or more, elements to be broken into. This example will suffice. It was meant simply to show the limited number of devices available to a novelist, and ultimately to a printer, for the readable conveyance of people's physical and intellectual activities, and this we can grasp at first sight.

A second look at the same page, however, will tell us:

(a) that a substantial part of the printed text is aimed at describing nonverbal activities which are produced either simultaneously with words or alternating with them;

(b) that the author, by so doing, openly acknowledges the limitations of his written-typographical presentation of verbal behavior to portray vividly the physical and psychological configurations of his characters;

(c) that the ratio between verbal and nonverbal activities must be an indication of certain stylistic characteristics more accentuated in some novelists than in others, and therefore an important touchstone for the analysis of the novel; and

(d) that, as I will specify later, the repertoire of nonverbal communication symbols is much more limited than the one symbolizing verbal language, that is, what traditionally — but perhaps not one hundred percent accurately — we call words.

1.2 Once the basic observations about a printed narrative text are made, the logical question is which human nonverbal communicative activities are acknowledged by novelists in general as elements complementary to their characters' verbal ones. The answer is those produced by the human body as a socializing organism, which, although psychomuscularly and chemically originated, we can contrast against the intellectual ones, and thus subsume under what elsewhere I have called *Total Body Communication* (Poyatos, 1974) as most of the semantic context of face-to-face interaction is conveyed by the body through motor, respiratory, dermal, thermal, and secretional channels, which includes four basic categories: acoustic (verbal language, paralanguage, and audible gestures, mainly); visual (gestures and postures, use of space, body appearance, dermal changes, and secretions); olfactory (body odors and perfumes); and tactile (contact movements and kinesthetic perception of others); which are distributed among Vocal-Verbal, Vocal-Nonverbal, and Nonvocal-Nonverbal forms of communication.

All bodily activities within those categories are present in narrative fiction, and writers, in greater or lesser degree, try to convey to their readers the perception of blushing and goose flesh, of perspiration and tears, of soft skin and body scents. Naturally, the degree in which bodily phenomena are granted true literary and intellectual values depends entirely on the artistry of the narrator, and this quality plus the activities themselves deserve serious attention.[2]

In this paper, however, I will present a perspective of narration which I consider rich enough, as it concentrates only on what I have termed the *Basic Triple Structure of Human Communication Behavior*,[3] that is, language-paralanguage-kinesics. I have argued on different occasions how it is unrealistic to try to isolate any of them in a serious study of the actual communication situation – either from a structural point of view or from a semantic one – for even the reader of narrative literature will consciously or unconsciously reconstruct, according to his sensitiveness and to the elements provided by the writer, words, 'tone of voice', and 'gestures'.

It is those three elements, jointly or independently, that the reader appreciates, above all others, in the fictional characters, and that is why I have so far excluded even *proxemic behavior* when analyzing nonverbal communication in the narrative text, in spite of its socio-psychological and cultural values.[4] Proxemic behavior can actually be absent when language, paralanguage and kinesics concur, even though imperceptibly at times, as when only the eyes, or a single muscle, move. As for *chronemic behavior*,[5] although time – including the duration of silences[6] – plays an important structural function in the interactive encounter being depicted in the text, and on some occasions defines certain social and cultural characteristics, it is not an essential element by which to judge the stylistic and technical qualities of a narrator, as are language, paralanguage, and kinesics.

1.3 After identifying nonverbal communication in the written text and acknowledging its preponderance among other forms of communication (just as it happens in real life), I would like to indicate briefly how writers and printers have managed heretofore to represent nonverbal elements, or rather, which ones they have represented, so that later I can discuss how the message is transmitted from the original author, or creator of characters, to the ultimate, but multiple, recreator, the reader. Although a semiotic discussion of the encoding and decoding of nonverbal communication since the first printed narrative texts would probably deserve a volume by itself, I will just refer in passing to the relatively simple and most arbitrary development of punctuation marks, originated in the Greek and Roman rhetorical signs devised for the reading aloud of texts, in medieval biblical and liturgical manuscripts read in churches and refectories, in the French and Italian printing shops of the Renaissance, and in seventeenth-century additions, like exclamation and quotation marks.

As for the role of the writers themselves, little or no attempt seems to have been made on their part to enrich the very poor repertoire at their disposal, although a reasonable number of additional symbols for representing certain features of human interactive behavior would be simply feasible. However, neither printers nor writers during the great periods of the modern novel – so concerned with physical and psychological realism – have shown much initiative for trying to represent many of the nonverbal qualities of speech and voice modifications that play such an important role in personal interaction, which would assist readers in their silent or audible reading of the characters' communicative peculiarities. Apart from some individual efforts to transcribe a few of what below I will refer to as paralinguistic alternants (*Er-*, *Ugh!*), exclamation and interrogation marks can be doubled, tripled, or combined (although ambiguity would be avoided in English in cases in which syntactical order does not indicate the interrogative or exclamative inflections, if the marks were placed also at the beginning of the sentence, as is done in Spanish); a long dash [–], or suspension or ellipsis points [...], are used to represent direct speech and indistinctively suggest the level juncture typical of hesitation and the true ellipsis caused by interruption or by the cutting-in of an interlocutor; a parenthesis suggests the lower pitch of an insertion; *italics* indicate emphasis, and hy-phen-a-ted words indicate emphasis and also the breathless rythm of accelerated speech. But no new symbols have been introduced in the traditional repertoire, and writers have gone as far only as changing the ize of the letters (to indicate VERY HIGH VOLUME or INDIGNATION), or using apostrophes to represent syncopated and apocopated rural speech. I would not just say that "writers are not linguists and have other needs and interests than that of making their writing a perfect image of their speech" (Bolinger, 1968:158), because the fact is that linguists do not seem to express serious concern about the limitations of written language, nor about a possible revision of the system itself.

2. PARALANGUAGE: LITERARY DESCRIPTION AND TRANSCRIPTION

2.1 Although some of the voice inflections represented by the established punctuation symbols would be visually perceived as gestures as well, that is, audible gestures, it is actually in paralanguage – the closest to audible verbal segmental and suprasegmental language – and not in kinesics, that we can trace an effort to transcribe certain speech qualities not revealed by written words, and where we can foresee ways to enrich the written and printed rendering of spoken language by means of both direct orthographic transcriptions similar to *Pst!* or *Tsk-tsk*, and indirect voice quality indicators for whispering (as opposed to the exclamation mark), sighing speech, panting speech, etc. It is quite obvious that if a few signs exist in written language to which authors resort in a true effort to represent, and not describe, certain sounds and paralinguistic features, but only a very small number of them, there is no reason why some additional ones could not be incorporated into the existing repertoire without interfering with the stylistic aims of literary works.

Thus, knowing that both the average letter-writing layman and the professional novelist strive, in different degrees, to achieve a certain paralinguistic realism, and that a few solutions have been used for centuries while others reflect today's concern, I would like to suggest the possible objectives in this endeavor by simply outlining the classification of paralinguistic phenomena I have differentiated.[7] The challenge it presents for the written representation of nonverbal-vocal interpersonal communicative behavior could generate much research on the part of linguists, and certainly some interest for a minimum of experimentation on the part of novelists. I have proposed so far the following taxonomy of paralanguage:

Primary Qualities: timbre, pitch level, pitch registers, pitch interval, intonation range, resonance, volume, syllabic duration, overall tempo, and general rhythm of speech.

"You've revolting," said Daisy. She turned to me, and her voice, *dropping an octave lower*, filled the room with thrilling scorn. (Fitzgerald, *GG*, VII, 100 [italics mine])

Modifiers: Qualifiers: glottalic control, velar control, articulatory control, articulatory tension, pharyngeal control, laryngeal control, labial control, maxillary control, and respiratory control.

"You don't know what it is to be a cripple. Of course you don't like me. I can't expect you to." / "Philip, I didn't mean that," she answered quickly, *with a sudden break of pity in her voice* ... / He was beginning to act now, and *his voice was husky* and low. (Maugham, *HB*, LXI, 367 [italics mine])

Modifiers: Differentiators: forms and degrees of whispering, of loud voice, of crying, of laughing, etc., when they override words.

"Go away," *she cried through her tears*, "go away." (Huxley, *PC*, XIII, 185 [italics mine])

Alternants: consonantal (bilabial, labiodental, whistling, clicking, velar), vocalic (mainly glottalized voiced central vowel-like sounds, with up to five pitch levels and varying nasalization, each of which has a closed-lip variant with identical or almost identical meaning), inarticulated (pharyngeal, nasopharyngeal, and nareal frictions), and pausal (modified speech pauses with different meanings).

her round eyes started and her mild mouth gaped. 'A gentleman?' *she gasped ... she broke into a breathless affirmative groan* (James, *TS*, V, 44 [italics mine])

"*Hmph!*" he murmured, with a movement of his head to one side ... It was totally unassured. / Mrs. Hurstwood noticed the lack of colour in it. (Dreiser, *SC*, XXII, 217 [italics mine])

2.2 Paralinguistic features are, therefore, determined by the anatomy and physiology of the individual's vocal tract and by the idiosyncratic use of the various possibilities; something perspicaciously acknowledged by the more perceptive novelists, who obviously make a point of specifying their characters' communicative behaviors, whether by doing so they succeed in individualizing them or not.

Primary qualities like pitch level (vaguely suggested, as I pointed out above, by [...], [!?], etc.), drawling and clipping, or modifiers like articulatory tension and overriding laughter or sobbing, could be easily indicated by new symbols preceding and/or following a sentence, just as we close it with a question mark or an exclamation mark.

It is within *alternants*,[8] however, that we find most of the existing forms of written paralanguage (*Ssh, Hm, Mh-hm, Ha-ha, Grr, Pshoo*) and also most of the nonverbal sounds which writers must describe with literary ability as the only way to include them in their narrative, thus lacking in the theater. The situation is rather absurd and merits serious investigation, for those sounds, although traditionally regarded as abnormal and nonspeech sounds from the point of view of our western languages, possess a perfectly 'normal' semantic value within our vocal communicative repertoire, form constructs that have as much lexical value as words, and are perfectly encoded and decoded by members of a culture as well as cross-culturally. Therefore, there is no reason to believe that, if they were consistently represented by the existing orthographic signs, complemented by some additional ones, they could not appear as dictionary entries and be used in literary as well as in non-literary writing. Why should not the novelist or the playwright be able to resort to a richer repertoire of vocally produced signs which actually exist in their minds when they are at work, which they have learned to use and perceive in their proper context, but which, due to restricting spelling and linguistic taboos, they cannot represent vividly on paper?

If we think, for instance, of Aldous Huxley's almost clinical descriptions of paralinguistic features, we realize that he is so conscious of their semantic and lexical properties that he makes a point of exercising his linguistic-stylistic ability, coupled to his acute perception of others, to describe how a person speaks and the 'non-words' that person utters. In fact, he seems to develope more than many others a rich linguistic style to write about his characters' paralinguistic one. One cannot help wondering how his style would have been affected had he been able to resort to established written forms of such message-conveying sounds as "a brief and snorting laugh", or "a rueful little laugh". But most of our paralinguistic utterances having no written form, nor a label (a verb and a noun) to refer to them in a standard way, Huxley appears as extremely conscious of the role played by them in personal interaction:

"Do you *really*?" It was an intense, emphatic voice, and the words came out in gushes, explosively, as though they were being forced through a narrow aperture under emotional pressure. (*PC*, IV, 53)

"Poor man!" repeated Lucy, and the words came out on a puff of explosive mirth. "He could hardly speak for terror." Suddenly changing her tone, she mimicked Lord Edward's deep blurred voice bidding her sit down, telling her (stammering and with painful hesitations) that he had something to talk about. (*PC*, XI, 146)

Polly pronounced the words in a sonorous monotone, as though she were reciting to an audience. She lingered lovingly over them, rolling the r's, hissing on the s's, humming like a bee on the m's, drawing out the long vowels and making them round and pure. "Ghost rattle of ghost rifles, in-fin-it-es-imal ghost cannonade." Lovely words! It gave her a peculiar satisfaction to be able to roll them out, to listen with an appreciative, a positively gluttonous ear to the rumble of the syllables as they were absorbed into silence. (*PC*, XI, 150)

In general, paralinguistic alternants, still constitute a sort of lexicon beyond the dictionary, but only, it seems, through lack of more appropriate orthographic representations (which obviously could be blamed on the lack of supporting phonetic transcriptions linguists should seek), for a modern desk dictionary like the second edition of the *Webster's New World Dictionary of the American Language* (1974) offers the average layman writer forms like *Er, Ha, Ha-ha, Psst, Tsk, Ugh, Uh-huh, Uh-uh,* and *Ugh*, defining them as "conventionalized pronunciations" or "natural interjections".[9]

That writers acknowledge the semantic importance of paralinguistic features in their characters' speech, and how their description contributes to convey their vitality as individuals, is amply demonstrated in their efforts, not only to represent, but failing this, to describe how they speak, and not only quote what they say in words. The study of alternants in literature, whether described or transcribed, would cover perhaps the most important part of the paralinguistic repertoires of the characters, apart from the overriding qualities of their voices.

'I'll tell 'ee what – [Sue] ought not to marry this man again!' said Mrs. Eldin indignantly ... / 'Pshoo! You be t' other man's. (Hardy, *JO*, VI, v, 372)

She breathed a vague relief. (James, *TS*, V, 41)

"H'm!" said Gerald, in disapproval. (Lawrence, *WL*, II, 33)

"Would you like to dine with me and my wife sometime?" / "Why... er... I'd be delighted." (Dos Passos, *MT*, III, 58)

"He's talkin' red, agitating trouble." / "Hm-m-m." The deputy moved slowly around to see Floyd's profile ... "Ever see 'im before?" the contractors insisted. / "Hmm, seems like I have." (Steinbeck, *GW*, XX, 235)

"You wouldn't want them nice molars all smashed, would you?" / "Aw-haw. Big talk ... " (O'Hara, *AS*, VI, 105)

"Wagh! Whoo!" howled Remi in the evening streets of Frisco. ... "Aaah-how!" he wrapped himself around a pole to laugh. (Kerouac, *OR*, XI, 63)

Extensive research could be done about paralanguage in narrative literature: the voice qualities that seem to appear more often, those associated with specific cultures or specific socioeconomic strata; how far novelists can go in the realistic portrayal of the people they create; and which literary tendencies are apt to give more weight to nonverbal communication. From a semantic point of view we find, for instance, how the same paralinguistic alternants, identically transcribed, reflect the variety of meanings and contextual situations found in real life.

3. KINESICS: THE CHARACTER THROUGH GESTURES, MAN-NERS, AND POSTURES

3.1 As for kinesics, its possible written representation would certainly be a controversial subject which does not fall within the aims of this paper, although it seems incredible that attempts to transcribe movements – other than Birdwhistell's (1970) and Kendon's (1969) kinegraphs[10] – should be, as far as I know, totally absent among those interested in written communication and its historical development.

If we widen the concept of language without limiting it to the signs emitted and perceived in the human vocal-auditory channel, but acknowledging the semantic value of those produced in the kinetic-visual one – which constitutes an essential element of the basic triple structure, as I discussed earlier –, we must admit that in real-life interaction the total message between sender and receiver is perceived fully only when nonverbal activities can be decoded along with verbal ones. Furthermore, there are countless situations, usually critical ones, in which messages are encoded only through nonverbal channels, particularly through kinesic behavior; and even when words are used, it may be in gestures and glances, in manners and in conscious or unconscious positions of the body that we find the real meaning of those words, because, as Merezhkovsky wrote in connection with *Anna Karenina's* descriptions of kinesic behavior:

The language of body gestures, while it may be less variable, is nevertheless more unmediated and expressive, endowed with a greater force of *suggestion* than the language of words. It is easier to lie with words than with body gestures and facial expressions. ... One glance, one frown, one quiver of a facial muscle, one movement of the body can express that which cannot be expressed with words.[11]

And referring to both paralanguage and kinesics, he notes:

But Anna and Vronsky speak not with words, but only with "the flash of glances and smiles", with the tone of their voices, their expressions, and the movements of their bodies, like animals in love. And how much deeper than all human words is this elemental and animal, wordless language of love![12]

Among other aspects of the communicative properties of nonverbal activities, one should not forget that the blind, who must rely solely on verbal and paralinguistic communication (occasionally complemented by olfactory one), miss an important part of the basic triple structure as perceived by physically unimpaired interactants; just as the deaf miss, above all, the nuances with which paralanguage colors the words they might read in their interlocutors' lips.

3.2 It is true that a written sign symbolizing 'standing', or 'sitting', or 'raised eyebrows', would still need a complementary verbal specification, unless a very refined transcription of kinesic activity were devised. In other words, such a system would require kinemes (as defined by Birdwhistell), and not just broad kinemorphemes and kinesyntactic constructs, in order to indicate with some accuracy the formation and development of the movement in question. Naturally, it is hard to imagine a kinealphabet side by side with the orthographic one on which we have built up a whole rhetorical and esthetic system and based our national literatures. The mere thought of it, we feel now, seems to destroy the concept of literary style as conceived today, by means of which a gesture can be described in many ways by speaking about it, and not writing it.

We could argue that while a verb, an adjective, or an adverb can stand by themselves and suggest a very specific idea — although the counterargument would be that an adverb like 'mildly' contains a gamut of degrees differently perceived by readers or listeners –, a kinegraphic construct would be a rougher representation. Again, if an ancient rebus broadly depicted certain kinesic activities, we can wonder why that system could have not gradually become more and more refined until it would have been able to represent kinemorphemes and kinemes, just as the representation of phonemes followed that of syllables, and syllables succeeded whole words in writing. After all, just as phonological elements are determined by phonetic articulations, we can refer to kinesic constructs as formed by kinesiological articulations, and even draw up an acoustic-kinetic chart of the head, in which the relationships of sound-movement, verbal language-gestural language, would be clearly demonstrated.[13]

In spite of the fact, however, that language or paralanguage is not always more important than eye contacts and other body movements – since a subtle gesture can modify a whole linguistic-paralinguistic compound – no kinegraphic symbols were devised after alphabets were used, not even (as one might desire at times) to indicate a basic overriding posture, or a facial affect display that may accompany a stretch of speech. The advantage of using a few basic kinegraphic markers is that the reader would be able to perceive the kinesic behavior of the characters, not before or after their linguistic one, as it happens with the author's descriptions, but actually synchronized with it.

3.3 At any rate, one must concede that whatever kinegraphs one could introduce in a literary text would undoubtedly replace the literary process itself (by which reality can be rendered in subtly varying forms), and that the artistic difference between two writers, based on their individual description and evocation through words, would be seriously curtailed. We only have to read the narrative production of various national literatures, from their epics to their contemporary novels, to realize the extreme importance of the kinesic descriptions with which authors, in different degrees,[14] endeavor to achieve, not only physical realism but psychological one as well:

... by the way he opened his eyes, staring down at the ground without batting a lash for quite a while, and how other times he closed them compressing his lips and arching his eyebrows, we easily knew that some kind of madness had come upon him. (Cervantes, *DQ*, I, xxiii, 223, translation mine) (1)

Mr. Weller planted his hands on his knees, and looked full in Mr. Winkle's face ... having accompanied this last sentiment with an emphatic slap on each knee, folded his arms with a look of great disgust, and threw himself back in his chair, as if awaiting the criminal's defence. (Dickens, *PP*, XXXV, 573)

She exerted all the powers of her mind to say what she ought; but instead she fixed on him her eyes filled with love and did not answer at all. (Tolstoy, *AK*, II, vii, 127)

That officer [policeman] yawned, stretched out his elbows, elevated himself an inch and a half on the balls of his toes, smiled and looked humorously at Jude. ... (Hardy, *JO*, II, vi, 123)

Lady Edward hailed her over the heads of the intervening crowd with a wave of her long feather and a smile. The late arrival smiled back, blew a kiss, laid a finger to her lips, pointed to an empty chair at the other side of the room, threw out both hands in a little gesture that was meant to express apologies for being late and despairing regret at being unable in the circumstance to come and speak to Lady Edwards, then, shrugging up her shoulders and shrinking into herself so as to occupy the smallest possible amount of space, tiptoed with extraodinary precautions down the gangway toward the vacant seat. (Huxley, *PC*, II, 29)

"Sure I et all right," said Bud and ran his tongue round his teeth dislodging a sliver of salt meat that he mashed against his palate with his tongue. (Dos Passos, *MT*, II, 34)

The proprietress, her hands in the pockets of her apron, her shoulders thrown back and her legs apart, calls him [Pepe, the waiter] in a dry, cracked voice. ... (Cela, *LC*, I, 53, translation mine) (2)

4. THE COMMUNICATION PROCESS BETWEEN AUTHOR AND READER: TRANSMISSION OF THE CHARACTER IN NARRATIVE LITERATURE

4.1 The fact that verbal communication in its written or printed forms has reached such a degree of refinement and versatility — in spite of its limitations as a surrogate of speech — forces us to recognize the communicative superiority of words over gestures and their unlimited possibilities for symbolizing, and reduce to visual signs, all existing signs, that is, for writing down things and ideas. Although, as I have just shown, a great amount of words are used to speak about gestures and about other non-lexical behaviors.

In written literature, spoken language (or vocal-auditory signs in general) and movements are evoked by means of written signs we call words and punctuation marks. In fact, the whole sensorial world which surrounds us in real life is transmitted to us through writing and printing, which in turn will elicit images of it in our intellect, according to the writer's skill. In a novel, accoustic, visual, tactile and kinesthetic, olfactory, and gustatory signs are all reduced to visually perceived ones. This is the limitation and wonder of the written word.

A film may show physical images, sounds and colors, thus avoiding their description, but will not reach — in spite of the lenses' play with angles, focus, colors and light — the lexical combination which is available to the writer. And yet, a cinematic or musical construct might express, we could argue, the ineffable.

From a semiotic point of view — not perhaps a literary one, unless the very concept 'literary' is revised — any novel, even a poorly written one, appears as a fascinating display of communicative power and of transmitting devices. Even if we concentrate only on how non-verbal communication is conveyed and perceived in the novel (as the subject of this paper), we must first delineate the process by which the character (along with his contextual elements) is transmitted to and perceived by the reader (also subject to his own circumstance). That creative-recreative process — some of whose aspects will be discussed here — are outlined in the accompaning chart "The Communication Process Between Author and Reader: Transmission of the Narrative Character." It develops through three main stages, as indicated in the chart:

Stage 1. The process is initiated when the writer, drawing from his own world of physical and intellectual experiences, begins to decode and select as his material all the signs related to those experiences. This he can do in two ways:

(a) directly, that is, sensorially, almost as he lives them, as with the narrator's own sensations, which he simultaneously grants his character, whether consciously or unconsciously, shaping him in a way similar to the artist who works in front of his model, or facing a landscape that will elicit peculiar reactions in that fictional human being; or

(b) in a delayed way, including whatever was directly experienced in the past or is recreated through other verbal and written stories, that is, in an intellectual and more selective manner.

It is in this phase that the writer, by accumulating signs of different origins, carries out a selection of linguistic, paralinguistic, kinesic, proxemic, and other nonverbal behaviors (more or less conscious of their technical and stylistic functions), besides psychological and ideological characteristics. In other words, he gives shape to his character, both physically and intellectually.

Stage 2. As that character acquires life in the mind of the narrator through somatic and intellectual features, codified now for the future reader, the second stage of his transmission to the latter takes place. It consists of a channel reduction, made possible only by words, since the whole multisensory and intellectual world directly experienced by the writer is going to be reduced to the morphologico-syntactical representation (supplemented by a few punctuation signs) which is the written text, that is, a visual form of expression. We could say that it is a sign metamorphosis, which the reader will later trigger again so that the inverse may take place in the decoding process of his reading.

In this phase the nonverbal repertoires, mainly paralanguage and kinesics — very often so important in narrative literature — are revealed as factors which must be considered in the analysis of the work because of the power of the written word for describing and evoking those repertoires in spite of the imposed sensory limitations. We, as readers, find the character's behaviors in two forms:

(a) explicit, in other words, the visual printed signs: morphologically and syntactically modified words, verbal descriptions of nonverbal activities, and punctuation marks; and

(b) implicit, not even visually present in the written or printed text, but rather latent 'between lines' and intellectually perceived, in which way they will, in a hidden dimension, complement the author's implicit repertoires, and also enrich the reader's own sensations according to his own sensitivity:[15] the paralinguistic modifications that correspond to certain linguistic constructs, the gestures, manners, and postures equally co-structured with language and paralanguage in real life, the spaces that separate people in their interactive encounters according to the contextual situation, the type of silences dictated by that situation, etc.; all of which is, in greater or lesser degree, grasped by the reader, thanks to those printed words, in what is actually the next stage. But the first two actually overlap at the point in which the writer's real world is changing into his created, transformed, or imagined one through the necessary channel reduction.

Stage 3. In what can be the last stage in the literary process between author and reader, a reverse sign metamorphosis takes place when the reader begins to act as such by transforming the printed visual signs, and those which he can intuit further through them — an indefinite series of secondary, tertiary, etc., signs mutually elicited according to certain semiotic patterns that deserve attention — into their original sources, that is, by mentally bringing them back to life and turning the written words into intimate imagined sensations of optical, auditive, tactile, olfactory, kinesthetic, and dermal experiences. The reader, in sum recreates the author's flesh-and-bone character, thus completing the intended cycle, or rather, the literary recycling of signs. This duality, the author's character and the reader's character, spans between the two end points, input and output, of the coding process, at both of which the individual's own personal and cultural conditioning background[16] affects the entire process. From a literary point of view, I will discuss later the important communicative and technical functions that the character's verbal and nonverbal repertoires, thus transmitted, plays in the narrative work.

4.2 Another angle from which to consider the process just outlined would be that of *interaction*. Although the silently read narration does not elicit actual personal interaction,[17] we can easily imagine a speaker-listener relationship in the case of the medieval poems whose characters and events we must appreciate today only through their printed evocation. But the living, direct audiences of the medieval minstrel or the local entertainer surely must have displayed a rich repertoire of verbal, and mostly nonverbal, feedback (approval-disapproval, surprise, disappointment, etc.) and listener's behaviors (mainly completion of key sentences or expected expressions, and anticipation of the characters' gestures).[18] Which implies that certain activities (mainly linguistic, paralinguistic, and kinesic) did not have to be decoded through the visually perceived text of the poem, as we must do today, but directly from the minstrel's own performance of those behaviors.

5. VITALITY, PLURALITY, AND CULTURE OF THE NARRATIVE CHARACTER

5.1 One can conclude from the aforegoing that the creation, transmission, and perception of the people in the fictional world of the novel is a process based on the author's own exclusive circumstance in the real world, at one end, and the individual reader's own exclusive circumstance, also in the real world, at the other; each of them occurring in a specific spatial and temporal situation.

From the literary as well as from the psychological point of view, this would deserve much elaboration if we were to probe as deeply as possible into the most hidden layers of the creative process, on the one hand, and of the re-creative process, on the other; that is, if we were to analyze the motivations, sensitivity and general contextual circumstances of both writer and reader. The exclusiveness that defines each of them as individual human beings is, I feel, an unfathomable abyss in which the relationship Author (real world)-Character (fictional world)-Reader (real world) lies partly hidden to our curiosity, and the basis for the three premises which constitute the backbone of the analysis of nonverbal communication as a new perspective of narrative technique, namely: the vitality of both writer and reader, and the in-between position of the character, whose own vitality, confirmed by each reading, confirms in turn his inherent plurality.

5.2 When we acknowledge the human attributes of the characters in a novel – in this paper, mostly their nonverbal repertoires – it is imperative to acknowledge also the novelist's own vitality, his contact with the real world, his cultural locus. Robbe-Grillet (1963:149), referring to the inevitable subjectivity of objectivism and to the fact that only God can be objective, says about the author that "c'est *un homme* qui voit, qui sent, qui imagine, un homme situé dans l'espace et le temps, conditionné par ses passions [and by his culture, with whatever that implies, I would add], un homme comme vous et moi"; and, among many other similar statements, Mendilow (1965: 89) asserts: "The most original mind does not work in a vacuum". Therefore, an imagined human being, created by a real human being, and later recreated by still another human being, will offer the literary critic at least a double image (the original character and the 'read' one), perhaps a triple one (when identifying the author's own personality and communicative repertoires, as it happens sometimes), and actually an infinitely multiple one as 'lived' by each reader, here and there, now and in a hundred years.

A character may have been given life mainly as a highly intellectual vehicle for the conveyance of the writer's philosophy, as in the case of Sartre's Roquentin in *La Nausée*, Unamuno's Augusto Pérez in *Niebla,* or Gregor Samsa in Kafka's *Die Verwandlung*; as the tool for a satire, like Swift's Gulliver, or Voltaire's Candide; as a sort of intermittent lecturer for encyclopedic novels like Huxley's *Point Counterpoint* (whose people are, however, highly individualized and deeply rooted in a mimetic world); or as a fictional individual being drawn from, and depicted in, the author's daily environment, like Richardson's Pamela, Dostoevsky's Raskolnikov, Zola's bourgeois, Dreiser's self-made men, or Dos Passos' city dwellers. But, in any case, no matter how intellectualized he is, a character is, or has been, a flesh-and-bone individual in his author's mind, and his vitality is always confirmed.

It is important to recognize, however, that this undisputed vitality appears at the completion of the semiotic process I have outlined before, that is, when the reader decodes the explicit and implicit signs in the literary text, bringing back to life the dormant, awaiting human being left in the pages of the narrative by his creator; and furthermore, that this process that begins as a consequence of the synchrony between the writer and his time, reflects in the end the disynchrony between the reader and the character's first version. In other words, the reader, conditioned by a new circumstance in a new time in his culture, will not reconstruct Cervantes' Don Quijote, Dicken's Pickwick, or Malamud's Yakob Bok exactly as their authors lived them during the creative process, not even as they lived them in the subsequent readings of their own work, for those readings would take place at an already different time, conditioned by a new set of circumstances.

On the other hand, we can suspect, in some cases, that the nonverbal repertoires of the characters are a reflection of the author's own behavior; and this, along with his whole personality is certainly an important asset for the true understanding of his work and the people in it.[19]

5.3 I hope that this brief discussion of the creative-recreative multiple process, as part of the semiotic process outlined in the accompanying chart, will have clearly suggested the existence of two basic intellectual forms: *the author's character* and *the readers's character*.

We have seen that whatever characters say and do can be determined, first of all, by the author's own vitality, for which reason the linguistic-paralinguistic-kinesic style of the character, and that of his author, become in themselves both tools and subjects of complementary scholarly endeavors. This close relationship suggests the need to consider what are actually the two basic dimensions of any human activity: space and time.

There is a *cultural setting* for a fictional character. Whether his creator wants it or not, he will almost always, if we look for it, give away a specific culture (even above a possible intended plurality of cultures), either his own or another one. This poses one more problem for the reader, since he might not need to interpret those cultural characteristics properly in order to fully understand (and we might question this) the character's ideas and general personality, but he would certainly need to if he is to relive that character as closely as possible to the original one.

On the other hand, there is also a *temporal setting* the novelist draws from during his creative process. It can be his own present time, in which case he is using first-hand material. He can project us into the future, as in Utopian and science-fiction works, or he can be trying to bring the past back to life, as in the historical novel. But even in the case of a historical novel, he will inevitably draw from his own time locus. In other words, he will dress his own contemporaries in sixteenth-century clothes, and will see them move in those clothes, but that will not make their movements the true kinesics of the sixteenth-century, as it was Cervantes' while making Don Quijote and Sancho display their magnificent repertoires of gestures, manners, and postures.[20]

The problem of recreation, therefore, and the probability of minimizing the plurality of the characters will depend much on those two dimensions, time and space (indicated in the chart), as much as the creative process does.

Signs (the spoken word, the accompanying voice modifications and paralinguistic sounds, the movements of the body, the proxemic behavior displayed in the novel) vary with time, but also through space, due to geographical differences, cultural settings, and racial differences. The author's time and space relationship with his readers needs much research, and a semiotic approach to this relationship, in terms of the encoding and decoding of the many messages contained in the narrative work, could be a very fruitful one.

We must not forget, however, that a number of signs decoded by the readers of a novel might have never been intentionally encoded by the writer, and that a very valid argument in favor of the literary work is precisely the plurality of interpretations and appreciations to which a piece of narrative, for instance, is subject once it is released by its author. But this is not a new subject. I am referring to the plurality of the character, not, in fact, as a virtue on the part of his creator, but as something he himself would like to avoid if he could, in many cases. A writer can say, of course, that his readers will bring his characters to life as he created them, but we know only too well that this is not true, that each new reading is like a genetic act in which a new person comes to life. Or, to put it more mildly, another Don Quijote in the endless series of Don Quijotes.

Finally, I would add that this unavoidable characteristic of the narrative character is determined, as I have tried to show, by the vitality of both author and reader and, in sum, because the written text is so dissociated from the sensory world it tries to depict.

5.4 This basic problem the central one to my topic, made me think many times of the advantageous position of the characters in the medieval poems, as I hinted earlier. The plurality of the epic heroes and their surrounding personages in pre-Gutenberg times must have been greatly minimized, since each minstrel, each time, would act the same Green Knight, or the same Cid for many people, conveying a very similar image for which tone of voice and body movements, particularly in important passages, would be not only almost automatically displayed, but much closer to reality; as in the case of El Cid (a living contemporary Spaniard in those days), or to the original Green Knight, or Sir Orfeo, as imagined by their authors. Authors, characters, minstrels, and audiences were dealing with the same, or very similar, space and time settings. What would not we give today to be able to see and hear the real-life *Poem of El Cid* as sang by its minstrels, when El Cid and his men leave Vivar and, upon seeing the raven fly on their right hand side, and then on the other, he makes the then prescribed head and shoulder movements to cast off the ill omen; or how Pedro Bermúdez and the Infante Don Fernando get ready to charge against each other.[21] Likewise, although not based on real events, the minstrel would act Sir Orfeo's gestures and tone of voice, as described in the poem, when he faces the demented queen, and the dramatic dialogue that ensues;[22] or the appearance of the Green Knight at Camelot, his challenge, and how, after Sir Gawain severs his head, he gropes for it, remounts his horse and leaves with a final fierce jerk on the reins.[23]

Besides considering the previous comments as a basis for an elaborate study of certain aspects of realism, as I will discuss later, I would also suggest — as a sort of *literary anthropology*, or historical social psychology — the systematic investigation of the historical and documentary value; not only of the language, paralanguage, kinesics, and proxemic behavior of other periods of a culture, as described in its older literary works, but of other nonverbal activities, such as body adaptors (clothes, jewelry, cosmetics), object adaptors (handling of arms, belts, and long disappeared artifacts), or affect-displays (as shown on many occasions by the characters).[24]

6. THE FATE OF NONVERBAL COMMUNICATION IN THE TRANSLATED TEXT

6.1 A serious and fascinating aspect of translation, although hardly acknowledged in the scholarly literature, is that of the problems encountered by the translator (whether a professional one who produces a text in the target language, or the common reader who, inadvertently perhaps, tries to translate and interpret) when confronted with the nonverbal behaviors of the characters, not only the explicit ones, but those hidden beyond the words of the written text.

Since I plan to elaborate on this topic elsewhere with the appropriate documentation, I will simply outline here what in the chart is indicated by *interlinguistic and intercultural translation,* which can be a fourth stage beyond the basic recreation of the original character by a reader who is not a member of the author's (or the character's) culture.

Referring to foreign-language students, diplomats, and serious travelers, I have often emphasized the need to seek not merely linguistic fluency, but *cultural fluency* as well. This implies, among other things, an ability to understand and/or produce the nonverbal behaviors that must be displayed along with verbal language, and that are rooted in ethnic, geographical, and socioeconomic factors. In the case of the novel, it is important for the translator to acknowledge his responsibility as mediator between author and reader and, therefore, as the conveyor of the literary character; but the author himself, who writes for an audience here and there, now and tomorrow, should perhaps be able to predict the fate of the nonverbal repertoires he grants his characters, for those repertoires may be conditioned by elements which vary through space (climate, race, clothes) and time (clothes, furniture, etiquette norms, moral values).

6.2 The concept of translation should not be applied only to the rendering of a text into another language, but also to the intellectual process I would call *intracultural translation.* A reader can appreicate his own language in a novel whose characters belong to a subculture which is not his subculture; but that does not mean that he is equipped to fully understand the explicit and implicit nonverbal behaviors (without counting the linguistic localisms) contained, for instance, in a regionalistic novel dealing with rural life and all its human and environmental elements, from paralanguage and kinesics through proxemic behavior to chronemic behavior, unexplained furniture arrangement, and local customs.

6.3 Even if we concentrate on explicit nonverbal communication as described in a foreign culture's literature, I would offer some tentative suggestions just to elicit scholarly interest as to:

(a) how the foreign reader decodes certain paralinguistic, kinesic, and proxemic behaviors which do not correspond to the behaviors displayed in his own culture in similar situations;

(b) how often he misses certain important nuances of meaning attached to some nonverbal activities, and whether or not these could be clarified by a translator's note when it might cause a gross misunderstanding;

(c) how to transcribe paralinguistic alternants for which there is an orthographic representation in the source language but not in the target one (English *Tsk-tsk, Whew!, Hm,* and *Uh-uh,* for instance, are not written in Spanish);[25] and

(d) how to internationalize the orthographic representation of some basic pancultural paralinguistic alternants, as suggested in part 2 of this paper.

A few more comments about nonverbal communication and translation could be made which would suggest the interrelationships of the elements mentioned so far. They would prove further how the subject of literary translation, particularly of the novel, is necessarily related to the study of nonverbal communication and communication in general; and that, as long as the nonverbal elements of human interaction are not studied in depth, and the professional translator and the student of literature do not strive to deal with a written text in an exhaustive way, we will not understand fully what is involved in translation; in fact, what translation is all about.

7. NONVERBAL COMMUNICATION AND REALISM

7.1 From the discussion of how nonverbal communication in narrative literature reveals the semiotic (or communicative) process which in turn shows the author-character-reader relationship, and of how the character's repertoires affect the literary text itself, both in its original version and in translation, we could conclude that the use of those repertoires is a necessity inherent to the author. It is, in different degrees, a mimetic goal which, disguised in ephemeral artistic currents at times, always pervaded the fictional narration, from *Satyricon* to the work of our contemporaries. To decide, however, why some 'realists' give so much weight to the nonverbal behavior of their characters while others do not, would not be simply an easy cataloguing task. We can, for sure, associate the specification of paralinguistic and kinesic behaviors with the great figures of nineteenth-century realism or with the authenticity of Dreiser's world, but it would take a very deep analysis of the most hidden layers of literary, esthetic, and personal characteristics to even attempt anything like a taxonomy of narrative literature based on the use of the representation and description of nonverbal communication.

Trying to come closer to the understanding of the forms and functions of this tendency, however, I would like to point out that the morphologico-syntactical-orthographical vehicle used by the writer for that purpose can be either *poetic*, that is, deliberately esthetic (sometimes evoking more than saying), or merely *functional*, as a significant stripped of any artistic intentions, expressing with the most indispensable elements the physical behaviors of the characters. And yet, because of the writer's basic poetic vein, we may find both forms side by side, giving us a straightforward but artistic image of the world:

Uncle Jeff leaned towards him across the table with bulging gray eyes. / Jimmy chokes on a piece of bread, blushes, at last stammers weakly, "Whatever you say Uncle Jeff." ... he stands back against the wall with his hands in his pockets, watching people elbow their way through the perpetually revolving doors; soft-cheeked girls chewing gum, hatchetfaced girls with bangs, creamefaced boys his own age, young toughs with their hats on one side ... fed in two endless tapes through the revolving doors out into Broadway, in off Broadway. (Dos Passos, *MT*, V, 94)

But the literary fusion of the two forms, the poetization of the functional description and the functionalization of the poetic, is felt by the sensitive reader as the truly artistic form of realism, as in the following description of Lucy Tantamount's kinesic style in *Point Counterpoint*:

The cigarette between her thin lips, she leaned forward to drink the flame. He had seen her leaning like this, with the same swift, graceful, and ravenous movement, leaning toward him to drink his kisses. And the face that approached him now was forcussed and intent on that flame, as he had seen it focussed and intent upon the inner illumination of approaching pleasure. (Huxley, *PC*, XII, 160)

7.2 Touching again on the difficult subject of the inclusion or exclusion of nonverbal repertoires, we can observe – from a stricter communicative point of view – that, regardless of which linguistic style is used, poetic or functional, in the physical and psychological descriptions of the characters, there exists in narrative literature a clear-cut dichotomy between total verbal and nonverbal indifferentiation of the characters, on the one hand, and extreme behaviorism on the other. But extreme behaviorism, yielding to a high degree of objectivism and objectualism, fails to really define the individuals's behavior (not perhaps the behavior of the group), as in *Manhattan Transfer*, where the author does not take full advantage of his constant verbal and nonverbal descriptions to help us identify his many recurrent characters (an important technical function, as I will mention later); or as in the internationally-prized *Tormenta de verano*, by Garcia Hortelano,[26] who certainly defines a specific social group, but hardly so the individuals, except for two who do not belong to that group.

Of these two tendencies, indifferentiation seems to be a permanent characteristic of some authors through different currents of narrative literature, even of some of those who call themselves 'realists', but whose characters seem to use all the same language, which, in fact, is the language of the narrator himself. To consider nonverbal communication as a touchstone for the analysis of true realism offers, therefore, some interesting possibilities.

On the other hand, we also find, as with poetic and functional styles, an eclectic, integrative *selectivism* that relates the physical and psychological activities of the people to the meaningful objectual observations of the environment, as in Steinbecks's *The Grapes of Wrath*, or Sánchez Ferlosio's *El Jarama*, the most celebrated Spanish social novel of the fifties.

Considering, then, the literary possibilities of poetic language and functional language, of differentiation and selectivism, a close look at what the narrator achieves, in the final analysis, through the use of verbal and nonverbal personal repertoires, reveals not only six important types of realism, but, in all, the three classes of functions that the verbal-nonverbal compound (what in 1.2 I referred to as the basic triple structure of human communication behavior) can play in narrative literature: realistic, communicative, and technical.

8. THE REALISTIC FUNCTIONS OF NONVERBAL COMMUNICATION

8.0 In all periods of narrative literature, from the national epics on, the depiction of the linguistic-paralinguistic-kinesic structure of the people involved in the story has conveyed a feeling of authenticity we could call *human realism*, which is usually, but not always, complemented by the *objectual* or environmental kind of realism.

A close analysis of what the authors achieve by letting us know what their characters say and how they say it, and how they move their bodies as they say it, or in their silences, reveals an interesting perspective, since we can differentiate six types of realism, that is, six *realistic functions* of nonverbal communication.

8.1 *Physical realism*, as differentiated from the psychological one, conveys the sensorial perception of people's behavior and, therefore, their intended authenticity:

They [the pilgrims] began to eat with the greatest gusto and very slowly, savoring each mouthful, which they took on the end of their knives, and very little of each thing, and then ... they raised their arms and winebags in the air, the mouths of the winebags on their mouths, their eyes nailed on the sky ... wagging their heads from side to side. ... (Cervantes, *DQ*, II, liv, 931, translation mine) (3)

"... and that's my sister, Miss Rachel Wardle. She's a Miss, she is; and yet she an't a Miss — eh, sir, eh?" And the stout gentleman playfully inserted his elbow between the ribs of Mr. Pickwick, and laughed heartily. (Dickens, *PP*, IV, 89)

Spandrell uttered a brief and snorting laugh, and letting his chair fall back on its four legs, leaned forward across the table. Pushing aside his coffee-cup and his half-emptied liqueur glass, he planted his elbows on the table and his chin in his hands. (Huxley, *PC*, VIII, 103)

"I never see the dawn," said Marco, his voice rattling in his throat," "that I don't say to myself perhaps ... perhaps today." He cleared his throat and spat against the base of a lamppost; then he moved away from them with his waddling step, taking hard short sniffs of the cool air. (Dos Passos, *MT*, II, 31)

As a variety within physical realism, it is interesting how the description of task-performing behaviors contribute to what I have classified as documentary or historical realism:

To ladies and gentlemen who are not in the habit of devoting themselves practically to the science of penmanship, writing a letter is no very easy task; it being always considered necessary in such cases for the writer to recline his head on his left arm, so as to place his eyes as nearly as possible on a level with the paper, while glancing sideways at the letters he is constructing, to form with his tongue imaginary characters to correspond. These motions, although unquestionably of the greatest assistance to original composition, retard in some degree the progress of the writer. (Dickens, *PP*, XXXIII, 485)[27]

He took the wineglass and put his nose into it, slowly smelling the wine. Then he raised it on a level with his eyes and, with a turn of his hand, he made the liquid slide toward the glass brim. He wetted his lips by taking a little sip, testing the thick coolness of that vintage. He finished the glass with short swallows. (Caballero Bonald, *TDS*, VII, 84, translation mine) (4)

The preceding description poses a problem of what earlier I called cultural translation, since it refers specifically to the ritualistic wine testing as performed by any connoisseur in the wine region of southern Spain.

8.2 *Distorting realism*, that is, the literary, or artistic, expressionistic rendering of physicopsychological reality, meant to ridicule, to offer a caricature of reality, to gratuitously exaggerate it, or, truly to show what the eyes cannot see.

When Sancho saw that he could not find the book, his face turned deadly pale; and feeling all over his body in great haste, he once more realized he could not find it, and suddenly he threw his fists to his beard and tore off half of it, and, hastely and without stopping, he gave himself half a dozen blows on the face and on the nose, until it was all drenched in blood. (Cervantes, *DQ*, I, xxvi 255, translation mine) (5)

8.3 *Individualizing realism*, which shows a conscious effort to differentiate the characters, as to their physical and psychological characteristics, by means of their verbal repertoires and, in the best cases, by their nonverbal ones as well.

The eloquent Pickwick, with one hand gracefully concealed behind his coat tails, and the other waving in air, to assist his glowing declamation. ... (Dickens, *PP*, I, 41) His nostrils dilated, and his fists clenched involuntarily, as he heard himself addressed by the villain. But he restrained himself again — and did *not* pulverize him. ... He panted for breath, and looked benignantly round upon his friends. (*Ibid.*, X, 170)

But Jude's mind seemed to grow confused soon, and he could not get on [declaiming the Nicene's creed]. He put his hand to his forehead, and his face assumed an expression of pain. (Hardy, *JO*, II, vii, 127) He [Jude] was leaning with his elbows on the table and his chin on his hands, looking into a futurity which seemed to be sketched out on the tablecloth. (*Ibid.*, III, vii, 171) "It is horrible how we are circumstanced, Sue — horrible!" he [Jude] said abruptly, with his eyes bent to the floor. (*Ibid.*, IV, ii, 216) He [Jude] shook his head hopelessly, his eyes wet. (VI, iv. 367)

I would add, just in passing, that a careful analysis of the nonverbal repertoires may reveal sometimes, behind an apparent individualization, a rather intriguing commonness among the main characters in a novel as, for instance, in Lawrence's *Women in Love*.[29]

8.4 *Psychological realism* is, of course, the conscious ultimate aim of individualizing realism, and includes also the sensorial world (as the perception of it may let us probe deeper into subtle inner reactions):

"But it was the devil who killed the old hag, not I [Raskolnikov]. ... Leave me alone!' he exclaimed in a sudden convulsion of anguish. ... He propped his elbows on his knees, and clutched his head tightly in his hands. ... "Well, tell me what to do now," he begged, raising his head and gazing at her face monstrously distorted with despair. (Dostoevsky, *CP*, V, iv, 355)

"Tst! Tst! Tst!," was the only sound he [Asa] made at first, a sucking sound of the tongue and the palate — most weak and inadequate, it seemed to Clyde.

Next there was another "Tst! Tst! Tst!," his head beginning to shake from side to side. Then "What do you suppose could have caused her to do that?" Then he turned and gazed at his wife, who gazed blankly in return. Then, walking to and fro, his hands behind him, his short legs taking unconscious and queerly long steps, his head moving again, he gave vent to another ineffectual "Tst! Tst! Tst!" (Dreiser, *AT*, III, 35)

"I was hoping now for a man to come along," Gudrun said, suddenly catching her underlip between her teeth, and making a strange grimace, half sly smiling, half anguish. Ursula was afraid. (Lawrence, *WL*, I, 8)

"Do you love me, Walter?" she [Marjorie] suddenly asked. Walter turned his brown eyes for a moment from the reflected tie and looked into the image of her sad intently gazing grey ones. He smiled. "But if only," he was thinking, "she would leave me in peace!" He pursed his lips and parted them again in the suggestion of a kiss. But Marjorie did not return his smile. Her eyes took on a tremulous brightness, and suddenly there were tears on her lashes. ... Through her closed eyelids the tears were welling out, drop by drop. Her face was trembling into the grimace of agony. (Huxley, *PC*, 1, 9-10)

8.5 *Interactive realism* is always a thoughtful depiction of the mechanism of conversation, mainly in face-to-face encounters, and its study offers an interesting socio-psychological angle of narration, as we observe whether that mechanism reflects reality or seems rather improbable. The latter is often the case, since the flow of conversation is falsely smooth, its participants taking turns in an orderly manner, not even showing feedback cues or turn-requesting signals.[30] Therefore, if the less obvious structural elements of interaction are indicated, suggested, or implied in a novel in a way the average reader can appreciate, it should be valued as much as the other types of realism outlined so far.

8.6 *Documentary realism* (or historical realism) through nonverbal behaviors, finally, is a logical result of physical realism, mostly, and another rich source of research material. It would be part of the area I referred to (5.4) as *literary anthropology*, which would not seek its material in narrative works only, but in different types of non-fiction works.[31]

As far as narrative is concerned, however, it is important to note that, although the documentary-historical value of certain descriptions increases in direct proportion to the aging of the work, the student of literature can also search in today's production for the documentary elements whose value will increase through the years. In addition, I should refer again to the problems of translation, since the value of documentary realism is subject not just to time, but to space as well, that is, to cultural differences; in which case the non-verbal documentary descriptions in the narrative production of cultures other than our own would constitute an interesting topic for a comparative study.

A serious study of documentary realism would require a classification of the various types of descriptions found according to the functions played by those activities, for example: ritualistic and etiquette behaviors, occupational activities, general task-performing activities, and activities conditioned by clothes, hairdo, furniture, etc. The following quotations illustrate ritualistic and etiquette-prescribed kinesic behaviors, from the eleventh to the late nineteenth century:

[When El Cid and his men meet the King upon their return from exile] he fell to the ground on his hands and knees, / the grass of the fields he took with his teeth, / welling his eyes from the great happiness. ... (*Poema del Cid*, v. 3031; translation mine) (6)

He [the gentleman] put his sword back in and fixed it in place, along with a string of large beads as belt. And with calm gait and erect, rocking his body and head very elegantly, throwing the end of his cloak over the shoulder, sometimes under his arm, and resting his right hand on his side, he left ... (*Lazarillo de Tormes*, III, 99, translation mine) (7)

[Don Quijote to Sancho] Do not eat garlic or onions, lest they should discover your rusticity by the smell. Walk slowly; speak calmly, but not in such a manner as to appear as if you were listening to yourself, for all affectation is bad. ... not to stuff your mouth with food, nor eruct in front of anyone. ... when riding, do not bent your body over the back of the saddle, nor carry your legs stiffly and straight, away from the horses's belly; but do not ride so limply that it may seem as if you were astride your donkey, for riding makes gentlemen of some and grooms of others. (Cervantes, *DQ*, II, xliii, 843-845, translation mine) (8)

Their daughters, who remembering the maternal injuction to make the best of their youth, had already commenced incipient flirtations in the mislaying of scarves, putting on gloves, setting down cups, and so forth; slight matters apparently, but which may be turned to surprisingly good account by expert practitioners. (Dickens, *PP*, XXXV, 534)

When Ana stretched out her hand at him, she was afraid he might dare to press it a little, but nothing like that happened; he gave it that firm jerk he always used, according to what in Madrid was beginning to be fashionable. (Alas, *LR*, XVI, 347, translation mine) (9)

9. COMMUNICATIVE FUNCTIONS OF NONVERBAL REPERTOIRES IN NARRATIVE LITERATURE

9.1 After having considered all other aspects of nonverbal communication in narrative literature — and before discussing the specific technical functions of the description and/or representation of nonverbal communication —, I would like to discuss briefly what exactly the nonverbal behaviors of the characters communicate to the reader.

We are faced again, first of all, with the two basic dimensions of time and space, in that order. Mostly through the objectual world of the narrative, the time locus is revealed — in an anthropological way, first — in works whose stories take place in other periods of history; and that sense of the past diminishes until it reaches the uncertain boundary felt as the transitional years before today's world, namely in the works of the twenties and thirties. Naturally, as the narrative becomes more a thing of the past its documentary value increases, as I pointed out earlier.

Secondly, there is a more difficult aspect of the novel that sometimes needs the assistance of the author: the space setting, or cultural context.

As for the characters themselves, what the average writer gives us about them is: their physical portrait and their psychological one, the latter either through their own behaviors and thoughts or straight from the creator, or both; their clothes, which so many disregard in spite of their communicative value; their linguistic-paralinguistic-kinesic activities, discussed earlier; and, subsuming some of those behaviors, and clothes as well, their cultural differentiating behaviors, but perhaps not as specified.

Those are, therefore, the basic elements for the individualization of the character, some of which could be absent. But through them, and by what we may know of their geographical location, we will gradually be able to complete the character as we learn about their whole conditioning background (or some of its constituent elements, at any rate), as outlined in note 16.

9.2 Concentrating on sensorially perceived nonverbal activities — but leaving aside some of the anthropoliterary elements, such as descriptions of interiors and the rest of the objectual environment — I will summarize and illustrate the four ways in which the author usually transmits the nonverbal behaviors through the narrative text:

(a) by describing the behavior and explaining its meanings (signifier and signified), obviously the most traditional method:

Now, although this question was put in the most careless tone imaginable, Mr. Job Trotter plainly showed by gestures, that he perceived his new friend's anxiety to draw forth an answer to [his question]. He emptied his glass, looked misteriously at his companion, winked both of his small eyes, one after the other, and finally made a motion with his arm, as if he were working an imaginary pump-handle: thereby intimating that he [Mr. Trotter] considered himself as undergoing the process of being pumped, by Mr. Samuel Weller [his master]. ... he turned his glass upside down, as a means of reminding his companion that he had nothing left wherewith to slake his thirst. Sam observed the hint and feeling the delicate manner in which it was conveyed, ordered the pewter vessel to be refilled, whereat the small eyes of the mulberry man glistened. (Dickens, *PP*, XVI, 251-252)

"Such an old magician!" Polly spoke in a thrilling whisper, leaning forward and opening her eyes very wide, as though to express in dramatic pantomine as well as words the mysteriousness of the magical old man. (Huxley, *PC*, III, 42)

(b) by describing the behaviour without explaining the meaning (signifier, but not signified), as in the prescribed kinesic behaviors described in the *Poema del Cid* (8.6), meant for a contemporary audience familiar with their meanings; or in the following brief mention of the kinesic behavior of the cynical and cold-blooded man who is the seducer of his interlocutor's sister, and his mortal enemy:

The other man [during a tense conversation] kept hitting the thyme plants with little strokes of his stick. (Cela, *PD*, III, 50, translation mine) (10)

(c) by explaining the meaning without describing the behavior (signified, but not signifier), which may or may not be fully understood by the reader, at least as meant by the author:

"Bidlake? The man who ... who painted the pictures?" Polly spoke hesitatingly, in the tone of one who is conscious of a hole in her education and is afraid of making a ridiculous mistake. (Huxley, *PC*, IV, 51)

(d) by providing a verbal expression always concurrent with the nonverbal one, which is important, but not referred to at all; as in the following very specific variant of the expression *It goes in one ear and out the other*, which does not mention *ear* because the gesture describes it:

"Me? It goes in this way and out the other." (Sánchez Ferlosio, *EJ*, 214, translation mine) (11)

10. TECHNICAL FUNCTIONS OF NONVERBAL REPERTOIRES IN NARRATIVE LITERATURE

Finally, but most important from the point of view of the craft of fiction, there is another interesting perspective of the narrative: the analysis of the technical functions played by the nonverbal behaviors represented or described in the text.

When the author creates a character, if he wants to make him live as a well-differentiated individual, he has at his disposal an array of psychobiological and culture-based characteristics with which to make him *that* character and no other. But those personal features, which are not at all difficult to invent and handle throughout the story, must be put to good use in two ways that represent some of the writer's most important responsibilities towards the readers.

First, those features must reflect, not a random inventory of easily replaceable linguistic, paralinguistic, or kinesic characteristics, but a conscious selection that may give the characters the necessary consistency as credible people. To say that a character *must* look real to us may be the personal view of many, and not of many others, but when the author himself wants the character to seem real and unique, we should expect him to maintain that unique personality from the beginning to the end of the story, in a progressive, logical way, just as we become gradually acquainted with real-life people.

With these otherwise commonplace aforethoughts I merely tried to bring home one point: that the nonverbal repertoires of the characters can play, and do play, in the novel — though not as widely as they ought to — four definite and important functions in narrative technique, which I will only outline here, but which certainly merit more attention when discussing a novel:

(a) *initial definition* of the character, by means of an idiosyncratic linguistic, paralinguistic, or kinesic feature: a verbal expletive or. personal choice of words, a particular tone of voice in certain situations, a gesture, a socially but individually conditioned way of greeting others, or eating (that may agree with what we will know about that person later), a typical posture we can identify as a recurrent behavior, etc.

(b) *progressive definition*, by means of still new additional features made noticeable gradually, as in real life, and not hastily at the onset of the story: a feature adds to another feature previously observed, complements it, builds up the physical as well as the psychological or cultural portrait, and assists the reader in the progressive total appreciation of the narration;

(c) *subsequent identification*, by means of a feature, or features, repeated for the first time, whose technical importance is that, not only does it bring back that image (the verbal expletive, the gesture, the peculiar tone of voice), but that it does it precisely at a point in the story when the author knows that the readers need to identify some characters, as they may begin to confuse them or forget their external personalities. For this reason, this function and the next one, recurrent identification, are especially useful in saga series, in voluminous novels peopled by many characters, and in the panoramic type of novel, like Dos Passos' *Manhattan Transfer*, or Cela's *The Hive*; or any other type of narration whose author may insist on certain defining, individualizing features, such as Hardy's;

(d) *recurrent identification*, by means of a known feature repeated as many times as necessary at varying intervals in the narration, when, as in *The Hive*, the enormous amount of characters makes it technically advisable, or rather, indispensable for the novelist to save us from becoming absolutely lost, at least in a first reading and without a true effort on our part; but Cela, for one thing, wisely presents Martin Marco, for instance, leaning his head on his hands on pages 24 and 44, walking in a peculiar way on pages 98, 148, and 315, etc.; the following is an example of some of the technical functions (which are also communicative) played by the implicit paralanguage and the explicit kinesics of Hardy's Arabella Donn, in *Jude the Obscure*, which define her throughout the novel as Jude's sensuous part of his personality, in opposition to the fragile and physically inferior Sue Bridehead:

she [Arabella] gave, without Jude perceiving it, an adroit little suck to the interior of each of her cheeks in succession, by which curious and original manoeuvre she brought as by magic upon its smooth and rotund surface a perfect dimple, which she was able to retain there as long as she continued to smile. [*Initial definition*] This production of dimples at will was a not unknown operation, which many attempted, but only a few succeeded in accomplishing. (I, vi, 45)

by artificially producing in each cheek the dimple before alluded to, a curious accomplishment of which she was mistress, effecting it by a momentary suction. [*Subsequent identification*] (I, ix, 66)

"O – how stupid this is! I thought my visitor was – your friend – your husband Mrs. Fowley, as I suppose you call yourself?" said Arabella, flinging her head back to retain the dimple she had just taken the trouble to retain. [*Recurrent identification*] (V, ii, 274)

Arabella smiled grimly as she resumed her way, and practised dimple-making all along the road from where the pollard willows begin to the old almhouses. ... [*Recurrent identification*] (VI, iv, 364)

*The Communication Process Between Writer and Reader
Transmission of the Narrative Character Through the Nonverbal Repertoires*

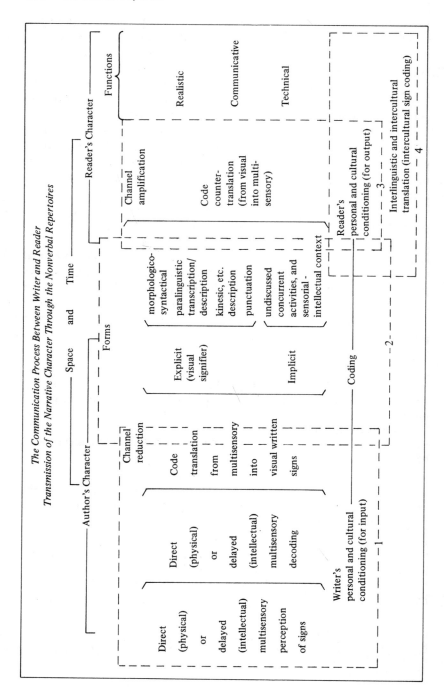

NOTES

*A few preliminary ideas in parts 5, 7, 8, 9, and 10 (but referring only to the Spanish novel) were read at the IIIrd Congress of the International Association of Hispanists (Salamanca, 1971), published as "Paralenguaje y kinésica del personaje novelesco: nueva perspectiva en el análisis de la narración" (*Revista de Occidente*, nos. 113-114, 1972, 148-170), and presented in a similar manner at the 1972 Symposium on the Modern Hispanic Novel Sponsored by the University of Toronto. A very reduced version of the present text was read at the 1975 joint meeting of the Canadian Comparative Literature Association and the Canadian Association of Semiotic Research (Edmonton), later as "Coding and Functions of Nonverbal Communication in the Novel" in *The Canadian Journal of Research in Semiotics* (3:2, 1976, 53-66).

**These are the literary works quoted. Original dates appear after the titles. Titles after the quotations are indicated by the initials shown here, and the original text of the translations appear after the Notes, numbered as throughout the article:

Alas, Leopoldo, *La Regenta*, 1884-5 (Madrid: Alianza Editorial, 1967) *LR*

Alemán, Mateo, *Guzmán de Alfarache*, 1599-1604, ed. S. Gil y Gaya (Madrid: Espasa-Calpe, Clássicos Castellanos, 1963) *GA*

Caballero Bonald, José, *Dos dias de setiembre*, 1962 (Barcelona, Seix-Barral, 1967) *TDS*

Cela, Camilo José, *La colmena*, 1951 (Barcelona-México: Editorial Noguer, 1962) *LC*

Cela, Camilo José, *La familia de Pascual Duarte*, 1942 (Barcelona: Ediciones Destino, 1968) *PD*

Cervantes, Miguel de, *Don Quijote de la Mancha*. 1605-15 (Barcelona: Editorial Juventud, 1965) *DQ*

Dickens, Charles, *Pickwick Papers*, 1836-7 (New York: Dell Publishing Co., 1964) *PP*

Dos Passos, John, *Manhattan Transfer*, 1925 (New York: Bantam Books, 1959) *MT*

Dostoevsky, Feodor, *Crime and Punishment*, 1866, ed. by George G. Gibian (New York: W. W. Norton Company, 1975) *CP*

Dreiser, Theodore, *An American Tragedy*, 1925 (New York: Dell Publishing Co., 1960) *AT*

Dreiser, Theodore, *Sister Carrie*, 1900 (New York: Dell Publishing Co., 1960) *SC*

Fitzgerald, F. Scott, *The Great Gatsby*, 1925 (New York: Charles Scribner's Sons, 1953) *GG*

Hardy, Thomas, *Jude the Obscure*, 1995 (New York: Dell Publishing Co., 1960) *JO*

Huxley, Aldous, *Point Counterpoint*, 1928 (New York: Avon Book Division, The Hearst Corporation) *PC*

James, Henry, *The Turn of the Screw*, 1998 (London: J. M. Dent & Sons Ltd., 1952) *TS*

Kerouac, Jack, *On the Road*, 1958 (New York: Signet Book, The New American Library, 1960) *OR*

Lawrence, D. H., *Women in Love*, 1921 (New York: Modern Library, Random House, 1950) *WL*

Lazarillo de Tormes, in *La novela picaresca española*, 1554 (Madrid: Editorial Aguilar, 1956) *LT*

Maugham, W. Somerset, *Of Human Bondage*, 1915 (New York: Modern Library, Random House, 1942) *HB*

O'Hara, John, *Appointment in Samarra*, 1934 (New York: Signet Books, The New American Library, 1961) *AS*

Poema de Mio Cid, 1140, ed. R. Menéndez Pidal (Madrid: Espasa-Calpe, Clásicos Castellanos, 1951) *PC*

Sánchez Ferlosio, Rafael, *El Jarama*, 1958 (Barcelona: Ediciones Destino, 1956) *EJ*

Sir Gawain and the Green Knight, 14th c., ed. R. Waldron, York Medieval Texts Series (Evanston: Northwestern University Press, 1970)

Steinbeck, John, *The Grapes of Wrath*, 1939 (New York: Bantam Books, 1964) *GW*

Tolstoy, Leo, *Anna Karenina*, 1873-7, ed. George Gibian (New York: W. W. Norton & Company, 1970) *AK*

---

[1]   Spandrell threw back his head and laughed, profoundly but, as was his custom, almost inaudibly, a muted explosion. "Admirable!" he said. "Admirable!" The first really good argument in favour of matrimony I ever heard. Almost thou persuadest me, Rampion. I've never actually carried it as far as marriage."

"Carried what?" asked Rampion, frowning a little. He disliked the other's rather melodramatically cynical way of talking. So damned pleased with his naughtinesses. Like a stupid child, really.

"The process of infection. I've always stopped this side of the registry office. But I'll cross the threshold next time." He drank some more brandy. "I'm like Socrates," he went on. "I'm divinely appointed to corrupt the youth, the female youth more particularly. I have a mission to educate them in the way they shouldn't go." He threw back his head to emit that voiceless laugh of his. Rampion looked at his distastefully. So theatrical. It was as though the man was overacting in order to convince himself he was there at all.

"But if you only knew what marriage would mean," Mary earnestly put in. "If you only knew..."

"But, my dear woman, of course he knows," Rampion interrupted with impatience.

"We've been married more than fifteen years now," she went on, the missionary spirit strong within her. "And I assure you ..."

"I wouldn't waste my breath, if I were you."

Mary glanced enquiringly at her husband. Wherever human relationships were concerned, she had an absolute trust in Rampion's judgement. Through those labyrinths he threaded his way with a sure tact which she could only envy, not imitate. "He can smell people's souls," she used to say of him. She herself had but an indifferent nose for souls. Wisely then, she allowed herself to be guided by him. She glanced at him. Rampion was staring into his coffee cup. His forehead was puckered into a frown; he had evidently spoken in earnest. "Oh, very well," she said, and lit another cigarette.

[2]   Etiemble, in his novel *Blason d'un corps* (Paris: Gallimard, 1961), carries to extremes the appreciation of the type of bodily messages that are usually not talked or written about in connection with the feeling of love, and rejected by

the average sensitivity. His narrator, besides his childhood enjoyment of the smell of his own sweat, relives in the letters to his dead lover: "je te vis, ma sirène, plonger dans l'écume incertaine, et t'enfouir le visage dans mes chemises. Les yeux clos, tu respirais fort, fort, fort" (p. 115), and her smelling his armpits and taking the hair with her teeth (p. 116); but above all, his tactile and olfactory enjoyment of her body, "le plaisir olfactif s'ajoutant au tactile" (p. 155), explaining that "C'est par les poiles qu'on aime, et pour la sueur; par et pour les odeurs des diverses parties du corps." (p. 155)

[3] "The Basic Triple Structure of Human Communication Behavior," paper read at the 1971 Annual Meeting of the Northeast Modern Language Association (Philadelphia). That which really shapes vocal language — around but not always simultaneously with words — is a series of structured elements subtly interrelated that support, emphasize, or contradict the essential message conveyed by words and sentences. Unrealistically considered as elements strange to 'language', one has hitherto tried to isolate a sentence as representing a complete unit of meaning, distinguishing patterns of stress, pitch, and juncture, but nothing else; when actually that combination of phonemes and morphemes acoustically perceived would appear quite lifeless if we only attached to it those suprasegmental elements, for any stretch of speech under normal circumstances carries some extralinguistic items which constitute what, for lack of a better term, we call paralanguage; and if visually perceived, that sentence is accompanied by certain kinesic constructs, hardly noticeable perhaps, but closely related to both the linguistic and the paralinguistic co-structures.

[4] Initiated by the anthropologist Edward T. Hall (1966), *proxemics* can be defined as people's conception, structuration and use of space, from their natural or built surrounding to the distances consciously or unconsciously kept in personal interaction. Proxemic behavior covers a very wide range of manifestations, both culture-specific and universal, but first of all biological, that is, displayed by human beings as living organism claiming, delimiting, and maintaining their own territory or occupying someone else's. As a body-originated system of communication in personal interaction, proxemic behavior seems to be patterned along with other message-conveying activities as a motor-based modality (not necessarily moving but resulting from movement shifts), perceived through vision, touch, olfaction, and also kinesthetically (through neuro-muscular appreciation of space and distance), and exercised as what is actually kinesic activity.

The analysis of proxemic behavior in the characters' interaction would reveal not only a specific psychological context, but often a cultural one as well (although the latter is in general less acknowledged by the writer), and it would be part of what here I suggest as literary anthropology (5.4 and 8.6). But whether or not the student of literature is interested in this additional anthropoliterary perspective, he should be aware — at least out of a certain interest in the psychosocial aspects of the story — of Hall's classification of interpersonal distances: public, social, personal, and intimate (plus the one I would call far-away distance, as it conditions the various communicative behaviors), particularly the last three. *Social distance* (far phase, 7 to 12 feet; close phase, 4 to 7), although subject, like the others, to many variables, is the distance kept at formal gatherings, in open-air public places, in very formal greetings, etc., although circumstances may cause people to reach a false personal, even intimate distance. *Personal distance* (far phase, 2.5 to 4; close phase, 1.5 to 2.5) implies more sensory involvement that is, smell, visual perception of subtle eye contact, of blemishes and dermal reactions; and, being within physical reach, the interactants' tactile perception of each other. *Intimate distance* (far phase, 6 to 8 inches; close phase, total contact) may be defined in narration by the more important role of deep glances, of breathy voice and embraces over that of words; and, in general, by the description of the characters' emotional involvement. What again becomes important from the anthropoliterary point of view is that the concepts 'personal' and 'intimate' can vary strongly from culture to culture, and we must be able to appreciate the cultural value of proxemic behaviors in different contexts, lest we should totally misinterpret those behaviors if the author is dealing with exotic cultures or simply with specific situations.

[5] I have suggested *chronemics* on different occasions (lately in "Towards an Exhaustive Intercultural Analysis of Human Communication,' paper read at the 1975 meeting of the International Communication Association [Chicago]) as an area of study that would deal with our conceptualization and handling of time as a biopsychological and cultural element lending specific characteristics to social relationships and to the many events linked within the communicative continuum, from linguistic syllables and flitting gestures to meaningful glances and silences. Since chronemic behavior identifies situational contexts, cultural backgrounds and personality and biological configurations, one could look for these elements in narrative literature, as complementary to the other communicative activities; not only 'social time' (time as handled in social relations within a culture as well as cross-culturally), but 'interactive time' (time used in the various forms of interactive encounters, and in the production of the different communicative activities themselves, not always easily measurable in the narrative text).

[6] Silences are indicated in the novel as breaks in speech, which the author may fill by describing the still continuing paralinguistic (sighs, hesitation ingressions), kinesic (gestures, postural shifts), or proxemic (distance shortening, orientation shift) behaviors. If he does not indicate silence verbally ("he gave a long sigh", "she paused", "there was a long pause/silence"), he can resort to a varying and eloquent series of suspension points that may take up to several lines.

Only from an acoustic point of view is silence the opposite of speech, but it is not complete as long as it is filled with consciously or unconsciously displayed paralinguistic sounds (hesitation clicks, nareal egression of contempt) that simply replace verbal expression. If there is a total absence of sound, however, the semantic context of that silence is then built up and defined by its duration and by the concomitant kinesic and/or proxemic behaviors; and those interactive breaks can carry many meanings, from the minimal pause of surprise or hesitation to the prolonged one that can become unbearable, or the infinitely expressive silences between Anna Karenina and her lover, in which case there is acoustic silence, but not communicative one, since Tolstoy tells us that they speak with "the flash of glances and smiles". We could refer to non-acoustic, non-visual silence (in a telephone conversation, or from adjoining rooms), and yet time would grant that silence its meanings, and we would respond to our interlocutor according to our decoding of it. The incisive narrator recognizes the semantic importance of silences, and uses them as interactive elements — in fact, as part of the repertoires of certain characters — and differentiates what we might call paralinguistically-filled silences, kinesically-filled silences, and proxemically-filled ones.

To study the use of silences in different authors and in different types of narration is, therefore, an interesting topic that can reveal various realistic, communicative and technical functions (as discussed in parts 8, 9, and 10) of what Thomas J. Bruneau, in a recent insightful and well documented article (Bruneau, 1976) has termed psycholinguistic silences, interactive silences, and socio-cultural silences (the latter also within the suggested literary anthropology (5.4 and 8.6). Cf. my latest paper on the topic of meaningful silence (Poyatos 1977b).

One can observe that the narrator sometimes exaggerates the duration of interactive silences: "The insinuating gentleman sighed deeply, fixed his eyes on the spinster aunt's face for a couple of minutes. ..." (Dickens, *PP*, VIII, 144)

[7] I have defined *paralanguage* as: nonverbal voice qualities, modifiers and sounds produced or conditioned in the areas covered by the supraglottal cavities (from the lips and the nares to the pharynx), the laryngeal cavity, and the infraglottal cavities, down to the abdominal muscles, which consciously or unconsciously man uses supporting or contradicting the linguistic, kinesic, or proxemic message mainly, either simultaneously or alternating with them.

[8] I have been studying *alternants* (Poyatos, 1975) as: ingressive or egressive nonverbal, marginal, and nonspeech sounds or clusters of sounds, articulated or not, produced or shaped in the areas covered by the supraglottal cavities (nares, nasal chamber, nasal pharynx, mouth, and pharynx), the laryngeal cavity (glottis friction or real voice), the infraglottal cavities, and the diaphragm and the abdominal muscles; which do not affect the verbal utterance (although they can be modified by primary qualities, qualifiers, and kinesic modifers), occurring either isolated or alternating with the verbal utterance and with the kinesic behavior. Today I would certainly question their 'non-verbality' and their "non speechness' for the reasons I merely suggest here, and because some, like clicks, are systematically studied by linguists as phonological elements of certain languages, such as that of African Bushmen. Besides, just as Philip Lieberman (1975) suspects that an advanced hominid species like classical Neanderthal man, while lacking many of today's segmental phonetic elements, probably used 'tone of voice' for different semantic constructs, and that the pretended "rigid dichotomy between 'linguistic' and 'paralinguistic'" is an artifice if something that cannot be transcribed with the International Phonetic Alphabet symbols is automatically called 'paralinguistic', I would think that phonetic-semantic constructs like alternants may have preceded the appearance of human language. At any rate, the exhaustive analysis of alternants may throw much light upon the narrator's possibilities and the direct realistic conveyance of the characters, and can suggest the semantic variations and development of an important part of man's vocal repertoire.

[9] Others included in the *Webster* are: *aha, ahem, hem/hum h'm, hep, hip, hist, ho, humph, oomph, poof, pooh, poop, pugh, shoo,* etc.; there being no reason, therefore, not to include more, and eventually increase the writer's expressive repertoire.

[10] Although the multidisciplinary and relatively new research area initiated as 'kinesics' by Birdwhistell is now constantly underrated by many journalistic and pseudoscientific writings dealing with 'body language', the interested reader should be aware of its more serious literature and of the truly scientic applications and work being carried out within anthropology, social psychology, psychiatry, semiotics, and, hopefully in this paper, in literary criticism.

Elsewhere (Poyatos, 1976, but mainly 1977a) I have attempted to offer a morphological and functional classification of kinesic behavior. I have differentiated *gestures* (conscious or unconscious body movements made mainly with the head, the face alone or the limbs, learned or somatogenic, and serving as a primary communicative tool, dependent or independent from verbal language, either simultaneous to or alternating with it, and modified by the conditioning background [smiles, eye movements, a gesture of beckoning, a tic]) *manners* (although similar to gestures, more or less dynamic body attitudes that, while somatogenically modified, are mainly learned and socially codified according to specific situations, either simultaneous to or alternating with verbal language [the way one eats, greets others, coughs]), and *postures* (conscious or unconscious positions of the body, more static than gesture, learned or somatogenic, either simultaneous to or alternating with verbal language, modified by social norms and by the rest of the conditioning background, and used less as a communicative tool, although they may reveal affective states and social status [sitting, standing]). I would define *kinesics* as: the systematic study of psychomuscularly-based body movements and/or their resulting positions, either learned or somatogenic, of visual, visual-acoustic, and tactile or kinesthetic perception, that whether isolated or combined with the linguistic-paralinguistic structures and with the situational context, possess communicative value, either in a conscious way or out of awareness. When applied to its analysis the methodology of linguistic structuralism, kinesics has revealed (in Birdwhistell's work) the smallest discrete element, the *kineme* (analogous to the phoneme), made up of various *alokines*. Kinemes combine into morphological constructs called *kinemorphs* and *kinemorphemes*, and these in turn form kinesyntactic structures. Birdwhistell has also reported certain suprasegmental elements, namely kinemes of stress and juncture, as appearing in the linguistic-kinesic stream, and has also studied the relationship between linguistic pitch and body movement; in addition, he identified parakinesic degrees of intensity, range and velocity (akin to stress and articulatory tension, syllabic duration, and speech tempo).

Paralanguage and kinesics complete, then, the basic triple structure one must analyze in narration. In the case of kinesics, the narrative text will reveal the ability of the writer to disynchronize it from the other two as little as possible (since a description must necessarily precede or follow the verbal expression), the ratio between kinesic repertoires and linguistic and paralinguistic ones, and which types of kinesic behaviors are consciously used as communicative vehicles in the story.

[11] Dimitri S. Merezhkovsky, *L. Tolstoi i Dostoevsky: Zhizn', tvortchesvo, i religiia* (St. Petersburg-Moscow, 1912), M. O. Volf Edition of Merezhkovsky's *Collected Works*, Vol. VII, pp. 154-157 and 193-201, as cited (with the title "Tolstoy's Physical Descriptions") by G. Gibian in his edition of *Ana Karenina* Norton Critical Editions (New York: W. W. Norton, 1970), p. 804.

[12] *Ibid.*, p. 805

[13] I have briefly suggested such a chart (Poyatos, 1976, 1977a) in relation to Birdwhistell's linguistic-kinesic analogy; but it would be particularly interesting should we attempt to elaborate a kinemic alphabet, not necessarily for its application to a literary text, but simply to work out a relatively refined transcription system, since it would show: internally, the speech organs (teeth, lips, tongue [tip, blade, front, back] etc.), and externally, the facial moving parts (eyebrows

[high, middle, low, knit], eyelids [raised, lowered], pupil [dilated, contracted], mouth, etc.).
[14] As I admit in 7.1, to arrive to any definite conclusions as to the notable differences among authors in their depiction of the characters' kinesic (or nonverbal) repertoires would take much research. The tendency to let the character define himself through his linguistic, paralinguistic, or kinesic behaviors seems quite understandable in behavioristic type of novels like Dos Passos', or in those of the great realists and naturalists (Dickens, Galdós, Dostoevsky, Dreiser). But one cannot hastily decide what prevents Salinger from showing the personality-revealing gestures and manners that the reader tends to attach to Holden Cauldfield's most realistic language; or why Lawrence insists so much on the slowness of glances and gait of *Women in Love's* Hermione, Gerald, Birkin, etc., without extending this apparently defining quality to other kinesic characteristics.
[15] My concern for the reader's decoding and re-creating end of the communication process is corroborated (I found after elaborating my own ideas) in Merezhkovsky's study of Tolstoi (note 13 [p. 804]): "we experience in the muscles and nerves directing the expressive gestures of our own bodies, upon reading similar descriptions, the beginning of those movements which the artist decribes in the external appearance of his characters. And, by means of this sympathetic experience involuntarily going on in our own bodies, this is, by means of the most realistic and shortest path, we enter into their internal world. We begin to live with them and in them."
[16] Whatever aspect of human communication one is dealing with I would always insist on the need to acknowledge what I have outlined on different occasions (e.g., Poyatos, 1976, but in a more refined way in Poyatos, 1977a) as the *Total Conditioning Background of Communication Behavior*, as a way not to overlook any of the possible factors that can affect our physical or intellectual activities. They are: biophysiopsychological (biological configuration, sex, age, physiological state, medical state, nutritional habits, psychological configuration, and emotional states), environmental (natural environment, built or modified environment, objectual environment, and socioeconomic environment), the degree of shareness (performer-spectator borrowing, that is, from an actor or public figure by others, the cohabiting couple, the nuclear or extended family, the social or occupational group, and the geographic or subcultural variety), cultural patterns (religious and moral values, relationships and role expectations, etiquette norms, and esthetic values), and socioeconomic levels (the superrefined, the average educated, the average middle-income employee, the low-income worker, the pseudo-educated, and the rustic). This would of course lead us to an aspect of the readership which is not discussed in this paper, namely the different interpretations of the narrative work by the various types of readers, and their specific relationships with both the author and the characters.
[17] Elsewhere (Poyatos, 1976) I have classified written literature as a cultural non-interactive form of delayed indirect communication (as against, for instance, epistolary communication, in which the receiver can become sender); and in *Man Beyond Words* (see Note 15) I have defined *non-interaction* as a situation in which, despite the lack of another interactant and of any external eliciting factors (except the printed text itself), bodily behaviors are developed which reflect the effect of one's own mental and/or physical activities (the phsyical activity, in this case, being the actual reading, which elicits, not just bodily activities, but mostly intellectual ones).

[18] The minstrel-audience encounter certainly deserves an anthropological and sociopsychological type of approach, which would include today's oral literature, transmitted in a similar fashion mostly. In an interactive encounter, even if it is not a typical conversational one, the listener displays a series of activities: mostly *feedback* verbal or nonverbal cues (words, smiles, hand gestures, laughter, postural shifts that may indicate attention or boredom, but something); and, in a lesser degree, *listener's secondary activities*, such as the ones indicated in the main text. In terms of the decoding process, one must consider the fact that individuals within the collectivity that constitutes the audience can be mutually influenced into a sort of collective decoding, quite different from the isolated private reading.

[19] I believe that direct acquaintance with a writer or, failing this, careful attention to his biography, may help us, to a certain degree, understand better the behaviors of his characters. In the nineteenth-century Spanish masterpiece *La Regenta* for instance, the frail and timid, yet very sensitive to women, provincial intellectual reveals much of Alas himself; and so does, in a sort of dreamed anti-Alas, the physically strong and sensuos, yet frustrated and repressed, male protagonist, whose nonverbal behaviors and reactions are most carefully described. In a similar fashion, Théodore Dreiser reveals himself through the passionate and ambitious Eugene Witla, of *The Genius*, and through other typical men in his novels.

[20] Human kinesic behavior has been modified through history by changes in furniture style (the series of more relaxed postures and accompanying manners determined by the eighteenth-century trend toward curved and softer sitting furniture), in clothes and hairdo (men's stockings and tight pants, jeans for both men and women, long or short hair in women, and long hair in men, all have produced conscious and unconscious gestures, manners, and postures), etc., and just as actors must make an effort to move naturally in the clothes of the past, so the non-contemporary writer must make an effort to make his characters move in strange clothes.

[21] *Poema de Mio Cid*, see**.

[22] *Sir Orfeo*, in *The Age of Chaucer, Vol. I of A Guide to English Literature* (Melbourne-London-Baltimore: Penguin Books, 1954).

[23] *Sir Gawain and the Green Knight*, see**.

[24] One of the most fruitful areas of literary anthropology could be developed through an exhaustive analysis of the various nonverbal categories, as classified by Ekman and Friesen (1969), although applied not only to kinesics but to any activity within total body communication (as in Poyatos, *Man Beyond Words*, n. 15), and even to objectual communication (the literary description of objects that indicate emotional states, such as black clothes for example; or a given socioeconomic status, such as domestic furniture and decorative items). *Emblems*, as cultural or personal substitutes for or alternatives to verbal expressions (The Cid's cast-off gesture upon seeing the raven, or any other agreed-upon movement or sound), *illustrators* (kinesic descriptions of objects, people, and ideas), *affect-displays* (how basic emotions, for instance, are exteriorized by the characters in different periods and cultures), *regulators* (verbal, paralinguistic, kinesic, or proxemic behaviors that act as hesitation fillers, turn-takers, feedback signals, etc.), and *adaptors*, that is, kinesic manipulation of or contact with one's own body (*self-adaptors*: holding one's head in dispair, pinching one's nose to muffle weeping), with someone else (*alter-adaptors*: in greetings, courting), with

objects (*object-adaptors*: arms, eating utensils), and, I would add, with things we attach to ourselves almost as parts of our own bodies (*body-adaptors*: jewelry, clothes, pipes, drinks, and food).

[25] The greater or lesser capability of different languages to accommodate paralinguistic sounds into their established phonemic-orthographic system is in itself an important subject of study, closely related to the problems and methodology of literary translation.

[26] Juan Garcìa Hortelano, *Tormenta de verano* (Barcelona: Seix Barral, 1962), Prix Formentor 1961.

[27] Dickens' most realistic description of such a common yet unthought of habit reminds one of Mateo Alemán's identical type of realism in his sixteenth-century picaresque novel *Guzmán de Alfarache*, in which he proposes the different types of penalty for the correction of various *necedades*, or 'foolish acts': "Those who, while bowling, if the ball goes to one side, twist their bodies in the same direction, thinking that the ball will do what they do ... and those who make odd faces when an object is knocked down. ... Those who make patterns with their urine while urinating, painting on the walls or sketching on the ground." (Alemán, *GA*, II, iii, i, 188-189, translation mine) (12) Whether meant to attack human follies or simply to humourously call the reader's attention toward such acts, the systematic and perhaps comparative or intercultural study of those descriptions would contribute to what in this paper I have suggested as literary anthropology or historical social psychology.

[28] Many similar culture-specific actions can go unnoticed by the foreign reader when the writer offers no indication of their being customary and characteristic of certain social groups or individuals. A translator's note would be in order.

[29] See Note 14.

[30] See 4.2 and Note 18.

[31] One of the contributions of literature to anthropology and some of its subareas is eloquently illustrated in Gordon Hewes (1974:1). Hewes' well known and insightful interest in glottogenesis and in gestural communication is the regular counterpart, for cross-linguistic, cross-cultural communication, of vocal language or speech" [p. 1]) from many logs and journals of different voyagers, from Columbus to James Cook and others in the eighteenth century.

(1) "por lo que hacía de abrir los ojos, estar fijo mirando al suelo sin mover pestaña gran rato, y otras veces cerrarlos, apretando los labios y enarcando las cejas, fácilmente conocimos que algún accidente de locura le había sobrevenido."

(2) "La dueña, que tiene las manos en los bolsillos del mandil, los hombros echados para atrás y las piernas separadas, lo llama. ..."

(3) "[los peregrinos] comenzaron a comer con grandísimo gusto y muy de espacio, saboreándose con cada bocado, que le tomaban con la punta del cuchillo, y muy poquito de cada cosa, y luego ... levantaron los brazos y las botas en el aire; puestas las bocas en su boca, clavados los ojos en el cielo ... meneando las cabezas a un lado y a otro. ..."

(4) "Cogió la copa y metió la nariz dentro, oliendo despaciosamente el vino. Luego la levantó a la altura de los ojos e hizo resbalar el líquido hacia los bordes del cristal, girando la mano. Se mojó los labios, dando un sorbito y paladeando la pastosa frialdad de la solera. Terminó la copa a pequeños tragos."

(5) "Cuando Sancho vio que no hallaba el libro, fuésele parando mortal el rostro; y tornándose a tentar todo el cuerpo muy apriesa, tornó a echar de ver que no le hallaba, y sin más ni más, se echó entrambos puños a las barbas,

y se arrancó la mitad de ellas, y luego, apriesa y sin cesar, se dio media docena de puñadas en el rostro y en las narices, que se las baño todas en sangre."

(6) "los inojos e las manos en tierra los fincó,/las yerbas del campo a dientes las tomó,/llorando de los ojos, tanto avie el gozo major."

(7) "el escudero Tornóla a meter la espada y ciñósela, y un sartal de cuentas gruesas de talabarte. Y con un paso sosegado y el cuerpo derecho, haciendo con él y con la cabeza muy gentiles meneos, echando el cabo de la capa sobre el hombro y a veces so el brazo, y poniendo la mano derecha en el costado, salió. ..."

(8) "No comas ajos y cebollas, porque no saquen por el olor tu villanería. Anda despacio; habla con reposo; pero no de manera que parezca que te escuchas a tí mismo; que toda efactación es mala ... no mascar a dos carrillos, ni de eructar delante de nadie ... a caballo, no vayas echando el cuerpo sobre el arzón postrero, ni lleves las piernas tiesas y tiradas y desviadas de la barriga del caballo, ni tampoco vayas tan flojo que parezca que vas sobre el rucio; que andar a caballo a unos hace caballeros; a otros caballerizos."

(9) "Ana, al darle la mano, tuvo miedo de que él se atreviera a apretarla un poco; pero no hubo tal; dio aquel tirón enérgico que él siempre daba, siguiendo la moda que en Madrid empezaba entonces."

(10) "El otro daba golpecitos con la vara sobre las matas de tomillo."

(11) "¿A mí? Por aquí me entra y por aquí me sale."

(12) "Los que jugando a los bolos, cuando acaso se les tuerce la bola, tuercen el cuerpo juntamente, pareciéndoles que, así como ellos lo hacen, lo hará ella. ... y los que semajantes visajes hacen, derribándose alguna cosa. ... Los que orinando hacen señales con la orina, pintando en las paredes o dibujando en el suelo."

REFERENCES

Birdwhistell, Ray L.
    1970 *Kinesics and Context*. Philadelphia: University of Pennsylvania Press; New York: Ballantine Books (1972).
Bolinger, Dwight
    1968 *Aspects of Language*. New York: Harcourt, Brace & World.
Ekman, Paul, and Wallace V. Friesen
    1969 "The Repertoire of Nonverbal Behavior: Categories, Origins, Usage, and Coding", *Semiotica*, 1, 49-98.
Hall, Edward T.
    1966 *The Hidden Dimension*. New York: Doubleday.
Hewes, Gordon W.
    1974 "Gesture Language in Culture Contact", *Sign Language Studies*, 1:4, 1-34.
Kendon, Adam
    1969 "Progress Report of an Investigation into Aspects of the Structure and Function of the Social Performance in Two-Person Encounters", in *Social Interaction*, by Michael Argyle.
Lieberman, Philip
    1975 "Linguistic and Paralinguistic Interchange", *The Organization of Behaviour in Face-to-Face Interaction*, ed. by A. Kendon, R. Harris and M. Key. The Hague: Mouton.

Mendilow, A. A.
1965 *Time and the Novel*. New York: Humanities Press.
Poyatos, Fernando
1974 "The Challenge of 'Total Body Communication' as an Interdisciplinary Field of Integrative Research", First Congress of the International Association of Semiotic Studies, Milano (*Proceedings*, in press).
1975 "Cross-Cultural Study of Paralinguistic 'Alternants' in Face-to-Face Interaction", *The Organization of Behavior in Face-to-Face Interaction*, ed. by A. Kendon, R. Harris and M. Key, 285-314. The Hague: Mouton.
1976 *Man Beyond Words: Theory and Methodology of Nonverbal Communication*. Oswego: New York State English Council.
1977a "The Morphological and Functional Approach to Kinesics in the Context of Interaction and Culture," *Semiotica* 20, 197-228.
1977b "Toward a Typology of Somatic Signs", in *Semiotik III. Zeichentypologie*. Munich/Salzburg: Wilhelm Fink.
Robe-Grillet, Alain
1963 *Pour un nouveau roman*. Paris: Gillimard.

NORBERT FREEDMAN*

Toward a Mathematization of Kinetic Behavior: A Review of Paul Bouissac's *La Mesure des Gestes***

In the quest to find an objective segmentation of the flow of behavior, the student of kinesics is confronted with an array of models which, much like the characters of Pirandello's play, all are in search of an author. In each case, the actions of the body, like the actions of the characters on the stage, are viewed as participants in a more encompassing lawful universe. Furthermore, much as in Pirandello's play, we have come to recognize six characters--six models: *an expressive behavior model* in which movements are embedded in personal strivings, conscious as well as unconscious drives; *a dyadic model* in which body movements are regulated by the forces inherent in the interpersonal relationships (frequently power relationships); *an ethnological model* in which the motions of the body are a dance regulated by the code of the culture; *an information processing model* in which movements are part and parcel of cognitive structure and of the processing of thought; a *choreographic model* in which the actions of the body are construed as an expression of the capabilities of skeletal musculature; and, most recently, Bouissac's attempt at what we shall only half-facetiously term *the acrobatic model*. Like all models, each is a myth, some more productive than others. Each of these models is tenable; each has its heuristic advantages; none can be viewed to be true or false; none is all encompassing.

Bouissac's treatise is essentially a methodological endeavor. Unlike the five other approaches enumerated above which Bouissac would view to rest on some 'mediation model,' his, in his view, is an attempt at formal structuralization independent of any mediation model. His overall goal is to arrive at a model for the quantitative and objective segmentation and representation of corporal sequences. His ideal model strives for the mathematization of body movements as construed in a volume of three-dimensional space so that behavioral sequences can be delineated as successive volumes. The behavioral

* The reviewer wishes to express gratitude for the informal translation of the French text conducted by Nicole Cox.
** (= *Approaches to Semiotics*, Paperback Series, 3) (The Hague: Mouton, 1973).

phenomenon that approximates this ideal is the acrobatic act, for truly these acts are suspended in space, reach the extreme points of corporal expansion, and entail a series of repeatable and articulated events. Such a flow of behavioral acts offers a terrain for the description of behavior relatively unencumbered by the biases of natural language, free from what Bouissac terms 'the perceptive-linguistic filters', or the unwarranted assumptions of anatomical substructure.

While this is a methodological treatise, there is no methodology without some substantive assumptions. While Bouissac seeks to arrive at purely formal structures, these structures must fit the reality of behavioral phenomena. Bouissac's very choice of the concept of three-dimensional space and his choice of the acrobat as embodying the quintessence of kinesics indicate that his theorizing must yield to the constraints of an objective reality. It is at this point that a reviewer must examine not the truth of a model, but its relevance, the potential validity of observations arising from it, and its productiveness. Before doing so, however, we must first, more carefully, examine the work itself, which is divided into four parts. In the first three parts, the author takes us through a selective critical historical review of various attempts at the objective representation of behavior before introducing us to his own ideal proposal.

DESCRIPTION OF CORPORAL SEQUENCES

The selective historical review proceeds from the attempt at representing behavior via description, transcription, and measurement. The distinction between description and transcription of corporal sequences inheres in the way in which a flow of behavior is analyzed using either natural language (description) or some notation system (transcription). In a selective survey of descriptive attempts, Bouissac passes through various historical antecedents: Tuccaro (1699), Master of Gymnastics; Berthez (1734-1806), anatomist; and Strehly (1892), philosopher and amateur acrobat. His introductory chapter of Tuccaro is particularly telling. In this chapter, Bouissac lays down his basic criticism of the description of behavior, but it is also not coincidental that he selects a book of acrobatic acts as the initial focus of his critique.

Tuccaro's book *The Three Dialogues on the Exercise of Jumping and Revolving in the Air: With Figures for the Perfect Demonstration and Intelligence of This Art* contains a review of 53 different jumps. The detailed description and charts provide Bouissac with an opportunity to effect the segmentation not of the behavior itself but of the linguistic account. A small segment of description roughly translated from the old French may be cited: "In order to effectuate this jump one will take a small space where there would be some distance from the limited place where the jump must begin, then one will run at ease, this jump being in itself easy to do; as soon as one will have arrived at the end of the run at the point where one has to place the hands, without any delay one will take the time with disjoint and open feet ..." (p. 23). Such an account offers an opportunity for the imposition of multiple levels of analysis starting with simple grammar, the description of anatomical parts, and ultimately entailing the invocation of more or less conscious mediation models. For instance, Bouissac suggests a political model, in which the movement is said to obey a central executive function; a geometric model in which it is recognized that the movement occurs in a spatial arrangement; and finally, a logico-mechanical model in which the dynamic sequences can be represented.

Bouissac arrives at the conclusion that the linguistic translation of corporal dynamic behavior is essentially ascientific because any description is a selective reconstruction of events: not only does it involve the selection of points of the body already contained in natural language (arms, legs, feet) but there is always a mix of models (political, geometric, etc.), each invoked as it suits the describer. Recognizing these limitations in the linguistic description of events, the question must nevertheless be raised that, in spite of the mix of models, natural description provides the investigator with the continuing resource for the discovery of intrinsic units of behavior and the discovery of functional relationship.

TRANSCRIPTION OF CORPORAL SEQUENCES

In Part II, Bouissac focuses on different systems of symbolic notation, or transcription. Transcription is an obvious advance over description in the sense that arbitrary symbols can be employed. Yet it is precisely the question of whether arbitrariness is achieved in transcription which leads Bouissac to conclude that most systems of symbolic notation are still rooted in natural language. There are three chapters: Polti (1892), a dramatist concerned with the exact notation of gestures; Conte (1955), choreographer; and Birdwhistell (1952), anthropologist. We shall focus on Bouissac's analysis of Birdwhistell's *Introduction to Kinesics* (1952) since this contribution is best known to contemporary theory of communication.

Bouissac's discussion of Birdwhistell focuses strictly on his sytem of notation and disregards the contextual significance of such notation as well as Birdwhistell's substantive contribution of viewing behavior in a context of interpersonal or cultural space. However, both Bouissac and Birdwhistell share the view that all behavioral acts must be recorded, must be unitized, as well as the belief that such units ultimately form the basis for a quasi-linguistic system of kinesics capable of an 'etic' and 'emic' level of articulation.

Bouissac's critique of Birdwhistell's sytem of notation focuses on the issue of arbitrariness. Birdwhistell defines his constitutive units, his kines, and his units of signification, his alokines, both in terms of the loci of the body and the culturel context in which they occur. The notation system is predominantly analogic in that its symbols for body actions of head, face, and torso are pictorial condensations of the physical act. In this sense, they are shorthand descriptions of units already given in natural language. Moreover, such analogic notation can only deal with two-, not with three-dimensional space (for instance, a spin of a superior limb cannot be represented by a line). Truly formal symbols are needed. It is this presence of an analogic code, the notation of events in two-dimensional space, and the hybrid use of analogic as well as arbitrary codes which give Birdwhistell's contribution essentially only a stenographic value, the illusion of transcription.

Birdwhistell's attempt toward creating a linguistic equivalent in kinesics can certainly be faced with skepticism as will be elaborated upon later in this review. But there are two substantive contributions in Birdwhistell's work which cannot be so readily dismissed. The first is that no structure of corporal sequences can be defined independent of the socio-cultural context (not the later imposition of context as Bouissac would have it); and secondly, that symbols rooted in an analogic code may indeed be an appropriate way of describing behavior. Bouissac would like to represent all behavioral sequences along digital dimensions, but such an attempt may force the code and may only serve to increase the gap between the notation system and objective reality.

MEASUREMENT OF CORPORAL SEQUENCES

The next step on the road toward objective segmentation is a review of efforts toward the rigorous measurement of corporal dynamic sequences. For the development of any science, the creation of a method for objective measurement of phenomena is, of course, a turning point. We thus move from arbitrary notation to the introduction of devices which dispense with the human eye as a source of observation and to the utilization of apparatus which can represent behavioral sequences in time and in space. Three contributions are considered: Muybridge (1901), Marey (1896), and Oseretzky (1931).

Muybridge, a photographer, around the turn of the century created an outdoor laboratory in which he sought to obtain an exact representation of the motions of the gait of a horse by setting up several cameras set off by an automatic timer at strictly equal time intervals. There were several sets, for front, back, and side positions much like the recording of a sporting event from different angles of a stadium. The result was an exact representation of the event. Yet, the different angles could not be synthesized since the model could not deal with three-dimensional space–Bouissac's ultimate objective. While there seems to be little practical scientific value in this enterprise, Muybridge's work is viewed as laying the foundation for the precise two-dimensional measurement of behavior over time. Marey, another photographer, who had knowledge of Muybridge's attempt, used yet a more sophisticated methodology, and introduced a space as well as a time dimension. Basically, he attempted to bring together the spread over pictures in a system of points and curves operating a geometrical synthesis. Muybridge's and Marey's methods can be considered essentially as attempting a two-dimensional spatialization of movement.

As a third representative in the effort toward direct measurement, Bouissac turns to the work of Oseretzky of whose tactic he approves, but of whose strategy he disapproves. Oseretzky, in his comprehensive review of motor phenomena as a source of observation (motoscopy), measurement (motometry), and coding (motography), insists on encompassing the totality of all body manifestations in its static and dynamic aspects. Oseretzky, far from the tracing of the gait by which a horse traverses a single plain, concerns himself with the measurement of a whole range of human expression from physical position (head, torso, shoulders, arms, legs) to attitude (impression given by the whole position), to facial expressions, to gesticulations, and ending with automatic movements. For each activity level, he proposes objective measurement, including the seismographic and oscillographic recording of direction, rhythm, or speed. It is this objective assessment which creates the necessary distance from direct perceptions and the subjective image of the body. It is noteworthy that Oseretzky's contribution toward measurement would not have taken place without some other encompassing view of behavior. Some 'other' myth guided his endeavor–not the myth of social context as with Birdwhistell, but the view that action systems reside in and are essential components of the personality. From the conception of the total personality, with its constituents of drive and structure, flow a series of hypotheses leading to discrete measurement, each appropriate to the function presumably assessed. Thus, measurement is used to assess a phenomenon previously discovered by naturalistic observation. Can measurement of this sort skip the stage of naturalistic observation? And, moreover, can measurement operate in a completely atheoretical universe?

Each of these contributors provided a building block for the adequate representation of corporal sequences: Muybridge–time; Marey–time and space; and Oseretzky–the concept of dynamic work. Each singled out only one variable, yet together they set the foundation for the integrative view which Bouissac seeks to set forth.

TOWARD A MATHEMATIZATION OF CORPORAL SEQUENCES

One of the tasks assigned by Francis Bacon to the human mind is the elaboration of a science of gestures. It seems now possible, Bouissac suggests at the conclusion of his methodological reflection, to spell out the birth of this science of gestures. The basic task is the segmentation of dynamic corporal sequences into elementary, measurable, and discrete units and to build a system which, in its initial phase, is truly independent of linguistic notation, of anatomy, or of social context.

In his first approximation of a model, Bouissac holds that "any movement describes a volume in space. The constitutive gestural units of the analyzed sequence are then defined by the intersections of successive volumes". (p. 174). Bouissac thus looks at the body as emitting articulated volumes, theoretically measurable. A sequence becomes an ordinated series of volumes independent of the body which defines them, and capable of mathematical expression.

In his proposed model, space, represented by three-dimensional geometrization, becomes the primary postulate of the system with time and dynamics having the status of variables. The distinction of body movements and gestures disappears since the aim at this stage of the game is to look at motor configurations rather than their symbolic meaning. The notation system is truly arbitrary. No symbolic notations for arms, legs, feet, etc., are used, these being replaced by mathematical symbols.

The entire vision is concretized for the reader by the introduction of a hypothetical laboratory which contains the requisite features of the model—an apparatus which in certain ways is reminiscent of a Cartesian machine. Such a laboratory could record behavioral events in three-dimensional space through the use of multiple sets of photoelectric cells (the nucleus of this could be found in the photography of the gait of horses described by Muybridge), through the transformation of the photoelectrically obtained input onto computer cards, and the derivation of two-dimensional matrices. Thus, the photoelectric cells are arranged in cubular fashion to allow for spatial representation; the cards provide for the recording of events by time and order, and the derived matrices constitute a translation from three- to two-dimensional space. At the end, a corporal dynamic sequence will be represented by a series of cards, each card representing a constitutive volume of the sequence.

In two concluding chapters, Bouissac attempts to integrate his model of successive intersecting volumes with the perplexing problems in semiotics: that of structure and that of meaning. He deals with the problem of structure under the broad heading of the syntagmatic aspects of gestures. Having defined the element for the analysis of movement as a constitutive volume in space, the next task is to elucidate a system of articulated volumes which may be definable by corporal sequences. The gestures of military salute, of removing a ·fly, or of relieving an itch may appear as identical gestures. Their distinctive character, however, is defined by the surrounding field. Another example of deriving units at a more complex level deals with situations of identical movements having different 'intentionalities', such as an acrobatic act or mimicking an acrobatic act. Both are identical in structure but different in sequence.

Any effort at unitizing behavior requires the delineation of starting points and end points. Bouissac proposes to deal with the problem of the sequential nature of acts by conceptualizing successive volumes as sentences, isomorphic in their own right but different from linguistic grammar. A sentence would be defined by two pauses which correspond to the state in which the basic volume (the body) is in stable equilibrium. Any sequence is conditioned by a breakdown of this equilibrium provoked by the displacement of the center of gravity. (Here enters Bouissac's substantive bias, namely, that the basic regulatory source of body movements is not the body, the information processing apparatus, or the social setting, but inheres in the gravitational forces of the universe.)

The designation of articulated sequences marked off by displacements of stable equilibrium would place the investigator in a position to sketch out sequences having different types of articulation: those having to do with coordination and those having to do with subordination. We thus have the units necessary for grammatical structure. Such a formalization of articulated volumes is an attempt to reestablish an 'emic' level, based this time on a more fully explored 'etic' level, providing units as successive volumes. The very choice of concepts such as disruption of equilibrium, leads Bouissac to recognize that the syntagmatic model is really an energetic model disguised as a quasi-linguistic model. What the syntagmatic approach cannot deal with is the problem of continual adaptation to modifications of a situation and, for this, a further level of analysis is required.

In a final chapter, Bouissac seeks to apply his concept of articulated successive volumes to the problems of change and meaning. The problem of change raises the issue of self-regulatory mechanisms and offers an opportunity to reintegrate the phenomena of corporal sequences with the phenomena of biology. The problem of meaning raises the issue of context and code. Bouissac resorts to a model provided by cybernetics as the only one capable of integrating an abstract syntax into a larger system which conditions its meaning. As a demonstration for this final level of analysis, he returns to his starting paradigm, the acrobatic act. Now, the acts of jumping and of spinning in mid-air are no longer given the linguistic description provided by Tuccaro, but are viewed anew in the context in which the movements of arms, legs, and torso are the curves recorded by photoelectric cells.

Cybernetics offers a set of higher order concepts dealing with the problem of change especially through the notion of transformation. A new kind of hypothetical machine is now created in which one could attempt to study the acrobatic sequence as a series of states of the system. From an initial state, the system goes through the same succession of states when the same operator is applied. A particular individual, however, only actualizes part of the possible which reduces the total variety of the machine. The main concepts, here, are control and regulation which reintegrate the acrobatic act into biological theory. Survival in this context is efficient control and regulation, through compensation of equilibrium whether the result of a correct anticipation from the subject or of an automatic correction or reflex. This new kind of machine is not a regression to the mechanical model used in linguistic description, because the machine now is considered as a producer of volumes, and, moreover, several machines (several transformations) interact and modify each other.

The new cybernetic syntax can be applied to an examination of context, and this step opens the pass to an examination of the meaning of the code. For the acrobatic act which has a well-defined structure (articulated volumes), differences in meaning can be defined by differences in the structure of the act in successive contexts. For instance, the clown's acrobatic act is not only described by a sequence of syntagmatic volumes, but also as a signification defined by the situation. Bouissac now enlarges the scope of the signifier from successive volumes of the acrobatic act itself to the costume, the linguistic environment, or the social behavior of the crowd (i.e., a measurement of the situation). The thing being signified can represent processes of biological superiority and inferiority, concepts which are indeed appropriate to the roles of the acrobat and the clown. By enlarging the class of signifiers to include the vicissitudes of the situation, Bouissac is forced back into using 'perceptive-linguistic' filters which he so much seeks to avoid.

IMPLICATIONS OF THE MODEL

In perusing these pages, the reader marvels at the sophistication, the historical scope, and the awareness of contemporary thought; and yet, the gnawing question emerges, is a three-dimensional machine a *Riesenspielzeug* or a castle in the air? Or does it present the essential ideas which point to vistas for the further development of kinetic research?

There is one clear and substantive contribution for which Bouissac's work will be known. This is the proposal to view all kinetic behavior in terms of three-dimensional geometric space. This is so patently true, for body movements are three-dimensional movements and linear representation (in-out, up-down, etc.), as they have been frequently used in the literature, only tell half the story. It is a notion that could be applied to all kinetic research, regardless of the particular model that is embraced.

Yet this is not the essence of the monograph. Its essence, rather, I suspect, is the application of structural analysis to the phenomena of body movements. This is evident in the progression from description to transcription to formal analysis. It is evident also in Bouissac's own model which seeks to arrive at the structure of kinesics quite independent of its correspondence with objective reality. He follows quite closely the prescription based on the analysis of language as it can be found, for instance, in the writings of Martinet (1965) and applies it to kinesics. Bouissac shares a bias with certain structural linguists of a movement away from the subject building its own structures and hence a de-emphasis of issues of development. But I would rather direct my comments to what this model will do to future research in nonverbal communication.

The creation of a hypothetical machine, much as in Descartes' days, must be taken not in the literal sense, but in the figurative sense. It points to the image of behavior that the author wishes to communicate. What will be the future of kinesics in kinetic research under the aegis of Bouissac's machine? In its application to empirical inquiry, the entire proposal encounters difficulty in relevance, feasibility, validity, and productiveness. One gets the impression that the proposal is based on a series of *mirages* which create the illusion of scientific structure without advancing knowledge.

1. *The mirage of the acrobatic act as a relevant model for social discourse.*

It is no coincidence that Bouissac's treatise begins and ends with an analysis of the acrobatic act. For him, the acrobatic act constitutes the essence of unified corporal articulation. Since, however, the acrobatic act is introduced as a model for the study of social discourse as well, it behooves us to question the relevance of the act to an interchange between people.

The essential features of the acrobatic act are that it is predominantly monologue in nature; that it is pure kinesics; that it emphasizes the gross muscles of the limb defying gravity and reaching for outer space; and that it tends to de-emphasize microkinetic activity such as facial display. Most important of these considerations is the exclusiveness of the kinetic vehicle, with language (except for some introductory comments) almost absent. Moreover, the act is well rehearsed with each movement constituting a carefully planned final product, the result of a studied program. The act is conducted by individuals with a high degree of body awareness.

Pragmatic situations are, of course, very useful in the development of science. For instance, animal research does reveal a good bit about cognition or affect of relevance to humans. Yet, the paradigmatic situation must be so chosen as to maintain the essential features of the phenomenon under study. The essential features of acrobatic behavior and social discourse are fundamentally different. In social discourse, kinesics are part of spontaneous dialogue, not studied monologue. Body movements emerge in support of verbalization; hence language constitutes the major vehicle of articulation. The movements themselves are not nearly as articulated; they generally do not entail limb extensions and emphasize the subtler movements of hand and face. Indeed, a large amount of body activity appears to have no communicative function (e.g., wiggles, twitches, and tics). All this is not to deny that there is a range of special conditions created by verbalization difficulty or by conditions in which the linguistic repertoire is insufficient (deaf mutes, bilingualism, etc.), conditions under which gestures do achieve a high degree of articulation. Yet, at the very moment when the verbal vehicle assumes dominance, the structural significance of body movements is fundamentally altered. In this sense, the machine which would represent the acrobatic act would appear to be essentially irrelevant as a representation of the structure of social discourse.

2. *The mirage that everything that is recordable is also interpretable.*
High speed electronics has given us the illusion that the recording of all behaviors in an event sequence constitutes a path toward the ordering of behavior. Yet this illusion comes up against both the feasibility of such recording and its interpretability.

The recording of a behavioral sequence, be it an acrobatic act or social interchange, comprises a tremendous range of phenomena infinitely more complex than the horse's gait in Muybridge's work. The movements range in locus, in size (from micro- to macrokinetic), in speed, and in rhythm. On strictly technical grounds. it seems difficult to envisage a machine which can appropriately record all these attributes of behavior. Can a machine simultaneously monitor posture, limb activity, eye blink, and facial display *and* describe all of these in terms of volumes in space? It would seem that each of these behaviors operates in very different space, time, and dynamic dimensions. Yet even if such a machine were feasible, can the resultant data be interpreted without reference to the anatomy of the behaving organism?

It is true that verbal accounts of body activity have been hampered by much subjective bias, but it is also true that body movements cluster around distinct muscle groups and these define a territory for focused observation. Each of these muscle groups, as we shall see later, pertains to relatively discrete psychological functions: facial display pertains to affect arousal; posture as well as abdominal and thoracic respiration deal with defensive organization; proxemics (the definition of interpersonal distance) deals with social status and power relation; eye glance deals with affiliative motivation; and head, hand, and foot movements deal with information processing. Random recording of behavior without programming the observation to focus on these systems could hardly lead to observations which have the property of regularity, repeatability, and structure. By creating a recording device which indiscriminately portrays all behaviors, large and small, fast or slow, it is hard to imagine how relatively uniform volumes can be derived.

3. *The mirage of pure corporal structures.*

Bouissac is quite correct when he seizes upon the issue of the objective segmentation of behavior as a central problem in kinetic research. One can share the concern of Pike that unitization often seems impossible because onset and termination of kinetic acts cannot clearly be delineated. Thus Bouissac's answer of defining units by articulation of volumes seems reasonable. The difficulty with his definition of units lies in three aspects of his proposal: the emphasis on exclusively corporal units, the reliance on digital definitions, and the assumption, in a section on syntagmatics, that units are constituents of quasi-linguistic structures.

There are a good many observations to indicate that an articulated kinetic unit in social discourse tends to involve *cross-channel* or *cross-vehicle* forms of behavior and does not reside in corporal sequences alone. Take the two examples of relieving an itch on the forehead or touching the same area in a reflective pause; both describe identical trajectories of the arm and may occur in identical postures. Yet the essential, distinguishable characteristic is the embeddedness in the verbal flow. When the forehead is touched in a reflective pause, it is likely to occur at the point of hesitation and hence is embedded in the phonemic rhythm. When the touching occurs to relieve an itch, its relationship to the verbal flow is likely to be random. The essential unit, here, is not the touching of the forehead *per se*, but its co-occurrence with defined aspects of the phonemic rhythm.

There are many examples in kinetic behavior research which point to cross-channel units. Dittmann (1973), for example, in describing listening behavior, has identified a listener-response(LR) as involving the contiguity of head nod by the listener and vocal pause by the speaker. The two events co-occurring may be presumed to lead to improved communication in a dyad. Yet when only a head nod occurs, regardless of its pause location, improved listening would not be expected. Sander and Condon (1974), studying mother-neonate dyads, defined units to consist of the sustained synchrony of organized correspondences between adult speech and neonate's body movements. In our own work, we have sought to define verbalization structures consisting of the co-occurrence of kinetic acts within units of language syntax, units which were not definable by the morphology of the act alone, and these indeed were predictive of certain affective states.

The emphasis on purely nonverbal (i.e., kinetic) units of behavior is quite prevalent in contemporary kinetic research. It can be found in the work of Birdwhistell, Scheflen, and notably Watzlawick. Yet for the latter, the kinetic phenomenon is viewed as following an analogic code. It has a Gestalt configuration often demanding anecdotal linguistic (stenographic) descriptions. Gestures often have the property of icons and emblems. They are thus not readily reducible to digital dimensions. Bouissac, on the other hand, by attempting to define his units along dimensions of space, time, and dynamic force would seek to describe an analogic phenomenon along the line of a continuous variable. One would suspect that such an attempt may involve a distortion of the data.

Finally, in his section on syntagmatic and cybernatic analysis, Bouissac proposes to regard the basic volumes as constitutive units in larger syntax-like structures. Such constitutive units must have the properties not only of discreteness but, as in grammar, of subordination or superordination as well. Is this possible? Dittman (1971), in his critique of Birdwhistell's work, has convincingly argued that much of kinetic behavior during social discourse lacks the properties which allow one to speak of kinesics as language. One convincing reason is that much kinetic activity lacks the quality of discreteness. For instance, continuous self-stimulation is an example in point. Once there is no discreteness, it is hard to speak of sub- or superordination.

In sum, the unitized corporal sequences derived by Bouissac's machine would lack validity for they do not encompass cross-channel units of behavior; they would tend to digitalize what is essentially analogic or metaphoric and would attribute a quasi-linguistic structure to kinesics which is often not warranted by the facts of behavior.

4. *The Mirage of Mathematization as a Substitute for Naturalistic Observation.*

In this day of cybernetics, of servomechanisms, one can hardly take a position against quantification, or mathematization. The representation of behavior in terms of arbitrary symbols does give us a degree of freedom from subjective experiences, or what Bouissac calls the perceptive-linguistic myth. Formalization is a necessary base for the exploration of higher order relationships. The question, however, is: At what point in the development of science is mathematization introduced? And what is the continuing status of naturalistic observation vis-à-vis formal structures? There is much to be said for the view that formalization, in principle desirable, when introduced prematurely, may stifle development, and especially discovery of functional relationships.

A cursory view of the significant discovery of functional relationships in our field has not come from mathematization but from naturalistic observation. Darwin (1904 [1872]) discovered that the angry frown and the protruding chin is a basic biological pattern of facial affect display, common to higher primates and man when confronted with survival situations. Hall (1966), following Lorenz, has discovered that proxemics, the definition of interpersonal space, is an intrinsic property of social status and distance. And more modestly, in our own research, we have noted, at first from casual observations from video-recorded interviews, that the common distinction between gestures which we have termed object-focused movements, inhere in their relationship to language structure. Each of these kinetic-linguistic structures refers to very different psychological processes, one having to do with enactment of thought, the other with body tension regulation.

As substantive contributions, these foregoing 'discoveries' have suggested distinct body movement systems, as already outlined, i.e., affect arousal systems, social status systems, etc. The discovery of such functional systems depends on the identification of empirically 'valid' structures; and it would seem that discoveries of structures having functional significance must come from observations of *kinesics in context*. Once the relevant variables have been charted out, even with a stenographic notation system, mathematization then becomes possible. For instance, proxemic distancing lends itself to mathematization in Bouissac's terms. Measures of facial affect display do so as well. Most recently, in a developmental study, the occurrence of object- and body-focused activity during specified information processing tasks could be represented as linear as well as curvilinear functions varying in successive age groups. Indeed we may now be ready for more formal mathematical analyses relating these measures to other kinetic as well as verbal functions. Yet this development occurred after the domains had been clarified, the domains being kinesics in affect-arousing situations, kinesics in social space, and kinesics in information processing.

The scientific methodologist is to the empirical investigator what a parent is to an offspring. The point at which formalization is introduced by the methodologist can be likened to the point at which formal logical communication is used by a parent in influencing the child. In infancy and early childhood, the growth of intelligence is mediated by motor exploration and the parent fosters development through communication which involves touching and simple imagery. The premature introduction of formal logic may stifle growth. Indeed, even in maturity the ability to revert to the primary experiences of visual imagery or tactile sensation remains a continuing nutriment for formal operations. In similar fashion, the 'imagery' of naturalistic observation must remain an ongoing companion for the investigator even if he strives towards formalization.

Bouissac writes his work manifestly as a scientific methodologist. Yet, is it really possible to divorce form from substance? Can we be concerned with the structure of behavior without a concern for what the behavior is all about? I suspect that he too has a substantive bias. The acrobatic act defies the laws of gravity and views the motions of the body as not governed by social forces or biological need, but in the literal physical sense of motions in space. Geometry is the language of Physics. Units are described in terms of equilibrium and desequilibrium; indeed, it seems that the acrobatic model is a physicist's model. If this is the case, can Physics, in spite of its high prestige value, be of help in the study of communication? From where we stand, *the raison d'être* of kinetic behavior has to do with the role of action in cognition. As such, the segmentation of behavior cannot be undertaken as separate from the delineation of cognitive structures.

In concluding, we suspect that Bouissac's machine is a brilliant exercise applied to the representation of the behavior of an acrobat -- an acrobat whose corpus is articulated; who defies the laws of gravity, and yet whose behavior has little to do with the functional human being in social discourse, be it in the interpersonal setting or in the processing of his thoughts. As such, Bouissac's model remains one of the characters in Pirandello's plays and does not become author itself.

REFERENCES

Birdwhistell, R.L.
   1952 *Introduction to Kinesics* (Louisville: University of Louisville Press).
Darwin, C.
   1904 *The Expression of the Emotions in Man and Animals*. (London: John Murray).
   [1872]
Dittmann, A.T.
   1971 "Review of R. Birdwhistell: Kinesics and Context", *Psychiatry* 34, No. 3.
   1973 "Developmental Factors in Conversational Behavior", personal communication.
Hall, E.T.
   1966 *The Hidden Dimension*. (New York: Doubleday).
Martinet, A.
   1965 *La linguistique synchronique* (Paris: Presses Universitaires de France).
Sander, L.W. and W.S. Condon
   1974 "Neonate Movement Is Synchronized with Adult Speech: Interactional Participation and Language Acquisition", *Science* 183, 99-101.

HENRY W. SEAFORD, JR.

Maximizing Replicability in Describing Facial Behavior

Man has inherited from the primitive anthropoids the ability to draw back his lips in anger, to open them in a laugh, or again, to protrude them into a funnel and so to confer kisses on the objects of his affection. How much dour literature, ancient and modern, might be lightened by this thought! (Gregory 1963)

Physical variation among humans has properly inspired, *inter alia,* generations of anthropologists. In days of yore, coerced by an insatiable desire to formulate human 'types', our intrepid professional ancestors deftly wielded anthropometer and caliper to collect computer-boggling lists of indices of head, face and body. Like *Oreopithecus,* many of those data with their related speculations, died without issue. Professional phylogeny shifted to the 'new physical anthropology', in which Washburn (1951) declared it was of infinitely more evolutionary significance to explore process rather than type. How is mandibular morphology determined by contractions of m. temporalis, m. pterygoideus, and the masseter? Later, other questions followed: What are the relations of face and dental morphology to culture? How is the face used in primate communication? Whatever the question, one is always faced with the corollary problem: how can facial behavior be best described? One answer to this question is the focus of this paper: viz., that description is most felicitously accomplished with reference to the contractions of the various muscles, a view which is by no means unique. By way of approaching this subject, a cursory review of some studies of the face will be made. In addition to artists, anatomists, and physiologists, the face has been studied by anthropologists, biologists (ethologists), and psychologists – each with a preference for how facial behavior should be described.

The study of the face by anthropologists can be viewed as coalescing from the two major foci of that discipline in America: biological and cultural. In 1936, Goldstein pointed out that, with all the voluminous, anthropologically-related literature on human growth, there had been relatively little on the face to that date. He summarized what there was. As early as 1866, Weckler had studied the development of the head and face. Hrdlicka (1900) and Connolly (1928) made inter-racial surveys. Boas (1911) studied morphological changes in immigrants. Hellman (1927, 1935) made important contributions. Schultz (1920) and Schaeffer (1935) wrote on ontogeny; Krogman (1930, 1931a, b, c.) on phylogeny.

Loth (1949) studied facial variation in the structure of facial muscles, and concluded there were differences between Caucasoids and Negroids, a conclusion that had been reached earlier by Huber (1931). Darwin (1872:18) had long before noted that "the observation of Expression is by no means easy", something Loth discovered for himself:

It is very hard to study facial muscles on the living subject, and is possible only with intelligent people with whom one can communicate to evoke the desired facial expression ... I ... gave up this study in Uganda. (1949:222)

Fortunately, later workers have been more persistent.

In 1946 Hooton, in his immortal *Up from the Ape*, stated: "I venture to predict, that another couple of decades may establish, upon a rigorously scientific base, some rather astounding associations of physiognomy with behavior" (1946:176).[1] Two decades from the year Hooton penned this prophecy, Steegmann (1965:355), in a stimulating reappraisal of facial morphology as it relates to climate, notes (echoing Goldstein's 1936 comment) that "the face has gone almost unexamined as an area of experimental physical anthropology", although he mentions some studies by physiologists in the 50's and 60's. In a publication by one of Hooton's students the same year, Carleton Coon (1965:258) includes a brief discussion of the muscles of expression and scattered references to their function in primates, a matter DeVore (1965) considers in more detail. A year later, Buettner-Janusch (1966:74-77) delineates facial muscles and their functions. Steegmann (1967, 1968, 1970, 1972) has continued his study of the face's adaptation to low temperature. Kohara (1968) has indicated that the inability of Japanese to contract the orbicularis oculi and frontalis unilatterally in the wink and one-eyebrow raising respectively is a biological phenomenon, not a cultural one. More recently, Chevalier-Skolnikoff (1973, 1974) provides information on the *Cercopithecidae* which corroborates some of the conclusions reached in the study of regional facial expression (Seaford 1975, 1976), in which pursing and lip smacking may have a rapport-establishing function.[2]

Curiously, Hooton's schedule was accurate.

A convenient, as well as symbolic, place to begin tracing the interest of cultural anthropology in facial expression is the work of Sir Edward Burnett Tylor. Musing over the face's response to mood, he wrote:

The ascertaining of the precise physical mode in which certain attitudes of the internal and external face come to correspond to certain moods and mind, is a physiological problem as yet little understood; but the fact that particular expressions of face are accompanied by corresponding and dependent expressions of emotional tone, only requires an observer or a looking-glass to prove it. The laugh made with a solemn, contemptuous, or sarcastic face, is quite different from that which comes from a joyous one; the ah! oh! oh! hey! and so on, change their modulations to match the expression of countenance. (1871:166)

Tylor noted the close association of speech with gesture. He thought that gesture in "the lower races" was relatively prominent, and that it assumed many of the functions of "articulate speech". Moreover a facial expression of emotion so-called can be quite affectless:

By turning these natural processes to account, men contrive to a certain extent to put on particular physical expressions, frowning or smiling for instance, in order to simulate the emotions which would naturally produce such expressions, or merely to convey the thought of such emotions to others. (1871:165)

Although Tylor seems to give preeminence to culture in the molding of expressions of emotion — "a certain action of our physical machinery shows symptoms which we have learnt by experience to refer to a mental cause" — his comments also suggest Ekman's concept of "display rules" (Ekman, Friesen, and Ellsworth 1972:23). That is, although emotions have universal modes of expression, they are elaborated upon in certain situations by culturally standardized procedures.

An early student of face and body gestures in America was Franz Boas. He was interested in demonstrating that gestures are not biologically determined, but artifacts of culture, changing "with great ease" (1938:125). His programmatic statement that "motor habits of groups of people are culturally determined and (are) not due to heredity" (1938:126), placed the whole matter beyond cavil in some minds, and provided a seemingly firm basis upon which to build subsequent anthropological perspectives, a bias which probably led anthropologists away from the Darwinian fold,[3] while psychologists were returning (Ekman *et al.* 1969, Ekman 1972, Izard 1968, 1971). His extensive observations of Northwest Coast culture indelibly influenced his students (Birdwhistell 1970a:38-39), among whom were Otto Klineberg, David Efron, Edward Sapir, and Margaret Mead.

In a book dedicated to Boas, Klineberg emphasizes the importance of culture in facial expressions: "There is ample evidence in ethnological literature that emotional expression varies in the same manner ... as language, and that it is also to some extent a conventionalized form of communication" (Klineberg 1935:282). At the same time Klineberg is careful to consider the possibility that pansapient expressions exist beneath cultural accouterment (1935: 285, 287-88): "There are undoubtedly certain types of expressive behavior which are common to all human societies" (1940:176).

David Efron, an Argentine and a Jew, who had traveled in Italy, had Italian friends in Argentina and had studied with Boas in New York, was uniquely sensitized to cultural differences in modes of expression. True to his mentor, Efron notes: "... one is never confronted with a purely physical movement in gesture, but always with gestural movement, i.e., meaningful movement, whether strictly 'linguistic' or 'discursive'" (1941:64).

That Edward Sapir attributed some body movements to a learned code is an indication of Boasian influence, according to Birdwhistell (1969:381), but sometimes the former seems less captivated by cultural relativism. With usual, uncanny intuition he perceived the nonverbal context of language in the familiar quotation:

In spite of ... difficulties of conscious analysis, we respond to gestures with an extreme alertness and, one might almost say, in accordance with an elaborate code that is written nowhere, known by none, and understood by all. (1949:556)

Such facial movements as the wrinkling of the brow can be 'unconscious symbolism' facilitating communication.

It is no coincidence that Margaret Mead wrote the preface for the 1955 edition of Darwin's *The Expression of the Emotions in Man and Animals,* the book from which my own interest sprang and which must be the single, most significant work inspiring modern research on facial expression. The pioneer photographic study of personality she did with Gregory Bateson (Bateson and Mead 1942) corroborates the Boasian dictum that human behavior is above all cultural, a notion which does not easily yield to refutation. Embued with cultural relativisitic perspective, Weston LaBarre (1947) impressively marshals ethnographic examples leading him to conclude that "there is no 'natural' language of emotional gesture". Even though the same expressions might be found cross-culturally, the meanings attached to them vary from one culture to the next.

The allegedly "instinctive" nature of such motor habits in personal relationships is difficult to maintain in the face of the fact that in many cases the same gesture means exactly opposite, or incommensurable things, in different cultures. Hissing in Japan is polite deference to social superiors. (1947:56)

Clearly the most active exponent of the Boasian tradition in the study of the cultural significance of behavior is Ray Birdwhistell. After acknowledging his debt to Boas, Efron, Sapir, and LaBarre, he attributes to descriptive linguistics the real impetus behind his founding of kinesics (1952), "the scientific investigation of the *structured* nature of body motion communication" (Birdwhistell 1968b:381). Spreading behavior on a linguistic model, body motion is compared to "kinesic building blocks (which) are ranges of movement, quanta of motion" (1968a). "Gestures are really *bound* morphs" (1966:183). Birdwhistell is concerned with isolating "kines" which are "least perceptible units of body motion" (1970a:166) in order to work out a kinic system upon which is based the kineme and kinemorpheme (1970a:193-200 *et passim*). He comments on the difficulty of delineating mouth kinemes.

The seven kinemes which make up the present circumoral complex are tentative. Only continued research will give us confidence that these represent complete assessment and that the list is composed of equivalent categories. The list includes "compressed lips," "protruded lips," "retracted lip," "apically withdrawn lips," "snarl," "lax open mouth," and "mouth overopen." I am particularly doubtful about the first two of these. Both may belong to some general midface category which we have thus far been unable to isolate.

To this list must also be added "anterior chin thrust," "lateral chin thrust," "puffed cheeks," and "sucked cheeks." "Chin drop" may gain kinemic status. (1970a:100-01)

From his statement that his "work was only complicated by assumptions about communication as an elaboration of a pan-human *code* emergent from the limited possibilities of physiological response" (1970b:19) it is evident that he maintains the traditional anthropological position of cultural preeminence.

DESCRIBING FACIAL EXPRESSIONS

The literature on facial behavior manifests some reluctance to formulate descriptions in terms of muscle contractions. Probably the main reason for this is the variability of the musculature making it impossible to discern, for example, if the risorius or the platysma is really retracting the corners of the mouth. Moreover, further ambiguity is introduced in the observation process itself, for who can be sure he is precisely delineating – without electromyography (or maybe even with it) – the contribution of every single muscle to a given facial expression? Darwin notes the problem of variability:

> The facial muscles blend much together, and, as I am informed, hardly appear on a dissected face so distinct as they are here represented. Some writers consider that these muscles consist of nineteen pairs, with one unpaired; but others make the number much larger, amounting even to fifty-five. ... They are ... very variable in structure ... they are hardly alike in half a dozen subjects. They are also variable in function. (Darwin 1955:23)

Yet the great naturalist himself did not refrain from referring to specific muscle contraction when describing facial expressions (e.g., Darwin 1955:148-49) for fear he might be attributing movement to a muscle which just happened not to be there. Surely muscles such as m. orbicularis oris, m. mentalis, m. triangularis, the zygomaticus, the quadratus labii superioris, the corrugator, m. frontalis, and the platysma must always be present on normal human faces for the very fact that most people's faces work as they should.

As for the objection that describing facial behavior in terms of specific muscle contractions on the grounds that it would be unscientific, since one is never quite sure whether the job is being done by the muscle which is supposed to do it or another, it is my contention that this is far out-weighed by the gain in observer replicability-potential. That is, if I know what usually happens when a particular muscle contracts, and so state that such a muscle is contracting, any future observer will know precisely what movement I describe. Moreover, my guess is that the muscles described as doing the contracting would be actually doing it most of the time. Tinbergen (1955:7), for one, appears undaunted by possibilities of ambiguities:

> Because it is our task to analyse behaviour as co-ordinated muscle activity, the ultimate aim of our description must be an accurate picture of the patterns of muscle action. Except in some especially simple cases, this has never been done, probably because most workers are only dimly aware of the necessity.

In 1862 Duchenne established the precedent for describing facial expression in terms of facial muscle contraction in his careful study of muscle physiology. Darwin relied heavily on this work (1955: 148-50, 200-02, *et passim*), and its procedure appears most useful in describing facial behavior today. Ekman, Friesen, and Tomkins (1971), in fact, point out the relevance of Duchenne's work and procede to base the Facial Affect Scoring Technique on it, at least up to a point. After quoting Darwin's comment about Duchenne that "no one has more carefully studied the contractions of each separate muscle and the consequent furrows produced on the skin", these authors opt for description by "furrows" rather than con-tractions".

Initial attempts to describe facial behavior in terms of muscle movements revealed that it was often quite difficult to determine which muscles had moved by looking at the face. A decision was made to describe the appearance of the face primarily in terms of wrinkles, ... (1971:40)

If, indeed, Duchenne's procedure was to be followed, and if the "wrinkles" referred to are the result of muscle contraction, why not go to the source rather than to the consequence? Furthermore, if it is so "difficult to determine which muscles" move, so that wrinkles have to be used instead, what has happened to Duchenne's procedure by now? For its originators FAST was successful — out of 51, 45 photographs were judged correctly — but the technique is unsuitable for behaviors which are not related to affect. If descriptions of facial expression are to be given in terms of "wrinkles" (especially if one does this because he is not quite sure what the facial muscles are doing), how can someone untrained in FAST definitions know for sure what behaviors are being effected?[4]

Recently, Kendon (1975) has stealthily studied kissing behavior. In a *tour de force* describing the amorous activities of the face, he rightfully points out that procedures used to categorize emotions are inadequate for general descriptions — a point which is well-taken even if one concedes that kissing is not nonemotional. The notations he devises, modified from Ex and Kendon (1969), are, notwithstand-ing, not unlike those of Birdwhistell (1952b:40-44) in their limited utility for other studies. For example, the category "mouth corners raised in definite smile", symbolized by the usual spread-U form, would have confused description of the southern smiles I studied which are characterized by *unraised* corners. Surely the most im-portant datum here is that a "definite smile" is being effected, which a category based on muscle contractions would have more amply described. This advantage is used in two of Kendon's notations which are based on muscle contractions. Interestingly, he finds female faces more expressive than males' – a phenomenon I also noted in the study of Virginia faces[5] (see below).

In an earlier study, Blurton Jones suggests that "precise descriptions" of facial muscle contraction can be best approximated by dividing the face into "segments" which are made up of "components" (1971:365). These segments are simply "guides to where to look on the face" (1971:372) having nothing to do with describing a whole facial expression. Alternatives for describing components are "location of shadows and lines" (cf. Ekman *et al.* 1971), reference to the assumed muscle contractions per se, or "positions of landmarks". Blurton Jones opts mainly for the latter device since, he reasons, one can never be absolutely sure he can accurately describe all muscle contractions by sheer observation, and, besides, why impose on the reader the necessity for learning names and functions of all the facial musculature (1971:368-69)? At the same time he notes it is "fairly easy to make a good interpretation of a face in terms of the muscle activity involved". Fortunately the 'landmark' emphasis (shortcomings of which are discussed below) is fortified with contraction data wherever this makes description more precise. Although his descriptive procedure appears quite adequate for the photographic materials illustrating his paper, my own preference would have been to include contraction data in every case, and force the serious student of facial expression to learn the facial muscles and their behavior – something he needs to know anyway! Moreover such data would make somewhat less tedious the 'component' system which tends to be confusingly atomistic sometimes.

Less flexible as a multipurpose system of description, but exemplifying the advantages of the muscle referent are Izard's categories (1971:242-45). While pertaining only to expressions of emotion, that worker nevertheless carefully delineates all muscle contractions usually involved in each expression.

Hjortsjo (1970) has recently provided a thorough treatment of facial muscle contractions. Although emphasizing expressions of emotion, that author follows the unabashed, detailed description of muscle contraction after the traditional manner of Duchenne (1862), Virchow (1908), Lightoller (1925, 1928), and Huber (1931), *inter alia.* The uninformed readers with whom Blurton Jones is concerned would never be the same after studying this little book.

If the phylogenetic and/or ontogenetic components of facial expressions are to be understood and sorted out from cultural phenomena, in the case of *Homo sapiens,* muscle contractions per se must be the significant units. If this be so, there is great value in standardizing descriptions of primate facial expressions in terms of muscular contractions. Many times this is not done. Take for example for 'pout face' which a chimpanzee displays if it wants to regain contact with its mother's body. The pout muscle par excellence is the mentalis — something every *Homo sapiens* infant instinctively 'knows'. But Goodall (1969:420) does not specify if that muscle is used — a datum which would corroborate her category and make interspecific comparison meaningful. Moreover, van Hooff (1969:59) in describing "the pout face" omits comment on muscles which might be associated with the lips which "are protruded; typically they stay pressed together near the mouth corners, but are lifted in the middle region, thus creating a small round opening". One could assume the configuration of "the middle region" is caused by the mentalis, but it is not clear if contractions are occurring in the chin or upper face.[6]

Andrew (1965:92) does mention the action of the orbicularis oris which "may round the lips or thrust them forward in a pout". However, although this is an "important human facial expression" which is shared by chimpanzees among other primates, no mention is made of whether or not the mentalis is participating. This is even more curious when he goes on to describe a primate threat (human indignation) expression which uses the same rounded lips but with an expulsion of air. Testing the pout and indignation expression on myself, I discover I use the mentalis effecting the former, but not the latter. This just could be a significant difference which simple, complete description would make available for future investigations.

Grant (1969) has suggested an "ethological check list" for human facial expressions. He considers the face to be divided into three relatively independent expressive areas: "gaze, eyebrow position and mouth position". To these he adds body posture. The lower part of the face "with the extreme mobility built into the lips and mouth has the greatest number of expressive positions". In determining a procedure for describing behavior, he questions whether a minimal element exists in nature. But description must go on, so he weighs the validity of patterns built up from muscle contractions against "functional" designations, "bits of behaviour which fulfil a particular function". He prefers the latter, since "many recognisable patterns of behaviour can be adequately described and may yet vary considerably in terms of muscular contraction", as, for example, a pecking bird will use different muscles according to the positioning of its prey, but that it is pecking is incontrovertible. He chooses, then, cutaneous, "functional" descriptions rather than muscular ones (Grant 1969:525-27, 535).

In trying to avoid one kind of misinterpretation, Grant's choice might well lead to others. One of his "flight" elements, for example, is "mouth corners down". The description of this element is: "The lips are closed and the corners of the mouth are drawn down. ... This element is frequently associated with 'Sad frown'" (1969:528). His plate 11a (Pl. I Fig. 1) illustrating this expression shows a double-chinned youngster looking quite serious, but with, apparently, no muscles contracting, with the possible exception of the corrugators, which of course accounts for the 'frown' component. His mouth indeed is bowed cranially, but this is apparently a natural stance, and the corners do not appear to be 'drawn' caudally. Blurton Jones (1971:372, 387) points out the difficulty of judging "mouth activity", one reason being that "the resting position of the mouth is with the corners just below the lower lip." Grant describes the "Sad frown", thusly: "The brow is wrinkled horizontally by the scalp being drawn forward. The eyebrow tilts down at the outside corner" (1969:527). Although Blurton Jones (1971:374) cautions that con-

PLATE I

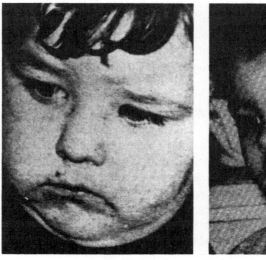 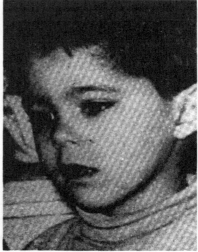

Fig. 1   Fig. 2

Fig. 1. "Sad frown" (Grant 1969: Pl. 11a)
Fig. 2. "Eyebrow raised" (Grant 1969: Pl. 10a)

tractions in this area are difficult to discern, I cannot avoid thinking that the photograph reveals none of the purported facial muscle contractions. Concerning "the scalp being drawn forward" Hjortsjo (1970:50) does mention this contraction, but Duchenne (in Tomkins 1962:239) and Gray (1959:415) refer only to the backward motion of the occipitofrontalis. It is this upward contraction which causes horizontal wrinkles. Moreover, the mesial action of corrugators causing barely perceptible vertical wrinkles is not mentioned at all. On the other hand, Grant's Plate 10a (Pl. I Fig. 2) is purported to show "eyebrow raised", although I am unable to determine any contraction of the frontalis. (Of course, Blurton Jones' previously mentioned point should be kept in mind.) These cases suggest that cutaneous topography can suggest muscular contractions when there are none, and lead to their nonobservance when they are present. Hinde (1966: 10-11), while pointing out the value of "descriptions by consequence" over sheer muscle contractions, also cautions that they may bias future hypotheses based upon them, and that they easily lend themselves to "overinterpretation". It would seem that a few of Grant's 'elements' are cases in point.

One other matter involved in observing human facial expression is the presence or absence of speech. Bilabial stops and nasals, for example, necessitate clamped lips, while high central or back vowels call for orbicular contractions. Failure to take these behaviors into account can cause ambiguities in description, a case of which occurs in a recent book on primate behavior. The 37th president of the United States is depicted displaying an "open-mouth threat" (Jolly 1972:161). Although the photograph appears to match the label eminently, the possibility of the presidential mandible's being dropped to articulate a low-front or central vowel cannot be overlooked. If this be the case, the main purpose of the mouth's being open is simply phonetic. Perhaps the photograph showing the "tense-mouth face" (1972:156) of the same president is more accurate, but this could represent the articulation of a bilabial consonant, even though the degree of contraction is abnormally exaggerated. Notation of speech behaviors should be salient in describing facial expressions. Only after accounting for these is one able to speculate about the non-verbal phenomena.

AN EXERCISE IN MUSCLE CONTRACTIONS

At the 1966 Annual Meeting of the Pennsylvania Sociological Society the results of a study of over 10,000 yearbook photographs (e.g.,

Pl. VI Fig. 2) exploring the possibility of regional patterns of facial expression was reported (Seaford 1966). Evidence that various muscular contractions were more typical of the southern U.S. than other places led to further research at the University of Virginia in 1969. The earlier study was fully supported by the new data, and these became the substance of a doctoral dissertation (Seaford 1971). Throughout this research the problem of description was salient. Birdwhistell's notation (1952b:40-44) based on facial topography was not suited to describing the kinds of facial behaviors encountered. The Facial Affect Scoring Technique (Ekman, Friesen, and Tomkins 1971) was considered, but that system, developed for describing expressions of emotions, provided no way to describe, for example, the simultaneity of the levator-depressor action of the face – a common phenomenon in the South. Description in terms of the facial muscle contractions themselves appeared to be the only answer (cf. Fig. 1).

In describing the facial expressions of 62 Virginians, categories based on muscular contractions were found useful in delineating recurring patterns in that sample. What has been called the "southern syndrome" (Seaford 1966, 1971, 1975, 1976) consists of the following patterns:

(1) Orbicular Clamp (Pls. II, III) is formed by contractions of the orbicularis oris superioris and inferioris, not infrequently assisted by m. mentalis, joining the lips together with varying degrees of firmness;

(2) Purse-Clamp (Pls. IV-VI) results from the clamping action just described, but elaborated by contractions of the caninus and triangularis (and/or modiolus) resulting in a mesial movement of the angles of the mouth;

(3) Pursed Smile (Pls. VII, VIII) is produced by contractions of the zygomaticus major and the various heads of the quadratus labii superioris which are countered by the orbicularis oris;

(4) Inferior Press Smile (Pl. IX) is a variant of the Pursed Smile effected when the quadratus labii inferioris is activated resulting in the squaring off of the lower lip as it is pressed against the mandibular alveolus and/or lower teeth;

(5) Angle Depression Smile (Pl. X) is caused by antagonistic contractions of the triangulares, sometimes assisted by the platysma, simultaneously with contractions of the levators of the upper face;

(6) The Tongue-Lips (formerly Tongue Display Type A) (Pls. XI, XII) pattern occurs as the tongue is discretely protruded by the posterior fibers of the genioglossi, while the apex is spread by the verticalis as it passes through the lips;

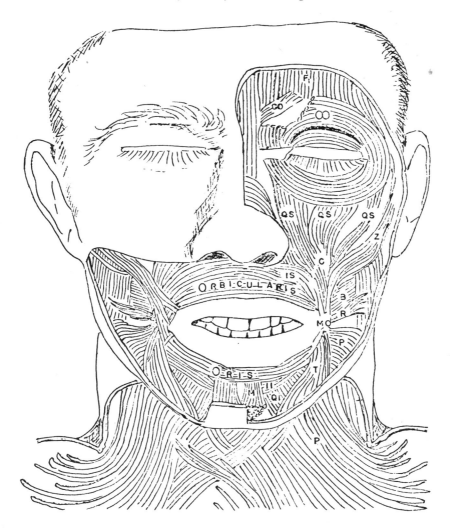

Fig. 1. Selected Facial Muscles

Buccinator (B); Caninus (C); Corrugator (CO); Frontalis (F); Incisivus Inferioris (II); Incisivus Superioris (IS); Mentalis (M); Modiolus (MO); Orbicularis Oculi (OO); Orbicularis Oris; Platysma (P); Quadratus Labii Inferioris (QI); Quadratus Labii Superioris (QS); Risorius (R); Triangularis (T); Zygomaticus (Z). Orbicularis Oculi cut to show Corrugator. (After Grant 1951: Figs. 448 and 499 with omissions and modifications from Shapiro 1947 and Gray 1959 – original sketch revised in Seaford 1976.)

PLATE II   Female Orbicular Clamp

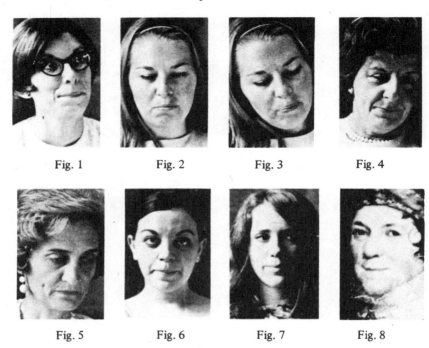

Fig. 1   Fig. 2   Fig. 3   Fig. 4

Fig. 5   Fig. 6   Fig. 7   Fig. 8

Fig. 3. Some mesial contraction of orbicularis oris; therefore, more properly a Purse-Clamp.

Fig. 8. Dorothea Payne Todd Madison (1768-1849) by Rembrandt Peale (Weddell 1930).

(7) Tongue Smile (Pl. XIII) patterns are formed either by the tip of the tongue touching the upper inscisors or the tongue's being curled behind the teeth simultaneously with contractions of the levators of the upper face;

(8) Mandibular Thrust (Pls. XIV), a result of contractions of the masseter and pterygoideus, is defined by its title.

The difference between the occurrence of these patterns in the Virginia sample and the Pennsylvania control is significant at the .01 level (Seaford 1976:620). Data were collected from yearbooks, photographs, historic paintings, as well as from informants during face-to-face interaction. Artifacts of articulation were considered unlikely in yearbook photographs and paintings. Other photographs taken during the fieldwork were synchronized with audio tape to ascertain moments of articulation. From portraits of colonial

PLATE III   Male Orbicular Clamp

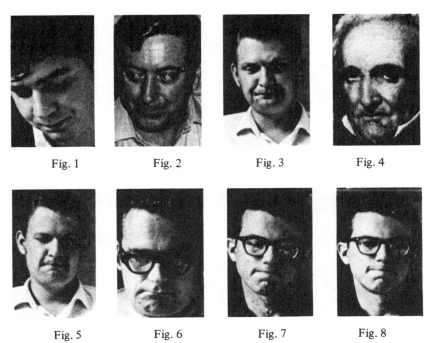

Fig. 1   Fig. 2   Fig. 3   Fig. 4

Fig. 5   Fig. 6   Fig. 7   Fig. 8

Figs. 1-3. Probable mentalis action.
Figs. 3, 8. Articulating "hmm".
Fig. 4.   Pattern possibly caused by clamping of orbicularis oris with mentalis assist, and/or loss of teeth. James Gibbon (1759-1835) by John B. Martin. Courtesy Virginia Historical Society.
Figs. 5-8. Strong mentalis action.

Virginians historic depth was suggested for Orbicular Clamp (Pl. II Fig. 8), and Purse-Clamp (Pls. IV Fig. 6; V Fig. 3; VI Fig. 1). The fact that the fourth president of the United States and some of his peers display these patterns suggests they have been part of proper Virginia bearing for some time.[7]

Although other workers may have been able to study and to describe these paintings without reference to muscular contractions (an improbable feat in my opinion), the fact that I was sensitized to behavior of the orbicularis oris and the levators and depressors in Virginia faces made me instantly aware of what was probably transpiring in the Madison physiognomy. By describing this behavior in terms of the contractions of the orbicularis oris, the caninus and the

PLATE IV   Female Purse-Clamp

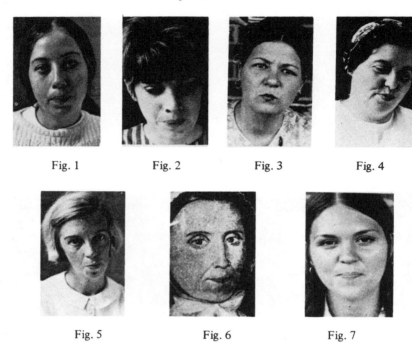

Fig. 1   Fig. 2   Fig. 3   Fig. 4

Fig. 5   Fig. 6   Fig. 7

Fig. 5. Slight alveolar prognathism could affect contraction of orbicularis oris.
Fig. 6. Probable mesial contraction of orbicularis oris. Lucy Gray Briggs (d. 1779)
   of Dinwiddle County (Weddell 1930).

triangularis and/or the modiolus — an emphasis on process rather than type — the possibility that other workers will be able to replicate it is maximized.

The advantages of describing facial behavior in terms of muscle contractions are:

1. In observation it provides a safeguard against subjective impressions about what behavior is, in fact, being effected;

2. In recording it furnishes enough information for the reader to precisely replicate the expression — with his own muscles if he wishes;

3. In making interspecific comparisons it addresses the most significant unit of structure and function;

4. It provides categories to describe cultural variations of primary expressions of affect; e.g., depressor-levator antagonism in Southern smiles.[8]

PLATE V   Male Purse-Clamp

Fig. 1   Fig. 2   Fig. 3   Fig. 4

Fig. 5   Fig. 6   Fig. 7   Fig. 8

Fig. 3. Possible locked modioli causing slight mesial movement of lips. John
       Buchanan (1743-1822), Episcopal rector in Richmond from University
       of Edinburgh. Courtesy Virginia Historical Society.
Fig. 8. Purse-Clamp with strong mentalis assist.

PLATE VI   Purse-Clamp

Fig. 1

Fig. 2

Fig. 1. James Madison (1751-1836) by Gilbert Stuart (Christian Science Monitor 1971).

Fig. 2. A Northcarolinian pictured in yearbook (Yackety Yack 1949:84).

PLATE VII   Female Pursed Smile

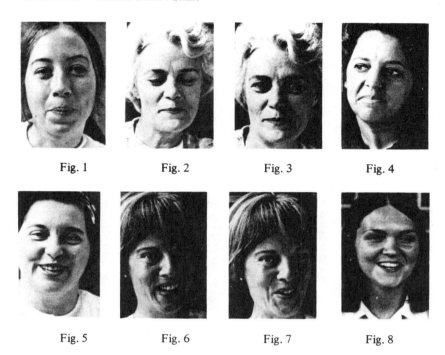

Fig. 1   Fig. 2   Fig. 3   Fig. 4

Fig. 5   Fig. 6   Fig. 7   Fig. 8

Fig. 1. Articulating "hmm".
Fig. 7. Articulating vowel of "cook", but triangularis (Angle Depression Smile)
     and platysma contractions in addition to those of the orbicularis oris not
     phonetically necessary.

PLATE VIII   Male Pursed Smile

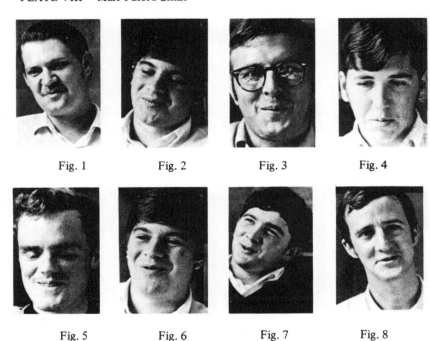

Fig. 1   Fig. 2   Fig. 3   Fig. 4

Fig. 5   Fig. 6   Fig. 7   Fig. 8

Fig. 1. Pursing artifact of articulating initial bilabial stop of "put", but smile and triangularis action not phonetically required.
Fig. 5. Articulating high *front* vowel of "deep".
Fig. 6. Orbicularis oris assisted by triangulares restraining levator contraction of upper face.
Fig. 7. Articulating "uh".
Fig. 8. Articulating last vowel of "begin".

PLATE IX   Inferior Press Smile

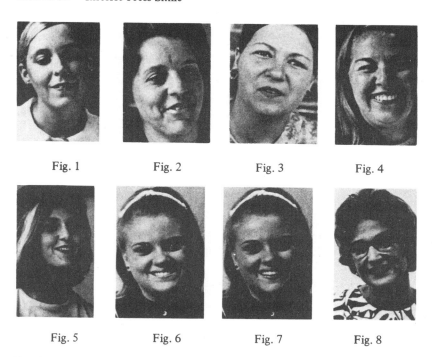

Fig. 1   Fig. 2   Fig. 3   Fig. 4

Fig. 5   Fig. 6   Fig. 7   Fig. 8

Fig. 5.   South Carolinian informant.
Figs. 6-8. Georgian informants.
Figs. 5, 8. Triangularis contraction also.

PLATE X   Angle Depression Smile

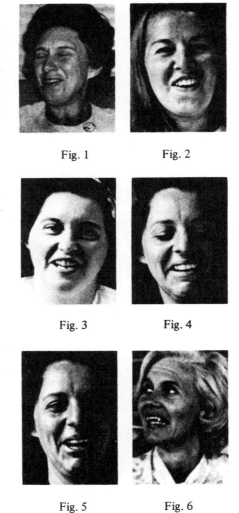

Fig. 1   Fig. 2

Fig. 3   Fig. 4

Fig. 5   Fig. 6

Fig. 1. Probably articulating initial dental fricative of "they".

Fig. 2. Angle Depression combined with Inferior Press.

Fig. 3. Articulating "ah".

Fig. 4. Lower face appears as if crying.

Fig. 5. Strong action of orbicularis oris, triangularis and mentalis countering levators of upper face.

Fig. 6. Angle Depression fortified by platysma. Frontalis also contracting.

PLATE XI   Female Tongue-Lips

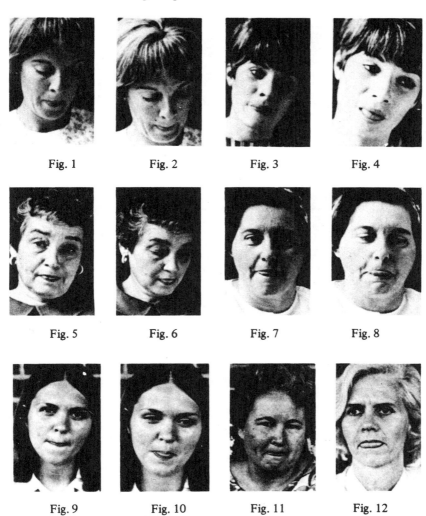

Fig. 1   Fig. 2   Fig. 3   Fig. 4

Fig. 5   Fig. 6   Fig. 7   Fig. 8

Fig. 9   Fig. 10   Fig. 11   Fig. 12

PLATE XII   Male Tongue-Lips

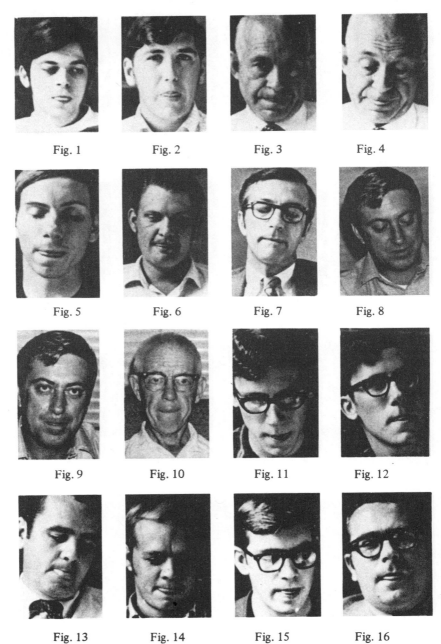

Fig. 1   Fig. 2   Fig. 3   Fig. 4

Fig. 5   Fig. 6   Fig. 7   Fig. 8

Fig. 9   Fig. 10   Fig. 11   Fig. 12

Fig. 13   Fig. 14   Fig. 15   Fig. 16

PLATE XII   Tongue Smile

Fig. 1

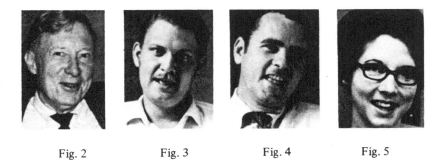

Fig. 2   Fig. 3   Fig. 4   Fig. 5

Fig. 1. Crowning Miss Albermarle County. Both women effecting Tongue Smiles.
(Courtsey "The Daily Progress").

Fig. 5. A South Carolinian.

PLATE XIV   Mandibular Thrust

Fig. 1   Fig. 2

Fig. 3   Fig. 4

Fig. 5   Fig. 6

Figs. 1-2. Combined with Orbicular Clamp.
Fig. 4.   Articulation uncertain, but Mandibular Thrust obviously elaboration
            of phonetic requirements.
Fig. 5.   Pause after articulating "time".
Fig. 6.   Articulating velar stop and low mid vowel of "calm".

NOTES

[1] Hooton is referring to constitutional anthropology.

[2] I have speculated (Seaford 1975, 1976) that if friendliness be highly valued in a subculture, the 'ready-made' primate patterns of pursing and lip-smacking could be 'marshalled' by the communication system as an appropriate way to express it.

[3] Although Darwin recognized that some expressions "apparently have been learnt like the words of a language" (1955:352), he emphasized that "all the chief expressions exhibited by man are the same throughout the world" (1955: 359). Among anthropologists, Earl Count (1958) is an early representative of a trend to theorize outside cultural limits without fear of 'reductionism'.

[4] Recently, Ekman and Friesen (1976) have published a significant statement in which they describe facial behavior by 'Action Units' based squarely on muscle contractions. The thoroughness of their approach should provide a well-organized, convenient method for describing facial expression. I hope it is widely adopted. The same authors promise an even more detailed treatment in *The Facial Atlas* (forthcoming).

[5] Out of a sample of 62 Virginians, 32 women effected 390 patterns of the southern syndrome; 30 men, only 288. Women were notably higher in Inferior Press Smile (17:4), Angle Depression Smile (66:28), and Tongue Smile (7:2).

[6] In the summer of 1973 I had the pleasure of chatting with van Hooff about descriptions of facial expression. If I remember correctly, he preferred not to refer to muscle action because of the impossibility of precisely documenting every contraction.

[7] Since Virginia was settled by people from the British Isles, it is possible that the typical English orbicular restraint could have been an imported cultural behavior which persisted in its New World variety. Darwin (1955:212) noted triangularis action during the laugh of one of his female compatriots and I have also noted it on English faces. A Dickinson colleague, Robert Cavenagh, informs me that pursing is common among his fellow Scots (cf. Pl. V Fig. 3). What all this might or might not have to do with the primate purse I am not prepared to say, nor am I sure that the British are notorious for their friendliness!

[8] Some of the very authors whose works I have used as illustrations herein have furnished me with enriching perspectives in print and in conversation. Some might not agree with my point about basing all descriptions of facial expression on muscle contractions. My own research was made possible by NSF Grant GS-2338 and grants from the Dickinson College Faculty Research Fund.

REFERENCES

Andrew, R. J.
1965   "The Origins of Facial Expression", *Scientific American* 213, 88.
Bateson, G., and M. Mead
1942   *Balinese Character*. New York: New York Academy of Sciences.
Birdwhistell, Ray L.
1952   "Field Methods and Techniques", *Human Organization* 11, 37-38.
1966   "Some Relations Between American Kinesics and Spoken American English", in *Communication and Culture*, ed. by Alfred G. Smith. New York: Holt, Rinehart and Winston.

1968a "Communication Without Words", in *L'aventure humaine,* Encyclopedie des Sciences de l'Homme 5, 157-66. Geneva: Kister.
1968b "Kinesics", in *International Encyclopedia of the Social Sciences,* ed. by David L. Sills. New York: Crowell, Collier and Macmillan.
1970a *Kinesics and Context.* Philadelphia: University of Pennsylvania Press.
1970b "Kinesics: Inter- and Intra-Channel Communication Research", *Social Science Information* 7, 9-26.
Blurton Jones, N. G.
1971 "Criteria for Use in Describing Facial Expression of Children", *Human Biology* 43, 365-413.
Boas, Franz
1911 *Changes in Bodily Form of Descendants of Immigrants.* Washington: Government Printing Office.
1938 *The Mind of Primitive Man.* New York: Macmillan.
Buettner-Janusch, John
1966 *Origins of Man: Physical Anthropology.* New York: John Wiley.
Chevalier-Skolnikoff, Suzanne
1973 "Visual and Tactile Communication in *Macaca arctoides* and Its Ontogenetic Development", *American Journal of Physical Anthropology* 38, 515-18.
1974 *The Ontogeny of Communication in the Macaque (Macaca arctoides).* *Contributions to Primatology* 2. Basel: S. Karger.
The Christian Science Monitor
1971 "Assaults on That Ageless Piece of Aging Parchment", January 20.
Connolly, C. J.
1928 "Growth of Face in Different Races", *American Journal of Physical Anthropology* 12, 197.
Coon, Carleton S.
1965 *The Living Races of Man.* New York: Alfred A. Knopf.
Count, Earl W.
1958 "The Biological Basis of Human Sociality", *American Anthropologist* 60, 1049-85.
Darwin, Charles
1955 *The Expression of the Emotions in Man and Animals.* New York: Philosophical Library.
DeVore, Irven, ed.
1965 *Primate Behavior: Field Studies of Monkeys and Apes.* New York: Holt, Rinehart and Winston.
Duchenne, G. B.
1862 *Mécanisme de la physionomie humaine, ou analyse électro-physiologique de l'expression des passions.* Paris: J.-B. Ballière et Fils.
Efron, David
1941 *Gesture and Environment.* New York: King's Crown Press.
Ekman, Paul
1972 "Universals and Cultural Differences in Facial Expressions of Emotion", in *Nebraska Symposium on Motivation,* ed. by James Cole. Lincoln: University of Nebraska Press.
Ekman, Paul, and Wallace V. Friesen
1969 "The Repertoire of Nonverbal Behavior: Categories, Origins, Usage and Coding", *Semiotica* 1, 49-98.

1976   "Measuring Facial Movement", *Environmental Psychology and Non-verbal Behavior* 1:1.
        forthcoming *The Facial Atlas.*
Ekman, Paul, Wallace V. Friesen, and Phoebe Ellsworth
1972   *Emotion in the Human Face: Guidelines for Research and an Integration of Findings.* New York: Pergamon Press.
Ekman, Paul, Wallace V. Friesen, and Silvan S. Tomkins
1971   "Facial Affect Scoring Technique: A First Validity Study", *Semiotica* 3, 37-58.
Ekman, Paul, E. R. Sorenson, and W. V. Friesen
1969   "Pan-cultural Elements in Facial Displays of Emotions", *Science* 164, 86-88.
Ex, J., and Adam Kendon
1969   "A Notation for Facial Positions and Bodily Postures", in *Social Interaction*, ed. by M. Argyle. New York: Atherton Press.
Goldstein, Marcus S.
1936   "Changes in Dimensions and Form of the Face and Head with Age", *American Journal of Physical Anthropology* 22, 37-89.
Goodall, Jane Van Lawick
1969   "Mother-offspring Relationships in Free-ranging Chimpanzee", in *Primate Ethology*, ed. by Desmond Morris. Garden City: Doubleday.
Grant, Ewan C.
1969   "Human Facial Expression", *Man* 4, 525-36.
Grant, J. C. Boileau
1951   *An Atlas of Anatomy.* Baltimore: William and Wilkins.
Gray, H.
1959   *Anatomy of the Human Body*, 27th ed., ed. by C. C. Goss. Philadelphia: Lea and Febiger.
Gregory, William K.
1929   *Our Face from Fish to Man: A Portrait of Our Ancient Ancestors and Kinsfolk Together with a Concise History of Our best Features.* New York: Capricorn [1963].
Hellman, Milo
1927   "Changes in the Human Face Brought About by Development", *International Journal of Orthodontics, Oral Surgery and Radiography* 20, 475.
1935   "The Face in Its Developmental Career", in *The Human Face: A Symposium.* Philadelphia: The Dental Cosmos.
Hinde, Robert A.
1966   *Animal Behaviour: A synthesis of Ethology and Comparative Psychology.* London: McGraw Hill.
Hjortsjo, Carl-Herman
1970   *Man's Face and Mimic Language.* Lund: Studentlitteratur.
Hooff, J. A. R. A. M. van
1969   "The Facial Displays of the Catarrhine Monkeys and Apes", in *Primate Ethology*, ed. by Desmond Morris. Garden City: Doubleday.
Hooton, Earnest A.
1946   *Up From the Ape*, revised edition. New York: Macmillan [1954].
Hrdlicka, Ales
1900   *Anthropological Investigation on 1000 White and Colored Children of Both Sexes. Anthropological Report.* New York: Juven Asylum.

Huber, Ernst
    1931   *Evolution of Facial Musculature and Facial Expression.* Baltimore:
            Johns Hopkins Press.
Izard, Carroll E.
    1968   *The Emotions as a Culture Common Framework of Motivational
            Experiences and Communicative Cues.* Technical Report 30.
            Washington, D.C.: Office of Naval Research.
    1971   *The Face of Emotion.* New York: Appleton.
Jolly, Alison
    1972   *The Evolution of Primate Behavior.* New York: Macmillan.
Kendon, Adam
    1975   "Some Functions of the Face in a Kissing Round", *Semiotica* 15,
            299-334.
Klineberg, Otto
    1935   *Race Differences.* New York: Harper.
    1940   *Social Psychology.* New York: Henry Holt.
Kohara Yukinari
    1968   "Racial Difference of Facial Expression; Unilateral Movement",
            paper Delivered at the VIIIth International Congress of Anthro-
            pological and Ethnological Sciences, Tokyo, September.
Krogman, W. M.
    1930   "The Problem of Growth Changes in the Face and Skull as Viewed
            from a Comparative Study of Anthropoids and Man", *Dental Cosmos*
            (June), 624.
    1931a   "Growth Changes in the Skull and Face of the Gorilla", *American
            Journal of Anthropology* 47, 89.
    1931b   "Growth Changes in the Skull and Face of the Chimpanzee", *American
            Journal of Anthropology* 47, 325.
    1931c   "Growth Changes in the Skull and Face of the Orangutan", *American
            Journal of Anthropology* 47, 343.
La Barre, Weston
    1947   "The Cultural Basis of Emotions and Gestures", *Journal of Personality*
            16, 49-68.
Lightoller, G. S.
    1925   "Facial Muscles", *Journal of Anatomy* 60, 1.
    1928   "The Action of the M. Mentalis in the Expression of the Emotion of
            Distress", *Journal of Anatomy* 62, 319.
Loth, Edward
    1949   "Anthropological Studies of Muscles of Living Uganda Negroes",
            Yearbook of Physical Anthropology 5.
Sapir, Edward
    1949   *Selected Writings of Edward Sapir,* ed. by David G. Mandelbaum.
            Berkeley: University of California Press.
Schaeffer, J. P.
    1935   "The Ontogenetic Development of the Human Face", in *The Human
            Face: A Symposium* Philadelphia: The Dental Cosmos.
Schultz, A. H.
    1920   "The Development of the External Nose in Whites and Negroes",
            Contributions to Embryology ix, 173. Washington: Carnegie
            Institution.

Seaford, Henry W., Jr.
  1966 "The Southern Syndrome: A Regional Pattern of Facial Muscle Contraction", paper delivered at the Annual Meeting of the Pennsylvania Sociological Society, Haverford College, Haverford, Pennsylvania.
  1971 *The Southern Syndrome: A Regional Patterning of Facial Muscle Contraction.* Ph.D. Thesis, Harvard University.
  1975 "Facial Expression Dialect: An Example", in *Organization of Behavior in Face-to-Face Interaction,* ed. by Adam Kendon, Richard M. Harris, and Mary Ritchie Key, 151-55. The Hague: Mouton.
  1976 "Cultural Facial Expression", in *The Measures of Man,* ed. by E. Giles and J. S. Friedlaender, 616-39. Cambridge, Mass.: Peabody Museum Press.
Shapiro, Harry H.
  1947 *Applied Anatomy of the Head and Neck.* Philadelphia: J. B. Lippincott.
Steegman, A. T., Jr.
  1965 "A Study of Relationships Between Facial Cold Responses and Some Variables of Facial Morphology", *American Journal of Physical Anthropology* 23, 355-62.
  1967 "Frost Bite of the Human Face as a Selective Force", *Human Biology* 39, 131-44.
  1970 "Cold Adaptation and the Human Face", *American Journal of Physical Anthropology* 32, 243.
  1972 "Cold Response, Body Form and Craniofacial Shape in Two Racial Groups in Hawaii", *American Journal of Physical Anthropology* 37, 193-221.
Steegman, A. T., Jr., and W. S. Platner
  1968 "Experimental Cold Modification of Craniofacial Morphology", *American Journal of Physical Anthropology* 28, 17.
Tinbergen, N.
  1955 *The Study of Instinct.* Oxford: Oxford University Press.
Tomkins, S. S.
  1962 *Affect, Imagery, Consciousness,* 1: *The Positive Affects.* New York: Springer.
Tylor, Edward Burnett
  1871 *Primitive Culture.* London: John Murray. [Republished 1958 as *The Origin of Culture.* New York: Harper and Row.]
Virchow, H.
  1908 "Gesichtsmuskeln und Gesichtsausdruck", *Archiv fur Anatomie und Physiologie, Anatomische Abteilung,* S. 371, 371-436.
Washburn, Sherwood L.
  1951 "The New Physical Anthropology", *Transactions of the New York Academy of Sciences* 13/7, 298-304.
Weddell, A. W., ed.
  1930 *A Memorial Volume of Virginia Historical Portraiture.* Richmond: The William Byrd Press.
Welcker, H.
  1866 "Kraniologische Mittheilungen", *Archiv fur Anthropologie* 1, 89.
The Yackety Yack
  1949 *The University of North Carolina.* Chapel Hill, North Carolina.

Part Two

Organization of Behavior in Social Encounters

PETER COLLETT and PETER MARSH*

Patterns of Public Behaviour:
Collision Avoidance on a Pedestrian Crossing

INTRODUCTION

One of the more remarkable aspects of public life in cities is the phenomenon of pedestrian routing. On almost any street corner one may daily
witness large numbers of people navigating their courses along the pavements without bumping into each other. What is especially interesting
about this complex avoidance behaviour is the apparent ease with which
it is effected. Yet it is performed in the absence of an explicit code and
with few, if any, individuals being able to specify the procedures whereby
they and other people avoid collisions.[1] Despite the everyday nature of
pedestrian avoidance behaviour, and the important questions which it
raises concerning interpersonal coordination, the phenomenon has not,
at least until very recently, received the attention it deserves.

Recent investigations in this area have looked at behaviour on pavements.[2] Most of these studies have proceeded from the observation of

* We would like to express appreciation to the S. S. R. C. for financial support, and
to Adrian Smith, Michael Argyle, Erving Goffman, and Michael Wolff for their
suggestions and comments.
[1] The city dweller's pedestrian skills are, in a sense, overlearned. The procedures
which he employs in traversing the pavements are second nature to him, something
in which he engages without undue effort or concentration. Against this one might
contrast the behaviour of country folk. Lyn Lofland (1966) points out that one of
the standard signals in movies and television for characterising the country boy,
newly arrived in the city, is his inability to walk down the street without bumping
into people.
[2] The two articles most frequently referred to in this paper are those by Goffman
(1972) and Wolff (1973). Other descriptions and studies of pedestrian behaviour

PEDESTRIAN STREAMING or what Goffman calls 'lane formation', and the fact that people on the pavement have a propensity for keeping to the right. This overriding tendency to 'keep to the right' is widespread. It is not however universal. Australians and New Zealanders walk on the left.[3] Pedestrian streaming is a highly fluid affair. To begin with, it is dependent upon pedestrian density, so that the more crowded the pavement, the greater the advantage afforded to the individual who slots in behind those ahead of him. The width and speed of approaching streams is also functionally related to the relative numbers of people moving in opposite directions, and to the presence of obtrusions such as construction works, street vendors, and people entering and leaving buildings. In the absence of these types of obstruction, the walking speeds of individuals who constitute the main body of a lane or stream will tend to be rather similar. Those pedestrians who wish to quicken their stride may either weave their way through their own lane or at the interface between opposing lanes or, and this seems to be more common practice on crowded pavements, take to the road where lane formation is absent.

Apart from instances of 'blind coordination' (that is, solutions achieved in the absence of 'monitoring'), the individual processes which simultaneously maintain lane formation and ensure against collision are the processes of MONITORING and what Goffman has termed EXTERNALISATION or BODY GLOSS. Body gloss refers to those observable body movements which, whether they be performed consciously or unconsciously, serve to offer an ongoing commentary on someone's likely behaviour to those who approach and those who follow him. A pedestrian's monitoring processes will therefore involve his watching (and possibly listening to) both people who move in the same direction as himself and those who approach him, and the more well-defined the streaming, the more easily he will be able to ignore oncomers. In this sense, streaming may be seen as a corporate and informally constituted means of reducing the monitoring and locomotor problems of individual pedestrians.

Monitoring consists predominantly of visual scanning of oncomers.

---

may be found in Lofland (1966), Morris (1967), Hirsch (1970), Stilitz (1970), Fruin (1971), Knowles (1972), Henderson and Lyons (1972), a report in *Time* Magazine (11th May 1970, p. 66), and what appears to be a tongue-in-cheek paper by Ryave and Schenkein (1974).

[3] Last summer there were several letters to the Editor of *The Times* (August, 1973) which mentioned the antipodean habit of walking on the left. It was contended that this habit is due, not, as one correspondent suggested, to the reversed Coriolis forces of the Southern hemisphere and the unsettling effects of an inverted environment, but rather to its enforcement by civic authorities who wished to ensure that, as in America, pedestrians walking beside the curb faced oncoming traffic.

Goffman has suggested that the scanning field takes the form of an elongated ellipse, narrow to either side of the individual and longest in front of him. The individual engages in what Goffman calls a 'body-check' as people enter this area in order to determine whether or not their course foretells collision. The focus of attention is thus cast beyond people in the immediate vicinity whose trajectories were calculated as they entered the ellipse. More can be said of monitoring. Wolff, for instance, has observed that the individual usually takes up a position which, while it protects him from oncomers, offers a relatively unobstructed view over the shoulders of those ahead of him, and minimises the likelihood of his stepping on their heels. He suggests that the individual also relies upon those approaching him to act as an 'early warning system'; the faces of oncomers function as a 'rearview mirror' in which he may observe what is happening behind him.

Goffman points out that where streaming is absent and collision seems likely, the individual "can introduce a large directional change through a small and therefore undemeaning angular correction" (1972:33). Goffman suggests, moreover, that where an early angular correction is deemed to be inadaquate to avert collision, the individual may do one of two things: he may display his intentions to take or hold a particular course or else, if assurances on the part of the other are sought, he may externalise his intentions and, by eyeing the other, invite some indication that his intentions have been noticed and approved of by the other. This collaborative procedure, what Goffman calls the 'checked-body-check', consists of two parts, namely a 'critical sign' indicating the other's acceptance of the individual's intentions, and an 'establishment point' at which each party realises that his displays have been observed and accepted, and where they "both appreciate that they both appreciate that this has occurred" (1972:33). For Goffman then, such accommodative patterns of avoidance are predicated upon a mutual interchange of signals which are intentionally communicated and whose receipt is intentionally confirmed, and for both Goffman and Wolff the role played by the eyes is central to this process of coordination. Goffman, for instance, suggests that after the individual has given a course direction, "he can make sure the signal has been picked up, either by meeting the other's eyes (although not for engagement) or by noting the other's direction of vision, in either case establishing that his course gesture has not been overlooked. In brief, he can check up on the other's eye check on him" (1972: 34). Similarly, Wolff writes of pedestrians scanning the faces of those coming towards them, and describes how couples look longer at people approaching them in order, as it were, to indicate their reluctance to engage in what, for them, would be more effortful avoidance behaviours. Wolff has observed that a characteristic avoidance movement in situations of relatively high density is the "step-and-slide", a movement which involves "a slight angling of the shoulders and an almost imperceptible side step" (1973: 37), all of which, he has suggested, is reciprocated by the oncoming pedestrian.

This then briefly summarises some of the observations that others have made concerning pedestrian behaviour. What follows is a report of a study of collision avoidance on a controlled pedestrian crossing.

THE OXFORD CIRCUS STUDY

This study arose out of an interest in pedestrian behaviour and, in particular, the relationship between collision avoidance and the processes of monitoring and externalisation. More generally, it offered an opportunity to observe instances of interpersonal coordination served by channels other than speech, where these occurred in a public setting. We began the study by observing pedestrians on the pavement. It soon became apparent, however, that situations of low density produced relatively uninteresting patterns of early avoidance, while in situations of high density where streaming occurred, pedestrians were obliged to make fewer accommodative movements. We therefore decided to shift our location, and chose instead to watch people on a controlled pedestrian crossing where one phalanx faces another across the road and where, after the lights have changed, pedestrians are forced to find a way past each other. The study took place on a controlled crossing at Oxford Circus in London. Recordings were made over a number of days with the aid of a portable videotape recorder and a powerful zoom lens from the seventh floor of a building overlooking the crossing. About four hours of videotape were collected and later subjected to coding and analysis.

We began by isolating 'passes' between single individuals.[4] This involved searching through the videotape for instances where two people advanced towards each other with an 'approach overlap' and where, instead of making an early course alteration, one or both parties was forced to take relatively late avoidance action by angling the body. Only unattached pedestrians and contextually unambiguous passes were considered. A contextually ambiguous pass might, for example, occur where a pedestrian took a gap between two approaching individuals or

4   'Pass' is Albert Scheflen's term.

where his course alternatives were constrained by the presence of others moving in the same direction as himself. A total of 94 passes (i.e., 188 persons) were selected from the tapes. For each pass, the videotape was 'frozen' at the moment of pass, and the following attributes and avoidance behaviours (with the exception of the antecedent 'approach overlap') of each pair and each person were coded.

For each pair:

1. DIRECTION OF PASS — People passed either to the right or the left of each other.

2. APPROACH OVERLAP — Three categories: minimum overlap (inside shoulders overlapping), intermediate overlap (head and inside shoulders overlapping), or total overlap (head and both shoulders overlapping).

For each person:

3. LINE OF APPROACH — A seven-point scale consisting of three $22\frac{1}{2}°$ intervals on either side of the line perpendicular to the pavements. (All but four people walked straight across.)

4. SEX — Male or female.

5. AGE — Four categories: 16-24 yrs, 25-34 yrs, 35-44 yrs, or 45 yrs and older.

6. POSITION — Either facing towards or away from the camera.

7. SHOULDER ORIENTATION — A seven-point scale consisting of three $22\frac{1}{2}°$ intervals on either side of the line perpendicular to the line of approach. This was taken to be a measure of body twist.

8. SHOULDER TILT — A three-point scale: right shoulder dipped, shoulders level, or left shoulder dipped, in the frontal plane.

9. HEAD ORIENTATION — A three-point scale: head to the right, head forward, or head to the left, in the transverse plane, relative to the shoulders.

10. HEAD DOWNWARD TILT	A three-point scale: head erect, head tilting down less than 20°, or head tilting down more than 20°, in the sagittal plane, relative to the shoulders.
11. HEAD SIDEWAYS TILT	A three-point scale: head tilting to the right, head upright, or head tilting to the left, in the frontal plane, relative to the shoulders.
12-17. FOR EACH ARM:	
(a) EXTENSION IN THE SAGITTAL PLANE	A three-point scale: arm extended in front of the body, arm by the side, or arm extended behind the body.
(b) EXTENSION IN THE FRONTAL PLANE	A three-point scale: arm extended away from the body, arm by the side, or arm extended across the body.
(c) CARRYING	Whether or not carrying an article.
18. LEG	Which leg forward at the moment of pass.

In the early stages of observation, it became apparent that the behaviour of men and women differed in several respects. The most striking difference seemed to be the manner in which men and women oriented themselves with respect to the person they were passing. To examine this difference more closely, we computed a new variable which we called the 'pass index'. The pass index is a composite measure derived from three of the original variables, namely 'line of approach', 'shoulder orientation', and 'direction of pass'. Negative values of the index indicate that the subject was turned towards, and positive values away from, the person that he or she was passing. We refer to these two orientations as 'open' and 'closed' passes respectively. A pass index of zero indicates a 'neutral' pass. The distributions of pass indices for the two sexes are shown in Fig. 1. Here we can see that the two distributions are strongly skewed in opposite directions, indicating that men predominantly make open passes, and women closed passes. Analysis showed this sex difference to be highly significant ($X^2 = 73.85$, d.f. $= 6$, $p < .001$). This dramatic difference in avoidance behaviour is displayed in Fig. 2, which illustrates the modal patterns of pass for the two sexes. The picture shows the same

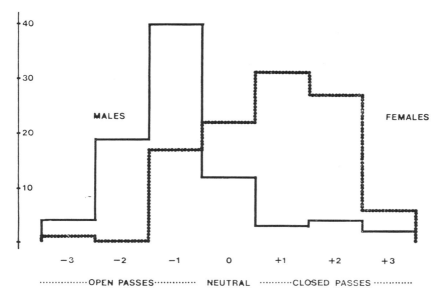

·············OPEN PASSES············· NEUTRAL ···········CLOSED PASSES ···········

Fig. 1. Distributions of pass indices for males and females.

Fig. 2. The modal patterns of pass for males and females.

man and woman viewed from opposite sides; the man making a typical open pass and the woman a typical closed pass.

This finding poses an obvious question: which type of pass requires explanation, the closed female pass or the open male pass? In other words, what should be the null hypothesis? In endeavouring to answer this question, we considered the relationship between type of pass and 'step' for the two sexes. A person was defined as being 'in-step' if his leg and opposite shoulder were both forward (as in the normal walking gait), and as 'out-of-step' when, for example, his right leg and right shoulder were both forward AT THE MOMENT OF PASS. People with both feet together and/or with no shoulder orientation at the moment of pass were not considered here. Since the morphologies of the in-step open pass and the in-step closed pass are almost identical, they can safely be assumed to involve the same degree of difficulty for pedestrians. This, however, is not the case for passes performed out-of-step. While the out-of-step open pass — what Wolff has termed the 'step-and-slide' — is executed with relative ease, the out-of-step closed pass consists of rather awkward movements. It involves bringing the leading leg across the other, which, together with the accompanying shoulder rotation, tends to throw the person off balance. Now, Table I shows that while most men who were

TABLE I. SEX BY STEP BY TYPE OF PASS

		OPEN	CLOSED	T
MALE	IN-STEP	17	4	21
	OUT-OF-STEP	39	6	45
FEMALE	IN-STEP	6	31	37
	OUT-OF-STEP	10	26	36
	T	72	67	139

Effect due to STEP: $X^2 = 5.42$, df $= 1$, p $< .02$

out-of-step performed open passes, most women who were out-of-step performed closed passes (effect due to step: $X^2 = 5.42$, d.f. $= 1$, p $< .02$). Since the out-of-step closed pass is more effortful, we can assume that women are, on the whole, performing more difficult avoidance movements than men. We therefore require some explanation as to why women are loathe to orient towards oncoming pedestrians. Put in these terms, an explanation is not too difficult to find: the obvious assumption to make is that women are concerned to protect their breasts.

Another finding which relates to this self-protective movement on the part of women is that concerning the 'armcross'. We noticed while recording that more women than men drew one or both of their arms across their bodies when passing another person. Analysis of the data in Table IIa showed this effect to be significant. Half our subjects had their

TABLE II. SEX BY ARMCROSS

(a) ALL PERSONS

	CROSSED	NOT CROSSED	T	
MALE	21	63	84	
FEMALE	53	51	104	$X^2 = 13.31$, df $= 1$, p $< .001$
T	74	114	188	

(b) 'COMERS'

	CROSSED	NOT CROSSED	T	
MALE	9	33	42	
FEMALE	25	27	52	$X^2 = 18.41$, df $= 1$, p $< .001$
T	34	60	94	

(c) 'GOERS'

	CROSSED	NOT CROSSED	T	
MALE	12	30	42	
FEMALE	28	34	52	$X^2 = 5.09$, df $= 1$, p $< .05$
T	40	64	94	

backs to the camera, and we are naturally concerned that our coding of their arm movements might be less reliable than for subjects facing the camera. We therefore separated subjects into two groups, 'comers' and 'goers', and tested the effects separately. As can be seen in Tables IIb and IIc, the effect is still present for goers, although the somewhat reduced value of the X^2 in Table IIc reflects our concern over loss of coding reliability for this group.

This sex difference for armcross is similar in some respects to that observed by Kendon and Ferber (1973) in their analysis of greetings. They found that significantly more women than men drew an arm across their bodies during the approach sequence prior to a close salutation. However, it seems reasonable to suppose that the 'body cross' noticed by these authors might simply be related to the transfer of articles from one hand to another in preparation for the close salutation.[5] This in itself could

[5] A suggestion made by Michael Argyle.

account for the observed sex difference, since women are more likely than men to be carrying articles such as handbags. As can be seen in Table IIIa, our own data showed that significantly more women than men were carrying something. It therefore seemed plausible that in our case the greater frequency of the armcross among women might similarly be related to carrying. However, when we removed from the analysis all those subjects who were carrying something in one or both hands, the sex difference remained, as shown in Table IIIb. Indeed, a separate test, shown in Table IIIc, confirmed that armcross was relatively independent of carrying.

TABLE III. SEX BY ARMCROSS BY CARRYING

(a) SEX BY CARRYING

	CARRYING	NOT CARRYING	T	
MALE	46	38	84	
FEMALE	83	21	104	$X^2 = 12.40$, df $= 1$, p $< .001$
T	129	59	188	

(b) SEX BY ARMCROSS (CARRIERS REMOVED)

	CROSSED	NOT CROSSED	T	
MALE	9	28	37	
FEMALE	13	7	20	$X^2 = 7.70$, df $= 1$, p $< .01$
T	22	35	57	

(c) ARMCROSS BY CARRYING

	CARRYING	NOT CARRYING	T	
MALE	52	22	74	
FEMALE	77	37	114	$X^2 = 0.054$, df $= 1$, p $> .80$
T	129	59	188	

There was yet another explanation concerning the relationship between sex and armcross that could not be dismissed; namely that the greater frequency of armcross among women was due to the fact that more women than men were engaged in closed passes, and the likelihood that closed passes are more easily performed when accompanied by an armcross. In other words, the relationship between sex and armcross could be related artefactually to the general morphology of the closed pass rather than to the morphology of women. Examination of the data in Table IV serves to clarify this issue. Analysis of the combined data for men and women showed that there was a significant relationship between

TABLE IV. SEX BY ARMCROSS BY TYPE OF PASS

(a) SEX BY ARMCROSS BY TYPE OF PASS

		OPEN	NEUTRAL	CLOSED	T
MALE	CROSSED	14	1	6	21
	NOT CROSSED	49	11	3	63
FEMALE	CROSSED	8	9	36	53
	NOT CROSSED	10	13	28	51
T		81	34	73	188

(b) ARMCROSS BY TYPE OF PASS

	OPEN	NEUTRAL	CLOSED	T
CROSSED	22	10	42	74
NOT CROSSED	59	24	31	114
T	81	34	73	188

$X^2 = 16.56$, df $= 2$, p $< .001$

(c) SEX BY ARMCROSS IN NEUTRAL AND OPEN PASSES

	CROSSED	NOT CROSSED	T
MALE	15	60	75
FEMALE	17	23	40
	32	83	115

$X^2 = 5.50$, df $= 1$, p $< .02$

type of pass and armcross. That is, more subjects drew one or both of their arms across themselves when effecting a closed pass. This suggests that the armcross may be one of the movements associated with the closed pass. However, if the armcross were SOLELY related to the closed pass, then we should expect to find men and women engaging in the armcross with equal frequency when performing either open or neutral passes — that is, those passes which do not afford the kind of protection offered by an orientation away from the other person. In fact, when we examine the relationship between sex and armcross in these types of pass we find this not to be the case. Table IVc shows that significantly more women than men cross themselves when effecting open or neutral passes. We can therefore conclude that since it is not linked to the act of carrying, nor solely explained by the nature of the closed pass, the armcross is another instance of breast protection on the part of women.

Thus far we have examined certain differences between the behaviours of men and women. We next turned our attention to the phenomenon of interaction, that is the manner in which pedestrians' avoidance behaviours are related to attributes of the person they are passing. First we considered whether or not the behaviour of a pedestrian was influenced by the sex of the person he or she was passing. Analysis of the data in Table V showed that the types of pass performed by men and women were independent of the sex of the person being passed. We also found that the step-and-slide movement is not, as Wolff has suggested, generally reciprocated by the other person. Of the 41 pedestrians who performed a step-and-slide, only 8 had their movements reciprocated. In other words, there were only four passes in which both pedestrians executed a step-and-slide.

TABLE V. SEX OF PASSER BY SEX OF PASSED BY TYPE OF PASS

PASSER	PASSED	OPEN	NEUTRAL	CLOSED	T
	MALE	31	6	5	42
MALE	FEMALE	32	6	4	42
	MALE	8	9	25	42
FEMALE	FEMALE	10	13	39	62
	T	81	34	73	188

For MALES: $X^2 = 0.126$, df $= 2$, p $> .90$
For FEMALES: $X^2 = 0.172$, df $= 2$, p $> .90$

The relationship between the types of pass and ages of approaching parties was also examined. Table VIa shows that the type of pass performed by one person was unrelated to the age of the other, and Table VIb

TABLE VI. AGE OF A BY AGE OF B BY TYPE OF PASS

(a) AGE OF A BY TYPE OF PASS OF B

		PASS OF B			
		OPEN	NEUTRAL	CLOSED	T
	16-24	14	5	14	33
AGE OF A	25-34	15	6	16	37
(years)	35-44	10	4	7	21
	45+	2	0	1	3
	T	41	15	38	94

$X^2 = 1.25$ (with rows 3 and 4 collapsed), df $= 4$, n.s.

(b) SEX BY AGE BY TYPE OF PASS

		OPEN	NEUTRAL	CLOSED	T
	16-24	14	5	4	23
MALES	25-34	38	3	3	44
	35+	11	4	2	17
	16-24	7	9	31	47
FEMALES	25-34	5	5	21	31
	35+	6	8	12	26

For MALES: Comparing row 2 with rows 1 and 3, $X^2 = 6.51$, df $= 2$, p $< .05$

shows that, with the exception of men deemed to be between the ages of 25 and 34, the type of pass performed by someone was unrelated to his or her own age. Proportionately more men in this group were found to engage in some body rotation, that is, they made neutral passes significantly less often than either older or younger males.

We have already noted reports by Goffman and Wolff concerning lane formation and the tendency for streams to form on the right. In this study we noticed that lanes formed on the crossing when pedestrian density reached a certain level. However, four streams occurred, resembling, as it were, two pavements placed side by side. Here again there was a clear pattern of walking on the right. Now, we were interested in discovering whether pedestrians avoiding collisions moved to the right when lane formation was absent. Of course, in those instances where approach overlap is less than total, the direction of pass is governed by the relative position of the approaching parties, so that if, for example, their right shoulders are overlapping, they will move to the left (in fact, not one pair moved in the unexpected direction; all pairs with left shoulders overlapping moved right, and all pairs with right shoulders overlapping moved left). Only where overlap is total, that is where two people approach each other head-on, is there any real choice to be made. Table VII shows that there is a significant overall relationship between

TABLE VII. DEGREE OF OVERLAP BY DIRECTION OF PASS

| | OVERLAP | | | |
	MIN.	INTER.	TOTAL	T
MOVING TO LEFT	29	10	6	45
MOVING TO RIGHT	19	19	11	49
T	48	29	17	94

$$X^2 = 6.19, \text{df} = 2, p < .05$$

degree of overlap and direction of pass. We can see that in cases where overlap was total, almost twice as many pairs moved to the right as to the left of each other, a finding which fits with the convention of streaming on the pavement. However, the table also shows that in instances of minimum overlap, most pairs moved to the left rather than to the right, that is, counter to the pavement convention. When pedestrians are obliged to move to the right of each other by virtue of the fact that their left shoulders overlap, their behaviour will accord with the pavement convention. Therefore no problem of interpretation arises. But when people are obliged to move to the left of each other by virtue of the fact that their right shoulders overlap, then they will act in accordance with a principle other than that governing the convention of moving to the right. Now we would suggest that in instances of 'intermediate' right shoulder overlap (i.e., where heads and right shoulders overlap), either one or both individuals will move further to the left, thereby reducing the overlap to 'minimum' overlap (i.e., where ONLY right shoulders overlap). Moving to the left in this fashion will serve to disambiguate the situation by offering evidence, either consciously or unconsciously, of a pedestrian's intentions to act in a manner other than that which accords with the pavement convention.[6] In other words, it is possible to make sense of Table VII by supposing that in the right shoulders overlapping condition, people moved from intermediate to minimum overlap prior to our having coded their approach overlap.

Before proceeding to a discussion of these findings, a note should be made concerning the statistical methods that were employed in this study. The kinds of data with which we have been working, namely a mixture of dichotomous and multiple-category variables, do not lend themselves readily to traditional analysis of variance or multiple regression procedures. Instead, we have simply drawn up appropriate contingency tables, and partitioned the degrees of freedom within them to yield X^2 values. Such a method is not only essential where distributions are not normal, but in the context of a naturalistic study, is one which results in clarity and ease of interpretation.

---

[6] A piece of recent research concerning collision avoidance between ships on the high seas is relevant to this interpretation. Using a marine radar simulator, Captain Kemp (1973) presented both experienced mariners and naive subjects (non-mariners) with a series of standardised encounters with another ship. Each subject could man-oeuvre his own ship and alter its speed on the radar screen. It was found that in head-on encounters, all the experienced mariners altered course to starboard, whereas naive subjects, who were ignorant of the rules governing collision avoidance, altered course either way. In encounters between ships on reciprocal and parallel courses, but offset by two nautical miles to starboard, both experienced and naive subjects maintained course and speed. Experienced subjects were also found to act with unpredictability over more cases of intermediate course displacement to starboard than naive subjects, suggesting that in their attempts to adhere to the rules of the road, experienced mariners increased the likelihood of their colliding with approaching vessels. What is more relevant to our concern, is the finding that in encounters between ships offset by less than two miles, those experienced mariners who altered course to port made earlier and more exaggerated detours than naive subjects, who either maintained course or steered slightly to port. This suggests that experienced mariners, like experienced pedestrians, provide more elaborate prefigurements of their intentions to act in a manner other than that which accords with normal convention.

DISCUSSION

Several issues need to be raised. The first concerns the assumptions that may be held, and therefore the explanations that may be offered, concerning the nature of interpersonal coordination between approaching pedestrians. As Goffman has correctly observed, coordinated solutions between individuals may have various antecedents. People may, for example, engage each other in open conversation, or they may reconcile their individual and mutual interests through some form of tacit communication other than speech. Of course not all communicative behaviour need be intended as such, and as we shall argue later, a great deal of pedestrian behaviour may be inadvertently rather than intentionally communicative. Coordinations may also arise in the absence of communication, through adherence to rule by convention or through actions, which are not culturally prescribed, but which have some type of biological or physical base.[7] These then define the various preconditions which, either singly or in concert, serve to bring about a coordinated solution for two individuals.

Now, as it so happens, pedestrians seldom resort to conversation when approaching each other. For our purposes we may therefore safely ignore the role of discussion, and consider instead how coordinations may evolve through pedestrians adhering to a rule, their responding to biological-physical factors, or their engaging in tacit communication of one sort or another.

When a pedestrian finds himself on a collision course with another person, there are several things he may do, depending on the nature of his spatial relationship with that person and other people in the vicinity. One obvious determinant of the course he chooses will be the type and extent of his approach overlap with the other. If, for example, he finds his right shoulder overlapping that of the other person, he will pass by on the left, thereby adopting a course which, it so happens, serves sensibly to minimise the effort required for avoidance. Thus in instances of partial

[7] Two important notions of 'rule' can be distinguished. First there is the idea of the rule as it can be said to guide behaviour. In this case members of a community must be able to articulate the rule and/or recognise instances of its breach. Some would argue that recognition of a breach is, in itself, a sufficient condition for saying that particular behaviours are rule-guided. The second sense of rule involves the idea of the rule as an explanatory device employed by professional observers to account for regularities in behaviour among the members of a community. For a full discussion of these and other aspects of 'rule', see Winch (1958), Lewis (1969), Quine (1972) and Collett (1974).

overlap, the direction of pass will be determined by a physical consideration, namely that of effort expended. The very regularity of this behaviour is likely to instil in pedestrians a set of expectations that others will likewise adhere to a principle of least effort. But whether or not failure to fulfil such expectations may rightly be regarded as breach of a social rule is of course a moot point. With that much said, it is worth noting that instances of total overlap present a special case which cannot be handled by the notion of minimal effort.

When an individual finds himself approaching someone with a total overlap, he cannot, unless contextual factors offer relative advantage to a particular course of action, rely on the other person to adopt the kind of course he would were he in a situation of partial overlap. In other words, uncluttered head-on confrontations are ambiguous with respect to the principle of least effort. For this reason, approaching parties must either act in accordance with convention, such as it is, or resort to some form of communication. There is, in a weak sense of the term, a convention governing direction of pass. This involves moving to the right. So an individual may conform to the convention, consciously or unconsciously anticipating that the other person, whom he takes to be similarly disposed, will do likewise. On the other hand, he may take the initiative and move with sufficient resoluteness both to obviate the need for decision on the part of the other and to discourage him from not cooperating. This type of solution is essentially 'preemptive' in character. It does not require, and seldom involves, overt endorsement by the other.[8] As Goffman points out, there may however be instances where a pedestrian seeks assurances on the part of the other as to the acceptability of his intended course. Here the individual will quite consciously signal his intentions, in the anticipation that what his signals prefigure will be endorsed by the oncoming person.

Already we can see that different types of collision avoidance, and even seemingly similar solutions, may arise through different processes. Collisions which involve partial overlap are invariably averted by one or both parties acting in accordance with a principle of least effort. On the other hand, collisions which involve total overlap are averted either through one or both parties adhering to the pavement convention, or through behaviours which, whether or not they fit with convention, involve one party taking the initiative, or both parties collaborating in

---

[8]   Goffman (personal communication) suggests that a preemptive solution is not unilateral in character. "It works because the attitude of the other can be assumed, and he can assume that the mover assumes he has this attitude."

order to avoid collision. Thus, cases of collision avoidance in situations of partial overlap are best explained by appealing to a biological-physical notion, whereas solutions which arise in situations of total overlap may be variously explained, depending on the details of the case. Insofar as adherence to convention mitigates against the need for communication, the relationship between an established convention and communication would seem to be one of substitution. Only where there is no conventional solution, or where there is doubt as to either knowledge of the convention on the part of the other person or its appropriateness in a given setting, will a solution need to be sought through communication.

A break-down in any one of the processes that ensures collision avoidance may of course result in a collision, or, if approaching parties are quick to notice their failure to coordinate, a pedestrian 'dance' or what Wolff (personal communication) has called a 'stutter-step'. Where one or both parties acts in a manner which is counter to convention without indicating an intention to do so, fails to notice the other, gives a course indication which is offered too late or not noticed, or, more typically, where both pedestrians signal their intentions to move in the same direction, there will be a greater likelihood of collision.

Both Goffman and Wolff have emphasised the collaborative aspects of collision avoidance and, in particular, the expressive and monitoring functions[9] performed by the eyes during encounters on the pavement[9]. Moreover, Goffman seems to be suggesting that whereas the behaviours of approaching parties are deliberately intended to communicate, the processes of monitoring are largely unconscious in character. At one stage he describes body gloss as "relatively self-conscious gesticulation an individual can perform with his whole body in order to give pointed evidence concerning some passing issue at hand" (1972: 160), and in much the same vein, he speaks of the pedestrian "providing this gestural prefigurement and commiting himself to what it foretells" (1972: 32).

9   Little evidence was found to support the suggestion by Goffman and Wolff that pedestrians scan the faces of oncoming people. In the early stages of the study we attempted to manipulate avoidance behaviour by having a confederate position himself at the crossing and, once the lights had changed, walk straight towards a pre-selected subject with his head and eyes oriented either to the left or to the right. Here we were interested in deictic gaze. It was expected that oncoming subjects would observe the orientation of the confederate's head, take this to be an 'intention display', and move accordingly in the opposite direction. A videotape record was made of each encounter, and it was found that in a large proportion of trials subjects did not raise their heads at all, let alone scan the confederate's face. This suggests that, in the main, pedestrians (or at least Londoners) glean information concerning the behaviour of oncomers by observing their more gross body movements. It also suggests that they do not necessarily rely on the line of regard as an indicator of where a person is going.

Scanning or monitoring, on the other hand, is seen as occurring "almost entirely out of awareness" (1972: 33). Although data are not readily available in this connection, nevertheless it is worth noting that instances of intentional communication are probably not representative of the behaviours in which pedestrians, for the most part, are engaged. True, there will be encounters, especially those characterised by ambiguity, in which pedestrians deliberately signal their intentions. But, more to the point, there will also be encounters in which seemingly intentional acts of communication are really no more than behaviour produced in and through the actual process of locomotion.

The problem of collision avoidance must resolve in a solution concerning direction of pass, that is whether pedestrians pass each other on the left or the right. However, the MANNER in which each pedestrian passes the other need not depend on the behaviour of the other. Unless one or both individuals gives the other a wide berth, the only requirement is that one or both individuals angles the body in order to reduce its effective width. We have found that men and women exhibit quite different styles of behaviour when passing other people, and that these styles are independent of the age of the person, and the age and sex of the other. Males were found to make open passes, and females were found to make closed passes. The closed pass and the sex difference in armcross can best be accounted for in terms of women endeavouring to protect their breasts, whether it be from painful collision or from violation of a body region which, in our culture, is ritually associated with the erotic. It seems that here both the natural inclination to avoid hurt, and the tendency to act with propriety, work together to produce behaviours which are characteristically female (cf. Morris, 1967: 86).

Although there have been several descriptive studies of pedestrian behaviour, this is one of the first to examine collision avoidance in a systematic fashion. This has enabled us to note behavioural regularities which might otherwise have escaped us, and allowed us to look at relationships between certain variables for different groups of pedestrians. The use of systematic procedures has also enabled us to both corroborate and question some earlier findings in this area from a position founded upon data rather than impression.

REFERENCES

Collett, P. (ed.)
   1974   *Social Rules and Social Behaviour* (Oxford: Dept. of Experimental Psychology). [mimeo.]

Fruin, J. J.
1971   *Pedestrian Planning and Design* (New York: Metropolitan Association of Urban Designers and Environmental Planners).
Goffman, E.
1972   *Relations in Public* (Harmondsworth: Pelican).
Henderson, L. F., and D. J. Lyons
1972   "Sexual differences in Human Crowd Motion", *Nature* 240, 353-55.
Hirsch, V.
1970   *A Study of Pedestrian Behavior* (New York: City University of New York).
Kendon, A., and A. Ferber
1973   "A Description of Some Human Greetings", in: R. P. Michael and J. H. Crook (eds.), *Comparative Ecology and Behaviour in Primates* (London: Academic Press), 591-668.
Kemp, J. F.
1973   "Behaviour Patterns in Encounters between Ships", *The Journal of Navigation* 26, 417-23.
Knowles, E.
1972   "Boundaries around Social Space: Dyadic Responses to an Invader", *Environment and Behaviour* 4, 437-45.
Lewis, D.
1969   "*Convention: A Philosophical Analysis* (Cambridge, Mass.: Harvard University Press).
Lofland, L.
1966   *In the Presence of Strangers: A Study of Behavior in Public Settings* (Ann Arbor: University of Michigan Center for Research in Social Organization).
Morris, D.
1967   *The Naked Ape* (London: Jonathan Cape).
Quine, W. von O.
1972   "Methodological Reflections on Current Linguistic Theory" in: G. Harman and B. Davidson (eds.), *The Semantics of Natural Language* (New York: Reidel Publishers)
Ryave, L.A., and J. N. Schenkein
1974   "Notes on the Art of Walking", in: R. Turner (ed.), *Ethnomethodology* (Harmondsworth: Penguin), 265-74.
Stilitz, I. B.
1970   "Pedestrian Congestion", in: D. Cantor (ed.), *Architectural Psychology* (London: Institute of British Architects), 61-72.
Winch, P.
1958   *The Idea of a Social Science and its Relation to Philosophy* (London: Routledge).
Wolff, M.
1973   "Notes on the Behaviour of Pedestrians", in: A. Birenbaum and E. Sagar (eds.), *People in Places: The Sociology of the Familiar* (New York: Praeger), 35-48.

Peter Collett (b. 1945, in Zambia) is senior research officer in the Department of Experimental Psychology, Oxford University. His interests are cross-cultural psychology, public behavior, and the study of objective classification.

Peter Marsh (b. 1946, in England) is a lecturer in the Oxford College of Further Education. His research interests are communalities of meaning within deviant subculture, and behavior in public.

DAVID GIVENS

Greeting a Stranger: Some Commonly Used Nonverbal Signals of Aversiveness

No social relationship is more stressful than the encounter with a stranger, an unknown and potentially threatening fellow human being. The nature of interpersonal stress is difficult to specify, but studies of the galvanic skin response (e.g., McBride *et al.* 1965) indicate that anxiety increases in subjects, i.e., skin resistance decreases, as they are approached by strangers. Fear of strangers originates in infants at approximately seven to nine months of age. The early ontogeny of a generalized fear system, apparently unrelated to the infant's rearing experiences, as well as its presence in a variety of socio-cultural settings, suggests a possible phylogenetic history (Emde *et al.* 1976). Anthropologists have described numerous standardized greetings, such as the Polynesian embrace, the Afro-American long distance greeting, the Papuan genital-pressing salutation, and Japanese bowing. These greeting activities, which can be used with friends and strangers, may be construed as cultural solutions to the problem of social tension, as standardized recognition signals serving partially to ease the anxiety of initial meeting periods.

Like LaBarre (1956) and Birdwhistell (1970), many anthropologists, aware of the tremendous cultural variation in greeting patterns, are suspicious of those who speak of 'instinctive' human gestures, facial expressions, and body movements. Nevertheless, in recent studies Ekman (1973) has demonstrated the existence of pancultural relationships between facial expressions and emotions. And in the area of greeting behavior Scheflen (1972) and Eibl-Eibesfeldt (1975) have alleged that activities such as the brow raise, smile, and head nod may represent universal signals indicative of bonding readiness and affiliation. It would be fruitless here to argue for the superiority of either perspective. But certainly the existence of cultural signal units neither implies nor denies the existence of culture-free expressive behaviors.

The present paper describes a naturalistic study of aversive greeting behaviors. One hundred and fifty observations of encounters between strangers were made in an effort to identify common nonverbal activities which appeared to signal an indisposition to initiate or maintain a social bond. Kendon and Ferber (1973), in an examination of 70 greeting episodes performed at a garden party, described several affiliative signals, such as the upper smile, saying "hi", the palm-upward waving gesture, and the embrace, which signaled an apparent readiness to bond. Most observers are familiar with such contact-readiness expressions. Less well known are expressive behaviors which contrast with these, the nonverbal activities used to communicate bonding avoidance or reluctance to establish social contact. The goal of this study was first, objectively, to find out what kinds of behaviors adult strangers performed while in one another's immediate presence, and then, more subjectively, to interpret the behaviors as possible signals of social pose, specifically, as messages about the degree of bonding volition in a relationship.

METHOD

Naturalistic observations were carried out in three metropolitan gathering areas, the Seattle Public Market, a popular Seattle Irish bar, and on the campus of the University of Washington. Each location imposed unique constraints on subjects' movements and interaction patterns. The Public Market houses a long walkway, 20' wide, bordered on the sides by open displays of fruit, vegetables, meats, and delicatessen items. Shoppers stroll leisurely up and down the walkway and, under crowded conditions which make close physical proximity unavoidable, often are constrained to acknowledge one another, to greet or otherwise recognize the presence of unfamiliar individuals. In the Irish pub patrons would situate themselves at the wide entryway, and stop and peer inward for several seconds before entering. The bar was crowded and noisy during the observation periods. Newly entering patrons were observed to perform characteristic body movements and facial expressions in the entryway. The behaviors appeared to have been elicited by the stressful setting, by the prospect of having to enter a room full of loud strangers. And the university setting offered lengthy stretches of uncrowded streets and sidewalks. Here people could be observed as they approached one another, one-on-one, from a distance. Fifty encounters between strangers were observed in each of the three settings.

An unobtrusive observational technique was used. Subjects were not overly aware of my presence, and I could record behavioral units in a small notebook as they occurred. Film or videotape would have added greatly to the study, but technical and legal difficulties made their use impossible. Of necessity detailed records were made of only one party in each encounter. Frequently when one person's face was visible the partner's face was turned away, and without film or videotape simultaneous observation of both subjects was not possible.

The study dealt with what Goffman (1961:7) has called 'unfocused' interaction "...those interpersonal communications that result solely by virtue of persons being in one another's presence...." Unfocused interaction was defined operationally here to include an identifiable *contact-phase*, a definite recognition or awareness by the subject that a stranger was present. Two criteria were taken to signify recognition: gaze contact and/or very close physical proximity. Gaze contact consisted of looking at the stranger and fixating his or her face. (In the bar setting gaze contact was defined as looking inward for at least five seconds.) Very close physical proximity consisted of having to alter one's path significantly to avoid physical collision. When either or both of these criteria were present between apparent strangers, social contact was considered to have been made, and an unfocused interaction was taken to have been initiated.

Using behavioral units defined in an earlier study (Givens, 1976) the author recorded only those facial expressions, body movements, and gaze patterns that were performed subsequent to the contact-phase, and further, that were terminated once the unfocused interaction was stopped. Only these activities, it was assumed, could be considered realistically as being possible social signals. They were analyzed as greeting behaviors, as contact signals that could be used by a receiver as meaningful clues of the sender's social-psychological orientation. In all three settings typical greetings between strangers conveyed an attitude of contact avoidance rather than contact readiness.

FINDINGS

The most general finding was that in over 90 percent of all cases

(137 out of 150) unfocused interaction, as evidenced by a definite phase of social contact, was accompanied by various combinations of the following activities: lip-compression, lip-bite, tongue-show, tongue-in-cheek; downward, lateral, and maximal-lateral gaze avoidance; hand-to-face, hand-to-hand, hand-to-body, and hand-behind-head automanipulations; and postures involving flexion and adduction of the upper limbs. These behaviors were initiated during the contact-phase and were terminated abruptly after social contact with the stranger was stopped. Unlike affiliative nonverbal units, such as smiling, touching, embracing, and so on, the above activities correlated with non-contact, and seemed to signal that contact would not be well received.

Facial Expressions. Common facial expressions performed in the presence of strangers, between the contact-phase and the subsequent separation, included the lip-compression (lips pressed tightly together and rolled inward), lip-bite (upper incisors contacting lower lip), tongue-show (slight protrusion of tongue between the lips), and tongue-in-cheek (tongue pressing visibly against the inside of the cheek). The first three units are equivalent respectively to Grant's (1969) 'lips-in', 'bite lip', and 'tongue'. Grant considered 'lips-in' to accompany fleeing or submissiveness; 'bite lip' and 'tongue' were not analyzed. Brannigan and Humphries' (1972) 'lips in', 'bite lips', and 'tongue between lips' are also equivalent; they were not interpreted by these authors. Neither notational scheme included a tongue-in-cheek component.

These facial expressions occurred with high frequency (over 50 percent) among adult men and women in the three settings. A typical incident at the Public Market involved a male, approximately 55 years old, who bit his lower lip while gazing at and approaching a younger male (30 years old). The lip-bite was terminated when they passed from one another's view. Another episode, a near collision between a female (25) and an adult male, involved the female showing the tongue. There had been no initial gaze contact. The tongue show was stopped once she had passed beyond him. At the Irish pub individuals would very frequently perform these facial expressions, especially the lip-compression, as they peered into the bar from the entryway. Once situated at a table the expressions would cease and would be replaced by affiliative smiling and by a neutral (blank-face) expression. At the university, tongue-showing, lip-compressing, and lip-biting were frequently performed when students passed closely in front of people seated at tables in cafeterias and in libraries — but only when the seated person was facing them. At both the Public

Market and the university the close-quarters approach elicited aversive facial behaviors only when the partners could look at one another, whether or not looking actually occurred. Facial expressions would not be performed by individuals who nearly collided with someone from the rear, nor by individuals as they passed closely behind someone who was seated.

In over half of all cases these facial expressions were accompanied by patterns of gaze aversion. The subject would glance at a stranger, perform the tongue or lip behavior, and avert the gaze. Smiling and upward or downward movements of the eyebrows were observed not to occur in these contexts. The tongue and lip expressions appeared to contrast significantly with smiling behaviors and with the mutual gazing and brow-raising that accompany smiling. Further, while smiling appears to invite social contact, lip-compressions and tongue-shows seem to discourage it. The strangers observed in the study neither signaled contact readiness, nor did they participate in a relationship beyond the rudimentary contact phase of recognition. For these reasons it seemed justifiable to interpret the behaviors as signals of social aversiveness.

In a naturalistic study of tongue-showing, Smith *et al.* (1974:203) alleged the expression to mean that "...the communicator is relatively unlikely to initiate or accept suitably social interactions, or particular features of them". From my own observations their conclusions, based on investigation of children and adults in the United States and the Canal Zone, would be valid additionally for the lip-compression, lip-bite, and tongue-in-cheek expressions. In an ethological study of children approaching a strange adult Stern and Bender (1974) found the tongue-show ('tongue between lips') and 'apprehensive' mouth behaviors such as 'bite lip' and 'lips in'. These facial expressions, along with various kinds of smiles, were observed in 3-to-5 year old children as they walked up to unknown, expressionless (blank-face) adults who maintained a steady gaze at the children. The smiles were interpreted as possible appeasement signals which, in boys and girls, were associated with a more direct facing orientation toward the adult. The apprehensive, non-smiling expressions were associated more with facing away and might be analyzed as aversive signal units. Significantly, the affiliative and the aversive behaviors are present and already fully operative in nursery school children in potentially threatening situations. Eibl-Eibesfeldt (1973) has reported the presence of fear-of-strangers responses even in congenitally deaf-and-blind children, and has observed lip-biting to be one behavioral reaction to frustration and conflict in the children (such as, in one example, after turning away from another person).

Often the aversive mouth behaviors were performed and terminated very rapidly. One encounter between a male and a female in the university library involved an ephemeral lip-compression that expressed a rather strongly negative reaction. Two 20-year-old females were standing and talking, facing one another and smiling as they conversed. One then introduced her male companion (20) who, though watching the conversation, had not been participating (neither woman had looked at him or addressed him before the introduction). The second female gazed at the male and, without smiling, performed a fleeting open-mouth compressed-lips expression, lasting approximately half a second, and abruptly averted the gaze maximally. Five seconds later, after saying goodbye's, the group split up. The male-female pair went one way and the aversive female went the opposite way. Plainly, something very negative obtained in that brief confrontation; the sudden splitting of the group appeared to have been announced or at least foreshadowed by the brief compressed-lips expression and the maximal-lateral gaze avoidance. The indisposition to interact was transmitted clearly, and little time was spent being friendly.

Gaze patterns. Goffman (1963) has suggested that direction of gaze can play a crucially important role in the initiation and maintenance of social encounters, and has alleged that gaze contact can signal a willingness to interact. In the present study observations of unfocused interactions between strangers yielded three distinct gaze-avoidance patterns that appeared to signal a clear aversion to social interaction. These were maximal-lateral gaze (turning the head all the way to the side), lateral gaze (turning the head slightly to one side, or moving the eyes to one side), and gaze-downward (tilting the head forward or lowering the eyes vertically).

Maximal-lateral gaze aversion represented a most frequent and very interesting reaction to strangers. Like the other behaviors it was performed between the contact and separation phases of the unfocused interactions. Both men and women used maximal-lateral gaze at the Public Market, the Irish pub, and on the university campus. At the market it was observed to be a usual reaction to impending collision. Individuals who nearly collided would abruptly avert the gaze maximally (turn the head completely away from the stranger) as they stopped and hastily got out of each other's way. And in all three settings maximal-lateral gaze was used to 'cut off' contact made initially by looking at a stranger's face, even when the stranger had not returned the eye contact. Patrons entering the bar, for instance, often would stand in the entryway and perform maximal-lateral gaze several times before entering to buy a drink. On the campus students would approach one another on an uncrowded sidewalk, and as they neared to within 10-to-20 feet would maximally turn the heads completely away from each other. As soon as they had negotiated the pass-by the heads would return quickly to the forward-facing position. There was one unique episode of what might be called maximal-lateral-body-positioning. At the Public Market a 50-year-old lady, who appeared to be disoriented and confused, would not only avert the gaze but would stop and turn the entire body to one side, completely away from oncoming shoppers. When the latter had passed from view she would once again face ahead and continue walking forward. The maximal body aversion seemed to represent a kind of temporary immobility, a typical childlike reaction to strangers.

Lateral gaze and gaze-downward occurred in similar circumstances. They would be executed very briefly between the contact and the separation phases by men and women. Lateral gaze was a predictable response in persons who were being stared at. At the market, for example, one woman (25) who sold vegetables spent a lot of idle time gazing at the faces of customers who walked by her stall. Occasionally a customer would glance in her direction and discover this attention. A typical reaction was that of another 25-year-old female who, noticing the fixed, nonsmiling gaze of the vendor, performed the tongue-in-cheek expression and averted the gaze slightly to one side. Once out of range the tongue-in-cheek and the lateral gaze were halted.

Although there are not enough data to identify a definite pattern, it was observed that young adult females (age 12 to 16) would tend to avert the gaze downward without lowering the head when approached by groups of males. In one episode a 12-year-old female tongue-showed and lowered her eyes while keeping her head in a fixed forward-facing position as she neared an all male group. This may indicate an exaggerated fear reaction, a combination of postural immobility, downward-gaze, and tongue-show functioning unambiguously to convey the message, "Do not approach!"

Euro-American gaze patterns have been well studied (see Nielsen 1962, Argyle and Dean 1965, Kendon 1967). Grant (1969) has identified 'look at', 'look away', and look down' variables, but has not given maximal-lateral gaze a specific label. Brannigan and Humphries (1972)⁻have specified identical units. In naturalistic studies Kendon and Ferber (1973) and Pitcairn and Eibl-Eibesfeldt (1976) have examined gaze as a kind of 'cut-off' behavior. Cut-off activities (gaze-downward, lateral, and maximal-lateral gaze) were observed in subjects as they greeted acquaintances. Kendon and Ferber (1973) found gazing downward ('dipping' the head and 'lowering') to occur between an initial long distance greeting (such as facing gaze plus upper smile) and a close greeting (facing gaze, upper smile, head tilt). Pitcairn and Eibl-Eibesfeldt (1976) have observed and filmed the same kinds of gaze cut-off activities in Europeans, infants, and non-human primates. Like Kendon and Ferber they found cut-off behaviors (such as 'complete cut-off, turning away') occurring characteristically after the distance salutation, during the approach, and then again after the close greeting. Unlike Kendon and Ferber, who interpreted gaze cut-off as a signal that can be used to disclaim unwarranted intimacy or threat, they withhold an interpretation, but claim that cut-off activities are unlearned:

> ...what is important here is, first, that these behaviors are maintained in the population of all primates (including man) examined and, second, that they occur in very young and visually deprived subjects. This latter argues for some central control of the pattern, as it is difficult to envisage how such behavior could then be learned. (Pitcairn and Eibl-Eibesfeldt 1976:98)

Some studies of infants and young children have found patterns of gaze avoidance in aversive social circumstances. Konner (1972) found gaze aversion to be one typical reaction of Bushman (*Zhun twasi*) infants to strangers. McGrew (1972) described gazing-downward as a frequent behavior in Scottish youngsters newly introduced into existing nursery school groups. And Stern and Benders' (1974) study of 3-to-5 year olds approaching strange adults, in which gaze avoidance was found to be a typical reaction, ascertained that standing adults, potentially more threatening than seated adults, elicited the most extreme lateral gaze aversion in the children. This may support the idea that the greater the degree of stress in a social relationship, the greater the amount of gaze avoidance.

Eibl-Eibesfeldt (1975) has hypothesized that the visual cut-off may function to control social arousal, and has cited a study of heartbeat rates in 6-to-10 month old infants who were approached by strange adult females. Heartbeat rate increased during the approach, but decreased by 10-to-15 beats per minute when the babies averted their gaze from the stranger. If heartbeat rate can be interpreted as one indication of fear/anxiety, then such infantile gaze avoidance can be seen both as a response to social stress and as a way of managing or controlling it. Gaze-aversion patterns among adult strangers may also relate closely to factors of interpersonal stress and anxiety. Maximal-lateral, lateral, and downward-gaze behaviors may even rest on innately predisposed tendencies to avoid stressful visual stimuli. To receivers, experienced after years of observing, these patterns may represent rather clear messages of a sender's less than enthusiastic presentation, a social pose that would appear to discourage rather than encourage or solicit approach.

Maximal-lateral gaze avoidance portrayed a clearly aversive signal in crowded university cafeteria settings. Typically, an individual would approach an occupied table, put down the food tray, glance at the seated occupants, and maximally avert the gaze before taking a seat. The behavior seemed to indicate that the new arrival would not attempt to start a conversation. Because sitting and eating together define a very sociable setting, strangers in cafeterias may have to use exaggeratedly aversive nonverbal behaviors to prevent social interaction, or make it clear that they do not expect the others to exercise undue friendliness. But whatever the rationalization, the fundamental message involves social aversiveness, an indisposition to bond.

Automanipulation. It has been established that automanipulation (self-touching activity such as hand-to-face, hand-to-neck, hair-preen, scratch, and so on) is a common behavioral reaction in aversive social situations in children (Blurton Jones 1972, McGrew 1972, Stern and Bender 1974). Certain automanipulations, notably hand-behind-head and hand-cover-mouth, have been interpreted firmly as expressions of dislike, negative reaction, and aversiveness in adults (Grant 1969, Brannigan and Humphries 1972, Scheflen 1972, Givens 1977). In the present study automanipulations were observed in males and females in each of the three settings.

Self-touching activity occurred most frequently in contact situations, in settings where interaction was more likely to be initiated or prolonged. When quick avoidance was possible there was little or no automanipulation. At the Public Market, head-scratching, hand-to-nose, hand-to-ear, adjust-glasses, and other automanipulations were performed when the initial contact phase of recognition was prolonged, i.e., when gaze contact was kept up beyond a few seconds or when close physical proximity was protracted somewhat longer than the quick pass-by. Men, for example, were observed to automanipulate as they gazed steadily at other shoppers while the latter walked by them. Or a shopper would automanipulate while facing and waiting for someone to move out of the way. In these cases there seemed to be more of a likelihood that waiting and/or gazing might elicit a reaction in the stranger, a reaction that could entail possibly uncomfortable social interaction.

Automanipulative activities were most common at the Irish pub. Entering a room full of noisy strangers, and the expectation of being looked at by many people at once, appeared to elicit considerable social stress in the patrons. Males and females typically would adjust clothing, preen hair, touch their necks, cover their mouths, reach a hand behind the head, or tug on earlobes. Men often would accompany these behaviors with performances of maximal-lateral gaze aversion, while females often would combine them with extreme lip-compression, tightly crossed arms (over the stomach), and sustained hand-to-neck postures. The automanipulative postures, the hand-to-neck and the arm-crossing (with the upper arms pulled closely in against the torso and the lower arms held snugly against the stomach, were attended by moderate supination of the shoulders and by a temporary immobility in body and head movement. Females exhibited greater flexion of elbows, greater flexion or extension of wrists, and more of a tendency to clutch the body tightly. Social anxiety appeared to be higher in the women than in the men but, in both sexes, the automanipulations seemed to derive from amplified stress, from the likelihood of having to interact with strangers, if only to secure a table and remain in the crowd, rather than of having simply to negotiate an escape by them as at the Public Market.

Two encounters observed on the campus of the university illustrate the relationship between automanipulation and these more 'focused' interactions with strangers. The first took place between a female student and an older male whom she approached to ask for help because her car had broken down. She approached submissively, gazing at the male with her head tilted downward, shoulders flexed forward, and aversively, with the lips tightly compressed and one hand held behind her head. The hand-behind-head seemed to express that she would not have approached the stranger in less needful circumstances. In the second example an adult female initiated an interaction with an adult male acquaintance by tapping him on the shoulder, tilting her head to one side, and smiling. He turned toward her, smiled, stretched the arms, and protruded the chest toward her as he spoke. A second male adult, presumably the woman's boyfriend (he had been holding her hand earlier), then approached the pair, with a nonsmiling, open-mouthed expression, and averted the gaze maximally as he neared them. The first male reacted to the approach by turning away from the female, averting the gaze maximally from the boyfriend, and reaching a hand behind the head. The maximal-lateral gaze and the hand-behind-head were used to express a strongly aversive social pose, an apparent indisposition to prolong the interaction. The initial chest-protrusion, open smile, and arm stretching defined a flirting or courtship relationship, an exaggerated affiliative social pose that likely would not have been performed had the boyfriend been standing next to the female from the start. When caught in the act, the flirtation was halted abruptly and a pose of aversiveness was assumed. The encounter was terminated shortly after introductions had been made.

Automanipulation was a common behavior in these lengthier confrontations between unacquainted adults. Subjects would preen the hair, scratch the stomach, rub the arm, and so on, when asking a stranger for the time, when asking to borrow a newspaper, or when making a friendly comment. They seemed to signal simultaneous tendencies of affiliation and aversion, a social pose that was both 'friendly' and 'reserved'. A typical encounter involved two male university students in the library. One gazed at the other and asked, "Do you have the time?" The second looked at his watch, then gazed at the petitioner and touched the hair on the frontal region of the scalp as he replied, "Five 'til three." They smiled briefly, the first said "Thanks", and both gazed downward. The automanipulator behaved in a sociable manner (smiling-facing-gaze), but the hair-preen seemed to betray a degree of anxiety, some small amount of social tension in the relationship with the stranger. Many automanipulations seemed to indicate an ambivalent reaction to the partner.

CONCLUSIONS

In all three social settings strange adults were observed to 'greet' one another with characteristic aversive-like nonverbal signals. Lip-compressions, tongue-shows, lip-bites, and tongue-in-cheek facial expressions; downward, lateral, and maximal-lateral gaze avoidance patterns; and automanipulative activities such as hand-to-neck, hand-to-ear, and hand-behind-head were performed in the presence of unknown adults, between the initial contact or recognition phase and the termination, separation, or spacing phase of the confrontation. These behaviors, observed in similar aversive social circumstances among children, some even among deaf-and-blind-born youngsters, appeared to contrast significantly with smiles, head-nods, waving, brow-raising, embracing, and other affiliative expressions that signal poses of contact-readiness or 'friendship'. The usage of automanipulations was most frequent in situations where interactions with the stranger was unavoidable, more likely to occur, or actually initiated.

The researcher was surprised that adult strangers, not linked by clear role relationships or expectations, would respond so frequently to one another with aversive rather than affiliative social signals. The most characteristic behavior pattern consisted simply of ignoring the stranger (i.e., no contact-phase observed). But when contact was made inadvertently, by gazing-at or by close physical proximity, contact-avoidance activities typically would be performed. The nonverbal message was clear — "I disaffirm the accidental social contact; I have no intention of approaching you." The significance of the performance for a receiver would be, "Stay away."

It would be tempting, but premature, to state that all of the aversive behaviors observed in this study are unlearned or innately predisposed. The temptation exists because so many of them are performed at an early age (e.g., gaze avoidance from 14 days, automanipulations and aversive mouth behaviors from 1-to-2 years) in many cultural settings, are found in the Hominoidea generally, and are exhibited by congenitally deprived youngsters. In Euro-American tradition contraction of the zygomaticus muscles is labeled with words that can be translated as 'smile'. Similarly, 'frown' and 'pout' are commonly designated, but the aversive behaviors typically are not named, even though they are quite as important as meaningful signals of social pose. In many cultures the smiling response in children is encouraged by parents and relatives. By contrast, tongue-showing, lip-compressing, and hand-behind-head (touching the region of the third cranial nerve) are not promoted, and do not receive the same cultural attention or embellishment. Nevertheless, they too seem to convey social information, and their meaning, from the receiver's perspective, may derive from the years of close observation humans give to one another. Like the smile and the frown, these activities correlate reliably with social disposition and can be used very effectively as mood signs in interaction. In a conversational setting, for example, the tongue-show or lip-compression can signal the performer's desire to get away, a negative reaction to the discussion topic, or a reluctance to answer a difficult personal question. Mahl (1968:305) has stated that 'autistic' actions, such as automanipulations, "...seem only to be manifestations of general personality traits and of momentary emotional-ideational states; they do not seem to have a communicative function." The present study would indicate that these actions are communicative in Kendon's (1973) sense of being available to the receiver for an interpretation. They appear to be correlated with contact avoidance in the same way that affiliative behaviors correlate with contact initiation and maintenance.

According to Goffman (1963) people sometimes greet one another with a kind of 'civil inattention'. Civil inattention consists first of gazing at the other to acknowledge the person's presence, then withdrawing the gaze to signal non-attention. "By according civil inattention, the individual implies that he has no reason to suspect the intentions of the others present and no reason to fear the others, be hostile to them, or wish to avoid them." (Goffman 1963:84). In the present study civil inattentiveness was rare. In over ninety percent of the 150 observations the contact or recognition phase was followed immediately by potentially aversive nonverbal behaviors, by tongue-shows, lip-compressions, hand-behind-head, maximal-lateral gaze avoidance, and so on. Civil inattention implies a kind of neutral social pose; the observations suggest that, among strangers, the partner is evaluated somewhat more negatively, suspiciously, or doubtfully.

The aim of this study was to identify the natural behavioral units used in face-to-face communication between strange adults. A more ambitious project would be to compute relative frequencies of occurence of the units. Specific frequencies were not tabulated here because the great variation in subjects (sex, age, health, nationality, sobriety, clothing, social class, familiarity with surroundings, and so on) and in settings (crowded vs. uncrowded, indoors vs. outdoors, close vs. more distant proximity). These variables would have to be controlled for frequency tabulations to be meaningful. For instance, the observation that females performed the compressed-lips expression more often than males would have to be tested in less complex settings with more homogeneous subjects.

As Bateson (1968) has suggested, human nonverbal communication appears to express information pertaining to the most fundamental contingencies of social relationships, to dominance, submission, affiliation, and aversion. It predates spoken language and is more closely related to other mammalian signaling systems than to linguistic behavior. Thus, studies such as this one should prove to be useful for analyzing the more basic human social poses.

Studies of normal infants and adults indicate that galvanic skin resistance decreases and heartbeat rate increases in subjects as they are approached by adult strangers. Ethological and social-psychological observations have established that characteristic tongue and lip expressions, gaze-avoidance patterns, and automanipulations occur in children and adults as they approach or are approached themselves by unknown adults. Both the physiological and the more visible nonverbal activities, indications of 'social stress', may be related to escape, flight, or avoidance tendencies in subjects. The stranger is potentially threatening in magnitudes ranging from very mild to extreme. Conceivably, the greater the felt threat, the greater the stress and the more remote the likelihood of establishing or maintaining a social bond.

In the context of interacting with a stranger, tongue-show, lip-compression, lip-bite, and tongue-in-cheek appear to be purely aversive signals. They are highly correlated with prolonged gaze avoidance and with noncontact or spacing, i.e., putting distance between individuals. In a similar way gaze avoidance, initiated immediately after the contact-phase and sustained while passing by the unacquainted partner, appears to be mainly aversive. This would be especially true for maximal-lateral gaze avoidance. These expressive units can be regarded as unambiguous messages of an avoidance bias in a performer.

The automanipulations can be interpreted as signals of a more ambiguous social attitude. Automanipulations occurred most frequently among subjects who, for a variety of reasons, found it necessary to interact and actually deal with a stranger. They were correlated with gazing-at, sustained physical proximity, and approach. Hand-to-neck, hand-behind-head, scratch, touch-eye, and so on, occurred when subjects became involved inadvertently or accidentally in relationships with strangers. The relationships typically were brief and did not include smiling, touching, and relaxed conversation. These self-touch behaviors, in some ways inappropriate to the social context, might be interpreted as displacement activites performed in response either to conflicting tendencies of approach/avoidance or to thwarted avoidance. In both cases the automanipulations appeared to express a strong avoidance tendency in the performer.

By way of pure speculation it might be hypothesized that the aversive signals are used most frequently by individuals who are more likely to use submissive-like nonverbal units, especially those held by the author to derive from the shoulder-shrugging complex (Givens 1977). That is, there may be an empirical relationship between submissive and aversive nonverbal presentations. By contrast, dominant-like individuals might be expected to experience less anxiety in the presence of strangers and would be less likely to automanipulate or to respond with aversive facial expressions and gaze avoidance. And in some cases the dominant or high status person experiencing little or no stress in the presence of a low status stranger, may withold all aversive activities and convey what Goffman (1963:84) has called 'nonperson' treatment — a behavior that "...may be seen in our society in the way we sometimes treat children, servants, Negroes, and mental patients". In the absence of social anxiety an individual would be likely to withhold all aversive/submissive reactions. Unaccompanied by smiling, such a presentation of self could be quite disturbing to a receiver.

Finally, it should be made clear that social aversion, an indisposition to approach or bond, does not necessarily imply dislike or negative reaction. This can be appreciated especially in an analysis of the nonverbal signals used in coy or shy poses of flirtation. Coyness seems to involve mixed messages of affiliation and aversiveness, and portrays a peculiar social relationship combining eager approach tendencies with tendencies to avoid. The individual is at once strongly attracted to the partner and yet fearful of approaching. Anxiety is high (rapid heartbeat, low GSR), and automanipulations are frequent (especially 'preening' activities; see Scheflen 1972), gaze alternates between looking at the partner and gazing-downward (see Eibl-Eibesfeldt 1971), and smiles or ambivalent smiles (smiling-tongue-show, compressed-lips-smile, smiling-lip-bite) are performed. Except for smiling and periods of direct gaze, the latter often from a forward or laterally tilted head position, the flirting display is identical to more purely aversive performances. Aversiveness and disliking apparently are not synonymous even though both may be responses to social anxiety or stress.

It may be hypothesized that the childhood fear-of-strangers phenomenon and its concomitant nonverbal reactions are carried into adulthood without significant alteration. Social aversiveness may represent one of our most fundamental interpersonal poses.

REFERENCES

Argyle, M., and J. Dean
   1965   "Eye-Contact, Distance, and Affiliation," *Sociometry* 28, 289-304.
Bateson, G.
   1968   "Redundancy and Coding," in T. A. Sebeok, ed., *Animal Communication*, 614-26. Bloomington: Indiana University Press.
Birdwhistell, R.
   1970   *Kinesics and Context.* Philadelphia: University of Pennsylvania Press.
Blurton Jones, N. G.
   1972   "Categories of Child-Child Interaction," in N. G. Blurton Jones, ed., *Ethological Studies of Child Behaviour,* 97-127. Cambridge: Cambridge University Press.

Brannigan, C., and D. Humphries
    1972   "Human Non-Verbal Behaviour, A Means of Communication," in N.
            G. Blurton Jones, ed., *Ethological Studies of Child Behaviour*, 37-64.
            Cambridge: Cambridge University Press.
Eibl-Eibesfeldt, I.
    1971   *Love and Hate*, San Fransisco: Holt, Rinehart, and Winston.
    1973   "The Expressive Behaviour of the Deaf-and-Blind-Born," in M. von
            Cranach and I. Vine, eds., *Social Communication and Movement*.
            (=European Monographs in Social Psychology 4), 163-94. New York:
            Academic Press.
    1975   *Ethology: The Biology of Behavior*. 2nd ed. San Fransisco: Holt,
            Rinehart, and Winston.
Ekman, P.
    1973   "Cross-Cultural Studies of Facial Expression," in P. Ekman, ed., *Darwin and Facial Expression*, 169-222. New York: Academic Press.
Emde, R., T. Gaensbauer, and R. Harmon
    1976   *Emotional Expression in Infancy: A Biobehavioral Study*. New York:
            International Universities Press.
Givens, D.
    1976   *An Ethological Approach to the Study of Human Nonverbal Communication*. Doctoral Dissertation, University of Washington.
    1977   "Shoulder-Shrugging: A Densely Communicative Expressive Behavior,"
            Semiotica 19/1-2, 13-28.
    1977   "Infantile Reflexive Behaviors and Nonverbal Communication", *Sign
            Language Studies* 16, 219-36.
Goffman, E.
    1961   *Encounters*. Indianapolis: Bobbs-Merrill.
    1963   *Behavior in Public Places*. New York: The Free Press.
Grant, E.
    1969   "Human Facial Expressions," *Man* 4, 525-36.
Kendon, A.
    1967   "Some Functions of Gaze-Direction in Social Interaction," *Acta Psychologica* 26, 22-63.
    1973   "The Role of Visible Behavior in the Organization of Social Interaction," in M. von Cranach and I. Vine, eds., *Social Communication
            and Movement*, (=European Monographs in Social Psychology 4), 29-
            74. New York: Academic Press.
Kendon, A., and A. Ferber
    1973   "A Description of Some Human Greetings," in P. Michael and J. Crook
            eds., *Comparative Ecology and Behaviour of Primates*, 591-668.
            London: Academic Press.
Konner, M.
    1972   "Infants of a Foraging People," in N. G. Blurton Jones, ed., *Ethological Studies of Child Behaviour*, 285-304. Cambridge: Cambridge
            University Press.

LaBarre, W.
1956 "The Cultural Basis of Emotions and Gestures," in D. Haring, ed., *Personal Character and Cultural Milieu*, 547-63. Syracuse, N.Y.: Syracuse University Press.

Mahl, G.
1968 "Gestures and Body Movements in Interviews," in J. Shlien, ed., *Research in Psychotherapy*, 295-346. Washington, D.C.: American Psychological Association.

McBride, G., M. King, and J. James
1965 "Social Proximity Effects on GSR in Adult Humans," *Journal of Psychology*, 61, 153-57.

McGrew, W.
1972 "Aspects of Social Development in Nursery School Children with Emphasis on Introduction to the Group," in N. Blurton Jones, ed., *Ethological Studies of Child Behaviour*, 129-56. Cambridge: Cambridge University Press.

Nielsen, G.
1962 *Studies in Self Confrontation*. Copenhagen: Munksgaard.

Pitcairn, T., and I. Eibl-Eibesfeldt
1976 "Concerning the Evolution of Nonverbal Communication in Man," in E, C, Simmel and M. Hahn, eds., *Communicative Behavior and Evolution*, 81-113. New York: Academic Press.

Scheflen, A.
1972 *Body Language and the Social Order*. Englewood Cliffs, N.J.: Prentice-Hall.

Smith, J., J. Chase, and A. Lieblich
1974 "Tongue Showing," *Semiotica* 11, 201-46.

Stern, D., and E. Bender
1974 "An Ethological Study of Children Approaching a Strange Adult," in R. Friedman et al., eds., *Sex Differences in Behavior*, 233-58. New York: John Wiley and Sons.

David Givens (b. 1944) is the Director of Interpersonal Communication Consulting Service, Inc., in Seattle, Washington. His principal research interest is in ethological studies of human communication. For recent publications consult the above list of References.

DEBORAH SCHIFFRIN

Handwork as Ceremony:
The Case of the Handshake

1. INTRODUCTION

When a student wants to speak in a classroom, he raises his hand. When the pledge of allegiance begins, the hand covers the heart. A soldier, upon greeting his officer, salutes. When parting at the train station, friends wave their last good-byes. An audience gives a standing ovation. "Uncle Sam wants you", and points a finger. "Pleased to meet you", he said, while extending his hand. Such performances are routine and commonplace, so that 'handwork', for the most part, goes unnoticed.

One way of approaching such handwork is in terms of its psychological functions, as an indicator of feeling, emotion or expression, used by and for the individual actor. An alternative perspective through which to view social performances such as handwork, the one used here, is that of the ritual ceremony. As phrased by Goffman (1971: 62), a ritual is "a perfunctory, conventionalized act through which an individual portrays his respect and regard for some object of ultimate value to that object of ultimate value or to its stand-in".

This study suggests that handwork is generated from the organization of social occasions and relationships. Occasion is being used in Goffman's sense, that is, as providing "the structuring social context in which many situations and their gatherings are likely to form, dissolve, and re-form" (1963: 18). Events such as cocktail parties, sewing get-togethers, business meetings, and afternoon tea are examples of occasions. Particular

* The author wishes to thank Dean MacCannell for helpful criticisms on earlier drafts of this paper.

encounters, or "the natural unit(s) of social organization in which inter-action occur" (Goffman, 1961: 8) are framed by occasions: for instance, introductions, greetings, and partings. A ritual ceremony is generated by such settings and events, and by requirements of the particular roles and relationships involved in a spate of activity. In short, the organization of occasions and relationships constitutes the dramatic context from which handwork derives its meaning, and, in turn, to which handwork gives meaning.

In this paper, I want to describe the handshake, a typical example of hand performances, as product of both a ritual and a social context, and its function as a sign of access and solidarity.

2. THE ANALYSIS

Considering the definition of ritual, it follows that there exist sacred entities in secular society that demand some display of deference, if they are to continue to fulfill certain societal requirements. Goffman (1967: 95) has further suggested that:

Durkheimian notions about primitive religion can be translated into concepts of deference and demeanor, and that these concepts help us to grasp some as-pects of urban secular living. The implication is that in one sense this secular world is not so irreligious as we might think. Many gods have been done away with, but the individual himself stubbornly remains as a deity of considerable importance. He walks with some dignity and is the recipient of many little offerings.

As suggested, the handshake falls under this rubric of ritual performed to the individual as a sacred object. Specifically, it is in a class of rituals that serves to provide brackets around a spate of activity, an occasion, undertaken by several participants, a 'meeting', 'gathering', and 'en-counter'. The handshake marks the beginning of the activity, or the period during which there is an increase in joint access. It also can be used at the end of such periods, as an indication that the access gained will extend over the following period of separation, and not be limited to that one occasion. Since there is some amount of regard being contained and conveyed in that offering of access to the self, such behavior may be designated as "access rituals" (Goffman, 1971: 80).

Whereas ritual is a symbolic attestation of respect and regard, the ex-pression and dramatization of such regard is found in ceremonialization. Thus when two people shake hands while being introduced "a little dance is likely to occur; faces light up, smiles are exchanged, eyes are addressed" (Goffman, 1971: 78). That such actions can be smoothly performed, is indicative of a "focused definition of the situation" (Young, 1970: 298), that is, a manifestation of solidarity. In short, if a ceremony such as handshaking is to appear 'smooth', there must be a coordinated effort between the two performers towards this end; such integration of effort is indicative of solidarity.

Recall however, that the handshake as an access ritual, precedes a period of INCREASED access. Thus, not only will signs of solidarity be required during handshaking itself, but will also be required in the upcoming period of heightened access. The successful completion of the handshake then, constitutes an implicit assurance that the interactions to follow will be similarly coordinated. In other words, if two individuals cannot coordinate their efforts to shake hands with one another, one might suspect that in sustaining a relationship they would be even less able.

One way in which the handshaking ceremony is uncompleted is when one participant ignores the other's outstretched hand. However, that a handshake not be returned is unlikely, because an obligation to respond to what is simultaneously being offered is built into the very process of handshaking. Such an obligatory exchange process, as Mauss (1967: 10) has suggested, is "total prestation". Prestation, or primitive gift exchange, had as its object "a friendly feeling between the two persons concerned, and unless it did this it failed of its purpose ... . No one was free to refuse a present offered to him" (Mauss, 1967: 18). To paraphrase Mauss, total prestation carried with it three obligations: to give presents, to receive them, and to repay them. Such obligations were incurred because the gift, in whatever form, carried along with it a portion of the giver; thus, even when it had been abandoned by him, it still contained a part of him. This provided the giver with some hold over the recipient, obliging him not only to accept the gift, but to offer one in return.

The obligation inherent in handshaking may be understood in much the same way. The interchange that occurs during such an access ritual, would have the following structure:

A: offer
B: accept

Note that in replying to the initial move, B has completed the act that A initiated. If the interchange were verbal, the following utterances might occur:

A: Do you want to come over Saturday night?
B: Sure, great!

Note that in the example, A, in offering access to himself, is requesting access to another. The interchange then, can further be described:

A: request
B: grant

In a handshake, a single initiating action contains both a request for access into another and an offer from that same initiator of access to the self. Thus there is a double presentation in one move. Not only is a request for something being made, but simultaneously, through that same action, an offer of something has been made. Another way of stating the nature of the ceremony is that these access rituals are the empirical side of a transformation of offers into requests, and acceptances into grants. If they did not function in this way, they could not serve as access rituals.

This transformation, whether embedded in gift-giving, utterances, or handshaking, is the fulfillment of the ritual. Since the self is being offered along with the request, then an obligation to grant that request by accepting the offer, is built into the interchange.

The development of the handshake parallels the breakdown of both primitive prestation and of a social structure based on kinship. In modern society, kinship position is no longer the main determinant of social relationships and behavior appropriate to those relationships; status in groups other than the family plays a greater role in determining one's range of contacts and relationships. Thus traditional avoidance signs and joking relationships are replaced, and then re-applied to individuals other than kin. Hat-tipping for example, may be read as a standard avoidance sign (MacCannell, 1973). The handshake is a sign of access and solidarity, similar to primitive prestation, but developed and re-applied beyond it: a handclasp in ancient Greece was a welcoming sign of trust and friendliness, in Medieval Europe, "a sign of mutual trust" (Wildeblood, 1965: 138) between knights and their king, and in the 19th century, a lady's sign of recognition to a gentleman acquaintance. The modern-day handshake serves as introduction, greeting, and farewell.

When so much social information is to be conveyed in a single gesture it is not surprising to find that this gesture, far from being simple, is really quite complex and protected by norms in many of its smallest details. "The proper handshake is made briefly: but there should be a feeling of strength and warmth in the clasp, and as in bowing, one should at the same time look into the countenance of the person whose hand one takes" (Post, 1940: 23). Therefore the handshake is not a side involvement: the complete involvement being signified by the strength and warmth of the clasp and the eye contact. But with too much pressure applied, the handshake may be misread as an offense: "It is annoying to have one's hand clutched aloft in grotesque affectation and shaken violently sideways, as though it were being used to clean a spot out of the atmosphere. What woman does not wince at the viselike grasp that cuts her rings into her flesh and temporarily paralyzes every finger" (Post, 1940: 23). Conversely a " 'boneless' hand, extended as though it were a spray of seaweed or a miniature boiled pudding" (Post, 1940: 23) may result in quite a different misreading, namely that the person is not a worthy end to the access being exchanged, indeed, is not a 'person' at all.

Clearly, the handshaking norms suggested by Emily Post are not heeded by everyone in our population: indeed, Afro-Americans, Southern sharecroppers, Japanese-Americans and 'hippies' in communes, do not shake hands according to blue-book etiquette. More exact specification as to which population does follow such norms, may, as Goffman (1963:5) suggests, "always be checked by research". Generally, however, the code of handshaking discussed in this paper is limited to the American middle class.

From a close examination of how the organization of the occasion and the structure of the relationship can frame the ritual, three types of handshaking can be designated: the collapse, the opener, and the closure.

2.1 *The Collapse*

Here, the occasion is a campaign rally, the relationship, one candidate and innumerable spectators. A crowd of 5,000 is expected and already, news reports are counting closer to 10,000. Everyone at the mall is waiting to see the Presidential candidate due soon to arrive. Amidst the blaring of loudspeakers, security forces clear a path through the crowd, and a single man, until now seen only via mass media, is escorted through. Hands shoot out from all directions to reach him, and as he slowly walks through the crowd, he continually extends both his right and left hands, in an effort to grab as many of those outstretched as possible.

In the campaign rally, there is no actual relationship either prior to, or following the occasion; thus, the entire event has been collapsed into the ritual. Due to the ritual's isolation, it is overly dramatized: both left and right hands are used for shaking, pleasant inquiries as to the other's health are issued repeatedly, and spectators jump, shout, squeal, and grab at the candidate's jacket. The implication is that the effusiveness of the ceremony can make up for the lack of a 'real relationship', and, singly attempt to guarantee that the object of the exchange, votes and policy promises, will be fulfilled.

Although the actualization of the handshake is avidly striven for, if the candidate cannot shake everyone's hands, the structure of the occasion transforms a potential ritual insult into an indication of the candidate's overwhelming popularity. The fact that the hands of many spectators are left dangling provides for the candidate an implicit proof of the extent to which he is 'in demand'. The candidate is more than worthy of having his offering of self accepted by the public; indeed, he is so worthy, that the amount of requests being made has superseded the amount of access available for the candidate to grant. Indeed, as all good political advance men know, it is the 'occasion' that makes the candidate seem popular.

The collapsed handshake of the campaign then, functions as an introduction, a greeting, and a farewell, collapsed into one ritual performance. Since not all occasions and relationships that frame the handshake are as collapsed as the campaign, such bracketing functions are more often spread out within the entire occasion.

2.2 *Openers*

Handshaking may open a focused system of activity for two already related participants. For example, when two former business partners, who are weaving their way through the lunchtime crowd on a downtown street, recognize each other, they stop, shake hands, and exchange inquiries as to the other's health and success in the new company. The implication is that the two participants had not seen each other for some time, and that their chance encounter has become an occasion. Or, when a young man, who is employed by his fiancée's father, enters the father's home for a dinner party, the two shake hands, even though they may have seen each other at work earlier in the day. Here, the implication is that although the two have recently been together, a home-cooked dinner offers MORE ACCESS than an ordinary workday.

The opening handshake in both of these situations functions as an access ritual in three ways: (1) it renews the mutual access previously shared in the relationship, (2) it prepares for the exchange of access which may occur during the immediately following occasion, and (3) it demonstrates that the separation has not damaged the relationship.

However, not every member of every relationship shakes hands with his counterpart at the beginning of every shared occasion. As suggested above, an opening handshake between two related participants is more likely to occur when the period of separation has been lengthier than is usual for that relationship, and/or when the occasion being opened affords more access that is usually shared. In either case, the handshake demonstrates that a relationship has held up in spite of a separation, and that it will be sustained during the heightened amount of access suddenly available. Thus, it is a manifestation of solidarity. This demonstration is carried to its extreme when a separation due to an argument or dis-agreement, had temporarily 'broken' the relationship. 'Shaking and making up' demonstrates that the relationship can be renewed and that access can once again be exchanged along complementary lines.

An interesting variation of the opening handshake occurs when it is not the separation, but the occasion itself, which may appear to threaten the relationship. For instance, if the occasion is a socially organized bout of fighting, such as a wrestling match or a boxing competition, the two participants will 'shake and come out fighting'. Their handshake affirms that they are not really fighting, and are thus expected to dis-continue such activity, as well as the relationship implied by it, when the referee ends the occasion with his whistle.

A second variation occurs when there is no shared activity or oc-casion at all. When it is obvious that the situation will afford no opportu-nities for further access, hands are not shaken. That is, if the two business partners are rushing by one another, to catch buses that are leaving in opposite directions, a nod, smile, wave, or any combination of these, may have to be substituted for a handshake. On the other hand, if the occasion is ambiguous as to a further exchange of access, the opening handshake need not be substituted. Thus, the young man and his fiancée's father need not co-participate in any activity other than co-presence, at dinner, for their handshake to remain an opener. And of course limitations in occasioned access can always be circumvented by the handshake, as when one participant shakes the other's hand, and does not let go, thereby forcing the other to remain, at least physically, in an occasion.

A third variation occurs when an occasion is suddenly reorganized, due to a 'special relationship' or the re-arrangement of situational equipment, to allow even further access. For instance, a man who recognizes an old childhood friend on a city bus, will reach across rows of people and seats to shake his hand, and then, when room is made for the two to sit on the same seat, will shake his hand again. In some cases, of course, even the handshake may not provide sufficient renewal, as when, for example, two long-lost brothers find themselves re-united and hug, kiss, cry, and promise never to separate again.

Opening handshakes may initiate not only an occasion, but a relationship as well, as when two professors are introduced by a third. Since there is no previous relationship being renewed, this handshake is purely future-oriented: it opens both an immediate occasion and a potential relationship, but closes no separation. Its function is more limited in some respects than the handshake between two related participants. However, since this handshake may open a RELATIONSHIP, there is a new dimension being added to the opening function, and its dramatic potential has increased. Thus not only are hands shaken, but eyes light up, smiles are exchanged, pleasant inquiries about the other's health are made, and one's own delight in participation is expressed: "Nice to meet you". Even the main occasion has been put aside for awhile.

The introductory handshake then, is more dramatic than the mere greeting, but less dramatic than the campaign. Campaign handshaking rarely precedes an actual relationship, and must therefore compress the recognition normally saved for a relationship into the ritual. It is pure drama. Whereas the collapsed handshake of the campaign is introduction, greeting, relationship, and farewell all packed into one ritual, the introductory handshake leaves room for another round of dramatization. Even at cocktail parties, where relationships are notoriously fleeting, hands may be shaken both at the beginning and the end of a round of conversation. And of course two individuals may suddenly discover that they attended the same college, or that they share an interest in the novels of Jacquelyn Susann, thereby refocusing their encounter, re-organizing the occasion, and redirecting it towards a future relationship: "Well, listen, why don't you come over some time?" "Okay, sure. What's your phone number?"

As a sign of solidarity, introductory handshakes have no recourse to previous definitions of the relationship, and thus nothing on which to base a future. Only minimal criteria provided by the immediate setting can be relied upon: physical characteristics (age, sex, race), specifically stated social identity ("This is my brother-in law.") and the nature of the occasion that has brought about co-presence (a wedding reception, a board meeting). Since such indicators guide the organization of the occasion, and the structure of the relationship, they also guide the performance of the ritual.

Young people, for instance, shake hands when being introduced, but not when being greeted. Relationships are opened, but not sustained, according to adult standards, providing a demonstration that a ten-year-old will someday be able to participate as an adult, but not yet.

By far, the most frequent restriction occurs in the cross-sexed handshake; in fact, this handshake is a rare occurrence. Emily Post (1940: 11) suggests that "when gentlemen are introduced to each other, they always shake hands", but that "when a gentleman is introduced to a lady ... it is her place to offer her hand or not". With 'gentlemen' then, either may initiate the handshake, and in fact, it is a duty to do so, but between a 'lady' and a 'gentleman', it is the 'lady's' choice.

It seems that the incumbent of a role which has duties attached to it may find that in fulfilling those duties, some amount of status or power has been attached to them, and is thus being automatically imputed to him. In adhering to the dutiful act of shaking hands then, the man has merely slipped into the position of worth previously designated as his. When the same act is a PRIVILEGE however, the worth that was previously designated as intrinsic to that act as a duty, also becomes transformed into a privilege. Since women do not incur the responsibility of fulfilling that duty and are not expected to, neither are they automatically expected to be worthy incumbents of the same situational role. Suppose a woman does extend her hand for a handshake. Then, she is assuming upon herself a designation of worth not already implied in the role, and more importantly, by submitting herself as a worthy participant, has been committed to a position not dutifully hers.[1]

If the relationship being initiated is egalitarian, that is, both ends are of equal worth, one might expect each interactant to participate at a relatively equal level of activeness or passiveness. Since men always shake hands WITH EACH OTHER, the relationship between them is one of relative equality. Since their participation is equally dramatic, the worth and power of these two interactants is being mutually celebrated. But when one of the interactants is a woman, who has the choice of participating

---

[1] Interestingly, middle-class European women always shake hands with men, suggesting that neither the occasion nor the position is as tightly bound as Americans might believe.

at a lesser level of dramatization in that same ceremony, then nothing implicitly guarantees to her the same amount of worth and power.

Indeed, since it is the woman's prerogative to offer her hand or not, the relationship being initiated already seems to be one of unequal status. Furthermore, even after the relationship has been in progress, "a woman should always allow a man who is only an acquaintance to shake her hand; she should never shake his. To a very old friend she gives a much firmer clasp, but he shakes her hand more than she shakes his" (Post, 1940: 24).

However, if the man extends his right hand first, thereby attributing worth to the woman not inherently demanded by the situation, the woman "of course gives him hers. Nothing could be more ill-bred than to treat any spontaneous friendliness curtly" (Post, 1940: 11). And nothing could be more conducive to a breakdown of either the relationship or the occasion, than to deny an assignation of worth that has been made to oneself, by not accepting another's offering of access to his self, and simultaneously, to deny the other's demonstration of his own worth, by not granting the other's request for access to one's own self.

2.3 *Closures*

Handshaking may close a focused system of shared activity, ending when the two participants take leave of one another. As Goffman (1971: 88) suggests, the main orientation of a farewell is to "the sharp decrease that is about to occur in the possibility of such comings-to-gether again occurring — at least for a time". As an access ritual, a farewell handshake is (1) an acknowledgement that the two individuals have just shared heightened access in a spate of activity together, and (2) an indication that such access may extend over the period of separation to be renewed in future occasions.

Closing handshakes then, need to be considered in light of the decrease in access about to occur, relative to the access normally shared in the relationship, and to the access recently shared in the occasion. For example, the young man, when departing from the dinner party given by his fiancée's father, shakes hands with his host, since the amount of access shared in dinner has been more than is normally shared at work. But "intimate friends rarely shake hands" (Post, 1940: 23), either when greeting or taking leave of one another, since their being 'intimate' entails their being able to frequently participate in occasions of high access. And finally, if the amount of access shared in the occasion is less than that normally shared in the relationship, as when two friends have a 'big fight' and do not talk to each other for the rest of the night, the decrease in access within the occasion may even preclude any further access or relationship. Thus the closing handshake could be accompanied by a "Good evening, Sir!", or it could be replaced by an 'exit', or no farewell at all, each of which would indicate just what kind of access was supposed to be shared, was in fact shared, and will NOT BE SHARED in the future.

2.4 *Deviants*

Like any bit of social behavior, handshaking collects its deviants: those who nod, smile, or wave, when being introduced, greeted, or bade farewell to. Before such gestures can be definitely established as functional equivalents however, a semiotic of 'substitutes' would have to be constructed. The problem lies in finding the exact form in which functional surrogates are exhibited, and establishing that the contexts are, in fact, the same. Acts that sometimes APPEAR to be substitutes actually do not occur in the exact situation. Generally, differences lie in the amount of access that is available and required for the interaction to begin, and the degree of solidarity that is available and required for the interaction to continue. Other acts that seem to be substitutes are limited to certain bounded subgroups, for example, the military, ethnic, or racial: the brisk salute between two Nazi commandoes, the double-cheeked kiss between two Italian brothers, the 'soul shake' between two Afro-Americans.

It is, however, implicit in the nature of encounters, occasions, and gatherings that an exchange of personal access is required for them to occur at all. If it is not handshaking that opens access, then something else, nods, smiles, or waves, must serve this function.

3. CONCLUSION

In the above remarks, a semiotic of handshaking has been proposed. It has been suggested that the handshake functions as a manifestation of the access and solidarity normally required for everyday social occasions and relationships. The handshake though, is but one example of the broader category of access rituals. In Saussure's terms, the handshake is merely a SIGNIFIER, through which an exchange of access and a focused bond of solidarity are SIGNIFIED. Thus the SIGN, that is, the combination of signifier and signified into a whole greater than either one of its parts, is the ritual ceremony, in particular, the access ritual.

The approach suggested by this paper however, is easily open for misinterpretation, namely that a particular instance of handwork, be it a grasp, a wave, or a handshake, will begin to carry a meaning all its own. Such an ethnography of handwork, although acknowledging cultural or even situational relativity, nevertheless becomes a dictionary of meaning. The approach suggested in this study surpasses the labelling of specific hand gestures, whether for inherently expressed meaning, or for some sort of symbolic meaning. Thus, rather than focusing initially on the meaning of handwork, we began with the organization of outside events in which the handwork is embedded. Once the overall organization is broken down, and layers of meaning are peeled away, handwork becomes more amenable to analysis as but another aspect of an ongoing social performance, as well as a social act in its own right. So the question of primary importance is not, what does handwork mean, but WHAT IS THE STRUCTURE OF AN ENVIRONMENT IN WHICH HANDWORK FUNCTIONS that gives a piece of handwork its meaning.

In order to grasp this point, it may be helpful to consider the meaning of social performances in general. The groundwork for the performance of a social act is laid out in the nature of the specific situation. A comparable delineation of the MEANING of the social situation however, is nowhere as readily available. Note then, that meaning is NOT dependent upon a collective interpretation of the situation that is rooted in a cohesive community of symbolic understandings.

With meaning thus separated from norms and from collective internalizations of them, what then would generate a responding move to the initial performance? The answer is in part meaning, but only insofar as this meaning is considered to reside in the relationships between various moves, or various performances, and the ways in which the totality of these are embedded in their social framework. Hence, what becomes seen as abnormal, improper, inappropriate, or MEANINGLESS, is a response that is incongruous in its relations to other events in the situation. Of course this leaves performances wide open for misreadings and uncertainties, but it is that ambiguity that makes the demand for social rituals more immediate.

How does handwork fit specifically into this realm? The answer is twofold. First, handwork is a part of a social performance when that performance is viewed *in toto*. It is an act, embedded in the context of the total scene. But when the scene is analyzed, with each unit described as to its place in the dramaturgy of events, then each unit can be broken down further into subunits. These subunits are also naturally occurring social units, and therefore they are just as viable as a unit of social organization in themselves, and subject to the same type of analysis.

In this perspective, handwork is now seen in its second mode, as a social fact, a social performance in its own right. Although it is never isolated from its context in meaning, if it is temporarily removed, for purposes of analysis, from a series of structurally alike situations in which it usually occurs, the function of the handwork as a social fact becomes clearer.

Handwork then, becomes visible as a vital 'sub-performance' within those encompassing situations, vital as a ritual move. It is both contributing to the meaning of the overall performance, yet organized enough to be considered as a social performance on its own. After all, when social performances are broken down, they become merely an organization of sub-performances, interrelated through certain occasions and relationships in structures, all of which give the social performance its meaning as ritual.

Activities such as handshaking may still appear mundane to the casual observer, or may even be attributed to 'rules of etiquette' by those who fancy themselves more astute. An examination of the 'casual', the 'commonplace' and the 'natural', can be revealing, and analyzing the meaning of such phenomena in their role of ritual ceremony is hoped to provide a line of inquiry that others will follow.

REFERENCES

Goffman, Erving
    1961   *Encounters* (New York: Bobbs-Merrill).
    1963   *Behavior in Public Places* (New York: Free Press).
    1967   "The Nature of Deference and Demeanor", in: *Interaction Ritual* (New York: Anchor Books), 47-95.
    1971   "Supportive Interchanges" in: *Relations in Public* (New York: Basic Books), 62-94.
MacCannell, Dean
    1973   "A Note on Hat Tipping", *Sémiotica* 7: 4, 300-12.
Mauss, Marcel
    1967   *The Gift* (New York: Norton Library).
Post, Emily
    1940   *Etiquette: The Blue Book of Social Usage* (New York: Funk and Wagnall).

Wildeblood, Joan
    1965   *The Polite World* (Oxford: Oxford University Press).
Young, Frank
    1970   "Reactive Subsystems", *American Sociological Review* 72, 297-308.

Deborah Schiffrin (b. 1951, USA) is a graduate student in the Sociology department of Temple University, Philadelphia. Her research interests are urban ethnography and comparative social organization.

ALTON J. DE LONG

Kinesic Signals at Utterance Boundaries in Preschool Children*

1.0 INTRODUCTION

The accommodation of the human animal to his social and physical environment is a process of increasing importance in a crowded, heterogeneous, urban environment.

The redundancy and predictability inherent in the recurrent patterns that characterize human communication have been documented across a variety of systems including paralinguistic (Trager, 1958), linguistic (Dinneen, 1967), kinesic (Birdwhistell, 1970), proxemic (Hall, 1968) and environmental (Barker, 1968; Willems, 1973). In addition, the incredible amount of sharing that takes place during communication applies not only to the discrete properties (i.e., classes of behavior) but to the continuous properties (i.e., the segmentation of the temporal continuum) as well (Condon and Ogston, 1967).

The communication process itself seems generically conservative, related in part to the evolutionary properties and emergence of the neurologic substrates (MacLean, 1967; Esser, 1972); and the importance of the small group in mammalian evolution (Hamburg, 1963; Calhoun, 1971; Esser, 1971). The short-circuiting of the ongoing communication process through the violation of expectancies both in terms of tactics (permissible order) and in terms of emics (appropriate classes) leads to the interruption of behavior. As Hall (1964) has suggested, such interruptions can have

---

* This paper is based on portions of a Doctoral dissertation of the same title submitted through the Division of Man-Environment Relations, Pennsylvania State University, September, 1972.

potentially disastrous consequences. The interruption of the behavioral sequence leads to emotional states which 'shut down' the organism, and gives him time to assess the uncertain situation (Pribram, 1967; Esser, 1972). If emotion can be viewed as the 'stop' mechanism, and motivation as the 'go' mechanism (Pribram, 1971), then communication can legitimately be viewed as a continual indication to the organism that it is 'safe to proceed'. It would seem that very fundamental properties of the communication process are closely related to the motivation-emotion mechanisms; and that communication itself provides the basis for mediation between the two states (Hall and Trager, 1953; McBride, 1964; De Long, 1972).

This poses potentially serious obstacles to the process of interpersonal accommodation, especially when accommodation is attempted across group boundaries; whether they be ethnic, subcultural or cultural. In a multifaceted, pluralistic society the entry of the child into the school environment underscores the importance of interpersonal accommodation, particularly in view of the fact that his previous experiences are normally confined to rather narrowly constrained homogeneous groups. In the early school environment, particularly within the urban context, it is quite likely the young child will be brought into contact with children from ethnic and/or subcultural groups he has no prior experience with. Given the estimate by Birdwhistell (1970) that as much as 65 % of the overall communication process may be related to nonverbal behavior — behavior which for the most part occurs entirely out-of-awareness — the accommodation process cannot be casually assumed and expected to be mediated principally by the enormous flexibility of the small child. The criticality of the accommodation process across group boundaries in the heterogeneous, early school environment would seem more evident if out-of-awareness communication patterns, such as aspects of kinesic signaling, could be shown to be reliably and predictably present before the child enters school, since the existence of such patterns constitute expectancies which if violated could short-circuit interpersonal accommodation processes and make intergroup communication tenuous.

The general question we have set out to investigate is simply, "Is the process of interpersonal accommodation during early school experience significantly affected and influenced by the prior internalization of out-of-awareness communication patterns?" An empirical answer, of course, requires several logical steps. First, do preschool children exhibit recurrent, internalized patterns of communicational behavior which occur out-of-awareness? Second, do these patterns vary across group boundaries? And third, do such differences interfere with, or short-circuit the accommodation process?

This paper deals empirically with the first step. Future research efforts will deal with the second and third steps.

2.0 STATEMENT OF PROBLEM

The delineation of the problem studied grew out of preliminary observations on interpersonal transactions among preschool children. Initially, the investigator set out to study the proxemic aspects of preschool transactions, such as body orientation, eye behavior, and spacing mechanisms. It soon became rather apparent, however, that contrary to popular stereotype, preschool children seldom interrupted one another. For the most part, observations among four and five year old children indicated that transactions went rather smoothly. Normally, a child played either the role of speaker or listener; and the exchange of these roles seemed a fairly congenial affair.

Now the value of this is easily overlooked. It is not at all clear why such transitions should be made smoothly and without difficulty. For it is not enough to simply know that someone else has stopped talking. There are numerous occasions in which people stop talking; but are not finished and, in fact, intend to continue. Some of these are unequivocally marked through the use of linguistic junctures and intonation contours; but others are not, and the question of how people know when their partner is finished speaking comes clearly to the fore.

If such boundaries in the transaction are not always clearly marked linguistically, then given the fact that disruptive interruptions are as rare as they are, they must be marked nonverbally. The efficient regulation, then, of speaker and listener roles, it can be hypothesized, is related to kinesic signaling at some level, presumably related to utterance boundaries. Additionally, if we are concerned generically with the accommodation process there is another advantage to looking for kinesic signals at the level of utterances. It is extremely unlikely that such signals would be associated with linguistic units the size of the word or smaller since linguistic-kinesic integration at those levels may well be under bioelectric control which means that all human organisms should be synchronously integrated once they begin interacting. And it seems clear that when interactants employ different linguistic and kinesic systems during a transaction, floor yielding signals are consistently missed. (W. S. Condon, personal communication, 1971). Evidently, temporal segmentation is not adequate. Therefore, we can expect such kinesic signaling to relate more to recurrent classes of movement which act as cues during the transactions.

In connection with this line of reasoning, a preliminary study was conducted analyzing, in a crude manner, the body movements of two four year old girls interacting with a teacher. The results, which will be discussed later, suggested that preschool children do, in fact, exhibit significant regularities in their kinesic behavior prior to and following verbalization. But since the sample was extremely restricted, and because work was conducted with video equipment which severely limits analytic flexibility, it was decided a more careful analysis was in order.

2.1 *Research Procedure*

2.1.1 *Sample*
The sample selected for the present study consisted of eight preschool children, of whom six were enrolled in the preschool nursery program in the College of Human Development at the Pennsylvania State University. The subsample from the nursery school contained two four year old males and four five year olds of whom two were male. The two additional subjects were preschool males, ages four and five, WITH NO PREVIOUS PRESCHOOL EXPERIENCE. There existed no preliminary selection criteria other than the stipulation that the children be between four and five years of age.

2.1.2 *Data Collection*
Raw data were collected by means of video tape recording utilizing a standard Panasonic 'video-corder' unit with 1/2″ tape. Subjects were seated in pairs at a rectangular table in full view of the television camera which was located in one corner of the room approximately 20 feet away. The camera was tripod mounted at a height of 5′-0″. The remaining video equipment was situated behind a screen to the right of the subjects and out of their view. During data collection, the investigator remained behind the screen monitoring the tape equipment. The environmental setting employed in data collection is shown in Fig. 1.

Preliminary to the taping, subjects were informed they would 'play a game'. They were given several nondescript blocks of wood varying in size and shape and asked to tell each other what they had, and additionally to make up a story about their pieces. The ensuing dialogue was then

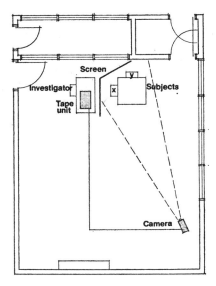

Fig. 1. Environmental setting.

taped. The average time of this task was approximately ten minutes. Subjects were informed they were being taped, and after each session the tape was played back for their viewing.

Raw data were then edited onto another tape with long stretches of silence and inactivity deleted. Prime consideration in the editing was governed by the desire to select those segments which were characterized by verbal and interactional spontaneity between subjects.

The final, edited tape was then played back through the video system in a dark room and filmed directly from the monitor with an Eastman Kodak Reflex 16 mm camera with a wild motor and a sound recording head in the camera. The motor was manually adjusted to approximately 30 frames per second in order to synchronize with the televised image. Film used was +X reversal, magnetic striped.

The final data used for analysis, then, consisted of sound film segments of each pair of subjects more or less spontaneously describing and discussing the blocks they had been given. In these sequences all subjects participated both as speaker and listener so that observations could be made regarding the regulation and transition from one role to the other under spontaneous circumstances.

2.1.3 *Data Analysis*

The equipment necessary for the micro analysis of the sound film data consisted of a standard 202 series 16 mm Bell and Howell sound projector modified with a handcrank assembly (four frames per sweep). This projector permits the manual control of the direction and speed of film movement so that segments of film of any length can be viewed and reviewed as many times as necessary to permit the detailed notation of body movements.

Data transcription involved two procedures. First, tapes were reviewed until all verbal content was transcribed phonemically. It was necessary to get this material from the tapes since the sound films were recorded at 30 frames per second but can be played back through the projector at only 24 frames per second. When the verbal notation was complete for each child, body movements were transcribed and correlated with the verbal record.

The transcription of body movement included the notation of eight basic movements across eight parts of the body. Basic movements recorded included up, down, left, right, forward, backward, and the tilting left and right of the head. Parts of the body transcribed were the head, left arm (forearm and upper arm), left hand, fingers of left hand, right arm, right hand, fingers of right hand and the trunk. While the quality of the film was good for observing movements in the above parts, it was not satisfactory for the consistent observation of eye behavior. Leg movements were occasionally noticeable, but generally the obstruction of the table where subjects were seated precluded notation of lower body segments.

Body parts were transcribed separately throughout utterances, so that all head movements were recorded before left arm movements were recorded, etc. The temporal correlation between body movement and speech is approximate since film frames were not numbered. Additionally there was some sound loss and distortion as a result of the transference of taped data to film. While these limitations would be crucial for a study of the precise synchronization of sound and movement, they are not particularly serious in the context of the present study. In the former, as Condon has shown, patterned regularities consist of points of change; and precise correlations in time become paramount. In the present study, however, the examination for patterned regularities is concerned with recurring configurations of movement, i.e., classes of movement, which are consistently related to the initiation and termination of verbalization. The important factor thus becomes the transcription of recurring patterns of movement. Precise temporal correlations become a secondary factor. Even so, the correlation between speech and movement within this study, while only approximate, is nonetheless tolerably close.

The segments transcribed in detail consist of 34 utterances which involve 24 changes in speaker and listener roles.

Data analysis from the transcribed notation of body movements was conducted by means of tracing paper overlays, in which the distribution across utterances of each type of movement were checked as well as configurations of movements. Typically, the data of one subject at a time were carefully analyzed for potential configurational patterns. Such patterns were then treated as working hypotheses and checked against the data of other subjects for verification. This process was continued until the range of hypotheses was considerably reduced and it was possible to begin considering types of movements and locations (i.e., sources) of movement which appeared mandatory at utterance boundaries. A sample of the raw transcribed data is shown in Fig. 2, and its overlay counterpart for leftward and rightward movements is shown in Fig. 3.

	ə i s	i z	ðɛr	ər	+uw	brɑwnz
Head	r	b r	r u,r		tl d tl	l,f d,l
L. Arm		u r			b,u b	
L. Hand			m m l		d u b d	d
Fingers						
R. Arm	u		d r		f	
R. Hand	u		d m r	b	u,b,d f	b b,r
Fingers						
Trunk		b r			b tl tw f	

tw= twisting, m= multidirectional motion

Fig. 2. Transcription of raw data.

	ə i s	i z	ðɛr	ər	+uw	brɑwnz
Head	R	R R R		L	L L L
L. Arm		R				
L. Hand				L		
Fingers						
R. Arm		R				
R. Hand						R
Fingers						
Trunk		R			L	

Fig. 3. Overlay distribution of left and right movements.

3.0 RESULTS

Preschool children in the present sample kinesically signal their intentions to terminate verbalization in several distinct ways. Additionally, verbal pausation such as an intention to change content during speech or the pausing to think about what will be said next is also marked kinesically. There did not seem to be any clear signaling related to the intention to initiate verbalization which was entirely consistent across all subjects. This seems compatible with the finding that kinesic activity increases as the utterance progresses so that relatively more movement is observed near the end of utterances than at the beginning.

3.1 *Termination Signals*

Termination of utterances is marked by a configuration of movement some of which is mandatory and some of which is optional. This leads to several types of signaling that may be employed during transactions. Further, such signals characteristically occupy certain positions relative to the overall utterance.

Three positions have been identified: postverbal, usually immediately following the termination of the utterance; final word position; and penultimate word position. Two movements have been identified that must occur if termination is to be signaled, and they must occur in tightly clustered bundles, usually simultaneously or in rapid succession. The first is a leftward movement of the head. While additional leftward movements in other parts of the body may also occur, examination of the corpus indicates that a leftward movement in the head must be present. The second movement is a downward shift which can occur in the head, arms or hands, individually or in any combination.

Additionally, these movements can be organized in several different ways. They can occur in rapid succession in the head, which we can refer to as SUCCESSIVE SIGNALING; or they can occur SIMULTANEOUSLY in different parts of the body. Successive and simultaneous signaling are often combined in various ways such that simultaneous signaling may occur successively or successive signaling in one body part may be repeated several times, or successive signaling may be followed by simultaneous signaling and *vice versa*.

Finally, one other phenomenon has been noted in connection with termination signaling. Occasionally one will find a 'massing' of specific movements across many body parts such that most of the body is moving in the same direction. With respect to termination boundaries, only leftward, downward, and backward massing have been observed. While still unclear, it seems that massing left or down may be sufficient by itself to signal termination. In the illustrations that follow, analysis has been concentrated on identifying configurations of movement associated with utterance position. Timing factors have not been examined, and since film frames are unnumbered the figures that follow do not incorporate information on temporal segmentation.

To illustrate these findings we will consider signaling according to position. Taking the postverbal signaling first we see three examples in Fig. 4. In the first, the child says, "But that's not brown crayon."

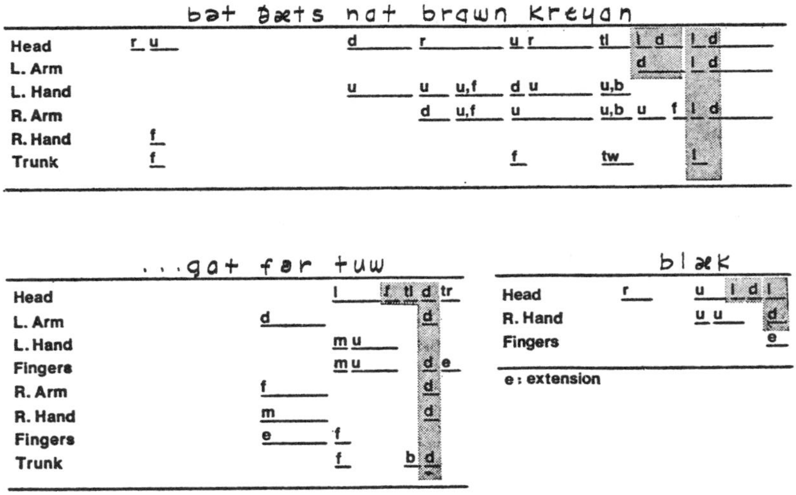

Fig. 4. Termination signals in postverbal position.

After finishing the word *crayon* he moves his head left and his left arm down (simultaneous) followed by a downward movement of the head (successive). This, in turn, is followed by successive left and downward movements in the head and both arms. In this example there exist four cases of successive signaling (two in the head) and one case of simultaneous signaling, all tightly clustered immediately following the utterance. The child with whom he is interacting then responds to the statement.

In the second example we find successive signaling in the head following the final word, *too*. In addition, the downward movement of the head is accompanied by a general massing of downward movements across body parts including the trunk and legs. In this case, then, termination is marked in two ways: first, through successive head movements, and second, through the massing of downward movements simultaneous with the down in the head.

Finally, in the third example we have a one word utterance, "Black". Here too, we find two signals. First, a successive signal in the head followed secondly by a simultaneous signaling involving a left in the head and a down in the right hand.

A more extended utterance is included in Fig. 5 to illustrate the lack of signals at a phrasal boundary when verbalization is intended to continue. The child is saying "… and this is a doggy, and this is a giraffe." Though a left and down configuration exists during the first phrase, it comes prior to penultimate position, occurring across "… this …" On the last word of the final phrase a left of the head occurs across the first syllable and a down right at the end of the word. But these two are not contiguously successive, being separated by a tilting right of the head. After the final word, however, we find a noninterrupted succession of down and left. Further, with the left of the head we simultaneously find a down in the left arm. Slight repositioning movements then occur, and we again find a left in the head simultaneous with a downward movement in the right hand. In this case we find a successive signal in the head followed by two simultaneous signals.

Signaling in the postverbal position, as shown by these examples, consists of more signaling than is minimally necessary; involving the combination of various types of signaling whether it be the combination of successive signals (example 1), successive + massing (example 2),

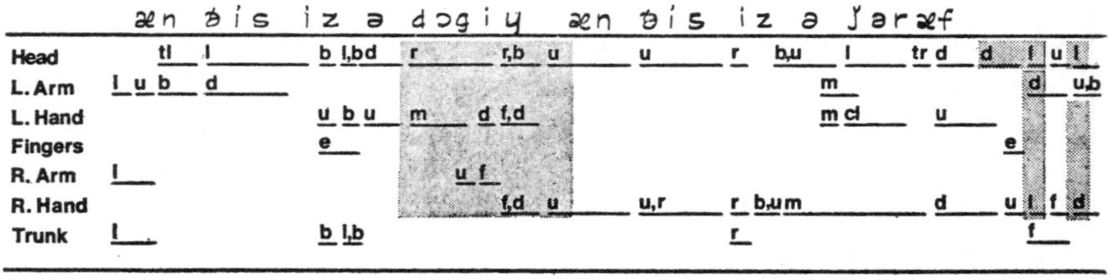

Fig. 5. Absence and presence of termination signals at phrasal boundaries.

successive + simultaneous (example 3) or successively simultaneous (example 4).

In the final position we can consider the three examples shown in Fig. 6 as being characteristic. In the first case, the child says, "This, this is a elephant." On the last word we find a leftward tilting of the head and a left in the left hand. This is immediately followed by a simultaneous left in the head and downward movements in the right arm and hand.

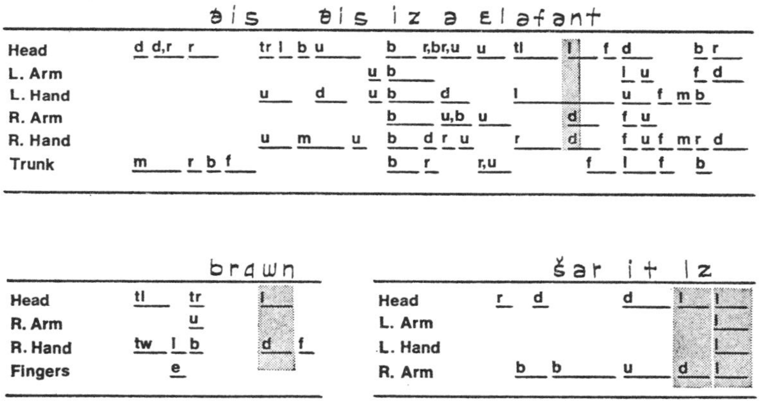

Fig. 6. Termination signals in final position.

In the second example we again have a one word utterance, "Brown", in which we find a left of the head and a down in the right hand across part of the vowel.

In the final example of final position signaling we have the short utterance, "Sure it is." Here we get a simultaneous signal on the final word followed by postverbal leftward massing. In contrast with the organization of termination signals we saw in the postverbal situation, with final position signaling there seems a tendency for more reliance on simultaneous signals, i.e., a left in the head concurrent with a down in other body parts.

Penultimate structuring seems again characteristic though this may be fortuitous, a function of the present sample. Examples of penultimate signals are illustrated in Fig. 7. In the first case, "I got a putty cat, too", we find successive signaling in the head (tilt left + down) followed by left over the final word in both the head and the left hand. In the

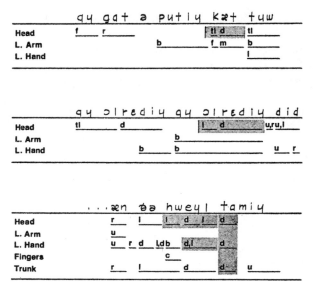

Fig. 7. Termination signals in penultimate position.

second example, "I already, I already did", we similarly find successive signaling in the head. In the last case we have the phrase, "... and the whale, Tommy". Here we find simultaneously occurring successive signaling in both the head and left hand followed by downward massing over the final word. Additionally, although it is initiated prior to the penultimate position, we also find a successive configuration of left and down in the trunk and left hand. After completing this phrase, the subject makes explicit his desire to terminate by a repetition of content, saying to his partner, "I got a whale!" His partner then takes the floor. But the interesting facet, even though unquestionably tentative, is the exclusive use of successive signals across the penultimate position.

We find the suggestive occurrence of successive signaling across the penultimate position, simultaneous signaling in final position, and combinations of the two postverbally. Regardless of position and with the exception of massing, the leftward movement in the head is mandatory, and is the only such body-part-specific movement uncovered. Taken together, this might suggest that the earlier signaling must involve both left and downward movements in the head. That this might be less than fortuitous seems reasonable if we consider the tendency of middle class whites to pay attention to eye behavior while listening (Kendon,

1967). Signals sent penultimately, i.e., during the verbal process would probably be less likely missed if they were located in head movement, since the listener will be intermittently gazing at the speaker's head. Upon completion, however, there is a tendency for the listener to look away and down which means that movement in the arms and hands would be more effective in signaling intention to yield the floor. Additionally, with the postverbal signals, there seems a great deal more redundancy present, particularly in contrast with the penultimate position. Such redundancy might well be related to shifting visual behavior on the part of the listener. Such redundancy could conceivably be related to changing eye behavior patterns in the listener since the probability of such cues being received would seemingly decrease if the listener dropped or shifted his gaze away from the speaker. Of course, the latter interpretation must remain speculative, since redundancy in communication systems is the norm rather than the exception.

To say that intention to terminate verbalization, willingness to yield the floor, is signaled by downward and leftward movements does not mean that every time a left in the head is accompanied by a down in the head or in other parts of the body the speaker intends to terminate. All it means is that when a speaker wants to terminate the types of movements previously described, it will occur in one of the three positions outlined. While this may seem paradoxical, it is not, as a simple linguistic example will show. In spoken English plurals are marked in a variety of ways. Two of the principal methods consist of adding /-s/ and /-z/ to the form to be pluralized. Thus with forms ending in voiceless consonants we add /-s/ and those ending in voiced consonants received /-z/. An example of the former is *hats*, of the latter *dogs*. But, as we all know, every form which ends in either /-s/ or /-z/ is not necessarily a plural. *Has* is not a plural form, nor are *bus* or *buzz*. And native speakers of English find no insurmountable confusion in signaling pluralization because nonpluralized forms often end in /-s/ or /-z/.

Returning to our discussion, for the tightly clustered display of left and down movements to signal intention to terminate, they must be DISTRIBUTED in one of the three positions previously discussed. An example which contains clustered leftward and downward movements that are irrelevant to termination is shown in Fig. 8. Here we have a child saying, "I'm gonna draw Johnny because he's brown ..." At the beginning we find a clear left and down in the head. Similarly, in the middle of the utterance we find left tilting in the head and a left in the hand. Finally, in postverbal position there is a slight left in the head, but no accompany-

·ɑɥn gənə dʰɔ ʃɑniɥ biɥkəz hiɥz brɑɯn...

Head	l d	u	tr f	d,f		tl	tl b	b	l
R. Arm			m u		m			r	
R. Hand							l	m	
Trunk			tw f		f			b	

Fig. 8. Left and down movements not signaling termination.

ing downward movements. The child pauses briefly, and then continues his utterance with, "I'm gonna draw you Johnny 'cause you're brown." In postverbal position following the utterance there are both simultaneous and successive termination signaling.

The examination of sections of utterances where speaker-listener transitions are not smoothly conducted reinforces our previous analysis. An utterance involving a significant delay, for example, between the end of the verbalization and signal emission is shown in Fig. 9. The child initially says, "No it isn't, I'll shown you what's brown." On the last word he tilts his head left without emitting accompanying downward signals. Following his head movements over the next several seconds we find intermittent lefts and down, but they are not tightly clustered. The other child remains silent. Finally, after no less than an eight second delay, we find left and downward successive signaling in the head. IMMEDIATELY FOLLOWING, the other child takes the floor and begins speaking.

. . . ɑɥl ʃoɯ ɥuɯ hwəts brɑɯn

Head	u	f			u		b	tl	b u f d		f r b tl d	
L. Arm	u						f		e b	8 sec. delay		
L. Hand	b d f			m	f			f			l	
Fingers			e			m						

Fig. 9. Postverbal termination signals following a long delay.

Observations with the present data and earlier data of a slightly different nature indicate that interruptions among preschool children when interacting with each other tend to be extremely rare. There is one such interruption in the present data, and its specific location is worth examining. The speaker says, "And this, this is a upside-down cake. Uh, that's a putty cat. And this." The listener interrupts after the speaker completes *this*. In Fig. 10 the kinesic accompaniment for a section of the verbalization is shown. Interestingly, at the point immediately preceding the interruption the speaker moves down across several body parts and emits a succession of downs and left in the head. Now examination of the kinesic behavior of the interruptor suggests that she is clearly aware of the fact that she has interrupted the speaker — her behavior is markedly constrained kinesically compared to her other utterances. She penultimately signals the termination of her brief utterance, and the original speaker continues smoothly. Reviewing of this transaction impresses one with how smoothly the interruption is conducted. What seems particularly odd, is the location of the interruption. One would normally suppose a more logical point for interruption would be after *cat*, which constitutes a logical semantic boundary. Instead, the interruption closely follows the clustering of left and downward movements in the head, arm, and hand.

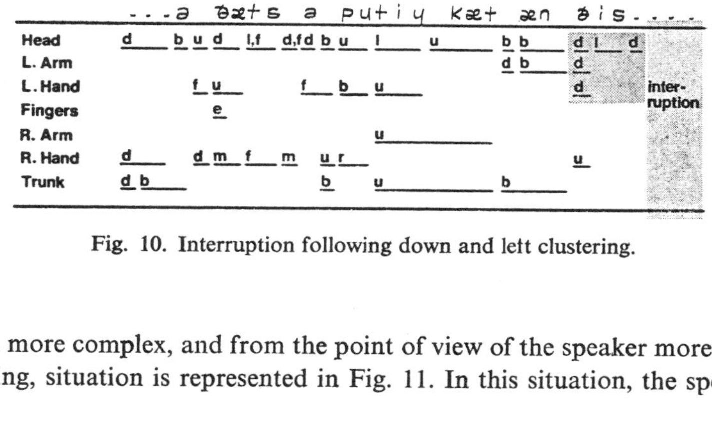

Fig. 10. Interruption following down and left clustering.

A more complex, and from the point of view of the speaker more frustrating, situation is represented in Fig. 11. In this situation, the speaker

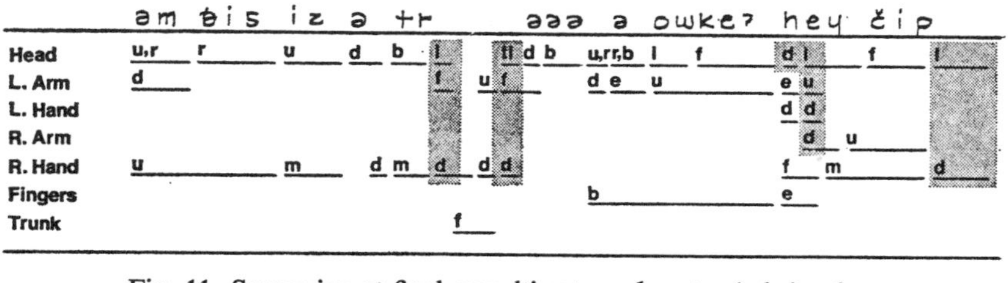

Fig. 11. Succession of final, penultimate and postverbal signals indicating a desire to yield the floor.

is clearly confused. He begins by uttering. "Um, this comes apart", after which he pauses briefly and changes to, "Um, this is a tr." He then changes content again with, "Uuuuh, uh, okay", after which he again pauses and looks frustrated. Finally, he utters, "Hey Chip", to his partner. Throughout this utterance the speaker is looking at and fondling a block, apparently trying to determine what it is. His confusion seems in part reflected by the presence of all three types of signaling across this utterance. First, we find a final position signal consisting of two successive simultaneous signals following "... tr." Across the next utterance he is clearly confused. He then signals penultimately across the word *Hey*, and again signals immediately after *Chip*. His partner comes in following the last set of signals. One gets the distinct impression that the speaker fully intended to yield the floor following his first set of final position signals. The speaker has unsuccessfully tried to signal termination (once in final position and once in penultimate position) before relying on explicit verbal content, "Hey, *Chip* (help me out)", and the kinesic postverbal signaling. The speaker is obviously frustrated and signals his frustration by multiply emitting termination patterns.

In connection with this example, there are indications that intention to signal termination is partially independent of decisions made on the verbal level, or at least occurs prior to decisions on the verbal level. In other words, the child may make his decision to kinesically signal termination prior to final verbal decisions. For example, in Fig. 12 we find a child changing his mind at the very last second regarding what he says. He says, "I'm draw this col, John that's braw, this is black." In this sequence he changes his mind twice, both at the last moment. First, he obviously interrupts his chain of thought on the first syllable of *color*, since he does not complete the second syllable. Despite this change, however, it appears that he had earlier made the decision to terminate his verbalization since we clearly find penultimate kinesic signals occurring across "... this ..." He seems to have changed his mind regard-

	...ðiŝ kəl	Jɑn ɓæts brɑʍ	ðiŝ iz blæk
Head	d tl d	tl r	f d d.l tl u b tr l d
R. Arm	l d l	b d	d d u u,f f d u
R. Hand		d m	f d u d
Trunk	f	m b	l b

Fig. 12. Penultimate, final and postverbal signals associated with changes in verbal content.

ing the particular color of the crayon he was going to use and proceeds now to inform his partner the crayon is brown. But he again changes his mind and does not complete what appears to have been intended the penultimate word, *brown*. Again, however, we find kinesic signals which would suggest he intended to terminate his utterance. Finally, he makes his last decision, "... this is black", and signals postverbally, and is followed by his partner.

It should be noted that the types of discontinuities or pauses we have just examined are not the cause of the termination signals. Rather, it seems the child genuinely intended to end his verbalization. This seems clear from other utterances by the same child in which he pauses, does not emit termination signals, and goes on for extensive, additional verbalization. Pausal phenomena and the accompanying signals will be discussed, but we defer consideration until after we examine the statistical topography of kinesics across utterances.

3.2 *Statistical Topography of Kinesics*

Thus far we have made several empirical conclusions. First, termination of utterances is signaled by leftward and downward movements in a variety of positions in a variety of ways. Second, we have suggested that activity increases as one approaches the termination of verbalization. And third, we have suggested that pausal phenomena are also signaled, though we have not yet specified this precisely.

For purposes of statistical analysis, utterances were divided into a number of 'positions'. First, preverbal and postverbal positions were identified. Next, depending upon whether the utterance contained pauses and/or a combination of phrases, the utterance itself was divided into several internal positions. With regard to direct, nonpausal utterances, the first and last words each constituted a position. The remaining verbal material was dichotomized into two positions — first and second halves of the utterance. Thus, for nonpausal utterances, there were six positions, as follows:

(1) Preverbal
(2) First word
(3) All material exclusive of first two positions in the first half of the utterance
(4) All material exclusive of last two positions in second half of utterance

(5) Last word of utterance

(6) Postverbal

Utterances containing pauses and more than one phrase were segmented in the following manner:

(1) Preverbal

(2) First word

(3) All material in the first half of the utterance exclusive of the first two positions and the last word before the pause

(4) Final word before the pause

(5) Pause

(6) First word after the pause

(7) All material in second half of the utterance exclusive of first word and final two positions

(8) Last word of utterance

(9) Postverbal

The eight types of movement previously described were then tabulated across the different utterance positions. Both types of utterances were classified into three topographical positions: an initial segment, a medial segment and a final segment. In the case of nonpausal utterances this meant that positions 1 and 2 were combined for initial position; positions 3 and 4 were considered representative of medial position; and positions 5 and 6 were combined for final position. For pausal data, positions 1, 2 and 3 were combined for initial position; 4, 5 and 6 were considered medial; and 7, 8 and 9 were combined for final position. This tripartite categorization, then, divided utterances into beginning, middle, and terminal segments for purposes of statistical analysis.

A variety of statistical tests were conducted, using the Kolmogorov-Smirnov and Chi-square statistics. Only the major statistical findings will be summarized here.

3.2.1 *Amount of Kinesic Activity across Utterances*

The most general finding uncovered through statistical analysis is that kinesic activity is not uniformly distributed across the entire length of utterances. This holds true for both pausal and nonpausal utterances, as can be seen through inspection of Fig. 13 and 14. Kolmogorov-Smirnov tests (Siegel, 1956) applied to both types of utterances were significant at the .01 level, indicating that kinesic activity increases as the end of utterances are approached.[1]

[1]   Movements were originally recorded per utterance per position per child and then

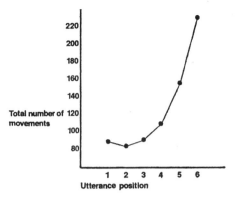

Fig. 13. Overall distribution of kinesic activity across nonpausal utterances.

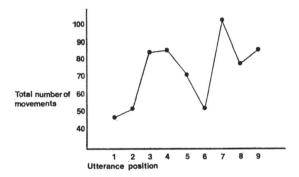

Fig. 14. Overall distribution of kinesic activity across pausal utterances.

The pausal utterances permitted additional testing potential, since they contained at least two utterances separated by a pause. The similarity between the first and second halves of pausal utterances is shown in Fig. 15. For purposes of additional analysis, position 5 was considered postverbal for the first half of the utterance and preverbal for the second half. K-S tests indicated that kinesic activity significantly increases toward the ends of both halves of the pausal utterance. A two-sample

averaged and totaled to eliminate bias from any particular child. Since the final graphs are essentially the same, total movements are shown in Fig. 13, 14 and 15. (Detailed tables illustrating the use of statistics in this study can be found in the original thesis.)

K-S test found the differences between both halves of the pausal utterance insignificant.[2]

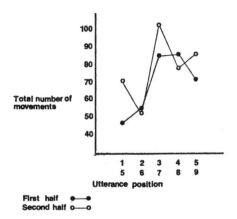

Fig. 15. Comparison of kinesic activity across first and second halves
of pausal utterances.

Summarizing the statistics thus far, we find kinesic activity significantly increases toward the ends of pausal and nonpausal utterances. Further, we find this pattern holds for both segments (first and second halves) of pausal utterances; and that PURELY IN TERMS OF THE GENERAL STATISTICAL TOPOGRAPHY OF KINESIC ACTIVITY when based upon positional analysis, the first and second halves of pausal utterances are indistinguishable from one another. Thus, the topography of the pausal utterance reinforces the findings obtained for nonpausal data in two distinct ways: in terms of the overall pausal utterance (analysis of initial-medial-final segments), and in terms of subdivisions within the pausal utterance (analysis of positions). The general pattern of increased activity toward the end of utterances would seem confirmed.

3.2.2 *Concentration of Left and Down Movements*
Turning to the statistical distribution of the specific movements, it was decided to apply the K-S test to the data to see if the movements

---

[2] The previous test that indicated kinesic activity increased across the overall pausal utterance was based upon lumping several positions to arrive at initial-medial-final segments.

we previously specified as being involved in termination signaling (i.e., left and down) occur significantly more frequently at terminal utterances since the AMOUNT of kinesic activity does not effectively differentiate between terminal (second half) and nonterminal (first half) parts of pausal utterances. Pausal and nonpausal utterances were divided into initial, medial and final segments as outlined previously, and K-S tests conducted. Results are shown in Tables I and II; and indicate that indeed left and downward movements do occur more prominently at the ends of both types of utterances, as can be seen by inspection of Fig. 16 and 17.

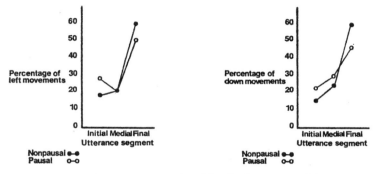

Fig. 16. Percentage of left movements across utterance segments.

Fig. 17. Percentage of down movements across utterance segments.

TABLE I

Summary of Movement Distribution across Initial, Medial and Final Positions for Nonpausal Utterances

	K-S Test Data			
	N	D value	Crit.value	Results
Right	87	.036	.145	n.s.
Tilt right	19	.087	.312	n.s.
Left	109	.266	.156	sig. .01
Tilt left	21	.094	.296	n.s.
Up	155	.092	.109	n.s.
Down	147	.265	.136	sig. .01
Forward	93	.181	.169	sig. .01
Back	94	.131	.140	n.s.

Additional X^2 tests were conducted for **pausal** utterances since they contain two utterance-final positions (5 and **9)** only one of which actually

TABLE II

Summary of Movement Distribution across Initial, Medial and Final Positions for Pausal Utterances

	K-S Test Data			
	N	D value	Crit.value	Results
Right	79	.080	.153	n.s.
Tilt right	27	.068	.248	n.s.
Left	67	.174	.166	sig. .05
Tilt left	22	.120	.279	n.s.
Up	148	.083	.112	n.s.
Down	155	.121	.106	sig. .05
Forward	76	.087	.158	n.s.
Back	99	.045	.133	n.s.

constitutes termination. As expected, left and downward movements are found concentrated only in position 9, and not in position 5.

3.2.3 *Rightward Movements across Pauses*

The distribution of rightward movements across both pausal and nonpausal utterances is shown in Fig. 18. As can be seen, the baseline of rightward movement seems fairly constant across nonpausal utterances. This baseline is deviated from only during the medial segment (the segment containing the pause position) of pausal utterances. Chi-square tests conducted across utterance segments of pausal utterances indicate this deviation is significant.

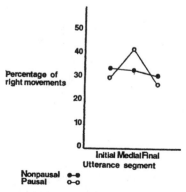

Fig. 18. Percentage of right movements across utterance segments.

3.2.4 *Self-directed versus Other-directed Speech*

A statistical test of the social significance of the left and down signals is possible through consideration of whether utterances are self-directed, or other-directed. In the current sample, three children emit utterances which seem primarily self-directed, as though they were speaking to themselves. Among the three children there are a total of five such utterances. The total sample represented by these children was tabulated into 'self' versus 'other' directed utterances each of which was segmented into initial, medial, and final positions and prepared for analysis by means of the K-S test. As previously found, kinesic activity tends to increase significantly toward the ends of utterances, BUT ONLY IN THE CASE OF OTHER-DIRECTED SPEECH. SELF-DIRECTED UTTERANCES DID NOT DISPLAY THIS CHARACTERISTIC! Additional tests were computed to determine if specific movements were distributed in nonrandom fashion across self-directed and other-directed utterances. The K-S tests summarized in Tables III and IV indicate that in other-directed utterances left and down

TABLE III

Summary of Movement Distribution across Initial, Medial and Final Positions for Self-directed Utterances

	K-S Test Data			
	N	D value	Crit. value	Results
Right	20	.090	.320	n.s.
Left	11	.121	.410	n.s.
Up	28	.097	.257	n.s.
Down	24	.206	.283	n.s.
Forward	15	.333	.350	n.s.
Back	25	.026	.272	n.s.

TABLE IV

Summary of Movement Distribution across Initial, Medial and Final Positions for Other-directed Utterances

	K-S Test Data			
	N	D value	Crit. value	Results
Right	32	.104	.241	n.s.
Left	33	.333	.294	sig. .01
Up	63	.085	.172	n.s.
Down	56	.236	.218	sig. .01
Forward	37	.090	.223	n.s.
Back	45	.043	.203	n.s.

movements were significantly clustered once again near the ends of utterances. Left and down activity in self-directed utterances, however, did not deviate from a random distribution.

3.2.5 *Seating Position and Termination Movement*

Finally, because 'forwardness' proved significant during nonpausal utterance termination, it was decided to test the possible effects of seating position on termination movement, since seating was not symmetrical. K-S tests prepared to measure potential seating position effects on termination movement all proved insignificant.

4.0 DISCUSSION

The most general, obvious, and unexpected finding associated with this research has been the realization that the amount of kinesic activity is not uniformly distributed across the length of utterances. For nonpausal and pausal other-directed utterances, the most consistent statistical finding is the significant increase in kinesic activity associated with the final segment of verbal utterances. Interestingly, it is only with self-directed utterances that this finding is not obtained.

When this research was initiated, it was expected that there would be kinesic signals marking both intentions to initiate and terminate verbalization. The latter have been discovered, but not the former. While the intention to initiate verbalization may well be signaled, it does not seem to reside in the configuration of specific types of body movements as does the signaling of willingness to yield the floor. Both Scheflen (1964) and Kendon (1970a, b) suggest that such signals may be present in the form of postural shifting which takes place while the individual occupies the role of listener. The lack of specific signaling in body movements to announce one's intention to initiate verbalization seems partially congruent with the RELATIVE lack of kinesic activity during preverbal and early verbal positions. Such signaling, like termination signaling, would presumably fare best if considerably redundant, or sent more than minimally necessary. This requires some modicum of kinesic activity. A shift in posture would be well suited in this instance since the speaker may not be looking directly at his auditor and gross movement would be better detected. Throughout a substantial portion of this research endeavor it was thought that upward and rightward movements functioned to signal utterance initiation. Closer scrutiny upon final analysis however, revealed substantial, unpredictable situations. Statistically, there exists no significant clustering of upward movements; and the only statistically significant clustering of rightward movements occurs in connection with verbal pauses.

The major finding of this research is the predictable patterning and clustering of leftward and downward kinesic activity to signal an intention to terminate verbalization. Termination signals appear to occur in one of two possible ways in any of three possible utterance positions. Signals may be successive or simultaneous. In the former, the same body part successively moves down and left or left and down several times. The only mandatory movement appears to be a leftward movement in the head. Downward movements can occur in the head or the arms and hands. Successive signaling is noticeably employed in the penultimate position (next to last word) where the head moves both left and down. Simultaneous signaling consists of a mandatory leftward movement in the head accompanied by simultaneous leftward and/or downward movements in the arms, hands or trunk. Simultaneous signaling seems to predominate in final word position, but is also present postverbally. Finally, combinations of successive and simultaneous signaling are frequently observed postverbally, usually immediately after verbalization is completed. Postverbal signals are characterized by noticeable redundancy, and it is not unusual to find termination signaled three or four times. In connection with this, it is interesting to note that in a study of floor yielding cues between a patient and a therapist, Duncan (1970: 230) writes,

The number of regular floor-yielding cues required to constitute a floor-yielding signal by the speaker is a number N, determined empirically, which can vary, probably within very small limits, among dyads. When $N-2$ cues are displayed, it is believed that the speaker is indicating a segmenting of his communication on a level lower than that of floor yielding.

In the current sample, while signals are generally sent more than once, especially in postverbal position; it has been noted that there is a tendency in longer utterances covering several phrases to mark the end of individual phrasal units with the left and down signal configuration. And normally such signaling is sent only once or twice. In other words, the ends of smaller units within the overall utterance are also often marked, but are done so with characteristically less kinesic activity than the termination of utterances. Duncan's findings (1970) suggest that the quantity of cues sent is functional, and our statistical tests would seem to confirm such a contention since left and down movements were statistically clustered in the postverbal position (9), but not in pausal position (5) which constitutes the postverbal position for phrases occurring earlier in the utterance.

Other observations by Duncan's study which seem consistent with the findings of this research include the specification of successive and simultaneous signaling and the fact that "... these behaviors ... sometimes occurred in larger clusters, typically at the end of a speaker's utterance" (Duncan, 1970: 228, 230). A characteristic of the termination signals not directly reflected in the statistical tests is the tightly clustered configuration of left and down movements. As we saw earlier, left and down movements occur throughout the utterances, but it is only when they accompany the end of the utterance in tight clusters that they appear to signal termination. Such clusters cannot be interrupted with other types of movements in successive signaling. There appear to be only two exceptions. First, on rare occasions when a rightward movement interrupts a left-down sequence it is always followed by a SHARP left or down. Second, as was uncovered in the statistical analysis, forward movements seem to be permissible in the left-down sequences during nonpausal utterances. Since forward movements do not hold up across pausal utterances, however, they seem an unnecessary addition to the termination signal configuration. The analysis as presented earlier is viable without reference to forward movements.

The introduction of a variety of nonparametric statistical tests seems to overwhelmingly support and reinforce the prior configurational analysis. Left and down movements prove to be clustered in a statistically significant manner at the end of utterances. That such distributions are not merely a function of the end points of phrases was clear from tests conducted on pausal utterances which indicated that left and down movements were not significantly clustered at the end of initial phrases within utterances.

Additionally, left-down clustering does not seem solely a function of ending an utterance. This became clear from comparison of self-directed and other-directed utterances. During the former, the statistical distribution of left and down movements across utterance positions was insignificant, whereas during the latter left and down distribution conformed to previous findings. This tends to suggest the left and down signal configuration is inherently a social signaling device, for quite obviously one need not signal an intention to terminate verbalization when talking to oneself.

Besides the statistical topography of kinesic activity across utterances, other internal data support the contention that left-down configurations constitute termination signaling. The delay sequences, in which considerable time expires between the end of verbalization and the display of the down-left signal, seem to offer support. It seems more than coincidental that when one child finishes talking there is an eight second period of silence; and that the other child begins to speak only after the previous speaker moves his head left and down in succession after the long delay. In addition, the sequences previously discussed in which speakers emit what appear to be final position signals and then at the last split second interrupt the content of the verbal activity, suggest that the left-down configuration functions as a termination signal. Finally, it seems less than fortuitous that the interruption we examined previously should occur precisely at that point where the speaker displays a cluster of leftward and downward movement; despite the fact that the verbal content clearly indicates she is not about to terminate her utterance.

Data external to the present sample which seem consistent and compatible with findings of this analysis come from several sources. First, the preliminary study conducted by this author on termination signaling in two preschool girls via videotape indicated that leftward movement in the head always accompanied the termination of utterances. While the data involved in the previous study were limited and undeniably crude compared to those of the current sample, those findings do reinforce the mandatory nature of leftward head movement in termination. Second, other data completely independent from the present analysis are remarkably similar to the findings presented here. In analyzing relationships between kinesics and speech, Kendon (1970b) reports how different hierarchical speech units are marked kinesically. Two in particular, the locution group and the locution deserve consideration. Says Kendon (1970b: 14),

... locution groups are distinguished from one another kinesically in a less obvious fashion than are other units of speech. Locutions which belong together in the same group appear to have a similar pattern of head movement. For example, both locution 6 and 7 ... start with the head cocked slightly to the right. The head is held still over the first few syllables, it then begins to move left, followed by a forward tilt, so that in each locution the terminal head position is one in which the head is tilted forward and cocked to the left. In contrast, for locutions 8, 9 and 10, (which all belong together ...), the initial head position is one in which the head is simply tilted forward.

Locution beginnings seem to be marked with an erect head held either centrally or cocked to the right. Locution terminations, however, are predominantly marked by a lowered head turned or cocked to the left. Locutions whose terminal points do not conform to this pattern are viewed by Kendon as being either corrections, floor accepting signals, or parenthetical in nature. From examination of the descriptions at the start and finish of locutions in terms of head position provided by Kendon it is clear that left and down head movements tend to predominate. And this is despite the fact that Kendon's data is based upon the discourse, the continual discourse, of one subject. As we discussed earlier in conjunction with Duncan's findings, the same cue configuration (namely left and down) when displayed N-2 times may function to segment lower levels of speech rather than functioning as a termination signal which indicates speech is about to end.

The suggestion by Kendon that locution groups may be kinesically marked by a characteristic head position at the beginning of locutions belonging to the group may, in part, explain why initiation signals were not found across all subjects in a consistent manner. Examining Kendon's reported data does suggest more head position variability at the beginning of locutions than at their end.

It is important to note that the consistency which does exist between certain findings of Kendon (1970a, b) and Duncan (1970) is not a function of intellectual cross-fertilization. The decision was made at the outset of this research not to read the few reports of previous research that might bear on the issue of termination or initiation signaling. For no matter how carefully objective a researcher may be, a prior knowledge of patterned relationships would almost assuredly bias the investigation. It was not until the present analysis had been completed that the reports of Kendon and Duncan were read in detail. A consequence is the virtual guarantee that any compatibility between findings can be considered genuinely independent.

The finding that termination and pausal signaling are specifically directional does not seem particularly surprising in view of Condon's work. Self synchrony and interactional synchrony involve not only the synchronized points of change, but sustained directionality as well. Condon has also noted a type of 'heightened synchrony' in which interactants not only share points of change, but also seem to be moving the same parts of the body isomorphically or in a mirror image. Kendon (1970a) has also noted that a listener will often manifest this mirror-imagery as the speaker concludes his utterance, perhaps as an indication that he will accept the floor next. Casual observation of the present data suggests that forms of mirror-image synchrony do often occur toward the ends of utterances, though without numbered frames it is difficult to specify the phenomenon precisely. Such activity, however, seems compatible with the general lack of specific directional signals accompanying intentions to initiate speech. Heightened synchrony could quite conceivably function effectively to signal a willingness to 'take over' the floor. If this proves a viable interpretation, then, it suggests that the intention to initiate may be signaled first through a heightened synchrony, and followed by the display of termination signals by the speaker if he wishes to relinquish the floor.

Kendon's work dealing with the initiation and termination of locutions was conducted with adults, as was the work reported by Duncan. Their data and findings seem consistent with those uncovered in this study; and, it would seem, provide at least a tentative longitudinal verification.

Once the basic configurational analyses were completed, they were treated as hypotheses and applied to additional data available on the present sample which were previously unanalyzed. Specifically, spot checks were made at points of transition between speaker and listener roles, or at points where one child concluded his verbalization. At least two such points were examined for each child, and this additional data confirmed the existence of clusters of left and downward movements at the ends of utterances. Exceptions to this signaling were consistent with those in the original data. Namely, the signal configuration may be lacking if the utterance constitutes an interrogative, or if it consists of a direct and short response to an interrogative. In both cases, termination expectations are implicit in the context.

REFERENCES

Barker, R. G.
1968   *Ecological Psychology* (Palo Alto: Stanford University Press).
Birdwhistell, R.
1970   *Kinesics and Context* (Philadelphia: University of Pennsylvania Press).
Calhoun, J.
1971   "Space and the Strategy of Life", in A. H. Esser (ed.), *Behavior and Environment* (New York: Plenum Press).
Condon, W. S., and W. D. Ogston
1967   "A Segmentation of Behavior", *Journal of Psychiatric Research* 5, 221-35.
De Long, A. J.
1972   "The Communication Process: A Generic Model for Man-Environment Relations", *Man-Environment Systems* 2, 263-313.
Dinneen, F.
1967   *An Introduction to General Linguistics* (New York: Holt, Rinehart and Winston).
Duncan, S.
1970   "Towards a Grammar for Floor Apportionment: A System Approach to Face-to-Face Interaction", in J. Archea and C. Eastman (eds.), *EDRA II* (Pittsburgh: Environmental Design Research Association).
Esser, A. H.
1971   "Social Pollution", *Social Education* 35, 10-18.
1972   "Evolving Neurologic Substrates of Essentic Forms", *General Systems Yearbook* 17, 33-41.
Hall, E. T.
1964   "Adumbration as a Feature of Intercultural Communication", *American Anthropologist* 66, 154-63.
1968   "Proxemics", *Current Anthropology* 9, 83-107.
Hall, E. T., and G. L. Trager
1953   *The Analysis of Culture* (Washington, D. C.: American Council of Learned Societies, Prepublication edition).
Hamburg, D. A.
1963   "Emotions in the Perspective of Human Evolution", in P. Knapp (ed.), *Expression of the Emotions in Man* (New York: International Universities Press).
Kendon, A.
1967   "Some Functions of Gaze-Direction in Social Interaction", *Acta Psychologica* 26, 22-63.
1970a   "Movement Coordination in Social Interaction: Some Examples Described", *Acta Psychologica* 32, 100-25.
1970b   "Some Relationships between Body Motions and Speech: An Analysis of an Example", in A. Siegman and B. Pope (eds.), *Studies in Dyadic Interaction* (New York: Pergamon Press).
MacLean, P.
1967   "The Brain in Relation to Empathy and Medical Education", *Journal of Nervous and Mental Disease* 144, 374-82.
McBride, G.
1964   "A General Theory of Social Organization and Behaviour", *University of Queensland Papers, Faculty of Veterinary Science* 1: 2, 75-110.

Pribram, K.
  1967 "The New Neurology and the Biology of Emotion", *American Psychologist* 22, 830-38.
  1971 *Languages of the Brain* (Englewood Cliffs, N.J.: Prentice Hall).
Scheflen, A.
  1964 "The Significance of Posture in Communication Systems", *Psychiatry* 27, 316-31.
Siegel, S.
  1956 *Nonparametric Statistics* (New York: McGraw-Hill).
Trager, G. L.
  1958 "Paralanguage: A First Approximation", *Studies in Linguistics* 13, 1-12.
Willems, E. P.
  1973 "Behavior-Environment Systems: An Ecological Approach", *Man-Environment Systems* 3, 79-110.

MICHAEL ARGYLE, ROGER INGHAM, FLORISSE ALKEMA,
and MARGARET McCALLIN

The Different Functions of Gaze

INTRODUCTION

Gaze has been said to have a number of different functions in social interaction. In this experiment an attempt was made to separate out these different functions, in order to study each one separately.

1. *Information Seeking*

Looking while talking (L_T) may be used to obtain immediate feedback on the reactions of listeners; looking while listening (L_L) may be used to supplement auditory information, by observing eye-movements and changes of facial expression. This function of gaze can be isolated in the situation where a subject interacts across a one-way screen, so that he can see and not be seen; he is unable to send any signals, so must look to collect information. Part of this information is about the other's timing of utterances and is used for synchronizing. This can be eliminated if the S delivers a monologue to his partner.

Hypothesis 1. Ss who can see through a one-way screen will look more than Ss who cannot see.

2. *Signalling*

(i) Signalling interpersonal attitudes. It has been found that people look more at those they like (Exline and Winters, 1965) and that Ss high in dominance look more in a competitive situation, Ss high in affiliative needs look more in a cooperative situation (Exline, Gray, and Schuette, 1965). Couples who scored high on a questionnaire measuring being in love spent somewhat more time in mutual gaze and a higher proportion of their gaze was mutual than for other couples during a discussion in the laboratory (Rubin, 1970). Mehrabian (1966) found that if an experimenter interviewed two Ss, the one whom he looked at more thought that the experimenter liked him. One function of gaze appears to be the communication of interpersonal attitudes. The signal that is sent also depends on the facial expression accompanying the gaze; it may be suggested that the intensity of the attitude communicated is a joint product of the length of gaze and the intensity of the expression. Interpersonal attitudes can also be signalled by looking AWAY, i.e., negative attitudes. However, this is a very uncertain form of communication, since the sender will not know if it has been received unless he looks himself.

(ii) Prosodic accompaniments of speech. Speech is accompanied by small movements of the hands, head, and eyes, which supplement the verbal contents by giving emphasis, comment, illustration, and displaying the structure of what is said (Kendon, 1970). These signals can modify or complete the meaning of what is being said, by providing emphasis, providing nonverbal comments, giving illustrations, etc. (Argyle, 1971; Crystal, 1969).

If gaze is used for signalling, it follows that a S who is on the wrong side of a one-way screen, and who can see nothing, will still gaze in the direction of the other some of the time. Again the use of gaze for synchronizing can be eliminated by using monologues. Goldberg and Mettee (1969) carried out an experiment in which Ss delivered monologues to another person who was invisible, but who could see the S through a slit. When the other person was there, Ss looked at the slit 8 % of the time and in a normal and deliberate manner; when the other person was NOT there they looked at the slit only 1 % of the time, and in an accidental manner.

Hypothesis 2: Ss who can see nothing will still look deliberately in the direction of the other for part of the time.

3. *Controlling the Synchronizing of Speech*

This depends on the sending of signals by gaze-shifts, and the perception of these signals by looking at the other. Kendon (1967) found that shifts of gaze are systematically coordinated with the timing of speech, and help with synchronizing. If one S does not look up at the end of an utterance there is a longer pause before the other replies. Argyle, Lalljee and Cook (1968) found that synchronizing was less good if eyes were concealed by dark glasses.

Hypothesis 3: Ss will gaze less during monologues than during conversations.

4. *Mutual Gaze and Intimacy*

Previous experiments suggest that gaze is used as a cue for intimacy, and that both gaze and mutual gaze decline with proximity, which is another cue for intimacy (Argyle and Dean, 1965; Argyle and Ingham, 1971). However it is not clear what are the precise conditions for affiliative satisfaction. If the decline of gaze with distance is taken as an index of affiliative effects, this should reveal what these conditions are: if there is no distance effect with the one-way screen, then EC is needed; if there is a distance effect, then sheer gaze will suffice. On the other hand gaze used for information-seeking may also increase with distance.

Hypothesis 4: If affiliation needs EC, there should be no effect of distance in this experiment. If some other feature of gaze is related to affiliation, this should be subject to the distance effect.

5. *Inhibition of Gaze — Avoiding Undue Intimacy*

Argyle and Dean (1965) proposed that gaze is affected both by approach and avoidance affiliative forces; the avoidance component would be expected to fall off more steeply with distance, as in other approach-avoidance conflicts, so that there is less gaze at closer distances, as was found both in that experiment and by Argyle and Ingham (1971). In the one-way screen condition it seems likely that the avoidance component will be eliminated, so that there should be more gaze than under normal conditions of vision. On the other hand it is also possible that the approach component is reduced — since we do not know whether this depends on simply seeing the other or on experiencing mutual gaze.

Hypothesis 5: There will be more gaze for Ss who can see but not be seen than under normal conditions.

6. *Distraction through Avoiding Excess Input of Information*

L_L is usually about twice as great as L_T, and this is thought to be mainly because a speaker does not want to be distracted. He particularly looks away at the beginning of an utterance, while he is planning it (Kendon, 1967).

It follows that a subject who can see but not be seen will not look all the time when talking, even though he could obtain more immediate feedback by doing so, and incur no mutual gaze.

Hypothesis 6: Ss who can see but not be seen will not gaze all of the time, especially while talking.

METHOD

Subjects talked to each other across a one-way screen, using throat microphones and loudspeakers, as shown in Fig. 1.

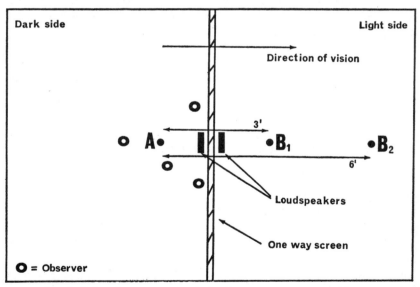

Fig. 1. Laboratory arrangements for the one-way screen experiment.

A was able to see, B was not. The lights on A's side were switched on temporarily so that B could see where A was, before each condition. A circle was drawn on B's side of the screen indicating where A was. Each pair of subjects went through 4 conditions, 2 each side of the screen, one at 3' the other at 6' separation. In each of these positions there was a monologue from A, a monologue from B and a conversation, in a counterbalanced design. There were 4 observers, all on A's side: (1) to observe B's looking at A — whenever B looked straight through the circle on the glass in the direction of A this was scored as looking, (2) to observe A's looking at B, (3) to record B's speech, and (4) to record A's speech. All were recorded on a 4-track Rustrak event recorder.

Each pair of Ss sat in 4 positions, i.e., each side of the one-way screen and at 3' and 6' for each, and had 2 monologues and a conversation in each position. For each position there was a single topic, chosen in random order from the following: Oxford, another town, travel and holidays, books and films. For the monologues notes were provided suggesting possible content areas, which Ss looked at before they started and could consult if they ran out of ideas. In fact very few Ss needed to consult the notes. They were asked to base their conversation on the preceding monologues. Eight MF pairs were used, 16 Ss in all. Ss were students, not of psychology, drawn from a panel of volunteers. The results were compared to those of a very similar experiment, conducted in the same laboratory, but with normal vision, and using different though similar subjects (Argyle and Ingham, 1971).

RESULTS

The average amounts of looking under different conditions are shown in Table I together with data from the previous experiment using normal conditions of vision for comparison purposes.

The analyses of variance are shown in Table II.

1. *Seeing vs. Not Seeing*

As Table II shows there was more L_L and L_T when S could see, both in the conversations ($P < .001$) and the monologues ($p < .01$), though the effect was greater for the conversations (67% vs. 23%). The difference was also greater when Ss were listening than when talking ($p < .01$) — differences of 52% (L_L), 35% (L_T) between see and cannot see for the conversations.

TABLE I

Total Gaze (%) at 3' and 6' under Normal and One-way Screen Conditions (MF only)

			Talk				Listen				Means						
			Male		Female		Male		Female								
			3'	6'	3'	6'	3'	6'	3'	6'	Talk	List-en	3'	6'	M	F	All
Normal	n = 8 pairs		26.7	52.3	28.6	36.5	58.0	76.3	54.8	69.0	36.0	64.5	42.0	58.5	53.2	47.2	50.2
One-way screen	Conver-sations	See	55.5	54.4	54.7	55.8	70.5	75.3	85.9	84.0	55.1	78.9	66.7	67.4	63.9	70.1	67.0
		cannot see	15.3	14.0	25.0	24.3	18.5	22.2	25.7	40.5	19.7	26.7	21.1	25.2	17.5	28.9	23.2
n = 16	Mono-logues	See	21.4	24.6	34.3	21.6	60.0	73.3	62.3	76.4	25.5	68.0	44.5	48.9	44.8	48.6	46.7
		cannot see	18.1	19.4	19.8	18.1	29.2	22.9	38.0	51.3	18.8	35.4	26.3	27.9	22.4	31.8	27.1

TABLE II

Summaries of Analyses of Variance on Looking and Talking Measures

Source	SS	df	MS	F
1. Total looking				
Between Ss	140344.23	15		
Sex (A)	13776.90	1	13776.90	1.52
Ss within groups	126567.34	14	9040.52	
Within Ss	266800.75	48		
Seeing (B)	213097.64	1	213097.64	94.05[a]
A × B	365.76	1	365.76	<1.00
B × Ss within groups	31719.85	14	2265.70	
Distance (C)	236.39	1	236.39	<1.00
A × C	15.01	1	15.01	<1.00
C × Ss within groups	11324.85	14	808.92	
B × C	199.51	1	199.51	<1.00
A × B × C	268.16	1	268.16	<1.00
BC × Ss within groups	9573.58	14	683.83	
2. Looking while listening				
Between Ss	21717.98	15		
Sex (A)	2465.12	1	2465.12	1.79
Ss within groups	19252.86	14	1375.20	
Within Ss	60010.25	48		
Seeing (B)	43607.88	1	43607.88	64.23[a]
A × B	2.03	1	2.03	<1.00
B × Ss within groups	9504.86	14	678.92	
Distance (C)	455.82	1	455.82	3.22
A × C	18.50	1	18.50	<1.00
C × Ss within groups	1980.14	14	141.44	
B × C	237.93	1	237.93	<1.00
A × B × C	315.95	1	315.95	1.14
BC × Ss within groups	3887.14	14	277.65	
3. Looking while talking				
Between Ss	17576.26	15		
Sex (A)	426.42	1	426.42	<1.00
Ss within groups	17419.84	14	1224.99	
Within Ss	30424.49	48		
Seeing (B)	20064.72	1	20064.72	45.8[a]
A × B	375.39	1	375.39	<1.00
B × Ss within groups	6133.18	14	438.08	
Distance (C)	4.00	1	4.00	<1.00
A × C	7.42	1	7.42	<1.00
C × Ss within groups	2438.74	14	174.19	
B × C	3.51	1	3.51	<1.00
A × B × C	2.42	1	2.42	<1.00
BC × Ss within groups	1395.11	14	99.65	

TABLE II CONTINUED

Source	SS	df	MS	F

4. Talking

Source	SS	df	MS	F
Between Ss	61086.98	15		
Sex (A)	3094.14	1	3094.14	0.75
Ss within groups	57992.84	14	4142.35	
Within Ss	79817.25	48	1662.86	
Seeing (B)	18462.01	1	18462.01	12.35[b]
A × B	70.14	1	70.14	.047
B × Ss within groups	20928.60	14	1494.90	
Distance (C)	6.89	1	6.89	<1.00
A × C	1164.51	1	1164.51	<1.00
C × Ss within groups	26052.35	14	1860.88	
B × C	43.89	1	43.89	<1.00
A × B × C	23.78	1	23.78	<1.00
BC × Ss within groups	13065.08	14	933.22	

5. Monologues

Source	SS	df	MS	F
Between Ss	118570.97	15		
Sex (A)	5751.28	1	5751.28	<1.00
Ss within groups	112819.69	14	8058.55	
Within Ss	365410.17	112		
Seeing (B)	50880.50	1	50880.50	14.69[b]
A × B	1035.13	1	1035.13	<1.00
B × Ss within groups	48503.12	14	3464.51	
Talking (C)	114960.13	1	114960.13	32.14[a]
A × C	2112.50	1	2112.50	<1.00
C × Ss within groups	50070.62	14	3576.47	
Distance (D)	1237.53	1	1237.53	1.19
A × D	5.29	1	5.29	<1.00
D × Ss within groups	14572.93	14	1040.92	
B × C	22313.28	1	22313.28	16.63[b]
A × B × C	3549.03	1	3549.03	2.64
BC × Ss within groups	18786.94	14	1341.92	
B × D	264.50	1	264.50	<1.00
A × B × D	2080.12	1	2080.12	2.16
BD × Ss within groups	13475.13	14	962.51	
C × D	4050.00	1	4050.00	10.48[b]
A × C × D	3160.12	1	3160.12	8.18[c]
CD × Ss within groups	5411.13	14	386.51	
B × C × D	1785.03	1	1785.03	3.53
A × B × C × D	69.03	1	69.03	<1.00
BCD × Ss within groups	7088.11	14	506.29	

[a] $p < .001$
[b] $p < .01$
[c] $p < .05$

2. *Gaze by Ss Who Cannot See*

As Table I shows Ss who cannot see look on average 23 % in the conversations, 27 % in the monologues. The observers in this experiment found that Ss looked quite definitely, deliberately and normally at the circle on the one-way screen, which showed where the other person was.

3. *Gaze When Seeing vs. Gaze under Normal Conditions*

Ss in the conversations who could see looked 67 % of the time, compared with 50 % in the normal conversations studied by Argyle and Ingham (1971). The difference was greater at 3' (24 %) than at 6' (9 %) and for females (23 %) than males (10 %). The relation between these scores and distance is shown in Fig. 2.

4. *Comparison of Monologues and Conversations*

It can be seen from Table I that there is more gaze in conversations, but only for SEE (67 % vs. 46 %), and not for CANNOT SEE. The effect is more marked for L_T (55 % vs. 26 % in SEE), than for L_L.

5. *Effects of Distance*

There is a significant interaction of distance with talking in the monologues; there is more L_L at 6' than 3' (p. $< .01$). In the conversations there was a nonsignificant trend in the same direction. In the monologues there was also a triple interaction: there was more looking at 6' while listening, by females (p. $< .05$); this was not found in the conversations.

DISCUSSION

We can learn something from this experiment about the different functions of gaze.

1. *Obtaining Information*

Hypothesis 1 is confirmed: Ss who can see look more than Ss who cannot see — 67 % vs. 23 % in the conversations. The effect of being able to see affected both L_L (79 % vs. 26 %) and L_T (55 % vs. 20 %), showing that information is sought both while talking and while listening.

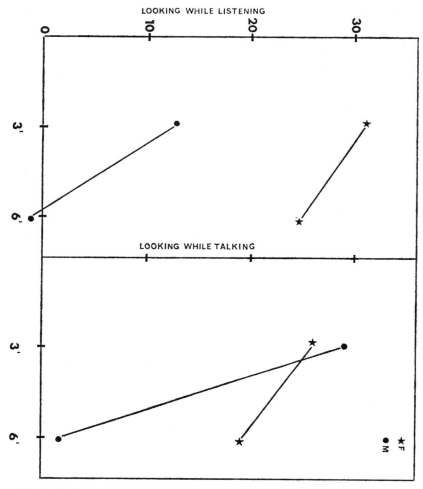

Fig. 2. Looking for one-way screen SEE minus looking under normal conditions, as a function of distance.

It is possible that some of the looking in SEE is for purely affiliative reasons — enjoying the sight of the other, but the absence of any consistent effect of distance on gaze here makes this unlikely.

2. *Signalling Interpersonal Attitudes and Prosodic Accompaniments*

It is not possible to separate these two kinds of signalling with this experiment, but their joint effects can be found. Hypothesis 2 is confirmed in CANNOT SEE Ss still looked 23% of the time in the conversations, 27% in the monologues. This is more than was found by Goldberg and Mettee (1969), whose Ss looked only 8% of the time. However their Ss just gave monologues whereas our Ss gave monologues as a prelude to a conversation on the same topic, which presumably generated rather more involvement with the other person. However Goldberg and Mettee's Ss looked 1% of the time when there was no-one behind the slit; we do not have the comparable figure for our situation, but presumably there would be some accidental looking or looking at the one-way screen itself so that 23% is an overestimate. This kind of looking may be partly out of habit, but it seems likely that it represents the signalling by means of gaze that is used under normal conditions. Gaze that is used to signal synchronizing can be eliminated by taking the figure for the monologues, where no synchronizing is needed. The amount of gaze in CANNOT SEE was greater while listening (35%) than talking (19%) and presumably consisted mainly of feedback signals commenting on the other's utterances.

3. *Synchronizing Speech*

The amount of gaze used for this purpose can be found by comparing the conversations and monologues. There was more gaze on average in the conversations, but only for the SEE condition (67% vs. 47%). Previous studies show that synchronizing depends partly on the sending of information by shifts of gaze (Kendon, 1967). There was no difference between our conversations and monologues in CANNOT SEE, perhaps because Ss do not realise that they send this kind of signal. The effect was greater in SEE for L_T (55% vs. 26%) than L_L. Ss look to obtain information to help with synchronizing — and part of the information they seek is obtained from the other's gaze behaviour; they obtain this information mainly by looking when talking.

4. *Gaze, Mutual Gaze, and Intimacy*

It was predicted that there should be no effect of distance on gaze in this experiment, on the assumption that distance affects only MUTUAL gaze, which was excluded here. There was however a small distance effect, for the monologues, for L_L only ($p < .01$), and especially for females ($p < .05$); there was a nonsignificant trend for the conversations, no effect for L_T, and little effect for males. The difference is in any case considerably less than under normal vision.

	3'	6'	Difference
L_L (normal)	56.4	72.6	16.2
L_L (OWS, all conditions)	48.8	55.8	7.0

This shows that there is a much reduced distance effect under one-way screen conditions, affecting L_L only (and females more than males). It may be a residue or carry-over from normal looking behaviour. However the results on the whole support the hypothesis, in that there is no effect of distance on L_T, and the effect on L_L is less than half of the effect under normal vision. This confirms that the distance effect is primarily due to MUTUAL gaze.

5. Inhibition to Avoid Intimacy

This hypothesis was confirmed: there was more gaze for OWS SEE than under normal conditions, 67% vs. 50%. The extent of this inhibition can be measured by subtracting the amounts of gaze under normal conditions from the OWS SEE scores for the conversations (though different Ss were involved). The effect falls off rapidly with distance, as shown in Fig. 2, and is greater for females than males.

These results confirm the existence of an avoidance component for gaze, which operates under normal vision, is eliminated by the one-way screen, and falls off rapidly with distance.

6. Inhibition by Avoidance of Distraction

This hypothesis was confirmed: in the conversations for Ss who could see L_L was 79%, L_T 55%: there was a greater difference in the monologues, where L_L was 68%, L_T 26%. Ss who could see without being seen looked more than under normal vision, but the amount of their looking did not become 100%. The highest percentage gaze found was for females in the conversations while listening — 85%. In the experiments by Argyle and Ingham (1971) gaze increased with distance, but at 10' was no more than 65%, and the curve for gaze against distance was approaching an asymptote at this level.

Summation of the different factors

We conclude that amount of gaze is a joint product of a number of approach and avoidance forces. However the different components do not appear to add up in any simple way, and it seems likely that two or more can operate simultaneously. For example A might look at B primarily for affiliative reasons, but he would also receive information. Or A might look up at the end of an utterance to collect immediate feedback, but this look will act as a synchronizing signal to B. And A cannot look at B to collect information without sending signals about his attitude to B.

REFERENCES

Argyle, M.
1971 "Non-verbal Communication in Human Social Interaction", *Non-verbal Communication*, ed. by R. Hinde (Royal Society and Cambridge University Press).
Argyle, M., and J. Dean
1965 "Eye-Contact, Distance and Affiliation", *Sociometry* 28, 289-304.
Argyle, M., and R. Ingham
1972 "Gaze, Mutual Gaze, and Proximity", *Semiotica* VI: 1, 32-49.
Argyle, M., M. G. Lalljee, and M. Cook
1968 "The Effects of Visibility on Interaction in a Dyad", *Human Relations* 21, 3-17.
Crystal, D.
1969 *Prosodic Systems and Intonation in English* (Cambridge University Press).
Exline, R. V., D. Gray, and D. Schuette
1965 "Visual Behavior in a Dyad as Affected by Interview Content and Sex of Respondent", *Affect, Cognition and Personality*, ed. by S. Tomkins and C. Izzard (New York: Springer).
Goldberg, G. N., and D. R. Mettee
1969 "Liking and Perceived Communication Potential as Determinants of Looking at Another", *Psychon. Sci.* 16, 277-78.
Kendon, A.
1967 "Some Functions of Gaze Direction in Social Interaction", *Acta Psychologica* 26:1, 1-47.
1970 "Some Relationships Between Body Motion and Speech: An Analysis of an Example", *Studies in Dyadic Communication*, ed. by A. Siegman and B. Pope (Elmsford, N.Y.: Pergamon).
Mehrabian, A.
1966 "Orientation Behaviors and Non-verbal Attitude Communication", U.C.L.A. (mimeo).
Rubin, A.
1970 "Measurement of Romantic Love", *J. Pers. Soc. Psychol.* 16, 265-73.

GEOFFREY W. BEATTIE

Sequential Temporal Patterns of Speech and Gaze in Dialogue*

INTRODUCTION

Although gaze has been the subject of much recent research in the area of non-verbal behavior (see Argyle and Cook 1976 for a recent review), the precise patterning of gaze and speech has been largely ignored. The small number of studies which have considered gaze patterns, in addition to overall amounts of gaze, have tended to employ rather ubiquitous language concepts, such as 'question' or 'remark', and have generally ignored the psychological subcomponents of these units which might be relevant to the speaker's visual behavior e.g., identifiable speech planning phases. As a result, the patterns of gaze which have been reported have displayed considerable variability. Libby (1970) observed that in an interview situation in which the interviewer gazed steadily at subjects who were replying to questions, 84.5% broke gaze during their reply (range 37.1-100%), although only 9.3% broke gaze before the end of the question (range 0-57.4%). Here embarrassing and non-embarrassing, personal and nonpersonal questions, demanding long and short answers, were combined in the analysis of gaze patterning. Nielsen (1962) observed that subjects broke gaze at the beginning of a 'remark' in conversation in 45.5% of all cases (range 8-84%) and they looked at their interlocutor at the end of a 'remark' in 50.5% of all cases (range 25-90%). Undoubtedly the ubiquitous nature of a concept like

* I would like to express my gratitude to Dr. B. Butterworth for his valuable criticism of an earlier draft of this paper.

'remark' is at least partly responsible for this variability, since the precise nature of the verbal exchanges must have varied considerably from dyad to dyad.

The most intensive analysis of the patterning of gaze in conversation, and the only study to focus on possible psychological units within speech, was a study of Kendon (1967), whose observations helped to elucidate the main functions of gaze. His main observations were that the speaker tended to look at the listener during fluent speech much more than during hesitant speech (50% of the time spent speaking fluently as compared to only 20.3% of the time spent speaking hesitantly). Hesitations in speech have been reliably shown to reflect the cognitive planning processes underlying speech (see Goldman-Eisler 1968) and thus gaze aversion, during hesitation, can be construed as a means of preventing an overload of information, on some central processer, if one accepts the hypothesis that gaze has a monitoring function. Hesitations in this study included both unfilled and filled pauses. However, Kendon failed to specify which kind of definition of UPs he employed − whether an objective temporal definition (e.g., pauses ⩾ 250 m sec; Goldman-Eisler 1968), or a subjective definition (e.g., "silences judged to be of unusual length"; Maclay and Osgood 1959). The latter type of definition would have resulted in many objective pauses, particularly pauses at grammatical junctures, being excluded from the analysis (Boomer and Dittmann 1962). Moreover, Kendon regarded hesitations as a unitary class of phenomena, failing to recognize that they serve planning functions at a number of levels (ideational, semantic, and lexical), and that they are organized into cohesive psychological units which are identifiable from changes in the pause/phonation ratio across time (Henderson, Goldman-Eisler, and Skarbek 1966; Goldman-Eisler 1967).

Kendon also described the patterning of gaze with respect to phrases and phrase boundary pauses. It is not clear, however, from Kendon's description of these phrases as "the minimally meaningful units of an utterance ... grammatically complete" (1967:41) what such phrases actually are, since presumably the spoken equivalent of a word (surely not what was intended) would satisfy these requirements. In his description of an utterance he gives more information about phrases:

... the utterance has been considered to consist of a series of phrases (identifiable as complete grammatical units), each phrase separated from the one that follows it by a short pause, the phrase boundary pause. (1967:39).

This description would suggest that the phrase is a unit whose length and form could vary enormously since pauses in speech segment speech into periods of very different length and form. However, since the number of phrase endings and phrase pausings are not identical (see Table 6, p. 39) it would appear that Kendon had not, in fact, built the phrase boundary pause into the operational definition of phrase which he himself used. Thus it is unclear exactly what such phrases actually are.

With respect to these phrases, Kendon found that the speaker tended to look at the listener as he approached the end of a phrase, and continued to look during the phrase boundary pause, but averted as the next phrase began. Similarly utterances were thought to terminate with prolonged gaze (note: utterance was not defined in this study). Kendon hypothesized that gaze had a signalling function at such points, specifically concerned with the transmission of information to the listener about the appropriateness of a listener response, either in the form of a turn-claiming attempt or in the form of an accompaniment signal (an assenting or attention signal), at these points. To support this hypothesis Kendon attempted to show that the probability of a listener response, at such loci, is affected by the presence or absence of gaze. In the case of accompaniment signals, Kendon failed to show that gaze had any effect over and above the effects of speech location *per se*. In the case of other listener responses (i.e., turn-taking attempts), the analysis was marred by a restricted data base and by an unsuitable concept of "utterance" ("all the speech of one participant until the other participant begins to speak"),[1] which would have resulted in interrupted (and incomplete) sequences of speech being included among the utterances ended and contributing to the observed relationship between gaze and the immediacy of a listener response (see Beattie 1978 for a detailed discussion).

An expressive function for gaze was also hypothesized, whereby the speaker was supposed to give expression to his feelings or attitudes on the basis of the observation that subjects avert gaze during points of high emotion in his speech. Kendon hypothesized that such gaze aversion may function as an indication to the listener that the speaker is embarrassed or over-aroused.

A number of other studies have sought to clarify the role of gaze in conversation and have, in general, supported Kendon's conclusions. Gaze aversion, presumably to prevent an overload of information (Argyle, Ingham, Alkema and McCallin 1973), has been observed during individual hesitation pauses in conversation, but not during pauses at syntactic clause junctures (Beattie 1976c), which may have a social rather than cognitive function (Goldman-Eisler 1972; Reich 1975). Gaze aversion has also been observed when subjects prepare arguments in conversation (Nielsen 1962) and when subjects are questioned; to a greater degree for reflective than factual questions (Day 1964; Duke 1968). The overall amount of gaze has also been found to be inversely related to the cognitive difficulty of the topic of conversation (Exline and Winter 1965). Thus there is considerable evidence for a monitoring function.

One of the signalling functions identified by Kendon, that of floor apportionment, has not been reliably demonstrated. Beattie (1978) failed to find any relationship between "complete" utterances (utterances terminating with one or more turn-yielding cues; Duncan 1972, 1973), accompanied by gaze or gaze aversion, and the duration of the succeeding switching pauses ("periods of joint silence bounded by the vocalization of different speakers"). Duncan (1975) has excluded gaze (or head turning) from the class of turn-yielding cues because "it failed to differentiate smooth exchanges of the speaking turn from instances of simultaneous claiming of the turn by the two participants" (p. 206). Furthermore, studies of conversation in no-vision conditions have tended to find fewer interruptions and shorter switching pauses in no-vision compared with face-to-face conditions (Cook and Lalljee 1972; Jaffe and Feldstein 1970). Only Argyle, Lalljee and Cook (1968) found interruption to be most frequent where there was least visibility. However, these no-vision condition studies cannot be considered to conclusively refute the hypothesis that gaze performs a floor apportionment function, since there is some evidence that functionally equivalent verbal signals (especially filled pauses) can, and do, substitute for gaze, when gaze is eliminated (Cook and Lalljee 1967; Kasl and Mahl 1965).

The other signalling function identified by Kendon – signalling about the appropriateness of certain listener responses, which do not constitute turn-claiming attempts – has received empirical support. Duncan (1972, 1973) found that auditor back-channel communications (a more extensive class than Kendon's accompaniment signals), all listener responses which do not constitute a claim for a turn (sentence completions, requests for clarification, brief restatements, and head nods and shakes), are systematically related to both gaze and grammatical clause completion. We can therefore conclude that the gaze accompanying speech does perform some function related to the transmission of information about the appropriateness of certain listener responses at critical loci in speech.

The empirical observations relevant to the expressive function as discussed by Kendon had previously been reported by Darwin (1872) and more recently by Goffman (1956). The level of emotionality or arousal necessary to cause gaze aversion has to be rather high, however, since subjects do not display less gaze when arguing for propositions with which they do not agree. (Mehrabian and Williams 1969; Mehrabian 1971).

The aim of the present study is to analyse the distribution of gaze with respect to speech units with demonstrable cognitive significance, and possible interactional importance, within low-emotionality dialogues, where gaze behavior should be largely a function of monitoring and signalling variables. The particular speech units are cognitive cycles, suprasentential units identified through changes in the hesitation rate across time (Goldman-Eisler 1967; Henderson, Goldman-Eisler and Skarbek 1966). The evidence suggests that cognitive processing load is asymmetrically distributed with respect to the alternating hesitant and fluent phases which constitute each cycle. Cognitive load is hypothesized to be higher in the hesitant phase of the cycle than in the fluent phase, since both proximal and distal decisions at the semantic and lexical level are made in the hesitant phase, whereas the evidence suggests that only proximal lexical decisions are made in the fluent phase (Butterworth and Beattie 1976). Moreover, the mean hesitancy of any phase should roughly reflect the magnitude of the cognitive load. Thus, from a cognitive perspective there should be an approximately inverse relationship, if gaze performs a monitoring function, between the main hesitancy of a phase and the proportion of the phase occupied by gaze.

Evidence also suggests that these cycles constitute semantic units in speech — cycles correspond to 'ideas' in the speech text where the 'idea' boundaries are determined by a number of judges (Butterworth 1975). Thus these cycles may act as important interactional units: the speaker may seek to avoid idea fragmentation, that is within-cycle interruption (understood in the broadest sense to include all back-channel communications other than attention signals), by inhibiting, where possible, turn-yielding and other listener-response cues during the cycles and displaying such cues, which should include gaze, at the boundaries of such units. Some support for this interactional hypothesis comes from a study by Butterworth and Beattie (1976) who found that changes in the basic equilibrium of the arms and hands of a speaker often corresponded with the terminal points of the phases constituting the cognitive cycles in his speech. Although such movements may have been primarily due to the processing underlying the speech, in some as yet unexplained way, they may acquire an interactional significance by indicating to the listener the termination of semantic units in the speech and therefore the arrival of an appropriate response point. Duncan (1972, 1973) has noted that the termination of any hand gesticulation, and the relaxation of a tensed hand position, can act as turn-yielding cues. Thus the equilibrium shifts observed by Butterworth and Beattie (1976), which would appear to be a rather specific subset of the cues discussed by Duncan, could function as turn-yielding cues. However, on the basis of the existing analyses the interactional importance of these cognitive cycles cannot be conclusively established, since, firstly, no analysis was performed on the distribution of attempt-suppression signals, which can override the effects of any number of turn-yielding cues (Duncan 1972, 1973). Secondly, many turn-yielding cues, consisting of the termination of a hand gesticulation, were excluded by the particular focus of the analysis. And, thirdly, it has not yet been demonstrated that listener responses are more probable at the ends of the cycles than at other points within the cycles. The present study includes a reanalysis of the original Butterworth and Beattie data in an attempt to answer these unsettled questions and establish, or refute, the interactional hypothesis of cognitive cycles.

The cognitive, and (possible) interactional, properties of these cognitive cycles allow us to make two sorts of predictions about the patterning of gaze in speech:

(i) Since gaze appears to perform a monitoring function, a general inverse relationship should obtain between the mean hesitancy of speech, which is a rough index of the amount of internal processing, and amount of gaze.

(ii) If gaze has the signalling functions outlined above, then appropriate listener response points should be marked by gaze. These marked response points may correspond to the semantic or syntactic units that comprise the total communication message. This study will focus on the analysis of gaze with respect to cognitive cycles, representing perhaps the minimal semantic units with interactional significance (this of course is being tested), and surface structure clauses as the minimal syntactic units. There are a number of pieces of evidence which suggest that clauses are important interactionally — clause completion has been found to act as a cue for a turn-taking attempt in conversation, as well as a cue for an auditor back-channel communication (Duncan 1972, 1973). However, clause boundaries are often marked by unfilled pauses (an estimated 43% of all clause junctures are occupied by UPs $\geqslant$ 200 ms; Beattie 1976), which themselves act as cues for turn-taking attempts (Beattie 1977; Jaffe and Feldstein 1970). Thus, the interactional properties of clauses may be partly attributable to the clause completion/UP confound, as well as to the fact that many clause endings are also the terminal points of a number of semantic units, notably sentences and cognitive cycles (Butterworth 1975). In this study, the incidence of gaze at clause junctures, at the end of cycles, is compared with the incidence of gaze at all other junctures in an attempt to determine the relative interactional importance of these two basic units. One last point which should be made about any lawful distribution which might obtain between surface clauses and gaze is that this could not be interpreted as simply reflecting the inhibition of the monitoring functions of gaze, since there is no conclusive evidence for the suggestion made by Valian (1971) and Fodor, Bever and Garrett (1974) that the clause is an important unit of encoding. A recent analysis of the distribution of hesitations across surface structure clauses suggests that such clauses are not important determinants of processing time (see Beattie 1976).

In the present study, these predictions about the distribution of gaze are tested in dialogues held to be relatively low in emotional content: supervisions (or tutorials).

PROCEDURE

Four interactions were filmed; three were hour-long supervisions involving either a graduate student or a member of staff as supervisor and an undergraduate. The remaining sample involved two participants of a seminar engaged in a prolonged interaction. All speakers were male; only one interaction involved a mixed sex pair. All of the sequences filmed were natural events, in that they were not arranged especially for the experiment. The supervisions and seminars took place in a comfortable observation room with video-cameras arranged as unobtrusively as possible. All subjects were informed that they were going to be filmed.

The present study involves an intensive analysis of the speech and gaze of five subjects. The speech samples analysed were selected at random from the speech corpus; the only constraint on this selection was that the speaker's turn in conversation had to be at least 30 secs in length so that temporal cycles could be identified.

Unfilled pauses (UPs) were defined as periods of silence $\geqslant 200$ m sec. and these were identified and measured using an Ediswan pen oscillograph and pause detector. A visual analogue of the speech identifying periods of silence and phonation was prepared in a manner described by several authors (e.g., Goldman-Eisler 1968; Henderson *et al*, 1966). The identification of the temporal or cognitive cycles was carried out in the manner described by Henderson *et al*. (1966:208). This procedure was checked by asking independent judges to decide on changes of slope in the graph. A transcript of the speech was made. Transition times between cycles and phases of the cycle were determined from the graphs, and mapped onto the transcripts using the timer on the video-screen to determine the precise temporal location of any given word in the speech corpus. Thus it was possible to determine which clauses constituted each cycle and each phase of the cycle. The amount of filled hesitation, consisting of filled pauses, FPs, a, ϵ, $æ$, τ, $ə$, m, repeats (all repetitions of any length judged non-significant semantically), false starts (all incomplete or self-interrupted utterances), and parenthetic remarks (e.g., "you know"), occurring in each cycle, and each phase of a cycle, was measured.

The occurrence or non-occurrence of speaker gaze (gaze at the head region or one's interlocutor) was noted at each word boundary in the transcript. The times of initiation and termination of each gaze sequence were also noted and these times were marked onto the pause/phonation graphs, so that the relationship between the cycles and gaze could be analysed.

Measurement of gaze has been the subject of much debate in the literature in recent years (see Argyle and Cook 1976, Chpt. 2). Evidence to date suggests that more accurate discriminations between eye-gaze and non eye-gaze can be achieved when judging actual interactions than is generally the case in the controlled fixation studies which have reported rather poor discrimination (Vine 1971). For greater accuracy and in an attempt to avoid the distance artifact in gaze judgement (Stephenson and Rutter 1970) gaze was judged from a video-screen rather than directly. Subjects were filmed using cameras with zoom lenses behind the head of the other person in the interaction and a split screen video-circuit was employed. Gaze aversion could be detected as deviations from the straight ahead look. High inter-observer reliability was obtained in judgements of the occurrence or non-occurrence of gaze (G) – 88.6%.

In order to describe changes in gaze pattern within cycles, the distribution of gaze with respect to syntactic (surface structure) clauses was noted. Surface structure clauses were defined as stretches of speech containing a subject and its predicate. The occurrence or non-occurrence of gaze at each boundary location (labelled by the ordinal number of the succeeding word) in the clause was recorded.

The gesticulatory behavior of the speaker at the ends of the hesitant and fluent phase of each cycle was analysed. The termination of any hand gesticulation was noted as was the display of any hand gesticulation, other than a self- or object-adaptor (see Duncan 1972: 287). The former behavior acts as a turn-yielding cue, the latter as an attempt-suppression signal.

The occurrence or non-occurrence of a listener response, either in the form of a turn-taking attempt or in the form of a back-channel communication (Duncan 1973:38) at each clause juncture nearest the phasal transition point, at other clause junctures and at non-clausal junctures, was noted. The two categories of listener response were combined because of the small number of examples of each category. Note: in the case of one of the dyads no information was available on the non-verbal behavior of the auditor and thus no data could be collected on the use of auditor head-nods and shakes in this dyad.

RESULTS

Physical Characteristics of Cycles

The alternating pattern of speech with different pause/phonation ratios, described by Henderson *et al.* (1966), was quite discernible in all of the samples of spontaneous speech studied. The mean cycle time was found to be 21.88 secs (S.D. = 15.68). Each cycle was found to contain a mean of 8.80 SS clauses; each fluent phase was found to contain a mean of 5.23 SS clauses; and each hesitant phase a mean of 3.57 SS clauses. In all 20 complete cycles (i.e., 20 cycles containing both a hesitant and a fluent phase) were observed, as well as 6 incomplete cycles bounded by speaker switches.

Cognitive Cycles and Listener Responses

The probability of the display of a hand gesticulation, which acts as an attempt-suppression signal, was compared with the probability of the termination of any hand gesticulation, which acts as a turn-yielding cue, in the clause junctures nearest the end of hesitant and fluent phases (see Table 1).

TABLE 1
Display versus termination of hand gesticulation in clause junctures nearest the terminal points of hesitant and fluent phases of cognitive cycles

		Number of phases accompanied by each type of gesticulatory behavior	Number of phases not accompanied by each type of gesticulatory behavior
End of hesitant phase	display of hand gesticulation	3	23
	termination of hand gesticulation	5	21
End of fluent phase	display of hand gesticulation	1	26
	termination of hand gesticulation	10	17

In the case of hesitant phases there was no significant difference in the type of gesticulatory behavior which occurred (G = 0.450, p ≫ 0.05; Sokal and Rohlf 1973). However, fluent phases were significantly more likely to terminate with a gesticulatory turn-yielding cue than with an attempt-suppression signal (G = 7.980, p. < 0.01).

The relationship between speech location, (specifically clause junctures nearest the termination of hesitant and fluent phases, other clause junctures, and non-clausal junctures) and listener responses, either in the form of turn-taking attempts or back-channel communications, was analysed (see Table 2).

Listener responses were significantly more likely to occur at clause junctures nearest the termination of fluent phases (i.e., at the end of cognitive cycles) than at other clause junctures (G = 6.676, p < 0.01), and significantly more likely at clause junctures than at non-clausal junctures (G = 12.236, p < 0.001). However, listener responses were

TABLE 2

Listener responses at the ends of hesitant and fluent phases, clause junctures and non-clausal junctures (others)

	Number of instances of each category accompanied by a listener response	Number of instances of each category not accompanied by a listener response
End of hesitant phase (nearest clause juncture)	2	20
End of fluent phase (nearest clause juncture)	5	19
Clause juncture (other than clause juncture nearest end of phase)	8	171
Other	10	1332

not significantly more probable at clause junctures nearest the terminal points of hesitant phases than at other clause junctures (G = 0.740, p > 0.05).

These results allow the conclusion that the cognitive cycle is an important unit in social interaction, as well as an important unit in the cognitive planning of an utterance.

Gaze and Mean Hesitancy of Phase

The number of hesitant and fluent phases dominated by gaze or gaze aversion (i.e., with more than, or less than, 50% gaze, respectively) were noted, as was the slope of each phase (measured in degrees; a 45° slope indicates an equal proportion of pausing and phonation, a 0° slope indicates uninterrupted phonation, a 90° slope indicates extended pausing). The number of changes in gaze state per phase, and the number of words separating each change of gaze state were also recorded (see Table 3).

A difference in the relative number of hesitant and fluent phases dominated by gaze did emerge, but this difference failed to reach significance (G = 2.512, p. < 0.2). There was a tendency for both types of phase to be accompanied by more gaze than gaze aversion;

however, in the case of fluent phases the trend was much more pronounced. The slopes (reflecting the mean percentage of hesitation per phase) of the various hesitant and fluent phases were then compared. In the case of fluent phases, those phases dominated by gaze aversion tended to be significantly more hesitant than the phases dominated by gaze (mean slopes 13.77° and 6.30° respectively, Mann-Whitney U test, U = 12, p < 0.05, 2-tailed test). In the case of hesitant phases there were no significant differences in the slopes of those phases dominated by gaze or gaze aversion (mean slopes 47.07° and 47.55° respectively, Mann-Whitney U test, U = 38½, p ≫ 0.05, 2-tail).

It should be noted that the dominance of a phase by gaze or gaze aversion is not simply attributable to there being more phonation or hesitation in the phase, since 6 of the 13 hesitant phases dominated by gaze had slopes which were greater than 45° (i.e., there was more pausing than phonation), and none of the fluent phases had slopes greater than 45°, although 4 of these phases were dominated by gaze aversion. In a number of cases the distribution of gaze can be clearly seen not to be optimal for cognitive purposes. For example, two hesitant phases had slopes of 90°, i.e., they consisted of prolonged pausing, but these were accompanied by uninterrupted gaze, and not gaze aversion. The psychological concomitants of such effects are discussed later. Thus, to summarize, in the case of fluent phases the dominance of the phase by gaze or gaze aversion was found to distinguish the degree of hesitancy of the phase, but this did not occur with hesitant phases. Moreover, some clear mismatches between cognitive load and gaze did occur in the case of hesitant phases.

Column 3, Table 3, seems to reveal differences in the stability of gaze in hesitant and fluent phases dominated by gaze or gaze aversion, but such differences largely disappear when the number of words are taken into consideration (column 4). There was an overall mean of 2.5 changes in gaze state per phase, which suggests that there was a change approximately every 1.76 clauses. One pertinent question is: how accurately do such changes reflect the transitions from individual hesitations to fluent periods and back. The hesitation analysis revealed that there was a UP, FP, or UP-FP cluster approximately every 8 words, which would suggest that gaze is somewhat less changeable than it should be it if were simply reflecting the location of every individual hesitation. However, some correction may be necessary, because hesitations at syntactic junctures may have a social rather than a cognitive function (see Beattie 1976). If this correction is carried out, we find a non-clausal hesitation every

TABLE 3
Patterns of gaze in cognitive cycles

PHASE TYPE		Phase dominated by gaze or gaze aversion	No. of H and F phases dominated by gaze or gaze aversion	Mean slope of each phase (in degrees)	Mean no. of changes in gaze state per phase	Mean no. of words separating each change in gaze states
Hesitant		gaze	13	47.07	2.39	10.04
		gaze aversion	9	47.55	1.67	11.51
Fluent		gaze	20	6.30	2.60	12.65
		gaze aversion	4	13.77	4.25	12.41

TABLE 4
Percentage of boundary locations in surface structure clauses accompanied by gaze

PHASE TYPE	BOUNDARY LOCATION											
	1	2	3	4	5	6	7	8	9	10	11	12
Hesitant	60.27	50.68	56.76	57.14	57.14	58.33	55.17	57.14	68.75	71.42	80.00	50.00
Fluent	60.61	64.65	59.79	65.85	66.15	69.09	72.73	72.73	75.00	70.00	76.92	85.71
Both	60.47	58.72	58.15	63.55	64.83	68.49	62.96	66.00	73.53	70.70	77.50	75.00

12.9 words, which would again suggest that gaze behavior is more stable than it should be, if it were simply reflecting each fluent-hesitant-fluent transition. There should be 2n changes in gaze state for every n hesitations, and thus we would predict a mean of approximately 6 words to separate each gaze state, if gaze were simply reflecting the location of individual hesitations.

Gaze and Syntactic Clauses

The analysis of gaze then focused on the syntactic clauses which comprised the cognitive cycles.

This analysis was carried out in two ways. Firstly, gaze across the first 12 boundary locations of clauses between 2 and 12 words in length (longer clauses were omitted as there were too few to yield reliable estimates) was analysed, and the percentage of each boundary location occupied by gaze was calculated (see Table 4).

The randomness of these percentages was tested using a one-sample runs test. When all clauses were considered, the distribution of gaze was found to be random ($r = 4$); similarly with clauses falling within hesitant phases ($r = 9$). However, in the case of clauses in fluent phases, the distribution was not random ($r = 2$, $p < 0.05$). The percentage of successive boundary locations occupied by gaze tended to increase in a non-random fashion. The mean percentage increase from boundary location 1 to boundary location 12 was 25.10%, in the case of syntactic clauses, within fluent phases. It should also be noted that clauses in fluent phases tended to have significantly more overall gaze than syntactic clauses in hesitant phases, when the percentage of gaze at each boundary location was compared. (Wilcoxon Matched-Pairs Sign Ranks Test, 2-tail, $T = 6$, $p < 0.01$).

The second analysis sought to determine if syntactic clauses tended to terminate with gaze. This time, the number of instances of gaze at the first and last position of clauses between 2 and 12 words in length were compared. This was carried out separately for clauses in the hesitant and fluent phases of the cycles. In neither case did a significant effect emerge, neither in the case of clauses in hesitant phases (Wilcoxon Test, $T = 16\frac{1}{2}$, $p \gg 0.05$), nor in the case of clauses in fluent phases (Wilcoxon Test, $T = 15$, $p \gg 0.05$). The mean percentage of gaze at clause junctures was found to be 60.47%.

These 2 analyses are perfectly compatible; the significant results in the first analysis but not in the second indicate that clause length is an important factor. The longer the clause, the more likely it is to terminate with gaze. This is especially the case with clauses in the fluent phases of cycles.

Gaze, Cognitive Cycles and Clause Junctures

The incidence of gaze at clause junctures nearest the terminal points of cognitive cycles was compared with the incidence of gaze at all other clause junctures (see Table 5).

TABLE 5
Incidence of gaze at clause junctures nearest termination of cognitive cycle compared with the incidence at all other clause junctures

	GAZE	GAZE AVERSION
Clause junctures nearest termination of cycle	18	4
Other clause junctures	100	71

Gaze was found to occur significantly more frequently at clause junctures nearest the terminal points of cognitive cycles than at other clause junctures (G = 3.836, p < 0.05). The mean percentage gaze at clause junctures nearest the terminal points of cognitive cycles was 81.82%.

The gaze which coincided with the ends of cognitive cycles was not a discrete cueing signal. This terminal gaze was initiated a mean of 1.83 syntactic clauses before the end of a cycle (a mean of 12.0 words earlier), and it continued into the subsequent cycle for a mean of 1.44 clauses (mean of 5.7 words). These figures suggest that such gaze does not function solely as a signal that an appropriate conversational switch point, or listener back-channel communication point, has been reached. Rather they suggest that such gaze performs a dual function: firstly, that of signalling and conversational regulation, and secondly, that of monitoring the reception of the semantic unit by the listener.

Filled Hesitation and Cognitive Cycles

The patterning of gaze and proportion of gaze within individual hesitant and fluent phases would appear not to be simply a function of a basic cognitive variable plus a compatible reciprocal social signalling function, since there is some degree of divergence between the actual patterns of gaze observed and the theoretical pattern if only the functions mentioned were operative. Some social explanation of the divergence between the observed and expected pattern will be attempted. But first an analysis is performed to determine if this divergence had any important cognitive consequences, i.e., if the gaze which accompanied planning periods had any significant effect on the content of the speech. Filled hesitation rate, an index which should prove sensitive to insufficient forward planning, was analysed, and the hesitation rates of two types of cycle were compared. G_0 G_1 type cycles (n = 7) are those cycles in which the hesitant phase is dominated by gaze aversion and the fluent phase by gaze, G_1 G_1 type cycles (n = 11) are those in which both phases are dominated by gaze (there were only 2 instances of G_1 G_0 type cycles, and no examples of a G_0 G_0 type cycle, in the present corpus). Since there is a tendency for gaze states to be relatively longer than individual periods of hesitancy and fluency, there should be some tendency for G_1 G_1 cycles to have more planning pauses occupied by gaze than G_0 G_1 cycles (since the slopes of G_0 and G_1 hesitant phase are very similar). Thus, if gaze does interfere with cognitive processing, there should be more filled hesitation in both phases of G_1 G_1 cycles than in G_0 G_1 cycles. Table 6 reveals that the false start variable was the most sensitive to the mismatch between gaze behavior and cognitive processing.

There were significantly more false starts in G_1 G_1 cycles than in G_0 G_1 cycles (Mann-Whitney U test, U = 15, p < 0.05, 2-tail). False starts were approximately 5 times as common, per unit word spoken, in G_1 G_1 cycles than in G_0 G_1 cycles. There was also an increase in rate of repeats and parenthetic remarks, per unit word, in G_1 G_1 cycles, although these differences failed to reach significance. Given the hypothesized ideational function of the hesitant phases of cycles, this result is encouraging, since the 'false start' variable is the one which should be most sensitive to a decrement in planning efficiency at the ideational level.

DISCUSSION AND CONCLUSIONS

The first result obtained in this study which requires comment was the high proportion of gaze whilst speaking. The mean percentage was 66.8%, which is rather higher than the percentages reported in

TABLE 6

Mean filled hesitation rate (measured in words) per phase, and FH rate per unit word spoken, within the hesitant and fluent phases of cycles with the H phases dominated by gaze aversion ($G_0 G_1$ cycles) or gaze ($G_1 G_1$ cycles)

	HESITATION TYPE	TYPE OF CYCLE					
		$G_0 G_1$ (n = 7)			$G_1 G_1$ (n = 11)		
		H	F	BOTH	H	F	BOTH
Hesitation rate (in words)	False starts	1.28	0	1.26	3.64	1.45	5.09
	Parenthetic remarks	0.86	1.43	2.29	0.73	1.27	2.00
	Repeats	0.14	0.57	0.71	0.27	0.37	0.64
	Filled pauses	0.86	1.28	2.14	0.55	0.73	1.28
Hesitation rate, per unit word spoken	False starts	0.0689	0	0.0221	0.1558	0.0609	0.179
	Parenthetic remarks	0.0463	0.0364	0.0396	0.0312	0.0533	0.0424
	Repeats	0.0075	0.0145	0.0123	0.0116	0.0155	0.0136
	Filled pauses	0.0463	0.0326	0.0370	0.0235	0.0306	0.0271

other studies. All speakers were male in the present study, and only one of the interactions involved a mixed sex pair. Thus the comparable figures from Argyle and Ingham (1972) for the percentage of gaze whilst talking was 31% for same sex (male) pairs, and 52% for mixed sex pairs, with the man talking. Nielsen (1962) reported a mean percentage of 52% gaze whilst talking. Furthermore, Exline and Winters' (1965) observation that amount of gaze in conversation is inversely related to the cognitive difficulty of the topic of conversation would lead one to predict a lower overall level of gaze in the present study, compared with other studies, since the topic under discussion in the present study was certainly more difficult than the conversational topics in many of the studies of gaze and speech. However, a number of social considerations can be used to account for the high rate. Firstly, subjects knew each other in the present study, whereas in most other studies of gaze and speech subjects were previously unacquainted. The level of gaze between intimates tends to be higher than between strangers (Argyle and Dean 1965). Furthermore, the distance between the interactants was fixed, for the purposes of filming, at a distance which would normally be considered to exceed the distance that subjects knowing each other would choose, if they had the choice (some subjects spontaneously commented on this fact). Thus if we evoke the intimacy equilibrium model of Argyle and Dean (1965), we can hypothesize that the high rate of gaze, whilst talking, was to compensate for the increased distance. The compensatory relationship between proximity and gaze, given a certain level of intimacy, has found considerable empirical support (Argyle and Ingham 1972; Knight, Langmeter and Landgren 1973; Schulze and Barefoot 1974; Stephenson, Rutter and Dore 1973; Patterson 1973). It may also be hypothesized that the high degree of listener attentiveness, produced by supervision-type situations, contributed to the high gaze rate, since Cook and Smith (1972) found that the amount of gaze whilst speaking increases when a confederate looks continuously. Thus the high rate of gaze observed would seem to be consistent with a number of other observations.

The analysis of the relationship between the cognitive cycles of speech and the macropatterns of gaze revealed a loosely coordinated system. The pattern of gaze did seem to reflect the gross temporal structure of the pause/phonation patterns in speech. These results appear to conflict with other studies, which have found that a Markov chain structure with a 0.3 sec transition state best accounts for the distribution of pausing and phonation in speech (Jaffe and

Feldstein 1970), and a Markov chain structure with a 0.6 sec transition state best accounts for the dyadic gaze of adults (Natale 1976), engaged in rather informal conversations (subjects were asked to have a 5-min. conversation on their impressions of life at the university). It should be added that such studies ignore the functional interdependence of speech and gaze by attempting to describe in isolation the pattern of two obviously related phenomena. It remains to be seen to what extent the Markov description of pause/phonation occurrences and of the gaze accompanying speech is compatible with the observations made in this study. It may be possible to reconcile the two sets of observations. For example, it can be suggested that the Markov structure of pausing and phonation in speech, reported by Jaffe and Feldstein (1970), may have resulted from gross averaging of samples of speech of different complexity, some of which may not have been sufficiently complex to involve a temporal rhythm (see Goldman-Eisler 1967). The Natale (1976) study, which imposed a Markov description on patterns of gaze, may well have been studying conversations which involved speech which did not display a temporal rhythm, given the rather simple topic of conversation. Alternatively, analyses which have shown that a first order, as opposed to an nth order, Markov process best accounts for the pattern of dyadic gaze may even be compatible with the results of the present study, by accounting for the local variation of gaze within the macropatterns observed. One point should be remembered about these macropatterns, namely, that variation in the overall length of the cycles was enormous (mean = 21.88 sec; S.D. = 15.68). Thus we cannot contend that a higher order Markov process, of any identifiable order, would be a better fit for the data given the enormous degree of temporal uncertainty in structure in the cycles. Only careful research in the future will determine which mathematical model best describes the patterning of gaze accompanying complex speech which displays a rhythmic structure.

The patterning of gaze and proportion of gaze within individual hesitant and fluent phases was shown not to be simply a function of a basic cognitive variable, plus a compatible, reciprocal social signalling function, since there was some divergence between the observed pattern and the pattern expected if only these functions were operative. One possible source of this divergence is the tendency for most individuals in conversations to attempt to create a favorable impression. Some research has been carried out on gaze patterning and listener evaluation; e.g., Argyle, Lefebvre and Cook (1974) found that subjects disliked continuous gaze. Exline and Eldridge

(1967) found that subjects thought that speakers were more likely to mean what they said if they looked at them. Kleck and Nuessle (1968) found that confederates, who looked only 15% of the time, were described as 'defensive' or 'evasive', whereas those who looked 80% of the time were described as 'friendly', 'mature', or 'sincere'. Cook and Smith (1975) found that there was a tendency for confederates who averted gaze to be seen as nervous and lacking in confidence. In fact, positive evaluation of the confederates was found to be positively related to the amount of gaze. Furthermore, Kendon and Cook (1969) found that subjects preferred individuals who gave long glances, and evaluated less favorably those who gazed frequently and with shorter glances. The tendency for gaze to be more stable then predicted, on cognitive grounds, was observed in the present study; thus it can be hypothesized that this gaze pattern is attributable to the fact that subjects were attempting to create a favourable impression by using relatively long glances. The high proportion of gaze accompanying certain hesitant periods may also be due to the same basic signalling effect. Total gaze aversion would have been the cognitively optimal strategy, in a number of cases, but zero gaze is disliked by subjects (Argyle *et al.* 1974). The fact that social factors may interfere with the cognitively-optimal patterning of gaze, and that this may result in decrements in verbal performance, would indicate that it may be fruitful to look closely at certain delineable populations who show marked abnormalities in both gaze behavior and speech, e.g., schizophrenics. The indication is that schizophrenics employ less gaze than do normals (see Rutter's 1973 review), but whether this is cognitively advantageous obviously depends on the precise patterning of gaze and speech. A careful analysis of the patterning of gaze and the accompanying speech may well prove fruitful.

Thus, to conclude, this study did demonstrate that gaze is organized in a coordinated system with the plans underlying speech, and the speech flow itself. Gaze was found to be more frequent in the fluent phases than in the hesitant phases of cognitive cycles (at least when the percentage of boundary locations occupied by gaze in syntactic clauses in both phases were compared). This result is presumably due to there being less ongoing cognitive processing to inhibit the gaze in the fluent phases. Furthermore, those fluent phases dominated by gaze aversion tended to be significantly more hesitant than those phases dominated by gaze. Gaze was also found to occur more frequently at each successive boundary location of a syntactic clause, in the fluent phase of a cycle, although no lawful relationship emerged between gaze and syntactic clauses falling within the hesitant phase of a cycle. Gaze was not significantly more probable in clause junctures than at boundary locations at the beginning of clauses, suggesting that the syntactic clause is not a major interactional unit. The high rate of gaze at clause junctures nearest the end of cognitive cycles, on the other hand, indicates that these cycles are important units of interaction in dialogue. The observed clustering of gesticulatory turn-yielding cues about such points, and the analysis of two types of listener response (back-channel communications and turn-taking attempts), support this conclusion.

Nevertheless, gaze patterning diverged from the predicted pattern in a number of important ways. Firstly, there was no significant difference in the degree of hesitancy of hesitant phases dominated by gaze or gaze aversion, and some clear mismatches between hypothetical cognitive load and gaze did occur, in the case of hesitant phases. And secondly, the gaze pattern was found to be more stable (i.e., subject to fewer changes in state) than one would predict if gaze simply reflected cognitive load, specifically each fluent-hesitant-fluent transition. It was also demonstrated that there were decrements in verbal performance in those cycles where hesitant phases were dominated by gaze. One possible explanation was offered for the observed diversions of gaze from the pattern which is optimal on cognitive grounds. It was suggested that there are certain social pressures on individuals in conversation to comply to certain behavioral standards regarding amount of gaze, and length of glances, if they wish to make a favorable impression. Other explanations are possible, however; for example, certain unusual behavioral acts on the part of the listener may have attracted the speaker's attention during the ideational planning phases. The present study cannot eliminate this alternative hypothesis, since data on the total behavior of the listener, in the dyadic conversations studied, was not available in every case. Clearly further research is necessary to explore which social variables can affect the intimate patterning of gaze and speech in dialogue.

NOTE

[1]   Kendon (1976) personal communication.

REFERENCES

Argyle, M., and M. Cook
    1976   *Gaze and Mutual Gaze*. Cambridge: Cambridge University Press.

318   *Geoffrey W. Beattie*

Argyle, M., and J. Dean
 1965   "Eye-contact, distance and affiliation", *Sociometry* 28, 289-304.
Argyle, M., and R. Ingham
 1972   "Gaze, mutual gaze and proximity", *Semiotica* 6, 32-49.
Argyle, M., R. Ingham, F. Alkema, and M. McCallin
 1973   "The different functions of gaze", *Semiotica* 7, 19-32.
Argyle, M., M. Lalljee, and M. Cook
 1968   "The effects of visibility on interaction in a dyad", *Human Relations* 21, 3-17.
Argyle, M., L. Lefebvre, and M. Cook
 1974   "The meaning of five patterns of gaze", *Eur. J. Soc. Psychol.* 4, 125-36.
Beattie, G. W.
 1976   "Hesitation and gaze as indicators of cognitive planning in speech". Unpublished paper, University of Cambridge.
 1977   "The dynamics of interruption and the filled pause", *Br. J. Soc. Clin. Psychol.* 16, 283-84.
 1978   "Floor apportionment and gaze in conversational dyads", *Br. J. Soc. Clin. Psychol.* 17, 7-16.
Boomer, D. S., and A. T. Dittmann
 1962   "Hesitation pauses and juncture pauses in speech", *Lang. Speech* 5, 215-220.
Butterworth, B.
 1975   "Hesitation and semantic planning in speech", *J. Psycholing. Res.* 4, 75-97.
Butterworth, B., and G. W. Beattie
 1976   "Gesture and silence as indicators of planning in speech". Paper presented at the Psychology of Language Conference, University of Stirling, June 1976. To appear in the Conference Proceedings.
Cook, M., and M. G. Lalljee
 1967   "The role of vision in interaction" (unpublished). University of Oxford.
 1972   "Verbal substitutes for visual signals in interaction", *Semiotica* 6, 212-21.
Cook, M., and J. M. C. Smith
 1972   "Studies in programmed gaze" (unpublished). University College of Swansea.
 1975   "The role of gaze in impression formation", *Brit. J. Soc. Clin. Psychol.* 14, 19-25.
Darwin, C.
 1872   *The Expression of Emotion in Man and Animals*. London: Murray.
Day, M. E.
 1964   "An eye-movement phenomenon relating to attention, thought and anxiety", *Perc. Mot. Skills* 19, 443-46.
Duke, J. D.
 1968   "Lateral eye movement behaviour", *J. Gen. Psychol.* 78, 189-95.
Duncan, S.
 1972   "Some signals and rules for taking speaking turns in conversations", *J. Pers. Soc. Psychol.* 23, 283-92.
 1973   "Toward a grammar for dyadic conversation", *Semiotica* 9, 29-47.

1975 "Interaction units during speaking turns in dyadic face-to-face conversations", in A. Kendon, R. M. Harris, & M. R. Key, eds., *The Organisation of Behaviour in Face-to-Face Interaction*. The Hague: Mouton.

Exline, R. V., and C. Eldridge
1967 "Effects of two patterns of a speaker's visual behaviour upon the authenticity of his verbal message". Paper presented to the Eastern Psychological Association, Boston (unpublished). University of Delaware.

Exline, R. V., and L. C. Winters
1965 "Effects of cognitive difficulty and cognitive style upon eye to eye contact in interviews". Paper read at Eastern Psychological Association Meeting, pp. 319-50.

Fodor, J. A., T. G. Bever, and M. F. Garrett
1974 *The Psychology of Language*. New York: McGraw-Hill.

Goffman, E.
1956 "Embarrassment and social organisation", *Amer. J. Sociol.* 62, 264-71.

Goldman-Eisler, F.
1967 "Sequential temporal patterns and cognitive processes in speech", *Lang. Speech* 10, 122-32.
1968 *Psycholinguistics: Experiments in Spontaneous Speech*. London: Academic Press.
1972 "Pauses, clauses, sentences", *Lang. Speech* 15, 103-13.

Henderson, A. I., F. Goldman-Eisler, and A. Skarbek
1966 "Sequential temporal patterns in spontaneous speech", *Lang. Speech* 9, 207-16.

Jaffe, J., and S. Feldstein
1970 *Rhythms of Dialogue*. New York: Academic Press.

Kasl, S. V., and G. E. Mahl
1965 "The relationship of disturbances and hesitations in spontaneous speech to anxiety", *J. Person. Soc. Psych.* 1, 425-33.

Kendon, A.
1967 "Some functions of gaze-direction in social interaction", *Acta Psychol.* 26, 22-63.

Kendon, A., and M. Cook
1969 "The consistency of gaze patterns in social interaction", *Brit. J. Psychol.* 69, 481-94.

Kleck, R. E., and W. Nuessle
1968 "Congruence between the indicative and communicative functions of eye-contact in interpersonal relations", *Brit. J. Soc. Clin. Psychol.* 7, 241-46.

Knight, D. J., D. L. Langmeter, and D. C. Landgren
1973 "Eye-contact, distance and affiliation: The role of observer bias", *Sociometry* 36, 390-401.

Libby, W. L.
1970 "Eye contact and direction of looking as stable individual differences", *J. Exp. Res. Pers.* 4, 303-12.

Maclay, H., and C. E. Osgood
1959 "Hesitation phenomena in English speech", *Word* 15, 19-44.

Mehrabian, A.
1971   "Nonverbal betrayal of feeling", *J. Exp. Res. Pers.* 5, 64-73.
Mehrabian, A., and M. Williams
1969   "Nonverbal concomitants of perceived and intended persuasiveness", *J. Pers. Soc. Psychol.* 13, 37-58.
Natale, M.
1976   "A markovian model of adult gaze behavior", *J. Psycholing. Res.* 5, 55-63.
Nielsen, G.
1962   *Studies in Self Confrontation*. Copenhagen: Munksgaard.
Patterson, M. L.
1973   "Stability of non-verbal immediacy behaviours", *J. Exp. Soc. Psychol.* 9, 97-109.
Reich, S. S.
1975   "The function of pauses for the decoding of speech". Unpublished Ph.D. thesis, University College, London.
Rutter, D. R.
1973   "Visual interaction in psychiatric patients: A review", *Brit. J. Psychiat.* 123, 193-202.
Schulze, R., and J. Barefoot
1974   "Non-verbal responses and affiliative conflict theory", *Brit. J. Soc. Clin. Psychol.* 13, 237-43.
Sokal, R. R., and F. J. Rohlf
1973   *Introduction to Biostatistics*. San Francisco: W. H. Freeman.
Stephenson, G. M., and D. R. Rutter
1970   "Eye-contact, distance and affiliation: A re-evaluation", *Brit. J. Psychol.* 61, 385-93.
Stephenson, G. M., D. R. Rutter, and S. R. Dore
1973   "Visual interaction and distance", *Brit. J. Psychol.* 64, 251-57.
Valian, V. V.
1971   "Talking, listening and linguistic structure". Unpublished Ph.D. thesis, Northeastern University.
Vine, I.
1971   "Judgement of direction of gaze – an interpretation of discrepant results", *Brit. J. Soc. Clin. Psychol.* 10, 320-31.

ADAM KENDON

Some Functions of the Face in a Kissing Round

INTRODUCTION

In this paper we will undertake a detailed analysis of a film specimen of a couple who are engaged in kissing one another. In undertaking this analysis we shall contribute to the study of kissing, but we shall also be able to show something of the subtlety and complexity of the role of the face in social interaction. Most studies of the face have considered it solely from the point of view of its role in emotional expression, and the focus of interest of these studies has been, accordingly, upon facial patterns as symptoms of affective states. In consequence, we have almost no systematic knowledge of how the face functions in social interaction. An important aim of this paper is to demonstrate how the behavior of the face may be studied within social interaction and how we may examine its integration with the other aspects of behavior that may be observed. In this way we shall be able to see what part the face plays in the interrelating of the behavior of the participants. The findings of the analysis will be discussed in relation to more traditional studies of the face, and also in the light of some more general theoretical considerations regarding the organization of behavior in face-to-face interaction. We may also note that, in using a kissing round for analysis, we shall be making a contribution to the as yet hardly existent literature on the behavior of human courtship. Although we deal with but a single couple and with but a very small fragment of their interaction, the close analysis we present here will enable us to raise questions appropriate for any further study of the behavior of human courtship.

The principal question that has been pursued in most studies of the human face has been whether or not observers can distinguish facial expressions reliably in terms of the different emotions which different facial expressions are presumed to be expressing. This line of inquiry is usually traced back to Darwin (1872), for he claimed that there are distinct patterns of behavior by which different emotions find expression. A very large proportion of the work done, mainly by psychologists, can be seen to have arisen in response to this claim. The main method that has been followed has been to present subjects with faces in various poses, portrayed either in diagrams, still photographs or, occasionally, moving pictures or live performances, and ask them to label the presentation in terms of an expressed emotion. In this work, which has been extensively reviewed several times (e.g., Bruner and Tagiuri, 1954; Woodworth and Scholsberg, 1954; Davitz, 1964; Izard, 1969; Vine, 1970; Ekman, 1973), it is always assumed that a facial expression is an expression of emotion. Many of these studies also assume that there are a limited number of discrete, primary emotions which can be defined in terms of behavioral, physiological and, occasionally, experiential features, quite apart from the way the behaving individual may be interrelated with the behavior of others. These studies are addressed, thus, to the significance of facial behavior to the state of the individual, and they are not concerned with how the facial behavior of one individual affects or is related to the behavior of others in the situation of a social encounter. As Vine (1970:304) concludes, from his review of the field: "Undoubtedly there is much that can be discovered from the results of the recognition studies, but they tell us little about the functioning of facial-visual communication in day-to-day social behavior."

This investigation will begin, therefore, not with emotions, but with behavior. It will start by looking at behavior from the point of view of how it functions in sustaining the patterns of behavioral interrelatedness that obtain between individuals when they are in each other's presence and which constitute occasions of interaction. With regard to the face one asks, thus, not what feelings does the face express or how it does so, but what does the face do? One then proceeds to determine, within the context of an ongoing interaction where, in relation to the rest of the behavior, the various patterns of behavior observed in the face can be seen to occur. The question at issue is, what functions *for the interaction* do these differentiable units of facial behavior have? From this point of view, in other words, the question of what organismic or affective state is supposedly made manifest in the face is not relevant. What is relevant is what difference different facial patterns make to the organization of the behavior in the occasions of interaction in which they occur.[1]

Remarkably little research on human facial behavior has been carried out from this point of view. Some of the work on the infant smile, summarized, for example, by Bowlby (1969) and Vine (1973), has examined the role of the smile in mother-infant interaction. Blurton Jones (1967), Grant (1969), Brannigan and Humphries (1972), and McGrew (1972) have reported observational studies of facial (and other) behavior, mainly in small children, and here a major interest has been in its signaling function. Eibl-Eibesfeldt (1970, 1971) has also reported extensive observations on several different patterns of facial behavior, collected from a wide range of cultural contexts, and here again the focus is upon its signaling, or communicational, function.

Reece and Whitman (1962) and Rosenfeld (1966a, b; 1967) have reported experimental studies in which the influence of smiling on other aspects of interaction has been studied. Kendon's (1967) study of the functions of gaze direction in interaction also includes some observations on the interactional functions of smiling. Finally, Birdwhistell (1970) has discussed the face from this point of view in several of his essays. Thus, in his essay on the smile, he points out how smiles have a wide variety of social functions, and that to consider them merely, in his phrase, as "visible transforms of underlying physiological states" (p. 32) would be to miss this aspect of their functioning entirely. In other essays he describes how the movements of the face may be brought into play in association with speech, and how these movements, along with movements of the head and limbs, have a complex relationship to the structuring of speech, both as an activity and with respect to its content. Facial displays can serve to mark out points of emphasis in speech, they can serve to mark off whole segments of speech as distinct units or as contained or embedded units, and they can also provide a commentary and supplement to what is being said. If we watch the faces of listeners too, we can see that nods, smiles, frowns, and raised eyebrows appear frequently in some circumstances. Such facial behavior probably plays an important part in the regulation of the behavior of the speaker.[2] Similar observations on the regulatory functions of facial behavior have been made by Ekman and Friesen (1969).

It will be seen, thus, that when one takes as a starting point the behavior of the face itself, and when one then considers what the relationship is between the behavior of the face and other aspects of behavior that may be going forward in interaction, it becomes apparent that the face is involved in a wide range of functions. The preoccupation with the face as it expresses, or in some other way manifests, emotion has left these other functions of the face unexplored. From the point of view of the development of a theory of the communicative functions of human behavior, however, it is of great importance to consider the face in all its various functions. It is hoped that the present paper will contribute to such a broader, communicative approach to the study of the face.

MATERIAL FOR THIS STUDY

If we are to study the behavior of the face in its natural context, it will be necessary to acquire some good specimens of facial behavior which can be examined in detail and at leisure. This is best done by the use of 16mm film, which allows both for the repeated study of the specimens and for one to see the behavior of the face as it develops in time. For our present interest, it is of great importance, in acquiring these specimens, that one should film in such a way that the faces of the individuals who are involved in interaction are always visible. If this is not done, one cannot hope to analyze the way in which the behavior of the face is integrated into the interaction. It should be noted that other workers who have used film in the study of the face, including Landis and Hunt (1936), Thompson (1940), Frijda (1953), Lynn (1940), Coleman (1949), Haggard and Isaacs (1966), Eibl-Eibesfeldt (1970), and Ekman (1972), have not been concerned with interaction and accordingly have only filmed individuals separately.

The analysis undertaken in this paper is of a four minute 16mm film record, here to be known as C14.1.[3] The couple filmed in C14.1 were observed sitting on a park bench and as they were seen to be actively engaged in a kissing round, the camera was set up. The camera was started as soon as possible thereafter and kept running continuously until the kissing round ended. The camera was restarted when the couple started a new round of kissing. C14.1 thus contains two segments, each approximately two minutes in length, showing a kissing round from very shortly after its beginning until its end. The first segment of this specimen was analyzed first. The second segment was examined in detail later as a way of checking some of the relationships we were able to observe in the first. Here we will present the details of the first segment only, although the second segment will be referred to for additional examples.

In filming the present specimen, a 500mm lens was used and the camera was placed about 100 yards away from the couple. No attempt was made to hide the camera. As far as can be told, the couple remained unaware that they were being filmed. The lens was focused in such a way that only the head and shoulders of the two were in frame and, since the camera was behind the bench on which they were sitting, their faces could be seen in profile whenever either of them turned to face the other. In the period during which they were filmed, the couple repeatedly turned to face one another, and they moved their faces closer together for kissing, nose rubbing, forehead touching, and neck nuzzling.

There are several limitations to the specimen used in the present analysis which should be noted. First, as we have just said, we see the faces of M or F only when either turns to face the other. That is, we see their faces only during certain phases of the interaction and not all of the time. Second, we are limited in that we can only see the heads and shoulders of F and M. A wider angle could have been used, perhaps, but had this been done we would have lost the extreme detail of facial behavior that we were able to acquire with this film. Ideally, a second camera should have been used at the same time. Given the circumstances under which the film was made, this was not possible. Third, we know nothing of the wider context of the behavior recorded. We do not know the place of this particular fragment of interaction within the larger period of time during which M and F were together, and, of course, we know nothing of their relationship. Finally, owing to the way that the cameraman started and stopped the film, we see the end of two kissing rounds, but not their beginning and we see nothing of the behavior between kissing rounds. Furthermore, no sound recording was attempted. At certain times in the specimen, we can tell where utterances occur from lip movements; however, these have been ignored in the present analysis.

Despite these limitations, we believe that the present analysis and discussion will prove useful, because it will serve to show how the face may function in interaction with a degree of detail that has not been achieved elsewhere. Also, the interaction recorded in this specimen is highly characteristic of one sort of human courting behavior. A detailed description is worthwhile, therefore, insofar as there are virtually no other accounts of the details of human courting behavior available.

ANALYSIS

In the account to follow, we shall consider first the *repertoire of facial patterns* observable in F and M. Second, we shall describe the action-sequence F and M engage in together. That is, we shall distinguish a number of 'action' elements' and describe how they are patterned in time. We shall see that in terms of these actions the kissing round can be divided into a number of phases according to differences in the way these actions are interrelated. Finally, we shall examine the *relationship between the different facial patterns and the action-sequence*. We shall see that whereas M's face shows very little change, F's face is highly variable, and that M's actions are highly interdependent with F's actions and with the behavior of her face. F's face, it will appear, functions to regulate M's behavior. We shall also be able to suggest what the different functions may be for the different kinds of facial patterns F displays.

1. *The repertoire of facial patterns*

There have been few attempts to develop a descriptive system for the behavior of the face. For the most part, the starting point has been the emotion the face is presumed to be showing, and the attempt is then made to describe how the face shows different emotions, rather than simply to describe what the face does. This is true even of the most recent and sophisticated attempts in this direction. Ekman, Friesen and Tomkins (1971), for example, developed a visual dictionary of facial behavior which they call the Facial Affect Scoring Technique (FAST), that consists of photographs of the brows, eyes, and mouth region of the face in numerous different positions. The positions depicted in these photographs, however, were selected in terms of a previously established set of categories of emotion. "The specific categories selected", Ekman *et al.* write, "were those that had been consistently found by all investigators within Western Cultures who had attempted to determine how many categories of emotion can be judged from the face ..." (40). Models were instructed to pose the various parts of their faces in specific ways, and these poses were then photographed. The poses they were instructed to assume, however, were dictated by the theoretical consideration that there are distinguishable categories of emotion. The different categories of facial behavior FAST allows one to score, thus, are classified according to the emotions the face is presumed to be showing. In its most recent development, however, FAST has been altered considerably to provide a system for measuring all facial behavior (Ekman, personal communication). When full details become available, it may well be that FAST will provide the comprehensive notation system for facial behavior that is so badly needed.

An alternative approach to the behavior of the face has emerged recently in the work of Blurton Jones (1967), Grant (1969), Brannigan and Humphries (1972), and McGrew (1972). These workers, influenced by the approach to behavior developed in ethology in dealing with the behavior of birds and fish, have independently provided lists of facial patterns, derived mostly from their observations of small children. This approach is closer to the one needed here, insofar as it is not tied to a specific theory of emotion and does not proceed from the assumption that the face serves only in affective functioning. However, since the descriptions are in terms of *categories* of facial patterns, it is not applicable as a system of notation for new material. What is needed is an approach in which the various moveable elements of the face are identified, and a notation system developed for writing their movements down. This would make it possible to describe specimens of facial behavior systematically and then, from these descriptions, an account of the various configurations of behavior in the face could be clearly arrived at.

Some beginnings along these lines have been made. An early attempt may be found in the work of Birdwhistell (1952, reprinted 1970), who presented a system of notation for bodily movements which included notations of the behavior of the face. This comprised fifty-three separate 'kinegraphs' that referred to actions of the eyes, brows, nose, and mouth. Birdwhistell's kinegraphs, however, are difficult to use as a notation system in systematic studies of the face, for what he has provided, in effect, amounts to an *ad hoc* list of actions that he has observed in the face. It is not a true notation system for it cannot be used to describe patterns of facial behavior that are not included in the list. The closest approach to a notation system for the face was developed by Ex and Kendon (1964, reprinted in Argyle, 1969). These authors recognized that the principal elements through which the behavior of the face could be described would be in terms of the movements of the brows, eyelids, and the mouth region. The notation was developed in reference to film specimens of people in conversation, and the glyphs of the notation were designed to accommodate the full range of behavior observed in each of three regions of the face: the brows, the eyes, and the mouth. This notation was used as a means of writing down what pose the face was in for each frame of the film being analyzed. From such a transcription, the phases of facial behavior could then be reconstructed. It is a fairly crude notation, though it has proved useful. The movements of the brows and eyelids can be described with some success with this notation, but a means of treating the extraordinarily variable mouth region was never satisfactorily arrived at. Recently, Blurton Jones (1971) has published a detailed account of the way the various components of the face have been observed to behave, based upon a very detailed study of a large number of photographs of children in natural situations. He does not present his findings as a notation system and the logic of the arrangement of his components of facial behavior leaves something to be desired. However, this work could be combined with an attempt such as that of Ex and Kendon, and a much more comprehensive system of notation could then be developed.

In this paper, a slightly modified version of the Ex and Kendon notation system has been used (see Table I). An examination of the film specimen' shows that the faces of the two individuals show periods of quite rapid change, alternating with periods in which the pattern of the face is more sustained. The Ex and Kendon notation system was found to be adequate for characterizing the more stable periods of facial patterning. A list of the patterns that were recorded in this way in the order in which they appeared and the length of time for which they were observed is provided in Table II.

It will be noted from Table II that M's face is almost the same each time it is observed. In contrast, F shows considerable variation in facial patterning. For F, twenty-three periods of relative stability were observed in the segment analyzed. Many of these periods are rather similar to one another, however, suggesting certain repetitions in the facial patterns of F. The twenty-three periods of relative stability have been grouped into nine classes of facial pattern. The groupings that we arrived at are as follows:[4]

    A. 'Normal face': 'Normal' brows, eyes, mouth. Occurs once in 14.
    B. 'Closed smile': 'Normal' brows, eyes; lips closed. with upper lip retracting to form smile. Occurs in 11, 13, and 17.
    C. 'Teeth smile': Brows normal to wrinkled; eyes normal to 'laughing' or 'screwed'; lips retracted to expose teeth and drawn laterally in smile. Occurs in 3, 5, 7, 10, 18 and 23, and in an extreme form in 6.
    D. 'Kiss face I': Brows normal; eyes closing by falling upper lid; lips parted and protruding slightly. Occurs in 4 and 8, both occasions when F is approaching to kiss M.
    E. 'Kiss face II': Brows drawn together somewhat; eyes 'tight'; lips

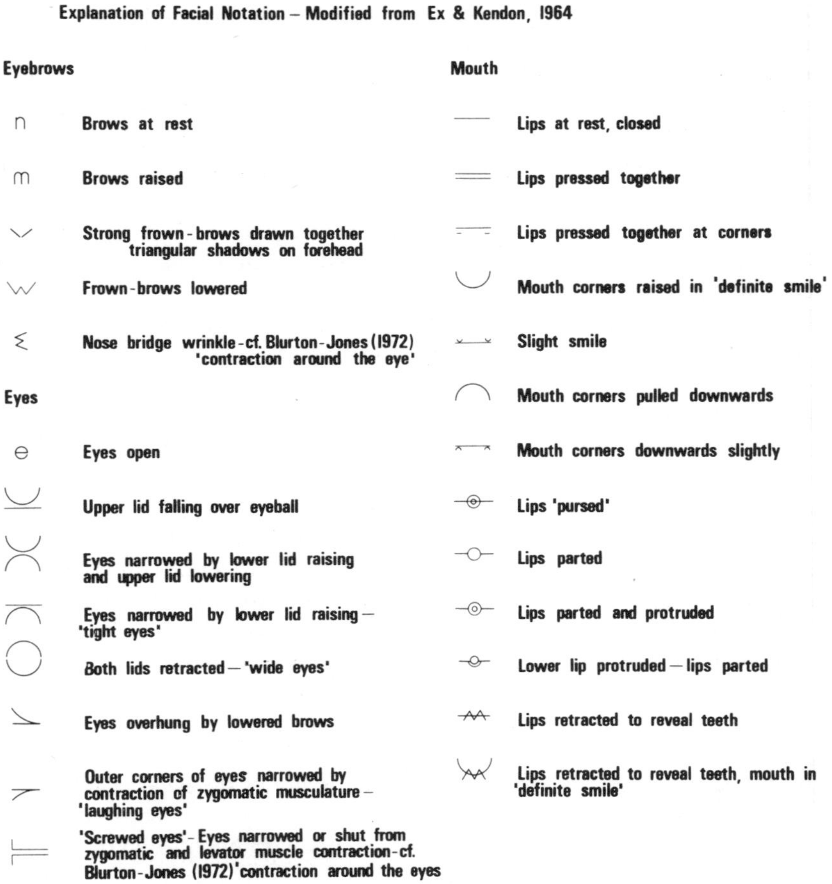
Explanation of Facial Notation – Modified from Ex & Kendon, 1964
Eyebrows
Brows at rest
Brows raised
Strong frown-brows drawn together triangular shadows on forehead
Frown-brows lowered
Nose bridge wrinkle-cf. Blurton-Jones (1972) 'contraction around the eye'
Eyes
Eyes open
Upper lid falling over eyeball
Eyes narrowed by lower lid raising and upper lid lowering
Eyes narrowed by lower lid raising – 'tight eyes'
Both lids retracted – 'wide eyes'
Eyes overhung by lowered brows
Outer corners of eyes narrowed by contraction of zygomatic musculature – 'laughing eyes'
'Screwed eyes'- Eyes narrowed or shut from zygomatic and levator muscle contraction-cf. Blurton-Jones (1972) 'contraction around the eyes
Mouth
Lips at rest, closed
Lips pressed together
Lips pressed together at corners
Mouth corners raised in 'definite smile'
Slight smile
Mouth corners pulled downwards
Mouth corners downwards slightly
Lips 'pursed'
Lips parted
Lips parted and protruded
Lower lip protruded – lips parted
Lips retracted to reveal teeth
Lips retracted to reveal teeth, mouth in 'definite smile'

TABLE I
EXPLANATION OF FACIAL NOTATION

The explanations given in this table are necessarily brief and we have given here only those notations used in the present study.

F's FACE

#	BROWS	EYES	MOUTH	GROUP	DURATION	#	BROWS	EYES	MOUTH	GROUP	DURATION
1.	n	∪	~⊙~	G	151-161	12.	n	e	—⊙—	A	1070-1074
2.	\/	⌐	——	I	179-196	13.	n	e	∪	B	1079-1090
3.	n	⌐	✕	C	197-261	14.	m	✕	⌐⊙⌐	F	1132-1235
4.	n	∪	⌣⊙⌣	D	266-278	15.	m	⌣	—⊙—	G	1551-1574
5.	n	⌐	✕	C	304-380	16.	n	e	——	A	1584-1586
6.	≲	⊨	✕	C	470-506	17.	n	e	∪	B	1587-1617
7.	n	e	✕	C	591-666	18.	w	⌐	✕	C	1862-1918
8.	n	∪	—⊙—	D	667-692	19.	w	⌐	✕	C	1931-2020
9.	n	∪	—⊙—	G	736-742	20.	\/	e	——	I	2130-2254
10.	n	⌐	✕	C	790-850	21.	n	✕	⌣⊙⌣	E	2259-2282
11.	n	e	∪	B	961-1026	22.	m	○	✕	H	2307-2338
						23.	m	e	✕	C	2715-2809

M's FACE

#	BROWS	EYES	MOUTH	DURATION	#	BROWS	EYES	MOUTH	DURATION
1.	⁄	⁄	—⊙—	188-235	5.	n	e	—⊙—	1120-1246
2.	⁄	⁄	⌣○⌣	313-360	6.	⁄	⁄	—⊙—	2147-2325
3.	⁄	⁄	—○—	553-569	7.	⁄	⁄	—⊙—	2694-2712
4.	n	e	—⊙—	1056-1103					

TABLE II
PERIODS OF SUSTAINED FACIAL PATTERN

Notations for each of the periods of sustained facial patterns for M and F in the First Segment of C.14. The duration of each pattern, as it could be seen in the film, is given in terms of numbers of frames, counted from the zero frame. Zero frame is explained in the text.

parted and slightly protruded, tight at corners with some slight smile. Occurs in 21, just prior to lips to lips kiss.

F. 'Dreamy face': Brows raised; eyes 'tight'; lips parted with some downward tension at the corners. Occurs in 14.

G. 'Lip forward': Brows normal, eyes closed by upper lid fully lowered over eye; lips parted with lower lip pushed forward slightly. Occurs in 1, 9 and 15 as F is turning away from M after being kissed.

H. 'Wide face': Brows raised; eyes over wide; lips parted smiling; mouth open. Occurs in 22.

I. 'Frown face': Brows drawn together; eyes 'frowning'; lips straight, tight at corners, upper lip retracted to reveal teeth. Occurs in 2 and 20.

If we may thus identify nine distinct facial arrangements, it may be remarked that F displays a considerable repertoire, even within such a short stretch of time and despite the repetitions already noted. If the face is to be regarded solely in terms of its affective functions, we would be led to remark on the range of feeling, or emotion, F has in this short period of time. Perhaps she does have such a range of affective experience here. However, to say this directs our interest to F and her inner states and away from the question as to whether these different facial patterns serve any function within the interaction. We turn, therefore, to look at the relationship between the appearance of these facial patterns and the other behavior that can be observed. To do this we must first consider the sequence of action.

2. *The Action-Sequence*

The specimen we are here concerned with is a specimen of what we have called a 'kissing round', which is a fairly common kind of interaction that can be observed in courting couples. This kissing round occurred while the couple was stationary, seated very closely side-by-side on a park bench. M and F were so close to one another that their bodies were in contact from the shoulder downwards. M had extended his left arm along the back of the seat and thus had his arm around F's shoulders. Such 'sitting together' within which kissing rounds often occur is, of course, a common pattern of behavior in couples in Western urban settings.

In a kissing round what we commonly observe is that the male or female, or both together, repeatedly orient their faces toward each other and move closer to make physical contact, either with the lips, the tip of the nose, the forehead, or the cheek. The point of physical contact is variable. In the present specimen, M and F contact each other's necks, earlobes, noses, foreheads, cheeks, and lips. Associated with such facial contacts, various huggings, strokings, and other kinds of contacts may be made with the limbs. In the present case we shall not be concerned with these, for none of this could be seen, owing to the way in which the film had been made.

For the purposes of the present analysis, five different head orientations were distinguished in terms of the different directions p was observed to point his face, relative to q's head. If p oriented his face fully toward q's head, he was said to be *facing* q; in this case, p's face could be seen in full profile in the film. If p's face could be seen in partial profile, p was said to be *quarter-facing forward*. If only p's cheek and tip of his nose could be seen, p was said to be *half-facing forward*. If none of the face could be seen and only the back of the head, p was said to be *facing forward*. Here, presumably, his face was oriented to the front of him and he was facing neither toward nor away from the head of the other. If p rotated his head any further in the direction that would point his face away from q, he was said to be *facing away*. P was said to *approach* if he moved his face closer to q. This would include approaches to physical contact. P was said to *back-off* if he moved his face away from q, at the same time maintaining his face in *facing* orientation. *Lean forward/lean away* was used to refer to forward and backward movements of the whole trunk. This occurs only in F who was observed to lean forward and towards M, thus leaning in front of him.

In terms of these phases of action, a diagram of the specimen has been constructed (see Fig. 1). This shows the relative temporal extent of the head orientations of *facing* and *quarter-facing* for M and F, periods of *approach* and *back-off* and *leaning* and periods of physical contact. It also shows, for F, the facial patterns that were observed. *Half-facing, facing forward* and *facing away* have not been marked in the diagram but their occurrence is included in Table III, which gives a detailed account of the action-sequence of the specimen.

3. *Analysis of the Action-Sequence*

We may begin by noting that there are periods of time within the segment being analysed during which F and M do not have their faces turned toward one another. They are either turned away from one another or both are facing forward. We shall refer to these periods as periods of *Disengagement*. Such periods of Disengagement separate periods of *Involvement*, in which either F or M, or both, are facing, or quarter-facing the other, approaching, leaning or touching. These periods of Involvement may be grouped into phases, which are distinguished from one another in terms of how M and F relate their actions to one another:

> PHASE I: In each period of Involvement in this phase, F faces M and then approaches him to kiss his neck, to touch noses with him or to touch foreheads with him. Each period of Involvement

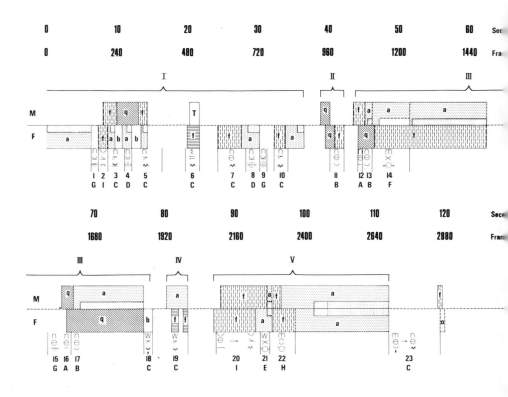

FIG. 1

This presents a map of the action-sequence of the first segment of C14.1, together with the locations of all of F's facial patterns. The map has been plotted to the nearest eight frames (1/3 of a second). In the interests of clarity of presentation, only the following units of head orientation have been plotted: Facing (vertical broken hatching labeled f), Quarter-Facing (diagonal hatching labeled q), Approach (dotted hatching labeled a). Lean-forward (horizontal hatching labeled f), Back-off (unhatched blocks labeled b), and Turn-away (unhatched block labeled o). T = Tilts head forward.

Hatched blocks on the center line = physical contact; broken outline block on center line = light physical contact. Exact time relations between M's and F's actions can be derived from Table III where boundary frame numbers are given.

is begun by F — that is, she is the first to begin facing or approaching M in each case.

PHASE II: M is the first to turn to F. F part-turns to M. There is no approach and no physical contact.

PHASE III: Periods of Involvement in this phase are begun by M, and he approaches F to kiss her neck or her cheek or to touch noses with her. In this phase, F faces or part-faces M but she does not approach him. Phase III, thus, is in some ways a reversal of Phase I.

PHASE IV: M initiates and approaches F as he does in Phase III. F, however, leans towards M, and in front of him. There is no physical contact.

PHASE V: F begins the single period of Involvement in this phase; M and F, facing each other, each approach and kiss lips to lips; each then kisses the other's neck. Except for the initial stage of F's approach to M, M and F show much greater symmetry in their behavior than they do in the other phases.

Following Phase V each turns 180^0 away from the other and then remains facing forward. Shortly after this the cameraman stopped the film, for the kissing bout was over.

It will be seen thus that in Phases I, III and V we have approach and physical contact which in Phase I is initiated by F, in Phase III by M, and in Phase V, it becomes mutual. Phases II and IV are very brief compared with the other phases. They are distinguished here because, though in both cases M initiates them, there is either no approach (as in Phase II) or the approach is not reciprocated by F in the way that it was in the preceding phase (Phase V). As we shall see later, there are other features of behavior in these phases which set them apart. We shall see that they are a special kind of phase and appear to bring about changes in established routines, rather than themselves being routines.

A more detailed account of the action-sequence of this kissing round can be found in Table III in which all the periods of Involvement and Disengagement that occur within the sub-phases are given. Since this account will be referred to throughout the discussion to follow, we have, accordingly, numbered the various sub-phases and other points of change within the action-sequence for ease of reference. This table should be read in conjunction with the diagram in Fig. 1.

TABLE III

ACTION-SEQUENCE OF C14.1, FIRST SEGMENT

Note: Numbers in parentheses give last frame following zero frame of each component.

PHASE I

1.   F kisses M's neck (0149)

DISENGAGE: F faces forward from M (0177)
                       M faces forward from F (0181)

2.   a.   F faces M (0200); M faces F (0214)
           F, still facing M, approaches M and they touch noses (0228)
      b.   F backs-off M (0258); M half-faces F (0304)
           F approaches, kisses M's neck (0295)
      c.   F backs off M (0321); M faces F (0323)
           F and M, facing each other, approach, touch foreheads (0356)

DISENGAGE: F faces forward from M (0416)
                       M faces forward from F (0445)

3.   F quarter-faces M (0477); M faces away from F (0477)
      F faces M (0501)
      F leans forward and toward M (0533); M lowers head in forward (0533)

DISENGAGE: F faces forward from M (0591)
                       M half-faces F (0601)

4.   F faces M (0653); M faces forward (0643); M faces away (0760)
      F approaches and kisses M's neck (0729)

DISENGAGE: F half-faces M (0787)
                       M faces away (0795)

5.   F faces M (0810); M faces forward (0931)
      F leans cheek against M' scheek (0876)

DISENGAGE: F faces forward (0937)
                       M faces forward (0931)

PHASE II

      M half-faces F (0958)

F quarter-faces M (0993); M faces forward (0989); M faces away (1047)

F faces M with head tilted back (1020)

DISENGAGE: F faces forward (1062)
M faces away from F (1047)

PHASE III

1.   M faces F (1077); F quarter-faces M (1132)
M kisses F's ear (1111)
F faces M (1250); M touches noses with F (1229)
M kisses F's ear (1505); F quarter-faces M (1514)

DISENGAGE: M faces away (1566)
F tilts head back and rotates rapidly ('shake'), and quarter-faces M (1571)

2.   M quarter-faces F (1606); F faces M (1858)
M approaches and kisses F's cheek, neck (1850)
F backs-off (1889)

DISENGAGE: M faces forward from F (1902)
F half-faces M (1934)

PHASE IV

M faces F and approaches (2009); F faces M (2017) and, while facing him, leans toward M (1967); leans away (1991); leans toward M (2011)

DISENGAGE: M leans away from F, faces forward (2111)
F leans back from M, faces fully away (2106)

PHASE V

F faces M (2239); M faces F (2244)

F approaches M, M approaches F (both facing), M and F kiss lips to lips (2383)

M and F kiss each other's necks (2686)

DISENGAGE: F backs off M, looks behind (2722), half-faces M (2870)
M backs off F, faces away (2855)

M faces F (2875); F faces away (2887), then turns to half-face M

KISSING ROUND ENDS: CAMERA STOPS

4. *The Relationship Between the Action-Sequence and Facial Patterns*

We shall now examine how F's face varies in relation to the phase of the kissing round and the action within the phase. We shall see how the role of F's face in the kissing round may be inferred from the contexts of occurrence of her various facial patterns.

(i) *Fa C ('Teeth smile') and Fa B ('Closed lips smile'): An Examination of Their Contexts of Occurrence*

We may begin by noting the contrast, in terms of F's facial displays, between Phase I and Phase III. In Phase I, F initiates each period of Involvement and, in each instance that she turns to M, she has some version of Fa C: smile with teeth showing, sometimes with open mouth as well. If M then faces F, as he does in I.2(a) and I.2(c), M and F approach each other and touch foreheads or noses, but they do not kiss. If M does not turn to F, but faces away from her as she turns to him (which he does in all the other periods of Involvement in this phase), then F approaches and kisses M's neck, leans in front of him, or leans her cheek against his.

In contrast, in Phase III, M begins each period of Involvement by first turning to F and when he does so, F does not move towards him but remains still. Here she shows Fa B ('closed smile'), and M then approaches her and kisses her. Fa B is thus associated with M kissing F, while when F shows Fa C ('teeth smile'), she is active in approaching M, and if M approaches her, he does not kiss her.

These observations suggest that Fa B functions as a signal to M that F is receptive to approaches and kisses from him, whereas Fa C is part of a configuration that serves to divert him from approaching and kissing. A closer examination of the relationship between the patterning of action and these facial arrangements of F serves to confirm this interpretation.

First, it can be seen that each time M kisses F, M waits before finally approaching her until she shows Fa B, as if the appearance of Fa B is the signal that gives M clearance for his final approach. Whenever M kisses F, he always proceeds in two steps: he turns to face F and then approaches her. On each occasion we may note that M does not begin his approach until *after* F has shown Fa B. In the first period of Involvement of Phase III, M turns to F and remains still, F part-turns to M with parted lips. Her lips then close to produce Fa B and only when she has completed this does M begin his approach. In the second period of Involvement in Phase III, this sequence is repeated, though here F changes to Fa B from Fa A ('neutral face'). Once again, however, M does not begin his approach until F has done so.

If we now look at the second segment of C14.1, we see exactly the same sequence again. That is, here, beginning at frame 4198, M turns his head

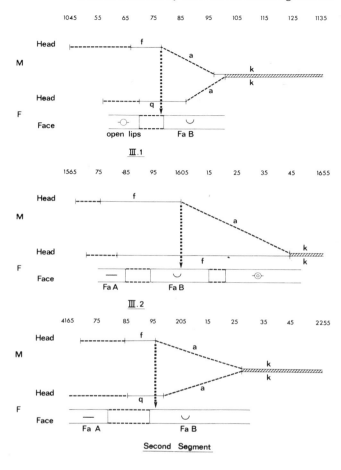

FIG. 2

These diagrams show the relationship in time between M's orientation and approach components and F's orientation and approach components and changes in F's face, for the beginning of kissing involvements at III.1, III.2 and the second segment.

For both F and M, the lines represent orientation components and their convergence represents approach. Broken lines represent movement. Line segment labeled f = face; q = quarter face; a = approach; k = physical contact. The boxes below F's head components indicate stable facial patterns when enclosed by continuous lines. Periods of change are represented by broken lines.

The perpendicular line beginning at the start of M's approach component indicates the relationship between the beginning of this and the state of F's face. Note that in each case M does not begin his approach until F has completed the formation of the facial pattern Fa B or 'closed lip smile'.

The diagram is begun in each case at the point where either F or M begins to change from Disengagement (facing forward) to Involvement quarter-facing or facing).

toward F, F turns to M and changes from Fa A to Fa B, whereupon M approaches and kisses her. These three sequences are diagrammed in Fig. 2, so that the exact time relations of these phases of behavior may be seen.

Let us now examine the contexts of occurence of Fa C, the 'teeth smile'. We have already observed how Fa C appears consistently throughout Phase I, where F is active in approaching M. Here, also, as we have seen, if M approaches F, he does not kiss her. We may now note that Fa C also appears at points which come just prior to changes in the relations of M's and F's actions, where the change is either to a relationship in which F again takes the initiative in beginning new periods of Involvement, or to one in which she turns away when M approaches her. Thus whereas at the end of III.1, F shows Fa G, and when M again turns to her, F responds with a part-turn and Fa B as she did before, at the end of III.2, she shows Fa C. This is also the end of Phase III, and in the next phase, though M approaches F again, he does not kiss her, and F now actively approaches M, showing Fa C throughout. Similarly, we may note how Fa C reappears as M and F disengage from mutual kissing at the end of Phase V. When M turns to F yet again, as he does beginning at 2856, F turns rapidly away from him and a prolonged period of Disengagement follows. It will be seen from these observations that the facial pattern F shows at the *end* of a period of Involvement gives an indication of how she will behave in the next period. When she shows Fa C in such a context, this indicates that she will next take the initiative in relation to M.

Further confirmation of our hypothesis about the functions of Fa C is derived from the second segment of the film. After a period in which M kisses F (already referred to above), and after a brief Disengagement, M again turns to F, but this time F turns to him with parted lips and exposed teeth. Here again, M does not commence any approach to F and they do not kiss.

We may conclude, thus, that these observations, when taken together, suggest that when F shows 'teeth smile' (Fa C) she will be behaving in relation to M in a way quite different from the way she behaves when she shows 'closed lips smile', or Fa B. Fa C signals that F is active in relation to M, and that M is not to kiss her; Fa B signals that F is receptive to kissing approaches from M.

(ii) *An Examination of Phases II and IV*

Further support for the functional role we have proposed for Fa C and Fa B in this kissing round may be derived from an analysis of Phases II and IV. This analysis will also suggest how these phases serve to bring about change in the relationship of M's and F's behavior. These phases are both much shorter than the others and they intervene between phases in which a repetitive pattern of interaction has been going on. Whereas Phases I and III have the character of routines, Phases II and IV appear to be negotiations.

In Phase II, for the first time in the sequence, M takes the initiative in starting a period of Involvement. He turns to F and F follows with a part-turn to M. Her lips are parted as she turns to M, but then she closes them to produce Fa B. As F closes her lips here, M turns away. F then turns somewhat more fully to M, still with Fa B, but now with her face tilted up slightly; then she also turns away. The next period of Involvement begins twenty-eight frames later (one and one-sixth seconds) at frame 1049. Here Phase III begins.

It can be seen that the pattern in Phase II is a partial version of the pattern in Phase III. Such a pre-enactment, we suggest, enables F and M to come to an agreement as to what the next routine of interaction will be. There are two possible ways in which this may be done. When M takes the initiative in turning to F at the beginning of Phase II, he is doing something new in relation to what has preceded this. He could thus be regarded as proposing that a new routine be established. F's part-turn and Fa B is then a reply to this proposal, a reply which serves to suggest what this new routine might be. Alternatively, M's initiative may be more specific. It may constitute a proposal that he should now do the kissing; F's part-turn and Fa B would, in this case, constitute her acceptance of this proposal. In either case, we may observe here how F's Fa B appears to serve as a signal to indicate what she is prepared to do next in relation to what M will do.

Turning to Phase IV, we may observe again how it partly foreshadows the pattern of interaction of Phase V. Here, however, it is not the specific routine of Phase V that is foreshadowed. It is, rather, that it will be F's turn to initiate periods of Involvement.

Phase IV is begun by M who turns to F in just the same way as he has been turning to her throughout Phase III. F responds, not by a part-turn and Fa B, but by leaning forward in front of M, with Fa C. Thus whereas in Phase II we had what, in effect, appeared to be a tryout for the pattern that was to follow, here one participant persists in the already established pattern while the other one now reciprocates differently. However, it will be seen that F, in reciprocating M's approach by leaning forward and with Fa C, is adopting a pattern of behavior which she has used in Phase I. Thus she refers back to an earlier behavioral interrelation, in which she is the initiator of Involvements, and in this way she sets the stage for re-establishing that relationship. And indeed, as may be seen, Phase V is initiated by F.

We may now observe that just as Phases II and IV appear to foreshadow the new routines that are to follow and so serve, as we suggest, to bring about the consensus upon which those new routines are based, so the occurrence of these phases is itself foreshadowed. There are features of F's behavior which immediately precede these phases that appear to hint at the new relationship that is to be established. Thus it will be seen how, in Phase I — in which F takes the initiative and is active in approaching M —in F's last approach to M *yeah?* [handwritten marginalia, top right]

(at I.5), she leans her cheek against M instead of kissing his neck or touching foreheads with him. In so doing, though she is active in her approach, she ceases to act *on* M, but leans on him, and so becomes passive in relation to him. Thus she hints at a new mode of relating to M and creates for him the opportunity of trying out, or proposing, a new routine.

Similarly, F does not switch to the mode of response she adopts in Phase IV without warning. We have already described how, at the end of III.2, as she moves away from M after his kiss, she displays Fa C. Fa C, as we have seen, occurs when F is the initiator of Involvements. Thus, in ending the second period of Involvement of Phase III with Fa C, in the facial pattern she adopts, she hints at the change in the relationship of her behavior to that of M that will be brought about through the enactment of Phase IV.

(iii) *Other Facial Patterns and Their Place in the Interaction*

We have noted so far that when F takes the initiative in facing M, and when M approaches F and kissing does not take place, F displays Fa C ('teeth smile'); whereas when M turns first to F and F then shows Fa B ('closed lip smile'), M approaches her and kisses her, while F remains relatively still. We adduced several observations to suggest that M's approach to F to kiss her was contingent upon F showing Fa B, whereas when F used Fa C, this served to signal that she was not receptive to the kissing approaches by M. We turn now to consider some of the other facial patterns F shows.

Phase III includes three approaches by M. In the first, M turns to F, F part-turns to M and displays Fa B. Thereupon M approaches and kisses her. M then pulls back a little, and M and F each face one another, M intermittently touching F's nose with his in a light brushing fashion. Here we observe Fa F, or 'dreamy' face. Following this, M re-approaches F for a further and, this time, very lengthy period of kissing. Fa F may therefore serve here to provide M with information about how F is responding to his kissing, and how she will behave in response to his continued advances. Notice that the first of M's three kissing contacts with F is very short. During the period of nose touching which follows, M would be able to perceive F's face and so, perhaps, check on how she is responding to his kissing. Here F's face serves as a source of information both on what she will do next and also on what she will let M do.

Phase V, in which lips-to-lips kissing and a mutual embrace occur, is very interesting from the point of view of F's facial behavior. She shows here a whole series of different patterns, each developing in a continuous fashion from the preceding one. The notation system employed in this paper was not adequate to describe all these changes, and only four patterns have been marked: two variants, both labeled I ('Frown face'), E ('Kiss face II') and H ('Wide face').

F initiates Phase V by shifting from a turned-away position to one facing

M. This turn is begun very abruptly and the movement is rapid. In this it is different from the other turns F makes. Once facing M, she moves slowly closer and closer to him. As she moves closer, she speaks and, at the same time, her brows are drawn together in a strong frown, her eyes are actively narrowed, and her lips are drawn back at the corners tightly. As she moves yet closer, she begins to retract her lips to show her teeth. Then, the extreme tension goes out of the eyebrows; the lips are momentarily inrolled, but then are parted and protruded forward slightly; the eyelids are partially lowered; and for a moment, just prior to the actual contact of her lips with M's, F's face shows a distinctive and recognizeable pattern, Fa E, which we have here nicknamed 'Active Kiss face II' but which could be called 'passionate kiss face' since it is the kind of face that is seen in females during kissing that is serious and erotically arousing. At the moment of osculation, however, F's face suddenly changes to Fa A, 'neutral face', and immediately after the kiss her eyes are opened 'overwide', the brows are raised, and the lips parted relaxedly. This is Fa H, which has a look of child-like, wide-eyed innocence about it. Thereupon, M and F fall with vigor on each other's necks, in what appears to be a rather intense mutual embrace.

The facial patterns F shows in this sequence are far different from what one expects to see in seriously erotic or passionate kissing. It is as if F is regulating the amount of arousal M can achieve by herself offering displays that do not otherwise fit the immediate context. Thus she turns to M with vigor and approaches him with 'fierce' faces. Yet, for but 9/24 of a second, just before their lips touch, F's face is posed for passionate, not for playful, kissing. Here, perhaps, she hints at passions someday (or sometime) to be aroused. Perhaps we see here an instance of what appears to be a common principle of courtship: the continued interest of the other partner is maintained, and even heightened, by fleeting displays of behavior that belong to later stages of the courtship program.[5] If F can hint to M what possibilities the future holds in store for him, she can hold his interest.

Two other facial patterns will now receive brief comment. Fa D ('Kiss face I') occurs twice, both times when F is approaching to kiss M. It is a facial pattern that arises as F prepares to perform an action that is carried out by the lips, and we see the lips preparing for the contact that they will make as she approaches. Fa G ('Lower lip forward') occurs twice as F is turning away from M after being kissed by him. As we shall note in a later section of this paper, this facial pattern is seen in precisely the same context in other kissing couples.

(iv) *A Note on Tongue Protrusion*

It is noteworthy that when F backs off from M at the end of Phase III, and when she turns sharply away from M at the end of Phase V, she protrudes her tongue from her mouth. The phenomenon of tongue showing has received extensive discussion by Smith, Chase and Lieblich (1974). They conclude that the common feature of all the contexts they observed in which the tongue is shown is that p is reducing, cutting off, or forestalling involvement with another or others. In the present specimen, F shows her tongue when she is backing off or withdrawing from M, on both occasions following a prolonged period of intensive kissing. What then follows is a period in which, despite M's approaches, F turns away from him (after Phase V) or does not permit kissing (as in Phase IV). The appearance of her tongue at these points is thus in accord with what might be expected in the light of the observations of Smith and his colleagues.

Another observer of tongue showing is Eibl-Eibesfeldt. His interpretation is quite different from Smith's. He refers to 'tongue flicking' in which the "tongue is put out fleetingly..." and observes that this serves as an invitation to flirtation. He states that girls of easy virtue in Central Europe signal their sexual availability by showing their tongues, and that among the Waika Indians it is used by both sexes as an indication of sexual interest. Eibl-Eibesfeldt (1971:141-42) suggests that this is a ritualized form of licking. And insofar as licking another entails great physical intimacy, to show the tongue in this way could function as a sexual signal since it suggests a readiness for closeness.

The observed instances of tongue protrusion in the present specimen and the contexts in which they occur are, as we have seen, associated with F's withdrawal from periods of intense Involvement. As we have mentioned above, this fits more closely to what might be expected in the light of the observations of Smith *et al.* Although on the basis of this alone, we are in no position to draw any conclusions about the validity of either Eibl-Eibesfeldt's or Smith's interpretation, we do suggest that very detailed analysis will be required even of such an apparently simple gesture as tongue showing, before speculation about its possible derivation becomes worthwhile. Since Eibl-Eibesfeldt supplies no details as to when, within the interaction sequences he has observed, tongue showing occurs, we cannot comment further. We would merely like to point out that the present specimen provides an example of tongue showing in a flirtatious or courting interaction which, although superficially, might seem to fit with the examples Eibl-Eibesfeldt has provided and so support his interpretation, yet an analysis of the context of occurrence of the tongue showing within the interaction shows that it could as well be seen to support the interpretations of Smith *et al.*

DISCUSSION

We shall now consider the foregoing analysis in relation to three questions.

First, we shall examine it from the point of view of its relationship to more general considerations about the organization of face-to-face interaction. Second, we shall discuss the implications of our approach for the study of the face. Third, we shall touch briefly upon the implications for the study of human courting behavior.

1. *The Kissing Round and the Organization of Interaction*

When individuals engage in face-to-face interaction, their behavior tends to become systemically interrelated. That is, each continuously adjusts his behavior in relation to that of the other, and together they tend to establish stable systems of relationship so that we may speak as if their behavior were governed by shared sets of rules. Goffman has dealt with this in his analysis of what he has called *focused interaction* (Goffman, 1957, 1961, 1963) where he has suggested that, on such occasions, participants come to govern their conduct in accordance with a jointly established 'working consensus'. Occasions of focused interaction are highly complex in their organization and, in attempting to analyse the way in which the behavior of participants in them functions, it is useful to regard an occasion of focused interaction as comprised of a system of systems of behavioral interrelations with many different levels of organization (see Kendon, forthcoming).

In reference to the specimen analyzed in this paper, we may see that the 'kissing round' dealt with here is but one small system of behavioral relationship that exists within the framework of other relationships which extend over much longer periods of time and which integrate such smaller subsystems into more inclusive organizations. Thus the 'kissing round' occurs within the framework of a 'sitting together' (a system of spatial-orientational relationship Kendon has referred to elsewhere as a 'formation system'). 'Sitting together', and the subsystems such as 'kissing rounds' that it integrates is itself part of another level of behavioral organization which we might call 'afternoon together' (a system of behavioral relationship which we might refer to, following Goffman (1971), as a 'with'). Such an 'afternoon together' may itself be a subsystem within a yet more inclusive system, which includes all the different occasions of togetherness M and F have with one another and which constitutes their participation in a system of organization we might refer to as the 'relationship' — here that of 'couple' or 'courtship'. At each level in this complex hierarchy of systems, we may identify a 'working consensus' and, for each, different observational procedures and descriptive strategies will be required. Here we are confined to the level of the kissing round and its internal organization. We assume, however, that interactive systems, at whatever level, share similar principles of organization, so that a close analysis of a system at one level will throw light on principles that apply more generally.

A central problem in any investigation of interaction from this point of view will be to see how, in terms of the functioning of observable behavior, the 'working consensus' for a given behavioral system is established and maintained. In particular, this means that we must identify those aspects of behavioral function which serve to control or regulate the behavior of the participants in relation to the currently established pattern of relationship. This requires that we not only look for regularities in a behavioral relationship, but also that we look closely at places where these regularities change.

Of particular interest, then, from the point of view of more general principles of interactional organization, is the analysis of the sub-routines of the kissing round and the way in which these routines change. Thus we observed three sub-routines: Phase I, where F takes the initiative in orienting to M and approaching him; Phase III where M assumes the initiative; and Phase V where F re-assumes the initiative, though here M's and F's behavior becomes much more symmetrical. In Phase I and Phase III, where two or three repetitive cycles of interaction could be observed, we saw how F's facial behavior appeared to function as a signal that confirmed the pattern of the current sub-routine. In the intervening phases, Phase II and Phase IV, we were able to observe the way in which sub-routines of interaction may be changed. Thus, in Phase II, the change was brought about by a pre-enactment of the pattern that was to follow in Phase III. Here M initiated a turn to F which was a fragment of the complete sequence of actions he would perform in Phase III, while F responded to this by showing the facial display she was to use in Phase III. We suggested that, in this way, F confirmed the new pattern of behavioral relationship. Thus the pre-enactment of Phase II allowed M and F to agree upon a new set of rules to govern their interaction. In Phase IV, F responded to an established pattern of behavior in M by a pattern of behavior that belonged to Phase I. In this way, F established her intention to re-assume the initiative in starting periods of Involvement. Once again, we saw behavior which served to forewarn what later behavior was to be, and so again Phase IV allowed for a change in the prevailing rules of the interaction.

A principle of importance that is being illustrated here, is that an established routine in interaction is not simply changed, but that, if a new routine is established, this is done as a joint achievement of the participants. The interactants must therefore have a way of doing this, a way of each bringing the other to the point where they can begin together in terms of the new routine. Each must signal what his next mode of behavioral interrelating might be, before he can actually begin to relate in this new fashion. Thus we can expect to see a pre-exchange before any exchange is carried out according to new rules.

This feature of interactional organization has been demonstrated in some recent work on closings. The closing of an interactional system may be regarded as a special case of changing a routine and, like changing a routine, it is a joint achievement. Schegloff and Sacks (1973), in a study of conversational systems, have shown how such systems are brought to an end by a terminal exchange — i.e., a pair of utterances, such as "good-bye: good-bye", whose special function it is to bring both participants to the point where each does not respond to the end of the other's last utterance as if it were then his turn to speak. But Schegloff and Sacks show that such terminal exchanges cannot occur anywhere in a conversational system. They must be preceded by a 'closing section'. Here p announces, by a variety of devices (such as "O.K.", "we-el", "So-o" — to give their examples) that he is ready to close; the terminal exchange will not take place until q has reciprocated, that is, matched p's closing section initiation with a closing section completion. Similarly, Kendon (forthcoming) has referred to some recently completed observations on the closing down of another kind of interactional system, the 'facing formation system'. This is a spatial-orientated system which participants in face-to-face conversations usually (though not always) establish and maintain and which they typically bring to a close concurrently with the closing of a conversation. In the observations reported, it also appears that closing is accomplished in two steps: first, one of the participants steps away, turns out, or in some other way lapses in his contribution to the facing formation system. This is then reciprocated by the other, so that for a short time the system is not being fully sustained. The participants then reconstitute the system, whereupon they may jointly turn and step away from one another. Similarly, Kendon and Ferber's (1973) analysis of greetings may be mentioned here, in which it was shown how greeting is often accomplished in two steps: a 'distance salutation' and a 'close salutation'. Once again we have an exchange which allows the individuals involved to attune themselves to one another, so that they can then proceed together according to a new behavioral relationship.

If, in the present analysis, Phases II and IV have a functional status similar to the pre-phases of greeting and of conversational and facing-formation system closure, as we are suggesting, we may observe here, however, how in the present specimen, at least, these pre-phases are themselves foreshadowed. As we have seen, the interaction in the kissing round could be segmented into periods of Involvement separated by periods of Disengagement. Within each period of Disengagement, either M or F will be the next to start a new period of Involvement. Whether this will be done in a new way, or not, and so whether a new Phase will be begun, is evidently indicated by how F behaves as she changes from Involvement to Disengagement. We pointed out how her action towards M in the last sub-phase of Phase I appeared to hint at her readiness for some change in routine. Likewise, as F moved away from the last period of Involvement in Phase III, her facial pattern was quite different from the one she showed at the end of the previous period of Involvement in

Phase III, but it was one that belonged to a pattern of relationship we had already seen, namely, one in which she takes the initiative in respect to M in beginning periods of Involvement.

We have said that pre-exchanges and foreshadowings arise in interaction because the participants, having jointly committed themselves to a particular kind of behavioral relationship must, if they are to change to a new one, have a means of changing together. In the case of the changes of routine in the kissing round we have examined here, it should be noted that what we have been concerned with are changes in routine *within* a kissing round. Another problem that arises for interactants when they change routines is that of maintaining (or changing) the boundaries of the system within which the change in routine is to take place. Thus, when a period of Involvement comes to an end, how do M and F ensure that this is not also the end of the kissing round, or how do they ensure that it is the end (as it is at the end of Phase V)? An important feature that these routine-changing phases (such as Phase II and Phase IV) must have, is a reference to the system of organization in which they are contained. In the present example we may find this, we believe, in (a) the way in which behavior at the end of the previous phase structures the context within which the next period of Involvement will begin; and (b) the behavior pattern employed in the routine-changing phase itself. We will now discuss these two features in order.

The way a phase of Involvement is ended creates the context for repetition or change, but where it is to be changed it will also refer to the system of behavioral organization of which the ending sub-phase has been a part. Thus, when F leans her cheek against M's in the last sub-phase of Phase III, we suggested that in doing so she no longer acts *on* M, but becomes passive in relation to him and so suggests a possible new mode of relation. However, the new mode of relation she is suggesting is one that is one of a kind of relation that can be incorporated into a kissing round. Thus any subsequent action that either of them takes will be responded to by the other as an action governed by the prevailing principles of the kissing round.

The behavior in the routine-changing phases can also be seen as having a reference to the system within which the change is to take place, and so contains the change within that level of organization. This is clear enough in Phase II where F's Fa B is a signal for kissing to continue. Like the cheek lean, it proposes a pattern of behavior that is wholly within the framework of the kissing round. In Phase IV, however, which, as we have seen, does not foreshadow the pattern of organization of the next phase, F behaves according to a pattern she has used in Phase I and so, we suggested, she hinted at her intention to regain the initiative in starting periods of Involvement. However, we may also note that by referring back to her behavior in Phase I, although she does not foreshadow the pattern of any subsequent phase, this does once again serve to maintain the context as being that of the kissing round.

We may now compare what happens at the end of the kissing round. We may expect here that F will behave differently as she ends the last period of Involvement of the kissing round from the way she behaves at the end of a period of Involvement within the round. We can see an ending to a kissing round at the end of Phase V and also at the end of the kissing round recorded in the second segment.

At the end of Phase V, as F backs off from M, she shows Fa C, as already noted, and she also protrudes her tongue, as we have noted also. At the same time she rotates her head backwards to look behind her. In doing this, she looks in a direction she has not looked in before — she looks out of the space that she and M have been using for the kissing round and to the wider surrounding environment, thus hinting at other variables to which her behavior may become linked. In this way, she shows that the kissing round frame is over for her. This interpretation appears to be confirmed when, shortly thereafter, M initiates a turn to F. F responds to this by facing away very sharply.

The kissing round recorded in the second segment of the film ends with a phase similar to Phase III. A period of Disengagement follows a period of Involvement that has the same structure as the periods of Involvement in Phase III, and this period of Disengagement is ended when M turns to F again. F responds with a part-turn to M as before but, as we noted above, she does not show Fa B as she did earlier. Her lips are parted slightly, with some exposure of teeth, and M does not continue his approach. F then pulls in her lower lip over her teeth and appears to lick it briefly and then, reverting to a smile with lips only very slightly parted, she glances over her shoulder. Thus she again looks to the wider world just as she did at the end of Phase V. She then faces forward, whereupon M shifts posture, leaning toward her but, at the same time, bending his left arm at the elbow to bring his hand up so that he can lean his head on it.

We see, thus, that F behaves in a similar way at the end of the last period of Involvement of each of these two kissing rounds, but in a way that is quite different from the way she behaves at the ends of periods of Involvement within either of them. In referring, with her glance, to spaces beyond the space used for the kissing round, we suggest that she indicates that the frame of the kissing round is ended for her, that her behavior is no longer going to be governed by its principles. We may note that 'looking out' in this way is something that is not uncommonly observed in individuals who are about to leave a facing formation system, as if one way of hinting an end to one's current involvement is to look at parts of the environment which are not incorporated into the focus of involvement one is currently related to.

In short, we see how F's behavior appears to address itself not only to 'what next', but also to the context within which that 'what next' is to take place. This is done either by keeping behavior within the bounds of the current context, in which case that context can continue to operate; or by referring outside that context, which can serve as a signal to the other inter-actant that the current context will now be terminated. M may thus be fore-warned and so, jointly, again, a system of behavioral relationship can be brought to an end or changed.

2. *Differential Functions of Facial Patterns*

We started our analysis by listing a number of different facial patterns dis-played by F and we have shown that, at least for some of these, we were able to see them repeated often enough for us to be able to compare the contexts of their occurrence and so propose what function they had within the inter-action sequence we were studying. We may now raise the question: Do the facial patterns we have observed in F occur in others and, if they do, within the context of other kissing rounds, do they have the same functions? With this question in mind, we have reviewed the other filmed examples of kissing and related types of courting interaction that we have collected. This material is still very limited, but it does suggest that the features of F's facial behavior we have observed in the kissing round in C14.1 are not idiosyncratic. The main question we have been able to look into is whether or not a 'closed lip smile' is characteristic of actual kissing, while a 'teeth smile' is characteristic of kissing round interactions where actual kissing nevertheless does not occur.

The material available to us for review consisted of three series of film specimens: the CO Series and the C14 Series, comprising seventy-seven couples filmed in public parks in New York City, and two couples filmed in Australia (AN 1, AN 2). Of these, only eight specimens included examples of kissing or of a kissing round where it was possible to examine facial behavior.

In the CO series we have three examples, CO 51, CO 59 and CO 75, where, as the couple walks along, F turns her face towards and up to M's, and M bends down and kisses her. In CO 51 and CO 59, F shows a facial pattern very similar to Fa B ('closed lip smile'). In CO 75, F shows relaxed part-closed eyes and relaxed, parted, slightly protruded lips; a facial pattern which, it may be noted, is very close to the one given by Eibl-Eibesfeldt (1971:142) of a Waika Indian girl inviting a kiss.

Finally, in AN 1, a five minute stretch of film of a seated couple, there are four instances where M and F orient to one another and where M moves his face in closer for kissing. In two of these instances, kissing does not take place, F turning away as M completes his approach. In both of these cases, F shows 'teeth smile'. In the two instances where kissing does occur, F shows no definitive smile, and she changes to a facial pattern very much like Fa D ('kiss face I').

These few examples suggest that in kissing round contexts or contexts closely similar to this, if F shows 'closed lip smile' or some variant of slightly protruded, parted lips, in turning to M or when M turns to her, kissing is likely to occur. If F shows 'teeth smile' at these same junctures, however, though M may begin an approach for kissing, actual kissing does not take place. The relationship between kissing or non-kissing and 'closed lip smiling' or 'teeth smiling' that we had discerned in C14.1 thus appears to obtain in other couples as well.

Several of the other facial patterns described for C14.1 may also be seen in other specimens, again in closely similar contexts. Thus Fa G (brows normal, upper lid lowered over eye, lips parted slightly with lower lip pushed forward slightly), which we see in F on two occasions in C14.1, as she turns from a kiss and where further kissing will follow, is also seen in F as she turns from the kiss in CO 51 and in CO 75. In both of these cases, we may note that, as F turns her head away from the kiss, she also tilts it forward. Fa E, which we have aleaday said could be described as a 'passionate kiss face', is very well illustrated in C14.3 — a specimen of a couple who appear to be engaged in quite intense kissing.

These few examples, drawn as they are almost at random from among couples observed in urban park settings, do suggest that females, at least, have a repertoire of facial patterns which is common to them and which functions in much the same way in kissing interactions, regardless of who the individuals are. We may well be able to build up a vocabulary of facial patterns used in kissing rounds, and be able to specify their functions within such interactions. However, an attempt along these lines will have to wait until a sufficiently large number of specimens has been acquired. For obvious reasons, this material is not very easy to obtain.

It should be clear, of course, that the facial patterns we have been describing here may not be confined in their occurrence to the context of kissing rounds. Fa C and its variants and Fa B, especially, occur much more widely. Thus we cannot infer, from the mere appearance of one of these facial patterns, what sort of an interactional context we are dealing with. A careful study of the range of contexts within which these different facial patterns can be observed to occur could be undertaken, however, and a systematic comparison of contexts might show that, for a given species of facial arrangement, the contexts of its occurrence all share some underlying similarity or, perhaps, at least some 'family resemblance'. This could then, perhaps, be summarized in some single concept. This procedure has been followed, for human facial behavior by Smith *et al.* (1974) in their study of tongue protrusion. As we have already mentioned, the common thread of all the contexts of occurrence of tongue protrusion studied by Smith and his colleagues was that p was reducing, withdrawing from, or fending off interaction with others. Smith *et al.* infer from this that the information another could gain from observing tongue protrusion without knowing anything of its context, is that of a tendency to withdraw from interaction. This information is referred to as the 'message' of the behavior (Smith, 1968, 1969a,b). 'Meaning' is the way in which a recipient organism behaves in response to the behavior. Here, however, the recipient responds not only to the 'message' of the behavior, but to its occurrence in a context. In Smith's terms, thus, in this paper, we have been attempting to give an account of the 'meanings' of F's facial displays within the context of a kissing round.

3. *Implications for the Study of Human Courtship*

Courtship is the process by which a more or less stable relationship is formed between two individuals of the opposite sex, within which mating can take place. Since the relationship is to be one within which mating occurs, many of the behaviors which serve to establish and maintain the pair-bond that is the outcome of courtship are similar to behaviors that precede mating. An important feature of the behavior of courtship, indeed, appears to be that it should create some degree of sexual arousal in the partners. It seems that the 'kissing round' of the sort we have studied in this paper, which is obviously so characteristic of a certain stage of courtship, has this function.

The detailed study of a single kissing round cannot allow us to draw any conclusions about this kind of interaction or its functioning in courtship. However, there are certain features of the organization of this kissing round that appear to illustrate a pattern of behavioral relationship that might be expected to be widely characteristic of courting interactions. From the point of view of the further study of human courtship behavior, therefore, the present analysis may suggest what may be looked for.

From this point of view, therefore, it is of interest to recall that throughout the kissing round, it is F's behavior and particularly that of her face, that appears to function as a regulator, modulating the approaches and orientations of M. Thus the interaction of Phases III and IV may be characterized by saying that M makes a series of highly similar approaches to F, while what comes of these approaches — that is, whether M continues kissing F or not, — depends upon how F responds to them. In Phases I and V, M does not initiate Involvement but waits for F to do so, and what he does then follows upon what F does. Throughout the interaction, M's behavior thus appears to be guided by F. It is not surprising, therefore, that we find that F's behavior is more highly differentiated than that of M.

This pattern, in which F appears to regulate and modulate the repetitive approaches of M, is of interest because it seems that this is what we might expect on the basis of a more general picture of human courtship. One such picture has been sketched by Crook (1972) in which, although a female may appear attractive to a male (because of her various secondary sexual characteristics, both biological and cultural), he will not approach her without some indication from her of her interest in him. In approaching her, however, the male must not only be sexually interested, but must at the same time be re-assured that the female will not be aggressive to him. Certain characteristics of females, such as relative hairlessness, smooth complexion and voice tone which have a childlike character may contribute to this. They may also serve to dispose the male toward care-taking and protective behaviors which are important, not only as a reassurance to the female that she also will not be attacked upon approach by the male, but also in regard to the role that the male will play in relation to the offspring that are the likely outcome of a successful courtship. However, once an association is established, specific-ally courting interaction may develop in which the male behaves toward the female in such a way as to arouse her sexually. However, how frequently and how extensively the male may do this will depend upon how the female responds. The male's behavior may consist of a succession of rounds of sexual advances – and this of course includes kissing – while the female will respond, in each round of sexual advances from the male, with behavior which serves to regulate this: she may show signs of sexual arousal, and so encourage the male to continue, or she may, in various ways, show a re-duction in sexual responsiveness and so discourage the male. However, in encouraging or discouraging him, the female is faced with a delicate task. Her encouragements must be carefully matched to the stage that has been reached in the pair-bond that may also be developing. Her discouragements must also be carefully managed if she is not to drive the male off altogether. It will appear, thus, that from the point of view of successful courtship, we may expect that it will be the female who will show a high degree of differ-entiation in her behavior. In courtship interactions, therefore, we may expect to see just the kind of behavioral relationship arising that we have found in the kissing round of C14.1.

We have noted that F's face showed great variety in its behavior. M's face, in comparison, appeared relatively monotonous. Is this difference character-istic? If the above picture of human courtship has been sketched along the right lines, it would not be surprising if there were a tendency for females to be more varied and subtle in their facial behavior than males.

CONCLUSION

We began this paper by suggesting that, in the study of the human face, far too much attention has been paid to the face in its function in emotion and that our understanding of the role of the face in interaction remained almost unexplored. We have now seen how, by looking at the patterning of facial behavior in the context of interaction, we may arrive at some detailed notions of how it functions. We have seen how F's face appears to function as a feed-back device, both regulating the relationship between M and F's behavior directly and also serving to refer to the wider context or frame within which this behavior is occurring, thus disambiguating F's actions and contributing to the maintenance of the current 'working consensus' which governs the kissing round or its particular sub-phase, or contributing to the process by which this consensus is modified.

We may conclude by remarking on the superb efficiency of the face for these communicative functions. It allows for shared sets of expectations to be established or to be confirmed with extreme rapidity. If a device like the face were not available, coordination of action in interaction would be far less delicate and rapid. The possibility of each misreading the other's behavior would be much greater and the chances of maintaining one level of inter-actional organization as a change is made at another level would be much less. It appears that the delicate tuning device that the face is here seen to be, makes possible the development of the kind of highly complex hierarchy of systems of interrelationship that are characteristic of human social inter-action. This, in turn, allows for the development of the elaborate systems of relationship in which individuals are enmeshed and which are so characteristic of human sociality. Thus we see how a detailed study of the interactional functioning of the face may help us to an understanding of the behavioral foundations from which the complexity and delicacy of human social life emerge.

Adam Kendon (b. 1934) is a Senior Research Fellow in the Department of Anthropology at The Australian National University.His research is centered on the organization and function of behavior in face-to-face interaction. Among his major articles are: "Some Functions of Gaze Direction in Social Interaction" (1967); "Some Relationships between Body Motion and Speech" (1972); "The Role of Visible Behavior in the Organization of Face-to-Face Interaction" (1972); and "A Description of Some Human Greetings" (with A. A. Ferber) (1973).

NOTES

1   The theoretical and methodological outlook of the approach being followed here owes most to the work of Bateson (1956), Scheflen (1966, 1973), Birdwhistell (1970), and Goffman (1957, 1961, 1963, 1971). For a recent re-statement of the central tenets of Birdwhistell's approach, see Kendon (1972). For a very useful treatment of Scheflen, see Bär (1974).
2   Students of the face of alloprimates have followed a method much closer to the one adopted in this paper. Since these animals cannot talk about their feelings or label with words pictures of the faces of others, it is inevitable, perhaps, that the study of their faces has had to resort to the observation of behavior in the face and to a study of the effects of different facial patterns on the behavior of con-specifics' in interactional situations. See Van Hoof (1962, 1967, 1972, 1973), Andrew (1963a, 1963b), Hinde and Rowell (1962) and Chevalier-Skolnikoff (1973). For a very interesting experimental approach, see Miller (1971).
3   I am indebted to Peter Jones and BBC Television for this film specimen. The specimen was originally part of some footage that was made for the film *What's in a Face*, directed by Peter Jones and first shown on BBC Television in 1973.
    The film was analyzed using a Bell & Howell 16mm sound projector modified for oper-

ation by a handcrank and an L-W Athena. The film was not frame-numbered and a frame counter was used. The frame counter was set at zero for the first frame of the film in which the couple appeared in a close 'two-shot'. The film was shot at twenty-four frames per second.

4 Scholars wishing a set of photographs illustrating each of the nine facial patterns distinguished here may write to the author at the Department of Anthropology, Research School of Pacific Studies, P.O. Box 4, Canberra ACT 2600, Australia. The photographs will be sent on the understanding that they are for private use only.

5 I am indebted to a conversation with Desmond Morris for this suggestion.

REFERENCES

Andrew, R.J.
    1963b   "The Evolution of Facial Expressions", *Science* 142, 1034-41.
    1963a   "The Origin and Evolution of the Calls and Facial Expressions of the Primates", *Behaviour* 20, 1-109.
Bär, E.
    1974   "Compte rendu: Context Analysis in Psychotherapy", *Semiotica* 10, 255-81.
Bateson, G.
    1956   Introduction in: *The Natural History of an Interview*, ed. by N. McQuown (= University of Chicago Library Microfilm Collections of Manuscripts in Cultural Anthropology, Series 15, Nos. 95-98, 1971).
Birdwhistell, R.L.
    1952   *Introduction to Kinesics* (Washington, D.C.: U.S. Department of State Foreign Service Institute).
    1970   *Kinesics and Context: Essays on Body Motion Communication* (Philadelphia: University of Pennsylvania Press).
Blurton Jones, N.G.
    1967   "An Ethological Study of Some Aspects of Social Behaviour of Children in Nursery School", in: *Primate Ethology,* ed. by D. Morris (Chicago: Aldine), 347-68.
    1971   "Criteria for Use in Describing Facial Expression of Children", *Human Biology* 43, 365-413.
Bowlby, J.
    1969   *Attachment and Loss: Vol. I, Attachment* (New York: Basic Books).
Brannigan, C.R., and D.A. Humphries
    1972   "Human Non-Verbal Behaviour, A Means of Communication", in: *Ethological Studies of Child Behaviour*, ed. by N.G. Blurton Jones (London: Cambridge University Press), 37-64.
Bruner, J.S., and R. Tagiuri
    1954   "The Perception of People", in: *Handbook of Social Psychology*", Vol. II, ed. by Gardner Lindzey (Reading, Mass.: Addison Wesley), 634-54.
Chevalier-Skolnikoff, Suzanne
    1973   "Facial Expressions of Emotion in Non-Human Primates", in: *Darwin and Facial Expression: A Century of Research in Review*, ed. by Paul Ekman (New York and London: Academic Press), 11-89.
Coleman, J.C.
    1949   *Facial Expression of Emotion* (= *Psychological Monographs*, Whole No. 296) (Washington, D.C.: American Psychological Association), 36 pp.
Crook, J.H.
    1972   "Sexual Selection in Primates", in: *Sexual Selection and the Descent of Man 1871-1971*, ed. by B. Campbell (Chicago: Aldine), 231-81.
Darwin, C.
    1872   *The Expression of the Emotions in Man and Animals* (London: John Murray).
Davitz, J.R.
    1964   *Communication of Emotional Meaning* (New York: McGraw-Hill).

Eibl-Eisenfeldt, I.
    1970   *Ethology: The Biology of Behavior* (New York: Holt, Rinehart and Winston).
    1971   *Love and Hate: On the Natural History of Basic Behavior Patterns* (London: Methuen).
Ekman, P.
    1972   "Universals and Cultural Differences in Facial Expressions of Emotion", in: *Nebraska Symposium on Motivation 1971,* ed. by J.K. Cole (Lincoln: University of Nebraska Press), 207-83.
Ekman, P. (ed.)
    1973   *Darwin and Facial Expression: A Century of Research in Review* (New York and London: Academic Press).
Ekman, P., and W.V. Friesen
    1969   "The Repertoire of Nonverbal Behavior: Categories, Origins, Usage and Coding", *Semiotica* 1, 49-98.
Ekman, P., W.V. Friesen and S.S. Tomkins
    1971   "Facial Affects Scoring Technique (FAST): A First Validity Study", *Semiotica* 3, 37-58.
Ex, J., and A. Kendon
    1964   "A Notation for Facial Positions and Bodily Postures". Appendix to Appendix II, Progress Report to D.S.I.R., Social Skills Project, Institute of Experimental Psychology, University of Oxford. Reprinted in: *Social Interaction,* ed. by M. Argyle (New York: Atherton Press, 1969).
Frijda, N.H.
    1953   "The Understanding of Facial Expression of Emotion", *Acta Psychologica* 9, 294-362.
Goffman, E.
    1957   "Alienation from Interaction", *Human Relations* 10, 47-60.
    1961   *Encounters* (Indianapolis: Bobbs-Merrill).
    1963   *Behavior in Public Places* (New York: The Free Press of Glencoe).
    1971   *Relations in Public* (New York: Basic Books).
Grant, E.C.
    1969   "Human Facial Expression", *Man* (N.S.) 4, 525-36.
Haggard, Ernest A., and K.S. Isaacs
    1966   "Micromomentary Facial Expressions as Indicators of Ego Mechanisms in Psychotherapy", in: *Methods of Research in Psychotherapy,* ed. by L.A. Gottschalk and A.H. Auerbach (New York: Appleton-Century-Crofts).
Hinde, R.A., and Thelma E. Rowell
    1962   "Communication by Postures and Facial Expressions in the Rhesus Monkey *(Macaca mulatta)*", *Proceedings of the Zoological Society of London* 138, 1-21.
Izard, C.
    1969   *The Face of Emotion* (New York: Appleton-Century-Crofts).
Kendon, A.
    1967   "Some Functions of Gaze Direction in Social Interaction", *Acta Psychologica* 26, 22-63.
    1972   "Review of R.L. Birdwhistell: *Kinesics and Context: Essays in Body Motion Communication",* *American Journal of Psychology* 85, 441-55.
    forth-   "The Facing-Formation System: Spatial-Orientational Relations in Face-to-
    coming   Face Interaction".
Kendon, A., and A. Ferber
    1973   "A Description of Some Human Greetings", in: *Comparative Ecology and Behaviour of Primates,* ed. by R.P. Michael and J.H. Crook (London and New York: Academic Press), 591-668.
Landis, C., and W.A. Hunt
    1936   "Studies of the Startle Pattern: III, Facial Pattern", *Journal of Psychology* 2, 215-19.

Lynn, J.G.
   1940   "An Apparatus and Method for Stimulating, Recording and Measuring Facial Expression", *Journal of Experimental Psychology* 27, 81-88.

McGrew, W.C.
   1972   *An Ethological Study of Children's Behavior* (New York and London: Academic Press).

Miller R.E.
   1971   "Experimental Studies of Communication in the Monkey", in: *Primate Behavior: Developments in Field and Laboratory Research*, Vol. II, ed. by A. Roseblum (New York: Academic Press), 139-75.

Reece, M.M., and N.R. Whitman
   1962   "Expressive Movement, Warmth and Verbal Reinforcement", *Journal of Abnormal and Social Psychology* 64, 234-36.

Rosenfeld, H.
   1966a   "Approval Seeking and Approval Inducing Function of Verbal and Non-Verbal Responses in the Dyad", *Journal of Personality and Social Psychology* 4, 597-605.
   1966b   "Instrumental Affiliative Functions of Facial and Gestural Expressions", *Journal of Personality and Social Psychology* 4, 65-72.
   1967   "Nonverbal Reciprocation of Approval: An Experimental Analysis", *Journal of Experimental Social Psychology* 3, 102-11.

Scheflen, A.E.
   1966   "Natural History Method in Psychotherapy: Communicational Research", in: *Methods of Research in Psychotherapy*, ed. by L.A. Gottschalk and A.H. Auerbach (New York: Appleton-Century-Crofts), 263-89.
   1973   *Communicational Structure: Analysis of a Psychotherapy Transaction* (Bloomington and London: Indiana University Press).

Schegloff, E.A., and H. Sacks
   1973   "Opening Up Closings", *Semiotica* 8, 289-327.

Smith, W.J.
   1968   "Message-Meaning Analysis", in: *Animal Communication: Techniques of Study and Results of Research*, ed. by T.A. Sebeok (Bloomington: Indiana University Press), 44-60.
   1969a   "Displays and Messages in Intra-Specific Communication", *Semiotica* 1, 357-69.
   1969b   "Messages of Vertebrate Communication", *Science* 165, 145-50.

Smith, W.J., Julia Chase, and Anna K. Lieblich
   1974   "Tongue Showing: A Facial Display of Humans and Other Primate Species", *Semiotica* 11, 201-46.

Thompson, Jane
   1940   "Development of Facial Expression of Emotion in Blind and Seeing Children", *Archives of Psychology* 37: 264, 1-47.

Van Hoof, J.A.R.A.M.
   1962   "Facial Expressions in Higher Primates", *Symposium of the Zoological Society of London* 8, 97-125.
   1967   "The Facial Displays of the Catarrhine Monkeys and Apes", in *Primate Ethology*, ed. by D. Morris (Chicago: Aldine), 7-68.
   1972   "A Comparative Approach to the Phylogeny of Laughter and Smiling", in: *Nonverbal Communication*, ed. by R.A. Hinde (London: Cambridge University Press), 209-41.
   1973   "A Structural Analysis of the Social Behavior of a Semi-Captive Group of Chimpanzees", in: *Social Communication and Movement: Studies of Interaction and Expression in Man and Chimpanzees*, ed. by M. Von Cranach and I. Vine (London and New York: Academic Press), 75-162.

Vine, I.
   1970   "Communication by Facial-Visual Signals", in: *Social Behavior in Birds and Mammals*, ed. by J.H. Crook (London: Academic Press), 279-354.

1973   "The Role of Facial-Visual Signalling in Early Social Development", in: *Social Communication and Movement: Studies of Interaction and Expression in Man and Chimpanzee,* ed. by M. von Cranach and I. Vine (London and New York: Academic Press), 195-298.
Woodworth, R., and H. Scholsberg
1954   *Experimental Psychology* (New York: Holt, Rinehart and Winston).

MARC ROSENBERG

The Case of the Apple Turnover: An Experiment in Multichannel Communication Analysis*

INTRODUCTION

The scientific study of human communication, as it has developed over the last quarter of a century, is today in the position of having at its disposal the beginnings of a rather powerful theoretical structure based on the calculus of relationships (Watzlawick, Beavin, and Jackson, 1967) and also an extensive body of partially analyzed data stored on audiotape, videotape, film, and paper. Between these two resources lies a gulf of uncertainty, speculation, and unconfirmed hypotheses at all levels of description. The difficulty, it seems, lies in finding adequate operational methods for achieving fit between data and theory.

For the most part, research strategies may be characterized as those which approach the data with coding systems, raters, and statistical operations and whose results achieve reliability only through a trivialization of the constructs which they are intended to illuminate; and those strategies which, while retaining the richness of the constructs and a certain descriptive flair for the texture of interpersonal experience, do so on a largely intuitive basis which typically lacks reliability, replicability, and usable operational procedures.

The research reported in this article was undertaken in an attempt to begin the building of a bridge between these two approaches. A fundamental goal was the generation of a *communicational* description of interpersonal behavior.

In keeping with this goal, two important constraints were placed on the observational and analytical procedures: (1) Descriptive generalizations must be arrived at through a sequence of low-inferential steps. This requirement in effect operationalizes the concepts used, since the communication analyst must be able to point to specific behaviors in support of his generalizations. In this regard, it should be emphasized that agreement, even among trained observers sharing the same theoretical model, is not a criterion of validity. However, the requirement that generalizations be tied to observable behavior does compel the observer to move beyond intuition and global impressions and to state what he means in a way that is convincing to others.

(2) Related to and implied by the first constraint is the second requirement, namely, that intrapsychic states (motives, feelings, intentions, etc.) *not* be invoked as causes or explanations of observed behavior. The emphasis here is *interactional*: one is concerned with what goes on between persons, not with what supposedly happens inside them.

The basic axiom on which this research rests is that metacommunication cannot *not* occur. The commonsense notion of interpersonal communication as synonymous with information sharing fails to take into account that people *label* their statements. That is, we not only make statements to each other, but we also (and necessarily) make statements about these statements. These labeling statements constitute the metacommunicational level of human interaction. By classifying the kind of statement that one is making, one also necessarily expresses an expectation of a particular (and appropriate) kind of response from the other. A joke implies a laugh, a question implies an answer, a move to 'change the subject' requires the agreement of the other, and so on.

By labeling one's own statements and thereby implying the expectation of a particular kind of response, a person acts to define his relationship with the other. If the expectation is met, then we say that the other has agreed to the proposed relationship definition. If the expectation is not met, it is because the other has proposed a different relationship definition. This, in turn, may be accepted or rejected by the first person, and so on throughout the stream of interaction.

In task-oriented situations, in which persons are attempting to reach some decision about a substantive issue, it is communicationally efficient to keep relationship battles (rejections of proposed relationship definitions and proposals of alternative definitions) to a minimum. Formal rules of procedure, such as those used in parliamentary debates or in classrooms, are intended to serve just this function. In less formal contexts, these rules often have to be negotiated and renegotiated throughout the interaction. It is clear, however, that with a finite amount of time in which to reach substantive decisions, the more time spent in negotiating the rules, the less time there will be for dealing with the issue.

Moreover, in interpersonal relationships of long duration, the facility with which persons achieve agreement on the metacommunicational level is a good indicator of the health of their relationship (Laing, *et al.*, 1966), while the *way* in which they achieve (or fail to achieve) agreement is indicative of their *interactional style*. (A typology of such styles is one of the goals of this research, though its realization still lies far in the future.) It should be emphasized here that metacommunicational agreement does not have to do with the content of communication, but rather with its relational component. People may — and do — agree to disagree, and our theoretical model takes this capacity well into account.

The context of the behavior analyzed in this report, although suitable for communication research, was not designed for it. The Family Socialization Project, under whose auspices this research was conducted, is studying the relationship between patterns of parental authority and the development of instrumental competence in children. The Project requires, as one of its procedures, that participating families (mother, father, and child) come into the office and engage in a three-way discussion. The topic of this discussion is invariant. The family is presented with two stories and a set of questions about them. The stories pose certain ethical problems, and the questions are intended to evoke ethical responses from the family members. The family is asked to try to reach a consensus, but the way in which they do this is left up to them.

It is a standard part of the procedure to allow the parents fifteen minutes alone in which to plan (or not to plan) a discussion strategy. This part of the procedure occurs without the presence of the child, and it is from the videotape record of this discussion that the data is derived.

No attempt has been made, either through photographs or illustrations, to represent the visible aspects of the interaction, although these have been taken into account in the analysis. However, a transcript of the lexical content of the interaction is included, as is a description of kinesic behavior. It is suggested that the reader familiarize himself with the transcript and the kinesic description before proceeding to the analysis.

LEXICAL TRANSCRIPT[1]

W: I got a hot apple turnover today and it was ghastly. I mean it was hot, but that's all you could say for it—just awful.

H: Did it turn over? (pause) I mean did it turn over in your stomach afterwards?   PUN

W: No, it wasn't that bad. It was just mushy.

H: (mumbles) 17 ?

W: They have this microwave oven. It's really great. They make hot sandwiches and they stick, I mean they make the sandwich and stick it in for about two seconds and its goes bing and it's done and the cheese is melted and it's hot and it's good.

H: Mm hm. [26]

W: But it sure didn't do anything for the turnovers. [28] I guess you have to have something to start with. [30]

(silence) [31-51]

W: (laugh) [52] God! [55] (laugh) [59]

H: Mm. [61]

W: "What would happen if there were no rules? [63.5] Please be specific." [66.5] (laugh) [62] Oh well. [68]

H: Mm. [72]

W: (whistle) Oh. [80]

H: Mm. [82]

W: Dick, what is it? [87] What kind of metal? [90]

KINESIC DESCRIPTION[2]

Both the husband and the wife have instruction sheets which contain the stories and the questions that they will be discussing. At the beginning of the sequence, the husband is sitting on the couch and the wife on the chair. Both are reading. At T_0, the wife slaps her papers down on the coffee table. This action coincides with the beginning of her speech. However, she does not look up at her husband until T_3. When she does look up, she finds him already looking at and attending to her. The cookie, which he has taken from a plate on the table, is held in his right hand. His left hand holds the corner of his papers, which are lying on the coffee table.

At T_4, the husband looks down. Immediately following this, the wife looks down and picks up her papers in both hands. As the husband finishes his punning statement, she releases the papers with her right hand and puts that hand to her forehead, while continuing to hold the papers in her left hand. As he repeats the pun ($T_{8.5}$-T_{10}), she turns her head away from him, smiles, and moves her right hand to a position covering her mouth. She maintains this posture throughout her next utterance. With *mushy* (T_{13}), she looks back at the paper while keeping her right hand at her mouth.

As his wife begins her next statement at T_{16}, she drops her left arm (and with it the papers) and moves her right hand away from her mouth. Simultaneous with this movement, the husband places on the table the coffee cup, which he had picked up at $T_{6.5}$ and sipped from at T_{10} (bracketing the elaboration of his pun). As she begins to speak, he moves the cookie in his right hand toward his mouth. At T_{17} he takes a bite from the cookie. At T_{18} he looks up at his wife, keeping the cookie in front of his mouth. At

T_{20} he bites the cookie again. At $T_{22.5}$ he looks down briefly, looking up again at $T_{23.5}$ and down at T_{25}.

As the wife ends her statement, and coinciding with his own *mm hm*, the husband begins a series of rapid head nods which continue until T_{28}. After the first three of these nods, the wife shifts her position for the first time since T_{16}. At $T_{27.5}$ her right hand returns to her mouth and her left arm raises the paper to a reading position. Although she does not stop speaking until T_{30}, she is completely oriented toward the paper by T_{28}. At T_{30}, as she stops talking, she leans forward in her chair, her right hand moving slightly around her mouth, and her left hand holding the papers in a reading position. She maintains this posture until her prelaughter signal at T_{51}.

The husband, too, is very still during this twenty-one seconds of silence. About two seconds after his wife finishes her statement (i.e., at about T_{32}), he picks up his instruction sheets in his left hand and continues to hold and look at them until T_{58}. During this time, he also holds the cookie in his right hand and takes three bites from it between T_{35} and T_{39}. Except for chewing motions, which continue uninterrupted until T_{56}, he does not move again until right after she says *God!* and leans forward, at which time he takes another three bites from the cookie.

This period of silence and stillness is terminated by the wife. At T_{51} she begins a laughter sequence by placing her right hand to her forehead. At T_{52} she begins to laugh and increases the volume until, at T_{56}, she leans back in her chair, shakes her head laterally, and says *God!* At T_{59} she leans forward in her chair and laughs again. It is at this point that her husband takes three more bites from the cookie and emits a barely audible *mm* (T_{61}) between the second and third bites. He does not, however, change his position or look up from the instruction sheets.

One and a half seconds after his *mm*, she begins to read the passage. The instruction sheets are on the table before her, and she looks down at them as she reads. Beginning with *rules* ($T_{63.5}$) and ending with her laugh ($T_{66.5}$), she picks up the papers before her, turns them over, and places them back on the table. But before she completes this move—as she says *specific*— her husband turns over the top sheet of his instructions and appears to read from the next page. She then says *Oh well* and gets up and leaves the room (T_{70}).

At T_{72}, while continuing to chew but without otherwise moving, the husband emits another low-volume *mm*. Six seconds later, although she is still off camera, we can hear the wife whistling. Immediately following the whistling (at T_{80}), she says *Oh*. Her husband then puts the last of the cookie in his mouth, glances up briefly, then down again. He reaches for the coffee cup with his left hand but does not touch it. He then says *mm* again, his left hand returns to the papers, and he resumes the same basic posture that he has held since T_{25} (left hand holding the corner of instruction sheets, head tilted down in a reading position).

He remains in this position until she returns with the metal cube at T_{87} and asks, "Dick, what is it? What kind of metal?" As she says *Dick*, he looks up at the cube in her hand, then up at her face, back at the cube and, as she finishes her question, he reaches for the cube, which she relinquishes.

DISCUSSION

From T_0 to T_5, the wife tells an anecdote and the husband responds appropriately with kinesic signals of appreciative attention. He orients toward her, maintains eye contact, and his right hand, which is holding a cookie, remains suspended and motionless.

At T_6 the husband suggests a change in the relationship. He will be a punster and she will be the appreciative audience. His pun ("Did it turn over?") is completed in less than a second, and she responds to it immediately by placing her right hand to her forehead. (We will see this same idiosyncratic prelaughter gesture again at T_{51}.)

Her response, however, is apparently insufficient for her husband who, after a two-second pause, elaborates on the pun (even to the extent of laughing at T_9). While he is making his pun more explicit, she acknowledges it by smiling, placing her hand over her mouth, and turning away from him.

By now, it is clear that she got the pun, but she refuses to acknowledge it verbally. In fact, her first verbalization following his pun (T_{11}) suggests that she heard no pun. Her response ("No, it wasn't that bad") labels his utterance as a straight question rather than a joke. In brief, what she has done here is to reject his classification of his own message, although (and she has signalled this kinesically) she is aware of his label and did indeed get the pun.

However, her response is not a simple matter of "I see how you label your statement and define our relationship, but I don't accept it." Her response is more complex and confusing than that. Verbally, she signals nonreceipt of his labeling. Kinesically, she signals receipt, appreciation, and a *feigned* unwillingness for the appreciation to be perceived (You don't cover your mouth to hide a smile without knowing that *they* know you are smiling.) In other words, she responds verbally and explicitly to the content of his statement but not to its label.

We cannot hear the husband's mumbled response to his wife's statement at T_{14}-T_{16}, and it is not clear whether or not she has heard it. But having rejected his relationship proposal, she continues her anecdote and the relationship implied by it. This time, however, he is not such an attentive audience. Compare his very quiet kinesic behavior during his wife's first speech with the movement we see now (T_{16}-T_{30}). His *Mm hm* in this context signals receipt of her signal but rejection of her relationship proposal: he is not going to be the appreciative audience of T_0-T_5. The cookie-eating (especially its rhythm, which is not ruminative chewing) and the glances toward the paper signal to her that there are other strong pulls on his attention. But probably the most compelling signal in this sequence is the series of head nods between T_{26} and T_{28}. The rhythm of these nods is too rapid to signal supportive affirmation. It is more like: "Okay, I heard you; now that's enough."[3] Even before he completes the head nod sequence, his wife responds to his signals of inattentiveness by turning her attention to the paper. She is oriented away from him a full two seconds before she stops speaking. In returning to her paper, she accepts his proposal, "Don't talk to me."

The ensuing twenty-one seconds of verbal silence point up one of the advantages of thinking in terms of *levels of communication*. For those who concern themselves solely with the content of communication, this duration must be seen as one in which the couple is 'not communicating'. From our viewpoint, however, communication cannot not occur. Or, to quote Birdwhistell, "Nothing never happens." ! *Shakespeare again* ——

This twenty-one seconds, however wrought with tensions it may be, marks the duration of a mutually agreed upon relationship definition. It is a difficult relationship to change. If we construe it as "We are not communicating", then we see this couple as enmeshed in one of the now classical paradoxes of communication.[4] If we see it as (H:) "Don't talk to me." – (W:) "Alright", then only the husband is in a position to change the relationship without reneging on their agreement. The wife, as we shall see, is sensitive to this dilemma and uses a variety of strategies to change the relationship while staying within the bounds of her agreement not to talk to him.

From T_{51} to T_{60}, the wife initiates a sequence of acts apparently designed to get her husband to change their relationship agreement by asking her to speak. Her laughter and movement here signal to him that she has found something which she wants to share. Note that, unlike before, she is not now signalling that she *is* a story-teller; she is signalling that she wants him to invite her to be a story-teller. At T_{51} she puts her right hand to her forehead (the same prelaughter signal that we saw at T_6). Then she laughs, increases the volume, says *God!* while sitting back in her chair (a modulation of the guffaw?), shakes her head, and then leans forward and stops laughing. In this brief sequence (T_{51}-T_{59}), neither the wife's laughter, her movement, nor her exclamation constitutes a breach of their agreement, but each of these acts provides an opportunity for the husband to ask her: "What's so funny?".

A question which arises when one attempts to do communication analysis based in part on formal considerations is the extent to which real persons actually exhibit an awareness of the logical structure of their behavior. From our point of view, in the sequence just described, the wife had backed herself into a corner by agreeing not to talk to her husband. This agreement, if strictly adhered to, could not be renegotiated by the wife, for to initiate a renegotiation of the rules would constitute a violation of those rules.

Although we need not hypothesize that the wife is conscious of these logical considerations, we can say that she acts in a way which is consistent with them. Her laughter, her movement, and even her exclamation can be construed as expressive rather than communicational, as signs rather than signals.[5] That is, should the husband respond to his wife's behavior by saying, "I thought you'd agreed not to talk to me", she has a safe way out. She can counter with: "I wasn't talking to you; I was just reacting spontaneously to something I read."

In fact, of course, any behavior by one person that is perceptible to another person is communicational in that the other must either respond or not respond, and in either case (meta)communication has occurred. Nonetheless, in the situation just described, the wife has adhered to her agreement and has recognized her husband's one-up position by inviting him to initiate a renegotiation of the rules.

He responds to this invitation with reluctant acceptance. His barely audible *mm* occurs ten seconds after his wife begins the sequence by putting her hand to her forehead and one and a half seconds after her final laugh. The timing and volume of the husband's verbal response in conjunction with his refusal to look up from the instruction sheets suggests a very grudging acquiescence to the wife's maneuver. Indeed, we may suppose that his ability to disattend his wife's invitation signals for a full ten seconds requires considerable effort and must have been perfected over many years of repeated practice.

At any rate, the one and a half seconds which he allows to elapse between the end of her laugh and his *mm* is matched by the pause which she allows to occur before reading the amusing passage (perhaps suggesting: "Maybe I won't tell you, after all"). One second after finishing her statement (quite long enough to realize that an *immediate* response is not forthcoming), the wife laughs, labelling her statement as funny (just as he did at T_9). Thus, she explicitly defines the relationship as one in which he is expected to be an appreciative audience. But this laugh, like his at T_9, is also an admission of failure. In both cases, a statement is made which implies the expectation of a particular kind of response. In neither case is the appropriate response given by the other, and the speaker must supply it him- (or her-)self.

Unlike his wife's response to his pun, however, there is nothing incongruent in the husband's reaction. Her laughter is greeted with silence, and kinesically he signals that he considers it an intrusion by turning a page of the instruction sheets in front of him. In other words, his response to her amusement (and her attempts to engage him) is to suggest that he has more important things to attend to.

After completing her laugh, she again allows one and a half seconds to elapse. When he does not respond within this time, she gives up with an *Oh well*, gets up from her chair and leaves the room. A full four seconds after her *Oh well*, after she has moved out of camera range, and at a level which is surely inaudible to her, the husband responds with another minimal *mm*. (Perhaps: "I responded to you. I can't help it if you didn't hear me. If you hadn't stalked out of the room, you would have".) In such relationships, it may be necessary to prepare for all contingencies.

Despite this setback, however, she does not give up. Returning to the room at T_{87}, she holds out a small metal cube and asks, "Dick, what is it? What kind of metal?". This is an interesting move on her part and quite different from her previous proposals. Unlike her anecdotal utterances, which propose that she will talk and he will listen, this question sets up a student-teacher relationship, implies that he has knowledge which she lacks, and suggests that she will now listen to what he has to say. In seeking information from him, she places herself in the complementary one-down position. But she is *giving* him the upper hand in this situation, and the upper hand can no more be given than can freedom or equality. The recipient of such a gift is placed in the position of the child ordered to be independent or the husband whose wife tells him that he must dominate her.

Although he takes the upper hand by agreeing that he is in a position to inform her (i.e., he tries to answer her question), the relationship itself is one that has been defined by her. This situation has been called 'metacomplementary' (Watzlawick, Beavin, and Jackson, 1967). With his acceptance of the teacher role (in which, interestingly, he fails), she regains control of the relationship.

CONCLUSIONS

In this ninety-second sequence, we see two people unable to reach mutual agreement about what sort of relationship is to exist between them. Their most enduring agreement lasts some twenty-one seconds, and it requires that they not talk to each other. Typically, relationship proposals are met with incongruent responses, which transmit contradictory information along the same or different infracommunicational channels.[6] We see this incongruence in the wife's response to her husband's pun and in his inattentive listening and minimal *mm*'s.

Of course, relationship proposals may be dealt with more openly. The wife could have said, "That's a terrible pun" (a type of response often cheerfully accepted by the inveterate punster), and the husband, later, could have said, "Let's not talk now; I want to read these instructions". But it is not this couple's style to be so direct, and so we may speak of *covert relationship battles*. We may assume, too, that these communicational moves and counter-moves must have some adaptive value in the family environment, or they would not have been learned. In other words, we may speculate that, in the history of this couple, there have been repeated instances of punishment associated with communicational commitment and that, as a result, both parties have learned how to avoid such commitment through the ambiguity and incongruity of their relationship signals. A back door is left open, and one may deny one's own message by referring to another, simultaneous one, which contradicts it.

It has been the main purpose of this preliminary phase of the research to demonstrate the feasibility of rendering intelligible those processes through which persons shape and modulate the interpersonal relationships existing among them. In keeping with this goal, we have attended to observable communication behavior recorded and stored on half-inch videotape. Despite the rather coarse grain and high noise level of the recording instrument, we have found it possible to pay relatively close attention to information coded lexically, kinesically, and paralinguistically. Our analysis demonstrates the necessity of looking at least at these three infracommunicational channels and especially at the relationships among them, at the way in which signals along one channel confirm, negate, or otherwise modify signals along some other channel.

Obviously, this report must be seen as a very preliminary account of work in progress. As such, it raises many more substantive questions than it even attempts to answer. We do not, for example, have sufficient knowledge of family dynamics or of the time structure of communicational events to judge the adequacy of a ninety-second sample of behavior. Nor do we know the extent to which a finer-grained analysis would yield more information, or the value of such information were it available. Nonetheless, the method outlined here provides at least a beginning of the necessary bridge-building between theory and data. The level of analysis at which we are working, while allowing for the non-trivial operationalization of such important concepts as relationship definition, metacommunicational labeling, and interchannel congruence and incongruence, does not require the painstaking and time-consuming techniques of the professional linguist or kinesicist. Although data stored on videotape or film is indispensable in freeing the researcher from the constraints of real time, the actual techniques require nothing unmanageable in the way of specialized training. Indeed, much of what is substantive in this analysis would be intuitively obvious to the trained clinician. But the method of analysis proposed here has the advantage of being able to translate intuition into operation, and of allowing one to know what he knows and to state this knowledge so that it can be known to others.

NOTES

* The research reported in this paper was supported by the National Institute of Child Health and Development, Research Grant HD-02228, and by The Grant Foundation, Inc. The author gratefully acknowledges the stimulating environment of controlled freedom supplied by Dr. Diana Baumrind and the fruitful disagreements with Steve Schultz.
1 The irregularities in the timing are due to the limitations imposed by the use of a hand-operated stopwatch.
2 See Birdwhistell, 1970: 173-79.
3 According to Birdwhistell (1970: 162): "If //nnn// is made up of //n// of less than .4 second, the communicatively normal speaker may stop vocalizing entirely or ask a question like 'What's the matter?'"
4 See, for example, Gregory Bateson (1952: 2): "You meet somebody in the street and he turns and looks into a shop window. You noticed that he saw you coming; you observed that he turned and looked into the shop window. He may be transmitting the very peculiar message: 'We are not communicating.' Whether he is or is not communicating is a question which brings us to Epimenides' paradoxes."
5 For this distinction, see Bateson (1972): "If we speculate about the evolution of communication, it is evident that a very important stage in this evolution occurs when the organism gradually ceases to respond quite 'automatically' to the mood-signs of another and becomes able to recognize the sign as a signal: that is, to recognize that the other individual's and its own signals are only signals, which can be trusted, distrusted, falsified, denied, amplified, corrected, and so forth."
6 This relates directly to Jay Haley's (1959) observation that "If people always qualified what they said in a congruent way, relationships would be defined simply and clearly, even though two levels of communication were functioning. However, when a statement indicating one sort of relationship is qualified by a contradictory communication, difficulties in interpersonal relations become inevitable".

REFERENCES

Bateson, G.
  1952 "The Position of Humor in Human Communication", in: *Cybernetics: Circular Causal and Feedback Mechanisms in Biological and Social Sciences; Transactions of the Ninth Conference*, ed. by Heinz von Foerster (New York: Josiah Macy, Jr. Foundation).
  1972 "A Theory of Play and Fantasy", in: *Steps to an Ecology of Mind* (New York: Ballantine Books).
Birdwhistell, R.
  1970 *Kinesics and Context* (Philadelphia: University of Pennsylvania Press).
Haley, J.
  1959 "An Interactional Description of Schizophrenia", *Psychiatry* 22, 321-22.

Laing, R.D., H. Phillipson, and A.R. Lee
  1966 *Interpersonal Perception: A Theory and a Method of Research* (London: Springer Publishing Co.).
Watzlawick, P., J.H. Beavin, and D.D. Jackson
  1967 *Pragmatics of Human Communication: A Study of Interactional Patterns, Pathologies, and Paradoxes* (New York: W.W. Norton).

Part Three

Gesture

FERNANDO POYATOS

Gesture Inventories:
Fieldwork Methodology and Problems*

0. In the last decade or so kinesics (more superficially and rather in its picturesque side than as a far-reaching area of study) has attracted the interest of foreign language specialists concerned with cultural fluency as much as with linguistic fluency. Although they have not gone far in understanding the true importance and necessity of integrating the various verbal and nonverbal systems of communication used in interpersonal relationships, they have at least recognized the role that body movements play in the total expressive repertoire of man, as well as the cultural clash resulting from the misunderstanding, misuse and ignorance of a foreign culture's gestures (though still underrating manners and postures).

~~good~~

And yet, in spite of the much-cited statements by Alfred Hayes (1964), and in spite of brief attempts at fostering the interest in a systematic study of gestures in foreign language journals (Brault, 1963; Poyatos, 1970),[1] there is still a great gap to be bridged between the teach-

---

*. Robert L. Saitz and Edward J. Cervenka, *Handbook of Gestures*: *Colombia and the United States* (= *Approaches to Semiotics* 31) (The Hague: Mouton, 1973).

David Efron, *Gesture, Race, and Culture*, revised edition (= *Approaches to Semiotics* 9): (The Hague: Mouton, 1972).

Jerald R. Green, *A Gesture Inventory for the Teaching of Spanish* (Philadelphia and New York: Chilton Books/Educational Division, 1968).

[1] Apart from other contributions of which I may not be aware, I personally dealt with paralanguage, kinesics, and nonverbal communication in general at several meetings of the International Association of Hispanists, the American Association of Teachers of Spanish and Portuguese, and at an international congress for the teaching of Spanish. After doing the same for the Northeast Modern Language Association, I was asked, due to the interest generated among linguists, to organize a new session on paralanguage, which I did in 1972. However, there is still a most unfortunate lack of information about nonverbal communication among foreign language teachers.

ing of the linguistic structures and the association of those structures with the paralinguistic and kinesic patterns (and also the proxemic and chrone-mic ones) that form the total communication situation. Classroom-oriented authors have recommended the teaching of gestures and their inclusion in foreign language textbooks, but that kinesic material is still lacking in them. If it were not it would still have to face the strongest variable, namely the teacher himself, who in many cases would be unable to reproduce foreign kinemorphemic constructs faithfully and, therefore, effectively. Even if he were he would have to master other contextual variables and know the patterns of synchrony and disynchrony, and how these gestures fit in a given situation. But this is precisely what textbooks do not explain. In other words, as far as language students are concerned they still have not been introduced to nonverbal communication in rela-tion to their own discipline. It is only now in the early seventies that kinesics, proxemics, paralanguage and other nonverbal modalities are attracting the interest of secondary schools in North America,[2] while some courses are being offered in different universities, and textbooks on nonverbal communication are beginning to proliferate,[3] although they are bound to reach English and foreign-language students only tangential-ly. So far the non-specialists are showing some curiosity and pseudo-scientific interest for what has been popularized as 'body language', while language students and teachers are being exposed to a few gesture inventories that are probably used by a few and ignored or snubbed by the rest.

The initiative of their authors is a very plausible one, and they would only need to offer more insights into the culture of that language and a realistic presentation of all the contextual variables that the foreign student or teacher must take into account.

1. The book on which this article is based is *Handbook of Gestures: Colombia and the United States*, the new *Approaches to Semiotics* series

[2]   I can certainly foresee the success of truly classroom-oriented kinesic inventories by the keen interest shown by high school teachers and students in the Canadian province of New Brunswick when first introduced to kinesics, paralanguage and proxemics, and by the reaction of some heterogeneous groups of academics in Canada and the U.S.
[3]   As far as the growing interest within the universities in kinesics and nonverbal communication, and new courses taught (my only student last year wrote a paper on the kinesic behavior of rural Pentecostal in New Brunswick), as well as new publica-tions and persons working in the field, the best source of information is the newsletter graciously prepared by Mary Ritchie Key, Program in Linguistics, University of California at Irvine, Irvine, California.

edition of the 1962 inventory by Robert L. Saitz and Edward J. Cervenka (hereafter S & C), although references will be made frequently to Jerald R. Green's *Gesture Inventory for the Teaching of Spanish* (1968) and to David Efron's *Gesture, Race and Culture* (ninth in Mouton's series *Approaches to Semiotics*, 1972),[4] in order to comment better on the methodology and problems of fieldwork and presentation from the point of view of the foreign observer-learner, come to some interesting conclusions and offer a few suggestions regarding the elaboration of this type of inventories.

The new edition of S & C's book (thirty-first in the same Mouton series) shows some interesting variants from its earlier edition by the Centro Colombo Americano in Bogotá, *Colombian and North American Gestures: A Contrastive Inventory.*

While the new edition says that the book "derived from the experience of the authors during their terms as Fulbright lecturers in Colombia, 1960 to 1962... originated in an effort to point out some of the more obvious gestural differences between cultures to a group of language teachers", the definite emphasis on teaching, characteristic of the original edition, has been minimized to the point of completely deleting the appendix entitled "Gestures in the Classroom", where the authors aimed their inventory at "the teachers of English and Spanish as second languages". In this appendix some interesting comments are made related to the teaching of kinesics in the classroom and to the cultural context of language, stating that the student will learn a second language more effectively "if he is required to produce and understand not only the articulations of the vocal apparatus but the articulations of the body as well". I feel that the *Approaches to Semiotics* series would have made quite a few more avid readers among foreign-language teachers if that appendix, rather than being deleted, had been expanded to a well-documented introduction on the present-day status of kinesics in the classroom, its methodological possibilities, and the problems to be solved in that area. Green's book on Spanish gestures, although it falls short of its expectations, offers, however, an interesting and documented initiation to the field of kinesics and to the work of Birdwhistell and others, while surveying some works on foreign culture studies and on the cultural approach to language teaching.

Far from the typed-copy edition of 1962, the new version has been

---

[4] First published as *Gesture and Environment* in 1941 by King's Crown Press, New York, and now prefaced by Paul Ekman and reviewed in *Semiotica* IX: 3 (1973) by Allen Dittmann.

stream-lined to Mouton standards and it offers a three-page "Introduction" on the type of material included, the method used and the rationale of the collection gathered, plus an up-to-date "Selected Bibliography" on nonverbal communication, with a special section on proxemics and on kinesics and teaching.

2. THE MATERIAL SELECTED

2.1 There seems to be a striking uniformity among the existing inventories regarding the selection of their material from life. While Green's collection attempts to include those gestures which almost exclusively accompany verbal behavior, and not those which replace it (although some of them perform both functions), and provides a written context for most of them, S & C's focuses on gestures which seem "discrete" (characterized by an essential physical movement) and are easily recognizable by an untrained observer, excluding, they say, specialized group gesture systems, "heavily iconic gestures" (actually Efron's kinetographs and pictographs) and body configuration and stance varying geographically as well as among communities. Green excluded autistic gestures and erotic ones, while S & C, who also deleted the latter from their first printed collection, now include them in the new one.

2.2 What actually diminishes the scope of these inventories is the fact that their authors deal with different kinds of kinesic categories under the common label of 'gestures', when in reality, from the cultural standpoint as well as considering the pedagogical possibilities, they should differentiate between gestures, manners, and postures. For the collectors of inventories of kinesic activity this differentiation is amply justified by the bibliography on kinesics and nonverbal communication they themselves suggest to their readers. They refer to Birdwhistell's latest work (1970) as stating that total, real communication consists of the interrelatedness of several aspects of kinesic behavior in their interactional use and according to specific communicative functions, and yet tend to disassociate verbal and nonverbal behaviors (the latter an unfortunate term, according to Birdwhistell's reviewer, Kendon, 1972) and, within kinesic activity, between gestures, manners, and postures. A differentiation that, from the cultural point of view, proves most necessary in the elaboration of a contrastive inventory like the one under discussion. It would be wise, in my opinion, to concretize the following definitions of those three categories I have often proposed:

yes

By GESTURE I understand a conscious or unconscious body movement made mainly with the head, the face alone, or the limbs, learned or soma- *explain!* togenic, and serving as a primary communicative tool, dependent or independent from verbal language; either simultaneous or alternating with it, and modified by the conditioning background (smiles, eye movements, a gesture of beckoning, a tic, etc.).

MANNER, although similar to gesture, is a more or less dynamic body *interesting* attitude that, (while somatogenically modified) is mainly learned and socially codified according to specific situations, either simultaneous or alternating with verbal language (the way one eats at the table, greets others, coughs, stretches, etc.).

POSTURE is a conscious or unconscious general position of the body, more static than gesture, learned or somatogenic, either simultaneous or alternating with verbal language, modified by social norms and by the rest of the conditioning background, and used less as a communicative tool, although it may reveal affective states and social status (sitting, standing, joining both hands behind one's back while walking, etc.).

2.2.1 Birdwhistell's view, according to which there are no universal facial expressions as far as their social meaning is concerned is well known, but both S & C and Green seem to be familiar with the opinions of opponents of this view, such as Ekman and Friesen (1969), who maintain that there are some patterns of facial muscular activity typical of specific emotions, and that, being common to all humans, exist in different societies with identical semantic values. They are actually emblematic gestures and affect displays, but S & C do not take full advantage of their observations. If they had they would have described the concomitant facial activities accompanying many of the gestures recorded in their inventory (i.e., important parts of inseparable kinemorphemic and kinesyntactic constructs). The striking thing about it is that many of the drawings illustrating such descriptions show a very realistic representation of the facial expression lacking in the text (for the quality of Mel Pekarsky's rich sketches is a great improvement over the first edition's un-anatomical and blank-faced people), for which reason I fail to understand why the authors do not describe fully the true kinesic complex. The explanation that feelings are shown on the face anyway would not be acceptable, since the accompanying facial expression may vary between two cultures, even when 'the other gesture' is identical.

The cultural value of such recorded observations would have enhanced the book's excellent repertoire, especially considering (a) what I have termed self-regulatory function among different communicative activities; under 'Anticipation' it says that "hands, palm to palm, are rubbed together briskly", but neglects to describe the facial expression depicted in the illustration: raised eyebrows, smiling mouth distension; actually, the faster the hands rub against each other, the higher the brows are raised; (b) the different kinesyntactic combinations according to specific cultures, even though one kinemorphemic construct may be the same; under 'Attention D' it describes that "neighbor is nudged with elbow. This gesture in both cultures is proper only with close friends"; but actually the North American speaker-actor tends to accentuate the unilateral mouth distension when uttering at the same time (as the book tells us) *Mira* 'look'; (c) the unquestionable interactional use of facial expression always accompanying the hand gestures described, among many others, for 'Termination', 'Victory', 'Strength' (physical prowess), etc., varying among cultures; (d) the affect displays carried out by facial expression, repeating, qualifying or contradicting, not only a lexically stated affect but another kinemorphemic construct of, say, the hands, or a postural shift; (e) the possibility of affect blends, or multiple emotions shown simultaneously by paralanguage, kinesics and proxemics; and (f) the display rules for those affects, socially learned according to certain techniques (to conceal the clues to a given affect, to overdo it, to look affectless, or to dissimulate it with another affect), which sometimes varies from culture to culture, as in the case of grief for a lost husband or child: the Latin wife or mother will, in general, show a more elaborate paralinguistic and kinesic series of semantic constructs, while the Anglo-Saxon ones (this I have witnessed a number of times) may smile while recalling the suffering last moments of a lost one, which is worth considering when presenting a kinesic repertoire because it can avoid many misunderstandings.

In sum, facial gestures should be given more emphasis in kinesic inventories. Neither S & C nor Green specify facial activity. The latter uses numerous quotations from contemporary Spanish novels, but novelists too fail to differentiate their characters by describing their kinesic expressiveness in detail when it should be necessary, and when they do they pay more attention to hand gestures, postures and stance, and much more to kinesics than to paralanguage.

2.2.2 As for manners, according to the definition I have offered, authors of inventories should follow the advice of Edward T. Hall (whom they always include in their bibliographies), apply to their fieldwork methodology many of his observations on manners and proxemics (noting their interrelationship), and remember that "The subject of manners is complex; if it were not, there would not be so many injured feelings and so much misunderstanding in international circles everywhere. In any society the code of manners tends to sum up the culture — to be a frame for all behavior" (Hall, 1955).

It is true that the boundary between gesture and manner becomes quite uncertain at times, that the socially codified patterns used at the table or in greetings are made up of discernible 'gestures'. However, we can isolate in each culture those patterns which are taught and learned, and that are even the subject of etiquette books.

In S & C's Table of Contents we can identify, among others, the following as socially codified manners: 'Approval' by clapping hands, which we could elaborate on, since it varies not only according to social status and protocol rules (apart from personal characteristics), but even between the two cultures discussed in the book, as in the case of younger and less educated Americans who applaud with hands and elbows at the same level, clapping more with the metacarpal region than with the fingers; 'Boredom' by yawning (not mentioning the hand-over-mouth kinemorpheme), of which we are only told that it may be used involuntarily or deliberately, when much could be said about its being a taboo in certain situations in one culture, but not in the other one, just as similar and informative comments could have been made about who stretches, when and how in the North-American classroom, but should never do it in a Spanish classroom; 'Full' (a very ambiguous label, in this case meaning 'of food'), when one, the authors say, "pats stomach gently", but actually in a circling motion typical of North America, although not common among the more refined people as an obliged complimentary display of satisfaction.

Much could be said (and something will be pointed out later) about 'Greetings', their parakinesic qualities of intensity, range and velocity, their proxemic variables as well as their chronemic aspects.[5]

Lacking, to my surprise, in S & C's and Green's inventories, but worth a detailed study, is the matter of 'table manners', that is, the way people in each culture handle knife and fork, bread, napkin, cups, salt shaker, etc., and the way they eat fish, fried eggs, a chicken leg, etc., how they use, or use not, their fingers for grabbing and pushing, etc. Whether the aim of an inventory is purely anthropological, sociological

---

[5] 'Chronemics' and 'chronemic' are the terms I have proposed before for the study of all the time aspects in personal interaction, just as proxemics deal with space.

or pedagogical, it should contain careful descriptions of these and other established patterns of manners in restaurants, churches, public vehicles, theaters, etc., since they are always clearly differentiated from intentional or unintentional gestures that we can, better or worse, translate linguistically.

2.2.3 Finally, both inventories acknowledge in their bibliographies (but specially S & C's well organized one, although not congruent with the contents of the book) the work on posture by Birdwhistell, Goffman, Mehrabian, and Scheflen, mainly, but a brief cross-cultural repertoire of postures is lacking in both of them. If, as Scheflen (1964) put it, "to understand the meaning of gestures, postures, inflections and even affective expressions, it is necessary to look critically across cultures, across classes, across institutions", it should follow that in order to understand and teach "a culture's behavior" one should look at the postural repertoire that is more conspicuously characteristic of its members, because just as English-speaking people move in English, in Scheflen's words, so Hispanic peoples move, sit and stand in Spanish.

To begin with, some of the statements and findings by the aforementioned authors could have very well been used by S & C and Green to their advantage. Mehrabian (1969), for instance, has observed that the arms-akimbo position is adopted more frequently in front of disliked persons and with persons of lower status, that leaning backward while sitting indicates a negative attitude, while a positive one is reflected in forward position. Any observer of either Colombian or Spanish speakers engaged in interaction will notice that (a) the arms-akimbo posture is adopted more by young people, (b) it is much more frequent among low-status people, mainly in the small towns, (c) it is more common among small-town women of all ages in Latin countries (or one forearm across the stomach, with the elbow of the other one perpendicular to it and the hand propping different points of the face), (d) in introductions, or simple confrontations, with persons of higher status, it is adopted by adolescents and young men who, at the same time, put one foot forward (and look down in embarrassment before older or higher-status people), besides being typical of athletes and players everywhere. Observations of this type included in cultural inventories would corroborate the fact that there exist certain postural indicators of certain relationships.

Goffman (1961) assures us that higher status individuals sit more relaxingly (feet on the desk, lying slumped on their seats, etc.). Since this also depends on social codes within each culture, any inventory should point out that those North Americans who may be used to putting their feet on the desk, or on another chair, lying slumped on their seats, or with one leg over a chair's arm, should not do the same in Spain, for those postures are taboos in any formal, or even informal, setting; besides the fact that higher-status persons do not take those positions in front of inferiors. An inventory that attempts to teach the gesture repertoire of another culture must offer, along with its manners, its more characteristic postures, and those belonging to the learner's repertoire which should not be displayed at a party, in the classroom, in church, at a restaurant, at a formal visit, etc. Once I saw a photograph of Dean Rusk sitting in front of Franco, and his posture struck me as quite unprotocolarian for El Pardo Palace: one leg horizontally crossed with the ankle resting on the other knee, his arms open in a gesture equally uncommon in such a place.

One of the books that have, somewhat distortingly, popularized the science of kinesics, by Nierenberg and Calero (1971), offers (labelling all three, gestures, manners, and postures, 'gestures') an excellent collection of postures that should incite authors of inventories to include a posture repertoire in a cross-cultural perspective. Following this book, vividly illustrated with the best drawings I have seen so far in kinesics, they would not agree with many of its generalizations, but they would find, for instance, that walking with hands clasped behind one's back, which Nierenberg and Calero associate with the preoccupied walker, is also a very common walking posture among Spanish males (apart from personality characteristics); that straddling a chair does not reveal superiority in Spain at all, since it is quite common among males, mainly lower-status ones, in informal situational contexts, such as an outside tavern or a small-town sidewalk gathering; that leaning back with hands laced behind the head is still a North-American posture not to be displayed in Spain unless in a very informal situation.

3. SOURCES OF DATA, SUBJECTS, AND RECORDING TECHNIQUES

What follows is a chart-like outline of the more salient features regarding the sources of data, the fieldwork and recording methods employed in the books by Saitz and Cervenka, Green, and Efron, in order that the presentation of the material itself may be discussed later (Chart 1). Here I shall simply make some observations about the methodology followed, or suggested, by the published inventories, and its results.

SOURCES OF DATA, SUBJECTS AND RECORDING TECHNIQUES OF THREE BOOKS ON GESTURES

methods, loci & subjects	1 life direct observations	2 sketches	3 film	4 informants	5 graphs & charts	6 counting	7 literature
Efron mid '30s	N.Y. City and nearby areas. Mainly male. Eastern Jews and Southern Italians. Natural, spontaneous situations in everyday environments	Drawn from life by Am. painter Stuyvesant Van Veen in natural situations	5,000 ft. of film, during a period of 2 years, of about 750 subjects of both sexes.	Who observed and judged the films.	About 1/3 of film projected on coordinate paper frame by frame	Rough counting, with a stopwatch, of the number of unit movements performed in a given time	
Green 1965-1966	Madrid. Students of both sexes and professors at the U. of Madrid. In daily activities Theater attendance	From written descriptions and preliminary sketches by the author		To verify gestures not fully described in fictional and dramatic literature.			Fictional and dramatic

Saitz & Cervenka 1960-1962 Cervenka (18 months)	Colombian and North-American friends in Bogotá. Upper, middle, and lower classes (of different ages), mainly from Bogotá and Tunja. The North-American gestures, from: a group of North Americans residing in Bogotá, of city and country backgrounds (businessmen, educators, students, and Foreign Service employees).	1972 edition: unspecified direct sources, By Mel Pekarsky (N.Y.). Line drawings. 1962 edition: Unspecified sources. By Renèe Bigio.	Interviews with Colombian inform-ants, young-adults and middle-aged, two male and two female, during a period of twelve months, for their recognition of the gestures and comments, and discussion and simulation of varied contexts in order to elicit further gestures. About twenty from the U. S., of different ages and geographical and social backgrounds	American publications.	Newspaper and magazine pictures in Colombia. Also North-American publications

Chart 1

3.1 *Direct Observations*

3.1.1 Basic to this part of the work, the most important one in the collection of a foreign culture's kinesic inventory, is the length of time devoted to it, that is, spent within that culture in daily interaction with, and not merely observation of, its members. Furthermore, while it is true that the fieldwork kinesicist can interpret correctly a number of national gestures, postures and manners recurring in given situations (anger, greetings, beckoning, etc.) without even speaking the language, he should have an excellent command of it if he is to appreciate, first of all, the linguistic context of the kinesic expressions he is trying to study, since many of them will repeat, emphasize, illustrate or contradict the words; but also a command of the paralinguistic features that may determine a given kinesic act. When Green (not S & C, unfortunately) explains, and wrongly too, how Spanish males embrace as a form of greeting, he could have given an accompanying verbal greeting, such as *¡Hombre, ¿cómo estás?!*, or *¡Me alegro de verte, Pepe!*, in which the syllables *hóm, bré, tás,* and *té,* respectively, are emphatically drawled as they coincide with firm pats on each other's back. Both the linguistic and the paralinguistic features of an expression like *¡Pero mamola!* should have been given by S & C as a typical Colombian verbal accompaniment of the gesture explained as 'Disagreement A', even specifying that the drawing back of the arms, which carries the kinesic accent, coincides with the word *mamola,* precisely with its emphatic syllable *mo.* Only a very good knowledge of the native tongue and its paralinguistic characteristics can truly reveal the full meaning of its concomitant kinesic repertoire.

3.1.2 To any interested observer most cultures offer two main groups of speakers, URBAN and RURAL, according to their two principal physical and socio-economic settings, and such a differentiation of these basic zones should, in my opinion, be essential for the kinesicist, or the student of communicative behavior in general. Within the urban area, which seems to have been the one experienced by the authors here discussed, the middle class offers the more standardized repertoire, and the emphasis should be placed on it. However, if an inventory of gestures is meant to contribute to mutual knowledge and understanding among men, it should undoubtedly help its users not only in detecting the more conspicuous levels of a society, but in performing their appropriate repertoires, and this could not be achieved unless the gestures, manners and postures of the rustic are observed, compared with those of the urbanites and recorded in each semantic or situational label (dismissal, beckoning; table manners, hand-shakes; sitting, standing) as separate culturemes. *wow* However, neither S & C nor Green seem to have been interested in the rural repertoires, in spite of their great psychosocial and cultural significance.

3.1.3 For the collector of a cultural kinesic inventory the NOTING should be based on direct observation and, to a certain extent, on readings of contemporary realistic fictional prose; but, in either case, mostly on direct observation of the natives' behavior. The authors discussed mention the loci of their observations, and S & C and Green tell us which groups they concentrated on, but nothing is said of how they carried out the actual collection of those observations on paper, whether they focused on individual situations one at a time, passing from one to the next in a selective way, or rearranged their material after having collected it with no deliberate order, in a general way.

3.1.4 Neither do they explain whether they consider REPETITIOUSNESS *yes — impt.* a required factor in the observation of a given behavior, before including it under a specific label and with a final description of its performance. This is quite essential, for a gesture could be observed in its more infrequent form and judged standard by the foreign observer. This is precisely the kind of exactness in field kinesics that one is inclined to doubt when, for instance, Green, for 'Embracing among men', presents a sketch of two males holding each other like two lovers would, and with no written description; or when, for 'Amount or quantity' and for 'Atmosphere or quality', he describes it as "raising the bunched fingers of one hand to the level of the chest", when actually the fingers are generally opened and closed twice in the first instance.

3.1.5 It seems to me that life direct observation should be a combination of the following corpus-collecting techniques:

A. Non-interactive { far-phase visual-acoustic observation

close-phase visual-acoustic observation { general selec- tive

B. Interactive $\begin{cases} \text{general} \\ \text{selective} \end{cases}$ $\begin{cases} \text{non-eliciting} \\ \text{eliciting} \rightarrow \text{informants} \end{cases}$ *we w not be, that*

The far-phase visual (or visual-acoustic if performers are talking loud-
ly) observation is the one that reveals the public kinesic style of a culture,
and certain contextual situations can be perfectly interpreted; while
the close-phase observation, but still non-interactive, gains the linguistic
and paralinguistic channels. The interactive approach, whether general
or selective, can be a non-eliciting one (and this is likely to be the one
a field investigator would use the most), or purely eliciting, in which case
the interlocutors, or co-actors, would perform as informants.

3.2 *Illustration*

3.2.1 There is no doubt that the ideal published kinesic inventory would
be the one accompanied by a SOUND FILM (or video-tape) companion reel
to the written material, that is, an edited part of the corpus. A candid-
camera type of recording is feasible only under special circumstances;
otherwise the filming equipment has to be installed with the subjects
being aware of it, the success of which depends upon their ability to ignore
it (the way Scheflen's subjects do in their own home for weeks). The
advantage of sound film or video-tape is that, from the right angle and
distance, it records quite well, if not to perfection, the basic triple structure of human communicative behavior (language-paralanguage-kinesics)
plus the proxemic and chronemic aspects of interaction.

3.2.2 Next comes STILL PHOTOGRAPHY, both collected by the investigator
and gathered from newspapers and magazines. S & C report having used
the latter. This may very well be, along with newsreels and TV docu-
mentaries, the only means available for observing the kinesic behavior
of diplomatic protocol, for instance. One still photograph taken by the
investigator can be accompanied by the linguistic context at least, and by
a paralinguistic notation, but it is only a fragment of a whole kinemorphemic or kinesyntactic construct, that is, just a kineme. Photographs,

therefore, require diverse lines indicating the range and direction of the
movement. If taken from film, several frames will illustrate it more
accurately. Efron had line drawings taken from film frames in this way.
There is the possibility, of course, of combining both film and still
pictures for illustrating a book, each type serving a special purpose:

Still photography $\left\{\begin{array}{l}\text{basic posture positions}\\\text{mono-kinemorphemic movements}\\\text{non-elaborate, simple gestures}\end{array}\right.$

Film $\left\{\begin{array}{l}\text{parakinesic qualities}\\\text{direction of movement}\\\text{formation of the movement}\\\text{multi-kinemorphemic movements}\\\text{elaborate kinesic constructs}\\\text{kinesic pausal features}\\\text{continuous eye movements}\end{array}\right.$

3.2.3 Unfortunately, the prevailing method (due no doubt to financial difficulties as much as to technical ones, together with the time factor involved) has been the use of SKETCHES, the quality of which varies considerably. The ones in S & C's first edition were like Green's, of the kind that entirely excludes facial expression and any subtleties (although Green's, published ten years later, are the poorest ones, entirely amateurish and lacking any anatomical proportions), while the new edition's betray the hand of an artist who knows how to suggest body stance and facial expression in simple but mature line drawings that certainly "capture the essence of the movement", as the authors claim. Although, as I pointed out before, facial expression is ignored throughout the inventory. Whether the new illustrator worked from the previous drawings or had the different gestures performed for him, is not specified. If he was not familiar with the Colombian culture, he was bound to lend his characters an American facial touch; and one can almost detect this facial and kinetic American style in Mel Pekarsky's vivid sketches.

When film recording is actually impossible, the investigator should procure the assistance of an artist familiar with the culture under analysis, a true co-fieldworker, not a home interpreter of the material collected. Photographs should be taken as often as possible, though, and a satisfactory combination of line drawings and pictures could be arrived at, always trying, however, not to miss the concomitant facial behavior.

3.3 *Literary Sources*

3.3.1 The more realistic type of NARRATIVE PROSE is always an excellent source for the study of the kinesic repertoire of a culture. Authors like Aldous Huxley and John Dos Passos (in spite of the obvious literary differences) are clear examples of this, and the kinesic and paralinguistic repertoires of their characters are rich enough to clearly differentiate them and, at the same time, reveal the style of the culture they belong to. If, besides having a good command of the language and the cultural fluency that helps understand the nonverbal behavior of his subjects, the field kinesicist gets to know the more representative writers of the narrative realism of his period, he will not only be able to document many of the items in his collection, very often accompanied by their linguistic context, but will, in addition, (a) probe into interesting stages of the creative process, (b) identify perhaps the author's own repertoire, (c) analyze the technical functions of the character's kinesic repertoire, and (d) more from the cultural point of view, learn much about obsolete gestures and the repertoires of the past by reading the classics (Poyatos, 1972b).

3.3.2 The problem for the foreign investigator when using literary quotations to provide his readers with a linguistic context is that he should clearly indicate with which word, or words, exactly, a particular gesture is synchronized, for sometimes a two- or three-sentence paragraph is given, but the reader cannot know when in that portion of speech the gesture really takes place; which is precisely what happens to a foreign reader of a novel, where the gesture in question, if described at all, is explained usually after the person has spoken. In Green's book, where we find many literary quotations, quite a few have the author's comments on the character's gesture, but some do not even have that.

3.4 *Informants*

Besides the non-eliciting techniques of direct observation and readings, field kinesicists like the ones under review have resorted to informants in order to verify the accuracy of their notes and the frequency of the gestures recorded. Such eliciting methods of collecting and ascertaining the body of data can be carried out in various ways, but it should be subjected to class, sex, and age of informants, and to their situational context, and it should aim at eliciting emblems, illustrators, basic affect displays (these less likely to be performed by informants out of certain particular contexts, such as grief, fear, etc.), self-adaptors (also better analyzed in non-eliciting direct observation, as in the case of preening behavior, hesitation scratching, thigh slapping, etc.), and object-adaptors (handling of pipe, glasses, etc., equally better in direct observation).

The advantages of using informants are that (a) the kinesicist does not have to wait for further occurrence of something already observed, (b) he can make his informants read and perform the literary quotations, and thus record the real synchrony between linguistic and kinesic behaviors, (c) he can ask for comments regarding social status, situational context, etc., and (d) he can show them the sketches or still photographs, if that is his illustrating method, and make sure that they identify the gesture in question and its possible situational contexts.

Naturally, the fieldworker will find informants who are good for the job, responsive, sensitive enough to suggest different contexts and to comment on social status and other variables, and, as Samarin (1967) pointed out, with the following social qualities: "patience, honesty, dependability, cheerfulness", plus "the ability to be analytical". But, as he also suggested, "when the linguist's [or kinesicist's] questions stimulate a whole array of associated responses, his corpus will be richer and more varied".

4. THE KINESICIST'S APPROACH TO CULTURE

One could conclude from the above comments on the fieldwork methods that the most sensible and organized framework for the kinesicist's corpus would be the analysis of a culture through its culturemes (Poyatos, 1973a). I have elsewhere proposed and defined the CULTUREME as: any portion of cultural activity sensorially or intellectually apprehended in signs of symbolic value, which can be divided up into smaller units or amalgamated into larger ones. Such an analysis of culture consists of several phases through which a progressive analysis is carried out from a broader view of a culture to an exhaustive and minute study of features, the flexibility of the cultural unit proposed depending on specific strategies. The kinesicist, who must acquire cultural fluency in a systematic fashion, would first differentiate (phase 1) what in many cultures are the four basic and indispensable frames of reference for his fieldwork: urban (exterior and interior) and rural (exterior and interior); next (phase 2) he would add two domains, the people themselves and their environment, this constituting eight primary culturemes (e.g., urban-exterior-human); then (phase 3), once aware of the broader aspects of the foreign culture, he would view each primary cultureme against the different settings (secondary culturemes), culture still viewed impressionistically at this point; it is as tertiary culturemes (phase 4) that each sensorial or intellectual area in secondary culturemes is analyzed as a separate unit in itself, a stage at which cultural systems and subsystems, as well as subcultures (geographically and socially), are discernible. After these four phases the kinesicist's acquisition of cultural fluency can gain in depth as the span of the analysis narrows into derived culturemes (in derived phases), concentrating on each sensorial or intellectual channel (e.g., kinesics in the home), after which derived culturemes 1, 2, 3, etc., specify even more (e.g., kinesics at the table, manners at the table, kinesics of upper-class hosts and middle-class guests, upper-class eye-contact behavior, kinesic turn markers in middle-class interaction, and so on). By regrouping table manners, for instance across a whole culture, we can build up a whole class and study it as such. In addition, the relationships between different systems can now be studied in great detail, as for example: relationship between kinesic and proxemic behavior at the table in a middle-class setting. Finally, one must consider at all times what I have called biophysicopsychological and socio-economic conditioning background of the speaker-actor (Poyatos, 1972a), against which each individual or collective behavior must be weighed. Certain factors, such as age, sex, socio-economic medium, geographical location, etc., will present elements for finer and exhaustive analysis, revealing, as they become discernible, individual, family, community, and national features within each communicative modality, from speech to object language to chronemics, none of which should be disassociated from kinesics when aiming at a well based inventory. Naturally, the collector must specify his goals, and then his work will be judged accordingly.

5. PRESENTATION OF THE MATERIAL

Along with the illustration of the kinesic repertoire of a culture, done by means of film, still photography or sketches, the success of a cultural kinesic inventory, once the material has been selected, depends upon its presentation to the reader and the practicability of the method used. I will comment on presentation in terms of classification, distribution and labelling, description, communicative contexts, conditioning background, table of contents, and indexing, and I shall point out some of the shortcomings that should be avoided.

5.1 The CLASSIFICATION of the kinesic material observed within a culture should establish a basic difference between non-interactive constructs and interactive ones. The two of them together would constitute the subject of analysis for the psychological, or psycho-cultural, kinesicist, while the latter would be the sole area covered by cultural kinesicists. Chart 2 suggests a practical classification which distinguishes, from the functional point of view: ritualistic, conversational, floor-apportioning, and receiver's feedback, applied to gestures, manners, and postures; and from the semiotic one, between free and bound constructs, taking into account the communicative context and the socio-economic one.

CLASSIFICATION OF THE KINESIC MATERIAL

FUNCTIONAL	SEMIOTIC		gestures	manners	postures
(1) ritualistic (2) conversational	free { emblems illustrators affect displays	Visual- Acoustic			
(3) floor- apportioning (4) receiver's feedback	bound { self- adaptors object- adaptors alter- adaptors	Visual			

COMMUNICATIVE CONTEXT: language, paralanguage, kinesics, proxemics, chronemics

SOCIO-ECONOMIC CONTEXT

Chart 2

Although Efron had previously distinguished several classes of non-verbal behavior, neither S & C nor Green explained whether they tried a similar classification of the material collected, apart from the fact that they concentrated on gestures mostly, did not isolate manners, and excluded national postures altogether.

5.2 By DISTRIBUTION AND LABELLING I mean the way in which the material collected and classified is presented to the reader in inventory form for both study and reference.

Green, after claiming that his gestures have been grouped and presented thematically, does not indicate when each group begins or ends, and his items are numbered from 'Heart of the matter' (number 1) to 'Bringing back to reality' (number 119); in other words, no clue is given to the reader who wishes to find, say, greetings, except through the alphabetical index at the end, although some labels in this index do not necessarily coincide with the reader's own conceptual labelling. Very few would look for some of Green's labels, such as 'Divine wisdom and testimony from above', 'Highly placed person and precursor', 'Masses or mass behavior', 'Heart of the matter', and the like, while others are ambiguous since they are much too arbitrary.

S & C have listed the following semantic labels alphabetically, which makes their book more practical because their labelling is more standard and objective:

Agreement, anger, anticipation, approval, attention, aversion, baby, bet, boredom, cigarette, cold, come, complication, cross, crowd, dance (invitation), delicacy, denial, directions, disagreement, disappointment, disapproval, disbelief, disgust, disinterest, drink, drunk, emphasis, encouragement, enthusiasm, excitement, fat, faux pas, favor, female, fight, flirtation (wink), following, food, friendship, frustration, full, go (traffic direction), goad, goodbye, gossip, graft, greetings, height, hitchhiking, hot, impatience, imprisonment, insanity, insults, intelligence, kiss, leave, luck, marriage, masculinity, memory, money, more or less, nervousness, no information, oath, perfection, photograph, pride, proximity & touching, punishment, quickly, recognition, regret-chagrin, repetition, requests, restaurant gestures, retribution, revenge, review, saintliness, self (me), sexual gestures, shame, silence, sit, sleep, slow down (traffic), small, smell, snobbishness, stand, stinginess, stop, strength, success, surprise, talk, telephone, termination, thief, thin, threat, time, tiredness, victory, wait, warning, what?, what happened?, yes/no.

With such a list the foreign reader can certainly learn a wealth of Colombian gestures, many of which, however, are common to North-American culture; but many others are of the kind he can learn and perform in Colombia, and groups like those of Peace Corps volunteers should use this inventory as a valuable piece of reference. Among the native gestures are those for: bet, smoking a cigarette, beckoning and goodbyes, disagreement, drinking, eating, greetings, oath, and the series of sexual signs that were not included in the first edition.

This thematic listing, however, seems to suffer from certain misleading shortcomings, in spite of its usefulness. In the first place, there are noun labels that should be adjectival labels ('Crowded', and not 'Crowd'), or gerundial labels ('Drinking' instead of 'Drink', while 'drink' has its own uses; or 'Hushing' instead of 'Silence') One notices that affects like surprise, anger, and disgust are listed, while others just as important, such as happiness, fear, sadness, and interest, are excluded. Something similar happens with certain functions of kinesic behavior. If 'Emphasis' is profusely illustrated as accompanying verbal communication, why not include also gestures that perform other functions in nonverbal communication, like 'Contradicting'?

Two more problems associated with labelling are ambiguity and misplacing. The former occurs, for instance, with the following entries: 'Anger B' (also threatening), 'Denial B' (also finished, matter concluded), 'Smell A (Bad)'. Misplaced labelling is represented in S & C's inventory by items like 'Full' (of food), which should perhaps go along with 'Eating', or rather, with 'manners at the table', not included in their book.

5.2.1 One must admit that the method used in distribution and labelling in the two inventories discussed does not take full advantage of the possibilities. Rather than a totally arbitrary and incomplete listing of topics or settings (Green), or an alphabetical inventory like S & C's, in which affects, situations, settings, semantic groups and partial culturemes are mixed, I would personally favor the systematic arrangement resulting from the study of culturemes as outlined above. Naturally, this study would be based on secondary culturemes, which specify the various settings: home, school (high school, boarding school, college, etc.), office (bank, university, etc.), restaurant (popular, out-of-doors, expensive, exclusive, etc.), bar (popular, hotel, club, etc.), church (Catholic, synagogue, Pentecostal, urban, rural, revival, etc.), and so on. Each of those settings shows, according to social and educational levels, typical kinesic repertoires observed, beyond standard usage, as extrastandard, infrastandard, and technical or group repertoire.

One could combine the observation and presentation of specific settings with their further classification into: basic affects, basic physical and mental states (disbelief, tiredness, thirst, hunger, heat, cold, etc.), qualities (physical, moral), and those which Efron called batons (movements that accent or emphasize verbal expression), ideographs (tracing the direction of thought), spatial movements, kinetographs and pictographs, plus the more common object-adaptors, self-adaptors and alter-adaptors. One would find, for instance, that the frequency and importance of emblematic behavior cross-culturally observed can be an interesting part of the inventory. In a Hispanic culture a great number of emblems are used, not when verbal expression is prevented, but simultaneously with it. We would also recognize pan-cultural emblems worth studying separately. Furthermore, there would be some highly identifiable cultural cues among the items in an inventory towards which the reader's attention should be called. Among them, probably, would be certain etiquette patterns which should be compared, making sure that some of them are not obsolete, or simply ignored and lacking an active value in the social life of the culture under study.

In addition, and this would be important from the point of view of social psychology, the cultural kinesicist could group together certain turn-claiming, turn-yielding, turn-taking and turn-suppressing gestures and postures that are possible to identify as culture-specific, as well as typical instances of simultaneous gesturing, or kinesic behavior in general, so common among Latins, plus some pausal kinesic markers and some culture-bound feedback cues.

5.3 In their DESCRIPTION of gestures, S & C have tried to show certain similarities and differences in Colombian and U.S. gestures, indicating when the same gestures have the same, or similar, meaning in both cultures (which we could call synonyms-homomorphs, indicated in the book by the designation 'common'; when the same meaning is represented by different gestures (that is, synonyms-antomorphs); when the same gestures carry a different meaning in each culture (antonyms-homomorphs); and when both form and meaning are culture-specific (designated as 'unique' in the 1962 edition).

5.3.1 All descriptions are accompanied by their corresponding illustrations and by additional cultural comments. In some instances, however, the description could have been more specific. For 'Telephone' (which should rather indicate the act of 'Telephoning'), it is said that "the fist rotates by the side of the ear", when it is actually the thumb against the index finger, as if grasping one of the old cranks, or the hand in the position of holding a receiver against the ear, with no crank-turning.[6] For 'Threat' it should be specified that the forearm with hand palm up moves, not back and forth, but rather from left to right and horizontally several times, slantingly, or with palm closely parallel to the performer's face when addressing children.

---

[6]   Although being a native of Spain I can appreciate another Hispanic culture, I had the privilege of using Dr. and Mrs. Gustavo Argáez, of Bogotá, as very sensitive informants when going through the book.

5.3.2 On the other hand, ELABORATION should be equally avoided. For 'Drink A' it is said that "hand is raised to mouth, thumb extended and pointing at mouth, little finger raised. Hand rocks back and forth in this position." The little finger is not necessarily raised, and the hand does not necessarily rock back and forth, but simply moves towards the mouth once.

5.3.3 AMBIGUITY OF USAGE is found sometimes in inventories. When S & C say for 'Emphasis D' that "fingers of both hands come to a point and tap chest", it is true, but this gesture is also used simultaneously with many verbal contexts. Green, explaining how men embrace in greeting or in leave-taking, shows, as I pointed out before, the least common way; he does not specify different situations (encounter, congratulatory, condolence, making up, agreement, etc.), nor does he indicate the parakinesic modifiers: range, intensity, and duration.

5.3.4 Sometimes it is INCOMPLETION that authors incur S & C, for 'More or less' should have described the gesture as combining both 'More or less A' and 'More or less B', specifying that hand rocks, head tilts to one side or both sides, lips are pursed as in disbelief, nose is puckered; in other words, a whole kinesyntagm must be explained. For 'No information' the drawing shows shoulder shrugging, as it actually happens, but the written description ignores it. When for 'Full' (of food) S & C wrote as "common" that "one hand pats stomach gently", they could have added that in North America the hand makes a circle on the stomach (while perhaps saying *It was good!*), which is done neither in Colombia nor in Spain.

5.3.5 It may happen that the author does not give the proper CULTURAL CONTEXT, as when S & C list only applause as common 'Approval' in both cultures, when it is well known that North Americans could never use their whistling at a Hispanic soccer game or at a bullfight; or when, trying to explain why guests linger at the doorstep while taking leave, they fail to say that goodbyes are prolonged all over the Spanish-speaking world, in some interesting stages, due to a certain chronemic behavior deeply ✳ hmm....
rooted in the Spanish personality, and not to the authors' belief that guests like to get accustomed to the temperature change before leaving because it can be harmful, according to many of them. Much could be said also about beckoning at a restaurant by means of hissing, clapping, finger-snapping, brow-lifting, hand-signalling, etc., according to the quality of the restaurant and other social variables.

5.3.6 Lack of context also exists in the LINGUISTIC side, as when S & C explain a gesture of 'Disagreement A' without giving *¡Pero mamola!* as a context more common in Colombia than the one they quote, which, as in other cases, carries some typical PARALINGUISTIC features.

5.3.7 One could refer also to certain INACCURATE COMMENTS, quite common in cultural inventories, as when Green, for 'Beckoning', assures his readers that the palm-down form of beckoning is "rarely observed in urban social contexts", when anyone can see a traffic officer calling the law-breaker that way; but, above all, in rural areas, and not only among "older madrileños" and "young children in the care of middle-age nannies"!

5.3.8 Closely related to it is the fact that often CULTURAL BORROWINGS are not identified as such. The palm-up way of beckoning, for instance, has been made popular in Spain through American movies and tourists.

5.3.9 One should also warn the kinesic collector against hasty statements regarding the FREQUENCY of a gesture and making the reader believe, for instance, as Green does, that a Spaniard always presses his lower eyelid down with his index finger to say, or signify, *Mira lo que hay allí* 'Look what's there', or that he takes the bunched fingers of one hand toward his mouth after saying, or to signify, *Vamos a comer* 'Let's eat'.

5.3.10 Finally, I would like to add to the above suggestions against some common failures the need to specify the SITUATIONAL context and the SOCIO-ECONOMIC STATUS. According to educated Colombian informants, the gesture listed by S & C under 'Regret D' is performed by low-class people, being typical of maids. The very important class of culturemes represented by the different types of restaurants require more specific comments about the socio-economic status of both the place and its customers.

5.4 I would like to mention, at least in passing, the five types of COMMUNICATIVE CONTEXTS that one should consider in a critical presentation of a kinesic inventory: linguistic, paralinguistic, kinesic, proxemic, and chronemic. The first two have been mentioned before simply as two of the indispensable factors often neglected by kinesic collectors.

5.4.1 The need for the LINGUISTIC context is obvious when it is present either preceding or following the kinesic act, or simultaneously with it.

It may happen that different verbal contexts give the same gesture different meanings. On the other hand, one has to know precisely the time relationship between the act and its context in terms of synchronization for there are instances in which the central kineme, or kinemorpheme, occurs exactly at one point and nowhere else. This synchronization, of course, applies to the other four contexts as well.

5.4.2 A gesture may determine the PARALINGUISTIC features of the verbal context just mentioned. In fact, attention should be given, first of all, to the parakinesic qualities of intensity (akin to stress and articulatory tension [overtense-tense-medium-lax-overlax]), range or extent of movement (similar to syllabic duration [overwide-wide-medium-narrow-overnarrow]), and velocity or temporal length (similar to tempo of speech [overfast-fast-medium-slow-overslow]). Both paralinguistic features and parakinesic features condition each other, and investigation is required in this area.

Apart from the paralinguistic qualities inherent to the concurrent verbal expression, there are a number of isolated paralinguistic "alternants" (Poyatos, 1973b) which may typically occur preceding, following, or simultaneously with, the kinesic expression: sighs, coughs, and throat-clearings; numerous clicks; hesitation vowels, clicks, ingressions, and egressions; and more specifically, for instance, a strong nareal ingression while stamping the foot in rage or impatience.

5.4.3 There is a KINESIC context to a kinesic act performed with a different part of the body, even within different parts of the face. While one could argue that such a concomitant act is not a context proper, but part of the whole semantic construct, it is also true, from the point of view of a gesture inventory, that it is anatomically independent from the basic gesture, and that, in fact, one can speak of that gesture without referring to the rest of the kinesic behavior. Such context, however, is culturally important in everyday gestures, like beckoning in a restaurant (with or without eyebrow lifting), or negation (with various facial constructs).

5.4.4 The PROXEMIC behavior displayed with specific body movements and positions is sufficiently meaningful to be recorded as an important contextual factor. Gestures of beckoning, for instance, vary with the distance kept from, say, a waiter; the gesture replacing *¿ Qué hay?* or *¿ Qué paso?* (S & C, p. 150) requires a long-phase public distance, or even farther. It is interesting to note that the same verbal expression, which would be whispered or muttered at a close-personal distance, and then fully voiced at normal social distances, is again muttered, not totally silenced, as it becomes replaced by an equivalent kinesic construct.

Proxemic context includes bodily orientation when performing certain gestures or taking certain postures. One may cite as an example the very Spanish way of emphasizing a verbal expression while driving a point home, or actually overemphasizing expressions equivalent to *Oh, come on!, Don't give me that!*: the standing speaker opens his arms, looks at you, turns away about 100 degrees and returns to the same point, his gesture still lingering. Also, while two Spanish males stroll along at a slow pace, each time there is an emphatic pause or an emphatic statement, the speaker stops, turns towards his listener and says the important thing, sometimes holding his arm.

5.4.5 Finally, by contextual CHRONEMIC behavior, I am referring, not only to the modification of the kinesic repertoire as time progresses (at a party, conditioned also by variables such as alcohol), but, for instance, to the time passed between the initiation of a gesture and its actual execution, as in the case of the masculine embrace among friends, which is initiated or anticipated while still at a distance.

5.5 Although the cultural kinesicist is likely to require less fine an analysis of behavior than the social psychologist, for instance, he would do well not to ignore that every act of behavior, no matter how insignificant it may seem, is connected to the biophysicopsychological and socio-economic conditioning background I mentioned earlier. I will just itemize its different components in Chart 3.

5.6 The table of contents and the index are, or rather, should be two very important parts of the reader-oriented apparatus in the kind of kinesic inventory I have discussed in this article.

The TABLE OF CONTENTS should reflect the distribution of the material as suggested in 5.2.1. Basic to this preliminary guide in the book should be the classification of culturemes, comprising, among others: settings (kinesics in the church [urban, rural], in the restaurant [different types], etc.), everyday situations (directions, in shops, bus, subway, table manners [educated upper and middle-class, lower and uneducated, the rustic, children, object-adaptors at the table], etc.), floor-apportioning (Spanish characteristics, grown-ups and children, arguments,

[handwritten margin notes: "Race.", "homo sexual"]

								CONDITIONING BACKGROUND					
BIOPHYSICOPSYCHOLOGICAL								SOCIAL					
								SOCIO-GEOGRAPHICAL					SOCIO-ECONOMIC
Sex	Age	Hereditary — Somatogenic	Physiology	Health	Psychology	Physical Medium	Socio-economic medium	Individual	Married Couple	Family — Clan	Social Group	Geographical variety	Refined
													Educated
													Modest employee
													Pseudo-educated
													Rustic

Chart 3

simultaneous talking and simultaneous gesturing, etc.), affect-displays (rage, threat, grief, boredom), physiological states (hunger, tiredness, pain, heat), psychological states (doubt, fear, confidence, etc.), physical qualities (strength, hardness, cold, etc.), illustrators for actions (speed, moving objects, mockery, etc.) and for objects and people (body shape, shape, size, etc.), spatial movement, etc. Let us not forget that some of these topics require an interesting differentiation of style between educated and rustic performers, and that in some cases the foreign observer and student would establish a better rapport if he adapts his own repertoire to his rustic co-interactants, for instance. As special groups indicated in the table of contents, one should offer a basic repertoire of kinesic markers and feedback-cues that occur in interaction, and that one can also learn for a better understanding of another people's idiosyncrasies.

As for the INDEX, this should be an exhaustive cross-reference tool so that the user of the book can, not only search for the expected, but discover the unexpected, being able to progress from the smallest cultturemes, such as fork, pipe, nose, feminine figure, to larger units of analysis, like restaurant, rustic repertoire (which refers the reader to items related to it), greetings, etc. Naturally, the index can be the most useful element in the book for quick finding and for practically exhausting the reader's needs concerning a specific topic.

[handwritten note: to get a "less studied" response?]

Only as I finish typing this paper I learn (too late to comment on it) about a detailed and photographically illustrated article on Arabic kinesics, containing an "Arabic gesture collection of 247 items, by anthropologist R. A. Barakat (1973). I am sure that, like the inventories here discussed, it will continue to foster the growing interest in kinesics, in how, why, when, and with whom people move, and in the great significance of this nonverbal behavior. These inventories will undoubtedly help develop the cultural aspects of research in this young science, and bridge the pervading gaps that prevent many people from really knowing their fellow men.

REFERENCES

Barakat, Robert A.
1973   "Arabic Gestures", *Journal of Popular Culture* 6, 749-892.
Birdwhistell, Ray
1970   *Kinesics and Context: Essays on Body Motion and Communication* (Philadelphia: University of Pennsylvania Press).
Brault, Gerard J.
1963   "Kinesics and the Classroom: Some Typical French Gestures", *The French Review* XXXVI, 374-82.
Ekman, Paul, and Wallace V. Friesen
1969   "The Repertoire of Nonverbal Behavior: Categories, Origins, Usage, and Coding", *Semiotica* 1, 49-98.
Goffman, Ervin
1961   *Encounters* (Indianapolis and New York: Bobbs-Merrill).
Hall, Edward T.
1955   "The Anthropology of Manners", *Scientific American* 192: 4, 84-90.
Hayes, Alfred S.
1964   "Paralinguistics and Kinesics: Pedagogical Perspectives", *Approaches to Semiotics*, ed. by Thomas A. Sebeok, *et al.* (The Hague: Mouton), 145-72.
Kendon, Adam
1972   Review of Birdwhistell's *Kinesics and Context*, *The American Journal of Psychology* 85: 3, 441-55.
Mehrabian, Albert
1969   "Significance of Posture and Position in the Communication of Attitude and Status Relationships", *Psychological Bulletin* 71, 359-72.
Nierenberg, Gerard I., and Henry H. Calero
1971   *How to Read a Person Like a Book* (New York: Hawthorn).
Poyatos, Fernando
1970   "Kinésica del español actual", *Hispania* 53: 3, 444-52.
1972a   "The Communication System of the Speaker-Actor and His Culture", *Linguistics* 83, 64-86.
1972b   "Paralenguaje y kinésica del personaje novelesco: Nueva perspectiva en el análisis de la narración", *Revista de Occidente* 113-14, 148-70.
1973a   "Analysis of a Culture Through Its Culturemes: Theory and Method", IXth ICAES International pre-Congress Conference on The Mutual Inter-

action of People and Their Built Environment, Racine, Wisconsin; to be published in *The Mutual Interaction of Man and His Built Environment*, ed. by Amos Rapoport (The Hague: Mouton, 1974).

1973b "Cross-Cultural Study of Paralinguistic 'Alternants' in Face-to-Face Interaction", IXth ICAES International pre-Congress Conference on The Organization of Behavior in Face-to-Face Interaction, Chicago; to be published in *Organization of Behavior in Face-to-Face Interaction*, ed. by Adam Kendon, Richard M. Harris, and Mary Key (The Hague: Mouton, 1974).

Samarin, William J.

1967 *Field Linguistics: A Guide to Linguistic Field Work* (New York: Holt, Rinehart and Winston).

Scheflen, Albert

1964 "The Significance of Posture in Communication Systems", *Psychiatry* 27, 316-31.

HAROLD G. JOHNSON, PAUL EKMAN,
and WALLACE V. FRIESEN

Communicative Body Movements: American Emblems[1]

In 1941 David Efron published his dissertation *Gesture and Environment* (re-issued as *Gesture, Race and Culture,* 1972). This pioneering study systematically explored differences between two cultural groups in their body movements during conversations. Efron's contributions were many. He combined both quantitative and qualitative methods of observation and analysis. He provided definitive evidence on how culture determines the pattern and type of certain body movements during conversation. And, he suggested the need to distinguish different classes of body movement. One such class of body movements which he termed *emblems* are the subject of this report.

Efron said that emblems were movement patterns that had a precise meaning. The pattern of the movement and its associated meaning are so precise that a glossary could be written visually depicting each action and message. Efron did, indeed, provide such an emblem glossary for immigrant Sicilians in the United States. Although recently there has been renewed interest in studies of body movement and facial expression (a number of representative articles have been published in this journal), few have been influenced by Efron's work and even fewer have been interested in the type behavior Efron termed emblems. Saitz and Cervenka (1962, 1973) were one exception, reporting a glossary of emblems (although they did not use this term), for Columbians and Americans. Ekman and Friesen are the other main exception. In the first issue of this journal (1969) they reported a theoretical classification of body movement which incorporated many of Efron's theoretical distinctions.

Their formulation distinguished among classes of body movements and facial expressions on the bases of their: (a) origin (how an action became part of the organism's repertoire); (b) coding (the principle underlying the relationship between action and significant); (c) usage (social contexts in which the action occurs). Ekman and Friesen proposed five classes of non-verbal behavior: facial expressions of emotion, regulators, adaptors, illustrators, and emblems. Emblems were said to be coded either arbitrarily or iconically, a disagreement with Efron who limited emblems to arbitrarily coded actions. Like illustrators (a class of movements which function to illustrate simultaneous speech), emblems occur in the presence of others and are rarely shown when someone is alone. Emblems differ in this way from adaptors (movements in which one part of the body manipulates another body part), since adaptors occur when alone as well as when *with*[2] another person. Emblems differ from illustrators, however, in that there need not be concomitant speech or any verbal conversation at all, although emblems can and do occur during conversation. Emblems are often used in social situations where speech is constrained or not possible, e.g., wartime patrol, hunters too distant to converse verbally or between students in a classroom.

Emblems differ from most other body movements or facial expressions in that the person observing the emblem, the decoder, assumes that the action was performed deliberately by the actor or encoder to provide the decoder with a message. The encoder typically acknowledges he is communicating; he usually takes responsibility for what he transmits, much as he would with his words. At the opposite extreme are movements classified as adaptors, such as scratching the face. Adaptors may be informative, but they are not regarded by encoder or decoder as deliberate, acknowledged, attempts to provide information. They are regarded by the participants in a conversation the way slips-of-the-tongue were considered before Freud.

Ekman and Friesen (1972) recently refined their definition of emblems:

> Emblems are those nonverbal acts (a) which have a direct verbal translation usually consisting of a word or two, or a phrase, (b) for which this precise meaning is known by most or all members of a group, class, subculture or culture, (c) which are most often deliberately used with the conscious intent to send a particular message to other person(s), (d) for which the person(s) who sees the emblem usually not only knows the emblem's message but also knows that it was deliberately sent to him, and (e) for which the sender usually takes responsibility for having made that communication. A further touchstone of an emblem is whether it can be replaced by a word or two, its message verbalized without substantially modifying the conversation.

There are a number of questions about emblems which should be of interest to students of nonverbal communication or semiotics. What is the ontogeny of emblems, at what point do different emblems become established in the infant's repertoire, and how does the acquisition of emblems interlace with the acquisition of verbal language? How are emblems utilized in conversation, are there regularities in which messages are transmitted emblematically, and do these emblems substitute, repeat or qualify the spoken messages? Are there any universal emblems, can we explain instances in which the same message is performed with a different motor action in two cultures? How are emblems related to American Sign Language? And, the phylogeny of emblems is of obvious interest.

We believe that the identification of the emblem repertoire is the most sensible first step which enables pursuit of all these questions. Once an emblem glossary has been established it would then be possible to observe when they first are shown by children, and how they appear in the structure of spoken conversation. Also the repertoire, structural characteristics and usage can be compared among different cultural groups, and with ASL. Without knowledge of the emblem repertoire, without a glossary, such observations are like searching for a needle in a haystack, since emblems are but one type of body movement or facial expression and usually they are not the most frequent type of nonverbal behavior emitted. This report describes a method of identifying the emblem repertoire for any group, literate or preliterate, which is usable with people once they reach the age where they comprehend a language.

METHOD

Neither Efron nor Saitz and Cervenka had provided much information about how they identified the repertoire of emblems. When Ekman and Friesen began their study of emblems in Japan and New Guinea (1969) they developed a method borrowing from anthropology (the use of informants), linguistics (back-translation), and psychology (quantification and rating scales). The techniques described here are a refinement and further elaboration of their methods. There are three separate steps: I. obtaining from informants the motor patterns which may be emblems (encoding emblem candidates); II. comparison of motor pattern performances across informants (visual analysis of encoding); III. obtaining judgments from a new group of informants about the semantic meaning and usage of the emblem candidates (emblem decoding).

I. *Encoding Emblem Candidates*

Ekman and Friesen found that simply asking people to perform the emblems they knew (once explaining the definition of an emblem) was unproductive. People remembered few. On the other hand, if people were read a list of messages and asked if they had an emblem for each message, it was easy for them to recall and perform emblems they knew. Importantly, this procedure also seemed to stimulate memory since informants frequently would volunteer emblems not on the list of messages read to them.

The message list utilized in this study included the list developed by Ekman and Friesen for use in Japan and the Fore of New Guinea. It included all emblems found for those two groups and many messages not emblems for either. Messages which were reported as emblems by Efron and Saitz and Cervenka were also included. The list was arranged so that messages concerned with a specific information domain (e.g. insults) were not all close to each other, although some clustering of messages seemed to be conducive in eliciting volunteered items for that domain. Each informant was presented with about 220 verbal messages one at a time. For each he was asked if he knew an emblem for the message. The instructions emphasized that he would not have an emblem for every message as the list had been compiled from many cultures. The instructions also emphasized that he should not give pantomimes, charades or on-the-spot inventions. "Give only those emblems which you have used or have seen other people use in your past experience."

Each informant was queried individually, with the entire procedure recorded on videotape. The investigator was very careful not to provide suggestions (verbal or nonverbal). Frequently he paused to ask the informant to volunteer emblems or alternate ways to convey the same message.

Since emblems might vary with age, sex, ethnic background, or social class a homogeneous pool of informants was selected for this initial survey in the United States. The informants selected were white, middle-class males between the ages of 21 to 35 years, at least third-generation United States, and living in an urban setting.

The performances of fifteen informants were videotaped. It is difficult to determine how many informants to use in a study such as this. The decision was made to stop when the informants did not volunteer any new items. After the tenth subject, only one or two new emblems were volunteered and it seemed reasonable to assume that we had exhausted what could be learned about the emblem repertoire using this procedure.

II. *Visual Analysis of Encoding*

If the majority of the informants did not perform any action for a particular message we assumed that there was no emblem in this cultural group for that message. Such messages were eliminated from further consideration. For those messages in which the majority said they knew an emblem, we required that the performance be visually similar among at least 70% of the informants. This requirement was intended to eliminate on-the-spot inventions or pantomimes which might be performed differently by various informants. Presumably, emblems are performed in much the same way by everyone. There might, of course, be more than one action pattern for a particular message, but informants were encouraged to provide more than one action for each message if they knew alternatives.

The visual analysis of the emblem performances to determine similarity did not involve precise measurement. Instead the assessment was a global judgment performed by the first author, and partially verified by the other authors. Decisions about similarity did not seem difficult. It seemed obvious that either the performances were minor variations on a particular action pattern, or they were markedly different in appearance. One hundred and thirty eight motor patterns met the criterion of visual similarity. This did not mean, however, that all 138 actions were necessarily emblems, but only that most people performed the same action for each of these messages. It was possible that most informants might invent the same movement for a message, yet that movement might not be an emblem. Take the example of the message "hammering a nail into the wall." If people are asked how to transmit this message, they usually will perform a similar motor action, involving a hammering movement with one hand while the other hand holds an invisible nail. If the informants followed our instruction to provide only actions they had seen in normal conversation, not pantomimes or charades, they would not make such an invention. But, there is no way to be certain simply on the basis of similar performances across informants. The third step of emblem decoding is needed.

III. *Emblem Decoding*

A different group of informants were shown each action and asked to decode the message. Here again, correct back-translation would not necessarily eliminate all pantomimes or charades. If the action was iconic its message might be obvious. Therefore, it was necessary to ask the informants to evaluate whether each action was currently in common everyday usage (natural), or used only in pantomimes or charades (artificial).

A new videotape was prepared showing one example of each of the 138 action patterns performed similarly by the first group of informants. Rather than use the original informants' behavior, which would vary with the physical characteristics of the 15 encoders, a single person (H.G.J.) performed each of the 138 actions. These performances were then examined by Ekman and a communications specialist (Randall Harrison) to insure that the performances were clear depictions of the informants' behavior. In addition to the 138 action patterns which emerged from the visual analysis, 14 other action patterns were added. These included nine action patterns thought by the authors to be emblems although they had not been on the message list nor volunteered by the informants and five actions known to be emblematic in France.[3]

This new videotape was shown to other informants who were asked to make four decisions after viewing each motor pattern:

(1) They wrote down, in their own words, the *Message* conveyed by the emblematic behavior pattern.

(2) They made a one to seven rating of their certainty about the message they derived from the behavior pattern, a *Message Certainty* score.

(3) They scored whether the pattern was used in everyday situations, a *Natural Usage* score; or, whether the pattern was used only for games of charades or in pantomime routines, an *Artificial Usage* score.

(4) They made a one to seven rating of their certainty about the *Natural-Artificial Usage* score they gave to the emblem, a *Usage Certainty* score.

Three groups of informants acted as decoders. Each group viewed 50 or 51 performances from the videotape. There was a total of 53 decoders who met the same cultural criteria as the encoder informants. Both females (26) and males (27) were members of the decoder groups. Subsequent analysis revealed no differences between male and female decoders.

Results

The majority of the decoders judged 32 of the action patterns as artificial; these were not considered further. There were ten action patterns for which less than 50% of the decoders agreed about the message. These also were discarded from further consideration. The remaining action patterns are listed in tables one through four.

Verified Emblems. Table 1 lists all the messages where the action patterns met the most stringent criteria:

– the message derived by at least 70% of the decoders matched exactly or almost exactly the message given to the encoder;

– at least 70% of the decoders judged the action pattern as natural in usage. These messages have been grouped according to information domains discussed below.

Probable Emblems. Table 2 lists messages where the action pattern met a less stringent criteria on the ratings of naturalness of usage:

– the message derived by at least 70% of the decoders matched exactly or almost exactly the message given to the encoders (same as for Verified Emblems);

— more than 50% but less than 70% of the decoders judged the action pattern as natural in usage.

Ambiguous Emblems. Table 3 lists messages where the action pattern met less stringent criteria on both message decoding and usage:

— the message derived by more than 50% but less than 70% of the decoders matched exactly or nearly exactly the message given to the encoders;

— more than 50% but less than 70% of the decoders judged the action pattern as natural in usage (same as for Probable Emblems).

Ambiguous Emblems. Table 4 lists messages where the action pattern encoded was not decoded as the same message, but the message decoded resembled the message encoded:

— the message derived by more than 50% of the decoders resembled the message given to the encoders;

— more than 50% of the decoders judged the action pattern as natural.

Discussion

Without replication of this study on a comparable group of informants we are uncertain whether the emblem repertoire should include items listed in all four tables or just those listed in Table 1. If the results shown in Tables 2, 3, and 4 were replicated these action patterns also should be considered emblems. Replication could add a few emblems not listed in these tables, but we consider it unlikely that there would be many new emblems uncovered by these same methods, within the same population.

We can not be certain whether the emblems listed in these tables are known and used by more than middle-class, white, college educated, third generation Americans living within the San Francisco Bay area. Comparison of our results with the emblems reported by Saitz and Cervenka (1962) for Americans, showed that about half of the emblems reported in Table 1 were also found in their study. The substantial *non*-overlap in emblem repertoires may be due to: time (their study was in 1962, ours in 1973), region (their informants were East coast, ours were West coast), and/or methods of study (they did not describe their methods in any detail). Study of another group within the U.S., utilizing the same methods we have employed is needed. The age, region, social class, ethnic background, should all be varied to determine the limits of generality for this emblem repertoire.

In his discussion of Indian Sign Language, Kroeber (1972) raised a number of questions which are relevant to ask about emblems. One issue he raised is whether any of the signs are compounds, built out of identifiable elements, which recombine into other compounds. If by elements we mean actions which themselves have some emblematic meaning, then the answer would be that there are few emblems which are compounds of such elements. Two exceptions help to illustrate. Pointing the finger or hand is an element which has emblematic meaning itself, and pointing is incorporated into a number of emblems together with other elements. The "shrug" compound can be performed with the wrists rotating so that the palms are turned facing up and then down (element one) and/or hunching upwards of the shoulders (element two). Either element when performed alone is an emblem as is the compound and the message is the same — "I don't know" or "I'm not certain."

These two examples are ones in which the elements contained in the compound are themselves emblems; the elements have meaning. And, we have said that there are few such emblem compounds. But, what of elements which are not themselves emblematic, which have no semantic meaning, but which combine and recombine into various compound elements? The answer to this question requires further work, but our judgment so far is that there are few such emblem elements.

In both American Sign Language and Indian Sign Language, the signs are usually emitted in strings or sequences. There has been considerable discussion of the principles governing such sequences and whether sign languages have a grammar similar to that of spoken languages (c.f., Tervoort, 1973; Stokoe, 1974 this journal). While there are occasions when emblems are used in sequential strings, these appear to be only those occasions when verbal conversation is some way constrained. For example, if while talking on the phone you notice a person come to the door of your office due for his appointment, you may emblematically signal that he will have to wait just a minute, and may follow this with an emblem that requests he come in and be seated. When two people are not constrained about the use of words, however, we have rarely observed a sequence of emblems.

Another question that can be asked about emblems (once the repertoire is known for a particular group), is whether there are common emblems across groups within a culture or across cultures. Efron claimed that emblem repertoires would differ across cultural groups, and Saitz and Cervenka reported a number of instances of differences in emblems between Columbians and Americans. Ekman and Friesen (1967, 1969) reasoned that as socially learned behavior emblems should be culture specific. They also suggested that there would be certain emblems common to a number of cultures. These would be "ones which involve a message describing a bodily activity which, for anatomical reasons, must be performed in similar ways." For example, if a culture has an emblem for sleeping, we have found it will involve moving the head into a lateral position, perpendicular to the body, with or without bringing one or both hands below the head as a kind of pillow" (Ekman, 1972, p. 364-365).

Comparison of our list of emblematic action patterns with those published by Saitz and Cervenka for Columbians and Efron for Sicilians suggested a surprising, unanticipated amount of overlap. Almost half of the messages listed in Table 1 are performed with the same action pattern in our U.S. sample and by the Sicilians and Columbians. Most of these presumably identical emblems in the U.S., Columbia and Sicily did *not* entail anatomically constrained bodily activity. The unusual amount of overlap may be explained by the high level of contact which U.S. citizens have with people from other cultures. The U.S. may have few indigenous emblems (as suggested by Efron), but may, more than most countries, incorporate a variety of emblems drawn from the immigrants from many different nations. Countries that have been extensively exposed to each other, particularly if that exposure is amplified by the media (as in TV's presentation of Italian emblems in crime stories) may show a great deal of overlap in emblem repertoires. Preliminary results from Ekman and Friesen's (1969) study of emblems in the South Fore of New Guinea, a group visually isolated from the U.S., showed very few emblems in common with the U.S. sample. Even their study of urban Japanese showed less overlap than the comparison of the U.S. with Columbia and Sicily. The matter is confounded, however, since the study of the South Fore and Japan utilized the same method of investigation as reported here, while Efron and Saitz and Cervenka presumably did not follow this method.

Cross cultural comparisons of emblems can consider not just equivalents in action patterns as we have just discussed, but also instances where a message is emblematic in more than one culture but with a totally different action. Approximately one third of the messages listed on Table 1 were also emblems in Sicily but performed with a different action. About a tenth of the messages in Table 1 were emblematic in Columbia but performed with a different action.

We also considered emblem repertoires in regard to the more abstract question of whether certain domains of information were emblematic in more than one culture, regardless of the specific message or motor action. For example, are there emblems for greeting and departure in each group studied? The answer to this is "yes," for the South Fore, urban Japan, U.S., Columbia and Sicily. Inspection of the messages listed in Table 1 suggested six other obvious categories or domains of information in addition to the greeting and departures, and the tables were organized in terms of these information domains.

Insults: e.g. fuck you, he's crazy, the hell with you.
Interpersonal Directions: stop, be silent, come here, go this way, hurry, etc.

Replies: yes, no, okay, I don't know, I doubt it, no way, etc.

Own Physical State: I'm hot, I'm cold, I've got a headache, toothache, etc.

Affect: I'm hungry, sad, surprised, etc.

Appearance: Woman – nice figure.

The categorization of information domains is a tricky matter, and best performed once a list of emblems from a number of cultures has been compiled. Such work is now in progress and will be reported in our forthcoming report (Ekman & Friesen, in preparation) of U.S., Japanese, South Fore, Iranian and Israeli emblems. In that report we discuss the issue of why certain domains of information are emblematic in one culture but not another, or are covered by many different emblems in one culture and only a few in another.

Another issue which needs discussion is the context within which emblems appear, and how that context modifies the semantic meaning of the emblem. Many emblems are performed with simultaneous facial expressions which serve to qualify the emblematic message. Posture, head position and other hand movements may also serve as such contextual qualifiers. Specifying how context influences the semantic content of emblems requires research of a different kind than we have done here. Research is needed which examines how other nonverbal behaviors, how location within the conversation, and how the semantic content of the speech provide contextual qualification of emblems.

In one such study of the conversational usage of hand movements (illustrators, adaptors as well as emblems), Ekman, Dittmann and Friesen (1975) learned about the usage of one emblem, the ubiquitous shrug. While many other hand movements occurred in the conversations, this was the only emblem which occurred with sufficient frequency to be systematically studied. They found that this emblem is used as a single action, not part of a string of hand movements. Typically it is made prior to a verbal reply or during an unfilled pause in speech. Much more rarely did it occur simultaneously with a spoken statement of uncertainty. As yet they do not know if this finding is limited to the particular social context and the speakers studied or to the particular emblem studied. With the establishment of a repertoire of at least 67 emblems it should be possible now to focus on a range of emblematic behaviors as they occur in natural conversation.

There are also many questions about the ontogeny of emblems. Some of the emblems listed on Table 1 are customarily employed only by adults to children (e.g. the finger-wagging no). Are there emblems which reverse this, and are used by children to adults? Are there emblems which are used by children to children but not part of the adult repertoire? (Probably the shame-on-you emblem.) Kumin and Lazar (1973) recently reported that 4-year-old children know how to decode more emblems than 3-year-old children. But they did not study the full list of emblems in Table 1. We do not yet know when emblems emerge in the child's repertoire, how they relate to language acquisition or the relationship between the point at which an emblem is decoded and when it is encoded by the child.

Unanswered questions about emblems abound. We have reported here but a first step in the study of this type of nonverbal communication.

NOTES

1. This research was supported by a grant from NIMH MH-11976, and is based in part on a doctoral dissertation by Harold G. Johnson conducted under Paul Ekman's sponsorship. Address reprint requests to: Paul Ekman, 401 Parnassus Avenue, San Francisco, California 94143.
2. Goffman (1971) characterizes situations where people are focused on the ongoing interaction as being in a "with." People waiting for a bus could be very close together physically but not in a "with" situation if they are not conversing or interacting.
3. Either a videotape (EIAJ-1, one-half inch) or a 16 mm film of the 152 motor pattern enactments will be made available within the next year in conjunction with a forthcoming book (Ekman and Friesen, in preparation) on cross-cultural studies of emblematic behavior.

REFERENCES

Efron, D.
    1941 *Gesture and Environment* (New York: King's Crown Press). Reissued as: *Gesture, Race and Culture.* The Hague: Mouton Press, 1972.
Ekman, P. & Friesen, W.
    1969 "The repertoire of nonverbal behavior: Categories, origin, usage and coding", *Semiotica* 1, 49-98.
    1972 "Hand movements", *Journal of Communication* 22, 353-374.
Ekman, P. & Friesen, W. (Eds.)
    — In preparation: *Communicative Body Movements: A Cross Cultural Study of Emblems.*
Ekman, P., Friesen, W. & Dittmann, A.
    — In preparation: "Hand movements and speech rhythms".
Goffman, E.
    1971 *Relations in Public* (New York: Basic Books, Inc.).
Kroeber, A.L.
    1972 "Sign language inquiry" (*Approaches to Semiotics* 14), ed. by T.A. Sebeok (The Hague, Paris: Mouton Press).
Kumin, L. & Lazar, M.
    1974 "Gestural communication in preschool children", *Perceptual and Motor Skills* 38, 708-710.
Saitz, R. & Cervenka, E.
    1962 "Columbian and North American gestures", *Centro Colombo Americano*, Carrera 7, 23-49 (Bogota, Columbia). Reissued as *Columbian and North American gestures* (The Hague: Mouton Press, 1973).
Stokoe, W.
    1974 "Motor signs as the first form of language", *Semiotica* 10, 117-130.
Trevoort, B.
    1974 "Could there be a human sign language?" *Semiotica* 9, 347-382.

Table 1   VERIFIED EMBLEMS

Encode Message	Decode Message	Decode Message %	Natural Usage %	Message Certainty	Usage Certainty
Interpersonal Directions (Commands)					
Sit down beside me	Sit down beside me	100	100	6.95	7.00
Be silent, hush	Be silent, hush	100	100	6.95	6.86
Come here	Come here	100	100	6.90	6.95
I can't hear you	I can't hear you	100	100	6.82	6.82
Wait-hold it	Wait-hold it	100	100	6.23	6.73
I warn you	I warn you	100	94	6.00	6.06
Get lost	*Get lost or get out or go away	100	93	6.53	6.20
Be calm	Be calm	100	93	6.20	6.00
Follow me	*Follow me or this way	100	88	6.56	6.44
++ Time to go	*Time to go or what time is it	100	87	6.27	5.60
Stop	*Stop or halt	100	81	6.81	6.44
Go the other way	*Go the other way or no − not that way	96	96	6.64	6.59
△I want to smoke and got a cigarette?	*I want to smoke or got a cigarette?	96	74	6.64	6.32
Look!	*Look or I see something or look over there	91	100	6.36	6.41
Go away	Go away or rejection or get out of here	91	96	6.24	6.23
Take it away	*Take it away or go away or get out of here	90	87	5.45	5.91
Go this way	*Go this way or over there or that way	89	86	6.38	6.13
Go ahead	*Go ahead or go on by	87	83	4.86	5.32
△Hurry and quickly	*Quickly or hurry or come here quickly	85	100	6.73	6.82
++ What time is it?	*What time is it? or time to go	77	100	6.45	6.64

Table 1 (continued)

Encode Message	Decode Message	Decode Message %	Natural Usage %	Message Certainty	Usage Certainty
Stay here	*Stay here or down here	77	100	5.64	6.05
Own Physical State					
△ I'm hot and it's hot	*I'm hot or hard work or a close shave	100	88	5.81	5.88
△ Hard work	*Hard work or I'm hot or a close shave	81	100	6.45	6.55
△ A close shave	*A close shave or I'm hot or hard work	81	100	5.53	5.67
△ It's cold and I'm cold	*It's cold or I'm cold	100	70	6.62	6.50
I'm full of food	I'm full of food	93	93	6.00	6.27
I've got a headache	I've got a headache	93	93	5.60	5.33
I've got a toothache	I've got a toothache	87	87	5.60	5.87
I've got an earache	I've got an earache	70	81	5.19	5.81
Tastes good	Tastes good	93	70	5.69	5.19
I am smart	I am smart	93	73	5.60	5.53
How could I be so dumb	How could I be so dumb	100	95	6.38	6.31
Insults					
+Fuck you (finger)	*Screw you or up yours or fuck you	100	100	7.00	6.86
+Fuck you (arm)	*Fuck you or up yours or screw you	100	81	6.50	6.63
△ The hell with you and rejection	*The hell with you or rejection	100	94	6.07	5.87
△ He's crazy and he's stupid	*He's crazy or he's stupid	100	75	6.67	6.27
Shame on you	Shame on you	100	70	6.81	6.62
Replies					
Okay (fingers)	Okay	100	100	6.80	6.60

Table 1 (continued)

Encode Message	Decode Message	Decode Message %	Natural Usage %	Message Certainty	Usage Certainty
△No (head) and I disagree	*No or I disagree	100	100	6.81	6.88
I don't know	I don't know	100	100	6.73	6.80
△Yes and I agree and I like it	*Yes or I agree or I like it	100	100	6.53	6.73
Absolutely no	*Absolutely no or no way	100	95	6.81	6.62
I dislike it	*I dislike it or no way	100	93	6.53	6.20
I promise	*I promise or cross my heart	100	74	6.67	5.73
Absolutely yes	Absolutely yes	93	81	5.33	6.13
△Hard to think about this and thinking	*Hard to think about this or puzzlement or thinking	89	100	6.06	6.44
I doubt it	I doubt it	70	81	4.62	5.06
Own Affect					
I'm angry	I'm angry	100	94	6.06	6.38
△I'm disgusted and something stinks	*Something stinks	100	81	6.88	6.56
I'm sad	*I'm sad or I'm ashamed	95	72	5.44	5.13
I'm surprised	I'm surprised	95	88	5.75	6.13
Whoopee	*Whoopee or hooray	88	74	4.06	5.19
Greetings and Departures					
Goodby	Goodby	94	100	6.60	6.53
Hello	Hello	80	100	6.20	6.13
Physical Appearance of Person					
△Woman and nice figure	*Woman or nice figure	100	100	6.90	6.77
Unclassified					
You (finger point)	You	100	100	6.81	6.75

Table 1 (continued)

Encode Message	Decode Message	Decode Message %	Natural Usage %	Message Certainty	Usage Certainty
Me (own chest)	Me	100	100	6.75	6.75
Hitch-hiking	Hitch-hiking	100	94	6.93	6.80
Counting	Counting	100	70	6.69	6.06
Gossip	*Gossip or talk-talk-talk	96	91	6.14	6.18
Fighting	Fighting	96	73	6.45	5.82
△Peace and victory	*Peace or victory	94	87	5.93	6.33
Good luck	Good luck	92	100	6.50	6.77
Money	Money	92	79	5.54	4.81
It's far away	*It's far away or over there	87	96	5.90	6.86
Suicide (gun)	*Suicide or shoot myself	83	73	5.95	5.95
Finished	*It's finished or that's enough	78	83	6.41	6.41

Code: Applicable for Tables 1, 2, 3, and 4.
* Either decode message was accepted, although the first message was given more often than the second.
△ The same action was performed for each encode message.
+ Two different actions were performed as alternatives for the same message.
++ Two subtly different actions were performed for two subtly different messages.

Table 2   PROBABLE EMBLEMS

Encode Message	Decode Message	Decode Message %	Natural Usage %	Message Certainty	Usage Certainty
Interpersonal					
Pleading	Pleading	95	62	6.19	5.81
Get up from there	Get up from there	70	68	5.06	5.56
Own Physical State					
I'm going to throw up	*I'm going to throw up or vomiting	100	68	6.88	6.34
I'm strong (bicep)	I'm strong	100	51	6.56	6.81
Insults					
None					
Replies					
None					
Own Affect					
I'm afraid	*I'm afraid or scared	100	57	6.00	6.00
I'm going to cry	*I'm going to cry or wiping a tear	88	64	5.69	6.13
Greetings and Departures					
None					
Physical Appearance of Person					
Fat	*Fat or pregnant	100	64	6.63	6.31
Pregnant	*Pregnant or fat	100	62	5.31	5.50
Unclassified					
Your fly is open	Your fly is open	82	55	5.55	5.32
Power to the people	Power to the people	82	50	5.80	4.93
Magnifique (French)	*Magnificent or great	80	68	5.73	5.60
I'm broke	*I'm broke or no money	78	50	4.59	4.54
I'm fed up	*I'm fed up or up to here	70	57	5.06	5.94

Table 3 AMBIGUOUS EMBLEMS: LOW DECODE MESSAGE AND NATURAL USAGE SCORES

Encode Message	Decode Message	Decode Message %	Natural Usage %	Message Certainty	Usage Certainty
Interpersonal					
Follow behind me	*Follow behind me or those in back come up here	63	69	3.86	4.36
Own Physical State					
△I want to eat and I'm hungry	*I want to eat or I'm hungry	53	60	5.53	5.13
Insults					
Up your ass	*Shove it or up your ass	68	61	5.93	5.40
Replies					
Only fooling	Only fooling	68	68	6.00	5.47
Own Affect					
Anticipation (rub hands)	Anticipation	62	57	4.25	4.94
Greetings and Departures					
None					
Physical Appearance of Persons					
None					
Unclassified					
He's safe (baseball)	He's safe	68	55	5.60	5.73
Bless you (religious)	*Bless you or a blessing	66	68	5.87	5.40
He's a snob	*He's a snob or stuck up	59	61	5.40	5.27

Table 4 AMBIGUOUS EMBLEMS: DECODE MESSAGE DIFFERS FROM ENCODE MESSAGE

Encode Message	Decode Message	Decode Message %	Natural Usage %	Message Certainty	Usage Certainty
Interpersonal					
You don't fool me	*Scolding or no-no-no	100	88	6.94	6.88
Go left	Move that way	100	88	6.27	6.93
Go right	Move over there	100	87	6.13	5.67
Shut the door	Move that way	74	78	5.68	6.09
Don't hit me	Look out	50	88	5.93	5.87
Own Physical State					
I'm tired	I give up	55	85	5.20	5.60
Insults					
Didn't get a sou (French)	*Fuck you or up yours	79	75	4.60	4.73
Replies					
What do you want?	*I don't know	100	100	6.75	6.94
So-so, about average	I don't know or uncertainty	75	95	6.19	6.12
I'm sorry	*Uncertainty or I don't know	50	87	5.00	5.00
Own Affect					
Look out!	*Fear or surprise	57	68	5.38	5.88
Greetings and Departures					
None					
Physical Appearance of Person					
Tall person	About this tall	100	100	6.50	6.68
Short person	About this tall	95	95	6.75	6.69
Thin person	It's narrow, it's straight up and down	59	79	4.54	4.59
Bald head	Fixing hair	54	51	3.90	4.05

Table 4   (continued)

Encode Message	Decode Message	Decode Message %	Natural Usage %	Message Certainty	Usage Certainty
Unclassified					
Something small	About this big, a little bit	100	100	6.36	6.73
It's near or close by	About this long or big	100	95	5.73	6.55
Proud of myself (beat chest)	Strong, tough	96	91	6.59	6.18
Happy (hands)	I give up	86	73	4.67	5.27
Surprise (hands)	Stop, hold it, wait	81	70	4.80	5.47
Brief	It's a snap, easy	67	100	6.36	6.68
Wash hands at a feast	Nervous, anxious	54	68	5.27	5.07

CAROL M. SPARHAWK

Contrastive-Identification Feature
of Persian Gesture

The following study concerns the application of linguistic analysis to the study of Iranian emblems, or hand gestures that have a specific verbal definition. In order to ensure that the emblems used in the study were indeed commonly used in Iran, the investigator both elicited gestures from informants in an *encoding* collection and presented the gestures back to informants for verification in a *decoding* collection. The data from the encoding collection forms the corpus for an analysis of the visual emic features of the Persian gestural system. The analysis is comparable to that performed by Stokoe (1960) for the American Sign Language.

Gestures and emblems have long held human interest. Many collections have been made (Rijnberk 1954, Mallory 1880, Saitz and Cervenka 1962, Efron 1941, Mehmandi-Mejad 1973, Johnson 1972, Barakat 1973); however, attempts at systematization are fewer. Wundt (ed. by Sebeok, 1973) was one of the first linguists to consider the systematic properties of gestures, classifying them on the basis of relationship to referent (meaning) and formal realization of that relationship (1973:74ff.) The most important distinction Wundt makes is between demonstrative or pointing gestures and descriptive or imitative gestures. Efron (ed. by Sebeok, 1972) examined Jewish and Italian immigrant gestures from spatiotemporal, interlocutional, and linguistic viewpoints. Catford (1940), Laban (1966), and Birdwhistell (1970) proposed notational systems for gesture. Bouissac (1973) suggests mathematical analysis of the spatial volumes created by gestural movement in space.

The works most relevant to the present study are Stokoe's application of phonemic analysis to the American Sign Language (ASL)

(1960), Ekman and Friesen's categorization of nonverbal behavior (1969a) and collection methodology for emblems, and Pike's *Phonemics* (1947). From *Phonemics* I derived the procedures of charting the gestures according to gross articulatory similarities and comparison of similar gestures for contrastive-identificational features (Pike 1947:8 and Pike 1947:73). Stokoe's work contributes a schematization of the articulatory system of gestures, and a series of 'cheremes' (analogous to phonemes) for sign language. The cheremes provide a useful basis for comparison and organization of Persian cheremic features. From Ekman and Friesen's work I derive the definition of *emblem* (1969a:63), one of five categories of nonverbal behavior, established on the basis of *origin* (innate, learned, and common to all members, or common to a culture), *coding* (arbitrary, intrinsic, or iconic), and usage (informative, interactive, or communicative). Emblems are communicative gestures often iconically coded, and learned through experience which varies with culture, class, and geographic region. They typically have a standardized meaning within a social group. Efron (1972:10) defines emblems as having no morphological relationship to their referents, but Ekman and Friesen note that emblem coding may be iconic as well as arbitrary (1969a:65). Finally, emblems are distinctive in that they can communicate meaning without use of the verbal channel.

The methodology used in the data collection also derives from Ekman and Friesen (1972:364). In the first, or *encoding,* phase of the collection, I presented fifteen informants with a *message* (derived from an unpublished list by Paul Ekman), in terms of word, phrase, or clause, and asked the informants if they knew of any emblems which conveyed that message. If they did, they performed the emblem and I recorded it by means of notes and sketches. I also asked the informants, usually at intervals of about ten emblems, to mention any other emblems which they had thought of. Their additions increase the inventory from one hundred eighty-five emblems to two hundred forty.

Only those emblems performed in the same way by at least half of the informants responding were used for the decoding phase of the collection.[1] Messages which produced no gestures or a variety of gestures were excluded from the decoding list. Judgment of the similarity of emblem performances was subjective, based on similarity of movement, shape, dynamics, point of reference, hand shape, and mimetic reference. If a two-hand emblem was symmetrical, a one- or two-hand performance could be judged as similar.

A decoding check properly requires that a different group of informants be used. However, due to limitations of willing volunteers, some of the same informants participated in the encoding and the decoding phase of the collection. However, a few months' time elapsed between each phase. Eight to ten informants judged each emblem. In the decoding phase, I performed the emblem for each informant separately, and he or she gave:

(1) the *message* conveyed by the emblem;

(2) a judgment on whether the emblem was commonly used, or *natural;* or whether it was used only in games and pantomines, or *artificial;*

(3) a judgment on their *certainty,* on a scale of seven to one, as to how certain they were that the emblem was natural or artifical.

The results of the decoding phase appear in *Appendix I.* In general, *verified* emblems must meet the following criteria:

(1) at least 70% of the decoding informants must give the same or almost the same message given by the encoding informant;

(2) at least 70% of the decoding informants must judge the gesture as natural in usage.

Probable emblems must meet the same criteria as verified emblems, except that more than 50% but less than 70% of the decoders must judge the emblem as natural. Finally, *ambiguous* emblems meet the following criteria:

(1) more than 50% but less than 70% of the decoders must give the same message given to the encoders;

(2) and more than 50% of the decoders must judge the message as natural.

Altogether, 98 emblems were verified, four were probable, and 24 were ambiguous. The list of verified and unverified emblems can be found in Appendix 1.

Perhaps informants would have verified more emblems had an Iranian informant performed them. Researchers on Japanese gesture have found that foreigners, for example Americans, will overlook certain features in the performance of Japanese emblems (Taylor 1976, personal communication). Cicourel (1974:137, 138) shows that deaf signers recognize more meaningful elements in the gestural communication of a deaf child than do hearing people who are familiar with American Sign Language. Admittedly a videotape presentation of native signers is more reliable. Lacking that facility, I took the following precautions: during the encoding phase, when an informant failed to identify an emblem I presented, I would tell him or her which message I had expected. He or she would then correct my performance if necessary. As one informant commented that she recognized the emblems I performed, I had an 'accent'. The performances on the whole, however, must have been recognizable.

The establishment of contrastive-identificational features is less conclusive when the minimal pairs presented as evidence include unverified emblems. Emblems 'borrowed' from Western films or learned in travels may add features to the set commonly used. This addition is valid when Iranians commonly recognize the emblem, as in the case of English 'no', but it is not valid for emblems like 'perfect' which are not commonly recogized. For this reason, it is helpful to keep the distinction between verified and unverified emblems in mind.

Fifteen informants contributed to the first two phases of the data collection, completed in Iran in 1974. Although all the informants were inhabitants of Tehran, some had come from outlying areas early in their lives. Eight women and seven men participated. Five of the women, between twenty and thirty years of age, taught English for a living, and only one of these had not traveled outside of Iran. One woman, who was over forty years old, spoke no English and had not traveled. Three of the seven men who participated were eighteen to nineteen years old. They had not traveled outside of Iran, although they did speak some English. Of the remaining four men, between twenty and thirty two years of age, only one, a teacher of English, had traveled to England and the United States.

The following analysis (the analysis under consideration) deals with the problem of choosing emblem features which must be accounted for in a recording or notational system. Analogical representation by drawing functions effectively as a preliminary means of recording gestures, but the development of a digital or symbolic notation corresponding to the users' perception of a communication system requires discernment of the perceived or emic units of the system and the contrastive-identificational features which comprise them. For Persian emblems, the establishment of contrastive-identificational features requires classification of emblems according to body part involved, and comparison of similar emblems within these classes. The more similar two emblems are, the more likely their dissimilar features are to be contrastive.

The data used for the following analysis includes all gestures collected in the encoding phase of the collection. Although these are not verified emblems they do provide a wider data base for the establishment of gestures.

A first classification of the gestures according to body part involved yielded the categories shown in Figure 1. This classification begins with the most obvious similarities.

I. Movement of a single body part

   A. hand alone or approaching or contacting another part.
   B. face, features
   C. head
   D. trunk
   E. leg or foot

II. Movement of two body parts

   A. hand and face, head, trunk, leg or foot
   B. two hands

III. Movement of three body parts or more

   A. two hands and face
   B. two hands, face and trunk

Fig. 1. The First Classification of Emblems

Differences within these groups are candidates for the contrastive feature system. This classification is analogous to the charting of phonetic segments according to place of articulation in the preliminary procedures for establishing the phonemic system of an unwritten language (Pike 1947:8). It ensures similarity of the most obvious features as a point of departure.

Other techniques and principles described in Pike 1947 may be extended to emblem study. Principles of preliminary procedures (Pike 1947:8) dictate the charting of segments according to productive type, or place and manner of articulation. Sounds of dissimilar productive type are probably separate phonemes. Similar sounds may be variants of the same phoneme, particularly if they appear in mutually exclusive environments (1947:73). In order to prove that similar sounds are not variants of the same phoneme, one must demonstrate that they occur in identical environments and result in a change of meaning (Pike 1947:80), or in enough analogous environments so that any possibility of mutually exclusive environments is eliminated.

The analysis presented here follows principles similar to those described in *Phonemics*. The characteristics which provided criteria for the preliminary classification of the data include: (1) the moving parts; (2) the shape of the moving parts; (3) the location of any approach or contact; (4) movement shape, direction and dynamics; and (5) the type of mime.

In order to clarify the feature system that exists in Persian, the following discussion presents the contrastive features established for

Persian emblems in comparison to the features established by Stokoe, Casterline and Croneberg (1965:x-xii) for the American Sign Language of the Deaf (ASL). It is true that ASL differs from Persian emblems in that ASL is a main-channel communicative system, while Persian emblems constitute an adjunct to spoken language. However, the ASL notation seems most appropriate for comparison with emblems, because Stokoe developed the notation of the linguistic principle of representing only that which is internally contrastive (Dr. H. M. Taylor, personal communication) or EMIC within a given linguistic community. Furthermore, ASL notation concentrates on movement in the upper body and facial area which also predominates in Persian emblems. In contrast, Labanotation (Laban 1966) was designed to account for any possibility of creative movement without reference to significance within a cultural community. Such a notation offers more possibilities than the study of emblems requires.

Stokoe analyzed the hand signs of the deaf in terms of three aspects: *tabula,* the locus or point of reference of a sign; *designator,* the shape or configuration of the signing hand; and *signation,* the movement performed by the signing hand (Stokoe 1960:41). This system works fairly well for the analysis of Persian emblems, with the addition of a dimension of facial activity and expression. In addition, the specific features manifesting each of the three aspects vary somewhat. In general more designator and direction (signation) features appear in ASL, and more tabula features appear in Persian emblems.

However, the application of the ASL analytical system must be slightly revised for examination of Persian emblems. *Tabula* seems to function in the same way for Persian emblems as it does for ASL signs. The hand may move in a certain area, or may direct attention to a particular locus. In addition, the signing hand may employ the other hand as tabula. We must define *designator* more broadly, however, for Persian emblems. According to Stokoe's definition, only the signing hand may constitute a designator; but in Persian emblems the face may be involved as well as the hands or, indeed, independently. Consequently, a definition of *designator* for the study of emblems must specify both the signing (element) and the configuration of that constituent. Furthermore, the identity of the signing element — say, arms or facial features as opposed to the hands — determines the range of configurations possible for that particular designator.

In fact, ASL itself may require such a definition: as Baker (1976: 24, 25) notes, facial movement does carry lexical significance in ASL.

Some of the features which she notes — raised head, puffed cheeks, eye direction, and openness — also carry meaning in Persian emblems.

We must define *signation* as well as *designator* slightly differently for the study of emblems. Stokoe, Casterline and Croneberg 1965 distinguishes thirty-two signation cheremes, which may be grouped into features of direction, shape, direction-shape contact, and dynamics. Perhaps a main-channel cheremic system can function on a limited amount of cheremes, but a descriptive system for emblems must allow for flexibility deriving from iconic imitation. For this reason, instead of specifying a limited number of cheremes, I specify a limited number of *parameters* of movement, as follows: *direction, dimension* (consisting of size and shape), and *dynamics* (consisting of *repetition, force*, and *contact*). Finally, while the symbols of ASL notation are arranged in the order TAB-DEZ-SIG, I propose that in notation of emblems that the symbols (when developed) be arranged DEZ-CONF-SIG-TABULA, since it is easiest to begin classification of emblems in terms of DEZ identity (Fig. 2).

The following discussion presents the internally contrastive features of Persian emblems, following the order of *tabula*, or emic point of reference; *designator*, or emic configuration of moving body part; and *signation*, or emic movement. In general, the discussion will begin with reference to the distinctive feature in Persian and conclude with a listing of gestures or minimally different pairs of gestures in which the feature appears. The data used for this analysis includes not only the verified emblems, but all gestures collected.

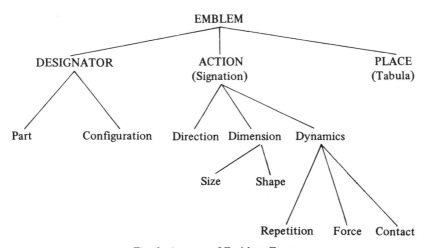

Fig. 2. Aspects of Emblem Form

TABULA FEATURES IN PERSIAN

Persian distinguishes fifteen tabula features, including five in the face area, one in the neck area, four in the trunk area, and four in the arm area. The first, 'zero tab', refers to the area in front of the hollow of the neck or upper chest. It contrasts with a side tab in 'stop' vs. 'hello' and in 'this size' vs. 'big'.

In the area of the upper face, Persian emblems demonstrate a distinction between the forehead and the eyes. In 'unfortunate fool' the hand covers the whole face, while in 'on my eyes' it covers on the eye. In 'think' the hand or index finger touches the forehead.

Evidence suggests that the eye and nose are emically distinct points of reference in Persian. If the investigator failed to cover the eye only in 'on my eyes', informants said that the sign was incorrect. Other signs such as 'burned your nose' and 'bad smell' involve hand-to-nose contact; however, the hand shape differs in these two signs.

A *lower face* or *chin* tab appears in Persian 'pleading', where the hand grasps the beard. This may contrast with 'bad smell', in which the hand grasps the nose.

The *temple* and *ear* are emically distinct in Persian gesture. In 'intelligence' the index finger taps and temple, but in 'deaf' the hand contacts the ear. The emic status of the tabulae is doubtful, however, as the two gestures involve different hand configurations.

A *neck* tab also functions emically. For example, in 'choke' the open hand grasps the throat, but in 'stomach-ache' it presses the stomach. 'Choke' also contrasts with a chin grasp in 'pleading' and with a nose grasp in 'bad smell'.

Within the trunk area, Persian gestures distinguish the *chest, stomach,* and *breast.* The hand lays on the chest in 'servant' and 'worry', on the stomach in 'full', 'hungry', and 'stomach ache', and on the breast for 'woman'.

Although gestures using the upper arm and forearm as points of reference appear in Persian, no minimal pairs exist to demonstrate their emic status. Two analogous pairs do appear, however. In 'strong' the open hand grasps the biceps; but in 'they caught him' the open hand seizes the lower arm or wrist area. The reason that this contrast is analogous rather than minimal is that the pair also differs in dynamics of movement; specifically, 'they caught him' involves more forceful contact. In another analogous opposition, a grasp of the upper arm in 'strong' contrasts with a grasp of the wrist in 'bracelet'. Again, the nature of the grasp differs slightly.

Pronation and *supination* refer to the direction of the palm as a result of wrist rotation. If the hands are positioned horizontally, *pronation* refers to downward (and inward) direction of the palms, and *supination* refers to upward (and outward) direction. (Evidence for the contrastiveness of palm direction will be presented in the discussion of *signation,* below). As for the wrist itself, *pronate wrist* appears as a point of reference in 'what time is it' and contrasts with the *whole wrist* in 'bracelet'. This constitutes only an analogous contrast, however, and no gesture involving contact with the 'palm side' of the wrist (*supinate wrist*) appears in this collection.

To summarize, in Persian emblems the forehead, eye, nose, temple, ear, and chin constitute contrastive points of reference. With regard to the trunk, the chest, stomach, and breast areas are contrastive. The upper arm and wrist areas are also contrastive, but no conclusive opposition establishes emic status for the upper arm vs. the forearm or for the pronate vs. the supinate wrist.

DESIGNATOR FEATURES IN ASL AND PERSIAN

Twenty-one designator features appear in Persian gestures. Of these, ten involve the hand, five involve the arm, and six apply to the face. In general, 'simple' hand forms such as flat hand, fist, or index hand (fist with index finger extended – pointing hand) predominate in Persian. Extensions of different fingers from the fist can also serve to distinguish one designator from another.

In the most common fist appearing among Persian gestures, the thumb lies along the side of the index finger and this finger, although curled, extends slightly to accomodate the thumb. This designator functions as a mime of holding something such as a pencil or key. A second configuration, in which the thumb protrudes between the index and middle fingers, appears in Persian 'intercourse'. It may be that this contrasts with 'protest', but dynamics may also distinguish these two gestures.

The open or flat hand designator frequently appears among Persian gestures. Open hand with fingers together, as in 'no', contrasts with open hand and spread fingers in 'five'. Open hand with fingers together also appears in 'this way', 'stop', and in emblems indicating a source of pain such as 'headache', 'toothache', 'earache', and 'stomach-ache'.

A curved open hand with fingers together appears in Persian 'prayer', 'come', and 'give'. As it appears in no minimal pairs, however, it is probably not emic in Persian. A tense curved hand, with fingers together, contrasts in Persian 'I'll strangle you' and 'this size', which requires the open hand

A thumb-and-forefinger circle with the other three fingers extended appears only in signs of foreign origin in Persian gestures, such as 'chic' and 'perfect'. Although neither of these are verified emblems, 'perfect' does contrast with one version of 'small'. In 'perfect' the thumb touches the tip of the bent forefinger, forming a circle; but in 'small' the thumb touches the base of the first or outermost phalange, forming a trapezoidal shape.

Persian gesture makes heavy use of the *index hand,* a closed fist with the index finger extended. This designator appears in 'intelligence', 'no brains', 'quiet', 'you', 'burned your nose (you goofed)', 'one', 'sign-line', 'drill', etc. It contrasts with flat hand in 'intelligence' vs. 'headache'.

An extension of the index, and middle fingers, with the other fingers curled, appears in Persian 'gun' in contrast with 'look', which utilizes only extension of the index finger. In 'gun' the index and middle finger are parallel; in 'two' they are separated, as in the American emblem 'peace'.

Extension of the little finger from the fist appears in one gesture 'thin', which is not a verified emblem. It contrasts with extension of the index finger in 'one'.

A loose fist, in which the curled fingers define a cylindrical space, appears in Persian 'pencil sharpener' and in 'intercourse'. This space allows penetration of a finger, but does not appear in opposition with a closed fist, so it may be said to be in complementary distribution with the normal closed fist. Signation features also distingish these gestures from others.

Certain features of arm extension and position appear to be contrastive in Persian. Total and partial arm extension contrast in 'big, fat' vs. 'this size'. Divergent, parallel, and convergent forearm alignment contrast in 'big', 'pray', and 'unity'.

Included among Persian designators, then, are the fist, spread hand, flat hand, and claw hand. Persian also employs extensions of the thumb, index, middle and little fingers to indicate contrast, as well as combination extensions of index and middle, or index, middle, and ring fingers.

Configuration of designator features appearing uniquely in Persian include total and partial arm extension and divergent, parallel and convergent arm alignment.

With regard to the face as designator, the following affect displays appear: 'pleasure' (a smile), 'anger', 'alarm', 'doubt', 'pain', 'grief' and 'sour'.[2] 'Pleasure' and 'anger' contrast in a joking ('naughty, naughty') vs. a serious ('I warn you, don't do it') shaking of the index finger. Presence or absence of the smile does cause the informant to assign a different gloss to the gesture. Displays of surprise appear in Persian, but without evidence of shared performance or of contrast. Several informants gave a similar performance for 'doubt' and for 'surprise', raising the eyebrows and protruding the lips slightly. 'Grief' contrasts with 'pleasure' when the signer places his palm on the chest. The former expression conveys 'worry', but the latter conveys the message 'I am your servant' (as a greeting or farewell). Finally 'sour', a tight closing of the eyes and smacking of the lips, contrasts with 'delicious', a smacking of the lips with smile and open eyes. 'Disgust' differs strikingly from 'sour' in that it involves contraction of the nose and upper lip area rather than closed eyes and smacking lips.

Ekman notes that six emotions – happiness, sadness, anger, fear, surprise, and disgust – have been found by all investigators who sought to determine what emotions could be judged from the face (Ekman 1973:53). Research on thirteen literate cultures and two visually isolated preliterate cultures has demonstrated that the same facial expressions are associated with the same emotions, regardless of the language (Ekman 1973:68). Ekman cautions, however, that the conditions giving rise to these emotions vary from culture to culture, as do the presence of facial displays representing the emotions in emblem inventories (Ekman 1973). In the Persian emblem inventory, 'pleasure', 'anger', 'alarm', 'disgust', and 'pain' are contrastive. Displays of 'doubt' and 'sour' appear in addition, but no single display appears for 'surprise' or 'fear'.

Expressions of affect displays involve all the features of the face, but individual features also signal emblematic meaning. Blowing from the mouth appears in 'chase away evil spirits after prayer'. The cheeks move in for 'weak' and out for 'fat'. Contrastive eye positions include the wink in 'let's go' and 'I'm kidding', closed eyes in 'sleep' and 'death', and squint in 'I didn't understand'. Raised eyebrows appear in 'surprise', 'doubt', and 'no'; lowered brows appear in 'anger' and 'disgust', and lowered brow raised slightly in the center appear in 'pain'.

In two-hand or two-arm emblems, configuration and action may be symmetrical, opposed, or asymmetrical. Symmetry may carry both referential and emotive significance. Referential significance of symmetry appears in 'nice figure', 'thin', and 'embrace'. To illustrate, 'nice figure' and 'thin' necessarily involve two hands, and 'embrace', performed with one hand becomes 'go this way'. Emotive significance of symmetry appears in 'please sit there', 'absolutely not', 'catch him', and 'don't hit me'. A signer may perform these four emblems with one or both hands. A two hand performance, however, conveys more emotional intensity in 'catch him', 'don't hit me', and 'absolutely not', and more politeness in 'please sit there'.

In general, hands, trunk, head and face function as designators in Persian. When the hand acts as designator, simple configurations predominate, such as open hand, fist, or pointing hand, so that the aspects of tabula and signation show a wider variety of features. Some evidence suggests limited contrasts in arm position, but these might be treated as features of hand position or movement. The face as a whole may act as designator, in representations of affect displays; in addition, activity of isolated features may convey emblematic meaning.

FEATURES OF SIGNATION IN PERSIAN GESTURE

Persian gesture includes twenty-eight signation features. Of these, seven involve direction, seven concern shape, seven involve contact, three involve dynamics, and four involve relative position or movement of the two hands.

Upward and downward movement are contrastive. For example, in 'wait' the palm faces downward; in 'get up' it faces upwards. Repeated up-and-down movement contrasts with side-to-side movement in 'straight ahead' vs. 'go'. Movement towards the signer, in 'come' and 'give', contrasts with movement away from the signer in 'go'. Repeated side-to side movement contrasts with repeated to-and-fro movement in 'absolutely not' vs. 'wait'. Surprisingly, rightward and leftward movement are not contrastive, as informants decode pointing either to the right or left as 'this way'. Finally, backwards hand movement as in 'yesterday' and 'come' (to signer from the front) appears in opposition with forwards movement in 'tomorrow' and 'follow me'.

Supinating and pronating rotation of the wrist appear in Persian, but without conclusive evidence of contrast. Supinating rotation appears in 'I don't know', 'prayer', 'twist ear', and 'take it away', while pronating rotation appears in 'secret' and 'follow me'. It seems, however, that palm direction and contact are sufficient to distinguish these gestures from others. Wrist rotation, however, appears to be contrastive. Back-and-forth rotation in 'drill' contrasts with no rotation in 'sit here'. A single rotation in 'I don't know' contrasts with a wrist cock or bend in 'no one'.

Wiggling action of the fingers appears only in one unverified gesture, 'walk', in Persian. Circular action, on the other hand, is fairly common. It contrasts with an s-shaped, amorphous action in 'cleaning' and 'drawing'. Interchanging action appears frequently, in 'drive', 'hurry', 'run', and 'swim', and contrasts with symmetrical action in 'crawl' vs. 'frog stroke'. Entering action appears in an opposition between 'eat', a verified emblem, and 'poor', 'no roof', an unverified gesture in which the signer 'blows' the index finger out of the mouth. Divergent action of the fingers, in 'enemies', contrasts with no action in an unverified variant of 'friends'. The action moreover, is iconically related to the meaning of 'enemies'. Finally, crossing action appears only in one Persian gesture, as follows in 'can you make change?': the signer holds up a bill and traces a cross on it as if dividing it into four parts. Informants say, however, that one could simply hold up the bill without tracing the cross. Probably, then, crossing action ('+') is not contrastive in Persian. However, one emblem, 'sign-line', involves the tracing of a diagonal 'x'. Informants take pains to clarify that tracing of '+' rather than 'x' fails to constitute proper performance of the gesture.

In the event of manual contact, grasping, discrete, and continuous touching are contrastive in Persian. Discrete touch (tap) in 'what time is it?' contrasts with a grasp of the wrist in 'they caught him'. Convergent position of the two hands in 'this size' contrast with mutual grasping in 'friendship'. Discrete contact contrasts with continuous contact in 'intelligence', where the hand taps the head, vs. 'headache', where the hand remains in contact with the head. Presence of rubbing is also contrastive in Persian, as a rubbing of the thumb and forefinger in 'money' contrasts with a wrist rotation in 'key', the hand configurations of these two gestures being otherwise the same.

With regard to relative hand positions in Persian, one hand *under* the other contrasts with hands *side by side facing* in 'thick book' vs. 'this size' The position of one hand *behind* the other appears in 'pregnant', but in no minimal pairs.

In dynamics Persian gesture includes a distinction of normal and fast movement in 'go' vs. 'get lost' and 'wait' vs. 'shut'. It is possible, as one informant mentions, that slow movement for polite 'wait' is also distinctive.

To summarize the Persian signation features, the directions *up, down, to self, away* from *self, forwards* and *backwards* are distinctive.

Supinating and pronating rotation of the wrist appear but are not conclusively contrastive. Back-and forth, to-and-fro, side-to-side, circular, bending, and twisting movement are contrastive. Opening and closing are contrastive for the eye as designator. Finger wiggling is not conclusively contrastive, as it appears in an opposition that includes one unverified emblem.

With regard to features involving approach or touch, four — grasping, crossing, interchanging, and discrete touch — are clearly contrastive. Diagonal crossing action, but not perpendicular crossing, is contrastive in Persian. Two relative hand positions are clearly contrastive. Forceful, normal, and perhaps slow movement dynamics are contrastive.

Five body signs, not conclusively contrastive, appear among Persian gestures. One variant of 'greeting' involves a rise from a seated position. Jumps appear in 'exitement' and fear. 'Indifference' and 'I don't know' include a shrug. In 'thinking', 'grief', 'sleepy', and 'bored', the signer leans the head on the hand and the body sags. Finally, a tense trunk with protruding chest appears in 'pride'.

When a relationship between sign and referent is arbitrary, as it is in spoken language and other digital systems, contrastive-identificational features must remain contrastive within a given communication system. They cannot function as contrastive features in one environment and as allophonic variations in another. In emblematic communication, however, some features slip in and out of contrastiveness on their function in iconic representations. For example, in Persian 'follow me', the direction *back-to-front,* with hand as designator and wrist rotation as signation, is significant. According to the variations given for this emblem, the signer may indicate the required movement with the forearm and apex of the hand pointing downwards and with supinating rotation of the wrist. He (she) may also direct the forearm and apex upwards and use a pronate wrist rotation, as long as he (she) clearly indicates the direction. In this emblem the distinctions *up-down* and *pronation-superination* are not in focus, so they appear in free variation. Nevertheless, ample contrastive evidence appears elsewhere for *up* vs. *down* (for example, in 'don't do it' vs. 'here'). No conclusive contrasts appear for *pronation-supination,* but a correct performance of 'I don't know' requires supinate rotation of the wrist. A few features, then, are contrastive when related to meaning, but may appear in free variation when not related to meaning.

A CONTRASTIVE ANALYSIS OF THE CHEREMES APPEARING
IN ASL AND PERSIAN

The following discussion contrasts the number and distribution of
tabula, designator-configuration, and signation features in American
Sign Language[3] and Persian gesture. The differences between the two
systems suggests ways in which an adjunct communicative system
(represented by Persian gesture) might develop into a main-channel
communicative system.

Tabula Features

Persian distinguishes fifteen tabula features, including five in the face
area, one in the neck area, five in the trunk area, and four in the arm
area. ASL distinguishes twelve tabula features, including four in the
face area, one neck tab, one trunk tab, and four arm and wrist tabs.
In Persian gesture the forehead, eye, nose, temple, ear, and chin
constitute contrastive points of reference, but ASL distinguishes
only the upper, lower, mid and side regions of the face. With regard
to the trunk, the chest, stomach, and breast are contrastive in Persian,
while ASL includes a single trunk tabula only. The upper arm and
wrist areas are distinctive in Persian, but no conclusive opposition
establishes contrast for the pronate and supinate wrist tabs which
are distinctive in ASL. To summarize, while Persian gestures display
more contrasts than ASL within the facial and trunk areas, they
display less contrasts than ASL with respect to the arm and wrist.

Designator Features

Twenty-one designator features appear in Persian gestures. Of these,
ten involve the hand, five involve the arm, and six apply to the face.
In general, 'simple' hand forms such as flat hand, fist, or hand with
index finger extended predominate in Persian, with tabula and signation carrying the bulk of the meaning load. ASL distinguishes
nineteen designator features, all of which involve the hand. Most of
these also represent letters in the manual alphabet of the deaf.
Extensions of different fingers or combinations of fingers from the
fist, combined with extended or curled thumb, serve to distinguish
one designator from another.

Both Persian and ASL distinguish the fist, spread hand, flat hand,
and claw hand. They also distinguish extensions of the thumb, index,

middle, and little fingers, and combination extensions of index and middle, or index, middle, and ring fingers. Although ASL distinguishes three thumb positions in combination with other finger extensions, Persian only distinguishes the thumb in isolation.

Designator features appearing in Persian but not in ASL include total and partial arm extension and divergent, parallel and convergent arm alignment. (Of course, these appear in ASL, but they do not figure as contrastive-identificational features. Rather, the parameter of touch/approach of the two hands is used.) Stokoe, Casterline and Croneberg (1965) do include features of convergence and divergence under the aspect of signation. However, the Persian emblems manifesting these features include no signation. It is the configuration alone that identifies the gesture.

Persian designator configurations for which there are no correspondents in ASL cheremes apply to the face. In the Persian emblem inventory, 'pleasure', 'anger', 'alarm', 'disgust', and 'pain' are contrastive. Displays of 'doubt' and 'sour' appear in addition, but no single display appears for 'surprise' or 'fear'.

In general, more body parts function as designators in Persian than in ASL, but there are less configuration possibilities for the hand in particular. Simple designators such as open hand, fist, or index hand predominate in Persian with place and signation carrying the bulk of the contrastive-identificational features. Some evidence suggests limited contrasts in arm position, but these may be subordinate to features of hand position in two-hand emblems. As for facial expressions which refer to emotion, displays for 'anger', 'pleasure', 'alarm', 'pain', and 'disgust' appear among Persian emblems as well as representations for 'sour' and 'doubt'.

In contrast, ASL distinguishes nineteen designator cheremes, all of which involve the hand. Most of these also represent letters in the manual alphabet of the deaf. Extensions of different fingers from the fist combined with extended or curled thumb serve to distinguish one designator from another. Earlier works (Stokoe, Casterline and Croneberg 1965, Stokoe 1972) make no mention of facial designators, but recent research (Baker 1976:24, 25) suggests that facial movement does indeed carry lexical and grammatical meaning in ASL.

Signation Features

Persian gesture employs twenty eight contrastive-identificational features of signation. Seven involve direction, seven involve shape, seven involve touch, three involve dynamics, and four involve relative position, contact, or movement of the two hands. ASL distinguishes thirty-two signation cheremes. Thirteen of these relate to shape of movement, nine to direction, two to touch, and one to dynamics. Only six of these fail to appear or to be contrastive in Persian. Thus there is more similarity between ASL and Persian with respect to signation than with respect to designator or tabula.

ASL and Persian employ the same directional contrasts, with the exception of back versus forward in Persian and left versus right in ASL. Persian includes diagonal cross shape and direction features which do not appear in ASL. ASL divergent and entering action appear in Persian, but are not conclusively contrastive. Persian distinguishes more features of contact and dynamics, but ASL distinguishes more features of two hand position. Finally, body signs appear in Persian but are not conclusively contrastive. On the whole, more features appear in Persian gesture except in the area of hand configuration A possible reason is that ASL as a main-channel system is more closely related to a digital system of communication (Watzlawick et al. 1967:61, 62), while Persian emblems are more closely related to an analogical system of communication.

The above comparison suggests the following differences between an adjunct and a main-channel system of visual communication. First, a greater degree of iconic representation occurs in an adjunct system. The main-channel system utilizes more subtle distinctions of hand configuration such as thumb position and varieties of finger extension. These represent not actions, objects, or feelings, but symbols – the letters of the manual alphabet. As cheremes, they come to participate in other, non alphabetic signs. Second, the contrastive features of Persian are not concentrated in hand configuration and signation. ASL researchers, on the other hand, have noted a strong historical tendency in ASL to concentrate information in the hands (Frishberg 1975). Finally, a few 'verb-verb' and 'noun-adjective' strings appear in the Persian data; but nothing parallels the more complex sentence conjunction and relative clause constructions found in ASL (Stokoe 1972:147). This property suggests that syntax in an adjunct visual system is at best rudimentary, becoming more complex as the system is used more heavily. This suggests that complex syntax is more likely to develop in main-channel systems like ASL than in adjunct systems like emblem inventories.

APPENDIX I: VERIFICATION OF EMBLEMS

The following table presents the list of verified emblems. On the left, the decode message appears. The encode message is not listed if it is the same as the decode message. Gestures with a different decode message are listed after the 'decode scores with less than 50% agreement'.

Starting from the left, the first column gives the per cent of informants who agreed on the decode message of the emblem; the second gives the per cent of agreement on whether the emblem was natural and commonly used; the third, a rating of the 'naturalness' of the emblem, from seven (very common) to one (rare). The fourth and fifth columns present a similar percentage of agreement and rating on the 'artificiality' of the emblem.

MESSAGE	%AGR	%NAT	RATING	%ART	RATING
VERIFIED EMBLEMS					
I'll twist your ear	100	100	7.00		
ridicule, defiance	100	100	5.50		
big	100	100	6.88		
no, nothing	100	100	5.72		
alarm	100	83	7.00	17	5.00
no (one hand)	100	75	6.86	12	7.00
kissing	100	100	6.86		
God bless you	100	100	7.00		
no (head raise)	100	100	7.00		
fat person	100	88	7.00	12	5.00
anger	100	100	7.00		
I'm hot (fan self)	100	100	6.75		
I'm hot (pull clothes)	100	100	7.00		
man	100	100	6.88		
I'm cold	100	100	7.00		
small	100	88	7.00	12	7.00
I'm strong	100	100	6.88		
I warn you	100	100	6.88		
sit by me	100	100	7.71		
sleepy	100	100	7.00		
wash hands of something (greedy tooth)	100	71	6.40	28	6.00
fuck you (thumb)	100	100	7.00		
fuck you (elbow)	100	100	5.50		
please go ahead	100	100	6.75		
no money (pull out pockets)	100	100	7.00		

	%AGR	%NAT	RATING	%ART	RATING
kiss my ass	100	100	6.80		
I didn't hear (hand)	100	100	6.88		
I didn't hear (head)	100	100	6.12		
Goodbye	100	80	6.50	(missed one informant)	
marriage, ring	100	88	7.00	12	7.00
agree, yes	100	100	6.75		
food, I want to eat	100	88	7.00	12	4.00
pleading (pulling beard)	100	100	7.00		
makeup (face)	100	100	7.00		
makeup (hair)	100	80	6.62	10	6.00
choking (one hand)	100	75	5.67	none	
walk slowly	100	100	6.67		
haha, you goofed	100	80	7.00	20	5.00
distaste (3 informants)	100	100	7.00		
just a little	100	100	7.00		
counting	100	75	7.00	25	6.00
delicious	100	100	6.43		
something stinks	100	100	7.00		
headache	100	100	5.88		
toothache	100	100	7.00		
get lost	100	100	6.88		
I want to drink	100	100	6.88		
threat	100	86	6.83		
wash hands	100	100	6.47		
ablutions (4 informants)	100	75	6.67	(one answer missing)	
playing cards (4 informants)	100	100	6.75		
he's crazy/stupid	100	100	7.00		
okay	100	100	6.75		
going to throw up	100	100	7.00		
be silent	100	100	7.00		
writing	100	75	6.67	25	6.00
give me a cigarette	100	100	6.62		
shoveling	100	88	7.00	12	7.00
tall person	100	100	6.62		
drive a car	100	88	7.00	12	7.00
short person	100	100	7.00		
thank God	90	90	6.67	(one response not given)	
follow me	89	88	6.47	12	6.00
shoot a man	89	100	6.62		

	%AGR	%NAT	RATING	%ART	RATING
what time is it	89	100	7.00		
money	89	100	6.33		
Do you have a match?	89	89	6.50	11	7.00
draw a bow	88	100	6.12		
come here	88	100	6.38		
drill a hole	88	75	5.57	25	6.00
reading	88	100	6.75		
I don't know	88	100	7.00		
enough, stop	88	75	7.00	12	7.00
you	88	88	6.86	12	7.00
pregnant	88	88	6.28	12	7.00
myself	88	100	6.71		
alarm (slap hand)	86	86	5.71	14	4.00
swimming	86	100	7.00		
rifle	86	100	6.00		
certainly I'll do it	80	80	7.00	10	7.00
clean a window	78	88	6.86	12	0.00
don't hit me	78	88	6.57	12	6.00
go away	75	88	6.57	12	2.00
earache	78	88	6.75		
drive away evil spirit	75	88	6.00	12	5.00
I dislike it	75	100	6.88		
get up	75	88	7.00	12	7.00
thinking	75	88	6.71	12	7.00
secret	75	100	6.50		
choking	75	100	6.12		
take it away	75	75	6.83	12	6.00
hello	75	100	6.88		
sharpen pencil	75	88	5.88	12	7.00
hunger/pain	75	75	6.83	12	7.00
				(one response missed)	
knock on wood	71	86	7.00	14	6.00
boxing	75	88	6.86	12	7.00
mock applause	71	71	6.60	28	6.50
sour	71	100	7.00		

PROBABLE EMBLEMS

	%AGR	%NAT	RATING	%ART	RATING
vagina	83	66	7.00	17	5.00
peeling fruit (cucumber)	78	75	7.00	12	7.00
				(N.B. Encode = 45%)	
grab collar (3 informants)	75	50	7.00	50	6.00
shut the door	75	62.5	6.00	38	5.67

	%AGR	%NAT	RATING	%ART	RATING
AMBIGUOUS EMBLEMS					
I am your servant	70	100	6.90		
eat with spoon	70	80	6.88		
he drove me out of my mind	70	100	6.50		
eat with hand	70	100	6.70	(Encode = 36%)	
big shot (thick neck)	67	62.5	5.60	38	5.00
go left/right: go this way	67	75	5.56	12	6.00
open the door	67	75	5.33	25	7.00
hanged	67	75	6.17	12	7.00
I'm full	62	75	6.50	25	5.50
I'm fed up	52	71	7.00	14	7.00
knock on door	67	75	6.83	none	
basketball	60	60	6.67	30	4.00
running	60	100	6.40		
key	57	57	6.00	28	6.00
bracelet	57	86	6.17	none	
go back	57	86	5.43	14	5.00
					(encode = 38%)
straight ahead	57	86	5.14	14	4.00
let's go (head)	57	100	6.86		
give	57	86	5.71	14	6.00
let's go (hand)	56	100	7.00		
kill	56	100	7.00		
look	60	100	6.50		
friends	50	100	7.00		
intercourse	50	60	7.00	17	7.00

DECODE SCORES WITH BELOW 50% AGREEMENT

MESSAGE	%AGR	MESSAGE	%AGR
shut up	43	ring doorbell	17
		seize/claw	14
be calm	38	throw a stone	14
it's far	33	pickpocket	11
wait a minute	33	he's bald	11
drawing	33	later	0
pinch	28	go this way	0
		handcuffs	0
I don't care (HS)	22	pleading (hand-to-cheek)	0
why? (HS) (rec. as 'what?')	20		

The following emblems were decoded with a message different from the encode message:

MESSAGE	%AGR	%NAT	RATING	%ART	RATING
why →what	100	100	6.70		
death → sleepy	89	100	6.12		
later → gone	75	100	4.67		
today → here	71	71	6.80	14	5.00
not speaking → friends	71	86	6.67	14	6.00
throw a stone → throw	71	100	6.88		
dirt on your head → get lost	50	75	7.00	25	5.00

The following messages were omitted from the decode list because of low encode scores:

MESSAGE	%AGR	ENCODE AGR%
a lot of money	90	none
call someone far away	100	44
peeling fruit	78	45
ward off evil eye	78	0
talks too much	75	50
suicide	75	38
polite no	75	28
anticipation	71	0
eat with hand	70	36
intelligent	67	30
attractive girl	67	33
we're equals	67	22
go back	57	38
fly open	56	40

APPENDIX II: ILLUSTRATION OF CONTRASTIVE FEATURES

The following appendix illustrates the contrastive features found in Persian gesture, and presents one minimally different pair to demonstrate the contrastiveness of each features. The appendix is arranged in the following manner: on the left-hand side of the page, the column labelled PERSIAN FEATURES includes the features, in capital letters; and on the right-hand side of the page, the column labelled OPPOSITIONS PROVIDING EVIDENCE presents two or three drawings which illustrate the features and the minimal pairs or oppositions in which they appear. Each drawing is labelled with the feature it illustrates, and with an English gloss of the Persian message.

A note advises the reader in case the gestures illustrated fail to constitute a true minimal pair. The note also specifies whether additional features distinguish the two gestures, or whether the feature in question simply appears in some gestures but does not appear in any contrastive oppositions.

The arrangement of features follows the order *tabula, designator, signation*. Tabula features begin with the 'zero ʿtab' and continue with the head and face, trunk and hand. Designator features begin with the hand and conclude with face and arm features. Finally, signation features begin with direction and conclude with shape, contact and dynamics.

A system of arrows in the drawings illustrates direction, shape and dynamics of movement in the following manner:

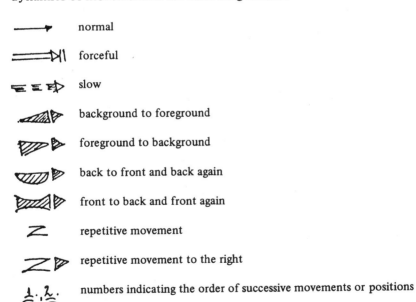

	normal
	forceful
	slow
	background to foreground
	foreground to background
	back to front and back again
	front to back and front again
	repetitive movement
	repetitive movement to the right
	numbers indicating the order of successive movements or positions

PERSIAN FEATURES   OPPOSITIONS PROVIDING EVIDENCE
Tabula Features
ZERO TAB
SIDE TAB

zero   side
'no'   'hello'

UPPER FACE
EYE

upper face   eye
'thinking'   'on my eyes I will do it'

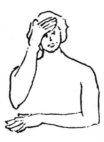

WHOLE FACE

whole face   upper face
'unfortunate fool'   'I'm thinking'

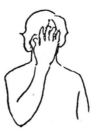

PERSIAN FEATURES OPPOSITIONS PROVIDING EVIDENCE
(Tabula, continued)
NOSE
CHIN
NECK

nose	chin	neck
'bad smell'	'for my sake'	'choking'

CHEST
STOMACH

chest	stomach	breast
'worry'	'hunger'	'woman'

UPPER ARM
WRIST

upper arm	wrist
'strong'	'caught him'

PERSIAN FEATURE   OPPOSITION PROVIDING EVIDENCE
(Tabula, continued)
PRONATE WRIST
WHOLE WRIST

pronate wrist   whole wrist
'what time is it'   'bracelet'

Hand and Fist Designator Features:

FLAT HAND

flat hand   spread hand
'no'   'five'

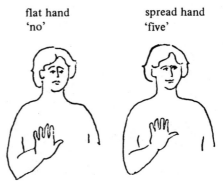

TENSE CURVED HAND

tense hand   flat hand
'strangle'   'this size'

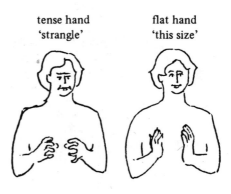

PERSIAN FEATURE
(Hand Designators,
   continued)

OPPOSITION PROVIDING EVIDENCE

FIST: thumb between
index and middle finger
FIST: thumb on side
of index finger

index and middle
'intercourse'

side of index
'money'

(This opposition does not provide conclusive evidence, as 'money' has an additional movement feature.)

FIST: with thumb
and forefinger
circle

'small'

(This feature appears but is not conclusively contrastive, as it appears in no oppositions or minimal pairs.)

FIST: index finger
extended (i.e.,
index or pointing
hand)

index hand
'intelligence'

flat hand
'headache'

PERSIAN DESIGNATOR
FEATURES

OPPOSITIONS PROVIDING EVIDENCE

FIST, EXTENSION OF
INDEX AND MIDDLE
FINGERS

index, middle
'gun'

index only
'look'

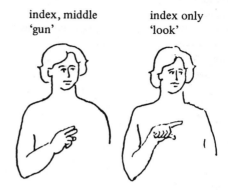

Arm Designator Features
TOTAL ARM
EXTENSION

total
'big'

partial
'this size'

PARTIAL ARM
EXTENSION

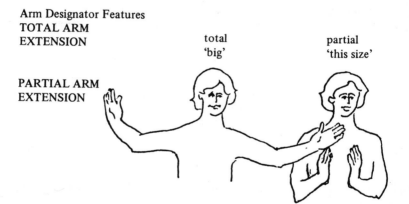

DIVERGENT EXTENSION
PARALLEL EXTENSION
CONVERGENT EXTENSION

convergent (not con-
clusive;
also has
grasp)

'unity'

divergent
'big'

parallel
'pray'

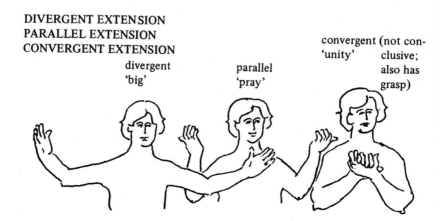

PERSIAN FEATURES   OPPOSITIONS PROVIDING EVIDENCE

Facial Designator Configurations

SMILE

GRIEF

smile
'your servant'

grief
'worry'

ANGER

anger
'I warn you'

joking, flirtatious
'naughty, naughty'

ALARM

alarm
'what did I do'

smile
'do it for my sake'

PERSIAN FEATURES   OPPOSITIONS PROVIDING EVIDENCE
(Facial Configurations)
SOUR (PUCKERED FACE)
DISGUST (FROWN,   puckered   smile   disgust
WRINKLED NOSE)   'sour'   'delicious'   'bad smell'

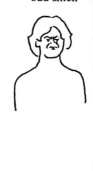

Symmetrical Emblems requiring both hands as designators:

   'nice figure'   'thin'   'embrace'

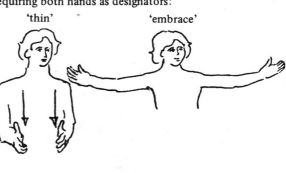

Emblems showing symmetrical designators with increased emotional involvement:

   'please sit there'   'absolutely not'   'don't hit me'

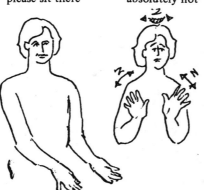

PERSIAN FEATURES   OPPOSITIONS PROVIDING EVIDENCE
Signation Features
PALM UP
PALM DOWN

palm up   palm down
'get up'   'wait'

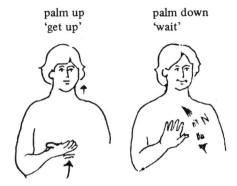

MOVEMENT TOWARDS
SIGNER
MOVEMENT AWAY   towards   towards   away
FROM SIGNER   'come' (V. 1)   'come' (V. 2) 'go, he went'

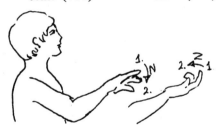

SIDE TO SIDE
TO AND FRO

side to side   to and fro
'absolutely no'   'wait, calm down'

PERSIAN FEATURES   OPPOSITIONS PROVIDING EVIDENCE
(Signation, continued)
FORWARD TO BACK
BACK TO FRONT

to back	to front
'come'	'follow me'

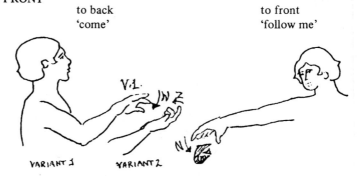

WRIST SUPINATION
WRIST PRONATION

supination	pronation
'I don't know'	'go away'

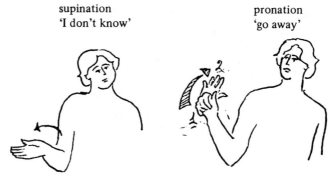

WRIST: twist
WRIST: cock

twist	cock
'I don't know'	'no'

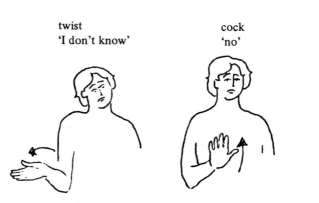

PERSIAN FEATURES
(Signation, continued)
ARM: CIRCULAR and
    S-SHAPED
MOVEMENT

ARM: INTERCHANGING
AND SYMMETRICAL
ACTION

CROSSING ACTION:
+ versus ×

OPPOSITIONS PROVIDING EVIDENCE

circular
'cleaning'

s-shaped
'drawing'

symmetrical
'frog stroke'

interchanging
'crawl'

+
'make change'

×
'sign-line'

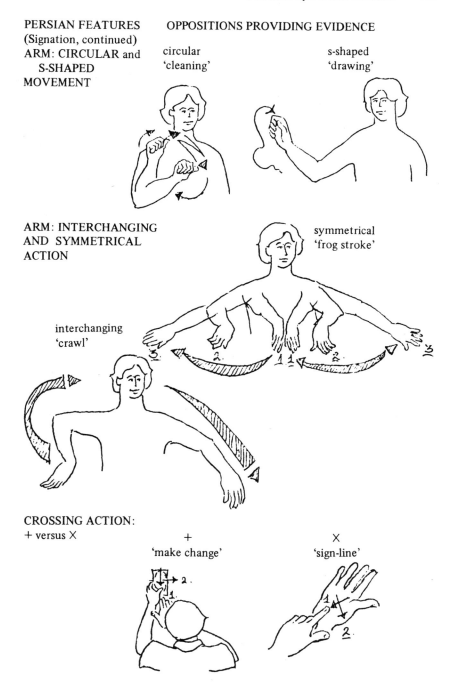

PERSIAN FEATURES   OPPOSITIONS PROVIDING EVIDENCE
(Signation, continued)
TOUCH   touch   grasp
GRASP   'What time is it?'   'they caught him'

CONVERGENCE
GRASP
                 convergence   grasp
                 'this size'   'unity, friendship'

DISCRETE CONTACT
CONTINUOUS CONTACT
                 discrete   continuous
                 'intelligence'   'headache'

PERSIAN FEATURES   OPPOSITIONS PROVIDING EVIDENCE
(signation, continued)
RUBBING

rubbing   rotation
'money'   'key'

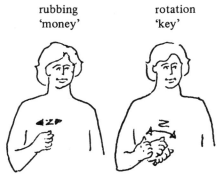

Relative Hand Position
FACING
FACING, UNDER
BEHIND

facing   under   behind
'this size'   'thick book'   'pregnant'

Features of Dynamics:
NORMAL   normal   fast
FAST   'go'   'get lost'

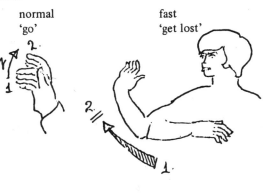

PERSIAN FEATURES   OPPOSITIONS PROVIDING EVIDENCE
(Dynamics, continued)
SLOW

slow	normal	fast
'don't get upset'	'wait'	'shut up'

(Body signs appearing but not conclusively contrastive – i.e., not appearing in any minimal pairs:)

RISE
TENSE, chest out
SHRUG

rise	tense	shrug
'greeting'	'pride'	

(Body movements, continued)
SAG

sag	sag
'bored'	'sleepy'

NOTES

[1] The procedure for emblem verification was developed by Paul Ekman and is detailed in Johnson 1972.

[2] For the sake of simplicity, I treat facial expressions as a unit. Actually they are composites of brow eyelid, nose, mouth and nasolabial fold configuration. For an analysis of the composites of the facial expressions recognized cross-culturally, see Ekman 1971:35ff.

[3] The information on ASL taken from (Stokoe et al. 1965:x-xii).

REFERENCES

Baker, Charlotte
    1976   "What's not on the other hand in American Sign Language", *Papers from the Twelfth Regional Meeting of the Chicago Linguistic Society*, 24-32. Chicago: University of Chicago Press.
Barakat, R.
    1973   "Arabic Gestures", *Journal of Popular Culture* 6/4, 749-93.
Birdwhistell, R. L.
    1970   *Kinesics in Context.* Philadelphia: University of Pennsylvania Press.
Bouissac, Paul
    1973   *La Mesure des gestes.* The Hague: Mouton.
Catford, J. C.
    1940   "Gestures and Gesture Notation". Unpublished paper.
Cicourel, Aaron V.
    1974   *Cognitive Sociology: Language and Meaning in Social Interaction.* New York: Free Press.
Efron, David
    1941   *Gesture and Environment.* New York: Kings Crown Press.
    1972   *Gesture, Race, and Culture*, ed. by Thomas A. Sebeok. The Hague: Mouton.
Ekman, Paul
    1971   *Universals and Cultural Differences in Facial Expressions of Emotion.* Omaha: University of Nebraska Press.
    1973   *Darwin and Facial Expression: A Century of Research in Review.* New York: Academic Press.
Ekman, Paul, and W. V. Friesen
    1969a   "The Repertoire of Nonverbal Behavior: Categories, Origins, Usage and Coding", *Semiotica* 1/1, 49-98.
    1972   "Hand Movements", *Journal of Communication* 22/4, 353-74.
Frishberg, Nancy
    1975   "Arbitrariness and Iconicity: Historical Change in American Sign Language", *Language* 51/3, 676-719.
Johnson, H. G.
    1972   *American Communicative Gestures: The emblem repertoire of white middle-class males in the western United States.* San Francisco: University of California Ph.D. dissertation.

Mallory, Garrick
    1880   *Introduction to the Study of Sign Language among the North American Indians.* Washington: Government Printing Office.
Mehmandi-Nejad, Mohammed-Javid
    1973   *Principles of Translation, English and Farsi.* Tehran: National Book Company.
Laban, R.
    1966   *Choreutics.* London: MacDonald and Evans.
Pike, Kenneth L.
    1947   *Phonemics: A Technique for Reducing Languages to Writing.* Ann Arbor: University of Michigan Press.
    1975   "On Kinesic Triadic Relationships in Turn-Taking", *Semiotica* 13/4, 389-95.
Poyatos, Ferdinand
    1975   "Gesture Inventories: Fieldwork, Methodology and Problems", *Semiotica* 13/2, 199-229.
Rijnberk, G. van
    1954   *Le Langage par signes chez les moines.* Amsterdam: North Holland.
Saitz, R. L., and E. J. Cervenka
    1962   *Colombian and North American Gestures: An Experimental Study.* Bogota: Centro Colombo Americano.
Stokoe, W. C.
    1960   *Sign Language Structure: An Outline of the Visual Communication Systems of the American Deaf.* Buffalo: State University of New York at Buffalo, Department of Anthropology and Linguistics.
    1972   *Semiotics and Human Sign Languages.* The Hague: Mouton.
Stokoe, W. C., Casterline, and Croneberg
    1965   *A Dictionary of American Sign Language on Linguistic Principles.* Washington, D.C: Gallaudet College Press.
Taylor, Alan Ross
    1975   "Nonverbal Communication Systems in Native North America", *Semiotica* 13/4, 329-75.
Taylor, H. M.
    1974   "Japanese Kinestics", *Journal of the Association of Teachers of Japanese* 9/1, 65-72.
Wazlawick, Paul, J. H. Beavin, and D. D. Jackson
    1967   *Pragmatics of Human Communication: A Study of Interactional Patterns and Paradoxes.* New York: W. W. Norton.
Wundt, Wilhelm
    1973   *The Language of Gestures,* ed. by Thomas A. Sebeok. The Hague: Mouton.

Carol Magda Sparhawk (b. 1945) is assistant director of the Intensive English Program at Cornell University. As her principal research interests she lists: gesture in social interaction, formal analysis of gesture, interaction structure, and discourse. She co-authored the textbook *English for Medical Students* (1973, 1974).

LORRAINE KIRK and MICHAEL BURTON

Physical versus Semantic Classification of Nonverbal Forms: A Cross-Cultural Experiment

INTRODUCTION

Judged similarity tests have been used with increasing frequency to study the cognitive organization of verbal materials. In this paper we extend the existing methodology to a new domain. Here we investigate judged similarities among nonverbal acts. One simple question motivating the research is whether or not the judged similarity test (in this case the triads test) can elicit nonrandom judgments of similarity among the elements of nonverbal behavior. A second question motivating the work is whether people will classify nonverbal acts on the basis of anatomy and motion or on the basis of semantics.

The elements of nonverbal behavior considered in this paper will be called emblems. Ekman and Friesen (1972) define emblems as:

> those nonverbal acts (a) which have a direct verbal translation usually consisting of a word or two, or a phrase, (b) for which this precise meaning is known by most or all members of a group, class, sub-culture, or culture, (c) which are most often deliberately used with the conscious intent to send a particular message to the other person(s), (d) for which the person(s) who sees the emblem usually not only knows tne emblem's message but also knows that it was deliberately sent to him, and (e) for which the sender usually takes responsibility for having made that communication. A further touchstone of an emblem is whether it can be replaced by a word or two, its message verbalized, without substantially modifying a conversation ... Emblems, as we have defined them, are communicative and interactive acts.

According to Ekman and Friesen's definition, an emblem can be interchanged with an equivalent verbal form. We have chosen to leave as an empirical question to be investigated here the extent to which emblems are interchangeable with verbal forms of communication. Related to this is a second empirical question concerning whether emblems have meanings which are independent of the context in which they occur. Clearly, if the meaning of an emblem is heavily dependent upon context, then it will be difficult to supply a word or phrase which can always replace it in speech. An example of extreme interchangeability would be a situation in which each emblem corresponded to one word or phrase, and in which the cognitive organization of the emblems was exactly the same as the cognitive organization of the corresponding lexical items. At another extreme would be a situation in which the emblems did not have any mapping onto verbal forms in terms of meaning, and in which the meaning of an emblem varied idiosyncratically with the context of its use. In the former case, we anticipate that people would make similarity judgments among emblems which are based on the semantics of the emblems. In the latter case it would be difficult to make similarity judgments based on semantics. Other criteria would take precedence, focusing on the visual/kinaesthetic mode of communication. Such criteria could include the body parts used or the kinds of motion involved in performing the emblems. The verbal/semantic and visual kinaesthetic criteria are, however, not mutually exclusive. It is conceivable that people would switch from one kind of criterion to another within a judged similarity task. The two kinds of criteria are also not necessarily independent. Semantic criteria may overlap with criteria based on parts of the body or kinds of motion. Emblems may be iconic in that they resemble their referents; by contrast, the meanings of spoken words are generally unrelated to the sounds of words.

Semantic Hypothesis

In order to test the hypothesis that emblems are classified according to semantic criteria, we elicited verbal labels for the emblems in the respondents' first language and administered two parallel judged similarity tests, one using the emblems and one using the corresponding verbal labels, to two groups of respondents from each of two cultures. Respondents to the verbal test were not told that the words presented had any relationship to body movements. Positive within-culture correlations between the results of these two tests would lend support to the hypothesis that semantic criteria are used to classify the emblems.[1]

Physical Performance Hypothesis

In order to test the hypothesis that emblems are classified according to visual/kinaesthetic criteria, we administered the verbal and kinesic triads tests to both Maasai and Kikuyu, who speak unrelated languages but who, probably due to their geographical contiguity, have a broad range of emblems which share kinesic representations. Because the two cultures share so many emblems, it was possible to design the test so that most of the emblems utilized in the test are in common use both in Maasai and Kikuyu.

Given that the Maasai language is unrelated to the Kikuyu language, it is unlikely that semantic judgments would be widely shared between the two cultures.2 However, to the extent that people classify emblems on visual/kinaesthetic criteria, it is conceivable that these criteria would be shared between the two cultures. We anticipate that some judgments based on physical performance attributes might include considerations of the body parts involved in performance of the emblems. In order to ascertain whether a classification of body parts has been used for such judgments, it is necessary to have knowledge of the folk classification of parts of the body. This has been obtained in another work (Burton and Kirk, unpublished) through triads tests on 13 body parts for Maasai and Kikuyu subjects. Results of hierarchical clustering of similarities from these triads tests are presented in Figures 7 and 8. For each test, a word which translates into English as 'body' was included in the test. The most striking result of the clusterings of body parts is that Maasai and Kikuyu differ in the location of 'body' with respect to other anatomical terms. The Maasai link 'body' with the head (most closely with 'mouth' and 'ear'). By contrast, the Kikuyu link their word for 'body' with the parts of the leg. Beyond this major difference, the two structures share a primary distinction between parts of the head and parts of the limbs, and a secondary distinction in the limbs between parts of the arm and parts of the leg. In both Maasai and Kikuyu, the words which translate into English as 'arm' and 'leg' actually refer to arm-hand-fingers and leg-foot-toes, respectively.

Given these structures, we would predict that any classification system utilizing body part criteria in the triads tests on emblems would indicate a primary distinction between parts of the head and parts of the limbs.

PROCEDURE

In order to compare the modes of classification which Maasai and Kikuyu respondents use in dealing with kinesic as opposed to verbal input, judged similarities tests were given to members of both cultures in kinesic and verbal form. Judged similarities were assessed here by means of triads tests, described below.

Triads Tests

In a triads test item, three stimuli are presented to the subject. The subject is asked to select from the three stimuli the one which is most different from the other two. A triads test typically consists of a number of such items (triads), chosen so as to make systematic similarity comparisons within a set of stimuli. Triads tests have been used extensively in cognitive anthropology using verbal stimuli (Romney and D'Andrade, 1964). A standard verbal triads test uses all of the possible triads among the words which comprise a semantic domain; in the present study we used a balanced block design (Burton and Nerlove, unpublished) in order to allow the inclusion in the test of a greater number of stimuli with no greater test length and negligible distortion in the reliability of the test. The balanced block design requires that each pair of stimuli appear in the same number of triads. In the present design, there are 24 triads using nine emblems. The 24 triads were randomized and presented in the same order for each subject and for each of the four tests (a kinesic and a verbal test in each of the two cultures).

Choice of Emblems

The emblems utilized in this study were selected in such a way as to maximize their distribution across a series of verbal/semantic and visual/anatomic variables. The verbal/semantic distinctions used included degree of deixis, indication of command, reference to supernatural forces, positive versus negative evaluation, and emphasis on social closeness versus agonistic behavior. Some visual/anatomic distinctions were the body parts involved in execution of the emblem, plurality of body parts used, plurality of movements within the emblem, repetitiveness of movement, and size and rate of movement. By selecting emblems so that they are distributed across both semantic and anatomical features, we allow for responses on the basis of either kind of criterion. It remains an empirical question which of the features will govern responses to the triads tests.

Definition of Terms

Nine emblems were chosen for the purposes of the present experiment; seven of these are the same in Maasai and Kikuyu. The remaining two emblems have some semantic and kinesic overlap between the two cultures, but remain distinct in both meaning and execution. Brief descriptions of the kinesic forms follow, under the headings of their English labels:

1. *Mouth Point*. This emblem is used to indicate an object or direction, very much as the finger is used for pointing in English. The core of this movement is a protrusion of the lips in the direction of the object or space indicated.

2. *Finger Point*. This emblem functions as does "mouth point", above. It is executed as in English, with a single finger pointing as an extension of an arm reach in the direction of the indicated object or direction; some head movement accompanies this movement in both cultures, with a slight additional trunk movement in Kikuyu.

3. *Blessing*. This movement is executed by pulling the clothes away from the chest with the hands, bending the head down so that the mouth reaches inside the clothing, and making a rapid succession of quiet, unvoiced spitting noises with the tongue and lips.

4. *Stop That*. This is executed by holding the arm extended toward the addressee palm forward, and rotating the forearm back and forth rapidly about 10-30 degrees. This shakes the fingers of the extended hand laterally.

5. *Swearing The Truth*. This emblem involves a sequence of movements: a finger touches the ground, then touches the tongue, then points to the sky.

6. *Come Here*. In this emblem the whole arm is extended toward the subject, with the palm of the hand forward and fingers pointing upwards; there follows a rapid flexion of the fingers to meet the heel of the hand.

7. *I Can't Hear*. In this emblem the hand is placed behind one ear, palm forward.

8. *Expression of Threat* (Maasai) /*Expression of Contempt* (Kikuyu). The Maasai emblem (*threat*) involves biting the forefinger, which is placed parallel to the lips and inside the teeth, followed by a shaking of the finger rapidly up and down while pointing at the recipient of the threat. A facial threat accompanies this movement. The Kikuyu emblem (*contempt*) involves thrusting five curved fingers forward toward the recipient of the abuse, palm forward, fingers above palm. The fingers are oriented during this movement as they would be if holding a ball of about five inches in diameter.

9. *Indication That a Secret is Being Communicated* (Maasai) / *Expression That Something is Funny* (Kikuyu). In the Maasai emblem (*secret*), the tongue touches the outside of the cheek on a horizontal plane. In the Kikuyu emblem (*funny*), the hand is placed over the mouth and the shoulders raised.

Administration of the Tests

In the kinesic version of the triads test, respondents were told that they were going to deal with how people say things without words. They were shown three movements, between which the tester would return to a standard home position and pause slightly. Respondents were asked to choose the movement which was most different from the other two. Respondents for the kinesic test were not given verbal labels for the emblems. Practice was given with emblems not included in the test itself (for example, a head shake, a head nod, and an emblem for 'go away').

For the verbal version of the test, the items consisted strictly of the verbal labels for the movements (emblems) elicited from speakers of the languages in which the tests were to be administered. Respondents for the verbal test were not told that the stimuli were labels for emblems. For each set of three words or phrases, respondents were asked to choose the word or phrase which was most different from the other two. Practice was given with triads not involving labels for emblems (for example: cow, boy, sheep). The tests were administered by Kikuyu and Maasai testers in their own languages.

Sampling

For each of the kinesic and verbal versions of the triads test, a sample of between 31 and 40 respondents were chosen from each of the two ethnic groups, for a total of four tests and 141 respondents. Respondents were selected to have little or no schooling, and were evenly distributed across age and sex categories. No respondent was given both the verbal and kinesic versions of the test, and care was taken to avoid exposure of respondents to any version of the test prior to testing.

Data Analysis

To examine the structure of the similarity relationships among the emblems, multidimensional scalings were done on the Kikuyu kinesic, Kikuyu verbal,, Maasai kinesic, and Maasai verbal data. Multidimensional scaling (Shepard, 1962; Kruskal, 1964) represents the stimuli as points in a space of one or more dimensions (see Figure 1). The multidimensional scaling program places the stimuli in a configuration so that small distances between stimuli correspond to high similarity between stimuli. The measures of similarity for the present experiment are computed from the aggregate triads judgments. Consider a hypothetical experiment containing the triad *man, woman, boy,* in which 45 people choose *woman* as most different, 45 people choose *boy* as most different, and 10 people choose *man* as most different. By choosing *woman* as most different, 45 out of 100 people judge *man* and *boy* to be similar, so the similarity index for *man* and *boy* is .45. If *man* and *boy* were also part of a second triad, the overall similarity measure for *man* and *boy* would be computed by averaging the similarity indices for the two triads. The multidimensional scalings were done in three and two dimensions, using the *TORSCA* program (Young and Torgerson, 1968).

In order to examine the hierarchical organization of the emblems, we performed hierarchical cluster analyses for the four sets of data. Hierarchical cluster analysis builds a binary tree structure from the bottom up. First the two most similar objects are placed together as a cluster. Then the next most similar objects or clusters are merged. This process continues until the tree structure has been connected at the top node. The hierarchical clustering procedure uses the same similarity measures as were used by the scaling analysis. Our clustering was done with D'Andrade's all-possible pairs program (D'Andrade, unpublished).

Both the scaling procedure and the hierarchical clustering procedure also compute measures of the degree of correspondence of the computed structure (multidimensional configuration or hierarchical structure) to the original data. For multidimensional scaling, the measure is called 'stress'. Zero stress indicates that a perfect correspondence between the model and the data has been achieved. For hierarchical clustering, the measure is referred to as 'number of taxonomic errors'; again, if this measure is zero, a perfect correspondence has been achieved.

To measure the degree to which the patterns of similarity across the tests are alike, the similarity matrices were intercorrelated, using Pearson's product-moment correlations. For the within-culture correlations, this was done with data on all nine emblems. However, since two of the emblems differ from the Maasai to the Kikuyu test, correlations of Maasai measures to Kikuyu measures were based on reduced similarity matrices using the seven emblems shared between the Maasai and Kikuyu tests.[3]

RESULTS

In this section are discussed results of (a) multidimensional scaling analyses, (b) hierarchical clustering analyses, and (c) correlations among dissimilarity matrices.

Multidimensional Scaling

In Table 1 are listed the stress values for two- and three-dimensional scalings of the four sets of data. The Kikuyu scalings have higher stress in two

TABLE 1

Stresses for Multidimensional Scalings

	Three Dimensions	Two Dimensions
KIKUYU KINESIC	.062	.183
KIKUYU VERBAL	.093	.183
MAASAI KINESIC	.064	.167
MAASAI VERBAL	.100	.155

dimensions than do the Maasai scalings. They also have lower stress in three dimensions than do the Maasai scalings. Thus the improvement in stress with the addition of the third dimension is much greater for the Kikuyu data than for the Maasai data. Comparison of the two-dimensional scalings for each data set with the three-dimensional scalings for the same data sets shows little change in the Maasai configurations with the addition of the third dimension. However, the Kikuyu configurations are changed substantually by the addition of the third dimension. Consequently, the Maasai configurations are represented here in two dimensions (Figures 1 and 2) whereas the Kikuyu configurations are represented in three dimensions (Figures 3-6).

Maasai Scaling Results

For the Maasai scalings, the most striking result is that the kinesic configuration is almost identical to the verbal configuration. For both configurations, the first dimension is a contrast between

> a. 'come', 'secret', 'mouth point', 'stop that' (positive on dimension one)
> b. 'threat' (neutral on dimension one)

and

> c. 'swear it's true', 'finger point', 'can't hear' (negative on dimension one).

For both configurations, 'threat' is extremely positive on dimension two and 'blessing' is extremely negative on dimension two.

Comparison of the graphs for Maasai kinesic forms and Maasai verbal forms reveals a shared structure for the first dimension. This structure shows a contrast between

and

a. 'come', 'mouth point', 'stop that', and 'secret' (positive on Dimension 1), henceforth referred to as cluster A.

c. 'swear it's true', 'finger point', and 'can't hear' (negative on Dimension 1).

Dimension 2, varying from 'threat' at one extreme to 'blessing' at the other, suggests the presence of an evaluative criterion. Dimension 1 appears in almost exactly the same form with nonverbal and verbal stimuli. Given that the verbal labels for the emblems are only approximate translations of what the emblems convey, there is much more overlap between the two Maasai structures than we had anticipated.

It is this shared structure which requires an interpretation. Below are listed some of the features of the emblems which we suspect enter into similarity judgments and result in the similarity structure which we have found for both Maasai kinesic and Maasai verbal data.

1 *Simple vs. Complex Motion.* Of the four emblems in cluster A, three of them (,come', 'secret', and 'mouth point') involve a single motion. The fourth, 'stop that', involves repetitions of a single motion. Emblems which involve a single motion or repetitions of a single motion we categorize as involving *simple* motion. These we contrast with emblems which involve *complex* motion, in which two or more distinct simple motions are strung together. Instances of complex motion are 'threat', 'swear it's true', and 'blessing'. None of the members of cluster A involve complex motion, whereas three of the nonmembers of cluster A do involve complex motion.

2. *Plurality of Body Parts.* Emblems employed in this experiment were designed to distribute themselves across a contrast between the use of only a single body area (e.g., head only, limb only) as opposed to the use of a combination of different areas of the body (e.g., simultaneous use of head and limbs) in the execution of an emblem. The four members of cluster A all involve either the head ('secret', 'mouth point') or the hand/arm ('come', 'stop that'), but not both. Of the five emblems which are not included in cluster A, all of them ('blessing', 'can't hear', 'swear it's true', 'finger point', and 'threat') involve both the hand/arm and the head.

3. *Finger Pointing.* All three emblems in the upper left of the configurations ('swear it's true', 'finger point', and 'threat') involve finger pointing. 'Finger point' is primarily a hand/arm motion, but the head is secondarily involved. We suspect that it has been pulled away from cluster A by the

facts (a) that the head is secondarily involved and (b) that two non-members of cluster A also involve finger pointing.

4.*Behavior Fostering Social Closeness versus Agonistic Behavior.* 'Threat' is an act with strong negative affect and 'blessing' is an act with strong positive affect. These are at opposite ends of the second dimension.

5.*Command.* 'Come' and 'stop that' are commands. They are both included in cluster A.

6. *Reference to Supernatural.* This is involved in both 'blessing' and 'swear it's true', and may also be involved in 'threat' (more ethnographic work would be required). All three of these emblems are outside of cluster A.

A surprising finding is that 'mouth point' and 'finger point' are not proximate either in the Maasai kinesic data or in the Maasai verbal data, in spite of the fact that their verbal forms are very similar (*awut tenkutok*, and *awut tolkimojino*).

Kikuyu Scaling Results

As with the Maasai scalings, the Kikuyu kinesic and Kikuyu verbal configurations are very similar. However, the degree of similarity of the two configurations is not as great as in the case of the Maasai data.

For Dimension 1, the two configurations are the same, with the exception of 'stop that'. The kinesic configuration assigns 'stop that' a negative value on Dimension 1, whereas for the verbal configuration it has a positive value. For dimension 2, the verbal and kinesic configurations differ on 'stop that', 'blessing', and 'come'. For dimension 3, the two configurations differ on 'blessing' and 'can't hear'. The differences in the two configurations are summarized in Table 2, which lists the octant location for each emblem in each of the three-dimensional spaces.

TABLE 2
Octant Location of the Emblems

	Kikuyu Kinesic	Kikuyu Verbal	Shared between Configurations
Contempt	+ + +	+ + +	+ + +
Mouth point	+ + −	+ + −	+ + −
Funny	+ − −	+ − −	+ − −
Swear it's true	+ − −	+ − −	+ − −
Can't hear	− − 0	− − +	− −
Come	− 0 +	− − +	− +
Blessing	− + +	− − −	−
Finger point	− + +	− + +	− + +
Stop that	− + −	+ − −	−

From this table it can be seen that the only major differences between the two configurations are in the locations of 'blessing' and 'stop that'.

Below are listed some criteria which appear to explain the similarity structures of the Kikuyu kinesic and verbal triads tests.

1. *Deixis.* Five of the Kikuyu emblems serve to locate a person or location in space. These are:

'Contempt': Directed towards the person being abused.
'Mouth point': Communicates the location of something.
'Finger point': Communicates the location of something.
'Stop that': Arm is extended in direction of person addressed.
'Come': Arm is extended in direction of person addressed.

Of these five emblems, four take on positive values on dimension 2 of the Kikuyu kinesic structure. The fifth ('come') is neutral on dimension 2 of the same structure. Of the five emblems, three ('contempt', 'come', 'finger point') share a strong positive value on dimension 3 of the kinesic structure. For the Kikuyu verbal structure, three of the five deictic emblems ('mouth point', 'finger point' and 'contempt') form a cluster at the positive end of dimension 2. The other two deictic emblems are located at the negative extreme of dimension 2. 'Mouth point', 'contempt', and 'finger point' form a more restrictive subset of deictic emblems defined by the property of *pointing action*. These three emblems form a cluster for both scaling configurations. However, that cluster is difficult to perceive for the kinesic configuration without the aid of a three dimensional model.

2. *Behavior Fostering Social Closeness versus Agonostic Behavior.* In the Kikuyu verbal configuration, 'contempt' and 'blessing' are at opposite poles on all three dimensions. In addition, 'blessing' forms a cluster with 'can't hear' and 'come'. These two emblems can be seen as requests for social closeness: 'communicate with me'; 'come closer'.

In the Kikuyu kinesic configuration, the contrast of 'contempt' with the triad of closeness emblems is not as clear. However, 'come', 'blessing', and 'can't hear' do form a cluster residing in the following region:

Dimension 1: negative
Dimension 2: negative to slightly positive
Dimension 3: neutral or positive.

3. *Body Parts.* There is some tendency for emblems which use the same parts of the body to be proximate in the kinesic structure. For example, the three most positive emblems on dimension three ('finger point', 'contempt', and 'come') all use only the hand-arm for their execution; 'mouth point'

and 'funny' are close together and both emphasize the mouth.

4. *Single Motion versus Repeated Motion.* 'Stop that' and 'blessing' both involve multiple rapid repetitions of small motions. They are proximate in the Kikuyu kinesic structure, but not in the Kikuyu verbal structure.

Hierarchical Clustering Analysis

Results of hierarchical clustering of the four sets of data are depicted in Figures 9-12. The Maasai cluster structures have considerably fewer taxonomic errors than do the Kikuyu structures, suggesting that the hierarchical model is more appropriate to the Maasai data than it is to the Kikuyu data. There is also more similarity between the two Maasai cluster structures than there is between the two Kikuyu cluster structures.

For both Maasai structures, the clusters are substantially the same as were found in the two-dimensional Maasai scaling. Cluster A ('mouth point', 'stop that', 'secret', and 'come') appears in both structures. The interpretation of the Maasai scaling structures accounts also for the Maasai cluster structures.

In contrast, the two Kikuyu cluster structures are very unlike each other, but both cluster structures can easily be mapped onto their respective scaling configurations. The cluster structures have brought out differences of emphasis between the Kikuyu kinesic data and the Kikuyu verbal data which the scaling structures tend to minimize. The Kikuyu verbal structure has a primary distinction between pointing actions ('mouth point', 'finger point', and 'contempt') and all other actions. These other emblems are divided into two groups. One group contains emblems which emphasize social closeness ('blessing', 'come', and 'can't hear'). The other group contains emblems which appear to have little in common other than that they all involve use of the hand ('stop that', 'swear it's true', 'funny'). The Kikuyu verbal structure appears to be based on semantic features (deixis and social closeness). The Kikuyu kinesic structure, by contrast, appears to be based mainly on body part and type of motion. This can be seen by four clusters which are created by cutting the tree two nodes from the top:

1. 'stop that', 'blessing'. Both involve repeated motion.
2. 'mouth point', 'funny'. Both emphasize the mouth.
3. 'swear it's true', 'can't hear'. Both involve the hand/arm in proximity to the head.
4. 'contempt', 'come', 'finger point'. All three involve only the hand/arm. Contempt can be distinguished from the other two on the semantic dimension of negative affect.

Although the cluster analysis emphasizes semantic dimensions among the

Kikuyu verbal data and visual/kinaesthetic dimensions among the Kikuyu kinesic data, examination of the multidimensional scaling configurations suggests that both kinds of criteria are present for both sets of data.

Correlational Analysis

Correlations of kinesic data to verbal data are listed in Table 3, along with results of statistical tests on the correlation coefficients.[4] For both cultures, the correlation of kinesic data to verbal data is high and significant, showing that subjects tended to make the same judgments of similarity among the emblems as they made among the corresponding verbal labels. These results lend support to the hypothesis that people use the same criteria for classifying the emblems as they use for classifying the verbal labels.

TABLE 3
Correlations of Kinesic Data to Verbal Data
(Based on all 24 triads)

Kikuyu kinesic to Kikuyu verbal	.491*
Maasai kinesic to Maasai verbal	.624**

* p < .01
** p < .001

Correlations among tests based on the reduced set of ten triads are presented in Table 4, along with results of significance tests on the correlation coefficients.[5]

TABLE 4
Correlations among Dissimilarity Measures,
Based on the Ten Triads which Contain only the Seven Emblems
Occurring Both in the Kikuyu Data and the Maasai Data

	Kikuyu kinesic	Kikuyu verbal	Maasai kinesic	Maasai verbal
Kikuyu kinesic	1.000	.478*	−.032	−.289
Kikuyu verbal	.478*	1.000	−.256	−.436*
Maasai kinesic	−.032	−.256	1.000	.497*
Maasai verbal	−.289	−.436*	.497*	1.000

* p < .05

The within-culture correlations show the same positive relationships of kinesic test data to verbal test data that were found for the full set of nine emblems. The between-culture correlations show no positive relationships between the Kikuyu data and the Maasai data.

CONCLUSIONS

This study had as its original objective to test two alternative, although not necessarily mutually exclusive, hypotheses: (a) that classification of emblems will focus on visual/anatomical criteria and (b) that classification of emblems will focus on semantic/verbal criteria. To test these hypotheses, verbal and nonverbal forms of triads tests were administered to two distinct samples of respondents within each of two cultures which share a considerable number of emblems but do not share either language or language family. The data from the resulting four sets of triads tests were examined in terms of correlational analysis, multidimensional scaling, and cluster analysis.

From the correlations data alone, it can be concluded that there is a strong relationship (about .5) between the emblems and their verbal labels within each of the languages studied, in sharp contrast with negligible or negative relationships both between the kinesic forms across language groups. The clarity of this contrast is surprising, as there is great room for error in obtaining labels (necessarily rough approximations) for the emblems and in administering the triads tests orally under field conditions.

Also from the correlations data: (a) It can be concluded that emblems are to a very great extent context independent. Some amount of context independence is generally assumed for emblems, but to our knowledge little if any empirical work has been done to support this. (b) The existence and context independence of emblems is demonstrated to be a cross-cultural phenomenon and to occur within the non-western world. (c) It is demonstrated that triads tests as a measure of judged similarity can be used successfully to produce nonrandom data with kinesic material.

From the multidimensional scaling and cluster analyses it can be concluded that:

(a) Within each culture, the organization of the verbal material is almost identical to the organization of the kinesic material.

(b) Both cultures utilize a dimension which can be broadly defined as deixis. This dimension appears both with the kinesic test and with the verbal test. However, the individual emblems which make up the dimension differ between Kikuyu and Maasai.

(c) Both cultures show a dimension which can be called evaluation, or more accurately, social closeness versus agonistic behavior.

(d) Both cultures do some sorting on the basis of body parts. In Maasai, several features augment the feature of plurality of body parts to account for the major cluster structures of the verbal and kinesic data. In Kikuyu, there is some classification by body parts within the kinesic data, reflecting a primary distinction between head and limbs, but this feature is not apparent in the verbal data. The sorting on the basis of body part may be a consequence of the iconic nature of many emblems.

*****

Given these findings, several hypotheses can be rejected:

(a) That the criteria used for sorting the emblems are mutually exclusive to the criteria used for sorting the verbal labels.

(b) That all sorting is done on the basis of meaning.

(c) That all sorting is done on the basis of physical performance attributes of the emblems.

(d) That no linkages exist between the verbal and kinesic criteria for sorting. The dimension of deixis is clearly a semantic dimension, but it is also a feature of physical performance.

The following hypotheses are supported:

(a) Members of the two cultures are able to respond to triads tests on body movements and, in so doing, to produce a structure which is clearly a product of shared organization of reality, rather than random or idiosyncratic responses.

(b) Kikuyu classification of emblems on the basis of body parts respects a primary distinction between the head and the limbs. This is consistent with Kikuyu body part classification (Burton and Kirk, unpublished).

(c) Both physical performance criteria and semantic criteria are used in the sorting of verbal as well as kinesic materials. The three modes of data analysis lend convergent support to this hypothesis. There appears to be at least a partial overlap between semantic and physical performance criteria, but the exact nature of the possible linkage is not yet apparent from the data.

(d) The organization of kinesic and verbal material is similar within languages; yet the organization of neither kinesic nor verbal material is similar across languages. Here we have two distinct languages. By a simplistic methodology involving elicitation of emblems for the two languages and elicitation of the indigenous and English labels for the emblems, it would be easy to jump to the conclusion that there were a number of emblematic universals, or, in the present case of a two-culture study, that there were a number of emblems which were shared by the two cultures. However, using the more sensitive tools of judged similarity analysis, we have shown that what appear to be the same emblems in terms of physical performance and elicited verbal labels are in fact distinct in the two language groups in terms of their cognitive organizations. That is, it appears here to be relatively inconsequential what the particular manifestation of the language: whether written, spoken, or emblematic — the cognitive organization seems to be consistent within languages and inconsistent across languages.

NOTES

1   Research on which this paper is based was done in Kenya between September, 1973 and July, 1974, supported by a grant from the Carnegie Foundation to the University of Nairobi. Triads tests in Kikuyu were administered by George Ndungu and Joseph Mwangi. Triads tests in Maasai were administered by Mosel ole Simel and Joseph ole Kipelian. We were also assisted in this project by Lydia Wangome, Edward Nganga and Rose Maina.
2   If there were a high degree of semantic sharing between Kikuyu and Maasai, then we would expect that the Kikuyu verbal test would have a positive correlation to the Maasai verbal test. As we shall see, this is not the case.
3   In order to do this, it is necessary to return to the raw frequency data, and re-compute it on the basis of triads which contain only these seven emblems. There are ten such triads out of the original 24 triads. Removal of the other 14 triads produces an unbalanced design. Some pairs of emblems are represented in two triads, some in one triad, and two in no triads. Consequently, correlations based on the reduced set of emblems are not as reliable as correlations based on the full set of emblems (Burton and Nerlove, unpublished).
4   Two-tailed test of null hypothesis that the correlation is zero.
5   Two-tailed test of null hypothesis that the correlation is zero.

REFERENCES

Burton, M.L. and L.Kirk
 Unpublished "Cognitive Organization of Body Parts".
Burton, M.L. and S.B.Nerlove
 Unpublished "Balanced Designs for Triads Tests: Two Examples from English".
D'Andrade, R.G.
 Unpublished "The All-Possible Pairs Method of Cluster Analysis".
Ekman, P. and W.V.Friesen
 1972 "Hand Movements", *The Journal of Communication*, 22: 353-374.
Johnson, S.C.
 1967 "Hierarchical Clustering Schemes", *Psychometrika*, 32: 241-254.
Kruskal, J.B.
 1964 "Multidimensional scaling by optimizing goodness of fit to a nonmetric hypothesis", *Psychometrika*, 29: 1-27.
Romney, A.K. and R.G.D'Andrade
 1964 "Cognitive Aspects of English Kin Terms", *American Anthropologist*, 66 (3), Part 2: 147-170.
Shepard, R.N.
 1962 "The Analysis of proximities", *Psychometrika*, 27: 125-140.
Young, F.W. and W.W.Torgerson
 1968 "*TORSCA*, a Fortran IV Program for Shepard-Kruskal Multidimensional Scaling Analysis", *Behavioral Science*, 12: 498.

476

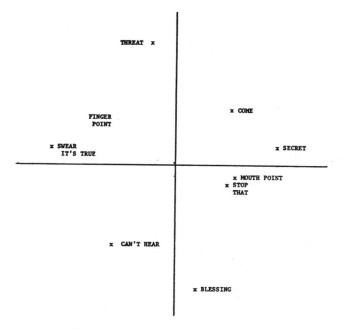

Fig. 1. Two-dimensional Scaling of Maasai Kinesic Data. Stress = .167

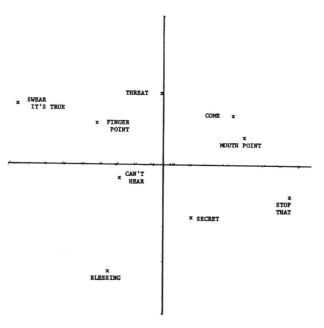

Fig. 2. Two-dimensional Scaling of Maasai Verbal Data Stress = .155

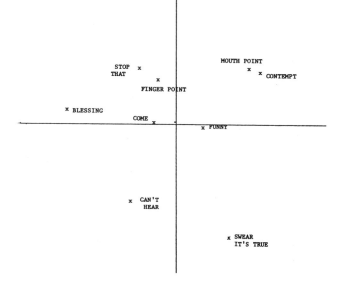

Fig. 3. Three-dimensional Scaling of Kikuyu Kinesic Data. Stress = .062
Plot of dimension 1 against dimension 2.

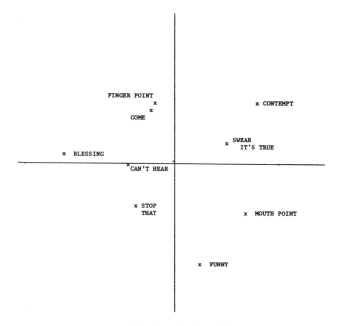

Fig. 4. Three-dimensional Scaling of Kikuyu Kinesic Data. Stress = .062
Plot of dimension 1 against dimension 3.

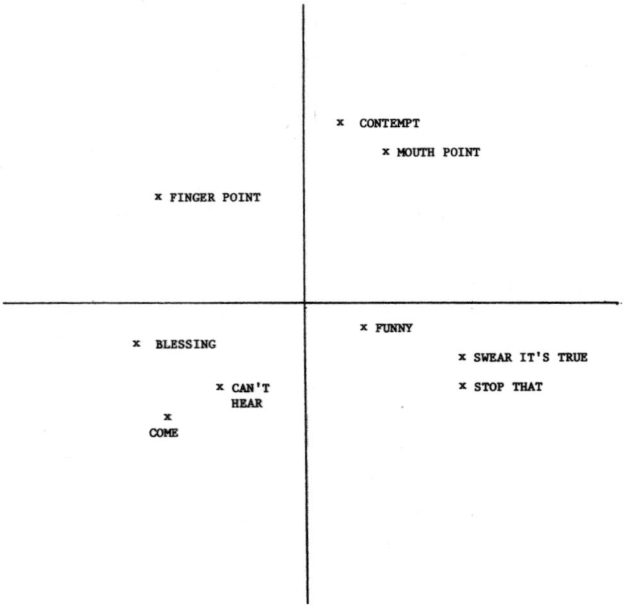

Fig. 5. Three-dimensional Scaling of Kikuyu Verbal Data. Stress = .093
Plot of dimension 1 against dimension 2.

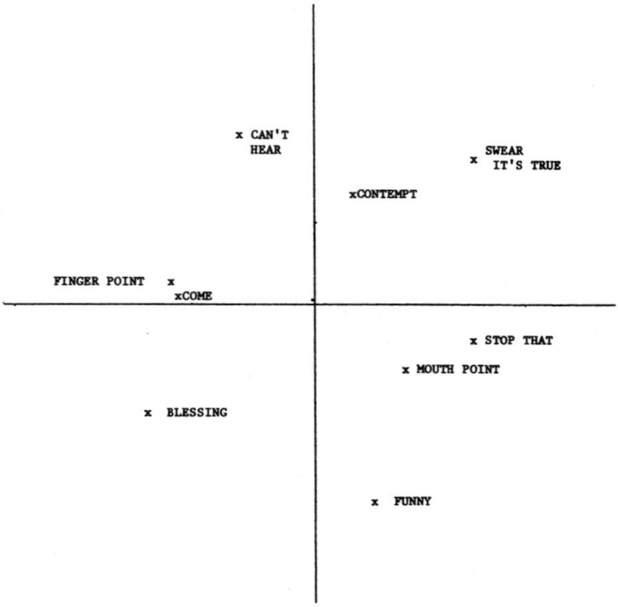

Fig. 6. Three-dimensional Scaling of Kikuyu Verbal Data. Stress = .093
Plot of dimension 1 against dimension 3.

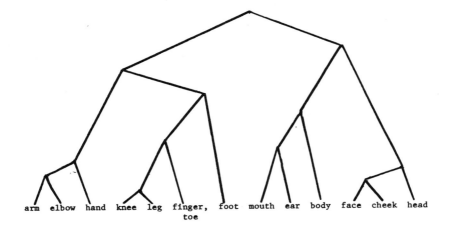

Fig. 7. Hierarchical Clustering of Body Parts (Maasai)

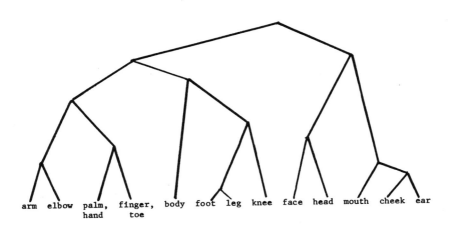

Fig. 8. Hierarchical Clustering of Body Parts (Kikuyu)

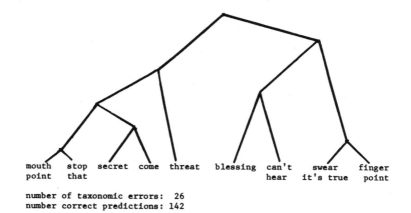

number of taxonomic errors: 26
number correct predictions: 142

Fig. 9. Hierarchical Clustering of Maasai Kinesic Data.

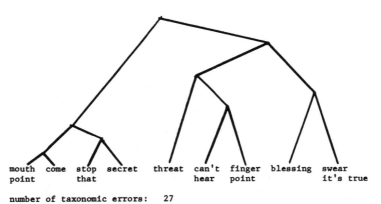

number of taxonomic errors: 27
number correct predictions: 141

Fig. 10. Hierarchical Clustering of Maasai Verbal Data.

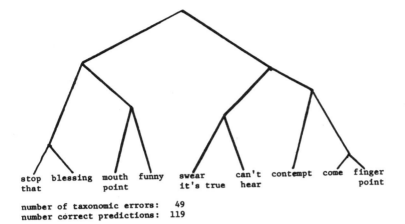

number of taxonomic errors: 49
number correct predictions: 119

Fig. 11. Hierarchical Clustering of Kikuyu Kinesic Data.

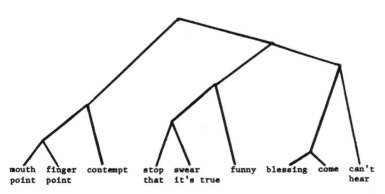

number of taxonomic errors: 51
number correct predictions: 117

Fig. 12. Hierarchical Clustering of Kikuyu Verbal Data.

HOWARD M. ROSENFELD, MARILYN SHEA,
and PAUL GREENBAUM

Facial Emblems of "Right" and "Wrong": Topographical Analysis and Derivation of a Recognition Test[1]

INTRODUCTION

The ability to determine when one's behavior evokes a positive or a negative reaction from other persons is fundamental for normal socialization and for satisfactory interpersonal relationships. Such information commonly is communicated via the verbal-vocal channels, kinesically, or combinatorially. When either consistent or conflicting evaluative messages are given over multiple channels, the kinesic tends to be most believable (Argyle, Alkema, and Gilmour 1972, Bugental, Kaswan, and Love 1970, Burns and Beier 1973, Levitt 1964, Mehrabian and Ferris 1967, Williams 1975, Zeidel and Mehrabian 1969). Whether the kinesic signals disconfirm associated verbal messages, or whether they accent, amplify, or substitute for them, clearly it is important to be able to decode them. The goals of the present study were to identify common kinesic forms of conveying positive and negative reactions and to derive from this normative information a test of ability to recognize such reactions. It was assumed that deficiency in this skill may account for some learning problems, and that competence generally is trainable.

To derive a comprehensive catalog of positive and negative reactions, a representative sampling of all classes of socially significant learning situations and occupants would be required. A more feasible and limited approach was selected for the present investigation. Positive and negative nonverbal reactions of normal adults were recorded in a specially constructed situation in which a substantial range of common forms was likely to be displayed and in which the forms could be interpreted unambiguously.

The situation itself was described in detail by Shea and Rosenfeld (1976). Briefly, it consisted of a two-way closed-circuit television network over which one person in each of 40 dyads tried to teach the other person to select the correct word in each of a consecutive set of ten word-pairs. To assure ample opportunities for the learner to give both correct and incorrect answers, the words in each pair were pretested to be equally likely to be selected. To evoke sufficient, but nonstereotypic, communication via the kinesic channel, the majority of the teachers were instructed to give feedback only in the form of positive and negative points to be delivered via hidden footpedals which actually were inoperative. Such teachers thereby were unobtrusively induced to display subtle nonverbal reactions in order to provide effective feedback to the student about his or her performance. Inasmuch as the head and face area is capable of the most differentiated expressions of positive and negative reactions (Ekman and Friesen 1969, Vine 1970), the video image of teachers presented to students was limited to that area of the body.

Shea and Rosenfeld demonstrated that approximately half of the 30 learners in the subtle conditions learned all of their items from their respective teachers, as did half of the 10 learners whose teachers were instructed to use nonverbal communication intentionally to aid in the learning process. Thus, it was necessary to infer that substantial nonverbal communication had occurred. Further confirmation was provided when two randomly selected blocks of ten responses from each of the 40 teachers were randomly edited from videotape records and subsequently presented to four independent judges who guessed whether each response indicated 'right' or 'wrong'. The degree of consensus among the judges of the 800 responses showed that there was more information about correct and incorrect performance available from the teachers' reactions than was utilized by the students.

The specific goals of the present study were to reliably code the consensually judged reactions of teachers for features and configurations of head and face movements, to determine statistically which of the coded response forms typically served as emblems of 'right' and 'wrong', to construct a brief but representative videotape test of ability to identify the emblems, and to validate the randomly-ordered items (behavioral episodes) of the test by administering it to new groups of judges. For clarity of presentation, our report of the attainment of these goals is arbitrarily subclassified into two studies.

STUDY I: IDENTIFICATION OF EMBLEMS OF 'RIGHT' AND 'WRONG'

First, to provide more substantial evidence of the consensual inter-pretability of the videotaped episodes of teacher reactions, a block of 10 of them from each of the 40 teachers was presented to a new group of 11 judges. The judges were recruited from an introductory psychology course at the University of Kansas. (The teacher-student dyads on the original learning study also were undergraduates from the same university, mostly majors in elementary education, human relations, and psychology.) The product-moment correlation between the mean judgments of 'right' or 'wrong' over the 400 items by the new 11 judges and the prior four judges was .77, indicating that a significant and substantial amount of emblematic information was contained in the tapes.

The two sequences of ten videotaped responses of 28 of the original 40 teachers were retained for further analysis. To be retained, at least 80% of a teacher's responses had to be correctly judged by three of the four initial judges. These 28 teachers constituted 20 of the 30 teachers from the subtle teaching conditions and eight of the ten from the more blatant condition. The two ratios are not significantly different $(X^2 (1df) = .16)$. Eighteen of the 28 retained teachers had succeeded in bringing their students to perfect performance, while only two of the 12 excluded teachers had students who mastered the task. These proportions are significantly different $(X^2 (1df) = 5.83, p < .02)$, indicating that the sample to be coded consisted primarily of the most effective nonverbal communicators from the original teaching situation. However, one clear bias resulted from the exclusion of the 12 ineffective teachers: fewer reactions to wrong than to right answers were included (184 versus 248). Thus, in the statistical analyses of nonverbal content of emblems of right and wrong, to be reported below, this disproportionality is taken into account. Otherwise the contents of emblems of right would be confounded with the greater overall activity levels of effective teachers.

Next, the coding of the remaining 560 teacher responses (20 per teacher) was initiated. The coding was accomplished by successive approximations. Initially, 36 definitions of kinesic movement and configuration were derived from the work of Birdwhistell (1970:259-60). A preliminary inspection of the teacher responses by the authors and two additional coders who were familiar with the scoring system indicated that 128 of the responses were not scorable due to insufficient quality of the video image. Thus, the final sample selected for coding consisted of 432 responses from the 28 teachers. Next the coders applied the 36-category scoring system to a subset of 50 of the responses to estimate both normative occurrences and scoring reliability. Events identified by coders were compared within .5 second intervals. In general, categories were eliminated if they occurred rarely, nearly always, or if intercoder reliability coefficients of agreement failed to reach 70 percent.[2] A final coding system consisting of 13 measures was adopted. While reliable coding of the starting and stopping times of most categories within one-half second agreement was found to be possible, the number and temporal distribution of data points (including repetitions of a form within an episode) proved to be excessively time-consuming to code and potentially unwieldy to analyze. Thus, a check-list coding system was selected, in which each episode of a teacher response was scored only as containing or not containing each of the 13 code categories.

The following code categories were employed:

Head movement:

NOD:	A multidirectional rotation along the vertical plane.
SHAKE:	A multidirectional rotation along the lateral plane.
TILT:	A discrete unidirectional diagonal displacement.

Mouth corners:

NORMAL:	Corners predominantly pointing in same direction as lip line; scored either as a continuation of a baseline position (prior to point of student response) or as a return from another corner position.
UP:	A movement upward from or past the normal position; omitted where smile configuration is scorable; includes continuation of baseline "up" position.
DOWN:	A movement downward from or past the normal position; includes continuation from baseline.

Lip pressure:

NORMAL (relaxed):	Absence of pressure; scored either as a continuation of a baseline position or as a return from another lip pressure position.
PRESS:	Pressing of lips together, without

changing distance between corners; not scored where smile configuration occurs; includes continuation from baseline.

SPREAD PRESS: Pressing of lips together along with increasing the distance between the corners; not scored where smile configuration occurs; includes continuation from baseline.

Other facial configurations:

OVAL: Horizontal separation of lips from a normal position; includes continuation from baseline.

SMILE(s): Raising or stretching of mouth corners along with upward movement of labial folds of cheeks, often resulting in pouching of skin below eyes; corners need not be up but configuration must give impression of 'smile' as colloquially comprehended by coder[3] (the resulting configuration is categorized into closed mouth or open mouth variety); includes continuation from baseline.

FALLEN FACE: A general relaxation of facial muscles from any configuration, resulting in a decrease in muscle tonus beyond normal or baseline level.

To determine the reliability of the check-list coding procedure, four coders applied 11 of the 13 categories to a substantial sample of the teacher responses. The closed-mouth variant of smile and the discrimination of spread-press from press were decided upon subsequent to the reliability check. Coders were unaware of the performance of the learner. Average intercoder coefficients of agreement for 10 of the 11 categories were 90% or greater. Insufficient tilts occurred in the reliability sample to permit valid computation. Data from the coder who agreed to the greatest degree with all other coders were selected as most valid. Although average intercoder consensus per item was an alternative possibility, it was decided that within-coder consistency was a preferred criterion, especially given the reasonably high overall reliability of the coders.

To determine the contributions of the coded nonverbal behaviors to the emblematic communication of right and wrong, three procedures were used: (1) the degree to which each nonverbal category was associated with teacher responses that followed right and wrong answers of students was assessed, regardless of possible co-occurrences among the categories; (2) a cluster analysis was performed on the categories, and the association of each cluster with 'right' and 'wrong' was computed; (3) a stepwise discriminant type of analysis was performed on expressions of 'right' versus 'wrong' to estimate the optimal cumulative contributions of categories and of possible inter-actions among them. The last procedure also was used to estimate optimal contributions of the nonverbal categories to the accuracy scores of the original four judges who had guessed the functions of the teacher responses but had not coded them. This permitted a com-parison of information that was available in the coded nonverbal responses to right and wrong performances — their *referential* func-tion — with the information attributed to them by judges — their *inferential* function. The greater the agreement between the two measures, the greater was the nonverbal *communication* of informa-tion from teachers to observers by means of the coded categories.[4]

The results of the first analysis — the referential functions of coded nonverbal categories — are displayed in Table 1. The head movement categories proved to have strong emblematic functions. Head nods were the most common head movements (24% of sample). Ninety-four percent of them followed right answers (p $<$.001 by Chi Square test comparing proportion of nod and proportion of non-nod teacher responses associated with right and with wrong student performances). Head shakes, which occurred in 11% of the sample, were associated with wrong responses 98% of the time (p $<$.001). Tilts, comprising a rare 2% (the minimum acceptable in the present study), indicated 'wrong' in 89% of their occurrences (p $<$.01).

Open-mouth smiles, which were coded in 13% of the sample, indicated 'right' 71% of the time (p $<$.05). Fallen faces, occurring in 3% of the sample, indicated 'wrong' 82% of the times they occurred (p $<$.01). Contrary to common conceptions, the closed-mouth smile was not a significant indicator of 'right'. Furthermore, upward move-ments of the lips in the absence of smiles were associated with wrong responses (p $<$.05). Spread pressed lips also were associated with wrong responses (p $<$.05).

The cluster analysis of the coded nonverbal responses was per-formed by the K-MEANS computer program (MacQueen 1967) in which clusters of components that tend to co-occur are separated from other clusters of components with which they tend not to overlap. Following the suggestions of MacQueen, parameters were

TABLE 1

Referential Functions of Nonverbal Components[a]

Nonverbal component	% of Rights (N = 248)	% of Wrongs (N = 184)	Chi Square	P
Head movement				
Nod	39	3	72.4	.001
Shake	0	25	63.4	.001
Tilt	0	4	8.1	.01
Mouth configuration				
Open smile	17	9	4.8	.05
Closed smile	16	13	0.6	NS
Fallen (slack)	1	5	7.1	.01
Oval	17	17	0.4	NS
Mouth corners				
Normal	59	63	0.6	NS
Up (nonsmile)	8	16	6.2	.05
Down	8	10	0.9	NS
Lip pressure				
Normal	43	48	0.9	NS
Press	15	13	0.5	NS
Spread press	4	9	4.9	.05

[a] Components listed occurred in at least 2% of 432 responses from the 28 teachers who provided emblematic information. Referential function refers to relative proportion of right and wrong performances of students that were followed by the component. Due to the higher association of low performing learners with the 12 excluded teachers, there were fewer wrong than right performances in the coded sample.

systematically varied so as to include the maximum number of teacher responses within the minimum number of clusters of components. The results of the parametric variant of the cluster analysis that provided optimal interpretable information (entry parameter set at .08 and collapse parameter at .04) are shown in Table 2. A given teacher response could occur in only one cluster. Decision rules for including a cluster in the table were that the cluster had to be repeated in at least five teacher responses and that it had to be 'significantly' associated with (follow) right or wrong answers of learners using the liberal criterion of $p < .10$ by Chi Square test.

Three clusters indicative of 'right' emerged, and four representing 'wrong'. Several of these clusters were heavily loaded with multiple components. Particularly noteworthy was that none of the clusters indicating 'right' was dominated by head nods. Rather, head nods tended to be distributed across clusters indicative of both right and wrong. Thus, atheoretical constructions of nonverbal response classes on the basis of co-occurrence would appear to be a non-optimal strategy for identifying emblems of right and wrong.

Still, several clusters provided useful information that was complementary to that derived from the prior analysis of individual components. Cluster No. 1, heavily based, respectively, on pressed lips, mouth corners down, and head nod, was indicative of 'right' in 100% of its 10 occurrences (p <.01). Thus, the addition of an emphatic mouth movement to the head nod made it a virtually unambiguous referent to right answers. Pressed lips in combination with a head shake had the opposite effect, as shown in Cluster 2 (p <.01). Cluster No. 5, which contained both spreadpressed lips and mouth corners down in all five occurrences, indicated 'wrong' in all but one instance (p <.10), and only the latter instance included the occurrence of a head nod. The combination of corners up and pressed lips in Cluster 6 was significantly indicative of wrong (p <.05). The remaining clusters reflected trends similar to those reported in the prior analysis of single components, except that the closed mouth smile reached marginal significance in Cluster 7 (p <.10).

The third method utilized the MAID program (Gillo 1972), a discriminant type of analysis of variance. In this procedure the component which accounts for the largest proportion of variance in the dependent variable (here, which best separates right from wrong responses) is listed first. Subsequently, a branching operation takes place, in which the two levels of the predictor (presence versus absence of the component) are themselves subdivided on the basis of the remaining variable which adds the next most discrimination. In this way it is possible to derive branches composed of sets of variables which are indicative of relatively optimal component and interactive-component discriminators of right and wrong. Results are shown in Table 3. Again, decision rules were applied to identify a predictor: It had to add at least two percent to the amount of variance accounted for prior to its emergence, and it had to be present in at least five responses, as well as absent in an additional five, at its level of occurrence in the tree structure.

In the prediction of right versus wrong answers of students, eight predictors met these criteria. Essentially, they provide information similar to that resulting from the earlier analysis of individual components. That is, most predictors were single variables; only one contained a combination or interaction of variables. But an advan-

TABLE 2

Referential Functions of Nonverbal Clusters[a]

Cluster components	% of Rights	% of Wrongs	Chi Square	P
1. Press (100), down (90), nod (80), up (20), normal closed (20), open smile (10), corners normal (10)	4	0	7.6	.01
2. Spread press (100), shake (80), corners normal (50), up (20), open smile (10)	0	5	9.4	.01
3. Fallen (100), corners normal (100), normal closed (100), open smile (17)	0	3	4.1	.05
4. Open smile (100), nod (40), up (7)	15	4	12.6	.001
5. Spread press (100), down (100), nod (20), shake (20), corners normal (20), up (20)	0	2	2.9	.10
6. Corners up (100), press (93), shake (47), nod (27), down (20)	2	6	6.0	.05
7. Closed smile (100), corners normal (29), normal closed (22), nod (22), shake (10)	14	9	3.0	.10

[a] Clusters were identified by the K-MEANS computer program (MacQueen 1967), with parameters arbitrarily set at 'entry' = .08 and 'collapse' = .04. Clusters are listed which include at least 5 teacher responses and which followed right or wrong learner performers at $p < .10$ level of significance by Chi Square test. Percent of items in cluster that contain component is indicated in parentheses.

tage of the discriminant procedure was that it indicated that the effects of the individual components generally were independent of each other. In essential agreement with the results of the individual component analysis, the discriminant analysis showed that the best predictors are respectively, head nod, head shake, and fallen face. Also open-mouthed smile and head tilt are included, although at lower levels in the predictive ladder. Additional information provided by the discriminant analysis is that spread-pressed lips tend to indicate 'wrong' when occurring in the absence of nods and shakes. Also mouth corners up, when they occur essentially in isolation from other categories (including most smiles, by our arbitrary definition), refer to wrong responses. But the single component and the cluster procedures had revealed a similar trend.

However, only the discriminant analysis showed that the combination of normal closed mouth and corners up is indicative of right responses. A possible explanation is that corners up by themselves tend to be continuations of a baseline expression indicative of amiable anticipation of an answer, which often turns out to be a wrong

TABLE 3

Cumulative Referential and Inferential Meanings Predictable from Nonverbal Components and Configurations[a]

Components and Configurations	Meaning	
	Referential	Inferential
	(N = 432)	
Head nod	15.4% R	9.9% R
Head shake	8.9 W	8.2 W
	(N = 150)	
Fallen	3.9 W	—
Spread press	3.4 W	—
Tilt	3.0 W	—
Corners up (CU)	7.7 W	7.3 W
Normal closed	—	2.6 W
Normal closed +CU	3.3 R	2.1 W
Open smile	2.4 R	2.8 R

[a] Referential meaning indicates conditions of usage by teacher; inferential meaning indicates judgments about teacher usage by observers. Predictors were identified by the MAID computer program (Gillo 1971). Each predictive component, occurring in the absence of the components listed above it, added the amount of predicted variance shown. Criteria for inclusion in the table were (1) augmentation of variance-accounted-for by at least 2%, (2) a minimum of 10 responses in the component category at the level listed, and (3) a minimum of 5 responses in each binary sub-category (occurrences and nonoccurrences). Only nod and shake met the criteria in the full sample of 432 responses. An additional analysis was done on the 150 responses that excluded nods and shakes, as well as neutrals and any responses consisting only of corners normal, normal closed, and/or oval in the absence of additional components. Dominant meaning symbolized by R for 'right', and W for 'wrong'.

answer, whereas the shift from a normal mouth line to corners up tends to occur in reaction to a correct answer.

Table 3 also uses the discriminant procedure to determine the communicative functions of the nonverbal forms. It shows the degree to which a group of observers of the teachers' responses used the nonverbal information in them (or unidentified correlated information) to correctly judge the emblematic meaning of the responses as 'right' or 'wrong'. Such communication occurred in the case of four predictors: head nod, head shake, open-mouth smile, and mouth corners up. However, the judges apparently failed to identify the head tilt, fallen face, or spread pressed lips at the levels at which their referential functions were revealed. Also, the judges apparently misinterpreted the combination of normal mouth and corners up which tended to be indicative of a right response, scoring it most often as wrong. Finally, it should be noted that only the judges apparently interpreted the normal closed mouth response in itself to be indicative of a wrong response.

STUDY II: DERIVATION AND VALIDATION OF A RECOGNITION TEST

The next step in this project was to construct a test of ability to recognize the nonverbal emblems of 'right' and 'wrong' which were identified in the preceding stages of research. Our goal was to identify a subset of the reliably-coded teacher behaviors which would be representative of their normative occurrences and in which each item would be accurately identifiable as an emblem of right or wrong at a significant level of consensus by normal adult observers. A major purpose for constructing the test was to identify groups and individuals who deviated from these normative adult performances. Consequently, a test length was sought that would be sufficiently short to maintain the attention of young children and other persons likely to have brief spans of attention or of task persistence. Also, two equivalent forms of the test were sought so that one could be used for testing and training, and the second for assessing generalization of training.

The first step in the procedure was to select 50 emblematic items from the 432 coded teacher responses. It will be recalled that all of the coded items had been judged as indicating 'right' or 'wrong' by four observers and that a random half of these same items also were judged by an additional 11 observers. From the latter half of the data, 30 items were selected, each of which was correctly judged by at least 3 of the 4 original judges as well as 10 of the 11 judges from the second group. From the other half of the items, 20 were selected in which all four of the judges accurately identified the emblematic meaning of the teacher's response. All of the selected items contained face and head activities that had been identified as reliably associated with emblematic usage in Study I, except for neutrals.

Items coded as neutral were selected for the test according to two additional criteria: (1) each was judged as indicating right and wrong equally often by the four original judges, and (2) each was selected from a block of 10 teacher responses in which all prior responses also were coded neutral, although the correctness of the prior responses varied. Thus, we refer to the selected items as *true neutrals* in that they were neutral not only topographically but further, as a class, they were not interpretable as 'right' or 'wrong' on the basis of the context of their prior usage.

The fifty responses were edited onto a new videotape, in random order, and presented to a new group of 10 college student judges. Using the criterion that at least seven of the 10 students had to correctly identify the emblematic meaning of the item, 11 items were eliminated. Their contents varied widely, including seven different configurations of nonverbal categories. Apparent reasons for their low interpretability were low quality of duplications, minimality of coded response in size or duration, confusion of particular teachers' characteristic forward leans during task presentation with head nods, and presentation of an item out of its 10-trial context. (Both of the previous judge groups had viewed each teacher response in the context of its original block of 10 consecutive responses, and thus had a 'baseline' of prior behaviors available for interpreting most items.) The current (third) judge group also rated the certainty of their decision to label each response 'right' of 'wrong', using a five-point scale ranging from 'very certain' to 'very uncertain'. The correlation between the percent correct judgment per item and its mean certainty rating was .87, indicating that the rejected items tended to be unclear to the judges. This conclusion was further supported by the absence of bimodality of judgments of the set of rejected items.[5]

A final version of the recognition test was constructed. The 39 items that were validated by the third judge group were retained. An additional 17 items were selected such that the total of 56 items contained two subsets of 28 items each, the subsets being matched for frequencies of occurrence of major emblematic features and configurations. Fourteen of the 17 additional items were selected on the basis of consensus of the first two judge groups. To make the two subtests apparently equivalent, three items had to be selected from original videotape records which had not been included in any prior judge or coding samples. These items were selected by the coder who previously had established the highest intercoder reliability. The 28 items in each subtest included 14 indicative of 'right', 12 meaning 'wrong', and 2 neutrals.

The 28 items within each of the two matched sets were randomly edited onto a new videotape. They were validated on two additional samples of available judges.[6] The fourth group of judges was comprised of 18 female undergraduates in a speech therapy class at the University of Kansas. The first nine students to arrive in class were presented the two subtests in the order AB, and the remaining nine subsequently received BA. As with the prior judge group, each judge marked her answer sheet for each item as 'right' or 'wrong' and also marked a five point scale indicating her certainty.

Mean accuracy and certainty over items correlated .66. Performances were submitted to analyses of variance due to test form, judge subgroup, and 'right' and 'wrong' item subsets. With neutrals scored as meaning 'wrong' (making 14 'rights' and 14 'wrongs' in each form), there were no significant differences between the test forms in accuracy of judgments of either neutral items considered as a separate category, or in total score. Nor were there significant differences in certainty ratings of neutrals, 'wrongs', 'rights', or total scores.

However, two unexpected significant differences were found. Wrongs were more accurately identified than 'rights' (p <.001), and the AB subgroup performed better than the BA subgroup (p <.05). Inspection of performances on the individual items showed that subjects had difficulty with five of the 28 'right' items. Three were head nods of low amplitude and two were smiles — one a relatively nonexcursive closed-mouth variant and the other a relatively toothy crescent that might have been interpreted as hostile. Also, one 'negative mouth' (corners down and lips pressed) in Form A was misjudged by the majority possibly because the downward movement of the mouth corners occurred at the end of the episode after a prolonged pressed-lip response, which could have been interpreted as 'not bad'. In five of the six problematic items, judge-group AB made more errors than did group BA, and the discrepancy was greatest in Form B. Our general interpretation is that the AB group, which included more 'latecomers' to the scheduled test-time and which had to wait for the BA group to finish, was likely to have been more unmotivated than the first-run group. Still, when items were collapsed into fourteen subsets (Table 4) based upon common emblematic components or configurations, all subsets were judged significantly accurately in both test forms by both judge groups (using 50% accuracy as random expected performance). Also none of the six problematic items was judged significantly opposite to prediction. In fact, with the exception of one neutral item scored as negative by only 78% of the subjects in Form A, the remaining 50 items ranged from a minimum of 89% of the judges being accurate to 100%. Thirty-one of these items were accurately identified by 100% of the judges.

Limitations of judge group 4 were its relatively small size, its monosexual make-up, and the likelihood that the AB subgroup lacked motivation, particularly by the time they reached the Form B items.

Consequently, a fifth judge group was tested. It consisted of 33 undergraduates in an advanced psychology class, approximately equally divided between males and females. Because of time restrictions, subjects were presented the items at one sitting, using a 21 inch (53.34 cm) video monitor, and in the order AB.

There were no significant differences in overall performance due to test form or sex of judge. Also no items were significantly misjudged, and only one item was not accurately judged by the majority — the delayed negative mouth in Form A which also was problematic for the prior judge group. The other five items that had been problematic for the prior AB judge group were all judged significantly accurately by the present judge group.

A nonsignificant trend in the fifth judge group that has procedural implications for future usage of the test was that students who sat at the rear and sides of the room (7.16 m deep by 7.92 m wide) had slightly more difficulty with subtle items such as low excursion head nods and neutrals than did students seated more toward the center and front of the room. Inability of more distantly situated students in classrooms to decode subtle facial cues of teachers may account for the finding by other researchers that such students are less involved, less successful, and less attracted to their teachers (Becker, Summer, Bee and Oxley 1973, Koneya 1976). Of course, it also is possible that student personality affects their selection of seats.

The students in the fifth judge group also rated each of the 56 items for the degree to which it expressed 'positivity' or 'negativity', using a 17-point scale with 9 as the midpoint. The mean ratings of all six subsets of items emblematic of 'right' were on the positive side, ranging from 10 to 13; all eight subsets emblematic of 'wrong' were rated on the negative side, ranging from 5 to 8. The mean ratings corresponded closely to the mean accuracy of judgments. However, it is particularly noteworthy that the modal rating of 'neutrals' was 9 (midpoint), even though neutrals were judged as emblematic of 'wrong' 78% of the time.

At this point in the project the investigators felt that sufficient evidence had been accumulated to indicate that the test was valid, that it provided a reasonably representative sample of the more characteristic and consensual emblems of 'right' and 'wrong' that had appeared in the original teaching situation explored by Shea and Rosenfeld (1976). The main structural features of the 56-item test are shown in Table 4, along with the unweighted average accuracy scores of judge groups 4 and 5 (total of 51 judges). It should be noted that the categorization of items and subsets of items is based

TABLE 4

Recognition of Nonverbal Feedback from Teachers: Test Structure and Performance of College Students

| Item Components | | Replications | | Mean % |
| Head | Mouth | N[a] | % Uninstructed[b] | Accuracy[c] |
(Dominant 'right')				
Nod	Smile-open	4	50	97
Nod	Smile-closed	4	50	97
Nod	Press	4	50	96
Nod	Normal	10	50	90
	Smile-open	4	75	82
	Smile-closed	2	100	69
(Dominant 'wrong')				
Shake	Smile-open	2	0	100
Shake	Smile-closed	4	50	98
Shake	Press	4	0	100
Shake	Normal	4	50	98
Tilt		2	100	98
	Negative	4	75	82
	Fallen	4	100	92
	Neutral	4	75	78

[a] Test items include 23 of the 28 teachers who reliably emitted nonverbal emblems.

[b] 'Uninstructed' indicates nonverbal behaviors that occurred under conditions in which they were implicitly prohibited.

[c] 'Accuracy' refers to agreement with dominant referential function (right, wrong). Percentages were obtained from test performances of 51 university students.

upon their inclusion of dominant emblematic features. Thus variations in topography (e.g., excursiveness and timing) and inclusion of additional emblematic information within a set of items were possible.

Salient features are that the items that represented emblems of 'right' were comprised mainly of head nods. These were subclassified into four sets according to concomitant mouth configurations. When the nod was displayed with an open or closed mouth smile or with pressed lips, the average correct judgment of 'right' was highest, ranging from 96% to 97% of the judges. When the nod was accompanied by a normal mouth, the consensus dropped to 90%. While one may be tempted to interpret the difference as due to the presence versus absence of mouth activity, another possible determinant is that the nods that accompany normal mouths are less blatant than are those that occur with active mouth movements. An additional study, in which larger samples of each of these two categories were analyzed, found support for both interpretations (Rosenfeld and MacRoberts 1977). The remaining items in the 'right' category, all containing smiles but no nods, were less consensually judged, with open-mouth smiles at 82% and closed-mouth smiles at 69%.

Of the items representing emblems of 'wrong' a rather parallel distribution of categories is apparent. Head shakes were included in half of these items and, in turn, were subclassified into the four varieties of mouth configuration that had accompanied nods (except that the lips under 'shake-press' were spread than the nod-press items). Shakes were virtually consensually identified as indicating 'wrong', regardless of mouth activity, with average percentages of judge agreement across subsets ranging from 98 to 100%. The one other head movement included in 'wrongs' was the tilt which also was accurately judged at 98%. The two active emblems of 'wrong' which lacked codable head movements were less consensually scored, with the fallen face judged accurately by 92% and the negative mouth by 82%. Finally, neutrals, which were included as emblematic of 'wrong' were so scored by 78% of the judges.

In interpreting the differences in percent agreement among judges across the different subcategories several points should be kept in mind. The percentages were closely related to ratings of certainty and attributions of positivity and negativity. Also the percentages corresponded quite closely to the actual consistencies of referential meaning of the categories. Study I showed that 98% of head shakes by teachers followed wrong responses of learners, as did 89% of tilts; and 94% of nods followed right responses. The facial categories correspondingly had less consistent emblematic usage, with 71% of open-mouth smiles and 62% of closed-mouth following right responses, and 82% of fallen faces following wrong responses. And 80% of negative mouths, represented by Configuration 5 of Table 2, followed wrong responses. Thus, although judges could only make a binary choice of 'right' or 'wrong' on a given item, average group judgements or pooled inferential meanings were amazingly close to actual probabilities of referential meaning of the various nonverbal subcategories.

Table 4 also shows that the majority of items in the test, particularly the more subtle ones, had occurred in social circumstances in which the teachers could reasonably be assumed not to have intentionally posed the responses. This is in contrast to typical conditions under which positive and negative nonverbal behaviors have been identified (e.g., Bugental, Kaswan, and Love 1970, Rosenthal, Archer, DiMatteo, Koivumaki, and Rogers 1974).[7] Consequently, performance on the present test should have considerable external validity in representing ability to identify typical variations in subtlety within each category.

Finally, the limited aims of the present approach to identification of emblems and test construction should be kept in mind. The primary purpose was to objectively identify dominant emblematic features and configurations that are clearly used by normal adults. The circumstances in which they occurred lend confidence that they reflect emblems that adults commonly communicate to each other. It is our tentative, but untested, assumption that adults also use such emblems when with children, both normal and nonnormal. At minimum, it is reasonable to assume that the ability of children to correctly interpret the emblems when they observe them in inter-adult communication is an important basis of modeling of normative forms of communication and of vicarious or incidental learning of socially desirable and undesirable behavior. The test is not intended to be a useful psychometric tool for assessing the ability of normal adults to recognize emblems, because the items were selected for their ceiling effects rather than their capacity to detect individual differences. Certainly more rare, subtle, probabilistic, and ambivalent (e.g., face versus voice) emblems of 'right' and 'wrong' could be identified.

The present test was constructed for the limited purpose of assessing ability to identify common and relatively unambiguous positive and negative emblems among younger subject groups, particularly those known to have difficulties in academic situations. Research in progress indicates that normal children up to the earliest grades of elementary school have considerable difficulty in identifying subtle negative emblems and that educable retarded children in public school systems have additional difficulties with subtle positive expressions. Other populations to which the test has been applied are children of normal intelligence who are either deaf or learning disabled. The different groups are showing both idiosyncratic problems in identifying subsets of emblems as well as developmental trends in common. While differences between such groups in performance on the test can be interpreted properly only within the context of their particular environments and histories, the results of applications to date suggest that the test has considerable promise as a tool for the diagnosis and improvement of a fundamental social skill.

NOTES

[1] The research reported herein was conducted in the Social Behavior Laboratory at the Kansas Center for Mental Retardation and Human Development. Partial support was provided by NICHHD Program Project Grant 00870, subproject on Extralinguistic Communication, OEC Grant 3-7-070706-3118, and University of Kansas General Research Grant 3909 and Biomedical Sciences Grant 4226.
[2] Examples of movements excluded due to infrequent usage are tongue thrust, circular mouth. tight closing of eyelids, raised brow, and furrowed brow. The aid of Ronald Warman and Philip McLaughlin in coding the data is gratefully acknowledged.
[3] Rosenfeld (1966) found that a subjective definition of smile produced better interobserver agreement than did several efforts at objective definition.
[4] The concept of 'emblem' as defined by Ekman and Friesen (1969) is based upon consensual interpretation in a population and thus emphasizes its inferential function. Weiner, Devoe, Rubinow, and Geller (1972) have recommended that the concept of nonverbal communication be limited to behaviors that are interpreted by receivers in accord with their meaning to senders. In the present research the referential meaning of emblems is inferred from objective criteria: the situational contexts in which the emblems are enacted. However, we do not assume that communicative emblems are necessarily consciously enacted, particularly the more subtle ones that contain components of affect displays.
[5] We are indebted to Dr. Paul Ekman for alerting us to the possibility that judges could split into subsets who attributed opposite meanings to an item, which would imply disagreement rather than lack of information.
[6] The authors appreciate the help of Dr. James Lingwall in the recruitment of Group 4, and of Robert McRoberts in the data analysis of Group 5.
[7] For further discussion of the implications of posed versus naturalistic expressions see Ekman, Friesen, and Ellsworth 1972:35-38, 95-102.

REFERENCES

Argyle, M., F. Alkema, and R. Gilmour
    1972   "The communication of friendly and hostile attitudes by verbal and
           non-verbal signals", *European Journal of Social Psychology* 1, 385-402.
Becker, F. D., R. Sommer, J. Bee, and B. Oxley
    1973   "College classroom ecology", *Sociometry* 36, 514-25.
Bugental, D. E., J. W. Kaswan, and L. R. Love
    1970   "Perception of contradictory meanings conveyed by verbal and non-
           verbal channels", *Journal of Personality and Social Psychology*
           16, 647-55.
Birdwhistell, R. L.
    1970   *Kinesics and Context: Essays on Body Motion Communication.*
           Philadelphia: University of Pennsylvania Press.
Burns, K. L., and E. G. Beier
    1973   "Significance of vocal and visual channels in the decoding of emotional
           meaning", *Journal of Communication* 28, 118-30.

Ekman, P., and W. V. Friesen
   1969   "The repertoire of nonverbal behavior: Categories, origins, usage, and coding", *Semiotica* 1, 49-98.
Ekman, P., W. V. Friesen, and P. Ellsworth
   1972   *Emotion in the Human Face*. New York: Pergamon.
Gillo, M. W.
   1972   "MAID, a Honeywell 600 program for an automized survey analysis", *Behavioral Science* 17, 251-52.
Koneya, M.
   1976   "Location and interaction in row-and-column seating arrangements", *Environment and Behavior* 8, 265-82.
Levitt, E. A.
   1964   "The relationship between vocal and facial communication abilities", in *The Communication of Emotional Meaning*, ed. by J. Davitz, 87-100. New York: McGraw-Hill.
MacQueen, J.
   1967   "Some methods for classification and analysis of multivariate observations", in *Proceeding of the Fifth Berkeley Symposium on Mathematical Statistics and Probability*, ed. by L. M. LeCam and J. Neyman, 281-97. Berkeley, California: University of California Press.
Mehrabian, A., and S. R. Ferris
   1967   "Inference of attitude from nonverbal communication in two channels", *Journal of Consulting Psychology* 31, 248-52.
Rosenthal, R., D. Archer, M. R. Dimatteo, J. H. Koivumaki, and P. L. Rogers
   1974   "Body talk and tone of voice: The language without words", *Psychology Today* 9, 64-68.
Rosenfeld, H. M.
   1966   "Instrumental affiliative functions of facial and gestural expressions", *Journal of Personality and Social Psychology* 4, 65-72.
Rosenfeld, H. M., and R. McRoberts
   1977   "Effects of topographical features and nonverbal context on ratings of teacher head nods". Unpublished manuscript, University of Kansas.
Shea, M., and H. M. Rosenfeld
   1976   "Functional employment of nonverbal social reinforcers in dyadic learning", *Journal of Personality and Social Psychology* 34, 228-39.
Vine, I.
   1970   "Communication by facial-visual signals", in *Social Behavior in Birds and Mammals: Essays on the Social Ethology of Animals and Man*, ed. by J. H. Crook. London: Academic Press.
Wiener, M., S. Devoe, S. Rubinow, and J. Geller
   1972   "Nonverbal behavior and nonverbal communication", *Psychological Review* 79, 185-214.
Williams, E.
   1975   "Medium or message: Communications medium as a determinant of interpersonal evaluation", *Sociometry* 38, 119-30.
Zeidel, S. F., and A. Mehrabian
   1969   "The ability to communicate and infer positive and negative attitudes facially and vocally", *Journal of Experimental Research in Personality* 3, 233-41.

W. JOHN SMITH, JULIA CHASE, and ANNA KATZ LIEBLICH

Tongue Showing: A Facil Display
of Humans and Other Primate Species

INTRODUCTION

Of the diversity of formalized, visible acts with which humans communicate, the intricately variable expressions assumed by the face are among the most consistently important. Indeed, the range and subtlety of facial expressions is basic in the conduct of what Goffman (1967) has designated 'face-to-face' interaction. Yet, while the forms of many facial expressions have been described and experiments have been done on associated 'affect states' and personality characteristics, no thorough, detailed study has been done of the use of any facial expression in a full range of naturally occurring situations. Without such studies we cannot know the capacity of facial expressions for informing us; that is, we cannot define what information these sources contribute to our social interactions.

Facial expressions can be reduced for analysis into sets of 'displays'. Displays are behavior patterns modified in form and/or employment to provide information to other individuals whose actions are pertinent for the communicator. That is, displays have become formally structured to function indirectly. Most facial displays are employed in diverse circumstances and vary in form within wide limits. For instance, a study of 'smiling' would require observation of its use in human behavior ranging from suffering to exultation, from anger to terror, from casual to intense, and would have to account not only for its contribution to such events, but also for its wide variability in form and its intergradation into other facial expressions. We chose to begin with a study of behavior in which the tongue is made visible.[1] 'Tongue showing' is not uncommon, but occurs in many fewer situations than does smiling. It most often appears to be employed spontaneously, although in some circumstances it (or acts perhaps derived from it) comes under volitional control. Tongue showing varies in form, but its relatively extreme manifestations may be formalized as well-marked variants with restricted ranges of employment. Finally, displays homologous with tongue showing are available in other primate species for comparative study. In particular, we have found a closely similar display is used by gorillas.

Human tongue showing enlarges the appearance of the mouth area by making the tongue visible between the lips. The conspicuousness of the act varies, as the mouth can be opened to different degrees and the tongue can merely be balled forward without protruding or can be protruded to different extents. In an abundantly used variant the tongue simply appears between the lips, becoming visible without being extended. When protruded farther it may loll down, remain approximately straight, or be curled upward or to the side. The tip can be pointed if the tongue is curled or thrust forward.

Tongue showing can be a single, brief flick out and in, or the tongue can be kept visible for a few seconds or even minutes. Movement, other than the single protrusion and retraction however, is NOT characteristic of the usual forms of this display. When the protruded tongue is moved, it may be repeatedly flicked or, more often, appears to lick the lips, wetting them and removing foreign matter or even serving as a signal of readiness to eat. We rarely saw rapid flicking, and feel it is probably a different display from 'tongue showing'. Licking movements are not uncommon; many occur in situations not characteristic of tongue showing, and although in many other cases they may combine the display with the act of wetting dry lips we did not tally any cases in which it appeared that the tongue could be serving directly to cleanse or wet the lips. In the vast majority of our observations there was no reason to suspect any direct function for the act of protruding the tongue.

As is true of other facial expressions, individuals differ greatly in the amount of tongue showing they do. Yet the display is found in all age groups, and in each ethnic group in which we have sought it. Children may do on the average relatively more, or more conspicuous, tongue

[1] Funding for this study was provided by National Science Foundation grant GB-6108, the Smithsonian Tropical Research Institute, Public Health Service National Institute of Mental Health grant MH-17216 at the Center for Urban Ethnology, University of Pennsylvania, and National Institute of Mental Health grant 5-25064, Comparative Social Behavior Program.

showing than do older persons, but we have not attempted to quantify this impression.

Our initial interest in tongue showing has been to determine its information content: i.e., the 'messages' it encodes. Following Smith (1965, 1968) we have sought to do this by studying how its use correlates with other behavior patterns of the individuals who employ it (the 'communicators'). This technique requires that all or most different kinds of natural employment of a display be studied, and that a common thread of information about the communicator's behavior be sought in them. It is held that this common information is what a recipient can know from having seen the display itself; all other information that a recipient uses in responding must come from sources other than the display.

Our main concern in this paper is to analyze the behavior with which we found human tongue showing to correlate; we shall suggest from this that tongue showing provides the message that the communicator is relatively unlikely to initiate or accept suitably social interactions, or particular features of them. This is the case whether the display is used by a child laboriously drawing with crayons on a piece of paper, an adult walking down the aisle of a bus looking for a seat, or a speaker pausing briefly without surrendering his speaking role. For conspicuous and well-marked variants of tongue showing such as those occurring in taunting behavior this message content may be altered by the addition of other information.

Finally, we shall show that some tongue showing displays of gorillas and other primate species are similar to human tongue showing, and may share evolutionary origins with it.

PROCEDURES

We observed naturally occurring human activities, and unobtrusively wrote or tape recorded whenever we saw tongue showing. We described the communicator's activities, events that correlated precisely with the onset, maintenance, and cessation of visibility of the tongue, and various aspects of the social circumstances of the communicator, such as how many other persons were interacting or at least closely present, their activities, and their social relationships (if known) to the communicator. Availability of such detail varied greatly, but we sought to record as much as possible.

The study had four phases: (1) detailed observations of nursery school children, (2) observations of all age groups in a broad range of situations, primarily in Philadelphia, (3) comparative observations in Panama and the Canal Zone, and (4) observations of captive gorillas and orang-utans, along with a survey of the primate literature.

(1) To reduce the effect of undetermined variables we wanted samples from a population whose membership we knew as individuals over an extended period, who engaged in a limited number of kinds of activities that recurred from day to day, who might tongue show reasonably often, and who would be minimally self-conscious of our watchful presence. We chose nursery school children, and at intervals during a 20-month period accumulated a large number of observations in the Mulberry Tree nursery school of Philadelphia. This school operated two classes, each with about 10-16 children, 3- and 4-year-olds in the morning, and 4- and 5-year-olds in the afternoon. Most were white middle-class children of students and faculty of the University of Pennsylvania, although each class included some black or Oriental children. Almost all were fluent in English and had lived all or most of their lives in the United States.[2]

The children were observed primarily during loosely organized activities such as free time, finger-painting, or when having juice and cookie snacks around a large table. Observations were made both during their improvised play, and during activities that centered around their teacher's leadership. We rarely interfered or intruded our presence upon them seeking responses, and after the first few sessions they appeared quite unconcerned by our presence. Toward the end of our work we did structure a few simple 'games' to obtain acts for which we had control of at least some of the situational variables.

(2) Despite its advantages, a nursery school class does not provide a sufficiently broad spectrum of activities to yield all major categories of usage of tongue showing. Older humans do engage in behavior patterns of greater complexity. We therefore observed in many other situations, in most of which we had much less knowledge of the individual subjects. We sought tongue showing in a very wide variety of public places: city streets, buses, waiting rooms, shops, sporting events, public meetings, and the like. A wide variety of usages was found.

Limited observations were also made of tongue showing by infants and children younger than nursery school age. Although the results must be considered preliminary, they contribute to rounding out the basis of our current understanding of this display.

[2]   We are grateful to Fran Bailey for her help in this phase of the study.

(3) Our search for tongue showing was not limited to the Philadelphia region, or to other parts of the United States visited briefly during the study. W. John Smith spent the academic year 1970-71 on leave in Panama and the Canal Zone and took advantage of this to observe tongue showing by Latin Americans, descendants of West Indian Negros, and various North Americans (military personnel, Canal Zone residents, scientists, etc.). With his wife and 18-month-old son he also visited Dr. and Mrs. Joel Sherzer in the Cuna Indian village on Mulatupo. Although observations of the Cuna were very brief, certain kinds of social interactions were facilitated by the Sherzers, and by the Indians' curiosity about the child.[3]

The observations made in Philadelphia, Panama, the Canal Zone, and on Mulatupo do not comprise a formal cross-cultural study, but do show that major categories of usage of tongue showing are represented and appear similar in each of these groups of people. We made no attempt to compare or contrast minor categories of usage among the groups.

(4) Finally, observations were made of captive young gorillas in the Philadelphia zoo to determine how they used an obviously similar display.[4] The range of behavior of such captives is necessarily limited, and it is entirely unlikely that we could observe the full spectrum of use of tongue showing by gorillas in this situation. Much of their social play, however, may have been performed fairly naturally despite the constraints of their environment.

General observations of gorilla display behavior began in April 1967 with the gorilla Kathy, then about five years of age, who was being raised with a young chimpanzee. To stimulate these two young apes to greater play activity during the autumn of 1967, W. John Smith often worked in their cage, usually with one of several students.[5] We customarily tried to engage the gorilla in rough-and-tumble activities similar to those employed when two gorillas played together. Observations were also obtained (autumn 1967 through spring 1968) from play sessions in which Kathy encountered a male gorilla of about her own age, N'Gui,

---

[3] Relevant information on the Cuna is available in Sherzer (1973) and references. We are indebted to Joel and Dina Sherzer for their help and hospitality.

The work in Panama profited from the help and encouragement of the following persons: M. H. Moynihan, A. S. Rand, N. G. Smith, A. Gomez, R. Kiester, and H. Feldmann.

[4] We are much indebted to the following personnel of the Philadelphia Zoological Society for assistance in various aspects of this work: H. Radcliffe, R. Snyder, C. Hamilton, and A. Hess, and to members of the zoo staff who facilitated our tasks.

[5] A. Maizel, H. Cantrell, C. (Ristau) Robbins, and L. Eliasoff.

sometimes in the presence of Fern and Bamboo II, a pair of gorillas about three years older than Kathy (April through November 1967).

More detailed observations, specifically concentrating on tongue showing, were made at intervals from October 1969 through March 1971 (primarily by A. K. Lieblich) on six younger gorillas as they played in groups of three or six.[6] For six hours each day these had the company of women who would play with them and adopt an 'adult' role toward them: keeping them from being too rough with each other, and providing a haven when they became frightened. Sometimes the women reprimanded a young gorilla by pushing it away if it was pestering them, or scolding and slapping it if it was hurting another gorilla or playing with feces.

A. K. Lieblich observed a five-month-old infant gorilla for a total of 14 hours in the Lincoln Park Zoo in Chicago, and several infant and young orang-utans in the Philadelphia and Chicago zoos, but the latter species was not studied extensively. We did not work with other primate species. Displays in which the tongue is protruded have been mentioned in the literature for several species, however, and are reviewed below in considering phylogeny.

THE USE OF TONGUE SHOWING IN THE NURSERY SCHOOL

Most of our observations of tongue showing by nursery school children can be categorized as correlated either with (1) involvement of the communicator in an activity that required attention, or with (2) a social interaction that had negative characteristics from the communicator's standpoint. A small number of observations can as yet be correlated only with (3) situations in which the communicator foregoes physical control. In any observation period we also noted cases of tongue showing that could not be categorized, although none that clearly required further categories. Usually we obtained too little information to enable us to grasp the child's role in these events, a recurrent problem when studying naturally occurring behavior. Uncategorizable observations were most frequent when we began our work and knew least about the children and their common activities; at no time were they more than a minority of our observations.

(1) The use of tongue showing during an involving activity. Some tasks

---

[6] These were three males and three females; when first studied the youngest was over six months old and the oldest at least one and one-half years.

require concentration because they are difficult (e.g., threading a needle) or risky (e.g., balancing and other precarious acts), or both. The task may be enjoyable or unpleasant, but not more than moderately distressing. Characteristically, social interaction can interrupt or interfere with the task; in some cases any social interaction could be detrimental and in others only a particular interaction or feature of an interaction could be.

We commonly saw a child totally absorbed, giving some task all of his attention. Often such individuals stared at their work, apparently oblivious to all other potential sources of sensory input. Their tongues were often visible throughout or at least during the initial portion of such rapt attention. While tongue showing might become less prominent as an event wore on, it might also recur if at times the child looked up from its task. In many cases of concentrating the tongue showing children neither looked at anyone nor were apparently aware if anyone looked at them; they looked at their tasks, or if their tasks did not demand constant visual attention they conspicuously disattended other individuals by taking a distant irrelevant fixation point. If such a child did become aware of another's attention or potential attention, he frequently tongue showed if not already doing so, and also conspicuously turned away with the eyes averted, sometimes lowered, and the chin often lowered. We triggered a great deal of tongue showing as we watched children concentrate.

A variety of involving, concentration-requiring activities was available to the nursery school children: e.g., painting or drawing with crayons, modelling with dough, working on puzzles, moving a chair, or kicking a ball. Children often tongue showed while pushing a large cart, a task that appeared to tax their strength and coordination. In particularly instructive cases an individual pushing this cart tongue showed only in correlation with events related to real or potential social interaction. For instance, one began to push the cart with tongue showing and gradually ceased the expression before becoming aware of one of us watching her. She then quickly looked down with a smile, began to tongue show again, and walked past with head averted and eyes down. That is, she tongue showed while continuing her activity at the point when she became aware of possible interruption. In a more complex case a different girl pushed the cart with tongue showing and stopped three times to turn and talk briefly with another girl. Each time she tongue showed again AS she turned back to pushing the cart. Her tongue showing thus correlated not with choosing to engage in social interaction, but with choosing to cease social interaction and to return to her individual task.

Some instructive cases comprised involvement in other kinds of demanding tasks. For instance, a 4-year-old girl began to run rapidly from one room to another and back again, quickly developing a specific and regularly repeated circuit about 12 meters long. Noting the regularity of the circuit, one of us moved to stand in her path. On her next run she simply detoured around him. For her ensuing pass he crouched and, smiling moderately, looked into her face from her eye level as she approached. She again detoured, but now averted her eyes and protruded her tongue from the beginning of the detour until just past him, withdrawing her tongue as she completed the maneuver. Two meters farther she turned at the end of her route then returned, protruding and withdrawing the tongue at the same relative points with respect to the observer during her detour. This whole procedure was repeated exactly through the next three circuits. Then the degree of tongue protrusion decreased and her gaze remained on the observer until she was nearer than previously. By her sixth circuit after the observer's crouching intrusion she was simply detouring as she had when he had been standing, with no tongue protrusion or conspicuous eye aversion.

Some activities requiring concentration are at least slightly risky — physical harm may result from failure. The children very often sucked in one or both lips (lip tucked, another display) or tongue showed during such activities. In various kinds of play balance was difficult: getting onto a rocking toy, stepping from one chair to another, climbing onto an elevated board, or onto a toy horse. One girl climbed to the fulcrum of a seesaw alone, tongue showed as she struggled to balance, and ceased to tongue show once she had firm balance. Another had hurt herself on a tricycle some months before and was just beginning to try to ride again; she was seen to tongue show as she mounted a tricycle. As in other involving tasks, we often noted that a child in a precarious situation might begin to tongue show only on becoming aware of someone watching or approaching him. For example, one boy rode a bicycle without tongue showing until he passed close to another child.

Tongue showing sometimes appeared only after completion of the most difficult aspect of a risky task. For instance, a boy stepped over a pile of blocks with lip tucking, then tongue showed; a girl lip tucked as she prepared to leap from a slippery board over a mud puddle, then tongue showed very briefly as she alighted on muddy ground. Perhaps in most of these cases the children had concentrated so much on the task that they were suddenly unsure of the properties of the situations prevailing afterward. On the whole, though, they much more commonly tongue showed during a risky task and ceased when the task (or the possibility of social intervention) had passed.

Children sometimes tongue showed when involved in an individual task while within the framework of a social interaction. For the nursery school children, most such cases involved a helping adult. Sometimes the child willingly accepted or sought the adult's help, but resisted further interaction. Examples were elicited by us through a task we designed, which was accepted as a new 'game'. We erected two piles of large wooden blocks to a height of about 3/4 meter, each pile with 3 steps of which the upper 2 steps were relatively narrow and difficult. A 3/4 meter wide board, was placed across the gap of 1 1/4 meters between the two piles. Children who asked were told that this was a bridge, and most promptly wanted to climb and cross it, usually over and over again. Where the task was most demanding and risky (the higher, narrower steps, both up and down, and the bridge crossing), it elicited at least twice as much tongue showing as did the first and last steps, and the tongue showing often correlated with obviously cautious behavior. Tongue showing usually coincided with staring at, starting onto, or taking a particularly difficult step, or with starting out across the bridge. One individual maintained a prominent tongue showing all the way up and down the steps, crossing the bridge with lip tucking, but several others failed to tongue show at all. We stood near the children to prevent them from falling, and this introduced a social variable. Up to a point our appearance seemed to make them more venturesome, but in the few cases in which we came closer they made slight avoiding movements and/or told us not to touch them, or to go away. Some would tongue show if we came too close; apparently they did not want us to hold them or prevent them from making the crossing alone, but did want us near enough to provide reassurance. (One small child crossed only while an adult held her outstretched hand, and tongue showed all the way.)

In further observations which may fall into this category the children were gathered on the floor, listening to an adult read a story. Most would usually appear attentive, and some occasionally did prolonged tongue showing. When some child interrupted, an attentive child might tongue show. In such story sessions, much tongue showing came during or at the start of interruptions, or sometimes immediately after — i.e., at times when the attentive children were concerned with a particular kind of social behavior that interfered with the availability of the story on which they were concentrating.

(2) The use of tongue showing with respect to a social interaction itself. Sometimes the children who tongue showed appeared to view a social interaction *qua* interaction with aversion, without necessarily being involved in a task requiring much concentration. For instance, they often tongue showed while being reprimanded for having engaged in some forbidden activity — a child who talked aloud while the teacher was telling a story might tongue show on being scolded. A boy tongue showed when he was stopped and scolded for carrying some blocks. Both the interference with chosen activities and the real or implicit scolding may be causally related to the tongue showing.

Characteristically, such scolding was only moderate; severe reprimand led to other kinds of signalling. Tongue showing sometimes appeared when scolding was merely implied, as in the order to 'Stop' some activity. In no case, however, did it appear that a child was being intentionally disrespectful and 'taunting' with the protruded tongue — a deliberate use that will be considered below. Tongue showing in events characterized as 'reprimand' did not appear different in form from that already described for events in which the subject was concentrating on a task.

Even without scolding or intervention, a child engaging in forbidden activity might tongue show if approaching a watching adult, or when being approached or stared at. Thus, one chasing two others with the announced intent of 'clubbing' one of them tongue showed as the chase neared adults, but the fleeing individuals did not tongue show. Similarly, a child tongue showed as she approached a pitcher of juice for the third time, having been told not to take any on both previous occasions; another hesitated with tongue showing on seeing the observer watch her as she got up from a table where she knew she should remain seated.

Children were sometimes singled out of a group and asked to sing, dance, answer a question, or perform in some other way. Some complied readily, while others showed signs of discomfort such as blushing or turning away, and might attempt to avoid the issue without complying. Often the task itself did not appear inherently aversive (as when the answer to "do you have a kitten?" was "yes"); perhaps having an audience was. In extreme cases avoidance led to crying with no tongue showing, but in many other cases the child would tongue show, and also sometimes complain of unwillingness ("I don't want to") or incompetence ("I can't"). The avoiding child may have feared criticism. The behavioral evidence for this was inconclusive, but criticism was meted out (and received with some tongue showing) for clumsy execution of 'easy' acts, as well as in reprimand for forbidden activities. Some tongue showing *wow!*

appeared to result simply from encounters with persons known to be critical frequently.

The nursery school children were cautious with strangers, and were relatively likely to tongue show during interactions with them. This happened to the observers at their first sessions. A child would note that he was being observed, and would avert his head and eyes with tongue showing or lip tucking. If addressed, such individuals might reply verbally, tongue show, and smile. This response to strangers may relate to the greater difficulty of predicting their behavior.

In a few cases children tongue showed while trying to avoid a particular interaction that might entail physical injury, although not through their own acts. For example, small children sometimes held back and showed aversion to larger children who were flailing about in an unpredictable fashion, or were riding tricycles recklessly. Children also tongue showed when approached by another child who was a bully.

The children were also sometimes quite hesitant about beginning social encounters with their peers. One child might approach another or a group and pause part way, looking and tongue showing while ambivalent about whether or not to join. Perhaps the process of coming to such a decision is an 'involving' task, or perhaps tongue showing in joining an interaction reflects preoccupation with possible undesirable results.

(3) The use of tongue showing when foregoing physical control. In a small number of observations children tongue showed in what might be 'involving' situations, but ones in which the child had foregone the physical control with which he could avoid or modify social interactions. For instance, children who made themselves dizzy by spinning in a circle with their eyes closed might tongue show while spinning; children picked up and swung by an adult sometimes tongue showed while being swung; in five cases (three involving the same individual) a child beginning to move down the ramp of a slide tongue showed; in several cases a child on a swing tongue showed when an observer stood close to the forward apex of a swing's trajectory. Situations such as these were relatively rare in the usual activities in the nursery school.

OTHER STUDIES OF HUMAN TONGUE SHOWING

Most of our observations of tongue showing fall into the same two categories that comprise most of the nursery school observations, although infants have special behavioral properties and will be treated separately. Within these general categories, however, many additional kinds of situations were encountered, reflecting the greater complexity of behavior that can characterize older individuals. In addition, we recognized at least one further category: the use of tongue showing in mocking and teasing.

(1) The use of tongue showing during an involving task. Using tools such as a screwdriver, negotiating unusual traffic while driving a car, backing a car into a narrow parking space, adding figures mentally, and making a choice when a number of factors or unknowns have to be taken into account (e.g., deciding which way to turn at a street corner) are but a few kinds of tasks in which we have seen older children and adults tongue show (see Fig. 1a and b). Competitive sports provide frequent examples: we have seen tongue showing by teen-aged American boys about to serve a tennis ball, and by Panamanian boys feinting past a guard to score in basketball. In attempting to sample crucial instants during games, sports photographers very often catch tongue protrusions: e.g., a baseball player conspicuously tongue showing while sliding into a base as another player reaches to tag him with a ball (see *Life* 72: 3; 72).

One of our students, Gary Owens, unobtrusively studied the use of tongue showing by his fellow University of Pennsylvania fraternity brothers as they played pool (pocket billiards). An experienced player himself, he ranked each individual as a good or poor player, and rated each shot as easy or difficult before glancing at the face of the player. The results are presented in Table I: his three best players did little tongue showing and his three worst did much more. The proportion of difficult shots made with tongue showing was over twice that of easy shots made with tongue showing. That is, the likelihood of tongue showing correlated directly with the need for concentration, which is greater for poor players and for difficult shots.

Like children, adults not infrequently tongue show in tasks in which balance is difficult. A Panamanian man briefly tongue showed while stepping carefully over rocks piled on a sidewalk. A Costa Rican graduate student balanced carefully and tongue showed broadly each time he searched with a foot for the next secure step while climbing down from a precarious stack of boxes. In a much more dangerous event a Panamanian man maneuvered intricately on a bicycle through a busy intersection on a four-lane highway. He crossed the first lane of cars and

TABLE I

Tongue Showing During Pocket Billiards

Players, by rank		No. of times they tongue showed during easy shots		hard shots		Total Tongue Showing	
good	1	1:22		6:16		7:38	
	2	1:22	2:61	5:19	13:45	6:41	15:106
	3	0:17		2:10		2:27	
poor	4	2: 5		7: 8		9:13	
	5	13:17	18:32	14:16	25:29	27:33	43:61
	5	3:10		4: 5		7:15	
Totals:		20:93		38:74		58:167	

Legend: For each player the number of cases of tongue showing in each category is expressed as a ratio of the total number of times he was seen to make a shot of that category. The hypothesis tested was that the amount of tongue showing would vary with the difficulty of each shot and the lack of skill of each player. Dividing the six players into three good and three poor (none was, in fact, mediocre in the sample observed) the following tests of the hypothesis can be made:

(1) For the good players, there was more tongue showing on hard than on easy shots, $\chi^2 = 12.0$, $p < 0.001$.
(2) For the poor players, there was not significantly more tongue showing on hard than on easy shots, $\chi^2 = 1.95$, $p > 0.10$ (they apparently found all shots difficult).
(3) On easy shots, good players tongue showed less than did poor players, $\chi^2 = 11.3$, $p < 0.001$.
(4) On hard shots, good players still tongue showed less than poor players, $\chi^2 = 6.1$, $p < 0.05$.
(5) Considering all shots combined, good players tongue showed less than poor players, $\chi^2 = 6.1$, $p < 0.05$.

then followed the white line on the pavement as he sought a break in the two oncoming lanes, then angled sharply across all three remaining lanes. This required speed to avoid nearby cars and accurate steering to stay between the first two lanes while monitoring a vehicle on his left behind him, then a precise decision about when to turn. He maintained throughout an extreme tongue showing, trapping the tip of his tongue behind his lower teeth and balling its body forward and out of his widely opened mouth. In an equally intricate but somewhat less risky maneuver, an adult Cuna Indian steered an outboard motor powered dug-out canoe in shallow water over sand bars across the mouth of a small river, with driftwood obstacles and turbid water intensifying the problem of steering into waves coming from the open sea. Alert but not tongue showing in the preceding hour's travel, he became more alert, tilted his head back, exposed his tongue broadly between slightly parted lips, and maintained this expression for about a minute and a half. Three minutes later shallows were again encountered, and he resumed the pose and tongue showing for another minute. A different maneuvering problem elicited about 10 seconds of similar tongue showing some minutes later. In every case he maintained his alertness and the tongue showing expression while concentrating on the difficult task.

Much as the nursery school children who tongue showed while attentive to a teacher reading a story to them, adults occasionally use this facial expression during a social interaction when trying to avoid the interference of a second social interaction. In a typical case a North American woman talked over a telephone while a companion repeatedly attempted to convey to her a question for the other party. She was trying to concentrate on her conversation and ignore her companion. Each time he intruded with the question she averted her eyes, tensed and slightly parted her lips, and showed her tongue broadly without protruding it far. Each tongue showing was sustained for some seconds after the cessation of an interruption. Similarly, a Panamanian store clerk, telephoning to a warehouse while engaged with a customer, visually disattended the customer and tongue showed while listening to his telephone party. Closely comparable events very often arise when an individual needs 'time-out' during a dyadic interaction such as a conversation; a speaker pausing to formulate a phrase usually averts his eyes and sometimes also tongue shows. And in an interaction that had become briefly dyadic, at least with respect to a temporary axis of interaction between a seminar speaker and a member of his audience, the latter turned away to write notes on his remarks, using a brief tongue show as she broke eye contact and turned.

(2) The use of tongue showing with respect to a social interaction itself. As with the nursery school children, tongue showing often occurred in aversive social interactions in which concentration on an involving task did not appear to be a primary, or even relevant, feature. Instances involving reprimand or anticipation of it were observed in younger children. For example, a 24-month-old Chinese Panamanian child maximally extended and depressed her tongue on entering an area where she was forbidden to play, although the maid supervising her was out of sight behind her back and not yet intervening. Older children and adults are less frequently reprimanded, but the implied or direct criticism in arguments is like a subtle form of reprimand. Individuals have been observed listening to their opponents expound views contrary to their own, observing the speaker with frowns or raised eyebrows and slightly

visible tongues; this may happen not only in open arguments but also in more subtle disagreements. Similarly, university students presenting seminar material sometimes tongue show as they listen to difficult questions with which they will have to deal. Tongue showing may even be done by a speaker after asking a difficult question, perhaps in anticipation of a negative reaction. Finally, adults sometimes tongue show when appearing 'thoughtful' in circumstances in which no other behavior seemed to occur consistently. By introspection and limited questioning it appears that in at least some such cases the subject is thinking about unpleasant social interactions. This ability to play or replay scenes in one's imagination makes the ethological study of human displays relatively difficult.

Tongue showing in response to the attentions of strangers was seen in children of various ages. The Chinese Panamanian child mentioned above tongue showed when, at the age of 22 months, she was approached by a 15-month-old boy whom she did not know — he walked up to her with his arm outstretched and touched her. In both Philadelphia and Panama City we very often found that staring at a child we did not know would elicit tongue showing and aversive behavior (lowering the chin and partially averting the head, eye aversion, twisting the trunk, hiding behind a parent or friend); such children tended to smile and remain in positions from which they could watch us. Many cases were also seen when Cuna Indian children from about 3 to 11 years of age gathered to watch a visiting child play. Usually the observer elicited the tongue showing by squatting down, smiling broadly, and looking back at the children one at a time from their eye level. Most evidenced 'shy' aversion, and perhaps a quarter of them also broadly exposed the tongue a short distance between the lips or teeth, darting it out briefly, or exposing it for about three seconds. Some individuals repeated the gesture several times. It seemed more frequently elicited when the observer stared at children through a camera lens (see Fig. 1c), as if they knew they should remain still for a photograph but wanted to turn away. For example, one mother told her 6- to 8-year-old daughter to stand for a photograph and the child contorted enormously in aversive twisting movements while smiling broadly, then conspicuously tongue showed — but kept facing the camera.

In both Panama City and Philadelphia children on mechanical rides in amusement parks often began to tongue show, lip tuck, or both if they became aware of being attended (see Fig. 1d). Particularly those children too young to be blasé about the rides and just old enough not to be terrified used both expressions a great deal in the initial parts of the rides, then slowly relaxed and smiled more; in the initial phase they often disattended all gazes, stared at infinity, and held their bodies rigid.

Adults sometimes tongue show when singled out for attention. When one of us photographed a Carnaval parade in Panama he noted that if he selected an individual and waited for a good pose the subject was likely to become aware of this attention and stare back. Some did not change expression, some smiled, and others smiled and briefly tongue showed. All individuals were performing, often doing quite intricate dance maneuvers.

Individuals sometimes tongue show at the instant of being surprised, although we do not know if surprise *per se* operates as a causal factor. For instance, Cuna children who suddenly noticed our direct attention, even from distances of up to 20 meters, might immediately tongue show. Whether this was the 'stranger effect', an effect of surprise, or both, we do not know. Klineberg (1938) in a preliminary report on figures of speech in Chinese literature says that the phrase "they stretched out their tongues" occurs very frequently in the long Chinese novel *The Dream of the Red Chamber*, and is meant to imply surprise. It is not clear that this usage is widespread in Chinese literature, but like the phrase "their jaws dropped" in western novels it may be an overly generalized literary device abstracted from common experience. Literary and anecdotal sources must be used only as suggestions about real behavior, however, and not construed as evidence, as La Barre (1964) does to his confusion.

The nursery school children sometimes tongue showed while trying to avoid an encounter that carried the risk of physical injury inflicted by the other party. In both Philadelphia and Panama City we have seen older children and adults tongue show while hurrying across wide streets in front of lines of waiting traffic. The converse, in which drivers of vehicles tongue show as they contend with unpredictable pedestrians while turning busy corners is probably an example of use of the expression while engaged in an involving task.

In the largest remaining group of observations in which tongue showing appeared to correlate with awareness of potentially aversive social encounters, the subject tried to avoid a particular interaction and then did something else. The alternative might or might not require concentration, but had not usually been begun at the time of the tongue showing — the subject was on his way to do it and not usually engaged in behavior that required much concentration. For example, five Cuna children lined up along a wall to watch a visiting child in the home compound of an Indian family. Their line blocked the access of a Cuna girl of 6 to 8 years who squeezed through in order to get a view. As she parted two of her playmates with her arms and passed between them she tongue showed very broadly, and began to stare intently at the visiting child. In cases with better temporal separation of the component events, people (in both Philadelphia and Panama City) have been seen hurrying to various tasks and tongue showing as they passed close by knots of friends.

Some such cases suggest that there are circumstances in which the gesture might function as a passing greeting, if it is used by persons aware of other parties but not about to accost or respond to them. In some cultures tongue showing may have become incorporated into a common greeting ceremony. For instance, Roosevelt and Roosevelt (1929) report the use of a protruded tongue, along with touching an ear, as a greeting in Tibet. J. F. Taylor (personal communication) has described this as a brief tug at the right ear with the right hand, with the tip of the tongue being protruded during the tug. He has seen it used in greetings by Tibetan schoolchildren (with and without smiles) along with a short bow-curtsy. He noticed that the ear tug-tongue show form was a common greeting among adult men of similar social status, and was used by men toward individuals of higher status. Often he saw the men greet women with a reduced hand-to-ear component, and adult women greeted each other and men with a tongue protrusion while their hands touched in front of their noses, instead of doing an ear tug. His observations were made on Tibetan refugees in Himachial Pradesh, India.

A further greeting-like case of tongue showing was seen at the initiation of a conversation which would become an undesired interaction. One American graduate student approached another and paused with a lowered chin in an oblique orientation toward the other. With a slight smile she announced that she had discovered inconsistencies in an hypothesis they had formulated the previous day. Immediately after this initial statement she very briefly tongue showed, while still smiling. Promptly questioned by the observer, she reported concern at having to devalue the hypothesis with which they had been pleased. The case illustrates a similarity between greeting situations and many situations in which we see tongue showing — both involve interactions that may subsequently develop in undesirable ways.

(3) The use of tongue showing in mocking and teasing. Tongue showing can at times be deliberate, although in most of the usages already described it is not so. Among usages that are borderline, deliberate, or often apparently not deliberate, are cases in which the subject tongue shows at another individual along with a verbal statement or other social act, and cases in which the subject tongue shows in response to some action of the other individual. For instance, in a not uncommon kind of event an individual violates the usual rules of social interaction by doing or saying something outrageous to a companion, often accompanying or following the insult with a smile, and then does a conspicuous, usually brief, tongue protrusion. By questioning or by studying the performance of communicators immediately after numerous such events we have always found that the communicator was jesting. Often he intended to make a compliment by what appeared to be a deliberate insult, and marked the false nature of the speech (or of a gesture, such as a raised and shaken fist) by the tongue showing. Other marking sometimes occurs: smiling, and elaborate flinching and a pantomime of warding off blows, for instance. Where an apparent insult is not so marked, its recipient may confirm his correct interpretation of the jest by tongue showing in reply. This good-humored behavior is commonly referred to as speaking or behaving 'with tongue in cheek'. In fact, pushing the tongue against the inside of the cheek often appeared to be relatively covert transformation of tongue showing in various usages, but it was difficult to detect and was deliberately excluded from this study.

These jesting usages have in common with the previous category correlation with a potentially aversive social interaction. However, in mocking or teasing the potential of unpleasantness is deliberately invoked as an expressive tactic. Functionally, tongue showing here appears to be one marker of the tactic, and it is appropriate for this if our message hypothesis (see below) is correct.

An individual who tongue shows when jesting is effectively mocking himself and is engaged in semi-collusive signalling (terms from Sherzer, 1973). Sherzer shows that the pointed lip gesture of the Cuna can be used as if one were a third person, commenting on the interaction between himself and a second person. By parallel interpretation, the implication of tongue showing would be that he who both tongue shows and insults holds an opinion very different from the one he stated. Similarly, cases in which it is the recipient of the infraction who tongue shows may also be semi-collusive, and imply conspiracy in the jest as the recipient mocks both himself and the other.

Tongue showing can probably be used as an admission that the state of a variety of types of interaction was not what was claimed if these develop in undesired ways. For instance, many Cuna Indian women wanted to take Smith's child to their houses. Mrs. Sherzer told one that the child was sleepy, whereupon the woman replied that she would take him home and sing him a lullaby. Mrs. Sherzer said: "sing it here, now" and the Cuna woman smiled and tongue showed — her interest was not in singing the lullaby but in keeping the baby, and she recognized that her bluff had been called.

Some mocking usages of tongue showing are best described as collusive. In these events one individual comments on the unacceptability of a second's performance to a third individual, without the second being made aware of the comment. Examples can be observed as university students respond to a lecture. One may turn to another and tongue show covertly after a lecturer has made a point badly, or has failed to carry off an attempt to be amusing. Yet other apparent mocking is done openly. For example, when a six-year-old Cuna girl was asked her name she gave a prompt but obviously incorrect reply (a Spanish name) unaccompanied by any clue that she was jesting. An adult walking beside her immediately protruded her tongue and let it loll conspicuously for several seconds, then turned directly to the observer and gave the girl's correct name.

Ambiguous cases of mocking may sometimes be related to teasing. In 'teasing' the communicator provides opposing messages simultaneously or in rapid succession, e.g., "leave me alone" (via tongue showing) and "come hither" (via other signals). Such subjects may be being coy, flirting, or maliciously or playfully inciting. A boy enticing his father into a chasing game may tongue show while challenging: "you can't catch me". A need to save face (Goffman, 1967) may operate in teasing; if opposing messages are offered, then different outcomes can be incorporated as results already defined as acceptable.

MODIFICATIONS OF TONGUE SHOWING

Consideration of the often deliberate use of tongue showing in mocking and teasing brings us to usages that are likely cultural stereotypes, and often involve extreme modification of the appearance of the protruded tongue. One of these modifications is commonly employed as a statement of dislike or disagreement. This is forward lolling down of a broad, flat, tongue, often accompanied by a vocalization such as "bleah" or "bluh", and sometimes by other facial expressions such as wrinkling the nose. It may be used to answer questions involving oral rejection (e.g., "do you like the taste of such-and-such a medicine?"), disagreement (e.g., "do you approve of this choice?"), and disdain (e.g., "what did you think of the acting in that play?"), or even offered as an unsolicited opinion (e.g., in the form known as the 'Bronx cheer' or 'raspberry', such as in disagreeing with an umpire's decision in baseball). The performance appears usually to function as a mocking rejection, and the form may encode somewhat different information from other tongue showing forms. Certainly, the vocalizations could bring additional messages to the performance.

In another variant the tongue is usually thrust maximally forward, aligned with a stare and accompanied by other agonistic signals, often including speech. This is commonly referred to as 'sticking one's tongue out at someone'. Individuals do this when taunting: i.e., when maliciously inciting others to respond aggressively. It likely adds information about the probability of attack to the basic message of tongue showing. Yet it is not simply an aggressive signal, as the taunting individual does not usually press an attack. This taunting display appears in children at least as young as our nursery school subjects, but its use is either regulated by training (i.e., through the application of what Ekman and Friesen [1969] call a display rule) or it originates entirely as a volitional variant of tongue showing. With our nursery school subjects, use of this taunting form sometimes became a game of sticking out tongues — i.e., became semi-collusive. This and the 'raspberry' are not independent; they are sometimes substituted for each other, although perhaps differently among cultures. For instance, Eibl-Eibesfeldt (1970: 424, fig. 270b) reproduces a drawing of two New Guinea warriors apparently using the depressed and lolled variant of tongue showing as a taunt.

Taunting may have social functions related to those both of mocking and of teasing. Another usage that is sometimes claimed for tongue showing may be functionally related primarily to teasing: it is said to occur in flirting, including solicitation by prostitutes, and perhaps in precopulatory behavior, in which there is use of the tongue in tactile signalling (Masters and Johnson, 1966; Morris, 1967). Descriptions of this behavior usually imply that the tongue is moved (Eibl-Eibesfeldt, 1972), perhaps flicked out and in repeatedly. This could conceivably be another variant of the tongue showing display, similar in its motions to precopulatory displays known from other primate species. However, a postulate can also be made that it has a different evolutionary origin from that of tongue showing (see below). Simple tongue showing, (i.e., a slight protrusion of the tongue between the lips, sustained for at least a few seconds) is sometimes used in at least posed portrayals implying 'sexiness', however, perhaps because of the ambivalent nature of teasing situations.

There thus appear to be two or more well-marked variant forms of tongue showing with relatively narrowly specialized usages (and modified messages), and there may be a second tongue display distinguished by flicking. All can intergrade in appearance with the less extreme forms of tongue showing. When intergrading forms are used, other sources of information provided by the communicator may at times reduce the ambiguity of the situation.

In practice, most individuals use extreme forms of tongue showing much less often than the other forms, but are nonetheless much more aware of the former unless they do a great deal of tongue showing. This may be because these stereotypes tend to be used deliberately, whereas individuals can be quite unaware both of their own employment of the more common forms and the use of these by the individuals with whom they interact. Such lack of awareness does not imply that tongue showing is not an efficient signal.

DIFFICULTIES IN CATEGORIZING EVENTS

The categories employed above were chosen primarily to summarize conveniently large numbers of observations. They are not intended as a constraining and conceptually rigid system. For various reasons, some of our observations do not fit them well.

(1) It is not always obvious to which category a case of tongue showing should be assigned. For instance, a child who tongue shows while passing a watching adult may anticipate interference with an activity on which he is concentrating, or a reprimand for engaging in it. An amateur performer in a pre-Lenten parade may respond to being singled out for attention, to becoming aware of the stare of a stranger, or may regard the taking of a photograph as a social indiscretion but not take it seriously, and tongue show to mock the event. In general, it is probably not important that such events be assigned to one category or another, and there is no reason that more than one category cannot be relevant in any given instance. What is important is that the categories that could fit all

have features in common; where this does not hold a single message interpretation cannot be made.

(2) When a social encounter appears to elicit aversion, the reasons for the aversion may not be apparent. Too few clues may be available: internalized codes and learned expectations of behavior may govern unseen. For instance, a nursery school child listening to the teacher read a story clapped her hand over her mouth and tongue showed immediately after laughing aloud; covering her mouth indicates that she may have understood the rules of silence enough to expect a reprimand. Other cases yield even less evidence. In one case, a 13-month-old girl was sitting in her mother's lap by a restaurant table. She scanned the objects on the table and tongue showed. Less than a minute later she again scanned them and tongue showed, this time leaning forward with slight forward and backward rocking motions as if in ambivalent attempts to reach the table. She then desisted. We knew that she had been taught not to grab things from tables. Presumably in the second instance her staring, rocking, and leaning indicated a tendency to risk reprimand, but in the first instance only her gaze provided any clue as to what she might be considering. Observation of only the first event would be uninterpretable; observation of the second event, taken with other information about the child, is tenuously interpretable.

Further, interactions can change and become aversive, leading a child to withdraw from the interaction. The withdrawal can be taken as an indicator of aversion, but the causes may not be readily apparent. The child may have become tired or bored, or have set out to do something else and not followed through. Even with a great deal of information about the social expectancies and customary behavioral predispositions of each individual subject, the study of naturally occurring events inevitably leaves some observations unexplained.

(3) Individuals may behave as if shifting in quick succession from one category to another, or different individuals may respond in different ways to the same event. These cases are difficult to categorize only because it is often difficult to obtain adequate information in the time available.

THE ONTOGENY OF HUMAN TONGUE SHOWING

Human infants are so different from older individuals in motor skills and types of social interactions that in a study based on behavioral analyses they comprise a special class. For example, J. Chase observed a six-week-old infant lying in her crib with tongue protruded between her lips. The mother remarked that the infant, too weak as yet to reject the breast by moving her head away, would terminate feeding by pushing the nipple from her mouth with her tongue, and let the tongue remain visible for some time thereafter. Since the mother recognized that the infant would not accept further attempts to be enticed to feed,[7] this continued visibility of the tongue functioned to reject a specific kind of social encounter. Darwin (1872) made comparable observations of a 6-month-old infant who pushed a novel solid food from his mouth with his tongue, an act which immediately suggested to him the 'lolling out of the tongue' by older humans which he felt was a formalized, pancultural signal of 'contempt'.

Most of our observations of infant tongue showing were made of a single individual.[8] He did not tongue show after feeding; however, unlike the first infant, he was bottle-fed. When seeking to feed during his first few weeks he would open his mouth into a vertical oval and swing his head through a roughly repetitive search pattern. By the sixth week his tongue would ball forward visibly and block the mouth during this pattern, and was periodically pulled downward off the dento-palatal surface as if suckling. Within a week this action sometimes yielded faint smacking noises. By the eighth week the behavior pattern was being used in a wider range of circumstances, but still in none that appeared to involve acts of rejection; if to some degree formalized, this visible tongue employment in suckling-like patterns may be initially a food-seeking signal.

In a study of space perception in infants of this age (4 to 8 weeks, mean 6 weeks) Aronson and Rosenbloom (1971) described behavioral indicators of 'distress' such as struggling, kicking, and facial grimacing. All the indicators were idiosyncratic with one exception: 'the sudden appearance of mouthing of the tongue' in which the tongue was moved both in the mouth and with intermittent periods of protrusion. The latter were sufficiently common that they employed visibility of the tongue as their indicator of distress. That is, they elicited tongue showing by producing distress — specifically, by confusing infants about the location of their mothers (while the mother remained visible through a glass barrier, the sound of her voice was shifted 90 degrees to one side). Although basically an experiment in perception, the results demonstrate

[7]   We are indebted to J. Taber for her observations.
[8]   We are indebted to Susan T. Smith who made many of the observations of this infant.

a quantitative correlation between tongue showing and the beginning of a discomforting social situation. Tongue protrusions were most evident in the first 20-30 seconds after the experimental shift, and as the discomfort persisted most of the infants eventually cried or whined.

In his tenth and eleventh weeks our principal infant subject sought and sustained eye contact with a parent for occasional periods of several minutes, mouth open and smiling, and sometimes struggled to produce simple vocalizations. Tongue balling or protrusion could then sometimes be elicited by tickling him. (Occasionally it was moderately common all through periods of several minutes with much eye contact and smiling — but these events did not include attempts to vocalize.) At the end of vocalizing periods he usually appeared to tire suddenly, and would avert his eyes and cease smiling. If we attempted to prolong the inter-action, he would ball his tongue forward or protrude and loll it, and, if not left alone, would begin to fret within the next minute. Never very common or easily elicited, this tongue showing behavior largely disap-peared in the twelfth week, about the time he appeared to be able to produce voluntary vocalizations easily. Although difficult to quantify, these episodes were his first known consistent use of tongue showing in discomforting social interactions. Another male infant was tested once at about the same age by dangling a necktie in his face; this elicited smiling and eye contact for somewhat over a minute, then elicited head and eye aversion and marked tongue balling.

In the 19th week the infant's behavior patterns began to change rapidly. He gained much more control of his arms and hands, could grasp and locate his mouth better, and would attempt to stand in one's lap. Tongue showing began to reappear, particularly at the start and sometimes the termination of vocalizing with eye contact. It was most easily observed when he was either drowsily awakening or becoming tired and fretful, both states in which he was somewhat reluctant to interact very directly. It remained most common when he was tired and being involved in dyadic interactions, or in our attempts to initiate or sustain them. By the 30th week he was crawling, and by the 33rd week occasionally pulled himself into a standing position. Now tongue showing was used fairly commonly when he attempted some difficult task, such as pulling himself onto a low lawn chair, or crawling on its yielding webbing. This tongue showing correlated with what for him were the most involving tasks, if these were neither too easy nor too hard but required skills he had yet to perfect. It was used whether or not his parents were nearby.

Tongue showing continued to occur in these circumstances, and also when he appeared to concentrate over a choice such as in which direction to crawl. It remained a moderately common response to unwanted interference with his activities, especially when he was relatively tired. Thus, if picked up while crawling or sidling he might struggle slightly and look back, and if put down promptly would return to what he had been doing. If he struggled forcibly he usually did not tongue show. In an instructive case during his 42nd week, he was sidling alongside a bed (moving while standing and holding onto the bed) when picked up by his mother. He struggled slightly without tongue showing, and then as she swung him about in a fashion he knew to be play he immediately protruded his tongue directly at her, then averted his head, shifted the protruded tongue to the side of his mouth away from her, arched his back and struggled more. She returned him to the floor where he immediately went back to the interrupted activity without further tongue showing. Tongue showing now also occurred (noted in the 46th week) when he was restrained from some act, such as pulling utensils from a table.

In his 49th week he tongue showed while crawling toward waves on an ocean beach, and stopped crawling as he reached them, although he had often played in waves if a parent remained nearby. That is, he tongue showed as he set out on what he may have regarded as a risky task. In his 54th week, this usage category was seen as he crawled up a stream bed, alternately passing through deep and shallow water. When in deep he had to lift his face to breathe, and proceeded slowly. Each time he lifted his face he would tongue show broadly and wrinkle his forehead — the more so as he tired. In shallower water he did neither.

Not until his 56th week did we begin to see food rejection as described by Darwin — pushing food from the mouth while frowning, then lolling the tongue while staring at the rejected food for a few seconds. Any subsequent attempts to get him to accept such food were avoided with lateral head-shaking, eye closing, arm swinging, and vocalizations, but not with tongue showing. This usage remained common for many months. He usually did it with the tip of the tongue at least initially trapped behind the lower gums, teeth, or lip. The resultant balling of the tongue might seem more functionally related to suckling than to pushing things from the mouth, but was used for ejection. In most observations of older individuals balling the tongue has been much less common than showing it tip foremost.

We made few observations of tongue showing by Panamanian infants. An infant of 3 to 4 months tongue showed as her father playfully swung her back and forth over his head, and the tongue protruded (tip foremost)

most conspicuously at the apices of the swing. Cuna Indian infants of about 2 to 6 months were observed both in their homes and outside when their mothers joined small crowds in the narrow passageways among the living compounds. Those inside did not tongue show when held up to be admired by their mothers, and could be cajoled into smiling if stared at with smiling and laughing (or if tickled). If attention was directed at them for more than a few tens of seconds, however, they would begin to show a balled tongue, usually making it broadly visible while still smiling. Many infants in their mothers' arms outside in the somewhat boisterous crowds of 20 to 30 people kept slightly balled tongues broadly exposed almost continuously. This may have been in response to the continuous jostling by individuals less familiar to them than were their mothers. Children around Philadelphia have often been seen to respond to the attention of strangers with avoidance movements and persisting tongue showing. An observation of our main subject after attending a Christmas party at the age of 60 weeks is comparable in the persistence with which the tongue remained visible. He had been greatly excited and by evening was extremely overtired and frenetically active. For the last eight minutes before he was put to bed his tongue was continuously balled forward slightly in his partially open mouth, he would occasionally protrude it farther, for example when suddenly picked up while otherwise engaged. He was thus still tongue showing in the usual situations, but had in effect established a new base-line in which the tongue was constantly visible.

In summary, these few observations suggest the following ontogeny for this display: tongue showing appears in some very young infants as a rejection of feeding, a fundamental social interaction. Others do not show it in such circumstances until months older, perhaps because of differences in the mode of feeding or in other individually different aspects of interactions with their parents. Further observations are needed in these early phases to distinguish tongue showing from open-mouthed behavior patterns used in food seeking. Tongue showing later appears in rejection of or discomfort over attentive dyadic interaction with parents at a time when infants have few motor skills but are able to stare at a face, and perhaps to struggle to vocalize. Gradually, as their developing motor skills lead them into more and more complex activities, they begin to tongue show in 'involving' activities that require concentration and the making of choices, and in instances where an adult restrains them from some action. Some circumstances may disturb them sufficiently to elicit a sustained but usually slight tongue showing beyond which they can still respond to appropriate events with further protrusion of the tongue.

(It may be a feature of later ontogeny that in most individuals the nondeliberate occurrences of this display become less frequent and are reduced to the less extreme forms. Extreme forms seem to be relatively frequently used by children, and may eventually become restricted largely to events in which they are deliberately employed. This might imply that adult usage is limited by what Ekman and Friesen (1969) call 'display rules', but we have not investigated the possibility.)

ANALYSIS OF TONGUE SHOWING AS A HUMAN DISPLAY

Since the act of showing the tongue correlates with a particular range of other behavior, it is available to serve signal functions in human interactions. We shall now treat it in terms of (1) its message content, and then consider more briefly (2) its probable range of meanings to recipients, (3) its functions, and (4) its distribution in human populations.

(1) The aim of this research has been to determine the information content or 'message' of tongue showing by studying how communicators employ it, as outlined in the Introduction and Procedures sections. This requires determining from what is common to all its uses the information that the occurrence just of the display makes available to a recipient. All other information used by recipients in diverse circumstances is treated as originating in sources contextual to tongue showing. There are always such sources, and they are absolutely necessary in permitting displays to function in particular events. But each kind of display makes its own, consistent, contribution of information (Smith, 1965, 1968, 1974).

We have employed categories of uses chosen for their convenience in summarizing the observations, as discussed above. Possibly better categories could be found, but if ours encompass the observations without concealing fundamental features of display usage they are adequate for the current purposes of analysis.

First, tongue showing was very often seen when the communicators were engaged in involving tasks. Many observations in this category suggest that something about social interaction is important in eliciting tongue showing. These include the many cases in which tongue showing began with the communicator's awareness of the proximity of another individual, or ended when other individuals became inattentive or more distant, as well as cases in which the communicator tongue showed while somehow avoiding interaction. Thus the act of concentrating may be simply one possible precondition for the display, placing the communicator in a state for which social interference would be disruptive.

The large second category of observations indicates that in many circumstances social interaction, or its possible initiation or alteration, leads to tongue showing by individuals who are NOT actively concentrating. Thus involvement in a demanding task is not necessary, whether or not it is sufficient. Further, it is usually evident from behavior in events fitting this category that social interactions, for quite varied reasons, are viewed by the communicator with some limited degree of aversion. The aversion may trace to the capacity of social interaction to interfere with communicator activities, or to inherently negative characteristics of the interactions themselves. Perhaps the most revealing incidents are those in which a child, responding to somewhat forceful attempts of a relatively unknown child or adult to interact, faces the other, shows its tongue broadly in or protruding slightly from its open mouth, often while smiling, and makes definite movements of avoidance with its head or its whole body. This is very commonly seen in children from a few months to a few years of age. There is no necessary interference with other activity, and the communicator may soon play with the other individual. But while showing the limited aversion, there is sustained tongue showing.

The greater part of our observations thus fall into two categories in which communicators probably view social interactions with limited aversion. The remaining observations have been categorized as comprising mocking or teasing, and most also involve social interaction that elicits aversion. In the seemingly most bizarre cases, an individual speaks 'tongue in cheek', deliberately creating a possible misunderstanding then seeking to change this with tongue showing.

Most tongue showing occurs when the communicating individual can best be served if permitted to choose his own behavioral alternatives. Social interaction, or some aspect of it, is likely to interfere or be otherwise unwelcome, and we should expect the communicator to be reluctant to accept or initiate interaction. However, it can be seen that he is not usually STRONGLY reluctant. For example, situations that generate strong aversion in children lead to displays such as crying, not to tongue showing. We do see behavioral indications of avoidance of social interaction by some tongue showing subjects — they turn or partially turn away from other persons, avert their eyes and conspicuously disattend so that they appear to ignore the others. At other times we see 'half-hearted' or resistant acceptance of social overtures. And yet simple acceptance of social interaction is commonly shown by tongue showing individuals, perhaps because there is often little choice available to them that does not involve worsening the situation. The probable consequences of active avoidance must often be less desirable than are the consequences of acquiescence. The measurement of a slight hesitance to interact is difficult or impossible in most naturally occurring events, and will have to be approached experimentally. It is also inordinately difficult to obtain control measures of how often hesitance is shown when the subject does not tongue show in otherwise 'identical' situations. Thus we can propose at this stage only an hypothesis about the message.

We propose that an individual who tongue shows has an enhanced probability of evidencing some form of rejection behavior, with respect either to any social interaction or to particular aspects of interaction.

This hypothesis encounters some difficulty when the aversive inter-action is not between two individuals. Examples are sometimes found in the relatively uncommon use of tongue showing as a comment of dislike or disagreement, the modified and perhaps culturally stereotyped behavior reaching its extreme in the Bronx cheer or raspberry. Loud, conspicuous, jeers used for social rejection may be distinctive in form, and if so their messages need not be identical with those of other tongue showing. But less extreme forms occur, e.g., as comments on the taste of a medicine or food, or on someone's taste in, say, clothing or decorum. As for taste *per se*, what is known of the ontogeny of tongue showing suggests that rejection of ingestible substances by infants is within the framework of a social interaction, but adults may generalize this employment to non-social rejection. Tongue showing as a comment on other persons' performances or tastes (their likes and dislikes) may imply rejection of the acts and the objects of taste. Alternatively, it may imply rejection of interaction with such people, if individuals usually seek to interact primarily with like-minded persons. The acceptability of other in-dividuals may be a pervasive although often implicit topic of conversa-tion: for instance, H. Sacks, in a personal communication, has shown that much conversing may function primarily to reaffirm commonality of experience among friends.

Shunning an interaction that is 'social' is also only a tentative inter-pretation of some of the small number of observations in which a tongue showing child had foregone physical control. Tests of potentially non-social rejection will be difficult, and we leave our contention as follows: all uses of 'typical' tongue showing, and most apparently modified uses, appear to inform that the communicator is relatively likely to reject some aspect(s) of social interaction. If the few remaining usages are not similarly interpretable, then the communicator rejects interactions that can be either social or with objects or concepts.

To conclude, the following is our provisional statement of the message content of the tongue showing display:

> The communicator may avoid or behave hesitantly if required either to accept or initiate a social interaction.

(2) As much of the use of tongue showing is evidently not deliberate, it is not necessary at this stage to investigate the 'intentions' of individuals who use the display. Something, however, should be said about what the display means to persons who see it, whether or not they usually make a reasoned assessment of its implications. Following Smith (1965, 1968) we shall operationally define the meanings of a signal to its recipients as the responses recipients select after receipt of the signal.

Used in different circumstances, tongue showing can be expected to lead to different recipient meanings, varying from ignoring the signal to delaying or avoiding completely social interaction with the communicator. In general, the 'appropriate' meanings generated would be expected to belong to the following class:

> Recipients should show an increased probability of avoiding or proceeding more cautiously with social interaction, or show increased efforts to gain the communicator's cooperation. That is, on seeing tongue showing a recipient should in some way treat the communicator as less available for interaction, or less easily understood, or both.
>
> The avoidance or caution predicted should not appear to be fearful. Tongue showing is not a threatening display, it does not indicate the communicator is about to behave aggressively, and is rarely used when the communicator is showing any strong agonistic behavior.

In selecting a response to a particular event, recipients will presumably employ the message made available by tongue showing differently with respect to at least the following variables: (i) whether or not they have reason to seek an interaction, or, granted reasons, (ii) the kind and importance of these reasons, (iii) the number of individuals present and the communicator's orientation and role with respect to these individuals, as well as (iv) any other contextual information that may be relevant.

In natural situations, recipients commonly proceed to interact with tongue showing communicators without obvious hesitance (i.e., respond 'inappropriately' from the communicator's standpoint) or appear to pay him no attention ('appropriate', but it is hard to know if this is in response to the tongue showing). Unfortunately, most naturally available situations in which tongue showing is seen do not provide sufficient control of the relevant variables; experimental procedures are being developed by A. K. Lieblich and J. Chase.

The usual forms of tongue showing are less extreme than are the variants that have more narrowly specialized employment, e.g., in taunting. Yet extreme forms of tongue showing are occasionally seen in situations not belonging to the special categories. Conversely, forms such as those used in taunting are sometimes done feebly; they are then not distinguishable from the 'typical' range of tongue showing, and also can be recognized only by context. A possibility of recipient error is thus engendered, but it usually lacks serious consequences. If a taunt is mistaken for a less specifically expressed unwillingness to interact, reasonably appropriate responses are still likely (a taunt with tongue showing is not a particularly aggressive threat). Similarly, if in the converse situation an unspecific expression of unwillingness to interact is mistaken for a taunt (with an attack message), responses are likely to be to a degree appropriate. The 'cost' of errors in such cases is not likely to be great if the social interactions falter slightly within a generally appropriate framework.

Recipient error might also occur should tongue showing be confused with either licking the lips to remove foreign matter or to moisten them, or with a signal indicating hunger or willingness to ingest (we have not studied the latter signal, but it appears to exist and to have a precedent in infant behavior patterns). Both differ from tongue showing in incorporating obvious lip-licking movements. They are always distinguishable from any tongue showing that is sustained for a couple of seconds or more. Confusion is likely both in cases in which the tongue is darted out and in again (these are relatively uncommon), and in cases in which tongue showing grades into lip-licking. In at least some cultures, people may parasitize directly functional lip-licking movements to disguise tongue showing when they feel it should not be made public. For instance, persons answering questions in public (e.g., contestants in televised 'beauty pagents' when listening to their questioners) often do more lip-licking than would seem necessary to moisten the driest of lips.

(3) Displays function in the regulation of social interactions. Employment of tongue showing should generate functions for each participant in an event, one for the communicator and one for each recipient. These can be expected to differ, often considerably, in different events, but in general should have the following characteristics:

> For a recipient, tongue showing should enable choice of an efficient course of action to take with a communicator who is less likely than usual to cooperate in the development of a social interaction.
>
> For a communicator, tongue showing should increase the likelihood that he will receive diffident treatment, increasing his opportunities to choose or complete a course of action, or enabling him to forestall an undesired interaction, to avoid its escalation, or to save face.

Goffman (1963) has explored the reasons why a person must both keep himself accessible to 'requests for face engagements' and also put limits on his accessibility. An 'implicit contract' appears to exist in society under which properly integrated members observe "situational proprieties ... [that] govern the allocation of the individual's involvement within the situation". Tongue showing is probably one of several behavioral devices that function to indicate temporarily reduced accessibility on the part of individuals, whether or not they are already interacting.

Many people with whom we have spoken do not believe tongue showing to be a commonly used facial expression, and because of this do not believe that it functions in social interactions. One need only watch for it deliberately to see that it does occur commonly. People are not consciously aware of a great deal of the use they make of display behavior, and if asked about even the commonest facial expressions (e.g., smiling) can give only very superficial analyses of both situations of use and manner of response in different circumstances. Yet a demonstration that recipients commonly take account of tongue showing is difficult when it cannot be determined in most events which information sources are important to recipients of the display. It is hard to imagine what forces would keep this behavior regular within human populations if it had no function, however, and we have found that tongue showing is done in a very regular selection of events.

Tongue showing by individuals who are concentrating might be interpreted as a behavior pattern that somehow acts to relieve motivational 'tension'. Such an attempt to explain causation at the level of the organism is not necessarily incompatible with a social-level interpretation of tongue showing as a display; a behavior pattern could function at both levels. A tension releasing hypothesis, however, leaves unexplained the formalization of the behavior. Why should individuals specifically tongue show instead of performing an unpredictable variety of behavior patterns in the circumstances we have described, and why restrict the use of tongue showing to such circumstances? Why should tension-releasing behavior be to any extent limited in form and similar among diverse individuals if it is JUST an emotional outlet? There seems to be no answer that does not imply signalling properties. This is true even if one argues that behavior evolved to relieve emotional stress and became secondarily restricted (i.e., formalized) to the forms of tongue showing so as not to be confused with already existing displays. Tongue showing would then have been formalized to indicate not the communicator states typical of those displays, but some residue of states — i.e., to correlate with a specific kind of information about the communicator. Any evolutionary pressures formalizing tongue showing would inevitably augment its communicative value, if it were not done only by solitary individuals. Finally, if tongue showing does in fact relieve 'tension' to some degree, it may be in part because it does serve in communication, protecting the communicator from interruption.

Tongue showing is very often done by individuals who are alone, or who appear to believe themselves alone, while concentrating on some task. It is by no means the only display known to be used frequently in the absence of obvious recipients, directed, as it were, 'to whom it may concern'. Some, like the loud 'songs' of many species of birds, appear to function primarily to broadcast information to potential, usually distant, recipients. Tongue showing is too inconspicuous to function at a distance, but is easy to sustain. It could be functional if used when there is a chance that if another individual appeared, the subject's opportunity to continue with his involvement would be jeopardized.

In many observed instances of tongue showing by individuals concentrating on tasks the subjects apparently ignored all other individuals and were not aware of being watched. In fact, on starting such tasks they often apparently disattended everything else: perceptually filtered all unnecessary, non-emergency input from ticking clocks to passing people, whether or not all their pertinent sensory receptors were preempted. It was as if they had put on 'blinkers'. It may be useful to tongue show when in this disattending state whether or not there are other individuals initially present, since the subject will not be aware of changes. (Some disattending actually begins when a subject becomes aware of another's attention, and in this case the subject is initially aware of the other's presence but may not be responsive to subsequent changes in the other's behavior.)

(4) Tongue showing was found in every age and ethnic group we examined. We did not attempt to be thorough, however, about examining either all age groups or a carefully selected spectrum of well-defined ethnic groups. Consequently we may have missed modifications of form or usage in each ethnic or age group, such as might be due to different cultural display rules. However, we feel we have shown that the display is widespread among age and ethnic groups; our basic categories of usage occur in each group, although there appear to be some age-specific limitations, and our interpretation seems consistent for the data from each group. This is perhaps not surprising since, as will be shown below, even gorillas have what appears to be the same display, encoding the same message.

TONGUE SHOWING BY OTHER PRIMATES

1. *Gorillas and Orang-utans*

In form, tongue showing by the young captive gorillas we observed usually looked very similar to the most common human forms of the display, although the gorillas' tongues were relatively conspicuous. Usually the tongue was shown broadly in a slightly opened mouth. It might be balled or not, but was not thrust far forward or pointed stiffly although it could be lolled far out; it was sometimes angled to one side of the mouth. Individuals differed considerably in the amounts they used tongue showing, and in the kinds of interactions that elicited it.

Gorilla tongue showing not only looks like the human display, it is also used in closely comparable circumstances. For instance, gorillas sometimes tongue showed while concentrating on 'involving tasks' such as balancing precariously atop an up-ended toy wagon, doing acrobatics on the chains which hang in their cages, or climbing while favoring an injured foot. These cases included both events in which no other gorillas were nearby as well as events in which social interaction was more likely.

More tongue showing was seen in events in which there was rejection of or withdrawal from social interaction. For example, when one gorilla reached for or pulled at another in an attempt at wrestling play the second might promptly grapple with the first, or might tongue show and then usually avoid wrestling. The gorilla attempting to initiate play might also tongue show, although we noted this only when N'Gui approached Fern at times when she was avoiding him; she was larger than he and sometimes reacted very roughly, and he was almost always cautious with her. Not infrequently a gorilla would leave another with whom he had been wrestling and sit a few feet away, disattending the other and tongue showing. This appeared to be resting behavior and such individuals sometimes could be seen to be breathing hard; sometimes they rejoined the other and engaged in further wrestling. Gorillas sitting alone within a few feet of others who were wrestling were also seen to tongue show while watching or disattending; they might get up and move farther away, still tongue showing. Tongue showing was never seen, however, during wrestling bouts when both participants were actively grappling and mock-biting each other.

Many other instances of tongue showing by the young gorillas appeared to relate to the likelihood that chasing or wrestling play bouts would be initiated, and were seen as one individual approached or passed by another. The tongue showing might be done either by an individual watching another approach or by an individual while approaching or passing near another, or sometimes standing looking obliquely at another (a pose that in play periods often preceded attempts to incite chases or wrestling). During or just after chases the chased individual might tongue show, although we recorded only one instance of tongue showing by an individual in the chasing role — and that came after he broke off the chase and sat down quietly, apparently resting.

Play with toys also often generated instances of tongue showing, usually by an individual watching but not joining as one of the others played with a toy. Many observations of this were made when the gorillas played with a ball; one would drop it and see it roll to another, or see the other get it, and tongue show without attempting to retrieve it.

Like the nursery school children, the young gorillas occasionally acted in ways that provoked verbal reprimand — in this case from one of the girls or keepers who was usually in their cage. A gorilla might tongue show on being shouted at for grabbing another gorilla, or on being lectured for playing too hard, or on turning to look back at the human after having been spanked. In other cases the tongue showing gorilla appeared to anticipate a reprimand: e.g., a male chased a small female and was verbally reprimanded, then soon turned to chase her again, saw that she was near the human, and stopped with tongue showing.

Several times gorillas tongue showed while in **contact** with a human but not being reprimanded. The human was sometimes doing a task to which the gorillas always showed aversion, such as using the hose to wash feces from the cage. In yet other cases a gorilla might tongue show while a human played with it roughly, dragging it on the floor or swinging it by its arms in a circle. These cases closely resemble the observations of human children tongue showing while engaged in activities in which they have foregone physical control.

As in other sets of observations, in a minority of cases we could correlate little other behavior with the use of the display. For instance, a gorilla might tongue show while sitting quietly with a human. We can correlate but not interpret a behavior pattern in a small number of additional cases. The front of the gorilla cage is a large glass window, electrified to discourage the gorillas from hitting it. It provides both a view of watching people and reflections of the interior of the cage. Tongue showing was seen several times as a gorilla approached the window or stood near it, apparently preoccupied with it.

Finally, tongue showing appeared a number of times during behavior for which we have no comparable observations of human children. All of these were done by the 5- to 6-year-old gorillas watched during 1967. The majority involved cases in which Kathy, the gorilla with whom we sometimes played, was extremely active, either highly ambivalent about playing with us in the cage, or thwarted by our visible presence outside the cage at times when we did not come in. Both circumstances elicited frenetic behavior in which she would run back and forth, throw excelsior and drape it over her shoulders and head (and sometimes mouth it), pirouette, roll, chest-beat, slap the floor, and flail her arms. Some of this looked remarkably like human tantrum behavior, but without aggressive components. When ambivalent about playing and yet pressed to play, she would often retreat to a ledge onto which we did not pursue her, and might extend one or both hands in an apparently specialized gesture (this gesture, the pirouetting, chest-beating, and related patterns that appear to be displays will be described in more detail elsewhere). If left alone on this ledge she usually calmed down. If approached there, however, particularly by one of us extending a hand (see Fig. 2) she was likely to tongue show and then to flail quite violently, sometimes letting her jaw hang slack as she waved her head from side to side with the tongue effectively flapping, and sometimes lolling the tongue grossly forward in an expression that appeared remarkably like a Bronx cheer. Very similar behavior sometimes built up, although with fewer retreats to the ledge, when she was thwarted by our presence outside the cage.

The occurrence of tongue showing during such highly agitated behavior suggests that its usage by gorillas may correlate with a somewhat broader range of emotional arousal than it does in humans. However, the gorillas were like nursery school children in using tongue showing in response to mild, but not severe reprimands.

A few possibly aberrant cases of tongue showing were seen in interactions between a male (N'Gui, when 5 to 6 years old) and the female Fern (approximately 9 years old) in the autumn of 1967. Fern began to have estrous periods in the summer of 1967 and N'Gui had learned to mount her after she began pulling him onto her back. Despite his immaturity he thereafter sought mounting when she was in estrus, and did pelvic thrusting (sometimes, however, while perched too high on her back). She appeared frustrated, and spent much time bumping her genital area against the wall; N'Gui would come to sites where she did this and press his face against them. He could have been sniffing, or licking at (tasting) a deposited pheromone. On three occasions, in three different periods of estrus, he was seen to approach or watch her while apparently licking his lips with an obviously protruded tongue. Conceivably, the tongue motions were 'intention movements' of pheromonal ingestion. While limited, these observations may indicate a display with a component of tongue movement encoding a message of copulatory behavior.

The infant gorilla observed in Chicago was being raised by its mother, and so was potentially in a more 'natural' situation than were the other gorillas. It tongue showed in the same kinds of situations as they did, for instance, as it maneuvered with difficulty along the bars of the cage, and when it was suddenly picked up by its mother. In several instances the infant protruded its tongue while staring at an object (food, the edge of a platform) and then leaned over and licked or bit the object. These cases were likely infantile anticipatory mouthing; nothing similar was shown by the older Philadelphia gorillas.

The young orang-utans had more diverse mouth and tongue movements than did the gorillas. These movements included tongue showing similar to that seen in gorillas and humans, and used in comparable situations. For example, a one and one-half year old female pulled on a one-year-old male as he hung on the chains in the cage. She pulled hard until she finally pulled him down and his face became visible; he was lip tucking and had his tongue far out to the side of his mouth. He sat, tongue showing, with his eyes averted; when the female walked away he watched her, still tongue showing. A six-month-old orang-utan raised by its mother in the Lincoln Park Zoo tongue showed as it pulled itself up farther on its mother's shoulders.

2. *Visible Use of the Tongue in Displays of Other Primates*

Apparently formalized protrusions of the tongue have been reported in a number of studies of captive and free-ranging primates. For apes, however, reports are as yet few: Reynolds and Reynolds (1965: 407) list "sticking out" of the tongue by chimpanzees "while two juveniles were playing"; Carpenter (1940) mentions that the tongue is shown in greetings of the gibbon *Hylobates lar.*

Andrew (1963) and Van Hooff (1967) both indicate that what Van Hooff calls the 'tongue-smacking face' is found in a range of Old World monkey genera, and is used by animals coming closer to one another: in greetings, approaches to allogroom, to huddle together or simply associate, to play, or to copulate. In most species the tongue-smacking face is an important preliminary to allogrooming and the tongue movements of the display are sometimes components of allogrooming *per se*, particularly early in a bout. The 'tongue-smacking face' display comprises opening the mouth, protruding the tongue, and withdrawing the tongue as the mouth closes shortly after; the cycle may be rapidly repeated. The tongue protrusions are apparently obvious in most Old World monkeys (and exaggerated in the gelada baboon *Theropithecus gelada*) but barely noticeable in the chimpanzee (*Pan troglodytes*), which may be the only ape having a facial expression that even resembles the tongue-smacking face in form and usage (Van Hooff, 1967). Many monkey species (particularly most macaques and baboons), however, have BOTH the tongue-smacking expression and a closely similar 'lip-smacking face' in which the tongue protrusions are made less obvious. Van Hooff (1967: 40) tentatively suggests that a communicator using the tongue showing form is less likely to approach than is one using the other — i.e., making the tongue conspicuous correlates with greater hesitancy to initiate a social interaction such as allogrooming. Nonetheless, all forms apparently function to "facilitate mutual approach" for friendly interaction, and indicate that while the communicator may either approach or flee, he is more likely to approach or permit the other to approach (Van Hooff, 1967: 52-53). In some cases, his choice may be between fleeing or trying to associate; for example, in the common langur Jay (1965) lists moving the tongue "in and out of the mouth" as a gesture used by submissive individuals.

Whether or not a visible tongue is widespread among primate species in precopulatory displays remains uncertain, as for a number of species only 'lip-smacking' has been mentioned. Lip-smacking may be a noise made largely or solely not by the lips but by the tongue and the dento-palatal surface. The moving tongue may be visible in this display in many species, but difficult to see at much distance. However, in at least some Old World monkeys (macaques and baboons), flicking of the protruded tongue is a prominent part of precopulatory behavior. It is also prominent in the precopulatory behavior of the New World howling monkey *Alouatta palliata* (Carpenter, 1934), accompanying allogrooming which the species uses only in this circumstance (Moynihan, 1967). In a New World tamarin, *Saguinus geoffroyi*, males may do exaggerated tongue protruding both before and during copulation; Moynihan (1970) reports an observation by M. Bernstein of a female using this display while RESISTING a male's attempt to copulate.

Most species of New World monkeys may use less tongue showing in greetings and allogrooming than do catarrhines. The best descriptions are for *Saguinus geoffroyi* (Moynihan, 1970) which employs a relatively inconspicuous form of 'tongue-protrusion' during some vocalizations, during allogrooming, and before or after feeding. Much more exaggerated forms are sometimes used by wild individuals "in apparent response to the approach of a human being", and occur when captives are "confronted by unfamiliar individuals of their own species". Moynihan also saw exaggerated tongue protrusions when a captive juvenile was caught and held in the hand for some minutes.

Some lemurs may also use a series of tongue protrusions in greeting. Andrew (1963) reports it for captive brown lemurs *Lemur fulvus*, Jolly (1966) says that the sifaka *Propithecus verreauxi* may lick the nose in a circumstance she describes as "to observer (in uncertainty)", and J. Chase has had tongue movements directed to her by an awakening captive ring-tailed lemur *L. catta*.

With respect to the ontogeny of visible tongue displays in monkeys, Andrew (1963) says that in *Macaca mullatta* the tongue movements seen in greeting "are exactly those of sucking or eating soft food" and that infants may pass from the use of these movements in a greeting into thumb-sucking. Anthony (1968) has traced a relationship between attempts by a weaned infant to suckle and the development of allogrooming as a tactic by which to get into a suckling position. Anthony's captive group of *Papio cynocephalus* (which did not include adult males) also provided evidence for an ontogenetic learning relationship between tongue showing and sexual behavior, in that females often responded to the approaches to suckle by male infants by sucking the infants' genitalia, inducing erections. In *Theropithecus gelada* Spivak (1968) found what may be an ontogenetic origin for the use of "Lippen-Zungen-bewegungen" by males to the anal-genital region of presenting females: females touch the anal-genital regions of other females' offspring with the same gesture.

3. *The Phylogeny of Tongue Showing*

The form and employment of tongue showing by young captive gorillas are closely similar to the form and employment of the human display. This suggests that the two behavior patterns are homologous, and in both species encode information that the communicator will likely behave hesitantly about social interaction, or some aspects of it. The very limited observations of orang-utans suggest that this species also has a homologous display with a similar message, although for both apes usages could possibly be found in wild, free-ranging populations that do not fit our limited understanding based on captives.

Insofar as displays revealing the tongue have been described for other primate species, all appear to correlate with circumstances in which the communicator is hesitant about social interactions. Such hesitation is usually evident in greetings, and is obvious when one individual is showing submission or resisting the attentions of another, is responding to the approach of a strange conspecific individual or a human, or is being held by a human. Further, there is abundant evidence that individuals coming together for 'friendly' contact behavior often do so very hesitantly. Moynihan (1967: 244) remarks that "physical contacts are always 'risky'. An individual approached or touched may become frightened, and retreat, or become irritated and start fighting"; other ethologists have made similar generalizations based on the study of a large variety of mammalian and avian species. Attempts by animals to copulate often go awry, with one individual fleeing from or attacking the other. Even approaching to allogroom is done with evident caution (e.g. see Van Hooff, 1967: 39), perhaps partly because it often involves animals differing in dominance status (see Sparks, 1967). Allogrooming often appears more easily initiated in a troop of primates once some individuals are already engaged in it than it is for the first individuals to begin a bout.

Thus, whatever additional information some species may encode in displays that show the tongue, some hesitancy to interact may be indicated. Added information may often be encoded in other displays that are used simultaneously. Other primates, like man, always employ tongue showing in a matrix of other facial expressions and informative behavior patterns.

Whether the forms of tongue protrusion diverge more among most primate species than between humans and gorillas is not clear. Descriptions of simple, unexaggerated protrusion are not common, perhaps because this is often hard to observe in the wild where the observer is usually farther from the communicator than are conspecific recipients. Much more commonly reported, usually in initiating allogrooming or precopulatory sequences, are displays involving a moving tongue. Neither man nor gorillas makes much use of the common primate forms of allogrooming. Both species may use visible tongue displays in precopulatory circumstances, and may be like most monkeys in using a form incorporating a flicking movement, but this remains to be established.

Very little can be said about the comparative ontogenetic origins of tongue showing displays. In each species for which we have some information (man, the rhesus macaque, and the olive baboon) there is an apparent relationship between the displays and suckling or food rejection movements. In the two monkey species there is also limited evidence for a relationship between early feeding experiences and subsequent use of tongue protrusions in sexual interactions. Repeated tongue protrusion-retraction cycles may derive from ingestive acts, just as non-cyclic protrusion may derive from oral rejection. Tongue flicking may also be ingestive if it is involved in the tasting of sexual pheromones. This may mean that two displays, distinguished by presence or absence of flicking movements, may have derived from precursor acts with effectively opposite functions. Nonetheless, some degree of hesitance to interact may typify a communicator using either display: for tongue showing interaction of an unspecified sort, for tongue flicking copulation is being sought, but cautiously.

In summary, displays in which the tongue is made visible may share common phylogenetic histories among primates, but there may be two lines of evolution. Tongue protrusions may, of course, antedate the evolution of primates as a set of mammalian displays. Much more detailed investigation of non-human species will be required before these possibilities can be clarified.

Fig. 1.

(A) A 15-year-old boy tongue showing while holding a small, squirming lizard against a ruler. He was measuring its length for a herpetologist whom he had recently begun to assist, and was not yet skilled in handling lizards.

(B) An adult Cuna Indian chief tongue showing while weaving a fishing net from heavy cord, a task at which he was not expert; he is sitting amongst a group of men from his village.

(C) A Cuna girl, 4 to 5 years old, averting her eyes and tongue showing as she reached back to touch a friend, while apprehensive about the photographer's attention.

(D) A Panamanian child of 4 to 5 years, tongue showing while looking obliquely at the photographer. She had just sat astride a wooden horse, and was waiting for a merry-go-round to begin to move.

Each line drawing was traced directly from a photograph. The photograph of the Cuna chief was taken by Joel Sherzer, the remaining photographs by W. J. Smith.

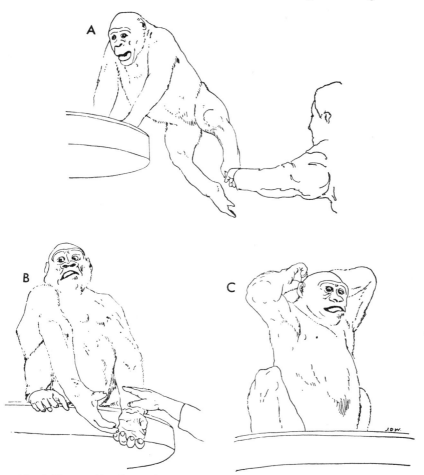

Fig. 2. Tongue Showing by a 5-year-old Gorilla (Kathy) in the Philadelphia Zoo.

(A) Tongue showing as she flees from the observer with whom she has been play-fighting. She was retreating to a ledge where she was always allowed to rest alone until ready to interact further.

(B) Tongue showing with head and eye aversion from her ledge as she reaches toward the observer in a palms-up gesture that appeared to correlate with seeking assurance. Observer's hand can be seen reaching forward to lie in hers, a procedure that usually calmed her.

(C) Tongue showing in a different sequence in which the observer did not take her proffered hand. She stood up on the ledge and went into behavior that looked very much like an unaggressive version of a human child's tantrums. As in this instance, the tantrum behavior often correlated with retreat after instensely active, rough, play, and the gorilla usually remained ambivalent about the observer for some minutes.

Each line drawing was traced directly from a photograph taken by R. Miselis.

SUMMARY

1. Among the facial expressions with which humans communicate are a number of ways of making the tongue visible. Most commonly, the tongue is inserted between the lips but not protruded far; it may, however, be further extended and lolled downward or variously pointed. All of these positions comprise a single tongue showing 'display' (an act formalized to function as an information source), of which the most common variants appear to be used spontaneously. In addition, special forms that are more often deliberately employed are probably also members of the display. However, acts incorporating formalized patterns of movement of the protruded tongue (rapid flicking or wagging, or licking of the lips) have not yet been studied and may or may not be specialized variants of the tongue showing display.

2. The principal objective of the study was to determine, through observation of the behavior of individuals who tongue show, what information this display contributes to social interaction. Observations were made in most detail on a group of nursery school children; humans of other ages were sampled in diverse, naturally-occurring situations.

Tongue showing is done while the communicators are engaged in or faced with the possibility of social interactions that are, in whole or in part, aversive for them. Often they are doing something that requires concentration, or are at least engaged in an activity that could be disrupted by social interference. At other times the social interactions themselves have negative characteristics: the individual may be being reprimanded, be losing or being misunderstood in an argument, be likely to lose his opportunity to speak in a conversation, being attended to by a stranger, and so forth. In some specialized, often deliberate, uses of tongue showing the individual may be teasing, and may have created a situation in which he could be misunderstood.

Because the display is not characteristically used in situations in which the communicator is prompted to strong avoidance, it is difficult to formulate precise predictions about the subsequent behavior of individuals who tongue show. Provisionally it appears that a tongue showing communicator may be likely to show some limited form of rejection: tongue showing appears to encode the information (the 'message') that the communicator may avoid or behave hesitantly if required to accept, initiate, or sustain a social interaction. This message of what we might call 'social interaction hesitance' is only broadly descriptive of the communicator's likely activities; it does not specify exactly how he will behave. In this respect the message resembles several other messages now known to be widespread among the displays of bird and mammal species. Each such broadly defined message is useful in a considerable range of circumstances, but requires that recipients use sources of information contexual to the display in selecting a response.

3. Tongue showing is used by humans of all ages. It initially appears in at least some infants after they reject food by pushing it from their mouths with the tongue; the tongue remains protruded, serving to indicate that they will not accept further attempts to feed them (or to feed them the same kind of food). This may provide a clue both to the ontogenetic origin of tongue showing in an act of oral rejection, and to the behavior that served as an evolutionary precursor for the display.

4. Tongue showing was used by humans wherever we sought it; in Philadelphia and other American cities, in Panama City and the Canal Zone, and among the Cuna Indians of the San Blas archipelago of Panama. We did not attempt to discover detailed differences, but conclude that the basic display is probably widespread among different ethnic groups.

5. Not only is tongue showing widespread among different human populations, but a closely similar display is used by gorillas. For other primates, displays have been described in which the tongue is protruded, but most appear to incorporate tongue movements that may derive from ingestive behavior rather than rejection; these appear to be used largely in pre-allogrooming and precopulatory behavior. Humans may have formalized tongue protrusion displays incorporating movements that resemble these other primate displays, and the static tongue showing we have observed in humans and gorillas could easily be missed in field studies of smaller primates. Further comparative studies are needed to determine the probable phylogeny of tongue showing.

REFERENCES

Andrew, R. J.
  1963 "The Origin and Evolution of the Calls and Facial Expressions of the Primates", *Behavior* 20, 1-109.
Anthony, T. R.
  1968 "The Ontogeny of Greeting, Grooming, and Sexual Motor Patterns in Captive Baboons (Superspecies *Papio cynocephalus*)", *Behaviour* 31, 358-72.
Aronson, E., and S. Rosenbloom
  1971 "Space Perception in Early Infancy; Perception within a Common Auditory-Visual Space", *Science* 172, 1161-63.
Carpenter, C. R.
  1934 "A Field Study of the Behavior and Social Relations of Howling Monkeys (*Alouatta palliata*)", *Comparative Psychology Monographs* 10: 2, 1-168.
  1940 "A Field Study in Siam of the Behavior and Social Relations of the Gibbon", *Comparative Psychology Monographs* 16: 5, 1-212.
Darwin, C.
  1872 *The Expression of the Emotions in Man and Animals* (reprinted 1965 by Phoenix Editions, University of Chicago Press, Chicago.)
Eibl-Eibesfeldt, I.
  1970 *Ethology: The Biology of Behavior* (New York: Holt, Rinehart and Winston).
  1972 "Similarities and Differences between Cultures in Expressive Movements", in: R. A. Hinde (ed.), *Non-verbal Communication* (Cambridge University Press), 291-312.
Ekman, P., and W. V. Friesen
  1969 "The Repertoire of Nonverbal Behavior: Categories, Origins, Usage, and Coding", *Semiotica* 1, 49-98.
Goffman, Erving
  1963 *Behavior in Public Places* (New York: Free Press).
  1967 *Interaction Ritual* (New York: Anchor Books).
Jay, Phyllis
  1965 "The Common Langur of North India", in: I. Devore (ed.), *Primate Behavior* (New York: Holt, Rinehart and Winston), 197-249.
Jolly, Allison
  1966 *Lemur Behavior: A Madagascar Field Study* (Chicago: University of Chicago Press).
Klineberg, Otto.
  1938 "Emotional Expression in Chinese Literature", *J. Abnorm. Soc. Psychol.* 33, 517-20.
LaBarre, W.
  1964 "Paralinguistics, Kinesics, and Cultural Anthropology", in: T. A. Sebeok, *et al.* (eds.), *Approaches to Semiotics* (The Hague: Mouton), 191-220.

Masters, W. H., and V. E. Johnson
  1966   *Human Sexual Response* (Boston: Little, Brown).
Morris, D.
  1967   *The Naked Ape* (New York: McGraw-Hill).
Moynihan, M.
  1967   "Comparative Aspects of Communication in New World Primates", in: D. Morris (ed.), *Primate Ethology* (London: Morrison and Gibb), 236-66.
  1970   "Some Behavior Patterns of Platyrrhine monkeys. II: *Saguinus geoffroyi* and Some Other Tamarins", *Smithson. Contrib. Zool.* 28, 1-77.
Reynolds, V., and F. Reynolds
  1965   "Chimpanzees of the Budongo Forest", in: I. DeVore (ed.), *Primate Behavior* (New York: Holt, Rinehart and Winston), 368-424.
Roosevelt, T., and K. Roosevelt
  1929   *Trailing the Giant Panda* (New York: Scribner's).
Sherzer, Joel
  1973   "The Pointed Lip Gesture among the San Blas Cuna", *Language in Society* 2, 117-31.
Smith, W. John
  1965   "Message, Meaning, and Context in Ethology", *American Naturalist* 99, 405-09.
  1968   "Message-Meaning Analyses of Animal Communication", in: T. A. Sebeok (ed.), *Animal Communication* (Bloomington: Indiana University Press), 44-60.
  1974   "Zoosemiotics: Ethology and the Theory of Signs", in: T. A. Sebeok (ed.), *Current Trends in Linguistics* 12 (The Hague: Mouton), 561-626. (In press.)
Sparks, J.
  1967   "Allogrooming in Primates: A Review", in: D. Morris (ed.), *Primate Ethology* (London: Morrison and Gibb), 148-75.
Spivak, H.
  1968   "Ausdruckformen und soziale Beziehungen in einer Dschelada-Gruppe (*Theropithecus gelada*) im Zoo", *Tierpsychologischen Abteilung der Universität Zürich am Zoologischen Garten* (Zürich: Juris Druck und Verlag), 1-137.
Van Hooff, J. A. R. A. M.
  1967   "The Facial Displays of Catarrhine Monkeys and Apes", in: D. Morris (ed.), *Primate Ethology* (London: Morrison and Gibb), 7-68.

Sources

The articles which appear in this volume are reprinted from the following issues of *Semiotica*.

Argyle, Michael, Roger Ingham, Florisse Alkema, Margaret McCallin 'The Different Functions of Gaze' (1973) 7: 19–32.

Beattie, Geoffrey W. 'Sequential Temporal Patterns of Speech and Gaze in Dialogue' (1978) 23: 27–52.

Collett, Peter, Peter Marsh 'Patterns of Public Behaviour: Collision Avoidance on a Pedestrian Crossing (1974) 12: 281–300.

De Long, Alton J. 'Kinesic Signals at Utterance Boundaries in Preschool Children' (1974) 11: 43–74.

Ekman, Paul, Wallace V. Friesen 'The Repertoire of Nonverbal Behavior: Categories, Origins, Usage, and Coding (1969) 1: 49–97.

Freedman, Norbert 'Toward a Mathematization of Kinetic Behavior: A Review of Paul Bouissac's *La Mesure des Gestes* (1975) 15: 83–96.

Givens, David 'Greeting a Stranger: Some Commonly Used Nonverbal Signals of Aversivenss' (1978) 22: 351–367.

Johnson, Harold G., Paul Ekman, Wallace V. Friesen 'Communicative Body Movements: American Emblems' (1975) 15: 335–354.

Kendon, Adam 'Some Functions of the Face in a Kissing Round' (1975) 15: 299–334.

Kirk, Lorraine, Michael Burton 'Physical versus Semantic Classification of Nonverbal Forms: A Cross-Cultural Experiment (1976) 17: 315–338.

Poyatos, Fernando 'Forms and Functions of Nonverbal Communication in the Novel: A New Perspective of the Author-Character-Reader Relationship' (1977) 21: 295–338.

Poyatos, Fernando 'Gesture Inventories: Fieldwork Methodology and Problems' (1975) 13: 199–227.

Rosenberg, Marc 'The Case of the Apple Turnover: An Experiment in Multichannel Communication Analysis' (1976) 16: 129–140.

Rosenfeld, Howard M., Marilyn Shea, Paul Greenbaum 'Facial Emblems of 'Right' and 'Wrong': Topographical Analysis and Derivation of a Recognition Test' (1979) 26: 15–34.

Schriffin, Deborah 'Handwork as Ceremony: The Case of the Handshake' (1974) 12: 189–202.

Seaford, Henry W. Jr. 'Maximizing Replicability in Describing Facial Behavior' (1978) 24: 1–32.

Smith, W. John, Julia Chase, Anna Katz Lieblich 'Tongue Showing: A Facial Display of Humans and Other Primate Species' (1974) 11: 201–246.

Sparhawk, Carol M. 'Constrastive-Indetificational Features of Persian Gesture' (1978) 24: 49–86.